murach's
ASP.NET
CORE MVC
2ND EDITION

Mary Delamater

Joel Murach

MIKE MURACH & ASSOCIATES, INC.
3730 W Swift Ave. • Fresno, CA 93722
www.murach.com • murachbooks@murach.com

Editorial team

Authors: Mary Delamater
                       Joel Murach

Editor: Anne Boehm

Contributor: John Baugh

Production: Juliette Baylon

Books for web developers

Murach's HTML and CSS

Murach's JavaScript and jQuery

Murach's ASP.NET Web Programming with C#

Murach's PHP and MySQL

Murach's Java Servlets and JSP

Books on data analysis

Murach's R for Data Analysis

Murach's Python for Data Analysis

Books on programming languages

Murach's C#

Murach's C++ Programming

Murach's Java Programming

Murach's Python Programming

Murach's Visual Basic

Books for database programmers

Murach's SQL Server for Developers

Murach's MySQL

Murach's Oracle SQL and PL/SQL for Developers

For more on Murach books, please visit us at www.murach.com

Contents

Expanded contents

Section 3 Add more skills as you need them

Introduction

If you want to learn how to develop ASP.NET Core MVC web applications, you've chosen the right book. The only prerequisites are that you already know the basics of C# and HTML/CSS. If you're new to web development, our self-paced approach helps you build competence and confidence at every turn of the page. If you're an experienced web developer, this same self-paced approach lets you learn ASP.NET Core MVC faster and more thoroughly than you've ever learned a web development framework before.

Either way, when you're through, you'll have mastered all the skills you need for developing web applications at a professional level. You'll also find that this book is the best on-the-job reference that money can buy.

What this book does

To make this book as effective as possible, it is divided into three sections:

- Section 1 presents a five-chapter course that's designed to get you off to a great start. It shows how to use ASP.NET Core MVC to develop a simple one-page MVC web application by the end of chapter 2, and it shows how to develop a multi-page MVC web application that uses a database by the end of chapter 4. Along the way, it shows how to use Bootstrap to create responsive web applications, and it shows how to test and debug your web applications, a part of the job that many books treat too lightly or too late. At that point, you're ready for rapid progress in the sections that follow.

- Section 2 presents essential skills that every ASP.NET Core MVC developer should have. To do that, this section reviews and expands on some skills that were introduced in section 1, such as routing, Razor views, model binding, data validation, and EF (Entity Framework) Core. It also adds new skills like working with session state and cookies. Then, it finishes by presenting a realistic website that shows how all these skills fit together.

- Section 3 presents more skills that you can learn as you need them. These skills take your web development to a professional level. To be specific, this section shows how to work with dependency injection (DI), unit testing, custom tag helpers, partial views, view components, authentication, and authorization. It also shows how to deploy an MVC web app and how to use the Visual Studio Code text editor, an increasingly popular alternative to the Visual Studio IDE.

Why you'll learn faster and better with this book

Like all our books, this one has features that you won't find in competing books. That's why we believe you'll learn faster and better with our book than with any other. Here are some of those features.

- Because section 1 presents a complete subset of ASP.NET Core MVC in just 5 chapters, you're ready for productive work right away. This section also uses a self-paced approach that lets experienced programmers move more quickly and beginners work at a pace that's right for them.

- Because sections 2 and 3 present the rest of the skills that you need for developing corporate and commercial web applications, you can go from beginner to professional in a single book.

- If you page through this book, you'll see that all of the information is presented in "paired pages," with the essential syntax, guidelines, and examples on the right page and the perspective and extra explanation on the left page. This helps you learn faster by reading less...and this is the ideal reference format when you need to refresh your memory about how to do something.

- To help you put the skills presented in this book into context, this book presents complete web applications that use these skills. These applications include the HTML, CSS, and JavaScript that runs on the client as well as the Razor and C# code that runs on the server. As we see it, studying applications like these is the best way to learn ASP.NET Core MVC.

What software you need

If you're using Windows, the only software you need for this book is Visual Studio Community, which is available for free from Microsoft's website. This provides the Visual Studio IDE, .NET Core, the C# language, a built-in web server called Kestrel, and a database server called SQL Server Express LocalDB, which is a scaled back version of SQL Server. For more information, please refer to appendix A.

If you're using macOS, the only software you need for this book is Visual Studio for Mac, which is available for free from Microsoft's website. This provides the Visual Studio IDE, .NET Core, the C# language, and a built-in web server called Kestrel. However, it doesn't include SQL Server Express LocalDB. Instead, you can use SQLite database files, which don't require installing a database server. Then, to view the database files, you may want to install DB Browser for SQLite, which you can download for free from the internet. For more information, please refer to appendix B.

How our downloadable files can help you learn

If you go to our website at www.murach.com, you can download all the files that you need for getting the most from this book. These files include:

* the source code for the applications presented in this book
* the starting code for the exercises at the ends of the chapters
* the solutions to these exercises

These files let you test, review, and copy the code for an application. If you have any problems with the exercises, the solutions are there to help you over the learning blocks, an essential part of the learning process. In some cases, the solutions may show you a more elegant way to handle a problem, even when you've come up with a solution that works. Here again, appendixes A and B show how to download and install these files on Windows and macOS systems.

3 companion books for ASP.NET Core programmers

As you read this book, you may discover that your C# skills aren't as strong as they ought to be. In that case, we recommend that you get a copy of *Murach's C#*. It will get you up-to-speed with the C# language, and it will show you how to work with the most useful .NET Core classes.

If you discover that your HTML and CSS skills aren't as strong as they ought to be, we recommend *Murach's HTML and CSS*. Or, if you want to learn more about JavaScript and jQuery, we recommend *Murach's JavaScript and jQuery*.

Support materials for instructors and trainers

If you're a college instructor or corporate trainer who would like to use this book as a course text, we offer a full set of the support materials you need for a turnkey course. That includes:

* instructional objectives that help your students focus on the skills that they need to develop
* projects that let your students demonstrate how well they have mastered those skills
* test banks that let you measure how well your students have mastered those skills
* a complete set of PowerPoint slides that you can use to review and reinforce the content of the book

Instructors tell us that this is everything they need for a course without all the busywork that you get from other publishers.

To learn more about our instructor's materials, please go to our website at www.murachforinstructors.com if you're an instructor. If you're a trainer, please go to www.murach.com and click on the *Courseware for Trainers* link, or contact Kelly at 1-800-221-5528 or kelly@murach.com.

Please remember, though, that the primary component for a successful ASP.NET Core MVC course is this book. Because your students will learn faster and more thoroughly when they use our book, they will have better questions and be more prepared when they come to class. And because our paired pages are so good for reference, your students will be able to review for tests and do their projects more efficiently.

Please let us know how this book works for you

When we started writing this book, we had two goals. First, we wanted to make this the best-ever book for learning how to develop ASP.NET Core MVC web applications. To do that right, we knew we had to make the book easy enough for beginners and yet still teach the skills needed by professionals.

Second, we wanted to make this the best-ever book for experienced developers who want to add ASP.NET Core MVC to their skillsets. To do that right, we've carefully selected the content, organized it from simple to complex in each chapter, and packed the book full of sample web applications. That's why we believe that this book will help experienced developers learn ASP.NET Core MVC faster and better than ever. And when they're done, this book will be their best-ever on-the-job reference.

Now, we hope we've succeeded. We thank you for buying this book. We wish you all the best with your ASP.NET Core MVC programming. And if you have any comments, we always appreciate hearing from you.

Mary Delamater
maryd@techknowsolve.com

Joel Murach
joel@murach.com

Section 1

Get off to a fast start

This section presents the essential skills for coding, testing, and debugging ASP.NET Core MVC (Model-View-Controller) web apps. After chapter 1 introduces you to the concepts and terms that you need to know for ASP.NET Core MVC programming, chapter 2 shows you how to develop a simple web app that consists of a single page. This includes writing the C# code for the model and controller classes as well as writing the HTML, CSS, and Razor code for the view files that are used to generate the user interface and present it to the user. That gets you off to a fast start!

Chapter 3 shows you how to use the CSS classes that are available from an open-source library known as Bootstrap to make an ASP.NET Core MVC app work well for all screen sizes. This is known as responsive design. Then, chapter 4 shows you how to develop a three-page Movie List app that works with data in a database. Finally, chapter 5 shows you how to manually test and debug ASP.NET Core MVC apps.

When you finish all five chapters, you'll be able to develop real-world apps of your own. You'll have a solid understanding of how ASP.NET Core MVC works. And you'll be ready for rapid progress as you read the other sections of the book.

1

An introduction to web programming and ASP.NET Core MVC

This chapter introduces you to the basic concepts of web programming and ASP.NET Core MVC. Here, you'll learn how web apps work, how ASP.NET Core MVC apps work, and what software you need for developing these apps. When you finish this chapter, you'll have the background that you need for learning how to develop ASP.NET Core MVC apps.

An introduction to web apps

A *web app*, also known as a *web application*, consists of a set of *web pages* that are generated in response to user requests. The internet has many different types of web apps such as search engines, online stores, news sites, social sites, music streaming, video streaming, and games.

The components of a web app

The diagram in figure 1-1 shows that web apps consist of *clients* and a *web server*. The clients are the computers and mobile devices that use the web apps. They often access the web pages through programs known as *web browsers*. The web server holds the files that generate the pages of a web app.

A *network* is a system that allows clients and servers to communicate. The *internet* is a large network that consists of many smaller networks. In a diagram like the one in this figure, the "cloud" represents the network or internet that connects the clients and servers.

Networks can be categorized by size. A *local area network* (*LAN*) is a small network of computers that are near each other and can communicate with each other over short distances. Computers in a LAN are typically in the same building or adjacent buildings. This type of network is often called an *intranet*, and it can run web apps that are used throughout a company.

By contrast, a *wide area network* (*WAN*) consists of multiple LANs that have been connected. To pass information from one client to another, a router determines which network is closest to the destination and sends the information over that network. A WAN can be owned privately by one company or it can be shared by multiple companies.

An *internet service provider* (*ISP*) is a company that owns a WAN that is connected to the internet. An ISP leases access to its network to companies that need to be connected to the internet. When you develop production web apps, you will often implement them through an ISP.

To access a web page from a browser, you can type a *URL* (*Uniform Resource Locator*) into the browser's address area and press Enter. The URL starts with the *protocol*, which is usually HTTPS. It is followed by the *domain name* and the folder or directory *path* to the file that is requested. If the filename is omitted from the URL, the web server looks for a default file in the specified directory. The default files usually include index.html, index.htm, default.html, and default.htm.

The components of a web app

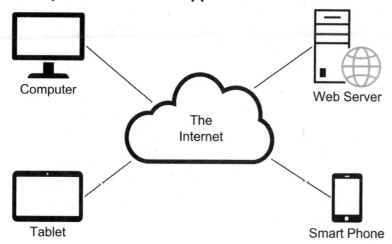

The components of an HTTP URL

Description

- A *web app*, also known as a *web application*, consists of clients, a web server, and a network.

- The *clients* often use *web browsers* to request web pages from the web server. Today, the clients are often computers, smart phones, or tablets.

- The *web server* returns the pages that are requested to the browser.

- A *network* connects the clients to the web server.

- To request a page from a web server, the user can type the address of a web page, called a *URL (Uniform Resource Locator)*, into the browser's address area and then press the Enter key.

- A URL consists of the *protocol* (usually, HTTPS), *domain name*, *path*, and *filename*. If you omit the protocol, HTTPS is assumed. If you omit the filename, the web server typically looks for a file named index.html, index.htm, default.html, or default.htm.

- An *intranet* is a *local area network* (*LAN*) that connects computers that are near each other, usually within the same building.

- The *internet* is a network that consists of many *wide area networks* (*WANs*), and each of those consists of two or more LANs.

- The *cloud* refers to software and services that run on the internet instead of locally on your computer. This term implies that you don't have to understand how it works to be able to use it.

- An *internet service provider* (*ISP*) owns a WAN that is connected to the internet.

Figure 1-1   The components of a web app

How static web pages are processed

A *static web page* is stored in a file that contains hard-coded content that doesn't change each time it is requested. This type of web page is sent directly from the web server to the web browser when the browser requests it. Static web pages were common in the early days of web programming but are less common today.

The diagram in figure 1-2 shows how a web server processes a request for a static web page. This process begins when a client requests a web page in a web browser. To do that, the user can either enter the URL of the page in the browser's address bar or click a link in the current page that specifies the next page to load.

In either case, the web browser builds a request for the web page and sends it to the web server. This request, known as an *HTTP request*, is formatted using the *Hypertext Transfer Protocol* (*HTTP*), which lets the web server know which file is being requested. To keep the communication over the network secure, most web apps use an extension of HTTP known as *Hypertext Transfer Protocol Secure* (*HTTPS*).

When the web server receives the HTTP request, it retrieves the requested file from the disk drive. This file contains the *HTML* (*Hypertext Markup Language*) for the requested page with references to any CSS or JavaScript files needed by the page. Then, the web server sends the HTML, CSS, and JavaScript back to the browser as part of an *HTTP response*.

When the browser receives the HTTP response, it *renders* (translates) the HTML, CSS, and JavaScript into a web page that is displayed in the browser. Then, the user can view the content. If the user requests another page, either by clicking a link or entering another URL into the browser's address bar, the process begins again.

In this figure, both the HTTP request and response use HTTP version 1.1. However, almost all browsers today support HTTP version 2, which is more efficient and secure than HTTP/1.1. HTTP/2 requests and responses are sent in binary, though, so they don't appear as shown here.

How a web server processes a static web page

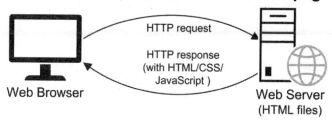

A simple HTTP request

```
GET / HTTP/1.1
Host: www.example.com
```

A simple HTTP response

```
HTTP/1.1 200 OK
Content-Type: text/html
Content-Length: 136

<html>
<head>
    <title>Example Web Page</title>
</head>
<body>
    <p>This is a sample web page</p>
</body>
</html>
```

Three protocols that web apps depend upon

- *Hypertext Transfer Protocol* (*HTTP*) is the protocol that web browsers and web servers use to communicate. It sets the specifications for HTTP requests and responses.
- *Hypertext Transfer Protocol Secure* (*HTTPS*) is an extension of the Hypertext Transfer Protocol (HTTP). It is used for secure communication over a network.
- *Transmission Control Protocol/Internet Protocol* (*TCP/IP*) is a suite of protocols that let two computers communicate over a network.

Description

- *Hypertext Markup Language* (*HTML*) is used to design the pages of a web app.
- A *static web page* is built from an HTML file that's stored on the web server and doesn't change. The filenames for static web pages usually have .htm or .html extensions.
- When the user requests a static web page, the browser sends an *HTTP request* to the web server that includes the name of the file that's being requested.
- When the web server receives the request, it retrieves the HTML, CSS, and JavaScript for the requested file and sends it back to the browser as part of an *HTTP response*.
- When the browser receives the HTTP response, it *renders* the HTML, CSS, and JavaScript into a web page that is displayed in the browser.

Figure 1-2   How static web pages are processed

How dynamic web pages are processed

A *dynamic web page* is a page that's generated by a program on an *application server*. This program uses the data that's sent with the HTTP request to generate the HTML that's returned to the server. For example, if the HTTP request includes a product code, the program can retrieve the data for that product from a *database server*. Then, it can insert that data into a web page and return it as part of an HTTP response.

The diagram in figure 1-3 shows how a web server processes a dynamic web page. The process begins when the user requests a page in a web browser. To do that, the user can click a link that specifies the dynamic page to load or click a button that submits a form that contains the data that the dynamic page should process.

In either case, the web browser builds an HTTP request and sends it to the web server. This request includes whatever data the app needs for processing the request. If, for example, the user has entered data into a form, that data is included in the HTTP request.

When the web server receives the HTTP request, the server examines the request to identify the application server that should process the request. The web server then forwards the request to that application server.

Next, the application server retrieves the appropriate program. It also loads any form data that the user submitted. Then, it executes the program. As the program executes, it generates the HTML, CSS, and JavaScript for the web page. If necessary, the program also requests data from a database server and uses that data as part of the web page it is generating.

When the program is finished, the application server sends the dynamically generated HTML back to the web server. Then, the web server sends the HTML, CSS, and JavaScript for the page back to the browser in an HTTP response.

When the web browser receives the HTTP response, it renders the HTML/CSS/JavaScript and displays the web page. To do that, the web browser doesn't need to know whether this HTML is for a static page or a dynamic page. Either way, it just renders the HTML/CSS/JavaScript.

When the page is displayed, the user can view the content. Then, when the user requests another page, the process begins again. The process that begins with the user requesting a web page and ends with the server sending a response back to the client is called a *round trip*.

ASP.NET Core apps use ASP.NET Core as the application server. In addition, they typically use a cross-platform web server known as *Kestrel* and a *DBMS (database management system)* named Microsoft SQL Server running on the database server.

Prior to ASP.NET Core, ASP.NET apps typically used a Windows-only web server known as *Internet Information Services (IIS)*. And, as you would expect, they used ASP.NET as the application server.

How a web server processes a dynamic web page

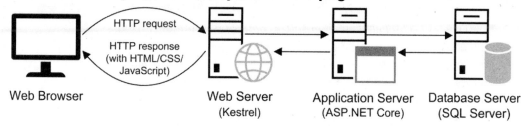

Web Browser   Web Server   Application Server   Database Server
                              (Kestrel)   (ASP.NET Core)   (SQL Server)

Description

- A *dynamic web page* is a web page that's generated by a program running on a server.

- When a web server receives a request for a dynamic web page, it examines the request to determine what *application server* should be used to process it and then passes the request to that application server.

- When the application server receives the request, it runs the appropriate program. Often, this program uses data that's sent in the HTTP request to get related data from a *database management system* (*DBMS*) running on a *database server*.

- When the application server finishes processing the data, it generates the HTML, CSS, and JavaScript for a web page and returns it to the web server. Then, the web server returns the HTML, CSS, and JavaScript to the web browser as part of an HTTP response.

- The process that starts when a client requests a page and ends when the page is returned to the browser is called a *round trip*.

- *Kestrel* is a cross-platform web server that also functions as an application server for ASP.NET Core apps.

- *Internet Information Services* (*IIS*) is an older Windows-only web server that also functions as an application server for older ASP.NET apps.

- SQL Server is typically used as the database server for ASP.NET Core and ASP.NET apps.

Figure 1-3   How dynamic web pages are processed

An introduction to the MVC pattern

The *MVC (Model-View-Controller) pattern* is commonly used to structure web apps that have significant processing requirements. Most modern web development frameworks today use some form of the MVC pattern. As you'll learn in this book, ASP.NET Core provides extensive support for the MVC pattern.

The MVC pattern divides an app into separate components where each component has a specific area of concern. This is known as *separation of concerns*. Although it requires a little more work to set up an app like this, it leads to many benefits. For example, it makes it easier to have different members of a team work on different components, it makes it possible to automate testing of individual components, and it makes it possible to swap out one component for another component. In short, it makes apps easier to code, test, debug, and maintain.

Figure 1-4 presents a diagram that shows the components of the MVC pattern and how they work together. To start, the *model* is in charge of data. Specifically, it gets and updates the data in a data store such as a database, it applies business rules to that data, and it validates that data.

The *view* is in charge of the user interface. Specifically, it creates the HTML, CSS, and JavaScript that the app sends to the browser in response to the browser's HTTP request.

The *controller* is in charge of controlling the flow of data between the model and the view. Specifically, it receives the HTTP request from the browser, determines what data to get from the model, and then sends the data from the model to the appropriate view.

It's important to note that each component should stick to its own area of concern and be as independent as possible. For example, the model should retrieve and validate data but it shouldn't have anything to do with formatting or displaying it. Similarly, the controller should move data between the model and the view but it shouldn't apply any business rules to it.

The MVC pattern

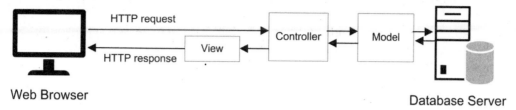

Web Browser   Database Server

Components of the MVC pattern

- The *model* consists of the code that provides the data access and business logic.
- The *view* consists of the code that generates the user interface and presents it to the user.
- The *controller* consists of the code that receives requests from users, gets the appropriate data from the model, and passes that data to the appropriate view.

Benefits of the MVC pattern

- Makes it easier to have different members of a team work on different components.
- Makes it possible to automate testing of individual components.
- Makes it possible to swap out one component for another component.
- Makes the app easier to maintain.

Drawbacks of the MVC pattern

- Requires more work to set up.

Description

- The *MVC (Model-View-Controller) pattern* is commonly used to structure web apps that have significant processing requirements.
- The MVC pattern breaks web apps into separate component parts. This is known as *separation of concerns*, and it leads to many benefits including making the app easier to code, test, debug, and maintain.

Figure 1-4   An introduction to the MVC pattern

An introduction to ASP.NET Core MVC

Now that you understand some concepts that apply to most web apps, you're ready to learn some concepts that are more specific to ASP.NET Core MVC apps.

Four ASP.NET programming models for web apps

Since 2002, Microsoft has developed many ASP.NET programming models. Figure 1-5 summarizes four of the most popular. Of these programming models, Web Forms is the oldest and most established, and Core MVC and Razor Pages are the newest and most cutting edge.

In 2002, Microsoft released ASP.NET Web Forms. It provides for *RAD* (*Rapid Application Development*) by letting developers build web pages by working with a design surface in a way that's similar to the way that developers build desktop apps with Windows Forms.

This approach made a lot of sense back in 2002 when many developers were switching from desktop development to web development. However, this approach has many problems including poor performance, inadequate separation of concerns, lack of support for automated testing, and limited control over the HTML/CSS/JavaScript that's returned to the browser. In addition, Web Forms uses the ASP.NET Framework, which is proprietary and only runs on Windows.

In 2007, Microsoft released ASP.NET MVC. It uses the MVC pattern that's used by many other web development platforms. It fixes many of the perceived problems with web forms to provide better performance, separation of concerns, support for automated testing, and a high degree of control over the HTML/CSS/JavaScript that's returned to the browser. However, it uses the same proprietary, Windows-only ASP.NET Framework as Web Forms. As a result, it can't run on internet servers that use other operating systems such as Linux, which is widely used for internet servers.

In 2015, Microsoft released ASP.NET Core MVC and ASP.NET Core Razor Pages. ASP.NET Core MVC uses an MVC service to implement the MVC pattern. It provides all of the functionality of ASP.NET MVC, but with better performance, more modularity, and cleaner code. In addition, it's built on the new ASP.NET Core platform that's open source and can run on multiple platforms including Windows, macOS, and Linux. As a result, it can run on most internet servers. Razor Pages is a model that's built on top of ASP.NET Core MVC.

While developing the different versions of MVC and Core MVC, Microsoft used different names and version numbers. For example, ASP.NET Core 1.0 was originally going to be called ASP.NET 5. But then Microsoft decided ASP.NET Core was a fundamentally different technology that should have a new name and number. Information on the internet sometimes uses the old names and version numbers that were used during development, not the official names and numbers

ASP.NET Web Forms
- Released in 2002.
- Provides for *RAD* (*Rapid Application Development*). Lets developers build web pages by working with a design surface in a way that's similar to Windows Forms.
- Has many problems including poor performance, inadequate separation of concerns, lack of support for automated testing, and limited control over the HTML/CSS/JavaScript that's returned to the browser.
- Uses the ASP.NET Framework, which is proprietary and only runs on Windows.

ASP.NET MVC
- Released in 2007.
- Uses the MVC pattern that's used by many other web development platforms.
- Fixes many of the perceived problems with web forms to provide better performance, separation of concerns, support for automated testing, and a high degree of control over the HTML/CSS/JavaScript that's returned to the browser.
- Uses the same proprietary, Windows-only ASP.NET Framework as Web Forms.

ASP.NET Core MVC
- Released in 2015.
- Uses a service to implement the MVC pattern that's used by many other web development platforms.
- Provides all of the functionality of ASP.NET MVC but with better performance, more modularity, and cleaner code.
- Is built on the open-source ASP.NET Core platform that can run on multiple platforms including Windows, macOS, and Linux.

ASP.NET Core Razor Pages
- Provides the same features as ASP.NET Core MVC, but accesses those features using a model that's built on top of MVC.

Description
- Since 2002, Microsoft has developed many ASP.NET programming models. Of these programming models, ASP.NET Core MVC and ASP.NET Core Razor Pages are the newest.
- While developing the different versions of MVC and Core MVC, Microsoft used different names and version numbers.
- Information on the internet sometimes uses the old names and version numbers that were used during development, not official names and numbers of the final release.
- ASP.NET Core has been stable since version 3.1, so most of the code for newer versions of ASP.NET Core should be compatible with version 3.1.

Figure 1-5   Four ASP.NET programming models for web apps

of the final release. So, be aware of this when you search for information about ASP.NET on the internet.

Although there were breaking changes between ASP.NET and ASP.NET Core and different versions of ASP.NET Core such as between 2.0 and 3.0, ASP.NET Core has been stable since version 3.1. As a result, most of the code for newer versions of ASP.NET Core should be compatible with code for ASP.NET Core 3.1.

Some web components of .NET Framework and .NET Core

Figure 1-6 shows some web components of the older *.NET Framework*. In addition, it shows some components of the newer *.NET Core* platform, now just called *.NET*.

There are several important differences between the .NET Framework and .NET. Most importantly, .NET is open source and supports multiple operating systems including Windows, macOS, and Linux. By contrast, the .NET Framework is proprietary and only supports the Windows operating system. If you want to develop Web Forms applications, of course, you have to use the .NET Framework. But for new program development, we don't recommend that. Instead, we recommend using ASP.NET Core MVC directly or using Razor Pages. That will result in improved performance and greater flexibility in where you can deploy your app.

In this book, you'll learn how to use the MVC model to develop ASP.NET Core MVC apps. This model is older and more established than the Razor Pages model, and many websites already use it. As a result, it's a skill that's likely to remain valuable for many years to come. However, the Razor Pages model is a newer approach that some programmers prefer. So, if you're developing a new website from scratch, you may want to learn more about Razor Pages before deciding which model to use.

Before going on, you should realize that the first version of .NET, .NET 5, was released in November of 2020. This was the latest release of .NET Core after 3.1. It was named .NET 5 to distinguish it from version 4.8 of the .NET Framework. In addition, Core was dropped from its name to indicate that it will be the main platform going forward. Since then, .NET 6 has been released, and it is the current version as of this writing. Note that to distinguish .NET from the .NET Framework, we sometimes refer to .NET as .NET Core in this book.

Some components of .NET Framework and .NET Core (.NET)

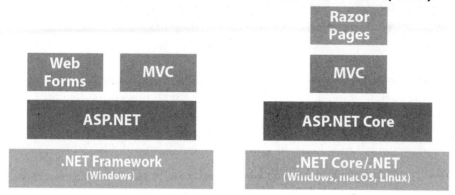

Description

- The *.NET Framework* only supports the Windows operating system.
- The *.NET Core* platform, now just called *.NET*, is open source and supports multiple operating systems including Windows, macOS, and Linux.
- ASP.NET Web Forms apps use services of the ASP.NET Framework, which uses services of the .NET Framework.
- ASP.NET MVC apps work by using services of the ASP.NET Framework.
- ASP.NET Core MVC apps work by using services of ASP.NET Core, which uses services of .NET.
- Although you can use MVC directly to develop ASP.NET Core MVC apps as shown in this book, another option is to use Razor Pages. When you use Razor Pages to develop ASP.NET Core apps, they use MVC under the hood.
- In November of 2020, Microsoft released a new version of .NET Core, called .NET 5. The previous version of .NET Core was 3.1, but version 4 was skipped so it would not be confused with .NET Framework 4.8.
- In November of 2021, Microsoft released .NET 6, which is the current version as of this writing.
- Although ASP.NET Core is based on .NET, it's name still includes "Core" to distinguish it from ASP.NET MVC.

Figure 1-6   Some web components of .NET Framework and .NET Core

An introduction to ASP.NET Core middleware

An ASP.NET Core app allows you to configure the *middleware* components that are in the HTTP request and response *pipeline*. This gives developers a lot of flexibility in how an app works.

Each middleware component can modify the HTTP request before passing it on to the next component in the pipeline. Similarly, each middleware component can modify the HTTP response before passing it to the next component in the pipeline.

The diagrams in figure 1-7 should give you an idea of how middleware works. To start, the authentication middleware authenticates the request by confirming the identity of the client making the request. To do that, it may need to edit the content of the request. Then, it passes the request on to the authorization middleware.

If the authorization middleware determines that the client is authorized to make the request, it passes the request on to the routing middleware. This middleware uses a controller to generate the content for a response by working with the model and view layers. Then, it passes the response back to the web server. Along the way, the authorization and authentication middleware can edit the content of the response.

If the authorization middleware determines that the client is not authorized to make the request, it short circuits the request by passing a response back to the web server. Along the way, the authentication middleware can edit the content of the response.

An ASP.NET Core app typically has a number of middleware components configured such as static files middleware, authorization middleware, and routing middleware. Near the end of this chapter, you'll be introduced to the code that configures the routing middleware for a simple ASP.NET Core MVC app. Most of the apps presented in this book configure this middleware. As you progress through this book, you'll learn how to configure additional middleware that's necessary to support the most important features of ASP.NET Core.

A request that makes it through all middleware in the pipeline

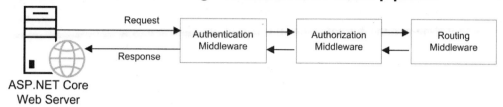

A request that's short circuited by a middleware component in the pipeline

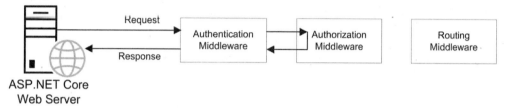

Middleware can...

- Generate the content for a response
- Edit the content of a request
- Edit the content of a response
- Short circuit a request

Description

- An ASP.NET Core app allows you to configure the *middleware* components that are in the HTTP request and response *pipeline*.

Figure 1-7   An introduction to ASP.NET Core middleware

How state works in a web app

State refers to the current status of the properties, variables, and other data maintained by an app for a single user. As an app runs, it must maintain a separate state for each user currently accessing the app.

Unlike some other protocols, HTTP is a *stateless protocol*. That means that it doesn't keep track of state between round trips. Once a browser makes a request and receives a response, the app terminates and its state is lost as shown by the diagram in figure 1-8. As a result, when the web browser makes a subsequent request, the web server has no way to associate the current request with the previous request.

ASP.NET Web Forms attempted to hide the stateless nature of a web app from developers by automatically maintaining state. This often resulted in large amounts of data being transferred with each request and response, which led to poor performance.

ASP.NET Core MVC does not attempt to hide the stateless nature of a web app from the developer. Instead, it provides features to handle state in a way that gives developers control over each HTTP request and response. When used wisely, this can lead to excellent performance.

Why state is difficult to track in a web app

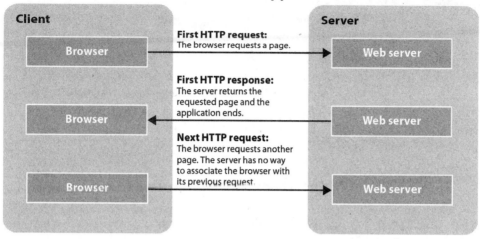

Concepts

- *State* refers to the current status of the properties, variables, and other data maintained by an app for a single user.
- HTTP is a *stateless protocol*. That means that it doesn't keep track of state between round trips. Once a browser makes a request and receives a response, the app terminates and its state is lost.

Description

- ASP.NET Web Forms attempted to hide the stateless nature of a web app from developers by automatically maintaining state. This led to poor performance.
- ASP.NET Core MVC does not attempt to hide the stateless nature of a web app from developers. Instead, it provides features to handle state in a way that gives developers control over each HTTP request and response.

Figure 1-8   How state works in a web app

Tools for working
with ASP.NET Core MVC apps

Now that you know some of the concepts behind ASP.NET Core MVC, you're ready to learn more about the tools that you can use to develop ASP.NET Core MVC apps. Some developers prefer to use an *integrated development environment* (*IDE*), which is a tool that provides all of the functionality that you need for developing an app in one place. Other developers prefer to use a code editor to enter and edit code and a command line to compile and run it. Each approach has its pros and cons. Fortunately, an excellent IDE and code editor are both available for free to ASP.NET Core developers.

An introduction to Visual Studio

Visual Studio, also known just as *VS*, is the most popular IDE for developing ASP.NET Core apps. Microsoft provides a Community Edition that's available for free and runs on Windows, as well as a free version that runs on macOS.

Figure 1-9 shows Visual Studio after it has opened an ASP.NET Core MVC app and displayed the code for one of its controllers. In addition, this figure lists some of the features provided by Visual Studio. For example, you can compile and run an app with a single keystroke.

Visual Studio is an established product that has been around for decades, and it's a great tool for learning. That's why we present it throughout this book, starting in the next chapter.

Visual Studio with an ASP.NET Core MVC app

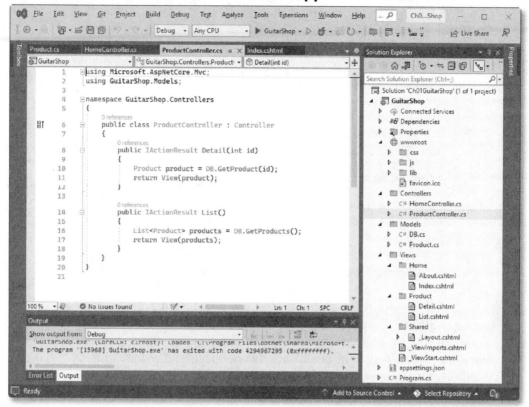

Features

- IntelliSense code completion makes it easy to enter code.
- Automatic compilation allows you to compile and run an app with a single keystroke.
- Integrated debugger makes it easy to find and fix bugs.
- Runs on Windows and macOS.

Description

- An *Integrated Development Environment* (*IDE*) is a tool that provides all of the functionality that you need for developing web apps.
- *Visual Studio*, also known as *VS*, is the most popular IDE for ASP.NET Core web development.
- Starting in the next chapter, this book shows how to use Visual Studio to develop ASP.NET Core MVC apps.

Figure 1-9   An introduction to Visual Studio

An introduction to Visual Studio Code

Visual Studio Code, also known as *VS Code,* is a *code editor* that's becoming popular with developers. Like Visual Studio, VS Code can be used to develop all types of .NET apps, including ASP.NET Core apps. Since it doesn't provide as many features as an IDE like Visual Studio, some developers find VS Code easier to use. In addition, VS Code typically starts and runs faster than Visual Studio, especially on slower computers.

Figure 1-10 shows VS Code after it has opened the same app as the previous figure. If you compare these two figures, you'll see that they look very similar. In short, both provide an Explorer window that lets you navigate through the files for an app, and both provide a code editor for editing the code for an app. The main difference is that Visual Studio provides more features than VS Code. That's either good or bad, depending on how you look at it.

This figure also lists some of the features provided by VS Code. If you compare this list of features with the list of features in the previous figure, you'll see that they're mostly the same. The main difference is that VS Code runs on Linux, and Visual Studio does not. So, even though Visual Studio provides more features, VS Code provides all of the most essential features that make it easy to develop ASP.NET Core apps.

When you use VS Code, you can use its Terminal window to use a *command line* to enter and execute the commands that build and run an app. With Windows, for example, you typically use the command line known as Windows PowerShell. In this figure, the Windows PowerShell command line is displayed across the bottom of the code editor window.

When you choose between Visual Studio and VS Code, you may want to consider that VS Code has a less restrictive license than the Community Edition of Visual Studio and adheres to a truly open-source, open-use model. As a result, you may want or need to use VS Code if licensing for commercial development becomes an issue.

As mentioned in the previous figure, this book shows how to use Visual Studio, starting in the next chapter. However, chapter 18 shows how to use VS Code. If you prefer using a code editor and command line to using a more full-featured IDE, you can use VS Code. Then, you can refer to chapter 18 whenever you need help with a task. This should make it easy to use VS Code with this book.

Visual Studio Code with an ASP.NET Core MVC app

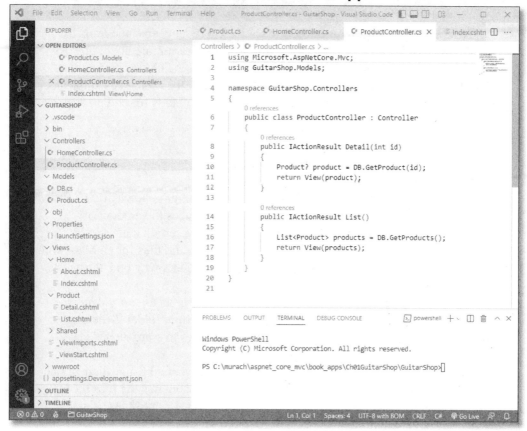

Features

- IntelliSense code completion makes it easy to enter code.
- Automatic compilation allows you to compile and run an app with a single keystroke.
- Integrated debugger makes it easy to find and fix bugs.
- Runs everywhere (Windows, macOS, and Linux).

Description

- *Visual Studio Code*, also known as *VS Code,* is a *code editor* that you can use to work with ASP.NET Core apps.
- When you use VS Code, you can use its Terminal window to use a *command line* to enter and execute the commands that build and run an app.
- VS Code has a less restrictive license than the Community Edition of Visual Studio and adheres to a truly open-source, open-use model.
- Chapter 18 shows how to use VS Code to develop ASP.NET Core apps.

Figure 1-10   An introduction to Visual Studio Code

How an ASP.NET Core MVC app works

Now that you've been introduced to some general concepts and tools for working with ASP.NET Core MVC, you're ready to learn more about how an ASP.NET Core MVC app works. To do that, the next few figures present the overall structure of an ASP.NET Core MVC app as well as some key snippets of code. Then, in the next chapter, you'll learn all of the details for coding such an app.

How coding by convention works

ASP.NET Core MVC uses a software design paradigm known as *convention over configuration*, or *coding by convention*. This reduces the amount of configuration that developers need to do if they follow certain conventions.

That's why figure 1-11 shows some of the folders and files for an MVC web app that follow the standard MVC conventions. And that's why this figure lists some of these conventions.

To start, the top-level folder for a web app is known as its *root folder*, also known as the *root directory*. In this figure, the GuitarShop folder is the root folder. Within the root folder, you typically use .cs files to store the C# classes that define controllers and models.

All controller classes should be stored in a folder named Controllers or one of its subfolders. In this figure, the Controllers folder contains the files for two classes named HomeController and ProductController. Both of these classes have a suffix of "Controller". This isn't required for controllers to work, but it's a standard convention that makes it easy for other programmers to quickly identify these classes as controller classes.

All model classes should be stored in a folder named Models or one of its subfolders. In this figure, the Models folder contains a single file for a model class named Product.

All view files should be stored in a folder named Views or one of its subfolders. In addition, the subfolders of the Views folder should correspond to the controller classes. For example, the Views/Home folder should store the view files for the HomeController class, and the Views/Product folder should store the view files for the ProductController class. These view files (.cshtml files) contain *Razor views* that define views for the app. In this figure, the views for the app are defined by view files named Home/Index.cshtml, Home/About.cshtml, Product/Detail.cshtml, and Product/List.cshtml files.

All static files such as image files, CSS files, and JavaScript files should be stored in a folder named wwwroot. The static files for an app can include CSS libraries such as Bootstrap or JavaScript libraries such as jQuery. In addition, they can include custom CSS or JavaScript files that override the code in these libraries.

Some of the folders and files for a web app

```
GuitarShop
    /Controllers
        /HomeController.cs
        /ProductController.cs
    /Models
        /Product.cs
    /Views
        /Home
            /About.cshtml
            /Index.cshtml
        /Product
            /Detail.cshtml
            /List.cshtml
    /wwwroot
        /css
            site.css
        /images
        /js
            custom.js
        /lib
            /boostrap
            /jquery
    /Program.cs
```

Some naming conventions for an ASP.NET Core MVC app

- All controller classes should be stored in a folder named Controllers or one of its subfolders.

- All model classes should be stored in a folder named Models or one of its subfolders.

- All view files should be stored in a folder named Views or one of its subfolders.

- All static files such as image files, CSS files, and JavaScript files should be stored in a folder named wwwroot or one of its subfolders.

- All controller classes should have a suffix of "Controller".

Description

- ASP.NET Core MVC uses a software design paradigm known as *convention over configuration*, or *coding by convention*. This reduces the amount of configuration that developers need to do if they follow certain conventions.

- The top-level folder for a web app is known as its *root folder* or *root directory*.

- You typically use C# classes (.cs files) to define controllers and models.

- You typically use *Razor views* (.cshtml files) to define views.

- The static files for an app can include CSS libraries such as Bootstrap or JavaScript libraries such as jQuery. In addition, they can include custom CSS or JavaScript files that override the code in these libraries.

Figure 1-11   How ASP.NET Core MVC uses coding by convention

How a controller passes a model to a view

In ASP.NET Core MVC, a *model* is a C# class that defines the data objects and business rules for the app. Figure 1-12 begins by showing the code for a model named Product. It contains three properties named ProductID, Name, and Price. This class is stored in the GuitarShop.Models namespace, and it defines a simple Product object.

In ASP.NET Core MVC, a *controller* is a C# class that typically inherits the Microsoft.AspNetCore.Mvc.Controller class. In this figure, the ProductController class inherits this class and defines two actions. In ASP.NET Core MVC, an *action* is a method of a controller that returns an *action result*. To do that, a method can use the built-in View() method to return a type of action result known as a *view result* that's created by merging the model (if there is one) into the HTML code specified in the view file.

In this figure, for example, the Detail() method is an action. It starts by using the parameter named id to get a Product object that corresponds to that id from the database. This Product object is the model for the view. Then, it passes this model to the view so the view can display its data.

Similarly, the List() method starts by getting the model, which is a List of Product objects, from the database. Then, it passes that List of Product objects to the view for display.

The code for a model class named Product

```
namespace GuitarShop.Models
{
    public class Product
    {
        public int ProductID { get; set; }
        public string Name { get; set; } = string.Empty;
        public decimal Price { get; set; }
    }
}
```

The code for a controller class named ProductController

```
using Microsoft.AspNetCore.Mvc;
using GuitarShop.Models;

namespace GuitarShop.Controllers
{
    public class ProductController : Controller
    {
        public IActionResult Detail(int id)
        {
            Product product = DB.GetProduct(id);
            return View(product);  // passes model to Product/Detail view
        }

        public IActionResult List()
        {
            List<Product> products = DB.GetProducts();
            return View(products); // passes model to Product/List view
        }
    }
}
```

Description

- A *model* is a C# class that defines the data objects and business rules for the app.
- With ASP.NET Core MVC, a *controller* is a C# class that typically inherits the Microsoft.AspNetCore.Mvc.Controller class.
- With ASP.NET Core MVC, an *action* is a method of a controller that returns an *action result*.
- An action method can use the View() method to return a type of action result known as a *view result* that's created by merging the model (if there is one) into the corresponding view file.

Figure 1-12   How a controller passes a model to a view

How a view uses Razor code, tag helpers, and Bootstrap CSS classes

Most of a typical view file consists of HTML elements. In figure 1-13, for example, the code uses an <h1> element to display a level-1 heading. It uses the <table>, <tr>, and <td> elements to display a table that has three rows and two columns. And it uses an <a> element to display a link that's formatted to look like a button.

However, a view file can also contain *Razor code* that allows you to use C# to get data from the model, format it, and display it. Razor code begins with an @ sign. In this figure, all of the Razor code is highlighted. As you can see, there are several different ways to work with Razor code.

To start, the @model directive specifies the class for the model, and the @Model property allows you to access a model object that's created from the specified class. In this figure, the @model directive at the top of the class specifies that this view uses the Product class as the model. Then, it uses the @Model property to get data from the ProductID, Name, and Price properties and insert this data into the HTML elements. In addition, it uses the ToString() method of the Price property to format the number as currency with 2 decimal places.

After the @model directive, there's an @ sign followed by braces ({ }) that identifies a block of C# statements. In this figure, the block of statements contains a single statement that uses the built-in ViewData object to set the title of the web page. However, if necessary, you could add other C# statements to this code block.

In a view, all HTML attributes that start with "asp-" are *tag helpers* that can make it easier to code HTML attributes. Tag helpers are defined by C# classes, and many are available from ASP.NET Core. As a result, you can use them to make coding HTML attributes easier. In this figure, for example, the <a> element uses the asp-controller and asp-action tag helpers to specify the controller and action method for the link. Alternately, you could code an href attribute that specified a URL to the correct controller and action. However, this isn't as flexible and easy to maintain as using the tag helpers.

In a view, it's common to use the class attribute of an HTML element to specify CSS classes from *Bootstrap*, a popular open-source CSS library that's often used with ASP.NET Core apps. In this figure, for example, the <table> element uses the class attribute to specify three CSS classes: table, table-bordered, and table-striped. That's why the table that's displayed in the browser looks so professional. Similarly, the <a> element uses the class attribute to specify two CSS classes: btn and btn-primary. That's why the link that's displayed in the browser looks like a button.

The code for a view file named Product/Detail.cshtml

```
@model Product
@{
    ViewData["Title"] = "Product Detail";
}
<h1>Product Detail</h1>
<table class="table table-bordered table-striped">
    <tr>
        <td>ID</td><td>@Model.ProductID</td>
    </tr>
    <tr>
        <td>Name</td><td>@Model.Name</td>
    </tr>
    <tr>
        <td>Price</td><td>@Model.Price.ToString("C2")</td>
    </tr>
</table>
<a asp-controller="Home" asp-action="Index"
    class="btn btn-primary">Home</a>
```

The view displayed in a browser

Description

- Most of a typical view file consists of standard HTML elements.
- The @model directive specifies the class for the model, and the @Model property allows you to access the model object that's passed to the view from the controller.
- The @ sign followed by braces ({}) identifies a block of C# statements. Within the block, you can code one or more C# statements.
- All HTML attributes that start with "asp-" are *tag helpers*. Tag helpers are defined by C# classes and make it easier to work with HTML elements. Many tag helpers are built into ASP.NET Core.
- The class attribute of an HTML element can specify CSS classes from *Bootstrap*, a popular open-source CSS library that's often used with ASP.NET Core.

Figure 1-13   How a view uses Razor code, tag helpers, and Bootstrap CSS classes

How the Program.cs file configures the middleware for an app

Figure 1-14 begins by showing the code that's generated for the Program.cs file when you create an ASP.NET Core MVC Web app. This is the code that's used for the Guitar Shop app, and it configures the middleware that's used by the app. This builds the middleware pipeline for the app. You'll learn more about this file in the next chapter, but here are some highlights.

The Program.cs file begins by creating a WebApplicationBuilder object. Then, it contains code that adds services to the app and then builds the app. For a simple ASP.NET Core MVC app like the Guitar Shop app, you only need to use the AddControllersWithViews() method to add services that support controllers, models, views, tag helpers, and so on.

Next, the Program.cs file contains the code that configures the services that have been added. In this figure, the if statement specifies the exception pages that the middleware should display if the page is run in a production environment rather than a development environment. The first statement after that indicates that the app should use a secure connection (HTTPS). The second statement specifies that the app can use the static files that are in the wwwroot directory such as the Bootstrap library. The third statement marks the position in the middleware pipeline where a routing decision is made for a URL. The fourth statement indicates that the app should use authorization middleware. And the fifth statement marks the position in the pipeline where the routing decision is executed.

This fifth statement consists of a MapControllerRoute() method that maps the controllers and their actions to a pattern for request URLs that's known as the default route. This route identifies the Home controller as the default controller and the Index() action method as the default action. As a result, if the request URL specifies the root folder (/), the app executes the Index() action method of the Home controller. However, if a request URL specifies /Product/Detail, the app executes the Detail() action method of the Product controller.

The default route also identifies a third segment of the URL that's a parameter named id, and it uses a question mark (?) to indicate that this parameter is optional. As a result, if a request URL specifies /Product/Detail/1, the app passes an id parameter of 1to the Detail() action method of the Product controller. This allows the Product controller to retrieve data about the product that has an ID of 1.

The Program.cs file

```
var builder = WebApplication.CreateBuilder(args);

// Add services to the container.
builder.Services.AddControllersWithViews();

var app = builder.Build();

// Configure the HTTP request pipeline.
if (!app.Environment.IsDevelopment())
{
    app.UseExceptionHandler("/Home/Error");
    // The default HSTS value is 30 days. You may want to change this
    // for production scenarios, see https://aka.ms/aspnetcore-hsts.
    app.UseHsts();
}

app.UseHttpsRedirection();
app.UseStaticFiles();

app.UseRouting();

app.UseAuthorization();

app.MapControllerRoute(
    name: "default",
    pattern: "{controller=Home}/{action=Index}/{id?}");

app.Run();
```

How request URLs map to controllers and actions by default

Request URL	Controller	Action
http://localhost	Home	Index
http://localhost/Home	Home	Index
http://localhost/Home/About	Home	About
http://localhost/Product/List	Product	List
http://localhost/Product/Detail	Product	Detail

Description

- The Program.cs file contains the code that configures the middleware that's used by the app. In other words, it builds the middleware pipeline for the app.
- The Program.cs file contains the code that identifies which services to use and provides additional configuration if necessary.
- By convention, the routing system identifies the Home controller as the default controller and the Index() action method as the default action.

Figure 1-14   How the Program.cs file configures the middleware for an app

Perspective

Now that you've read this chapter, you should have a general understanding of how ASP.NET Core MVC apps work and what software you need for developing these apps. With that as background, you're ready to gain valuable hands-on experience by learning how to develop an ASP.NET Core MVC app as shown in the next chapter.

Terms

web app
web application
web page
client
web browser
web server
network
URL (Uniform Resource Locator)
protocol
domain name
path
filename
intranet
internet
LAN (local area network)
WAN (wide area network)
cloud
ISP (internet service provider)
HTTP (Hypertext Transfer Protocol)
HTTPS (Hypertext Transfer Protocol Secure)
TCP/IP (Transmission Control Protocol/Internet Protocol)
HTML (Hypertext Markup Language)
static web page
HTTP request
HTTP response
dynamic web page
application server
database management system (DBMS)
database server
round trip

Kestrel
Internet Information Services (IIS)
MVC (Model-View-Controller)
pattern
model
view
controller
separation of concerns
RAD (Rapid Application Development)
.NET
.NET Framework
.NET Core
middleware
pipeline
state
stateless protocol
IDE (Integrated Development Environment)
VS (Visual Studio)
VS Code (Visual Studio Code)
code editor
command line
convention over configuration
coding by convention
root folder
root directory
Razor view
action
action result
view result
tag helper
Bootstrap

Summary

- A *web app*, also known as a *web application*, consists of a set of *web pages* that are run by clients, a web server, and a network. *Clients* often use *web browsers* to request web pages from the web server. The *web server* returns the requested pages.

- A *local area network* (*LAN*), or *intranet*, connects computers that are near each other. By contrast, the *internet* consists of many *wide area networks* (*WANs*).

- One way to access a web page is to type a *URL* (*Uniform Resource Locator*) into the address area of a browser and press Enter. A URL consists of the *protocol* (usually, HTTPS), *domain name*, *path*, and *filename*.

- To request a web page, the web browser sends an *HTTP request* to the web server. Then, the web server gets the HTML/CSS/JavaScript for the requested page and sends it back to the browser in an *HTTP response*. Last, the browser *renders* the HTML/CSS/JavaScript into a web page.

- A *static web page* is a page that is the same each time it's retrieved. By contrast, the HTML/CSS/JavaScript for a *dynamic web page* is generated by a server-side program, so its HTML/CSS/JavaScript can change from one request to another. Either way, HTML/CSS/JavaScript is returned to the browser.

- For ASP.NET Core MVC apps, the application server is ASP.NET Core, the web server is usually *Kestrel*, and the database server usually runs a *database management system* (*DBMS*) like SQL Server.

- One way to develop ASP.NET apps is to use Web Forms. This is similar to using Windows Forms and encourages *Rapid Application Development* (*RAD*). Web Forms are supported by the .NET Framework but not by .NET Core.

- Another way to develop ASP.NET apps is to use ASP.NET Core *MVC* (*Model-View-Controller*). It provides better *separation of concerns*, which leads to many benefits including making the app easier to code, test, debug, and maintain.

- The older *.NET Framework* only supports the Windows operating system. The newer *.NET Core* platform, now just called .NET, is open source and supports Windows, macOS, and Linux.

- An ASP.NET Core app allows you to configure the *middleware* components that are in the HTTP request and response *pipeline*.

- HTTP is called a *stateless protocol* because it doesn't keep track of the data (*state*) between *round trips*. However, ASP.NET Core provides features to handle state in a way that gives developers control over each HTTP request and response.

- *Visual Studio*, also known as just *VS*, is an *integrated development environment* (*IDE*) that that provides all of the functionality that you need for developing web apps.

- *Visual Studio Code*, also known as *VS Code,* is a *code editor* that you can use to develop ASP.NET Core apps.

- With ASP.NET Core MVC, you typically use *Razor views* (.cshtml files) to define the user interface and present it to the user.

- A *model* is a C# class that defines the data objects and business rules for the app.

- A *controller* is a C# class that controls the flow of data between the model and the view. A controller typically inherits the Microsoft. AspNetCore.Mvc.Controller class.

- With ASP.NET Core MVC, an *action* is a method of a controller that returns an *action result*. To do that, it's common to use the View() method to return a type of action result known as a *view result* that's typically created by merging the model into the corresponding view file.

- All HTML attributes that start with "asp-" are *tag helpers*. Tag helpers are defined by C# classes and make it easier to work with HTML elements. Many tag helpers are built into ASP.NET Core.

- The class attribute of an HTML element can specify CSS classes from *Bootstrap*, a popular open-source CSS library that's often used with ASP.NET Core.

Before you do the exercises for this book...

Before you do the exercises for this book, you should install the software that's required for this book, and you should download the source code for this book. Appendixes A (Windows) and B (macOS) show how to do that.

Exercise 1-1   Use Visual Studio to run the Guitar Shop app

In this exercise, you'll run the Guitar Shop app. This will test whether you've successfully installed the software and source code for this book.

Start Visual Studio and open the Guitar Shop app

1. Start Visual Studio.

2. From the menu system, select the File→Open→Project/Solution item. Or, if you are in the Start window for Visual Studio, you can click the "Open a project or solution" button. In the dialog box that's displayed, navigate to this folder:

    `/aspnet_core_mvc/book_apps/Ch01GuitarShop`

    Then, select the Ch01GuitarShop.sln file and click the Open button.

Run the Guitar Shop app

3. Press Ctrl+F5 to run the app. That should display the Home page for the Guitar Shop app in Visual Studio's default web browser. If you get messages about trusting and installing an SSL certificate, you can click Yes. And if a web page is displayed indicating that the connection is not private, you can click the link to proceed.

4. Click the "View Fender Stratocaster" link. This should display the Product Detail page for that product.

5. Click the Home button to return to the Home page.

6. Click the "View Products" link. This should display a list of products.

7. Click the View link for the product named Gibson Les Paul. This should display the Product Detail page for that product.

8. Close the browser tab or window for the app, and then switch back to Visual Studio.

9. In the Solution Explorer, expand the Controllers, Models, and Views folders and review some of the code.

Close the Guitar Shop app and exit Visual Studio

10. Use the File→Close Solution command to close the solution.

11. Exit Visual Studio.

Exercise 1-2   Use Visual Studio Code to run the Guitar Shop app (optional)

This exercise is optional. However, if you want to use Visual Studio Code instead of Visual Studio, or if you just want to see how VS Code compares to VS, you can use this exercise to take VS Code for a test drive. But first, you should install and configure VS Code as described in chapter 18.

Start VS Code and open the Guitar Shop app

1. Start VS Code.

2. From the menus, select the File→Open Folder item. In the dialog box that's displayed, navigate to this folder:

   `/aspnet_core_mvc/book_apps/Ch01GuitarShop/GuitarShop`

   Then, click the Select Folder button.

   If the "Do you trust the authors of the files in this folder" dialog is displayed, select Yes. This should open the GuitarShop project that's in this folder.

3. If you get any error messages, click on the appropriate buttons to fix them. VS Code should be able to do this for you.

Run the Guitar Shop app

4. Press Ctrl+F5 to run the app. That should display the Home page for the Guitar Shop app in your default web browser.

5. Click the "View Fender Stratocaster" link. This should display the Product Detail page for that product.

6. Click the Home button to return to the Home page.

7. Click the "View Products" link. This should display a list of products.

8. Click the View link for the product named Gibson Les Paul. This should display the Product Detail page for that product.

9. Close the browser tab or window for the app, and then switch back to VS Code.

10. In the Explorer window, expand the Controllers, Models, and Views folders and review some of the code.

Close the Guitar Shop app and exit VS Code

11. Select the File→Close Folder item to close the folder. This should close the Guitar Shop project that's in this folder.

12. Exit VS Code.

2

How to develop a
one-page MVC web app

In the last chapter, you were introduced to the basic concepts of web
programming and ASP.NET Core MVC. Now, this chapter shows you how to
develop a one-page ASP.NET Core MVC web app that calculates the future
value of a series of investments. To do that, this chapter shows how to use
Visual Studio because it's the most established tool for working with .NET
apps. However, if you prefer to use Visual Studio Code instead, you can refer to
chapter 18 to learn how to work with Visual Studio Code.

How to create a Core MVC web app

This chapter starts by showing how to create a new ASP.NET Core MVC web app. This includes all the skills you need to set up the folders and files for a simple MVC app that uses a controller to pass some data to a view that displays the data on a web page.

How to start a new web app

To create a web app, you start by creating a new project as shown in figure 2-1. When creating a new project, Visual Studio provides several *templates* that you can use. These templates are displayed by the dialog shown in this figure.

In general, we recommend using the ASP.NET Core Web App (Model-View-Controller) template because it makes it easy to start an MVC web app. However, if you want to manually build your web app from scratch, you can use the ASP.NET Core Empty template. Either template should work fine for the Future Value app presented in this chapter.

The template you choose determines the folders and files that Visual Studio adds to the project when it creates your web app. In this book, you'll learn how to use the two templates summarized in this figure.

The Web App MVC template sets up the starting folders and files for an ASP.NET Core MVC web app, including a configuration file that configures the default routing for the app. When you use this template, you typically start by deleting files and code that you don't need. Then, as you develop the app, you add the files and code you do need.

The Empty template provides two starting files for an ASP.NET Core app. When you use this template, you must manually add the folders and files for an MVC web app and configure the middleware for the request pipeline. Although we recommend using the MVC template for this chapter, you can also use the Empty template if you prefer to add the folders and files you need instead of deleting the ones that you don't need.

Although you won't learn how to use any of the other templates in this book, you might want to experiment with them. For example, the ASP.NET Core API template sets up the starting folders and files for a RESTful web service. Also, the ASP.NET Core Web App template sets up an ASP.NET Core app that uses Razor Pages.

The dialog that displays the project templates

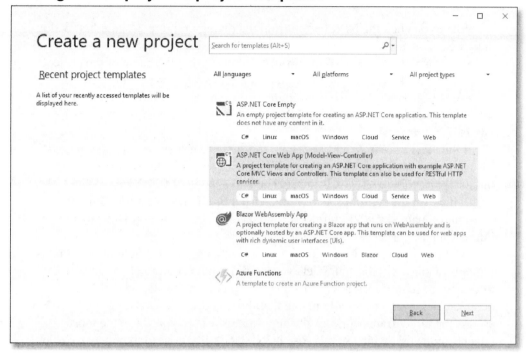

The templates presented in this book

Template	Contains...
Web App MVC	Starting folders and files for an ASP.NET Core MVC web app.
Empty	Two starting files for an ASP.NET Core app.

How to create a new project

- Select File→New→Project from the menu system, select the template you want to use, and then click the Next button.

Description

- When creating an ASP.NET Core web app, Visual Studio provides several *templates* that you can use.

- For this chapter, we recommend using the ASP.NET Core Web App (Model-View-Controller) template, also known as the MVC template, because it makes it easy to start an ASP.NET Core MVC web app.

- If you want to manually build your web app from scratch, you can use the ASP.NET Core Empty template.

Figure 2-1   How to start a new web app

How to configure a web app

When you click the Next button from the dialog in figure 2-1, the first dialog in figure 2-2 is displayed. Then, you can use the dialog to specify the name of the project and the location of the project. In this figure, the name of the project is FutureValue. To specify the location of the project, you typically click the Browse button to select a different folder or use the Location drop-down list to select a location you've used recently. In this figure, the folder is C:\murach\ aspnet_core_mvc.

If the "Place solution and project in the same directory" box is unchecked, Visual Studio creates a folder for the solution and a subfolder for the project. In this figure, this check box is unchecked and a name of Ch02FutureValue is specified for the solution. As a result, Visual Studio creates a folder for the solution named Ch02FutureValue and a subfolder for the project named FutureValue.

When you click the Next button from this dialog, the second dialog in this figure is displayed. This dialog lets you provide some additional configuration information. In most cases, you'll leave the options in this dialog at their defaults. However, you should notice that the first drop-down list lets you choose the target framework for the app. In most cases, you'll use the most recent framework, which in this case is .NET 6.0. If you need to target an earlier framework, you select it from the drop-down list. You may want to do that, for example, if you add a project to a solution that uses an earlier framework.

The dialog for configuring a new web app

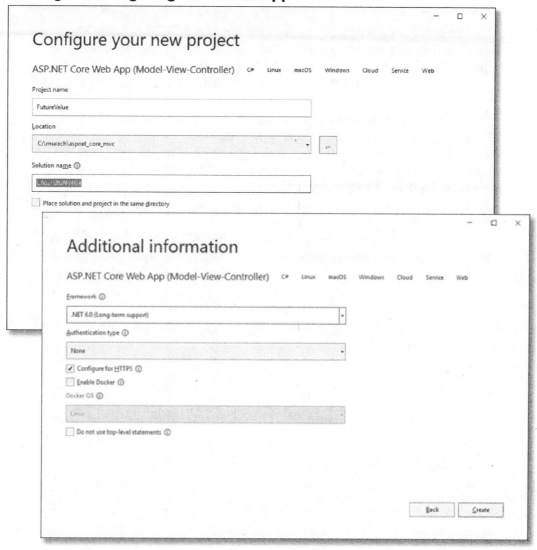

How to configure a new ASP.NET Core MVC web app

1. Enter a project name.
2. Specify the location (folder). To do that, you can click the Browse [...] button.
3. Edit the solution name if necessary, and then click the Next button.
4. Use the resulting dialog to provide any additional information for the web app and click Create.

Description

*   If the "Place solution and project in the same directory" box is unchecked, Visual Studio creates a folder for the solution and a subfolder for the project. Otherwise, these files are stored in the same folder.

Figure 2-2   How to configure a new web app

How to set up the MVC folders

The procedures in figure 2-3 show how to set up the folders for an MVC web app. The procedure you use depends on whether you started the web app from the Web App MVC template or the Empty template.

If you started from the Web App MVC template, you can delete all files from the folders named Models, Views, and Controllers. In addition, you can delete all files from the Home and Shared subfolders of the Views folder. This is an excellent approach when you're getting started.

Alternately, you can leave these files and edit them as described later in this chapter. However, this approach leaves extra files and code that can lead to errors, and it doesn't give you practice adding the files described in this chapter. As a result, it's better to use this approach later, after you've learned more about developing MVC web apps.

If you started from the Empty template, you need to add the folders named Models, Views, and Controllers. Then, you need to add the Home and Shared subfolders of the Views folder.

Visual Studio after the folders have been set up for an MVC web app

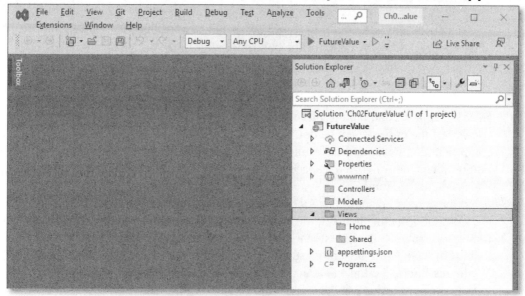

How to delete unnecessary files from the MVC template

1. Expand the Controllers folder and delete all files in that folder.
2. Expand the Models folder and delete all files in that folder.
3. Expand the Views folder and its subfolders and delete all files in those folders, but don't delete the folders.

How to add folders to the Empty template

1. Add the Controllers, Models, and Views folders.
2. Within the Views folder, add the Home and Shared folders.

Description

- To add a folder, you can right-click a node and select Add→New Folder.
- To delete a folder or file, you can right-click the folder or file and select Delete.

Figure 2-3   How to set up the MVC folders

How to add a controller

The procedure in figure 2-4 shows how to add a controller file to a web app. In addition, it shows the code for the controller after it has been edited so it's a good starting point for the Future Value app presented in this chapter.

A *controller* is a C# class that inherits from the Controller class that's available from the Microsoft.AspNetCore.Mvc namespace. When you develop an MVC app, it's common to place controller classes in a namespace that consists of the project name, a dot, and the name of the folder that stores the controllers. In this figure, for example, the HomeController class is stored in the FutureValue.Controllers namespace. If you follow the procedure in this figure, this is where the HomeController class is placed by default.

If a method of a controller runs in response to HTTP action verbs such as GET or POST, the method is known as an *action method*, or an *action*. In this figure, for example, the Index() method is an action because it runs in response to an HTTP GET or POST request. You'll learn more about how this works later.

In this figure, the Index() action begins by setting two properties of the ViewBag property that's automatically available to controllers and views. To do that, the first statement sets the Name property of the ViewBag to a string value of "Mary". Then, the second statement sets the FV property to a decimal value of 99999.99. This works because the ViewBag property uses dynamic properties to get and set values. As a result, you can dynamically create a property by specifying any property name that you want.

After the Index() action has stored some data in the ViewBag, it uses the View() method to return a ViewResult object for the view associated with the action method. For the Index() action of the Home controller, this returns a ViewResult object for the view in the Views/Home/Index.cshtml file like the one shown in the next figure. This works because a ViewResult object is a type of IActionResult object. As a result, the Index() method can return a ViewResult object.

Because specifying the IActionResult interface as the return type for an action method allows you to return any type of action result, it provides a flexible way to code an action method. Then, if you later decide to return a different type of action result, you can do that. However, if you know that you are definitely going to return a ViewResult object, you can change the return type of the method to ViewResult. Some programmers think this makes your code easier to read.

The dialogs for adding a controller

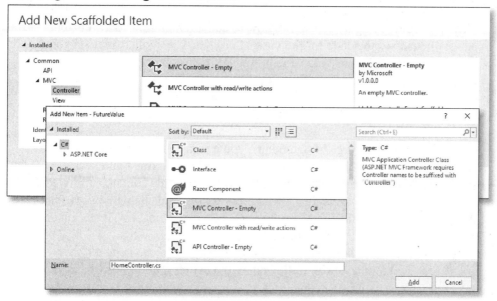

How to add a file for a controller

1. Right-click the Controllers folder and select Add→Controller.

2. In the Add New Scaffolded Item dialog, select "MVC Controller – Empty" and click Add.

3. In the Add New Item dialog, name the controller and click Add.

The HomeController.cs file

```
using Microsoft.AspNetCore.Mvc;

namespace FutureValue.Controllers
{
    public class HomeController : Controller
    {
        public IActionResult Index()
        {
            ViewBag.Name = "Mary";
            ViewBag.FV = 99999.99;
            return View();
        }
    }
}
```

Description

- A method of a *controller* that runs in response to HTTP action verbs such as GET or POST is known as an *action method*, or an *action*.

- The ViewBag property is automatically available to controllers and views. It uses dynamic properties to get and set values.

- The View() method returns a ViewResult object for the view associated with an action method.

Figure 2-4   How to add a controller

How to add a Razor view

The procedure in figure 2-5 shows how to add a Razor view to a web app. In addition, it shows the code for the view after it has been edited so it's a good starting point for the Future Value app presented in this chapter.

A *Razor view* contains both C# and HTML code. That's why its file extension is .cshtml. In ASP.NET Core MVC, the *Razor view engine* uses server-side code to embed C# code within the HTML. Razor code is preceded by the @ sign.

To execute one or more C# statements, you can declare a *Razor code block* by coding the @ sign followed by a pair of braces ({ }). In this figure, for example, the Index.cshtml file begins with a code block that contains a single C# statement. This statement sets the Layout property that's available to all views to null. This indicates that the view doesn't have a Razor layout. You'll learn more about Razor layouts later in this chapter.

To evaluate a C# expression and display its result, you can code a *Razor expression* by coding the @ sign followed by the expression. In this figure, for example, the view uses Razor expressions to access the ViewBag property that's available to all views and display the two properties that were set by the controller in the previous figure. Here, the first expression just displays the Name property. However, the second expression gets the FV property and calls the ToString() method to convert the decimal value to a string that uses the currency format with 2 decimal places. To do that, this code supplies a format specifier of "C2".

Besides the Razor code, the rest of the code for this view consists of simple HTML elements. As a result, if you have some experience with HTML, you shouldn't have any trouble understanding this page. If you don't understand the HTML on this page, you need to learn basic HTML skills like the ones presented in the first eight chapters of *Murach's HTML and CSS*.

The dialogs for adding a Razor view

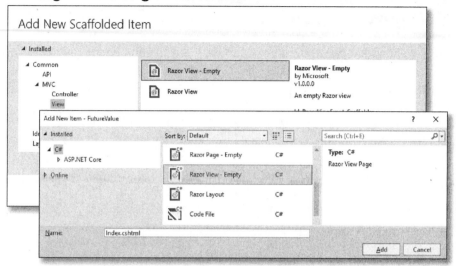

How to add a view to the Views/Home folder

1. In the Solution Explorer, right-click the Views/Home folder and select Add→View.

2. In the Add New Scaffolded Item dialog, select Razor View – Empty and click Add.

3. In Add New Item dialog, name the view Index and click Add.

The Home/Index.cshtml view

```
@{
    Layout = null;
}
<!DOCTYPE html>
<html>
<head>
    <meta name="viewport" content="width=device-width" />
    <title>Home Page</title>
</head>
<body>
    <h1>Future Value Calculator</h1>
    <p>Customer Name: @ViewBag.Name</p>
    <p>Future Value: @ViewBag.FV.ToString("C2")</p>
</body>
</html>
```

Description

*   A *Razor view* contains both C# code and HTML. That's why its file extension is .cshtml.

*   In ASP.NET Core MVC, the *Razor view engine* uses server-side code to embed C# code within HTML elements.

*   To execute one or more C# statements, you can declare a *Razor code block* by coding the @ sign followed by a pair of braces ({ }).

*   To evaluate a C# expression and display its result, you can code a *Razor expression* by coding the @ sign followed by the expression.

Figure 2-5   How to add a Razor view

How to configure the middleware for an HTTP request pipeline

Figure 2-6 shows how to configure a simple MVC web app like the Future Value app presented in this chapter. To do that, you can edit the Program.cs file so it configures the middleware for the HTTP request pipeline correctly. If you're starting from the MVC template, you can usually just accept the default configuration that it generates, which is shown in this figure. Or, if you're starting from the Empty template, you can add the statements shown in this figure.

The code for the Program.cs file that's generated by the MVC template starts by creating a WebApplicationBuilder object named builder. Then, it calls the AddControllersWithViews() method of the builder object's Services property. This enables the services required by the controllers and Razor views of an MVC app. As you move through this book, you'll use the Services property of the builder object to add other services as well.

Once the services that the application needs are added, the code calls the Build() method of the builder object and assigns the WebApplication object it returns to a variable named app. Then, it uses this object to configure the pipeline.

To start, the code checks whether the web hosting environment is a development environment. If it isn't, the middleware handles exceptions by displaying a page that the developer customizes for end users. That's typically what you want for a production environment. In addition, this code calls the UseHsts() method to configure the middleware to send HTTP Strict Transport Security (HSTS) headers to clients, which is a recommended practice for production apps.

Otherwise, the middleware handles exceptions by displaying a web page that's designed for developers, not end users. That's typically what you want when you're in a development environment as described throughout this book.

Next are several statements that configure the middleware components that are common to development and production environments. Of these statements, it's important to note that the MapControllerRoute() method sets the default controller for the app to the Home controller, and it sets the default action to the Index() action. As a result, when the app starts, it calls the Index() action method of the Home controller. This displays the Index view, which is usually what you want.

The Program.cs file that's generated by the MVC template

```
var builder = WebApplication.CreateBuilder(args);

// Add services to the container.
builder.Services.AddControllersWithViews();

var app = builder.Build();

// Configure the HTTP request pipeline.
if (!app.Environment.IsDevelopment())
{
    app.UseExceptionHandler("/Home/Error");
    // The default HSTS value is 30 days. You may want to change this
    // for production scenarios, see https://aka.ms/aspnetcore-hsts.
    app.UseHsts();
}

app.UseHttpsRedirection();
app.UseStaticFiles();

app.UseRouting();

app.UseAuthorization();

app.MapControllerRoute(
    name: "default",
    pattern: "{controller=Home}/{action=Index}/{id?}");

app.Run();
```

Description

- The Program.cs file contains code that configures the middleware for the HTTP request pipeline and then starts the program.
- The code generated by default by the MVC template begins by checking whether the web hosting environment is a development environment. If it isn't, it configures the middleware for a production environment.
- The MapControllerRoute() method in this figure sets the default controller for the app to the Home controller, and it sets the default action to the Index() action. As a result, when the app starts, it calls the Index() action method of the Home controller.

Figure 2-6   How to configure the middleware for an HTTP request pipeline

How to run a web app and fix errors

After you write the C# and HTML code shown in the previous figures, you need to test it to be sure it works properly. Then, if you encounter any errors, you need to fix them and test the app again. For now, you can do that with the basic skills presented in the next two figures. Later, in chapter 5, you'll learn more skills for testing and debugging.

How to run a web app

To run a web app, you can use one of the techniques presented in figure 2-7. For example, you can press Ctrl+F5 to run the web app without the debugger. Then, you can stop the app by clicking the close button in the browser's upper right corner.

However, you can also run the web app with the debugger by pressing F5. When you do that, you can use Visual Studio's debugger as described in chapter 5. Then, you can stop the app by clicking the Stop Debugging button in the Debug toolbar.

When you run an app, you need to decide whether to run it on the older Windows-only IIS Express server or the newer cross-platform Kestrel server. Since the Kestrel server runs faster than the IIS Express server, it's excellent for getting started with ASP.NET Core development. As a result, we recommend that you use it with this book.

If you view the drop-down list to the right of the Start button, you'll see that the project name is selected by default. This indicates that the project will use the Kestrel server. If you want to use IIS Express instead, you'll need to select the IIS Express item.

If you run the app with Kestrel, Visual Studio starts the server and uses a console window to display information about the status of each HTTP request. To stop the server, you can close this window.

In addition to testing whether a web app runs correctly, you should also check whether it displays correctly in different browsers. Visual Studio makes it easy to change the default browser for this purpose by providing a drop-down browser list. After you use that list to change the default browser, you can run the web app again to test it in that browser.

Before Visual Studio runs an app, it builds the project by compiling the necessary code. Then, if the code compiles without errors, Visual Studio runs the app and displays the starting page in your default browser. At that point, you can test the app to make sure that it works correctly. For now, the app is working correctly if it displays a web page that looks like the one shown in this figure that displays a customer name of "Mary" and a future value of $99,999.99.

The first time you run a web app, you may get a series of dialogs that display security warnings that indicate that you are about to install two SSL certificates. The IIS Express certificate is used by Visual Studio's Hot Reload feature to create a secure connection to the browser. As you'll learn in chapter 5, this is a

The Start button drop-down list in Visual Studio

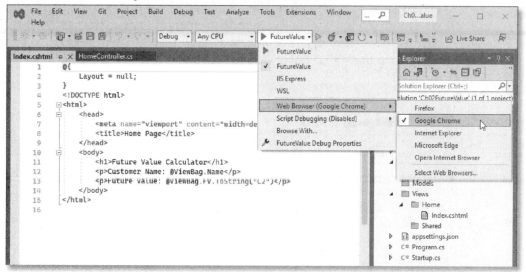

The Future Value app in the Chrome browser

Description

- To run an app in the default browser, press Ctrl+F5. This starts the app without debugging.
- To stop an app, click the close button in the browser's upper right corner.
- To change the default browser for the app, display the drop-down list for the Start button, select the Web Browser item, and select the default web browser from the list.
- By default, Visual Studio uses the Kestrel web server, which is usually what you want. To change the web server to the IIS Express server, display the drop-down list for the Start button and select IIS Express.
- When Visual Studio runs the app on the Kestrel server, it uses a console window to display information about the server. To stop the server, you can close the command line window.
- If you press F5 or click the Start button in the toolbar, Visual Studio starts the app with debugging. This is another way to run an app that's especially useful if you need to debug an app as described in chapter 5. Then, to stop the app, you can click the Stop Debugging button in the Debug toolbar.

Figure 2-7   How to run a web app

time-saving feature that you'll want to use while testing your projects. Because of that, you'll want to be sure to install this certificate.

ASP.NET Core needs the second certificate to configure a development environment, so you can install this certificate as well. Then, if a web page is displayed indicating that it may not be safe to proceed, you can click the link or button to proceed.

How to find and fix errors

If any errors are detected as part of the compilation, Visual Studio opens the Error List window and displays the errors as shown in figure 2-8. These errors can consist of *syntax errors* that have to be corrected before the app can be compiled, as well as warning messages. In this figure, just one error message and no warning messages are displayed.

To fix an error, you can double-click it in the Error List window. This moves the cursor into the code editor and to the line of code that caused the error. By moving from the Error List window to the code editor for all of the messages, you should be able to find the coding problems and fix them. In this figure, the error message accurately indicates that the name ViewBags doesn't exist. That's because the name of the property that's available to controllers and views is ViewBag, not ViewBags.

Keep in mind, though, that the error message might not be accurate, and its link might not jump to the line of code that's causing the problem. For example, it's common to need to fix a related statement such as a statement that declares a variable. Still, the error message and the line of code that it links to should help you find the statement that's causing the problem.

After you fix all of the syntax errors and run the app, you may still encounter an *exception*. That happens when ASP.NET Core can't execute one of the compiled C# statements correctly at runtime. Then, if you're running the app without debugging, ASP.NET Core MVC displays a description of the exception in the web browser. At that point, you can stop the app. Then, you can fix the problem and test again.

Alternately, if you're running the app with debugging, ASP.NET Core MVC switches to the code editor and highlights the statement that caused the exception. At that point, you can stop the app by clicking on the Stop Debugging button in the Debug toolbar. Then, you can fix the problem and test again.

Visual Studio with the Error List window displayed

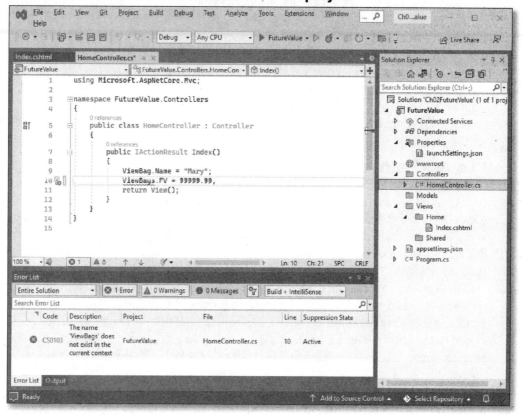

Description

- If a *syntax error* is detected as you enter code or when you attempt to build and run an app, a dialog asks whether you want to continue by running the last successful build. If you click No, the app isn't run and an Error List window is displayed.

- The Error List window provides information about the errors in your app.

- To go to the statement that caused a syntax error, double-click the error in the Error List window. This should help you find the cause of the error.

- If a compiled statement can't be executed when you run a web app, an *exception* occurs. Then, you can use the information that's displayed in the browser to attempt to fix this exception, or you can debug the exception as described in chapter 5.

Figure 2-8   How to find and fix errors

How to work with a model

Once you're sure that the controller and view are working correctly, you're ready to add a model to your app. Then, you can modify the controller and view to work with this model. When you're done, the app should get data from the user, pass that data to the model, use the model to perform a calculation, and display the result of the calculation. Along the way, you'll learn a lot about how an ASP.NET Core MVC app works.

How to add a model

A *model* is a regular C# class that defines the data objects for a page and is typically stored in the Models folder. As a result, to add a model to your app, you just need to add a C# class to the Models folder as shown in figure 2-9. In this figure, the model class has a name of FutureValueModel. Here, the "Model" suffix is optional.

To keep the name of the model short, some programmers would prefer to drop the "Model" suffix and give the model a name of FutureValue. However, a model can't have the same name as a namespace, and this particular model is stored in the FutureValue namespace. As a result, this class uses the "Model" suffix to create a name for the model that doesn't conflict with the name of the namespace.

The model shown in this figure is a standard C# class. It provides three properties that can be used to get and set the monthly investment, yearly interest rate, and number of years for a future value. In addition, it provides a method named CalculateFutureValue() that calculates and returns the future value for the specified properties. To do that, this method converts the yearly values to monthly values and uses a loop to calculate the future value.

The dialog for adding a class

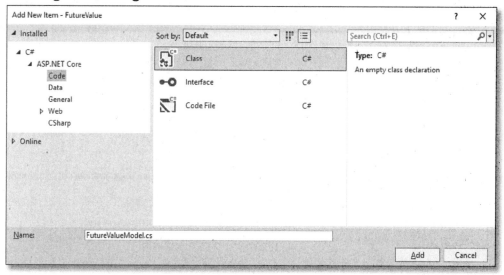

How to add a file for a model class

1. In the Solution Explorer, right-click the Models folder and select Add→Class.
2. In the resulting dialog, enter the name of the class, and click the Add button.

The FutureValueModel class with three properties and a method

```
namespace FutureValue.Models
{
    public class FutureValueModel
    {
        public decimal MonthlyInvestment { get; set; }
        public decimal YearlyInterestRate { get; set; }
        public int Years { get; set; }

        public decimal CalculateFutureValue()
        {
            int months = Years * 12;
            decimal monthlyInterestRate = YearlyInterestRate / 12 / 100;
            decimal futureValue = 0;
            for (int i = 0; i < months; i++)
            {
                futureValue = (futureValue + MonthlyInvestment) *
                              (1 + monthlyInterestRate);
            }
            return futureValue;
        }
    }
}
```

Description

- A *model* is a regular C# class that models the data for the app. The class for a model is typically stored in the Models folder.
- A model can't have the same name as the namespace.

Figure 2-9   How to add a model

How to add a Razor view imports page

A *Razor view imports page* makes it easier to work with models and tag helpers. As a result, most web apps include this page.

The procedure in figure 2-10 shows how to add a Razor view imports page to your web app. This adds a file named _ViewImports.cshtml to your app that contains Razor directives that are applied to all views in your app.

To give you an idea of how a Razor view imports page works, this figure shows the code for the Razor view imports page of the Future Value app. Here, the first line imports the namespace for your model classes. That way, you can use classes from that namespace in your views using code like this:

```
@model FutureValueModel
```

The next figure shows how that works.

If you don't import the namespace for a model class, you can still use the model in your views. However, you'll need to fully qualify its name like this:

```
@model FutureValue.Models.FutureValueModel
```

As a result, you typically want to include a Razor view imports page that imports the model.

The second line of the Razor view imports page enables all tag helpers that are available from the ASP.NET Core framework. That way, you can use these tag helpers in your views. If you don't enable the tag helpers, you can still use them in your views. However, you need to add a @addTagHelper directive to the top of each view that uses tag helpers. As a result, it typically makes sense to include this directive in a Razor view imports page. That way, you don't have to specify this directive for each view.

The dialog for adding a Razor view imports page

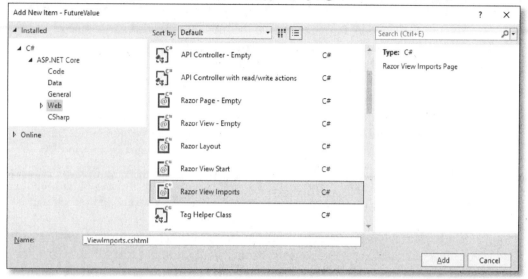

How to add a Razor view imports page

1. In the Solution Explorer, right-click the Views folder and select Add→New Item.
2. In the resulting dialog, select the Installed→ASP.NET Core→Web category, select the Razor View Imports item, and click the Add button.

The Views/_ViewImports.cshtml file for the Future Value app

```
@using FutureValue.Models
@addTagHelper *, Microsoft.AspNetCore.Mvc.TagHelpers
```

A Razor view imports page makes it easier to work with...

*   Model classes.
*   Tag helpers.

Description

*   Most apps include a *Razor view imports page* that makes it easier to work with your model classes and the tag helpers that are available from ASP.NET Core.

Figure 2-10   How to add a Razor view imports page

How to code a strongly-typed view

You use the @model directive to *bind* the model to the view. This kind of view is called a *strongly-typed view*. In figure 2-11, for example, the @model directive at the top of the view binds the view to the model class named FutureValueModel.

After binding the model to the view, this view uses the asp-for *tag helper* to *bind* HTML elements to the corresponding properties of the object. In particular, this tag helper binds the MonthlyInvestment, YearlyInterestRate, and Years properties to corresponding <label> and <input> elements in the view. As a result, when the user enters values into the <input> elements and clicks the Calculate button, ASP.NET Core MVC automatically updates the model with the values entered by the user. Then, the controller can access those values as shown in the next figure.

The asp-for tag helper automatically generates attributes for these HTML elements. For example, it generates the name and id attributes that MVC needs to be able to access these HTML elements. It also generates a type attribute that indicates the type of field to display.

The asp-action tag helper generates an action attribute for the <form> element. Instead of using this tag helper, you could just specify an action attribute that refers to the root directory like this:

```
<form action="/" method="post">
```

This maps to the Index action of the Home controller. However, using the asp-action tag helper makes your code more flexible and easier to maintain.

In this figure, the form only uses the asp-action tag helper to specify the action. As a result, MVC uses the Index() action method of the current controller, which is the Home controller. However, if you want to call an action from another controller, you can use the asp-controller tag helper to specify the name of that controller. As you progress through this book, you'll see plenty of examples of that.

The code in this figure uses the asp-for tag helper to access the properties of the model object. Since this tag helper is designed to bind a model object to HTML elements, you can access the properties of the model object just by specifying their names.

However, if you want to access a property of the model object outside of an asp-for tag helper, you must start by coding the @Model property (not the @model directive) to access the model object. Then, you access any property or method from that object. For example, you can use the @Model property to access the MonthlyInvestment property of the FutureValueModel model object like this:

```
<div>@Model.MonthlyInvestment</div>
```

Before you go on to the next figure, note that this view includes a <style> element within its <head> element. To save space, this <style> element just contains a comment that indicates that it includes all of the same CSS styles shown in figure 2-14. These styles apply some basic formatting to the <body>, <h1>, <label>, and <div> elements so this page appears as shown later in this chapter.

Common tag helpers for forms

Tag helper	HTML tags	Description
asp-for	`<label> <input>`	Binds the HTML element to the specified model property.
asp-action	`<form> <a>`	Specifies the action for the URL. If no controller is specified, MVC uses the current controller.
asp-controller	`<form> <a>`	Specifies the controller for the URL.

A strongly-typed Index view with tag helpers

```
@model FutureValueModel
@{
    Layout = null;
}
<!DOCTYPE html>
<html>
<head>
    <meta name="viewport" content="width=device-width, initial-scale=1.0" />
    <title>Future Value Calculator</title>
    <style>
        /* all of the CSS styles from figure 2-14 go here */
    </style>
</head>
<body>
    <h1>Future Value Calculator</h1>
    <form asp-action="Index" method="post">
        <div>
            <label asp-for="MonthlyInvestment">Monthly Investment:</label>
            <input asp-for="MonthlyInvestment" />
        </div>
        <div>
            <label asp-for="YearlyInterestRate">Yearly Interest Rate:</label>
            <input asp-for="YearlyInterestRate" />
        </div>
        <div>
            <label asp-for="Years">Number of Years:</label>
            <input asp-for="Years" />
        </div>
        <div>
            <label>Future Value:</label>
            <input value="@ViewBag.FV.ToString("C2")" readonly>
        </div>
        <button type="submit">Calculate</button>
        <a asp-action="Index">Clear</a>
    </form>
</body>
</html>
```

Description

- You use the @model directive to *bind* the model to the view. This kind of view is called a *strongly-typed* view.

- ASP.NET Core MVC *tag helpers* are used to automatically generate *attributes* for some HTML elements. They are also used to *bind* HTML elements to the properties of the object that's the *model* for the view.

Figure 2-11   How to code a strongly-typed view

How to handle GET and POST requests

Figure 2-12 begins by showing how to use the HttpGet and HttpPost attributes to create one Index() method that handles an HTTP GET request and another Index() method that handles an HTTP POST request. This is a common pattern in web development.

For example, it's common for a GET request to display a blank input form to the user. That happens by default when an ASP.NET Core MVC app starts, and it happens when a link like the Clear link on the Future Value form is clicked. Then, when the user clicks the submit button, the app sends a POST request to the same URL to process the data entered by the user. If you look back at figure 2-11, you'll see that the method attribute of the <form> element determines the type of request that's sent. In this case, it's a POST request.

In MVC, you can use overloaded action methods to handle both GET and POST requests for a page. In this figure, for example, the first Index() method doesn't accept any arguments. However, the second Index() method accepts a FutureValueModel object as an argument. Since each Index() method has a unique signature, you can use HTTP attributes to specify the HTTP verb for each method. When you use an attribute like this to provide information about a method, it is often referred to as *decorating* the method.

If you don't provide a unique signature for each version of the action method, you'll get a compiler error. For example, what if both versions of the action method need to specify the model as a parameter? In that case, you can solve the issue by specifying a dummy parameter like this:

```
public IActionResult Index(FutureValueModel model,
    string dummy)
```

Here, the second argument isn't used by the Index() method. However, it provides a unique signature for the method.

When an action method accepts a model object as an argument, MVC uses the data stored in the GET or POST request to set the properties of the model object. In this figure, for example, MVC automatically sets the properties of the model object that's passed to the POST version of the Index() method.

As a result, the action method can use the model object to work with the posted data. In this figure, the code just calls the CalculateFutureValue() method from the model to get the result of the future value calculation. However, this shows that the other three properties of the model were set automatically, which is what you want.

In addition, the POST version of the Index() method can use the View() method to pass the model on to the view. In this figure, that's what the second statement does. That way, the strongly-typed view in the previous figure can display the correct values for the properties of the model.

Two attributes that indicate the HTTP verb an action method handles

Attribute	Description
HttpGet	Specifies that the action method handles a GET request.
HttpPost	Specifies that the action method handles a POST request.

Two methods you can use to return a view from a controller

Method	Description
View()	Returns the view that corresponds to the current controller and action.
View(model)	Passes the specified model to the view that corresponds to the current controller and action so the view can bind to the model.

An overloaded Index() action method that handles GET and POST requests

```
using Microsoft.AspNetCore.Mvc;
using FutureValue.Models;

public class HomeController : Controller
{
    [HttpGet]
    public IActionResult Index()
    {
        ViewBag.FV = 0;
        return View();
    }

    [HttpPost]
    public IActionResult Index(FutureValueModel model)
    {
        ViewBag.FV = model.CalculateFutureValue();
        return View(model);
    }
}
```

Description

- A common pattern in web development is for the same URL to handle HTTP GET and POST requests. In particular, it's common to use a GET request for a URL to display a blank input form to the user. Then, a POST request for the same URL can process the data that's submitted when the user fills out the form and submits it.

- In MVC, you can use overloaded action methods to handle both GET and POST requests for a page. When you do, you use HTTP attributes to indicate which action method handles which request.

- When an action method accepts a model object as an argument, MVC uses the data stored in the GET or POST request to set the properties of the model object. Then, the action method can use the model object to work with the posted data, and it can use the View() method to pass the model on to the view.

Figure 2-12   How to handle GET and POST requests

The Future Value app after handling GET and POST requests

Figure 2-13 shows the Future Value app that has been presented so far in this chapter after it has handled GET and POST requests.

When this app starts, it sends a GET request to the Index() action of the Home controller. As a result, the app displays a screen like the first one shown in this figure. This page doesn't contain values for the first three fields, and it displays a value of $0.00 for the fourth field, which is a read-only field.

When the user enters data in the form and clicks the Calculate button, the app sends a POST request to the Index() action of the Home controller. As a result, the app calculates the future value and displays it in the fourth text field as shown by the second screen in this figure.

At this point, the user can edit the values and click the Calculate button again to calculate and display a different future value. Or, the user can click the Clear link. Then, the app sends a GET request to the Index() action of the Home controller. Since this GET request doesn't include a model, it clears the form as shown by the first screen.

The Future Value app after a GET request

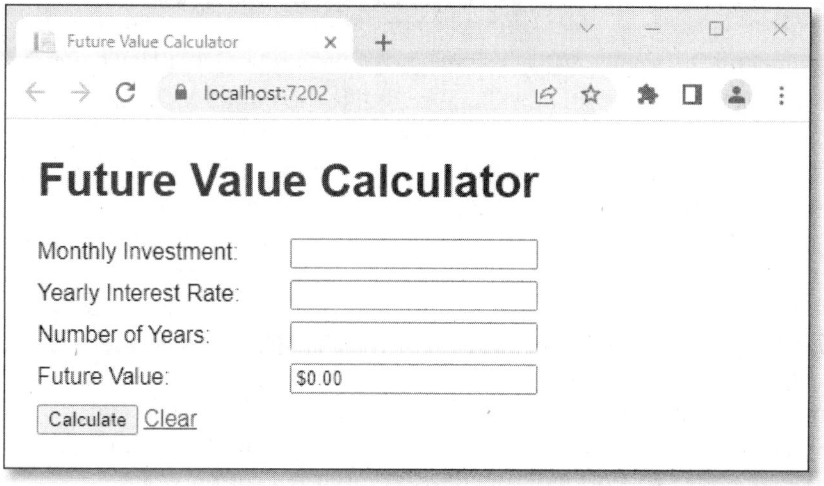

The Future Value app after a POST request

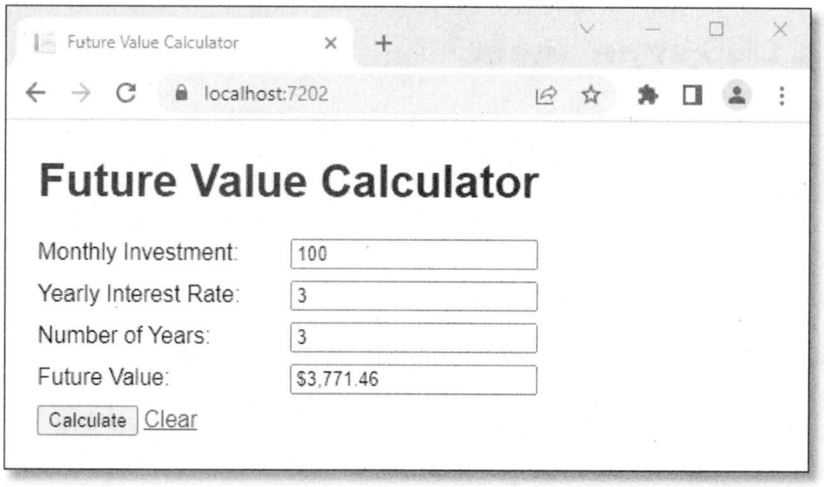

Description

- When the Future Value app starts, it sends a GET request to the Index() action of the Home controller.

- When the user clicks the Clear link, the app sends a GET request to the Index() action of the Home controller.

- When the user clicks the Calculate button, the app sends a POST request to the Index() action of the Home controller. If the user has filled out the form correctly, this automatically sets the three properties of the model object.

Figure 2-13   The Future Value app after handling GET and POST requests

How to organize the files for a view

So far, the view for the Future Value app consists of a single view file. That's adequate for a web app that consists of a single page like the Future Value app presented in this chapter. However, most web apps consist of multiple pages. When that's the case, it makes sense to split the view for a web app into multiple files. That way, you can store HTML elements and CSS styles that are common to multiple pages in their own files. Then, you can use the common HTML elements and CSS styles in other pages as shown in the next three figures.

If it's adequate to store the view for a one-page app in a single file, why does this chapter show how to split the view for the Future Value app into multiple files? Well, in the real world, multi-page apps are more common than one-page apps. Even for a simple app like this Future Value app, you might want to add pages such as an About page or a Contact Us page. As a result, it often makes sense to set up your app to support multiple pages, even if it's currently a one-page app.

How to add a CSS style sheet

Figure 2-14 shows how to add a file for a *CSS style sheet*. This provides a way to store the formatting for multiple web pages in a single external file.

When you add a style sheet to a project, you typically add it to the css folder of the wwwroot folder. In this figure, for example, a style sheet named site.css is added to the wwwroot/css folder. If your project is based on the MVC template, this folder and file should already exist. However, if they don't exist, you need to create them.

This figure also shows the styles that are stored in the site.css file. These styles format the Future Value app so it looks the way it does in the previous figure. If you're familiar with CSS, you shouldn't have any trouble understanding this code.

The four style rules in this figure select elements by type. These are referred to as type selectors. To code a type selector, you just code the name of the element. As a result, the first style rule in this group selects the <body> element, the second selects all <h1> elements, the third selects all <label> elements, and the fourth selects all <div> elements.

Each style rule also includes one or more declarations enclosed in braces that specify the formatting for the selected element. In this figure, the declarations for the <body> element set the font family for all elements nested within that element and set the padding for that element. The declarations for the <h1> element set the top margin and color for all <h1> elements on the page. The declarations for the <label> element cause it to be displayed on the same line as the following element and set the width and padding for all <label> elements on the page. And the declaration for the <div> element sets the bottom margin for all <div> elements on the page.

The dialog for adding a CSS style sheet

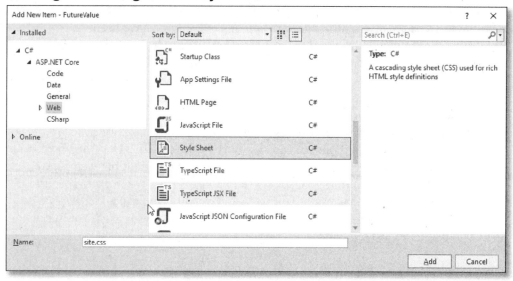

How to add a CSS style sheet

1. If the wwwroot/css folder doesn't exist, create it.

2. Right-click the wwwroot/css folder and select Add→New Item.

3. Select the ASP.NET Core→Web category, select the Style Sheet item, enter a name for the CSS file, and click the Add button.

The site.css file for the Future Value app

```css
body {
    padding: 1em;
    font-family: Arial, Helvetica, sans-serif;
}
h1 {
    margin-top: 0;
    color: navy;
}
label {
    display: inline-block;
    width: 10em;
    padding-right: 1em;
}
div {
    margin-bottom: .5em;
}
```

Description

- A *CSS style sheet* provides a way to store the formatting for multiple web pages in a single external file.

- By default, an ASP.NET Core web app includes a style sheet named site.css in the wwwroot/css folder. You can modify this style sheet or create one of your own.

Figure 2-14   How to add a CSS style sheet

How to add a Razor layout and view start

When you create a multi-page web app, it's common to have headers, footers, and navigation bars that are displayed on all or most pages of a web app. In other words, it's common to have HTML elements that are common to all pages. In that case, it's a good practice to store the elements that are common to multiple pages in separate files. This allows you to keep a consistent look across all pages, and it makes your app easier to maintain.

To store elements that are common to multiple pages in a separate file, you can add a Razor layout to your web app as described in figure 2-15. A *Razor layout* provides a way to store elements that are common to multiple web pages in a single file. Then, it usually makes sense to add a *Razor view start* to specify the default layout for the views of your web app. Finally, you can add a *Razor view* to provide a way to store elements that are unique to a web page. You'll see how to do that in just a minute.

The dialog for adding a Razor layout or view start

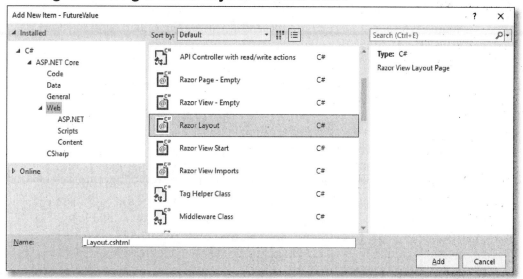

How to add a Razor layout

1. Right-click the Views/Shared folder and select Add→New Item.
2. Select the ASP.NET Core→Web category, select the Razor Layout item, and click the Add button.

How to add a Razor view start

1. Right-click the Views folder (not the Views/Shared folder) and select Add→New Item.
2. Select the ASP.NET Core→Web category, select the Razor View Start item, and click the Add button.

Description

*   A *Razor layout* provides a way to store elements that are common to multiple web pages in a single file.
*   A *Razor view start* lets you specify the default Razor layout for the Razor views of a web app.

Figure 2-15   How to add a Razor layout and view start

The code for a Razor layout and view start

Figure 2-16 shows the code for a Razor layout and view start for the Future Value app. If you study this code, you should see how it provides code that can be used by any Razor view in the app. When combined with the view shown in the next figure, you'll see how this code all fits together to form the same strongly-typed view as the one presented earlier in this chapter. The only differences are that it has been split up into the three Razor files and it uses the external CSS file shown earlier in this chapter.

The code for the layout is stored in a Razor file named _Layout. This code stores the HTML elements that are common to all pages such as the <html>, <head>, and <body> elements. In addition, it uses Razor code to do some processing. For example, it uses Razor code to get the title for the page from the Title property of the ViewBag property that's automatically available to all layouts and views. In addition, it uses Razor code to call the RenderBody() method that's available to all layouts. This inserts the code from any view file that uses this layout.

The code for the layout also uses a <link> element to link to the CSS style sheet shown earlier in this chapter. To do that, it specifies a rel attribute of "stylesheet" and an href attribute of "~/css/site.css". As a result, all of the pages of the web app use the styles from that style sheet.

The code for the view start is stored in a Razor file named _ViewStart. This code defines a block of C# statements that are executed before the view is rendered. In this example, the block contains a single statement that sets the Layout property to "_Layout". In other words, it sets the default layout for all views in the app to the _Layout view shown in the first example.

The Views/Shared/_Layout.cshtml file

```
<!DOCTYPE html>

<html>
<head>
    <meta name="viewport" content="width=device-width, initial-scale=1.0" />
    <title>@ViewBag.Title</title>
    <link rel="stylesheet" href="~/css/site.css" />
</head>
<body>
    <div>
        @RenderBody()
    </div>
</body>
</html>
```

The Views/_ViewStart.cshtml file

```
@{
    Layout = "_Layout";
}
```

Description

- You can use the Razor file named _ViewStart to set the default layout for all the views in your app. However, if necessary, you can use the Layout property of a view to override the default layout.

Figure 2-16   The code for a Razor layout and view start

How to add a Razor view when using a layout with a view start

Figure 2-17 shows how to add a Razor view that works with the Razor layout and view start shown in the previous figure. To do that, you select the Razor View item from the Add New Scaffolded Item dialog instead of the Razor View - Empty item as shown earlier in this chapter. Then, the dialog in this figure is displayed, which lets you name the view and indicate that you want to use a layout page with it.

Here, the code for the view is stored in a Razor file named Index. When combined with the _Layout.cshtml and _ViewStart.cshtml files shown in the previous figure, this code works much like the strongly-typed view presented earlier in this chapter. The main difference is that it uses a Razor code block to set the title for the page. To do that, it sets the Title property of the ViewData object to "Future Value Calculator". As you'll learn in chapter 8, ViewBag uses ViewData under the hood to store its data. As a result, the layout for the page can use ViewBag to get the value of the Title property and display it as the title of the page.

In general, it's considered a good practice to use a view start to set the default layout for all the views in your app. However, if necessary, you can use the Layout property of a view to override the default layout. To do that, you can add a statement below the statement that sets the title for the page like this:

```
@{
    ViewData["Title"] = "Future Value Calculator";
    Layout = "_LayoutCalculator";
}
```

Here, the page is using a hypothetical Razor layout named _LayoutCalculator that's designed especially for all of the calculator pages of the web app.

For now, that's all you need to know about Razor layouts, view starts, and views. In chapter 7, however, you'll learn more about working with layouts and views.

The dialog for adding a Razor view

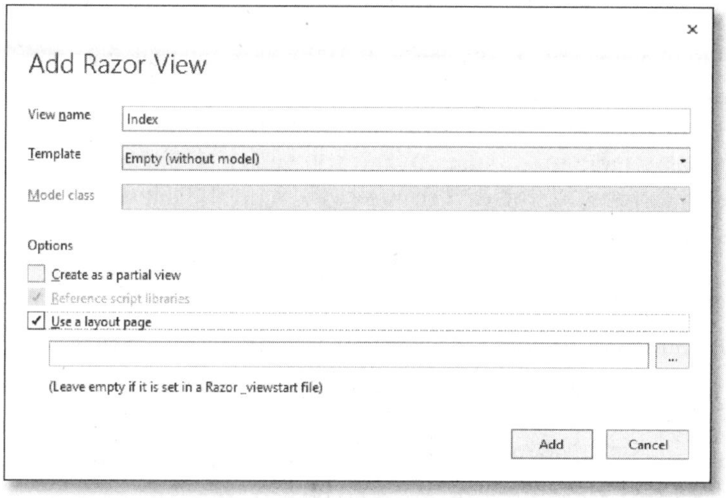

How to add a Razor view

1. Right-click the folder for the view (Views/Home, for example) and select Add→View.

2. Use the Add New Scaffolded Item dialog from figure 2-5 to select Razor View, and then click Add.

3. Use the Add Razor View dialog to enter a name for the view, make sure that the "Use a layout page" item is selected, but don't specify a name for the layout page.

The Views/Home/Index.cshtml file

```
@model FutureValueModel
@{
    ViewData["Title"] = "Future Value Calculator";
}
<h1>Future Value Calculator</h1>
<form asp-action="Index" method="post">
    <div>
        <label asp-for="MonthlyInvestment">Monthly Investment:</label>
        <input asp-for="MonthlyInvestment" /></div>
    <div>
        <label asp-for="YearlyInterestRate">Yearly Interest Rate:</label>
        <input asp-for="YearlyInterestRate" /></div>
    <div>
        <label asp-for="Years">Number of Years:</label>
        <input asp-for="Years" /></div>
    <div>
        <label>Future Value:</label>
        <label>@ViewBag.FV.ToString("c2")</label></div>
    <button type="submit">Calculate</button>
    <a asp-action="Index">Clear</a>
</form>
```

Description

- A *Razor view* provides a way to store elements that are unique to a web page.

Figure 2-17   How to add a Razor view when using a layout with a view start

How to validate user input

At this point, the Future Value app works correctly if the user enters valid data. However, if the user enters invalid data and clicks the Calculate button, the app just displays a future value of 0 without displaying any error messages to indicate that the user has entered invalid data. When you code a web app, you typically want to display error messages if the user enters invalid data. Fortunately, ASP.NET Core MVC makes it easy to validate data and display error messages as shown in the next three figures. This is known as *data validation*, and it's an important part of developing most apps.

How to set data validation rules in the model

The first step in validating the data that a user enters is to set data *validation rules* in the model as described in figure 2-18. To start, you can import the DataAnnotations namespace. Then, you can use the *validation attributes* from that namespace to set the data validation rules.

The table in this figure describes two of the most common validation attributes. First, you can decorate a model property with the Required attribute to indicate that a value is required for that property. Second, you can decorate a property with the Range attribute to indicate that the value for that property must be within the specified range of values.

When you code the Required attribute, the data type for the property must be nullable for the validation to work properly. To make a non-nullable data type nullable, you can code a question mark (?) after the data type as shown in the first example. Then, if the user doesn't enter a value for this property, the MVC framework generates a default error message.

The second example shows that you can decorate a property with more than one validation attribute. In this example, both the Required and Range attributes are used to decorate the property. Here, the Required attribute works the same as it did in the first example. In addition, the Range attribute specifies a minimum value of 1 and a maximum value of 500. As a result, if the user doesn't enter a value that's within the specified range, the MVC framework generates a default error message.

Although the default error messages generated by the MVC framework are adequate in some cases, it's a good practice to specify user-friendly error messages as shown in the third example. To do that, you can pass an argument named ErrorMessage as the last argument of the attribute. In this example, the Required attribute specifies an error message of "Please enter a monthly investment amount." This is more user-friendly than the default message of "The field MonthlyInvestment is required." Similarly, the Range attribute specifies an error message of "Monthly investment amount must be between 1 and 500." This is more user-friendly than the default message of "The field MonthlyInvestment must be between 1 and 500."

How to import the DataAnnotations namespace

```
using System.ComponentModel.DataAnnotations;
```

Two common validation attributes

Attribute	Description
Required	Indicates that a value is required for the property.
Range(min, max)	Indicates that the value for the property must be within a specified range of values.

A model property with a validation attribute

```
[Required]
public decimal? MonthlyInvestment { get; set; }
```

The default error message if the property isn't set

```
The field MonthlyInvestment is required.
```

A model property with two validation attributes

```
[Required]
[Range(1, 500)]
public decimal? MonthlyInvestment { get; set; }
```

The default error message if the property isn't in a valid range

```
The field MonthlyInvestment must be between 1 and 500.
```

A model property with user-friendly error messages

```
[Required(ErrorMessage = "Please enter a monthly investment amount.")]
[Range(1, 500, ErrorMessage =
        "Monthly investment amount must be between 1 and 500.")]
public decimal? MonthlyInvestment { get; set; }
```

Description

- The process of checking data to make sure it's valid is known as *data validation*.
- You can use the *validation attributes* of the DataAnnotations namespace to add *validation rules* to your model.
- For the Required attribute to work properly, the data type for the property must be nullable.
- If you don't specify an error message, the data validation attributes generate a default error message.
- To specify a custom error message, you can pass an argument named ErrorMessage as the last argument of the attribute.

Figure 2-18   How to set data validation rules in the model

The model class with data validation

Figure 2-19 shows the entire model class after data validation attributes have been added to its three properties. In addition, since these properties now use nullable data types, the result of any calculation that uses these properties must be assigned to a nullable type, and the return type for the CalculateFutureValue() method must also be nullable. Other than that, you shouldn't have much trouble understanding this model class. All three of the properties are decorated with both the Required and Range attributes. In addition, all three of the properties specify user-friendly error messages.

The model class with data validation attributes

```
using System.ComponentModel.DataAnnotations;

namespace FutureValue.Models
{
    public class FutureValueModel
    {
        [Required(ErrorMessage = "Please enter a monthly investment.")]
        [Range(1, 500, ErrorMessage =
               "Monthly investment amount must be between 1 and 500.")]
        public decimal? MonthlyInvestment { get; set; }

        [Required(ErrorMessage = "Please enter a yearly interest rate.")]
        [Range(0.1, 10.0, ErrorMessage =
               "Yearly interest rate must be between 0.1 and 10.0.")]
        public decimal? YearlyInterestRate { get; set; }

        [Required(ErrorMessage = "Please enter a number of years.")]
        [Range(1, 50, ErrorMessage =
               "Number of years must be between 1 and 50.")]
        public int? Years { get; set; }

        public decimal? CalculateFutureValue()
        {
            int? months = Years * 12;
            decimal? monthlyInterestRate = YearlyInterestRate / 12 / 100;
            decimal? futureValue = 0;
            for (int i = 0; i < months; i++)
            {
                futureValue = (futureValue + MonthlyInvestment) *
                              (1 + monthlyInterestRate);
            }
            return futureValue;
        }
    }
}
```

Description

- When you use a property with a nullable type in a calculation, the result must be assigned to a nullable type.

- If a method returns a nullable type, the return type must be defined as nullable in the method declaration.

Figure 2-19   The model class with data validation

How to check the data validation

The first example in figure 2-20 shows the Index() action for a POST request in the Home controller. Here, the code has been modified so it uses the ModelState property that's available from the controller class to check whether the data in the model is valid. If so, this code calculates the future value and sets the FV property of the ViewBag to the result of the calculation. Otherwise, this code sets the FV property of the ViewBag to 0. That way, the view can display the result of the calculation or the error messages depending on the state of the model. Either way, it passes the model object to the view so the values entered by the user are redisplayed.

How to display validation error messages

The second example shows the <form> element of the Index view. Here, the view includes code that displays a summary of all data validation errors in the model. In particular, within the <form> element, the first <div> element includes a tag helper named asp-validation-summary that specifies a value of "All". As a result, if the user enters valid data, the MVC framework hides this <div> element. However, if the user doesn't enter valid data, the MVC framework displays this <div> element and fills it with a list of all validation error messages that apply to the current model.

The Future Value app after validating data

The third example shows that the Future Value app displays validation error messages above the form when a user enters invalid data. Here, the messages indicate that the monthly investment is required, the yearly interest rate is out of range, and the number of years is out of range.

For now, that's all you need to know about validating data in your web apps. Later, in chapter 11, you'll learn more about data validation.

An action method that checks for invalid data

```
[HttpPost]
public IActionResult Index(FutureValueModel model)
{
    if (ModelState.IsValid)
    {
        ViewBag.FV = model.CalculateFutureValue();
    }
    else
    {
        ViewBag.FV = 0;
    }
    return View(model);
}
```

A view that displays a summary of validation messages

```
<form asp-action="Index" method="post">
    <div asp-validation-summary="All"></div>
    <div>
        <label asp-for="MonthlyInvestment">Monthly Investment:</label>
        <input asp-for="MonthlyInvestment" />
    </div>
    <!-- rest of input form -->
</form>
```

The Future Value app with invalid data

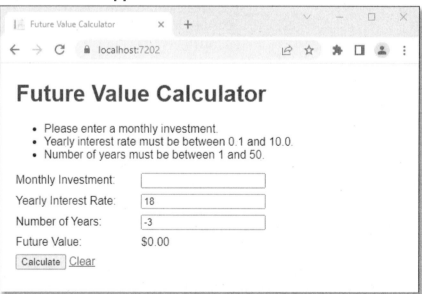

Description

- A controller can use the ModelState property that's available from the controller class to check whether the data in the model is valid.

- A view can use the tag helper named asp-validation-summary to display a summary of all data validation errors in the model.

Figure 2-20   How to check data validation and display error messages

Perspective

The purpose of this chapter has been to teach you the basic skills for creating a one-page ASP.NET Core MVC app with Visual Studio. If you've already used Visual Studio and C# to develop other apps, such as Windows Forms apps, and you have basic HTML and CSS skills, you shouldn't have any trouble mastering these skills.

In the next chapter, you'll learn the basics of using Bootstrap. This open-source library provides CSS and JavaScript classes that make it easy to give your pages a professional appearance. In addition, Bootstrap makes it possible to display your web pages on devices of varying sizes.

Terms

Visual Studio template	Razor view imports page
controller	strongly-typed view
action method	decorate a method or property
action	tag helper
Razor view engine	CSS style sheet
Razor view	Razor layout
Razor code block	Razor view start
Razor expression	data validation
syntax error	validation attributes
exception	validation rules
model	

Summary

- You create a web app from a *Visual Studio template* that determines the folders and files for the project.

- A method of a *controller* class that runs in response to HTTP action verbs such as GET or POST is known as an *action method*, or an *action*.

- In ASP.NET Core, the *Razor view engine* uses server-side code to embed C# code within HTML elements.

- A *Razor view* contains both C# and HTML code. That's why its file extension is .cshtml. A Razor view typically stores elements that are unique to a web page.

- To execute one or more C# statements, you can declare a *Razor code block* by coding the @ sign followed by a pair of braces ({ }). Within the braces, you can code one or more C# statements.

- To evaluate a C# expression and display its result, you can code a *Razor expression* by coding the @ sign followed by the expression.

- When you enter code or attempt to build and run an app, Visual Studio may display *syntax errors* that have to be corrected before the app can be compiled.

- If a compiled statement can't be executed when you run a web app, an *exception* occurs. Then, you can use the information that's displayed in the browser to attempt to fix the exception.

- A *model* is a regular C# class that models the data for the app. The class for a model is typically stored in the Models folder.

- A *Razor view imports page* makes it easier to work with models and tag helpers. As a result, most web apps include a Razor view imports page.

- You use the @model directive to *bind* a model to a view. This kind of view is called a *strongly-typed view*.

- You can use the @Model property to access the properties and methods of the model object that's specified by the @model directive.

- *Tag helpers* automatically generate attributes for some HTML elements. They can also *bind* HTML elements to the properties of the object that's the model for the view.

- A *CSS style sheet* provides a way to store the formatting for multiple web pages in a single external file.

- A *Razor layout* provides a way to store elements that are common to multiple web pages in a single file.

- A *Razor view start* lets you specify the default Razor layout for the Razor views of a web app.

- The process of checking data to make sure it's valid is known as *data validation*.

- You can use the *validation attributes* to add *validation rules* to your model.

Before you do the exercises for this book...

If you haven't already done so, you should install the software that's required for this book, and you should download the source code for this book. Appendixes A (Windows) and B (macOS) show how to do that.

Exercise 2-1   Build the Future Value app using the MVC template

This exercise guides you through the development of the Future Value app that's presented in this chapter. This gives you some hands-on experience using Visual Studio to build a web app.

Create and set up a web app using the MVC template

1. Start a web app that's based on the ASP.NET Core MVC template as shown in figures 2-1 and 2-2. Use a project name of FutureValue and a solution name of Ch02Ex1FutureValue and store it in this directory:

   `/aspnet_core_mvc/ex_starts`

2. Delete all the files inside the Controllers, Models, and Views folders, including the files inside the Views/Home and Views/Shared folders, but don't delete the Home and Shared folders themselves.

3. Add a controller named HomeController to the Controllers folder and modify it so it contains the code from figure 2-4.

4. Add a new empty Razor view named Index to the Views/Home folder and modify it so it contains the code from figure 2-5.

5. Press Ctrl+F5 to run the app. This should start the default web browser and display the Home/Index view, including the data that the HomeController stored in the ViewBag. Be sure to install any SSL certificates if you're asked to do that.

Add the model, Razor view imports page, and a strongly typed view

6. Add a class named FutureValueModel to the Models folder and modify it so it contains the code from figure 2-9.

7. Add the Razor view imports page to the Views folder and modify it so it contains the code shown in figure 2-10.

8. Modify the code of the Home/Index view so it contains the code from figure 2-11. Make sure to include all the CSS style rules from figure 2-14 within the <style> element.

9. Modify the HomeController class to handle both GET and POST requests as shown in figure 2-12.

10. Run the app. If you enter valid data, it should calculate and display a future value. However, if you enter invalid data, you may get unexpected results.

Add the Razor layout and view start, and modify the Razor view

11. Modify the site.css file in the wwwroot/css folder so it contains the CSS style rules shown in figure 2-14. To do that, you can cut the CSS style rules from the Home/Index file and paste them into the custom.css file.

12. Add a Razor layout named _Layout.cshtml to the Views/Shared folder and modify it so it contains the code shown in figure 2-16. Make sure to include a <link> element that points to the site.css file.

13. Add a Razor view start named _ViewStart to the Views folder (not the Views/Shared folder) and modify it so it contains the code shown in figure 2-16.

14. Modify the code in Home/Index view so it contains the code shown in figure 2-17. To do that, you can cut all elements that are already specified by the Razor layout. Note that you do not need to change the code that sets the Title property of the ViewBag so it uses ViewData, since either of these objects will work.

15. Run the app. It should work the same as it did before.

Add data validation to the Future Value app

16. Modify the FutureValueModel class so it imports the DataAnnotations namespace. Then, decorate each property with the Required and Range attributes as shown in figure 2-19. To do that, you must use nullable types for the properties and the method.

17. Modify the HomeController class so it checks for invalid data as shown in figure 2-20.

18. Modify the Home/Index view so it displays a summary of validation messages as shown in figure 2-20.

19. Run the app. It should work correctly if you enter valid data, and it should display appropriate messages if you enter invalid data.

Exercise 2-2   Build the Future Value app using the Empty template

This exercise guides you through the development of the Future Value app that's presented in this chapter if you start from the Empty template instead of the MVC template.

Create and set up a web app using the Empty template

1. Start a web app that's based on the Empty template as shown in figures 2-1 and 2-2. Use a project name of FutureValue and a solution name of Ch02Ex2FutureValue and store it in this directory:

   `/aspnet_core_mvc/ex_starts`

2. Add the Controllers, Models, and Views folders to the project.

3. Add a Home folder and Shared folder within the Views folder that you just created.

4. Follow exercise 2-1 starting at step 3. In step 11, you'll need to add the wwwroot folder and the css subfolder before you can add the site.css file.

3

How to make a web app responsive with Bootstrap

In chapter 2, you learned how to build the Future Value app using HTML and CSS to format the view for the app so it looks good on devices such as computers that have large screens. However, since so many users browse websites with devices such as phones that have small screens, it's important to make sure your web apps look good on devices of every size. To do that, you can use CSS and JavaScript provided by a client-side library such as Bootstrap to make your web apps responsive as described in this chapter. This can improve the appearance of your apps and make them more user friendly.

An introduction to responsive web design

Due to the popularity of phones and tablets, it's important to make sure your web apps look good on devices of every size. This is called *responsive web design*. An app that uses responsive web design doesn't just look good on phones and tablets, it's easier to use too. That's because you don't have to scroll and resize on a small screen. In fact, this is so important that apps that are mobile friendly perform better in Google's search results.

One way to make your web apps responsive is to use CSS3 *media queries*. Media queries let you adjust the layout of a page based on conditions, such as the width of the screen. Because it can be time consuming to develop media queries, though, frameworks have been developed to automate this process.

A *framework* contains general code for common situations and can be customized to meet the needs of individual projects. *Bootstrap* is a popular framework for responsive web design that was originally developed by Twitter. Bootstrap uses CSS and JavaScript to make a web page automatically adjust for different screen sizes.

A responsive user interface

Figure 3-1 shows a version of the Future Value app that uses Bootstrap to make it responsive. Here, the first screen is wide enough to accommodate labels, controls, and validation messages in individual rows.

The second screen shows what happens as the screen is narrowed so the labels, controls, and validation messages can no longer fit in individual rows. Then, the labels, controls, and validation messages are stacked on top of each other. This narrows the page to match the narrowed screen, and makes it so you don't need to scroll from side to side to see the whole page. The controls also span the width of the screen to make them easier to use on touch screens.

The third screen shows that as the screen continues to get narrower, the controls are also narrowed so they fit on the screen. In addition, when the validation messages no longer fit, they roll over to the next line.

One more thing to notice about these screens is that the size of the heading is reduced as the screen gets smaller. This happens automatically using a feature of Bootstrap called *Responsive Font Sizes* (*RFS*). Although this feature was available with previous versions of Bootstrap, it was disabled by default. Now, with the current version of Bootstrap (Bootstrap 5), this feature is enabled by default. In addition, it has been enhanced to include resizing of margins and padding, as well as other CSS properties.

When you use Bootstrap, these changes take place automatically when you narrow or widen the browser window or when you display the page on devices with different screen sizes. All you have to do is add Bootstrap to your app and then use the classes it provides.

The responsive Future Value app at different screen widths

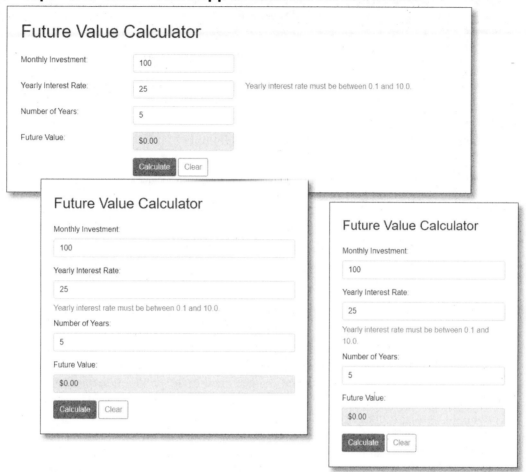

Description

- A web app should adapt to every screen size. This is called *responsive web design*.
- You can use the open-source *Bootstrap* library to implement a responsive web design with your ASP.NET Core MVC apps.

Figure 3-1   A responsive user interface

How to add client-side libraries such as Bootstrap and jQuery

The MVC template that you learned about in the previous chapter includes a version of Bootstrap by default. However, this version of Bootstrap might be different than the version presented in this chapter. All of the apps presented in this book have been tested against the version of Bootstrap specified in this figure. As a result, if you want this library to work as described in this book, you should use this version for your apps too. If you prefer to use the newest version of this library, you may need to modify the code presented in this book to get it to work correctly with the newer library.

Figure 3-2 shows how to add the Bootstrap library and the Popper.js library that it depends on. To do that, you can use the *Library Manager*, also known as *LibMan*. To start, the procedure shows how to add the Bootstrap library. Then, it shows how to add Popper.js, which is a JavaScript library that Bootstrap depends on for some of its components.

In addition to these two libraries, the MVC template includes the three jQuery libraries listed in this figure. Bootstrap versions before 5.0 were dependent on the main jQuery library, so you had to include it to use Bootstrap. However, Bootstrap 5.0 and later no longer depend on this library. So, you don't need to include it unless your app uses other jQuery libraries like the two listed here. These libraries are necessary to enable client-side data validation. This allows data validation like the validation described in the previous chapter to run on the client without needing to make an HTTP request to the server. If you're going to use these libraries, it's common to add them to your app at the same time that you add Bootstrap and Popper.js.

One thing to note is that the MVC template stores the jquery-validation library in a folder named jquery-validation. If you delete this folder and add a different version of the jquery-validation library using the Library Manager, however, the library is stored in a folder named jquery-validate. You'll need to be sure that you refer to the correct folder when you enable this library as shown in figure 3-4.

By convention, an ASP.NET Core MVC app stores all client-side libraries in the wwwroot/lib folder as shown in this figure. In addition, when you use the procedure in this figure to add client-side libraries, Visual Studio creates a file named libman.json. If you want, you can edit this file to easily manage the versions or locations of your client-side libraries as described in the next figure.

The dialog boxes for adding client-side libraries

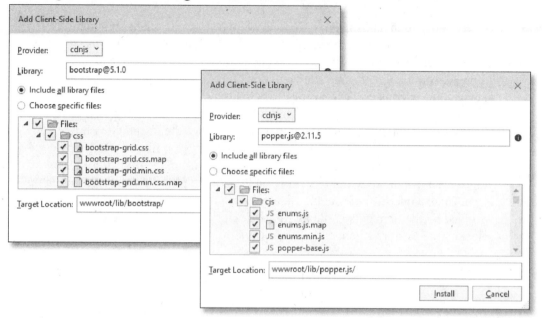

Client-side libraries included by the MVC template

- twitter-bootstrap 5.1.0
- jquery 3.5.1
- jquery-validation 1.17.0
- jquery-validation-unobtrusive 3.2.11

How to add the Bootstrap and Popper libraries to a web app

1. Start Visual Studio and open a project. In the Solution Explorer, expand the wwwroot/lib folder and delete any Bootstrap libraries.
2. In the Solution Explorer, right-click on the project name and select the Add→Client-Side Library item.
3. In the dialog that appears, type "twitter-bootstrap@5.1.0", change the target location to "wwwroot/lib/bootstrap", and click the Install button.
4. Repeat steps 2 and 3 for the library named "popper.js@2.11.5", but don't change the target location.

Description

- You can use the *Library Manager*, also known as *LibMan*, to add client-side libraries such as Bootstrap and Popper to a project.
- The MVC template that you learned about in the previous chapter includes a version of Bootstrap by default. However, this version of Bootstrap might be different than the version presented in this chapter.
- To determine the version of a library, display one of its files.

Figure 3-2   How to add client-side libraries such as Bootstrap and Popper

How to manage client-side libraries with LibMan

By convention, an ASP.NET Core MVC app stores its client-side libraries in the wwwroot/lib folder shown in figure 3-3. In addition, when you use the procedure in the previous figure to add client-side libraries, Visual Studio creates a libman.json file like the one shown in this figure. If you want, you can easily manage the versions or locations of your client-side libraries by editing the contents of this file. Then, you can right-click on this file and select the Restore Client-Side Libraries item. This automatically updates the client-side libraries on your system so they match the contents of the libman.json file.

If your app contains client-side libraries that aren't in the libman.json file, you can remove them by right-clicking on the libman.json file and selecting the Clean Client-Side Libraries item. Then, you can restore the client-side libraries specified by the libman.json file by right-clicking the libman.json file and selecting the Restore Client-Side Libraries item.

The libman.json file that's created when you add a client-side library

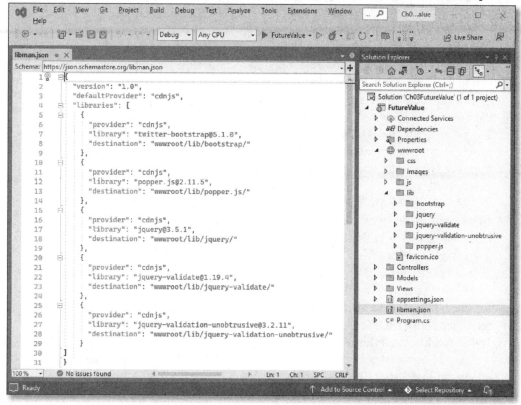

Description

- To manage client-side libraries, you can open the libman.json file and edit it to specify the correct versions and locations for your client-side libraries.

- To update all client-side libraries so they match the libman.json file, you can right-click on the libman.json file and select the Restore Client-Side Libraries item.

- To remove all client-side libraries, you can right-click on the libman.json file and select the Clean Client-Side Libraries item.

Figure 3-3   How to manage client-side libraries with LibMan

How to enable client-side libraries

Once you've added the Bootstrap and Popper.js libraries to your app, you can enable those libraries by adding some HTML elements to the view. Fortunately, most views use a Razor layout. As a result, you typically just need to add these elements to the view's layout. For example, figure 3-4 shows how to add the necessary elements to the layout for the Future Value app presented in the previous chapter.

To start, you need to add a *meta tag* to the <head> element. A meta tag provides information about your web app to browsers but isn't displayed to the user. For Bootstrap, you need to add a meta tag whose name attribute is set to "viewport".

The *viewport* is the part of the web page that's visible to a viewer, and its size varies by device. When you use Bootstrap, you should set the viewport meta tag as shown in this figure. This meta tag makes sure that the width of the page corresponds to the width of the device and that the content doesn't appear zoomed in or out.

Next, you code two <link> elements to attach the external style sheets for the app. For these elements to work properly, you must code them in the sequence shown in this figure. That way, the site style sheet can override existing styles or add new styles to the Bootstrap style sheet.

In addition to the <link> elements, you code two <script> elements that attach the JavaScript libraries for Popper.js and Bootstrap. Again, you must code these elements in the sequence shown in this figure. That's because the Bootstrap library depends on the Popper.js library.

The last three <script> elements attach the JavaScript library for jQuery, as well as the libraries necessary for client-side data validation. As mentioned earlier, these libraries aren't necessary for Bootstrap to work properly. However, you typically want to add these libraries to any views that perform data validation.

The folders for these client-side libraries contain many more files than those that are specified in this figure. For example, all of these libraries include a *minified* version and a regular version. In most cases, you use the minified files as shown in this figure because they load faster. However, if you want to examine or debug the code that Bootstrap provides, you can use the regular files because they're easier for humans to read and understand.

Once you've made the elements for Bootstrap available to a view, Visual Studio provides IntelliSense support for the various CSS classes provided by Bootstrap. That makes it easy to discover and enter the names of the Bootstrap classes as you add them to a view.

In this figure, the <script> elements are coded at the end of the <head> element. However, many programmers prefer to code the <script> elements at the end of the <body> element. That way, the browser loads most of the HTML before it loads the JavaScript libraries. This allows the HTML to load faster.

A project that's based on the MVC template includes an extra /dist folder in the paths to the Bootstrap, jQuery, and jQuery validation libraries. As a result, if you use the libraries from this template, you'll need to modify the <link> and <script> elements shown here so they point to the correct folders.

How to use a Razor layout to enable client-side libraries

```
<!DOCTYPE html>
<html>
<head>
    <meta name="viewport" content="width=device-width, initial-scale=1.0" />
    <title>@ViewBag.Title</title>
    <link rel="stylesheet" href="~/lib/bootstrap/css/bootstrap.min.css" />
    <link rel="stylesheet" href="~/css/site.css" />

    <script src="~/lib/popper.js/umd/popper.min.js"></script>
    <script src="~/lib/bootstrap/js/bootstrap.js"></script>

    <script src="~/lib/jquery/jquery.min.js"></script>
    <script src="~/lib/jquery-validation/jquery.validation.min.js">
    </script>
    <script src="~/lib/jquery-validation-unobtrusive/
                    jquery.validate.unobtrusive.min.js"></script>
</head>
<body>
    @RenderBody()
</body>
</html>
```

An extra directory that's included by the MVC template

```
<link rel="stylesheet" href="~/lib/bootstrap/dist/css/bootstrap.min.css" />
```

Description

- To make client-side CSS libraries such as Bootstrap available to the views in your web app, you can add the <link> elements for the CSS files to the <head> element in the Razor layout for the view.

- The <link> element for the Bootstrap CSS file should be coded before the <link> element for your own custom CSS files. That way, your CSS styles override the Bootstrap styles. Creating a separate style sheet is the preferred way of making changes to Bootstrap.

- To make client-side JavaScript libraries such as Bootstrap and Popper.js available to the views in your web app, you can add the <script> elements for those libraries to the <head> or <body> element in the Razor layout for the view. The <script> element for the Popper.js library should come before the <script> element for the Bootstrap library.

- If an app uses the jQuery library, you'll also need to include a <script> element for that library. That element should come before the <script> elements for other jQuery libraries.

- Most of these libraries include a *minified* version of the library that has removed unnecessary characters such as spaces and indentation. This decreases the size of the file and improves load time but makes it more difficult for humans to read the library. Minified libraries are typically identified with a suffix of .min.css or .min.js.

- After you've added the necessary <link> and <script> elements to your web form, Visual Studio provides IntelliSense for the Bootstrap CSS classes.

- The *viewport* is the part of the page that is visible to viewers. The *viewport meta tag* controls the width of the viewport.

Figure 3-4   How to enable client-side libraries

How to get started with Bootstrap

So far, you have learned how to install and enable the client-side libraries necessary to support Bootstrap. Now, you'll learn how to use some of the CSS classes available from Bootstrap to style the view for the Future Value app.

The classes of the Bootstrap grid system

To create responsive web apps, Bootstrap uses a grid system that's based on containers, rows, and columns. A container contains one or more rows, and a row can contain up to 12 columns. Bootstrap provides predefined CSS classes to work with its grid system. The most important of these classes are presented in the first table in figure 3-5.

To start, you use the container and container-fluid classes to identify the main content of the page. The difference between them is that an element that uses the container class is centered in the screen and has a specific width in pixels based on the viewport's width. This is sometimes called a *boxed layout*. An element that uses the container-fluid class, by contrast, is always the same width as the viewport. This is sometimes called a *full width layout*.

The main content of a page should be divided into rows using the row class. Then, within each row, you can code elements with one or more of the column classes that control how the content in the row is displayed. If you use the col class, the width of the column is automatically sized. In the first example, for instance, this class is used on two columns so the columns are sized the same.

If that's not what you want, you can specify a class with one of the screen sizes listed in the second table in this figure, along with the number of columns that the element should span. To understand how this works, the second example shows a <div> element that uses the col-md-4 class. This means that when the element is displayed on a medium-size screen (md), it occupies four columns.

The third example is similar, except that it specifies a second class for a large screen (lg). Then, the element occupies only three columns. However, it still occupies four columns on a medium-size (md) screen.

Neither of these examples includes classes for small (sm) and extra small (none) devices. Because of that, the element occupies all twelve columns on those devices, since that's the default. Classes for extra-large (xl) and extra, extra-large (xxl) devices are also omitted from these examples. Because of that, the class for the next smallest screen size that's specified will be used. Note that the xxl size is new with Bootstrap 5.

You can also use CSS classes to move an element a specified number of columns to the right. To do that, you use a class that indicates the screen size and the number of columns that the element should be offset as is illustrated in the fourth example. Here, the element occupies four columns on a medium-size screen just as in the first two examples. However, the element is moved one column to the right.

If you have a hard time visualizing this, don't worry. The next figure presents an example that demonstrates how the grid system works.

The URL for the Bootstrap documentation

`https://getbootstrap.com/docs/`

Valid class values

Class	Description
`container`	Contains rows or other content. Centered in the \<body> element, with a specific width based on the viewport size.
`container-fluid`	Contains rows or other content. Set to 100% of the width of the viewport.
`row`	Contains columns inside a container.
`col`	A column inside a row that will be automatically sized.
`col-`*size*`-`*count*	The number of columns an element should span on the specified screen size. The number of columns in a row should not exceed 12.
`offset-`*size*`-`*count*	The number of columns an element should be moved to the right on the specified screen size.

Valid size values

Size	Description
`xxl`	An extra, extra-large screen with a width greater than or equal to 1400 pixels.
`xl`	An extra-large screen with a width greater than or equal to 1200 pixels.
`lg`	A large screen with a width greater than or equal to 992 pixels.
`md`	A medium screen with a width greater than or equal to 768 pixels.
`sm`	A small screen with a width greater than or equal to 576 pixels.
(none)	An extra small screen with a width less than 576 pixels.

Two columns that are automatically sized

```
<div class="col">Column 1</div><div class="col">Column 2</div>
```

An element that spans four columns on medium and larger screens

```
<div class="col-md-4">This element spans four columns</div>
```

An element that spans 4 columns on medium screens and 3 on large

```
<div class="col-md-4 col-lg-3">This element spans three or four columns</div>
```

An element that is moved one column to the right on medium screens

```
<div class="col-md-4 offset-md-1">This element is offset by one column</div>
```

Description

- Bootstrap uses a grid system based on containers, rows, and columns. All rows should be inside a container, and each row must contain no more than 12 columns.
- You can assign a different column class to an element for each screen size to specify the number of columns the element should span at those sizes.
- If you don't assign a column class for a screen size, the class for the next smallest screen size will be used.

Figure 3-5   The classes of the Bootstrap grid system

How the Bootstrap grid system works

To help you understand how the Bootstrap grid system works, figure 3-6 shows an example of a simple grid that contains three rows. Here, the grid is shown as it would appear on three different screen sizes. In the HTML, each row is defined by a <div> element that's assigned the class named "row". In addition, the <div> elements that define the rows are coded within a <main> element that's assigned the class named "container". Each row in the grid contains two <div> elements that are used to define the columns.

In the first row, each <div> element specifies a width of twelve columns for the extra small size (none). As a result, each column spans all twelve columns of the row, or the entire width of the container, regardless of the screen size. That causes the columns to be stacked vertically as shown here.

In the second row, each <div> element specifies a class for the medium-size viewport (md). Here, the first <div> element specifies a width of four columns and the second element specifies a width of eight columns. This causes the <div> elements to be displayed side by side at the medium width. It also causes these elements to be displayed side by side at the large, extra-large, and extra, extra-large widths, since no classes are specified for those widths (lg, xl, and xxl). In that case, Bootstrap uses the width of the next smallest screen size that's specified, in this case, the medium size. By contrast, Bootstrap stacks the <div> elements at the small (sm) and extra-small (none) sizes. That's because this code doesn't specify column classes for these viewport sizes. In that case, each <div> element spans all twelve columns.

In the third row, the <div> elements specify the same column classes for the medium viewport as the <div> elements in the second row. In addition, they're assigned column classes for the small (sm) viewport. These classes specify a width of six columns for each <div> element. As a result, medium and larger devices display these <div> elements side by side at the same widths as the <div> elements in the second row. However, small devices display these <div> elements side by side but at equal widths as shown by the second screen. Finally, extra small devices stack these <div> elements vertically as shown by the third screen.

This figure also presents some custom CSS classes that override the Bootstrap CSS classes. This custom CSS makes it easy to see the rows and columns in the grid by providing custom margins, padding, borders, and a background color. As you review this CSS, you may notice that the margin-bottom and padding attributes use a rem unit to specify size instead of using the more traditional em unit. *Rem units* work similarly to em units. The main difference is that the size of an em is relative to the immediate container element, and the size of a rem, which stands for "root em", is relative to the root element of the document. In short, rems are used by Bootstrap 5 instead of ems. As a result, when you override Bootstrap classes, it usually makes sense to use rems, not ems.

A Bootstrap grid on medium, small, and extra small screens

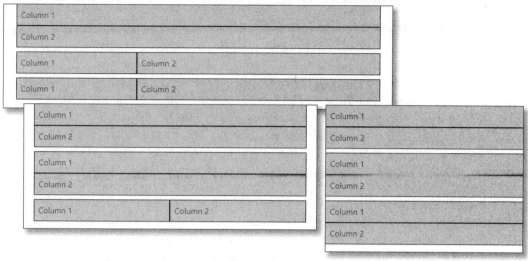

The HTML for the grid example

```html
<main class="container">
    <div class="row">
        <div class="col-12">Column 1</div>
        <div class="col-12">Column 2</div>
    </div>
    <div class="row">
        <div class="col-md-4">Column 1</div>
        <div class="col-md-8">Column 2</div>
    </div>
    <div class="row">
        <div class="col-md-4 col-sm-6">Column 1</div>
        <div class="col-md-8 col-sm-6">Column 2</div>
    </div>
</main>
```

Custom CSS classes that override the Bootstrap CSS classes

```css
.row {                              /* custom row styles */
    margin-bottom: 0.5rem;
}
.row div {                          /* custom column styles */
    border: 1px solid black;
    padding: 0.5rem;
    background-color: lightsteelblue;
}
```

Note

- Bootstrap CSS classes uses *rem units* for sizing. A rem (root em) unit works similarly to the more traditional em unit, but its size is relative to the root element rather than the current element.

Figure 3-6   How the Bootstrap grid system works

How to work with forms

Bootstrap also provides some predefined CSS classes for working with the labels and controls of a form. The table in figure 3-7 presents some of the most important of these classes.

By default, forms use a vertical layout. That means that the labels and controls in a form stack on top of each other and the controls span the width of the viewport. This is illustrated by the first example in this figure.

To apply styling to <input> elements like the ones in this figure, you use the form-control class. This class improves the appearance of these elements, and it makes them easier to use on mobile devices. For example, it improves their appearance by making them taller and by rounding their corners. And it makes them easier to use on mobile devices by making them span the width of the viewport in a vertical layout or the width of the column span in a horizontal layout. You'll learn more about horizontal layouts in a minute.

You can also use the form-label class to apply styling to <label> elements. By default, this class simply adds a margin to the bottom of the label. This is particularly useful when you're creating a vertical layout.

Before going on, you should notice that the first two <div> elements in this figure use the mb-3 class to add space below them. You'll learn more about how that works later in this chapter.

Some Bootstrap CSS classes for working with forms

Class	Description
form-label	Applies styling to labels in a form.
form-control	Applies styling to input or textarea controls in a form.
form-select	Applies styling to select controls in a form.
form-floating	Displays a label inside input, textarea, and select controls.
col-form-label	Applies styling to labels of a row within a form with a horizontal layout.

A form with two text boxes and a drop-down list in vertical layout

The HTML for the form

```
<form asp-action="Login" method="post">
    <div class="mb-3">
        <label for="email" class="form-label">Email</label>
        <input id="email" type="email" class="form-control" />
    </div>
    <div class="mb-3">
        <label for="pwd" class="form-label">Password</label>
        <input id="pwd" type="password" class="form-control" />
    </div>
    <div>
        <label for="major" class="form-label">Major:</label>
        <select id="major" class="form-select">
            <option value="Computer Science">Computer Science</option>
            ...
            <option value="Psychology">Psychology</option>
        </select>
    </div>
</form>
```

Description

- By default, the labels and controls in a form have a vertical layout.
- To create a text area instead of a text box, use the <textarea> element and specify the height of the control using the height property.
- To create a list box instead of a drop-down list, code the size attribute to indicate the number of items to be displayed in the list.

Figure 3-7   How to work with forms (part 1)

When you use a vertical layout, the labels are displayed above the controls by default. However, Bootstrap 5 also lets you create *floating labels*. When you use floating labels, the labels are displayed inside the control, as shown in the first example in part 2 of figure 3-7. This is similar to using a placeholder. Unlike a placeholder, however, a floating label is still displayed when data is entered into the control.

To use a floating label, you assign the form-floating class to the <div> element that contains the label and control. In addition, you must code the control element before the label element. Although the control elements shown here are <input> elements for text boxes, you should know that you can also use floating labels with <textarea> and <select> elements.

To align the controls in the horizontal layout, you use the grid system that you learned about in the previous figure. In the HTML for the horizontal layout in this figure, for example, the <div> elements use the row class to identify the rows in the form. Within these <div> elements, the <label> elements use the col-md-2 class, and the <input> elements that define the text boxes are coded within <div> elements that use the col-md-10 class. That way, the labels each span two columns on medium and larger viewports, and the controls each span ten columns. Because a column class isn't assigned for small or extra small viewports, though, Bootstrap stacks the labels and controls vertically on the smallest devices. In other words, since the layout uses the grid system, it is responsive.

Notice that because you use the grid system to create a horizontal layout, you don't code the form-label class for the labels. Instead, you code the col-form-label class. This class causes the labels to be centered vertically in the controls.

A form with two text boxes and floating labels

```
Email

Password
```

The HTML for the form

```
<form asp-action="Login" method="post">
    <div class="form floating mb-3">
        <input id="email" type="email" class="form-control" />
        <label for="email">Email</label>
    </div>
    <div class="form-floating">
        <input id="pwd" type="password" class="form-control" />
        <label for="pwd">Password</label>
    </div>
</form>
```

A form with two text boxes in horizontal layout

```
Email:

Password:
```

The HTML for the form

```
<form asp-action="Login" method="post">
    <div class="row mb-3">
        <label for="email" class="col-form-label col-md-2">Email:</label>
        <div class="col-md-10">
            <input id="email" type="email" class="form-control" />
        </div>
    </div>
    <div class="row">
        <label for="pwd" class="col-form-label col-md-2">Password:</label>
        <div class="col-md-10">
            <input id="pwd" type="password" class="form-control" />
        </div>
    </div>
</form>
```

Description

- Floating labels are a new feature of Bootstrap 5. A floating label appears inside the text box as shown above. You can also use floating labels with textarea and select controls.

- To align labels and controls horizontally, you use the grid system to define each row and the number of columns that each label or control occupies.

Figure 3-7   How to work with forms (part 2)

How to work with buttons and images

The grid and form classes that you have learned about so far allow you to set the basic structure of a web page and control the layout for different viewport sizes. Bootstrap also provides many CSS classes for styling individual elements and components that you'll learn about later in this chapter. But first, figure 3-8 presents some of the most common classes, like those for styling buttons and images.

In this example, the HTML starts with a <div> element that uses the container class. This centers the content and adjusts its size based on the size of the viewport. Then, the <header> element includes an <img> element to display an image.

To style the image, this code uses two classes. First, the img-fluid class causes the size of the image to be adjusted as the size of the viewport changes. That way, the entire image is always visible in the viewport. Then, the rounded class causes the image to be displayed with rounded corners, even though the original image doesn't have rounded corners.

Within the <main> element, the HTML uses Bootstrap classes to provide appropriate styling for the elements in the form. Here, the elements in the form aren't full screen and vertically stacked like they were in the vertical form example of the previous figure. That's because the form controls in this example don't use the form-control class. This shows that you can use just the CSS classes you need to get the look you want.

Within the <form> element, the HTML uses some of the button classes to style the Yes and No buttons. The btn class provides the basic size and rounded corners. The btn-primary class adds emphasis to the Yes button by making it blue with white text. And the btn-outline-secondary class makes the No button white with grey text and a grey border.

Notice that the Yes button in this example is created by styling a <button> element, while the No button is created by styling an <a> element. Throughout this book, buttons that cause a form to post to the server are coded as <button> elements with their type attribute set to "submit". By contrast, buttons that cause a GET request rather than a POST request are coded as an <a> element with an asp-action attribute that specifies the action to be executed. Both <button> and <a> elements can be styled with the Bootstrap CSS classes for buttons as shown here.

Some of the Bootstrap CSS classes for working with buttons

Class	Description
btn	Produces a simple button with rounded corners.
btn-primary	Sets the background color to blue and the text to white.
btn-secondary	Sets the background color to grey and the text to white.
btn-outline-primary	Sets the background color to white and the border and text to blue.
btn-outline-secondary	Sets the background color to white and the border and text to grey.

Some of the Bootstrap CSS classes for working with images

Class	Description
img-fluid	Makes the image automatically adjust to fit the size of the viewport.
rounded	Rounds the corners of the image.

A form with an image and two buttons

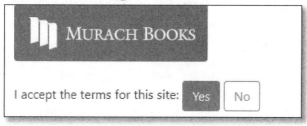

The HTML

```
<div class="container">
    <header>
        <img id="logo" alt="Murach logo" src="~/images/MurachLogo.jpg"
            class="img-fluid rounded" />
    </header>
    <br />
    <main>
        <form asp-action="Index" method="post">
            <span>I accept the terms for this site:</span>
            <button type="submit" class="btn btn-primary">Yes</button>
            <a asp-action="Index" class="btn btn-outline-secondary">No</a>
        </form>
    </main>
</div>
```

Figure 3-8   How to work with buttons and images

How to work with margins and padding

Figure 3-9 shows how to use the Bootstrap CSS classes for setting the margins and padding of an element. Here, the classes use m or p to specify margin or padding. Then, they use t, e, b, or s to specify the top, ending, bottom, and starting side of an element. Or, if the class doesn't specify a side, the class applies to all four sides of the element.

The example in this figure begins by setting the p (padding) class for the <header> element to a size of 4. This adds padding of 1.5 rems around the content of the header. Next, it sets the mt (margin top) class for the header to a size of 2, which adds a small margin of .5 rems between the header and the top of the page. It also sets the mb (margin bottom) class for the header to a size of 4 to add 1.5 rems between the header and the <main> element that follows. That's why no <br /> element is required to add space like it was in the previous figure.

The header also includes bg-light, rounded, and border classes. These three classes, along with the p-4 class, add the light gray, rounded, bordered background around the image within the header. Versions of Bootstrap before version 5 included a component called a jumbotron that produced a similar effect. However, this component has now been dropped since you can create it with classes as shown here.

This example continues by setting the me (margin end) class for the <span> element within the <main> element to a size of 2. This adds a small margin of .5 rems to the right of the text in the <span> element and before the first button. Similarly, this example adds a small margin to the right of the first button and before the second button. That's why there's more space between these three elements than there was in the previous figure.

This example finishes by setting the p (padding) class for both buttons to a size of 3. Since it doesn't specify a side, this adds padding of 1 rem to all four sides of these buttons. That's why these buttons appear larger than the buttons shown in the previous figure.

Note that the classes for margins and padding with Bootstrap 5.0 and later use "s" for start and "e" for end instead of "l" for left and "r" for right as with previous versions of Bootstrap. That's because Bootstrap 5.0 and later provide support for a right-to-left (RTL) layout instead of the default left-to-right layout. In either case, "s" refers to the starting side of an element and "e" refers to the ending side of an element, but the actual side differs depending on which layout you're using. To learn more about Bootstrap's support for right-to-left layout, see the Bootstrap documentation for RTL.

Some Bootstrap CSS classes for working with margins

Class	Description
mt-*size*	Sets the margin for the top to a specified size from 0 to 5. By default, these sizes correspond to rem unit values of 0, .25, .5, 1, 1.5, and 3.
mb-*size*	Sets the margin for the bottom to the specified size.
ms-*size*	Sets the margin for the starting side to the specified size.
me-*size*	Sets the margin for the ending side to the specified size.
m-*size*	Sets all four margins to the specified size.

Some Bootstrap CSS classes for working with padding

Class	Description
pt-*size*	Sets the padding for the top to the specified size from 0 to 5. By default, these sizes correspond to rem unit values of 0, .25, .5, 1, 1.5, and 3.
pb-*size*	Sets the padding for the bottom to the specified size.
ps-*size*	Sets the padding for the starting side to the specified size.
pe-*size*	Sets the padding for the ending side to the specified size.
p-*size*	Sets the padding for all four sides to the specified size.

Some elements that use margins and padding

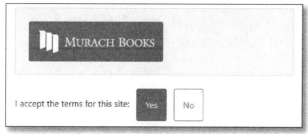

The HTML

```
<div class="container">
    <header class="p-4 mt-2 mb-4 bg-light rounded border">
        <img id="logo" alt="Murach logo" src="~/images/MurachLogo.jpg"
             class="img-fluid rounded" />
    </header>
    <main>
        <form asp-action="Index" method="post">
            <span class="me-2">I accept the terms for this site:</span>
            <button type="submit"
                    class="btn btn-primary p-3 me-2">Yes</button>
            <a asp-action="Index"
                class="btn btn-outline-secondary p-3">No</a>
        </form>
    </main>
</div>
```

Figure 3-9   How to work with margins and padding

The code for the view of the Future Value app

Now that you understand how the basic Bootstrap classes work, you should be able to understand the code for the view of the responsive Future Value app. Figure 3-10 shows this code. This results in a Future Value app that works on different screens sizes as shown in figure 3-1. Of course, this assumes that the view uses a Razor layout like the one shown in figure 3-4.

To start, the view begins with a <div> element that uses the container class to center the page and adjust its width to the viewport. This <div> element contains an <h1> element and a <for> element. The <h1> element displays the Title property of the ViewBag. This element uses the mt-*size* and mb-*size* classes to increase the size of the top and bottom margins for the heading.

This <form> element contains five <div> elements that use the row class to identify the five rows of the form. The first row contains the monthly investment label, a text box, and a validation message. Here, the label uses the col-md-3 class so it spans three columns on medium and larger devices. It also uses the form-label class for styling.

Next, the text box uses the form-control class for styling. In addition, it's coded within a <div> element that uses the col-md-3 class. That way, it spans three columns just like the label.

Finally, the validation message uses the col class so that it spans the remaining six columns. To display this message, a <span> element uses the asp-validation-for tag helper that you'll learn about in chapter 11. In addition, this <span> element uses the text-danger class that's presented later in this chapter to display the error message in red.

The second and third rows display the text boxes for the interest rate and number of years. The code for these two rows works much like the first row. As a result, you shouldn't have much trouble understanding how they work.

The fourth row also works similarly. However, it doesn't display an error message. As a result, it only specifies six out of twelve possible columns. This shows that you don't have to specify all columns when you work with a grid.

The fifth row contains the Calculate and Clear buttons. The <div> element that contains these buttons uses the col and offset-md-3 classes. The offset class moves the buttons three columns to the right, which aligns them with the controls in the previous rows. Then, the buttons use the btn, btn-primary, and btn-outline-secondary classes for styling.

Note that no column classes are included for small and extra small devices. As a result, on those devices, Bootstrap stacks the form elements vertically and makes them as wide as the screen as shown by the second and third screens in figure 3-1.

The code for the Index view

```
@model FutureValueModel
@{
    ViewData["Title"] = "Future Value Calculator";
}

<div class="container">
    <h1 class="mt-3 mb-4">@ViewBag.Title</h1>
    <form asp-action="Index" method="post">
        <div class="row">
            <label asp-for="MonthlyInvestment"
                   class="col-md-3 col-form-label">
                   Monthly Investment: </label>
            <div class="col-md-3">
                <input asp-for="MonthlyInvestment" class="form-control" />
            </div>
            <span asp-validation-for="MonthlyInvestment"
                  class="col text-danger"></span>
        </div>
        <div class="row">
            <label asp-for="YearlyInterestRate" class="col-md-3
                col-form-label">
                Yearly Interest Rate:</label>
            <div class="col-md-3">
                <input asp-for="YearlyInterestRate" class="form-control" />
            </div>
            <span asp-validation-for="YearlyInterestRate"
                  class="col text-danger"></span>
        </div>
        <div class="row">
            <label asp-for="Years" class="col-md-3 col-form-label">
                Number of Years: </label>
            <div class="col-md-3">
                <input asp-for="Years" class="form-control" /></div>
            <span asp-validation-for="Years"
                  class="col text-danger"></span>
        </div>
        <div class="row">
            <label class="col-md-3 col-form-label">Future Value:</label>
            <div class="col-md-3">
                <input value="@ViewBag.FutureValue" readonly
                       class="form-control" />
            </div>
        </div>
        <div class="row">
            <div class="col offset-md-3">
                <button type="submit" class="btn btn-primary">
                    Calculate</button>
                <a asp-action="Index"
                   class="btn btn-outline-secondary">Clear</a>
            </div>
        </div>
    </form>
</div>
```

Figure 3-10   The code for the view of the Future Value app

More skills for Bootstrap CSS classes

So far, this chapter has presented the skills you need to use Bootstrap to create the responsive version of the Future Value app. These skills include using Bootstrap CSS classes to style buttons, text boxes, and drop-down lists. Now, you're ready to learn how to use some other Bootstrap CSS classes to make other apps responsive. For example, you're ready to learn the skills you need to make the Movie List app presented in the next chapter responsive.

How to format HTML tables

The table in figure 3-11 shows some of the Bootstrap CSS classes for working with HTML tables. Then, the first example shows an HTML table that uses the default Bootstrap styling. For these Bootstrap table classes to work correctly, an HTML table must have <thead> and <tbody> elements as shown in this figure.

The second example shows the same table with additional table classes applied. Here, the table-striped class applies alternating colors to the rows of the table. The table-bordered class adds a border around the table and between cells. And the table-hover class makes the color of a row change when you hover the mouse pointer over it.

The table-responsive class works differently than the other CSS classes for working with tables. Instead of applying this class directly to a <table> element, you apply it to a <div> element that contains a <table> element that has one or more of the Bootstrap table classes applied to it. Then, if the viewport narrows so the data in each cell of the table can't be displayed, horizontal scrolling is added to the table.

When working with tables, you may sometimes need to specify the width of a column. To do that, you can use the w-*size* class to specify the size of a column as a percent of the parent element. For example, you can specify that a column for a table heading should be 25% of the width of the table by adding a class like this one:

```
<th class="w-25">Department</th>
```

Then, the table uses that width for the column in the heading and the body of the table.

Common CSS classes for working with HTML tables

Class	Description
`table`	Provides default styling for an HTML <table> element.
`table-bordered`	Adds a border around the table and between cells.
`table-striped`	Adds alternating colors to the table rows.
`table-hover`	Makes the color of a row change when you hover over it.
`table-responsive`	Adds horizontal scrolling to the table when the viewport narrows. Applied to a <div> element that contains a <table> element with the table class.
`w-size`	The width of a column as a percent of the parent element. Valid values are 25, 50, 75, 100, and auto. The default is auto.

A table with default styling

Department	Phone Number	Extension
General	555-555-5555	1
Customer Service	555-555-5556	2
Billing and Accounts	555-555-5557	3

```html
<table class="table">
    <thead>
        <tr><th>Department</th><th>Phone Number</th><th>Extension</th></tr>
    </thead>
    <tbody>
        <tr><td>General</td><td>555-555-5555</td><td>1</td></tr>
        <tr><td>Customer Service</td><td>555-555-5556</td><td>2</td></tr>
        <tr><td>Billing and Accounts</td><td>555-555-5557</td><td>3</td></tr>
    </tbody>
</table>
```

A table with alternating stripes and borders

Department	Phone Number	Extension
General	555-555-5555	1
Customer Service	555-555-5556	2
Billing and Accounts	555-555-5557	3

```html
<table class="table table-striped table-bordered table-hover">...
```

Description

- You must include the <thead> and <tbody> elements in your table for the Bootstrap table classes to work properly.

Figure 3-11   How to format HTML tables

How to align and capitalize text

The table in figure 3-12 shows some of the Bootstrap CSS classes for working with text. The classes shown here consist of alignment classes and transformation classes.

The alignment classes control where the text of an element displays on the page relative to the element that contains it. For instance, assume the <p> elements in the example below the table are coded within a <div> element that spans six Bootstrap columns. Then, the first <p> element is aligned at the right side of the <div> element, the second <p> element is centered, and the third <p> element is aligned at the left side.

Like the classes used for margins and padding, the alignment classes now refer to the starting or ending side of an element rather than the left or right side of an element. That way, these classes can be used with a right-to-left layout as well as the default left-to-right layout.

The transformation classes control how the text of an element is capitalized. For instance, the text in the first <span> element displays in all uppercase letters, even though the text in the HTML is in lowercase letters. Similarly, the text in the second <span> element displays with the first letter of each word capitalized, and the text in the third <span> element displays in all lowercase letters.

Common CSS classes for text

Class	Description
text-start	Aligns text at the starting side of the parent element.
text-end	Aligns text at the ending side of the parent element.
text-center	Aligns text in the center of the parent element.
text-lowercase	Makes all text in the element lower case.
text-uppercase	Makes all text in the element upper case.
text-capitalize	Capitalizes the first letter of every word in the element.

Some examples of the CSS classes for text

```
                                      This text is RIGHT-ALIGNED.

                      This Text Is Centered.

This text is left-aligned.
```

```
<p class="text-end">
    This text is <span class="text-uppercase">right-aligned</span>.
</p>
<p class="text-center">
    <span class="text-capitalize">This text is centered.</span>
</p>
<p class="text-start">
    This text is <span class="text-lowercase">LEFT-ALIGNED</span>.
</p>
```

Description

- The Bootstrap classes for text control the alignment and capitalization for the text.
- The alignment classes, text-start, text-end, and text-center, control where the text of an element is displayed on the page relative to the element that contains it.
- By default, Bootstrap lays out text from left to right. To provide for laying out text from right to left, Bootstrap classes now use -start and -end instead of -left and -right.
- The transformation classes, text-lowercase, text-uppercase, and text-capitalize, control the capitalization for the text of an element.

Figure 3-12   How to align and capitalize text

How to provide context

Figure 3-13 presents the context classes that are available with Bootstrap. These classes apply a color to an element depending on its context.

The table in this figure shows the eight main CSS classes for providing context. These classes are available to most elements.

The examples in this figure show how to use some of these context classes. The first example shows how six buttons appear with six different classes applied. Here, each context class is prefixed with *btn-* to indicate that the context is being applied to a button. You can use Visual Studio's IntelliSense feature to find out what prefixes you can use with the context classes.

The second example shows how the success class is applied to the text in a <p> element. Here, the text-success class indicates that the color for the success class, which is usually green, should be applied to the text within the <p> element.

By contrast, the third example shows how the warning class is applied to the background of a <p> element. Here, the bg-warning class indicates that the color for the warning class, which is usually orange, should be applied to the background of the <p> element. In addition, this element uses the p-2 class to add .5 rems of padding, and it uses the rounded class to round its corners.

The context classes available to most elements

Class	Description	Default color
primary	Specifies that the element is a primary element.	Dark blue
secondary	Specifies that the element is a secondary element.	Gray
success	Indicates a successful or positive outcome or action.	Green
info	Indicates neutral information.	Light blue
warning	Indicates something that might need attention.	Orange
danger	Indicates a dangerous or negative outcome or action.	Red
light	Uses a light background.	Light gray
dark	Uses a dark background.	Gray

Some examples of the context classes applied to buttons

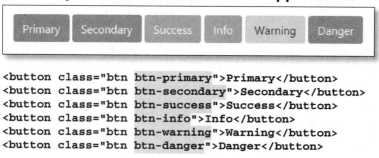

```
<button class="btn btn-primary">Primary</button>
<button class="btn btn-secondary">Secondary</button>
<button class="btn btn-success">Success</button>
<button class="btn btn-info">Info</button>
<button class="btn btn-warning">Warning</button>
<button class="btn btn-danger">Danger</button>
```

The success class applied to the text of an element

Congratulations! You are now registered.

```
<p class="text-success">Congratulations! You are now registered.</p>
```

The warning class applied to the background of an element

Warning! Some required fields are empty.

```
<p class="bg-warning p-2 rounded">
    Warning! Some required fields are empty.
</p>
```

Description

- The context classes are typically combined with a prefix that indicates the element or component being styled. For example, btn- specifies button, text- specifies text, bg- specifies background, and so on. However, the context classes can be applied without a prefix to some elements.

Figure 3-13   How to provide context

More skills for Bootstrap components

Up until now, this chapter has focused on showing how to apply Bootstrap CSS classes to standard HTML elements. However, Bootstrap also provides its own *components* that use predefined HTML elements and CSS classes to create a user interface element. Now, you'll learn how to use other Bootstrap components such as button groups, icons, badges, breadcrumbs, and alerts.

How to work with button groups

The table in figure 3-14 shows some of the Bootstrap CSS classes that create *button groups*, and the two examples show some of the ways to use these classes. In the first example, four links styled as buttons are grouped together within a <div> element that has the btn-group class applied to it. This class provides the formatting that makes the buttons in the group look like a menu bar.

In the second example, two <div> elements each with two links styled as buttons are coded as button groups. Then, these two <div> elements are coded within another <div> element that has the btn-toolbar class applied to it. This class combines the two button groups. In addition, the first button group uses the me-2 class to set its right margin to .5 rems. This adds a little space between these button groups to make it easy to identify each button group.

For assistive technologies such as screen readers to work correctly with button groups, you need to set the role attribute for button groups and toolbars correctly. In this figure, for instance, the first example sets the role attribute to group, and the second example sets the role attribute to toolbar for the outer <div> element and to group for the inner <div> elements. In addition, you should specify an aria-label attribute that accurately describes each element as shown in this figure.

Common CSS classes for creating button groups

Class	Description
btn-group	Groups two or more buttons with no padding between them.
btn-toolbar	Combines button groups with appropriate padding between groups.
btn-group-*size*	Applies sizing to all buttons in a group. Example: btn-group-lg.
btn-group-vertical	Stacks buttons in a group vertically rather than horizontally.

A basic button group

```
<div class="btn-group" role="group" aria-label="Button group">
    <a href="/" class="btn btn-outline-primary">Home</a>
    <a href="/cart" class="btn btn-outline-primary">Cart</a>
    <a href="/products" class="btn btn-outline-primary">Products</a>
    <a href="/contact-us" class="btn btn-outline-primary">Contact Us</a>
</div>
```

A toolbar with two button groups

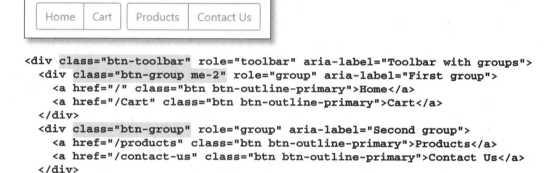

```
<div class="btn-toolbar" role="toolbar" aria-label="Toolbar with groups">
  <div class="btn-group me-2" role="group" aria-label="First group">
    <a href="/" class="btn btn-outline-primary">Home</a>
    <a href="/Cart" class="btn btn-outline-primary">Cart</a>
  </div>
  <div class="btn-group" role="group" aria-label="Second group">
    <a href="/products" class="btn btn-outline-primary">Products</a>
    <a href="/contact-us" class="btn btn-outline-primary">Contact Us</a>
  </div>
</div>
```

Description

- A *button group* lets you display a group of buttons.
- For assistive technologies such as screen readers to work correctly with button groups, you need to set the role attribute for button groups and toolbars. In addition, you should specify the aria-label attribute.

Figure 3-14   How to work with button groups

How to work with icons and badges

An *icon* is a symbol that decorates or adds meaning to an element. For example, you can add an icon to a button or link to indicate its purpose. To do that, you can use the free icons available from Font Awesome with the solid style.

The easiest way to enable the icons that are available from Font Awesome is to include a <link> element that links to the CSS file from the Font Awesome website as shown in the first example in figure 3-15. Typically, you can place this <link> element just below the element that links to the Bootstrap CSS file. The hash code for the integrity attribute is too long to display, but you can copy it from the Font Awesome website. This attribute helps verify that the Font Awesome website has delivered the resource securely.

To use an icon, you include the base fas (Font Awesome Solid) class along with the class for the individual icon you want to use. In this figure, the examples use the fa-home class for the Home icon and the fa-shopping-cart class for the Cart icon.

It's important to note that you can't code the Font Awesome classes directly on other components. For instance, in the first example, you might think that you could code the fas and fa-home classes on an <a> element. However, you must code these classes on an element such as a <span> element that's coded within another element such as an <a> element. In addition, the <span> element that specifies the icon classes can't include any other content such as text.

If you use icons, you should be aware that they don't have any padding by default. As a result, if you're going to use an icon with text as shown in the second example, you need to add space between the icon and the text. To do that, you can add a nonbreaking space entity ( ) to the HTML as shown in this figure. Or, if you prefer, you can use Bootstrap classes or CSS to add space.

When you use icons, you should make them accessible. This is particularly important if an icon isn't accompanied by text. In that case, make sure to include content that reflects the meaning of the icon and that can be read by screen readers. On the other hand, if an icon is accompanied by text, it should be hidden so it doesn't confuse screen readers.

A *badge* component lets you highlight text within an element. This is illustrated in the second example in this figure. Here, the <a> element contains text of "Cart" and a badge with the number 2. Here, the content of the badge is coded in a <span> element that uses the badge and bg-primary classes. As a result, the badge is blue with white text. In addition, the badge collapses so it's hidden if it doesn't contain any text. This is common when you use code to set the content of a badge when an app is running.

The third example shows that you can combine icons and badges within a single element, such as a link that's styled as a button. Here, the first <span> element displays the Cart icon, and the second <span> element displays the badge that indicates how many items are in the cart. Between these <span> elements, the HTML specifies text of "Cart" with a nonbreaking space before and after.

The URL for the Font Awesome website

```
https://fontawesome.com/
```

A typical <link> element that enables Font Awesome icons

```
<link rel="stylesheet"
      href="https://use.fontawesome.com/releases/v6.1.1/css/all.css"
      integrity="sha-long-hash_code" crossorigin="anonymous">
```

A button group that includes icons for both of its buttons

```
<div class="btn-group" role="group" aria-label="Button group">
    <a href="/" class="btn btn-outline-primary">
        <span class="fas fa-home"></span> Home 
    </a>
    <a href="/cart" class="btn btn-outline-primary">
        <span class="fas fa-shopping-cart"></span> Cart 
    </a>
</div>
```

A button with a badge

```
<a href="/cart" class="btn btn-outline-primary">
     Cart <span class="badge bg-primary">2</span>
</a>
```

A button with an icon and a badge

```
<a href="/cart" class="btn btn-outline-primary">
    <span class="fas fa-shopping-cart"></span> Cart 
    <span class="badge bg-primary">2</span>
</a>
```

Description

- An *icon* is a symbol that you use to decorate or add meaning to an element.
- A *badge* provides for highlighting text within a component.
- The classes for icons and badges are typically coded in a <span> element that's coded within another element.
- You can add an icon to a button or link using the free icons available from the Font Awesome solid (fas) style. For more details, please visit the Font Awesome website.

Figure 3-15   How to work with icons and badges

How to work with button dropdowns

Figure 3-16 shows how to create a *button dropdown*. When the user clicks a button dropdown, it displays a menu and lets the user select an item from that menu. To create a button dropdown, you use the CSS classes and the HTML data attribute summarized by the table in this figure.

Under this table, the example presents a button dropdown. To start, a <div> element uses the dropdown class to specify the start and end of the button dropdown. Within this <div> element, the code specifies a <button> element for the button and another <div> element that contains a dropdown menu.

The <button> element uses the dropdown-toggle class to style the button as a dropdown. This displays a caret to the right of the text on the button. This caret indicates that the button is a dropdown, not a standard button. Then, the <button> element sets its data-bs-toggle attribute to "dropdown" so the button behaves like a dropdown menu. Here, the "bs" portion of the attribute stands for Bootstrap, and it was added to all the Bootstrap data attributes with Bootstrap 5.

The second <div> element defines the items in the menu. To start, it uses the dropdown-menu class to style this element as a dropdown menu. Then, each <a> element within the list uses the dropdown-item class to style each link as a menu item. Each of these links specifies the URL to be requested when the user clicks the item.

A button dropdown needs the Popper.js library to work. That's because the Popper.js library contains the JavaScript that displays the menu when the user clicks on the button. As a result, the page must include the Popper.js library as described in figure 3-4. Alternately, the page can include the bootstrap.bundle library since that library includes the Popper.js library.

To keep this example simple, the menu uses <a> elements for all of the dropdown menu items since that's the most common scenario. However, it's possible to include most types of components in a dropdown menu. For example, you can include text boxes that allow the user to enter search terms. Or, you can include forms such as login forms. More commonly, though, you might want to include a checkbox menu item, a radio button group, or a submenu.

To make the dropdown menu work with assistive technologies, you can include the aria- attributes shown in this figure. For this to work, the dropdown menu can only contain menu items, checkbox menu items, radio button menu items, radio button groups, and submenus.

CSS classes and an HTML data attribute for creating button dropdowns

Class	Description
dropdown	Marks the start and end of a dropdown list of items.
dropdown-toggle	Applies styling to a button that will function as a dropdown.
dropdown-menu	Applies styling to a dropdown menu.
dropdown-item	Applies styling to the items in a menu.
dropup	Works like the dropdown class but makes the list items drop up.

Attribute	Description
data-bs-toggle	If set to "dropdown", makes a button dropdown.

A button dropdown

```
<div class="dropdown">
    <button type="button" class="btn btn-primary dropdown-toggle"
        id="productsDropdown" data-bs-toggle="dropdown"
        aria-haspopup="true" aria-expanded="false">
        Products
    </button>
    <div class="dropdown-menu" aria-labelledby="productsDropdown">
        <a class="dropdown-item" href="/product/list/guitars">Guitars</a>
        <a class="dropdown-item" href="/product/list/drums">Drums</a>
    </div>
</div>
```

Description

- You can use the classes and attribute shown above to create a *button dropdown*. When you click on a button dropdown, it displays a dropdown menu.
- To create a button dropdown, you must code a button for the button and a dropdown menu that includes the items for the menu.
- A button dropdown needs the Popper.js library to work.
- To make the dropdown menu work with assistive technologies, you can include the aria- attributes shown in this figure. For this to work, the dropdown menu can only contain menu items, checkbox menu items, radio button menu items, radio button groups, and submenus.

Figure 3-16   How to work with button dropdowns

How to work with list groups

The table in figure 3-17 shows some of the Bootstrap CSS classes that you can use to create *list groups*. As its name implies, a list group is simply a group of items displayed in a list.

In the first example, the items in an unordered list are styled as a list group. Here, the list-group class is applied to the <ul> element, and the list-group-item class is applied to each <li> element in the list. It's common to use a list like this when you just want to display information.

Although it's not shown here, Bootstrap 5 also provides for numbering the items in a list. To do that, you apply the list-group-numbered class to a <ul> or <ol> element.

If you want to display links or buttons in a list, you should code them within a <div> element that uses the list-group class as shown by the second example. Here, the list consists of a three <a> elements, and the list-group-item class is applied to each of these elements. In addition, the active class is applied to the first link. This highlights the link to show that it's the active link.

It's common to write code that sets the active class when the app is running. That way, you can change the active link depending on the user's actions. Similarly, you can use the disabled class to disable a link depending on the user's actions.

Common CSS classes for creating list groups

Class	Description
list-group	Groups two or more items in a <ul>, <ol>, or <div> element.
list-group-numbered	Groups and numbers two or more items in a <ul> or <ol> element.
list-group-item	Styles the individual items in a list group.
active	Highlights the list group item.
disabled	Grays out the list group item.

A basic list group

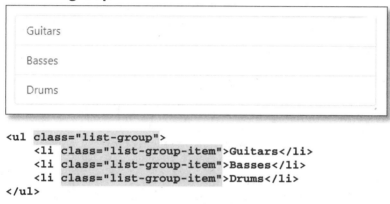

```
<ul class="list-group">
    <li class="list-group-item">Guitars</li>
    <li class="list-group-item">Basses</li>
    <li class="list-group-item">Drums</li>
</ul>
```

Another basic list group with an active item

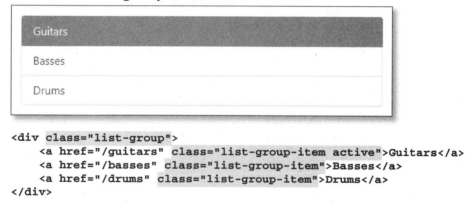

```
<div class="list-group">
    <a href="/guitars" class="list-group-item active">Guitars</a>
    <a href="/basses" class="list-group-item">Basses</a>
    <a href="/drums" class="list-group-item">Drums</a>
</div>
```

Description

- The CSS classes for *list groups* let you display a list of items such as links, buttons, and list items. You can also nest a list group within another list group.

- To create a numbered list group, you can include the list-group-numbered class on a <ul> or <ol> element.

Figure 3-17   How to work with list groups

How to work with alerts and breadcrumbs

The first table in figure 3-18 shows some of the Bootstrap CSS classes and an HTML data attribute that you can use to work with *alerts*. In its simplest form, an alert can consist of an element such as a <div> that contains text and has the alert class applied to it. In most cases, though, an alert contains additional components such as a close button and a link like the alert shown in this figure.

There are three things to notice about this alert. First, the alert class is applied to the <div> element that contains the alert. In addition, an alert-*context* class that provides the appropriate color for the alert is also applied to this <div>, as well as the alert-dismissible class that provides for closing the alert.

Second, within the <div> element, the btn-close class is applied to the HTML button. This class provides for closing the alert. Also, the data-bs-dismiss data attribute of this button tells Bootstrap to dismiss the alert when the button is clicked.

Third, the alert-link class is applied to the link in the alert so the link matches the styling of the alert itself. In this case, since the alert uses the success context class, the alert-link class styles the link to match that context.

This figure also shows how to create *breadcrumbs*. Breadcrumbs provide navigation links that are relative to the user's current location in a website. Here, the breadcrumbs are coded as an ordered list. In addition, the active class has been applied to the last item in the list. This class indicates the current page, and it displays the text of the item in a different color than the other items. Also, the last item doesn't contain a link.

It's common to write code that creates breadcrumbs when the app is running. That way, you can update the breadcrumbs as the user navigates through the website.

Because the breadcrumbs are a navigation component, it's a good practice to code them within a <nav> element as shown in this figure. In addition, to make breadcrumbs work with assistive technologies, you can include an aria-label attribute on this element as shown in this figure.

Common CSS classes and an HTML data attribute for creating alerts

Class	Description
alert	Wraps text and HTML in a context message area.
alert-*context*	Applies a context class to an alert. Example: alert-warning.
alert-dismissible	Makes an alert dismissible. The div for the alert should include a button that uses the close class and the data-bs-dismiss attribute.
alert-link	Styles links to match the styling of the alert that contains the link.
btn-close	Provides for closing an alert.

Attribute	Description
data-bs-dismiss	Tells Bootstrap to dismiss the alert.

A dismissible alert with a link

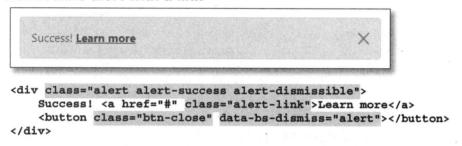

```
<div class="alert alert-success alert-dismissible">
    Success! <a href="#" class="alert-link">Learn more</a>
    <button class="btn-close" data-bs-dismiss="alert"></button>
</div>
```

Common CSS classes for creating breadcrumbs

Class	Description
breadcrumb	Makes an ordered list element display inline with separators between items.
breadcrumb-item	Identifies a list item as a breadcrumb.
active	Indicates the current page.

A breadcrumb with three segments

Home / Products / Guitars

```
<nav aria-label="breadcrumb">
    <ol class="breadcrumb">
        <li class="breadcrumb-item"><a href="/">Home</a></li>
        <li class="breadcrumb-item"><a href="/Products">Products</a></li>
        <li class="breadcrumb-item active" aria-current="page">Guitars</li>
    </ol>
</nav>
```

Description

- *Alerts* let you provide contextual feedback in your app.
- *Breadcrumbs* display navigation links that are relative to the user's current location.

Figure 3-18   How to work with alerts and breadcrumbs

How to work with navigation bars

Bootstrap provides an easy way to create a responsive menu bar known as a navigation bar that collapses to a dropdown menu on narrower viewports. To do that, you often code one or more nav components within a navbar component.

How to create navs

The table in figure 3-19 shows some of the Bootstrap CSS classes that you can use to create *nav* components. Nav components provide a way to create a simple menu bar. However, they're more commonly used as part of a navbar component as shown in the next figure.

In this figure, the first example shows how to create a nav component that contains navigation links styled as tabs, and the second example shows how to create the same navigation component with the links styled as pills. These examples show that the only difference between a tab and a pill is in the appearance of the active item.

For both examples, the navigation links are coded within an HTML <nav> element. This provides accessibility for the items. If for some reason you need to put a nav component within an element other than a <nav> element, you should include the role="navigation" attribute on that element.

To create a nav component, it's common to use an HTML <ul> element that contains <li> elements that contain <a> elements as shown in the third example. However, when you use Bootstrap, you don't need to include the <ul> or <li> elements. Instead, you can just apply the nav-item and nav-link classes directly to the <a> element as shown by the first two examples in this figure.

You can also add button dropdowns to a nav component. To do that, you just nest the code for the button dropdown within the nav component. Then, you can change the styling for the button so it looks good in the navigation bar. For example, you may want to use an outline style for the button when you place it in a navigation bar.

Common CSS classes for creating navs

Class	Description
nav	Groups two or more nav items.
nav-tabs	Styles the nav items in a single line with the active item displayed as a tab.
nav-pills	Styles the nav items in a single line with the active item displayed as a pill.
nav-item	Identifies a nav item such as an <li> element that contains a nav link. However, if you want, you can code nav links outside of an <li> element. In that case, you may need to use this class to identify the link as a nav item.
nav-link	Specifies that the nav item is a link.
active	Styles the active nav item or link differently than the other nav items.

Nav links styled as tabs

Home   Products   Cart

```
<nav class="nav nav-tabs">
    <a class="nav-item nav-link active" href="/">Home</a>
    <a class="nav-item nav-link" href="/products">Products</a>
    <a class="nav-item nav-link" href="/cart">Cart</a>
</nav>
```

The same nav links styled as pills

Home   Products   Cart

```
<nav class="nav nav-pills">
    <a class="nav-item nav-link active" href="/">Home</a>
    <a class="nav-item nav-link" href="/products">Products</a>
    <a class="nav-item nav-link" href="/cart">Cart</a>
</nav>
```

A more verbose way of coding the same nav links

```
<ul class="nav nav-pills">
  <li class="nav-item">
    <a class="nav-link active" href="/">Home</a>
  </li>
  <li class="nav-item">
    <a class="nav-link" href="/products">Products</a>
  </li>
  <li class="nav-item">
    <a class="nav-link" href="/cart">Cart</a>
  </li>
</ul>
```

Description

* You can use the CSS classes for *navs* to create tabs and pills. The difference between a tab and a pill is in the appearance of the active item.

Figure 3-19   How to create navs

How to create navbars

The Bootstrap *navbar* component creates a responsive menu bar that collapses to a dropdown menu on narrower viewports. The table in figure 3-20 presents some of the Bootstrap CSS classes and HTML data attributes that you can use to create a navbar. To get a navbar to work correctly, you don't need to understand exactly what each class and attribute does. Instead, you can often cut and paste code for an existing navbar and modify it as necessary. That's why this figure focuses on the most important Bootstrap classes for creating navbars.

This figure begins by showing the same navbar at two different viewport widths. Here, a wide screen displays the brand and all the links in the menu bar across the top of the page. By contrast, a small screen only displays the brand and a toggle button that you can use to display and hide the menu items.

After showing this navbar, this figure shows the HTML that creates it. To start, the navbar is coded within a <nav> element for accessibility. Then, four classes are applied to the <nav> element. The navbar class identifies it as a navigation bar, the navbar-expand-md class expands the navbar on medium and larger screens, the navbar-dark class sets the color scheme for a dark background, and the bg-primary sets the background color to the primary color, which is usually dark blue.

Within the <nav> element, the first <a> element uses the navbar-brand class to style the text for the brand with a larger font than the other navigation links. The brand is typically text or an image that displays the home page when clicked. By default, it's displayed at the left side of the navbar.

After the brand link, a <button> element defines the toggle button that's displayed when the navbar is collapsed. By default, this button is displayed at the right side of the navbar. This button uses the navbar-toggler class and the data-bs-toggle and data-bs-target attributes. This class and these attributes provide for collapsing the navbar and displaying and hiding the navigation links on small screens. In addition, this button uses the aria- classes that provide for accessibility.

After the toggle button, the nested <nav> element contains the links for the navbar. This element uses the collapse and navbar-collapse classes so the navbar collapses properly on small screen sizes. It also includes an id attribute whose value is identified by the data-bs-target attribute of the element for the toggle button.

The links for the navbar shown here are coded within two <div> elements. The navbar-nav class is applied to both of these elements. In addition, the me-auto class is applied to the first <div> element so the right margin can be set automatically, and the ms-auto class is applied to the second <div> element so the left margin can be set automatically. As you can see, this aligns the links in the first <div> element at the left side of the navbar and the links in the second <div> element at the right side of the navbar.

Common CSS classes and HTML data attributes for creating navbars

Class	Description
navbar	Creates a responsive navigation bar that collapses in smaller viewports.
navbar-expand-*size*	Sets the minimum size for the navbar to be expanded.
navbar-*light-or-dark*	Sets the color scheme for a light or dark background color.
navbar-brand	Identifies the brand for your navbar.
navbar-toggler	Identifies and styles the toggler button.
navbar-collapse	Identifies and styles the parts of the navbar that collapse.
collapse	Collapses the navbar until the user clicks on the toggler button.
navbar-nav	Identifies and styles part of a navbar.

Attribute	Description
data-bs-toggle	If set to "collapse", makes a navbar collapsible.
data-bs-target	Identifies the HTML element that will be changed.

A navbar expanded on a wide screen and collapsed on a small screen

The HTML

```
<nav class="navbar navbar-expand-md navbar-dark bg-primary">
    <div class="container-fluid">
        <a class="navbar-brand" href="/">My Guitar Shop</a>
        <button class="navbar-toggler" type="button"
                data-bs-toggle="collapse"
                data-bs-target="#navbarSupportedContent"
                aria-controls="navbarSupportedContent" aria-expanded="false"
                aria-label="Toggle navigation">
            <span class="navbar-toggler-icon"></span>
        </button>
        <nav class="collapse navbar-collapse" id="navbarSupportedContent">
            <div class="navbar-nav me-auto">
                <a class="nav-item nav-link active" href="/">Home</a>
                <a class="nav-item nav-link" href="/products">Products</a>
                <a class="nav-item nav-link" href="/about">About</a>
            </div>
            <div class="navbar-nav ms-auto">
                <a class="nav-item nav-link" href="/cart">
                    <span class="fas fa-shopping-cart"></span> Cart 
                    <span class="badge badge-primary ms-2">2</span>
                </a>
            </div>
        </nav>
    </div>
</nav>
```

Figure 3-20   How to create navbars

How to position navbars

When you code a navbar, you can code it as the first element in the <body> element. In that case, the navbar stretches across the entire viewport. However, you can also nest the navbar within a container element such as a <div> element. This causes the navbar to span the width of the container element.

In the previous figure, the navbar is coded as the first element of the <body> element. As a result, it's positioned at the top of the screen and stretches across the entire viewport. However, when the user scrolls down, the navbar will scroll off the screen. In many cases, that's how you want your navbars to work. In other cases, you may want your navbar to always be displayed at the top of the screen, even when the user scrolls down. Or, you may want to display a navbar at the bottom of the screen. To do that, you can use the skills shown in figure 3-21.

The table in this figure shows some of the Bootstrap CSS classes that you can use to create *fixed navbars*. Then, this figure shows a navbar that's fixed at the top of the screen and the code that's used to create it. Here, the <nav> element that defines the navbar component is coded as the first element of the <body> element. As a result, it spans the entire width of the viewport.

In this figure, the <nav> element includes the fixed-top class. Otherwise, the rest of the HTML is the same as for the <nav> element shown in the previous figure.

When fixing a navbar to the top of the screen, you typically need to adjust the top margin of the <body> element. If you don't, the navbar covers the content at the top of the page and makes it unreadable. In this figure, for example, the custom CSS adds 70 pixels to the top margin. Of these pixels, 50 accommodate the height of the navbar and an additional 20 pixels provide space between the page's content and the navbar.

If you want, you can easily modify the HTML and CSS code shown in this figure so it fixes the navbar to the bottom of the screen. First, edit the <nav> element so it uses the fixed-bottom class instead of the fixed-top class. Then, edit the custom CSS class so it sets the bottom margin to 70px. This should position the navbar at the bottom of the page as shown by the second screen in this figure.

Although the examples in this figure and the previous figure should get you off to a good start, there's a lot more you can do with navbars. For example, you can add brand images, buttons, search forms, and more. For more information, please see the Bootstrap documentation.

More CSS classes for positioning navbars

Class	Description
`fixed-top`	Makes the navbar stay at the top of the screen even when the user scrolls. Will overlay other content unless you add enough margin to the top of the body.
`fixed-bottom`	Makes the navbar stay at the bottom of the screen even when the user scrolls. Will overlay other content unless you add margin to the bottom of the body.

A navbar that's fixed at the top of the screen

The HTML that displays the navbar

```
<body>
    <nav class="navbar navbar-expand-md navbar-dark bg-primary fixed-top">
        <div class="container-fluid">
            <!-- navbar items go here -->
        </div>
    </nav>
    <div class="container">
        <!-- container items go here -->
    </div>
</body>
```

The CSS that sets the top margin

```
body {
    margin-top: 70px;
}
```

A navbar that's fixed at the bottom of the screen

Description

- A navbar can be coded as the first element in the <body> element, in which case it stretches across the entire viewport. By contrast, if a navbar is coded within a container such as a <div> element, it spans the width of that container.

- A *fixed navbar* remains displayed at either the top or bottom of the screen when the user scrolls up or down.

Figure 3-21   How to position navbars

Perspective

Now that you've completed this chapter, you know the right way to use Bootstrap in an ASP.NET Core MVC web app. That means using HTML for the content and structure of a page, using Bootstrap for responsive web design, and using a custom CSS style sheet whenever necessary. That separates the content and structure of each page from its formatting. And that makes it easier to create and maintain a mobile-friendly web app.

Of course, there's a lot more to Bootstrap than what's presented in this chapter. That includes more classes and components, as well as best practices for making Bootstrap accessible. Fortunately, the documentation for Bootstrap is excellent. As a result, if you need to learn more about Bootstrap, you can start by checking out the official Bootstrap documentation.

Terms

responsive web design	rem unit
framework	floating label
Bootstrap	button group
Responsive Font Sizes (RFS)	icon
Library Manager	badge
LibMan	button dropdown
minified	list group
viewport	alert
meta tag	breadcrumbs
boxed layout	nav
full width layout	navbar
Bootstrap CSS classes	fixed navbar
Bootstrap components	

Summary

- *Responsive web design* helps you create web apps that look good and are easy to use on all screen sizes.

- One way to create a responsive web design is to use a *framework* like *Bootstrap*, which uses CSS and JavaScript to make your web pages automatically adjust to different screen sizes.

- Bootstrap uses *Responsive Font Sizes* (*RFS*) to size fonts, margins, and paddings so they're appropriate for the screen size.

- With Visual Studio, you can use the *Library Manager* tool, also known as *LibMan*, to add client-side libraries such as Bootstrap and jQuery to a project.

- A *minified* version of a CSS or JavaScript library has removed unnecessary characters such as spaces and indentation. This improves load time but makes it more difficult for humans to read.

- The *viewport* is the part of the page that is visible to viewers. The *viewport meta tag* controls the width of the viewport.

- Bootstrap uses a grid system based on containers, rows, and columns.

- In a *boxed layout*, a container is centered in the screen and has a specific width in pixels based on the viewport's width. In a *full width layout*, a container is always the same width as the viewport.

- *Bootstrap CSS classes* let you style HTML elements such as buttons, images, and tables.

- *Bootstrap components* let you create user interface elements such as button groups, icons, and navbars.

- Bootstrap CSS classes often use *rem units* for sizing. A rem unit is similar to the more traditional em unit, which is commonly used in CSS.

- A *button group* lets you display a group of buttons.

- An *icon* is a symbol that you can use to decorate or add meaning to an element.

- A *badge* provides for highlighting text within a component.

- A *button dropdown* is a button that displays a dropdown menu when it's clicked.

- A *list group* displays a list of items such as links, buttons, and list items.

- *Alerts* let you provide contextual feedback in your app.

- *Breadcrumbs* display navigation links for the user's current location.

- A *nav* component creates a simple menu bar.

- A *navbar* component can be used to create a responsive menu bar that collapses to a dropdown menu on narrower viewports.

- A *fixed navbar* remains displayed at either the top or bottom of the screen when the user scrolls up or down.

Exercise 3-1   Work with the Bootstrap classes in the Future Value app

In this exercise, you'll review the Bootstrap files and classes that are used by the responsive version of the Future Value app. Then, you'll modify some of the classes to see how those changes affect the app.

Open the Future Value app and set up the client-side libraries

1. Open the Ch03Ex1FutureValue web app that's in the ex_starts folder.

2. In the Solution Explorer, expand the wwwroot folder and the lib folder to view the files for the client-side libraries. Note that these files include the Bootstrap CSS library.

3. Use the procedure in figure 3-3 to display the LibMan file and note the version numbers and file paths for the Bootstrap CSS library and the other client-side libraries.

4. Open the _Layout.cshtml file and note that the first <link> element specifies a path that leads to the Bootstrap CSS library. Also, note that the <script> element specifies a path that leads to the client-side JavaScript library for Bootstrap.

Review and modify the Bootstrap classes for the grid system

5. Open the Index.cshtml file and review the Bootstrap classes that are applied to various elements in this page.

6. Run the app. With the text fields empty, click the Calculate button so the validation messages are displayed.

7. Narrow and widen the browser window to see how the layout responds. Pay attention to when the labels and controls change from being displayed side-by-side to being stacked. When you're done, close the browser.

8. Locate the Bootstrap column classes and change the size from medium (col-md-*size*) to small (col-sm-*size*). Then, repeat steps 6 and 7 to see how the changes you've made impact the page.

9. If you're feeling adventurous, experiment with using the column classes so the elements display the way you want them on all screen sizes.

Experiment with some other the Bootstrap classes

10. Modify the HTML for the Clear button so it uses the Bootstrap btn-secondary class. This should display the Clear button with a gray background.

11. Before the form element, add a dismissible alert like the one shown in figure 3-18. This alert should say, "This site uses cookies". In addition, it should have a link that says, "View cookie policy". However, the link doesn't need to do anything.

12. Run the app and test your changes. When your changes are working correctly, close the app.

Exercise 3-2   Work with the Bootstrap classes in the Movie List app

In this exercise, you'll run the Movie List app that's presented in the next chapter. In addition, you'll modify some of the Bootstrap classes that it uses.

Open the Movie List app, review its Bootstrap files, and run it

1. Open the Ch03Ex2MovieList web app that's in the ex_starts folder.

2. In the Solution Explorer, expand the wwwroot folder and the lib folder to view the files for the client-side libraries including Bootstrap.

3. Open the _Layout.cshtml file and note that it includes a <link> element that includes a path to the Bootstrap CSS library. However, it doesn't link to any other client-side libraries. That shows that this app only needs the Bootstrap CSS library.

4. Press Ctrl+F5 to run this app. If you get an error message that says the app cannot open the Movies database, you need to create the database as described in appendix A (Windows) or B (macOS).

5. When the app starts, it should display a list of movies in a table. Note how the rows in the table alternate from white to a light gray. Also, note the border around the table and its cells.

Review and modify the Bootstrap classes

6. In the Views/Home folder, open the Index.cshtml file and review the Bootstrap classes that are applied to the table on this page.

7. Remove the classes that make the table bordered and striped.

8. Run the app. The table should display using Bootstrap's default settings for a table.

9. Add the table-hover class to the table.

10. Run the app again. If you hover the mouse pointer over a row, it should change the color of the row.

11. Modify the Edit and Delete links so they use the btn and btn-primary classes.

12. Run the app. The Edit and Delete links should now appear as buttons.

13. In the Views/Movie folder, open the Edit.cshtml file and edit the code for the Cancel link so it uses the btn and btn-outline-secondary classes.

14. Run the app and click on an Edit button. The Cancel button on the Edit Movie page should now appear white with a gray outline.

15. Repeat steps 13 and 14 for the Delete.cshtml file. This should change the appearance of the Cancel button on the Delete Movie page.

16. Close the app.

4

How to develop a data-driven MVC web app

In this chapter, you'll learn how to build a multi-page, data-driven MVC web app. This app displays data that's stored in a database and allows users to add, update, and delete that data. To do that, this app uses Microsoft's Entity Framework (EF) Core to work with two related tables in a SQL Server database.

An introduction to the Movie List app

This chapter shows how to create web apps that work with data that's stored in a database. To illustrate, it presents a simple Movie List app that stores data about movies in a SQL Server LocalDB database.

The pages of the app

Figure 4-1 shows the four pages of the Movie List app. To start, the Movie List page displays the movie data in a table. Above the table, the page displays a link that users can click when they want to add a new movie. Within the table, each row displays two links users can click when they want to edit or delete an existing movie.

If the user clicks the Add New Movie link, the app displays the Add Movie page. This page displays a form with text boxes that let the user enter the name, year, and rating for a movie. In addition, it displays a drop-down list that allows users to select a genre for the movie. The bottom of this form displays two buttons. As you might expect, the Save button adds the new movie to the database, and the Cancel button cancels the operation and displays the Movie List page.

If the user clicks one of the Edit links in the table on the Movie List page, the app displays the Edit Movie page. This page also contains a form with the same fields as the Add Movie page, as well as Save and Cancel buttons. In fact, since the Add and Edit pages require the same fields, they both use the same view. But, they have different URLs, and the Edit Movie page has data while the Add Movie page is blank. Later in this chapter, you'll see how this works.

If the user clicks one of the Delete links in the table on the Movie List page, the app displays the Delete Movie page. This page simply asks users to confirm that they really want to delete the selected movie. If they do, they click the Delete button to delete the movie from the database. If they don't, they click the Cancel button to return to the Movie List page.

Each of these pages communicates with a database that stores movie data. The Movie List page selects data, the Add Movie page inserts data, the Edit Movie page selects and then updates data, and the Delete Movie page selects and then deletes data. You'll learn how this works as you read this chapter.

The pages of the Movie List app

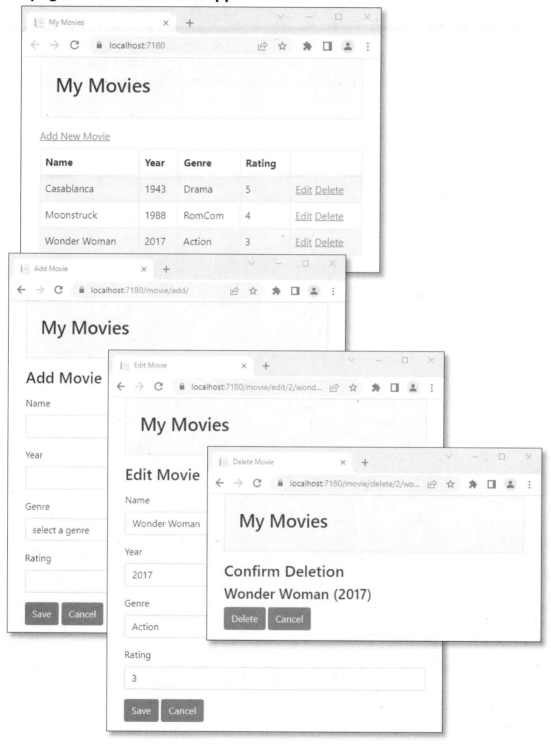

Figure 4-1   The pages of the Movie List app

The folders and files of the app

Before you learn the details of working with a database, you should learn a little more about the structure of the app presented in this chapter. Figure 4-2 presents the Solution Explorer window for the Movie List app. This window displays the folders and files found in the app's root directory.

The Solution Explorer contains the Models, Views, and Controllers folders that you would expect in an MVC app. In addition, it contains a folder named Migrations that you haven't seen before. This folder contains files that are used to create and update the underlying database. You'll learn how to work with the files in the Migrations folder as you progress through this chapter.

The last table in this figure describes two of the files in the Solution Explorer. As you'll see in this chapter, both of these files are important for apps that access a database.

The Solution Explorer for the Movie List app

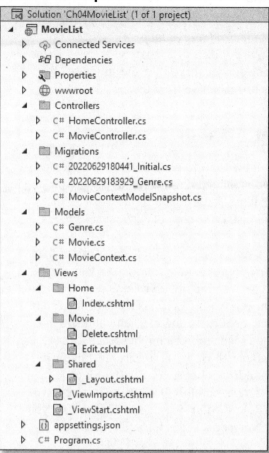

Folders in the Movie List app

Folder	Contains
Models	The files that define the Movie and Genre classes. Also, a MovieContext class that handles communication with the database.
Views	The view files associated with action methods in the Home and Movie controllers. Also, the Shared folder contains a layout that's used by the views.
Controllers	The files that define the Home controller that gets a list of movies, and the Movie controller that handles adding, editing, and deleting movies.
Migrations	Files that create a SQL Server LocalDB database and seed it with initial data.

Files in the Movie List app

File	Description
appsettings.json	A configuration file that stores static configuration settings such as database connection strings.
Program.cs	Code that runs when the app starts and configures the middleware for the app, including the objects that controllers need to communicate with the database.

Figure 4-2   The folders and files of the Movie List app

How to use EF Core

Entity Framework (EF) Core is an *object-relational mapping (ORM)* framework that allows you to work with the objects of a database in code. In the next few figures, you'll learn how to code classes that define the structure of a database. Then, you'll learn how to create a database from this code.

How to add EF Core to your project

Prior to .NET Core 3.0, EF Core and the tools to work with it were included with ASP.NET Core by default. However, with .NET Core 3.0 and later, you must manually add EF Core and the EF Core Tools to your project. To do that with Visual Studio, you need to find and install the correct NuGet packages as described in figure 4-3.

If you try to install a version of EF Core or EF Core Tools that's newer than the version of .NET Core you installed, you might get errors. That's why step 4 says to select the version that matches your version of .NET Core.

In addition, there are many different versions of EF. This means you need to make sure to select the right NuGet package. For example, when you first click on the Browse link in the NuGet Package Manager, you might see a package named EntityFramework in the left-hand panel. However, this is most likely an older version known as EF6. If you install EF6, almost none of the EF code in this chapter will work correctly. So, be sure to carefully follow the instructions presented here, especially the searches described in steps 2 and 7. That way, you can be sure to find the correct EF Core NuGet packages for .NET Core.

How to open the NuGet Package Manager

- Select Tools→Nuget Package Manager→Manage NuGet Packages for Solution.

The NuGet Package Manager

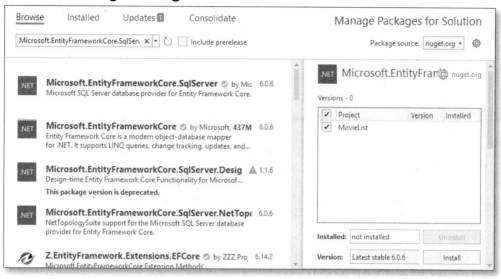

How to install the EF Core and EF Core Tools NuGet packages

1. Click the Browse link in the upper left of the window.
2. Type "Microsoft.EntityFrameworkCore.SqlServer" in the search box.
3. Click on the appropriate package from the list that appears in the left-hand panel.
4. In the right-hand panel, check the project name, select the version that matches the version of .NET you're running, and click Install.
5. Review the Preview Changes dialog that comes up and click OK.
6. Review the License Acceptance dialog that comes up and click I Accept.
7. Type "Microsoft.EntityFrameworkCore.Tools" in the search box.
8. Repeat steps 3 through 6.

Description

- With .NET Core 3.0 and later, you must manually add EF Core and EF Core Tools to your project.

Figure 4-3   How to add EF Core to your project

How to create a DbContext class

The most common way to work with EF Core is to code your model classes first. Then, you can use EF Core to generate a database from those classes. This approach is known as *EF Code First*.

Figure 4-4 begins by presenting a table that describes three classes provided by EF Core. The DbContext class is the primary class for communicating with a database. The DbContextOptions class provides configuration information to the DbContext class. And the DbSet class represents a collection of model classes, also known as *entity classes* or *domain model classes*, that map to a database table.

The first code example in this figure shows a DbContext class named MovieContext. This class inherits the DbContext base class, which is in the Microsoft.EntityFrameworkCore namespace.

The MovieContext class has a constructor that accepts a DbContextOptions object and passes it to the constructor of the base class, which is the DbContext class. In a moment, you'll learn how the Program.cs file passes the context options to the constructor.

To enable your DbContext class to work with collections of your entity classes, you need to add properties of the DbSet<Entity> type. For instance, the MovieContext class has a Movies property of the DbSet<Movie> type. EF Core uses DbSet properties like this one to generate database tables with the specified names. In addition, you can use LINQ to query a DbSet property.

Notice here that a value of null! is assigned to the Movies property. Because nullable reference types are enabled by default when you create a new MVC app, reference types can't contain null values. To allow the assignment of a null value, you can code null followed by the *null-forgiving operator* (!). This operator tells the compiler that it's okay to assign a null value, which suppresses any compiler warnings that would typically be displayed if you assign a null value to a non-nullable type.

The second code example shows the Movie class. This class defines four public properties and supplies data validation attributes for three of those properties. Two of these properties, Year and Rating, are value types, and one, Name, is a reference type.

When you use the Required attribute with a value type, the property must have a nullable data type to work properly. To make the int types for the Year and Rating properties nullable, a question mark (?) is coded after them.

You can also code a question mark after a reference type to make it nullable. However, that can lead to bugs that can be difficult to find. An alternative is to assign an initial value to the property. In this figure, for example, a value of string.Empty is assigned to the Name property.

When you use EF Core to create the database, it uses the Movie class to create a database table. As you review this class, you need to understand two things about the database creation process.

First, EF Core automatically treats a property with a name of Id (or ID) or the entity name followed by Id (or ID) as a primary key. A *primary key* value

Three classes provided by EF Core

Class	Description
`DbContext`	The primary class for communicating with a database.
`DbContextOptions`	Configuration options for the DbContext object.
`DbSet<Entity>`	A collection of objects created from the specified entity.

A MovieContext class that inherits the DbContext class

```csharp
using Microsoft.EntityFrameworkCore;

namespace MovieList.Models
{
    public class MovieContext : DbContext
    {
        public MovieContext(DbContextOptions<MovieContext> options)
            : base(options)
        { }

        public DbSet<Movie> Movies { get; set; } = null!;
    }
}
```

A Movie class with a property whose value is generated by the database

```csharp
using System.ComponentModel.DataAnnotations;

namespace MovieList.Models
{
    public class Movie
    {
        // EF Core will configure the database to generate this value
        public int MovieId { get; set; }

        [Required(ErrorMessage = "Please enter a name.")]
        public string Name { get; set; } = string.Empty;

        [Required(ErrorMessage = "Please enter a year.")]
        [Range(1889, 2999, ErrorMessage = "Year must be after 1889.")]
        public int? Year { get; set; }

        [Required(ErrorMessage = "Please enter a rating.")]
        [Range(1, 5, ErrorMessage = "Rating must be between 1 and 5.")]
        public int? Rating { get; set; }
    }
}
```

Description

- Within the DbContext class, you can use DbSet<Entity> properties to work with the model classes that map to database tables. These classes are also known as *entity classes*, or *domain model classes*.

- Any property in your entity with a name of Id (or ID) or the entity name followed by Id (or ID) is a *primary key*. If this property is also of the int type, the corresponding column is an *identity column* whose value is automatically generated by the database.

Figure 4-4   How to create a DbContext class

uniquely identifies an entity. This value is often used to select a specific entity from the database. If the Id property is also of the int type, EF Core configures the corresponding column in the database as an *identity column*. This means that the database automatically generates a value for new entities, so you don't need to do that in your code. In most cases, that's what you want. If it isn't, you can configure your code so the database doesn't automatically generate this value. You'll learn how to do that in chapter 12.

Second, EF Core uses some of the data validation attributes to configure the database table it creates. For instance, string properties typically create columns in the table that can accept nulls. But since the Name property shown here is decorated with a Required attribute, EF Core configures the Name field in the table to not accept nulls. Again, you'll learn more about how this works in chapter 12.

How to seed initial data

Sometimes you want to include, or *seed*, some initial data in the database tables that EF Core creates. For example, you might want to include a few initial records for test purposes. Or, you might want to include *lookup data* such as a list of states or movie genres that an app can use to look up data that it needs.

The DbContext class has an OnModelCreating() method that you can override to configure your context. You'll learn more about this in chapter 12. For now, all you need to know is that one of the things you can do when you override this method is seed initial data in your database.

The example in figure 4-5 shows the MovieContext class updated to seed initial Movie data. Here, the OnModelCreating() method overrides the method in the base class. Within this method, the code passes an array of new Movie objects to the HasData() method of the Entity<Movie>() method of the ModelBuilder object. This code runs when the database is created, and it inserts this data into the table that's created from the Movie class.

Since the MovieId attribute is a primary key and an identity column, EF Core automatically generates a value for the MovieId property when new movies are inserted. However, this doesn't apply to seeding initial data in the DbContext class. Instead, you need to specifically provide a value for the MovieId property of each Movie object as shown in this example.

The process of seeding initial data in Entity Framework has gone through many changes. As a result, it's easy to be confused by older examples. To keep this from happening, be sure to search for version 3.0 or higher when you're looking for help or examples online.

As you review this example, note that the OnModelCreating() method accepts a ModelBuilder object. This ModelBuilder object provides an Entity<T>() method that returns an EntityTypeBuilder<T> object. In this figure, for instance, the Entity<Movie>() method returns an EntityTypeBuilder<Movie> object. This object, in turn, provides a HasData() method that accepts an array of entity objects.

One method of the DbContext class

Method	Description
`OnModelCreating(builder)`	Called by the framework when the context is created. You can override it to configure your context.

The MovieContext class updated to seed initial Movie data

```
public class MovieContext : DbContext
{
    public MovieContext(DbContextOptions<MovieContext> options)
        : base(options)
    { }

    public DbSet<Movie> Movies { get; set; } = null!;

    protected override void OnModelCreating(ModelBuilder modelBuilder)
    {
        modelBuilder.Entity<Movie>().HasData(
            new Movie {
                MovieId = 1,
                Name = "Casablanca",
                Year = 1942,
                Rating = 5
            },
            new Movie {
                MovieId = 2,
                Name = "Wonder Woman",
                Year = 2017,
                Rating = 3
            },
            new Movie {
                MovieId = 3,
                Name = "Moonstruck",
                Year = 1988,
                Rating = 4
            }
        );
    }
}
```

Description

- The DbContext class has an OnModelCreating() method that you can override to configure the context.

- The OnModelCreating() method accepts a ModelBuilder object as an argument. You can use the Entity().HasData() method of this object to seed initial data in the database.

- When you use the HasData() method to seed data, you need to provide values for the Id properties, even the ones that will be configured as identity columns.

Figure 4-5   How to seed initial data in the DbContext class

How to add a connection string

A *connection string* is a string that specifies information that an app needs to connect to a database or other data source. Although you can hard-code connection strings in the code for your app, it's generally considered a best practice to store them in a configuration file. That way, if you move the database to another server or make some other change that affects the connection string, you won't have to change the code for the app. Instead, you can simply change the connection string in the configuration file.

For ASP.NET Core MVC apps, you typically use the configuration file named appsettings.json. This file is a text file that uses JSON to provide static configuration information for your app.

The first example in figure 4-6 presents an appsettings.json file with a connection string named MovieContext for a SQL Server LocalDB database named Movies. To fit this connection string on the page, it's shown here on two lines. For this string to work correctly, though, it must be coded on one line.

How to enable dependency injection

Dependency injection is a design pattern in which the services an object needs are passed to it rather than being hard coded as part of the object. In other words, the dependencies of an object are injected into it. This *decouples* the object from its dependencies and makes it easier to test.

ASP.NET Core MVC uses dependency injection to pass DbContext objects to the controllers that need them. To enable this, you can add code to the Program.cs file like the code shown in the second example in figure 4-6.

To enable injection of DbContext objects, you need to call the AddDbContext() method of the Services property of the builder object. Typically, you pass this method a lambda expression that creates a DbContextOptions object. In turn, this object gets passed to the constructor of the DbContext class so it can provide information about the database server. In addition, this lambda expression uses the GetConnectionString() method of the Configuration property of the builder object to get the connection string from the appsettings.json file.

Once you've configured dependency injection in the Program.cs file like this, MVC automatically creates and passes a DbContext object to any controller whose constructor has a DbContext parameter. In the next few figures, you'll see how this works.

A connection string in the appsettings.json file

```
{
  "Logging": {
    "LogLevel": {
      "Default": "Information",
      "Microsoft.AspNetCore": "Warning"
    }
  },
  "AllowedHosts": "*",
  "ConnectionStrings": {
    "MovieContext": "Server=(localdb)\\mssqllocaldb;Database=Movies;
                     Trusted_Connection=True;MultipleActiveResultSets=true"
  }
}
```

Code that enables dependency injection for DbContext objects

```
using Microsoft.EntityFrameworkCore;
using MovieList.Models;

var builder = WebApplication.CreateBuilder(args);

// Add services to the container.
builder.Services.AddControllersWithViews();

// Add EF Core DI
builder.Services.AddDbContext<MovieContext>(options =>
    options.UseSqlServer(
        builder.Configuration.GetConnectionString("MovieContext")));

var app = builder.Build();
...
```

Description

- A *connection string* contains information that an app needs to connect to a database or other data source.
- The appsettings.json file stores configuration settings for your app.
- *Dependency injection* is a design pattern in which the services an object needs are passed to it rather than being hard coded as part of the object. ASP.NET Core MVC uses dependency injection to pass DbContext objects to the controllers that need them.
- To inject DbContext objects into a controller, call the AddDbContext() method of the Services property of the builder object in the Program.cs file.
- The lambda expression that's passed to AddDbContext() creates a DbContextOptions object with information about what database server and connection string to use.
- Once you've configured dependency injection, MVC automatically creates and passes a DbContext object to any controller whose constructor has a DbContext parameter.

Figure 4-6   How to add a connection string and enable dependency injection

How to use migrations to create the database

Once you've coded your DbContext class and your entity classes, you need to tell EF Core to translate them into a database. With Windows, you can use Visual Studio to do that by executing PowerShell commands in the Package Manager Console (PMC) window.

If you run an app before you create its database, you'll get an error message that indicates that app can't open the database. For example, if you try to run the Movie List app presented in this chapter and you haven't created its database, you'll get an error message that says:

```
Cannot open database "Movies" requested by the login.
```

Figure 4-7 explains how to use the PMC window to create a database from your code. Before you can do that, you need to add a connection string and enable dependency injection as described in the previous figure.

The first PowerShell command you execute, Add-Migration, creates a migration file in a folder named Migrations. If the Migrations folder doesn't already exist in your project, it's created the first time you run the Add-Migration command.

A *migration* is a file that contains C# code for creating, modifying, or deleting database objects. More specifically, it has an Up() method with C# code that implements a migration, and it has a Down() method with C# code that rolls back a migration. Both of these methods accept a MigrationBuilder object to do their work.

This figure shows the code in the Up() method of the Initial migration file that's created by the Add-Migration command. This method creates a table based on the Movie entity and seeds it with initial data. In general, it's a good idea to review every migration file you generate. That way, you can make sure your DbContext and entity class code has been translated the way you want.

The second PowerShell command you run, Update-Database, applies the migration file. That is, it executes the Up() method of the migration file and creates, modifies, or deletes database objects. But first, if the database with the name specified in the connection string doesn't yet exist, the Up() method creates it. If you're using SQL Server LocalDB, you can make sure the database was created correctly by using the procedure described at the bottom of this figure to view the database.

If you don't understand the details of how this works, don't worry! You'll learn more about migrations in chapter 12.

If you're using Visual Studio on macOS, or if you're using Visual Studio Code instead of Visual Studio, the procedure shown in this figure won't work for you. Instead, you'll need to use the CLI to execute the migration commands as described in chapter 18.

The Package Manager Console (PMC) window in Visual Studio

```
Package Manager Console                                          ▼ ₽ ×
Package source: All              ▼ ⚙ Default project: MovieList        ▼
Each package is licensed to you by its owner. NuGet is not responsible for, nor does it grant
any licenses to, third-party packages. Some packages may include dependencies which are governed
 by additional licenses. Follow the package source (feed) URL to determine any dependencies.

Package Manager Console Host Version 6.2.0.146

Type 'get-help NuGet' to see all available NuGet commands.

PM> add-migration Initial|
```

How to open the Package Manager Console window

- Select the Tools→NuGet Package Manager→Package Manager Console command.

How to create the Movies database based on your code files

1. Make sure the connection string and dependency injection are set up.
2. Type "Add-Migration Initial" in the PMC at the command prompt and press Enter.
3. Type "Update-Database" at the command prompt and press Enter.

The code in the Up() method of the Initial migration file

```
protected override void Up(MigrationBuilder migrationBuilder)
{
    migrationBuilder.CreateTable(
        name: "Movies",
        columns: table => new {
            MovieId = table.Column<int>(type: "int", nullable: false)
                .Annotation("SqlServer:Identity", "1, 1"),
            Name = table.Column<string>(type: "nvarchar(max)",
                                        nullable: false),
            Year = table.Column<int>(type: "int", nullable: false),
            Rating = table.Column<int>(type: "int", nullable: false)
        },
        constraints: table => {
            table.PrimaryKey("PK_Movies", x => x.MovieId);
        });

    migrationBuilder.InsertData(
        table: "Movies",
        columns: new[] { "MovieId", "Name", "Rating", "Year" },
        values: new object[] { 1, "Casablanca", 5, 1942 });

    // code that inserts the other two movies
}
```

How to view the database once it's created

1. Choose the View→SQL Server Object Explorer command in Visual Studio.
2. Expand the (localdb)\MSSQLLocalDB node, then expand the Databases node.
3. Expand the Movies node, then expand the Tables node.
4. To view the table columns, expand a table node and then its Columns node.
5. To view the table data, right-click a table and select the ViewData command.

Figure 4-7   How to use migrations to create the database

How to work with data

Now that you know how to create a database and seed it with data, you're ready to learn how to work with that data. In the next two figures, you'll learn how to use *Language-Integrated Query (LINQ)* to select data, and you'll learn how to use methods of the DbSet and DbContext classes to insert, update, and delete data.

In these figures, the examples use a private property named context to get a MovieContext object. This property is created by a controller class as shown in figure 4-10.

How to select data

There are two steps to using LINQ and EF Core to select data from a database. First, you build a *query expression*. Then, you execute that query expression at the database.

The first table in figure 4-8 presents four methods for working with query expressions. You use the first two to build query expressions. These methods accept a lambda expression and have a return type of IQueryable<T>. The Where() method allows you to filter data according to the logic of the lambda expression, and the OrderBy() method allows you to sort data.

The third and fourth methods in this table execute query expressions and retrieve data. The FirstOrDefault() method returns either the first entity found or null if nothing is found. The ToList() method returns a List<T> object that stores zero or more entities of the specified type.

The second table in this figure presents a method of the DbSet<Entity> class that you can use to retrieve an entity. Like the FirstOrDefault() method, the Find() method returns either the first entity found or null if nothing is found. However, with Find(), you can only search by primary key.

The code examples below the tables show how to build and execute query expressions. The first example uses the Movies property and the OrderBy() method to build a query and store it in an IQueryable<Movie> object. Then, the second example uses the ToList() method to execute that query and return a list of Movie objects that contains the data in the result set.

The third example shows how to combine the first and second examples into a single statement. To do that, this example chains the two method calls together. In addition, it shows how to use the dynamic var type. As a result, the compiler determines the data type for the variable at runtime. This results in code that's shorter and more flexible. The only downside is that the data type for the movies variable isn't as clear.

The fourth and fifth examples show how to build a more complex query expression. Here, the fourth example chains methods calls, and the fifth example uses multiple lines of code.

A DbContext property that's used in the following examples

```
private MovieContext context { get; set; }
```

LINQ methods that build or execute a query expression

Method	Description
Where(lambda)	Filters the entities according to the logic of the lambda expression.
OrderBy(lambda)	Orders the entities according to the logic of the lambda expression.
FirstOrDefault(lambda)	Returns the first instance of the entity identified by the lambda expression parameter, or null if nothing is found.
ToList()	Returns a List<T> object with zero or more entities.

A method of the DbSet<Entity> class that gets an entity by its id

Method	Description
Find(id)	Returns the first instance of the entity identified by the id value for its primary key, or null if nothing is found.

Code that builds a query expression

```
IQueryable<Movie> query = context.Movies.OrderBy(m => m.Name);
```

Code that executes a query expression

```
List<Movie> movies = query.ToList();
```

Code that builds and executes a query expression

```
var movies = context.Movies.OrderBy(m => m.Name).ToList();
```

Code that builds a query expression by chaining LINQ methods

```
var query = context.Movies.Where(m => m.Rating > 3).OrderBy(m => m.Name);
```

Code that builds a query expression on multiple lines

```
IQueryable<Movie> query = context.Movies;
query = query.Where(m => m.Year > 1970);
query = query.Where(m => m.Rating > 3);
query = query.OrderBy(m => m.Name);
```

Three ways to select a movie by its id

```
int id = 1;
var movie = context.Movies.Where(m => m.MovieId == id).FirstOrDefault();
var movie = context.Movies.FirstOrDefault(m => m.MovieId == id);
var movie = context.Movies.Find(id);
```

Description

- *Language-Integrated Query (LINQ)* is a .NET component that allows you to query data in code. You can use LINQ to query the data in a DbSet property.

Figure 4-8   How to select data

The last example shows three C# statements that translate to the same SQL statement. In other words, each of these statements is functionally the same as the others. Here, using Find() leads to the shortest and cleanest code. However, if you aren't searching on a primary key, you will need to use one of the other techniques.

When you combine the building and executing of a query expression, make sure the method that executes the query comes last. That way, the filtering and sorting can be performed by the database server. Otherwise, the database server returns an unfiltered and unsorted collection to the web app, and the web app performs the filtering and sorting. In general, it's better to have the database server perform these filter and sort operations, especially if you're dealing with a large number of rows.

How to insert, update, and delete data

The first table in figure 4-9 presents three methods of the DbSet class that mark the specified entity for insertion, update, or deletion in the database. The Add() method also adds the specified entity to the DbSet collection. However, these methods don't execute code against the database. Instead, they mark the entities that require database action.

The second table presents the SaveChanges() method of the DbContext class. This method executes the operations at the database. For example, if the Update() method has marked a row for update, the SaveChanges() method executes that update operation at the database.

The first example shows how to use EF Core to add a new movie to the database. Here, the first statement creates a new Movie entity. Then, the second statement passes the Movie entity to the Add() method. This adds the movie to the DbSet property named Movies and marks it as Added. Next, the third statement calls the SaveChanges() method to execute this insertion at the database. The code for editing and deleting movies looks similar as you'll see in figure 4-11.

How to view the generated SQL statements

When you use EF Core, it generates SQL statements that it executes at the database. Sometimes it's helpful to view these SQL statements. To do that, you can add a logging setting to the appsettings.json file like the one shown in the second example of figure 4-9. Then, the generated SQL statements are displayed in the Output window of Visual Studio.

The third example in this figure shows a code statement that builds and executes a simple select query. Then, the fourth example shows the SQL statement this code executes at the database.

When you no longer want to see the SQL that EF Core generates, you can delete this setting. Or, to make it easy to enable EF Core logging again in the future, you can change its value to "Warning".

Three methods of the DbSet class

Method	Description
Add(entity)	Adds an entity to the DbSet collection and marks it as Added.
Update(entity)	Marks an entity as Modified.
Remove(entity)	Marks an entity as Deleted.

One method of the DbContext class

Method	Description
SaveChanges()	Saves changes to the database.

Code that adds a new movie to the database

```
var movie = new Movie { Name = "Taxi Driver", Year = 1976, Rating = 4 };
context.Movies.Add(movie);
context.SaveChanges();
```

An appsettings.json file that displays the generated SQL statements

```
{
  "Logging": {
    "LogLevel": {
      "Default": "Information",
      "Microsoft.AspNetCore": "Warning",
      "Microsoft.EntityFrameworkCore.Database.Command":  "Debug"
    }
    ...
}
```

Code that selects movies from the database

```
var movies = context.Movies.OrderBy(m => m.Name).ToList();
```

The generated SQL statement

```
SELECT [m].[MovieId], [m].[Name], [m].[Rating], [m].[Year]
FROM [Movies] AS [m]
ORDER BY [m].[Name]
```

Description

- You use the methods of the DbSet and DbContext classes to add, update, or delete entities.
- You can add a logging setting to the appsettings.json file to see the SQL that EF Core executes at the database. This SQL is displayed in the Output window of Visual Studio.

Figure 4-9   How to insert, update, and delete data and view the generated SQL

The Movie List app

So far, you have learned how to code an entity class and a DbContext class. Then, you learned how to use them to create a database for storing data about movies. Next, you learned how to select, add, update, and delete data from that database.

Now, you'll learn how to code the controllers and views used by the Movie List app presented at the beginning of this chapter. However, the code in the next few topics displays slightly simpler pages than the ones presented in figure 4-1. That's because this Movie List app won't be complete until the end of the chapter.

The Home controller

Figure 4-10 starts by presenting the code for the Home controller of the Movie List app. This controller starts with a private property named context of the MovieContext type. Then, the constructor accepts a MovieContext object and assigns it to the context property. As a result, the other methods in this class can easily access the MovieContext object.

This constructor works because of the dependency injection code in the Program.cs file presented in figure 4-6. That's because the constructor specifies that it needs an instance of the MovieContext class. As a result, the MVC framework creates one based on the options specified in the Program.cs file and passes it to that constructor.

The Index() action method of the Home controller uses the context property to get a collection of Movie objects from the database, sorted alphabetically by movie name. Then, it passes that collection to the view.

The Home/Index view

This figure also presents the code for the Home/Index view of the Movie List app. This view begins by using the @model directive to specify that the model for this view is a collection of Movie objects because that's what the Index() action method of the Home controller passes to this view.

Most of the HTML in this view displays a table of movie data. Just above the table, a link requests the Add() action method of the Movie controller. This link allows the user to add a new movie.

Within the body of the table, an inline foreach statement loops through the collection of Movie objects and displays each one in a row. Within that loop, the fourth column adds links that request the Edit() and Delete() action methods of the Movie controller for that specific movie. These links also use the asp-route-id tag helper to pass the ID for each movie. You'll learn more about how this tag helper works in chapter 7. For now, all you need to know is that it appends the MovieId value for the selected movie to the end of the URL.

The Home controller

```
using Microsoft.AspNetCore.Mvc;
using MovieList.Models;

namespace MovieList.Controllers
{
    public class HomeController : Controller
    {
        private MovieContext context { get; set; }

        public HomeController(MovieContext ctx) =>  context = ctx;

        public IActionResult Index() {
            var movies = context.Movies.OrderBy(m => m.Name).ToList();
            return View(movies);
        }
    }
}
```

The Home/Index view

```
@model List<Movie>
@{ ViewData["Title"] = "My Movies"; }

<div class="mb-2">
    <a asp-controller="Movie" asp-action="Add">Add New Movie</a>
</div>

<table class="table table-bordered table-striped">
    <thead>
        <tr>
            <th>Name</th>
            <th>Year</th>
            <th>Rating</th>
            <th></th>
        </tr>
    </thead>
    <tbody>
        @foreach (var movie in Model) {
            <tr>
                <td>@movie.Name</td>
                <td>@movie.Year</td>
                <td>@movie.Rating</td>
                <td>
                    <a asp-controller="Movie" asp-action="Edit"
                        asp-route-id="@movie.MovieId">Edit</a>
                    <a asp-controller="Movie" asp-action="Delete"
                        asp-route-id="@movie.MovieId">Delete</a>
                </td>
            </tr>
        }
    </tbody>
</table>
```

Figure 4-10   The Home controller and the Home/Index view

The Movie controller

Figure 4-11 presents the code for the Movie controller of the Movie List app. This controller starts by defining a private MovieContext property named context. Then, it uses its constructor to set that property. This works the same as it does for the Home controller described in the previous figure.

The Movie controller has three action methods: Add(), Edit(), and Delete(). In addition, the Edit() and Delete() actions have overloads that handle both GET and POST requests. The Add() action, by contrast, only handles GET requests. That's because the Add() and Edit() actions both use the Movie/Edit view.

For a GET request, both the Add() and Edit() actions set a ViewBag property named Action and pass a Movie object to the view. However, the Add() action passes an empty Movie object, and the Edit() action passes a Movie object with data for an existing movie. To do that, the Edit() action passes its id parameter to the Find() method to retrieve a movie from the database. This is possible because the Edit link in the Home/Index view uses the asp-route-id tag helper to specify a value for the id argument.

To be able to use the same view as the Edit() action, the Add() action passes "Edit" as the first argument to the View() method. As a result, the Add() action displays the same view as the Edit() action.

Because the Edit() and Add() actions both use the Movie/Edit view, the Edit() action method for a POST request must be able to add new movies and update existing ones. To do that, it starts by checking whether the user entered valid data for the model.

If the user entered valid data, the code checks the value of the MovieId property of the Movie object it receives from the view. If the value is zero, it's a new movie. In that case, the code passes it to the Add() action of the Movies property. Otherwise, it's an existing movie. In that case, the code passes it to the Update() action of the Movies property.

After marking the Movie object for insertion or update, the Edit() action calls the SaveChanges() method of the MovieContext property. This causes the movie data to be inserted or updated in the database. Then, the code redirects the user back to the Index() action of the Home controller, which displays the Home/Index view.

However, if the user didn't enter valid data for the model, the code resets the Action property of the ViewBag to "Add" or "Edit". Then, it sends the data the user entered back to the view to be redisplayed.

The Delete() action for a GET request uses its id parameter to retrieve a Movie object for the specified movie from the database. Then, it passes that Movie object to the view. Again, this is possible because the Delete link in the Home/Index view specifies a value for the id argument.

The Delete() action for a POST request passes the Movie object it receives from the view to the Remove() method of the Movies property. After that, it calls the SaveChanges() method of the MovieContext property to delete the movie from the database. Finally, it redirects the user back to the Index action of the Home controller.

The Movie controller

```csharp
using Microsoft.AspNetCore.Mvc;
using MovieList.Models;

namespace MovieList.Controllers
{
    public class MovieController : Controller
    {
        private MovieContext context { get; set; }

        public MovieController(MovieContext ctx) => context = ctx;

        [HttpGet]
        public IActionResult Add() {
            ViewBag.Action = "Add";
            return View("Edit", new Movie());
        }

        [HttpGet]
        public IActionResult Edit(int id) {
            ViewBag.Action = "Edit";
            var movie = context.Movies.Find(id);
            return View(movie);
        }

        [HttpPost]
        public IActionResult Edit(Movie movie) {
            if (ModelState.IsValid) {
                if (movie.MovieId == 0)
                    context.Movies.Add(movie);
                else
                    context.Movies.Update(movie);
                context.SaveChanges();
                return RedirectToAction("Index", "Home");
            } else {
                ViewBag.Action = (movie.MovieId == 0) ? "Add": "Edit";
                return View(movie);
            }
        }

        [HttpGet]
        public IActionResult Delete(int id) {
            var movie = context.Movies.Find(id);
            return View(movie);
        }

        [HttpPost]
        public IActionResult Delete(Movie movie) {
            context.Movies.Remove(movie);
            context.SaveChanges();
            return RedirectToAction("Index", "Home");
        }
    }
}
```

Description

- The Add() and Edit() action methods both display the Movie/Edit view.

Figure 4-11   The Movie controller

The Movie/Edit view

Figure 4-12 presents the code for the Movie/Edit view of the Movie List app. This view begins by using the @model directive to specify that the model for this view is a Movie object because that's what the Add() and Edit() actions for a GET request pass to this view.

In the Razor code block, a string variable named title is used to store the value of the ViewBag.Action property followed by a space and "Movie". This creates a title variable of "Add Movie" for the Add() action and a title of "Edit Movie" for the Edit() action. Then, this code uses the title variable to set the ViewBag.Title property that's used by the layout for the view and as the text of the <h2> element.

The Edit view contains a form that posts to the Edit() action for a POST request. This form uses an asp-action tag helper but not an asp-controller one. As a result, the form posts to the Edit() action of the current controller, which is the Movie controller.

This form begins with a <div> element that displays any data validation messages. Then, it displays labels and text boxes for the movie name, year, and rating. In addition, it uses a hidden field to store the movie ID.

If the Add() action method served this view, the text boxes are blank and the value of the hidden field is zero. That's because that action method passes an empty Movie object to this view. However, if the Edit() action method served this view, these fields contain data for the selected movie. Either way, the values in these fields are posted to the Edit() action that handles POST requests. By the way, this code binds the MovieId value to a hidden field rather than a text box because it's a primary key value, and you don't usually want to allow users to change a primary key.

The bottom of the form displays a button and a link that's formatted as a button. The first button is a submit button. As a result, it posts the form to the Edit() action method when the user clicks it.

The link that's formatted as a button allows the user to cancel the operation. It uses tag helpers to request the Index() action of the Home controller. This displays the Home/Index view.

The Movie/Edit view

```
@model Movie
@{
    string title = ViewBag.Action + " Movie";
    ViewData["Title"] = title;
}

<h2>@ViewBag.Title</h2>

<form asp-action="Edit" method="post">
    <div asp-validation-summary="All" class="text-danger"></div>

    <div class="mb-3">
        <label asp-for="Name" class="form-label">Name</label>
        <input asp-for="Name" class="form-control">
    </div>

    <div class="mb-3">
        <label asp-for="Year" class="form-label">Year</label>
        <input asp-for="Year" class="form-control">
    </div>

    <div class="mb-3">
        <label asp-for="Rating" class="form-label">Rating</label>
        <input asp-for="Rating" class="form-control">
    </div>

    <input type="hidden" asp-for="MovieId" />

    <button type="submit" class="btn btn-primary">Save</button>
    <a asp-controller="Home" asp-action="Index"
        class="btn btn-primary">Cancel</a>
</form>
```

Description

- The Edit view uses a Movie object as its model and binds HTML elements to the properties of the Movie object.

- The Edit view uses the ViewBag.Action property to set the text of the <title> and <h2> elements. This makes it possible for this view to work for both the Add() and Edit() actions.

- The MovieId value is bound to a hidden field. As a result, users can't change this value.

- When an empty Movie object is passed to the view by the Add() action method, the text boxes are blank. When a Movie object with data is passed to the view by the Edit() action method, the data in that object is displayed in the text boxes.

- The form uses tag helpers to specify the action but not the controller. As a result, the submit button posts the form to the Edit() action of the current controller, which is the Movie controller.

- The Cancel link uses tag helpers to request the Index() action of the Home controller. This displays the Home/Index view.

Figure 4-12   The Movie/Edit view

The Movie/Delete view

Figure 4-13 presents the code for the Movie/Delete view. This view begins with code that uses the @model directive to specify that the model for this view is a Movie object, because that's what the Delete() action for a GET request passes to this view.

The Delete view contains a form that posts to the Delete() action method for a POST request. Like the form in the Edit view, this form specifies an asp-action tag helper but not an asp-controller one. As a result, the form posts to the Delete() action of the current controller, which is the Movie controller.

Unlike the Edit form, this form doesn't contain any labels or text boxes. That's because it doesn't ask the user to input any data. Instead, it asks the user to confirm the deletion by clicking a button.

This form begins by binding the MovieId value to a hidden field. That way, the form posts the primary key of the movie to be deleted to the Delete() action.

The Delete() action method for a POST request expects to receive a Movie object from this view. However, if you look at the code presented here, you can see that this view only posts the MovieId value to that action method. This means the Movie object that the Delete() action method receives has null values for all the properties except MovieId. That's OK, though, because the Remove() method of the Movies property only needs the MovieId value to mark the selected entity for deletion.

Like the Edit form, the bottom of this form displays a button and a link that's formatted as a button. The first button is a submit button. As a result, it posts the form to the Delete() action when the user clicks it.

Like the Edit form, the link that's formatted as a button allows the user to cancel the operation. To do that, it uses tag helpers to request the Index() action of the Home controller. This displays the Home/Index view.

The Movie/Delete view

```
@model Movie
@{
    ViewData["Title"] = "Delete Movie";
}

<h2>Confirm Deletion</h2>
<h3>@Model.Name (@Model.Year)</h3>

<form asp-action="Delete" method="post">

    <input type="hidden" asp-for="MovieId" />

    <button type="submit" class="btn btn-primary">Delete</button>
    <a asp-controller="Home" asp-action="Index"
        class="btn btn-primary">Cancel</a>
</form>
```

Description

- The Delete view uses a Movie object as its model and displays properties of that Movie object to the user to confirm deletion.

- The MovieId value is bound to a hidden field. That way, it is passed to the Delete() action method when the user clicks the submit button and the form is posted.

- The form uses tag helpers to specify the action but not the controller. As a result, the submit button posts the form to the Delete() action of the current controller, which is the Movie controller.

- The Cancel link uses tag helpers to request the Index() action of the Home controller. This displays the Home/Index view.

Figure 4-13   The Movie/Delete view

How to work with related data

So far, you've learned how to create a data-driven web app that uses a Movie entity class to generate a Movie table in a database. Now, you'll learn how to add another entity class and generate another database table. In addition, you'll learn how to relate this new entity to the existing one. As you learn how to do this, you should know that working with related data like this is a big topic that you'll learn more about in chapter 12.

How to relate one entity to another

You can relate one entity to another by making one a property of another. To do this, you code a property with a data type of the entity you want to relate. Figure 4-14 shows how this works.

The first example presents a Genre class that has two properties: GenreId and Name. Here, the GenreId property is the primary key of this class. Because this property uses the string type instead of the int type, the database doesn't generate values for it.

The second example shows the Movie class used earlier in this chapter after it has been updated to contain a property named Genre of the Genre type. This is a simple way to relate the Genre class to the Movie class. In cases where you only need to read and display related data, this technique is adequate.

However, you often need to do more than just display related data. For example, you might want to seed related data, update related data, validate related data, or include related data in a query. In cases like these, your entity classes are easier to work with if you also add a *foreign key property* that refers to the primary key property in the related entity.

The third example shows how this works. Here, a GenreId property is added to the Movie class just before the Genre property. This GenreId property has the same data type as the primary key property in the Genre entity and specifically links the two entities on that value. In addition, this foreign key property is decorated with the Required attribute for data validation.

When you use a foreign key property, MVC will sometimes perform unexpected or unwanted data validation on the related entity property. For the Movie List app, for example, an error message will be displayed indicating that the Genre field is required even if the user selects a genre from the drop-down list on the Add or Edit Movie page. That's because selecting a genre sets the GenreId property, not the Genre property.

One way to prevent this validation is to decorate the related entity property with the ValidateNever attribute. The fourth example shows how this works. Here, the Genre property is decorated with this attribute. Because of that, MVC will ignore the Genre property when it validates a Movie object. However, it will still validate the GenreId foreign key property to be sure the user selects a genre.

The Genre class

```
public class Genre
{
    public string GenreId { get; set; } = string.Empty;
    public string Name { get; set; } = string.Empty;
}
```

How to add a Genre property to the Movie class

```
public class Movie
{
    /* MovieId, Name, Year, and Rating properties same as before */

    public Genre Genre { get; set; } = null!;
}
```

How to specify a foreign key property when adding a Genre property

```
public class Movie
{
    /* MovieId, Name, Year, and Rating properties same as before */

    [Required(ErrorMessage = "Please enter a genre.")]
    public string GenreId { get; set; } = string.Empty;

    public Genre Genre { get; set; } = null!;
}
```

How to turn off data validation for the Genre property

```
using Microsoft.AspNetCore.Mvc.ModelBinding.Validation;
...
public class Movie
{
    /* MovieId, Name, Year, and Rating properties same as before */

    [Required(ErrorMessage = "Please enter a genre.")]
    public string GenreId { get; set; } = string.Empty;

    [ValidateNever]
    public Genre Genre { get; set; } = null!;
}
```

Description

- You can relate one entity to another by coding a property with that entity class as its data type.

- A *foreign key property* indicates the property that's the primary key in the related class.

- Using a foreign key property makes it easier to seed, update, validate, or query related data. As a result, it's considered a best practice to use a foreign key property when you need to perform these operations.

- To avoid unexpected data validation results, you can decorate the related entity with the ValidateNever attribute in the Microsoft.AspNetCore.Mvc.Model-Binding.Validation namespace.

- You'll learn more about primary and foreign keys in chapter 12.

Figure 4-14   How to relate one entity to another

How to update the DbContext class and the seed data

When developing an app, it's common to need to update the database with new entities and seed initial data. Luckily, EF Core and migrations make this easy to do. For example, the Movie List app in this chapter started with just a Movie entity and some initial movie data. But now, a Genre entity has been added to the app. As a result, the MovieContext class needs to be updated to add this new entity with some initial data.

Figure 4-15 shows the MovieContext class after it has been updated to add the Genre entity. To start, this class adds a second DbSet property named Genres. EF Core can use this property to create a Genres table in the database. In addition, EF Core can use it with LINQ queries to select genre data from the database.

Next, the MovieContext class uses the HasData() method to seed initial genre data in the new table. This works similarly to the way that movie data is seeded, so you shouldn't have much trouble understanding how it works.

Finally, the MovieContext class updates the HasData() method for the Movie table. It does this by adding a GenreId field to each movie object with the ID value of the appropriate genre. This is possible because the Movie entity has a foreign key property.

The MovieContext class updated to add the Genre model with initial data

```
public class MovieContext : DbContext {
    public MovieContext(DbContextOptions<MovieContext> options)
        : base(options)
    { }

    public DbSet<Movie> Movies { get; set; } = null!;
    public DbSet<Genre> Genres { get; set; } = null!;

    protected override void OnModelCreating(ModelBuilder modelBuilder) {
        base.OnModelCreating(modelBuilder);

        modelBuilder.Entity<Genre>().HasData(
            new Genre { GenreId = "A", Name = "Action" },
            new Genre { GenreId = "C", Name = "Comedy" },
            new Genre { GenreId = "D", Name = "Drama" },
            new Genre { GenreId = "H", Name = "Horror" },
            new Genre { GenreId = "M", Name = "Musical" },
            new Genre { GenreId = "R", Name = "RomCom" },
            new Genre { GenreId = "S", Name = "SciFi" }
        );

        modelBuilder.Entity<Movie>().HasData(
            new Movie { MovieId = 1, Name = "Casablanca", Year = 1942,
                Rating = 5, GenreId = "D"
            },
            new Movie { MovieId = 2, Name = "Wonder Woman", Year = 2017,
                Rating = 3, GenreId = "A"
            },
            new Movie { MovieId = 3, Name = "Moonstruck", Year = 1988,
                Rating = 4, GenreId = "R"
            }
        );
    }
}
```

Description

- When you add new entities to your app, you also add them to your DbContext class as DbSet properties.

- You can also seed initial data for the new entities. And, if the new entities are related to existing ones, you can update the seed data for the existing entities.

- EF Core uses the updated DbContext class and seed data to change the database.

Figure 4-15   How to update the DbContext class and the seed data

How to use migrations to update the database

After you update the MovieContext class, you need to update the database to add a table and initial data for the new Genre entity. To do that, you can use the procedure presented in figure 4-16.

This procedure is similar to the procedure that you used to create a table for the Movie entity as described earlier in this chapter. To start, you display the Package Manager Console window. Then, you enter the Add-Migration command followed by a name for the migration file.

In this figure, the Add-Migration command specifies a name of "Genre" since that's the name of the entity being added. However, if you want, you can use a more descriptive name such as "AddGenreField". The more descriptive the names, the more the Migrations folder becomes self-documenting. In other words, if you use descriptive names, reading the names in the Migrations folder gives you a sense of the history of the database.

This figure presents some of the code in the Up() method of the Genre migration file that's produced by the Add-Migration command. This file has more work to do than the Up() method presented in figure 4-7. Like that method, this method creates a table based on an entity and seeds it with initial data for the Genre entity. But, it also adds a GenreId column to the Movies table, updates each movie with a value for GenreId, makes the GenreId column in the Movies table a foreign key, and creates an index for that column. For now, don't worry if you don't understand all the foreign key code shown here. You'll learn more about it in chapter 12.

If the migration file looks good, you can finish the procedure by running the Update-Database command. This executes the Up() method of the most recently created migration file, which in this case is the Genre file. If you're using SQL Server LocalDB, you can use the procedure described in figure 4-7 to view the database and see the changes you made.

How to update the database with the new Genre model and seed data

1. Select Tools→NuGet Package Manager→Package Manager Console to open the Package Manager Console window.

2. Type "Add-Migration Genre" at the command prompt and press Enter.

3. Type "Update-Database" at the command prompt and press Enter.

Some of the code in the Up() method of the Genre migration file

```
protected override void Up(MigrationBuilder migrationBuilder)
{
    migrationBuilder.AddColumn<string>(
        name: "GenreId",
        table: "Movies",
        type: "nvarchar(450)",
        nullable: false,
        defaultValue: "");
    migrationBuilder.CreateTable(
        name: "Genres",
        columns: table => new {
            GenreId = table.Column<string>(type: "nvarchar(450)",
                                            nullable: false),
            Name = table.Column<string>(type: "nvarchar(max)",
                                         nullable: true)
        }, constraints: table => {
            table.PrimaryKey("PK_Genres", x => x.GenreId);
        });
    migrationBuilder.InsertData(
        table: "Genres",
        columns: new[] { "GenreId", "Name" },
        values: new object[,] {
            { "A", "Action" },
            { "C", "Comedy" },
            ...
            { "S", "SciFi" }
        });
    migrationBuilder.UpdateData(
        table: "Movies",
        keyColumn: "MovieId",
        keyValue: 1,
        column: "GenreId",
        value: "D");
    // code that updates the other two movies
    migrationBuilder.CreateIndex(
        name: "IX_Movies_GenreId",
        table: "Movies",
        column: "GenreId");
    migrationBuilder.AddForeignKey(
        name: "FK_Movies_Genres_GenreId",
        table: "Movies",
        column: "GenreId",
        principalTable: "Genres",
        principalColumn: "GenreId",
        onDelete: ReferentialAction.Cascade);
    ...
}
```

Figure 4-16   How to use migrations to update the database

How to select related data and display it on the Movie List page

At this point, you're ready to update the Movie List app so it displays this new Genre data. That's why figure 4-17 shows how to add each movie's genre to the table on the Movie List page. In other words, this figure shows how to make the Movie List page look like the one presented in figure 4-1.

The first example in this figure shows how to update the controller for the Movie List page. To start, this controller adds a using directive for the EF Core namespace. Then, the Index() action uses the Include() method of the EF Core namespace to select the genre data related to each movie.

The Include() method accepts a lambda expression that specifies the related entity. Whenever necessary, you can chain the Include() method as part of a longer LINQ query. Like the OrderBy() method, the Include() method doesn't execute at the database. Instead, it helps build the query expression that the ToList() method eventually executes.

If you only need the GenreId value, not the data for the entire entity, you don't need to use the Include() method. That's because the Movie entity contains a foreign key property named GenreId. In other words, the GenreId value is automatically included when you select a Movie object. In this case, however, you want to get all the Genre data, not just the GenreId value. As a result, you need to use Include().

Once you've selected the related data, you use regular C# dot notation to work with it. In the second example, for instance, the Home/Index view adds a Genre column to the movie table. Within the foreach loop, it uses dot notation to display the Name property of the Genre property of the Movie object.

Another LINQ method that builds a query expression

Method	Description
`Include(lambda)`	Includes a related entity according to the logic of the lambda expression.

The Index() action method of the Home controller

```
using Microsoft.EntityFrameworkCore;
...
public class HomeController : Controller {
...
    public IActionResult Index() {
        var movies = context.Movies.Include(m => m.Genre)
            .OrderBy(m => m.Name).ToList();
        return View(movies);
    }
}
```

The <table> element of the Home/Index view

```
<table class="table table-bordered table-striped">
    <thead>
        <tr>
            <th>Name</th>
            <th>Year</th>
            <th>Genre</th>
            <th>Rating</th><th></th>
        </tr>
    </thead>
    <tbody>
        @foreach (var movie in Model) {
            <tr>
                <td>@movie.Name</td>
                <td>@movie.Year</td>
                <td>@movie.Genre.Name</td>
                <td>@movie.Rating</td>
                <td><!-- Edit/Delete links same as before --></td>
            </tr>
        }
    </tbody>
</table>
```

Figure 4-17   How to select related data and display it on the Movie List page

How to display related data on the Add and Edit Movie pages

Once you're done displaying the related data on the Movie List page, you need to modify the Movie/Edit view to add a Genre drop-down list as shown in figure 4-18. This makes the Add and Edit Movie pages look like the ones presented in figure 4-1.

For this to work properly, the Add() and Edit() actions of the Movie controller must get a collection of Genre objects sorted in alphabetical order by name. Then, they must assign that collection to the Genres property of the ViewBag object. In this figure, the first three examples all contain a line of code that does this. That way, the Add() and Edit() actions for GET requests provide the data that the Add and Edit Movie pages need to be able to display a drop-down list of genres when they're first displayed. However, the Edit() action for POST requests only needs to provide the genre data for the drop-down list of genres if the user enters invalid data. That's because the Edit() action for a POST request redirects to the Home/Index action if the user enters valid data.

In the Edit() action for GET requests, the code selects a Movie object by primary key as before. Although you might think that you would have to use the Include() method here to include the entire Genre entity, that's not the case. That's because the Edit Movie page only needs the GenreId value, not the entire Genre entity.

The Movie/Edit view receives a Movie object as a model and a collection of Genre objects in the ViewBag. Remember, it receives these objects from both the Add() and Edit() action methods. Then, it uses them to create a Genre drop-down list. To do that, this code binds the <select> element to the GenreId property of the model object, which is a Movie object. Then, a foreach statement loops through the Genre objects in the ViewBag to create a drop-down item for each Genre.

Since the <select> element is bound to the GenreId property of the model, the Genre drop-down list on the Edit Movie page selects the genre of the selected movie. For the Add Movie page, none of the items in the Genre down-down match the GenreId property. As a result, the drop-down list displays the first option in the list that says "select a genre".

The Add() action method of the Movie controller

```
[HttpGet]
public IActionResult Add()
{
    ViewBag.Action = "Add";
    ViewBag.Genres = context.Genres.OrderBy(g => g.Name).ToList();
    return View("Edit", new Movie());
}
```

The Edit() action method of the Movie controller for GET requests

```
[HttpGet]
public IActionResult Edit(int id) {
    ViewBag.Action = "Edit";
    ViewBag.Genres = context.Genres.OrderBy(g => g.Name).ToList();
    var movie = context.Movies.Find(id);
    return View(movie);
}
```

The Edit() action method of the Movie controller for POST requests

```
[HttpPost]
public IActionResult Edit(Movie movie)
{
    if (ModelState.IsValid)
    {
        if (movie.MovieId == 0)
            context.Movies.Add(movie);
        else
            context.Movies.Update(movie);
        context.SaveChanges();
        return RedirectToAction("Index", "Home");
    }
    else
    {
        ViewBag.Action = (movie.MovieId == 0) ? "Add": "Edit";
        ViewBag.Genres = context.Genres.OrderBy(g => g.Name).ToList();
        return View(movie);
    }
}
```

The form tag of the Movie/Edit view

```
<form asp-action="Edit" method="post">
    ...
    <div class="mb-3">
        <label asp-for="GenreId" class="form-label">Genre</label>
        <select asp-for="GenreId" class="form-select">
            <option value="">select a genre</option>
            @foreach (Genre g in ViewBag.Genres)
            {
                <option value="@g.GenreId">@g.Name</option>
            }
        </select>
    </div>
    ...
</form>
```

Figure 4-18   How to display related data on the Add and Edit Movie pages

How to make user-friendly URLs

If you've made it this far, you've learned how to create a data-driven web app that works with related data. That's a significant accomplishment! However, there are a few more things you can do to make the URLs that your app produces more friendly to your users.

How to make URLs lowercase with a trailing slash

By default, MVC uses the names of the controllers and their action methods to create the URLs of the app. By convention, these names begin with an uppercase letter. This produces URLs that use some uppercase letters like those shown at the top of figure 4-19.

However, there's also a convention that URLs should be lowercase. This makes them easier for users to type. In addition, some developers like to include a trailing slash after a URL. This makes it easy for users to add text to the end of a URL.

Fortunately, it's easy to make your MVC app produce URLs that are lowercase and have a trailing slash. To do that, you just need to add the code shown in this figure to the Program.cs file. Once you've done that, your app will produce URLs that look like those shown at the bottom of this figure. This is a good example of how you can customize your app by configuring the middleware pipeline.

The default URLs of an MVC app

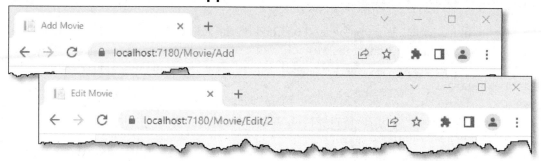

The Program.cs file updated to make URLs lowercase and end with a trailing slash

```
...
builder.Services.AddRouting(options =>
{
    options.LowercaseUrls = true;
    options.AppendTrailingSlash = true;
});
...
```

The same MVC pages after changing the URL configuration

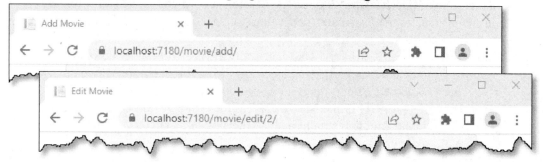

Description

- By default, MVC uses the names of the controllers and their action methods to create the URLs of the app. By convention, these names begin with an uppercase letter.

- It's generally considered a good practice to use lowercase letters for URLs.

- Some developers like to include a trailing slash after each URL to make it easy for users to type text at the end of a URL.

- You can modify the Program.cs file to make URLs lowercase with a trailing slash.

Figure 4-19   How to make URLs lowercase with a trailing slash

How to add a slug

In the Movie List app, when you click on the Edit or Delete link for a movie on the Product List page, the MovieId value of the selected movie is appended to the URL. For example, the URLs at the top of figure 4-20 include the ID values for movies.

These URLs work fine. In fact, many websites use URLs like these. However, some developers prefer to make their URLs more descriptive by adding a slug to them.

A *slug* is a descriptive section that comes at the end of a URL, often after URL sections that are used to look up data, such as a primary key value or a date. Adding a slug to a URL can make it easier for a user to predict the content of the page. This, in turn, can make a link more attractive for a user to click. This is particularly true when links are included in emails or text messages.

This figure presents one way to add slugs to the URLs in the Movie List app. First, you add a second optional parameter named slug to the default route in the Program.cs file. To do that, you can add a segment named slug followed by a question mark (?) to indicate that it's optional. For now, that's all you need to understand. You'll learn more about routing and the default route in chapter 6.

After you add an optional parameter named slug to the routing, you can add a read-only property named Slug to the Movie class. In this figure, this property just concatenates the Name and Year values into a single string, connected by a dash. In addition, it replaces any spaces in the Name value with dashes. In the real world, such a property would probably also perform other tasks like removing punctuation and returning an empty string for an empty Movie object.

After you add the Slug property, you can update the Edit and Delete links to add the Slug property of the Movie class as the optional slug URL parameter. Once you do that, your app should include the slug in its URLs as shown at the bottom of this figure.

The Edit page with numeric ID values only in the URL

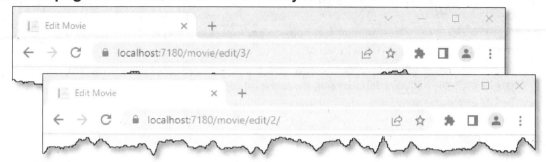

The default route in the Program.cs file updated to include a second optional parameter

```
app.MapControllerRoute(
    name: "default",
    pattern: "{controller=Home}/{action=Index}/{id?}/{slug?}");
```

A read-only property named Slug in the Movie class

```
public string Slug =>
    Name?.Replace(' ', '-').ToLower() + '-' + Year?.ToString();
```

The Edit/Delete links in the Home/Index view

```
<a asp-controller="Movie" asp-action="Edit"
    asp-route-id="@movie.MovieId"
    asp-route-slug="@movie.Slug">Edit</a>
<a asp-controller="Movie" asp-action="Delete"
    asp-route-id="@movie.MovieId"
    asp-route-slug="@movie.Slug">Delete</a>
```

The Edit page after updating the code to add a slug to the URL

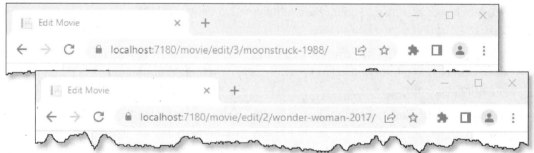

Description

- A *slug* is a descriptive section at the end of a URL. You can add a slug by adding an optional parameter named slug to the default route in the Program.cs file, adding a Slug property to the entity class, and including the Slug property on a link.

Figure 4-20   How to add a slug

Perspective

The purpose of this chapter has been to get you started with learning how to develop multi-page, data-driven MVC web apps. Now, if this chapter has succeeded, you should be able to develop apps of your own that use multiple pages to work with a database. Yes, there's a lot more to learn, but you should be off to a good start.

Terms

Entity Framework (EF) Core
Object-relational mapping (ORM)
EF Code First
entity classes
domain model classes
null-forgiving operator
primary key
identity column
seed data

lookup data
connection string
dependency injection
migration
Language-Integrated Query (LINQ)
query expression
foreign key property
slug

Summary

- *Entity Framework (EF) Core* is an *object-relational mapping (ORM)* framework that allows you to work with the objects of a database in code.

- When you use the *EF Code First* approach, you code your model classes first and then create the database from those classes.

- Model classes that map to a database table are also known as *entity classes*, or *domain model classes*.

- When using EF Core, any property in an entity with a name of Id (or ID) or the entity name followed by Id (or ID) is a *primary key* that uniquely identifies the entity.

- When using EF Core, a primary key property of the int type specifies an *identity column* whose value is automatically generated by the database.

- When using EF Core to create a database, you can include, or *seed*, some initial data in the database tables.

- *Lookup data* is data such as a list of states or movie genres that an app can use to look up data that it needs.

- A *connection string* contains information that an app needs to connect to a database or other data source.

- *Dependency injection* is a design pattern in which the services an object needs are passed to it, or injected, rather than being hard coded as part of the object.

- A *migration* is a file that contains C# code for creating, modifying, or deleting database objects.

- *Language-Integrated Query (LINQ)* is a .NET component that allows you to query data in code. You can use LINQ to query the data in a DbSet property.

- Some LINQ methods build a *query expression.* Other LINQ methods execute those expressions at the database.

- A *foreign key property* indicates the primary key property in the related class.

- A *slug* is a descriptive section that comes at the end of a URL.

Exercise 4-1   Create the Movie List app

This exercise guides you through the development of the Movie List app that's presented in this chapter. This will give you a chance to generate a database from entity classes.

Set up the file structure

1. Create a new ASP.NET Core Web Application in the ex_starts folder with a project name of MovieList and a solution name of Ch04Ex1MovieList. Base this app on the Web App (Model-View-Controller) template.

2. Using figure 4-2 as a guide, remove all unnecessary files such as Models/ ErrorViewModel.cs, Views/Home/Privacy.cshtml, and so on.

3. Using figure 4-3 as a guide, install the EF Core and EF Core Tools NuGet packages.

4. If necessary, use LibMan as described in figure 3-2 to install version 5.1.0 of the Bootstrap CSS library. In the Solution Explorer, expand the wwwroot/lib folder and make a note of the path to the bootstrap.min.css file.

Modify existing files

5. Modify the Views/Shared/_Layout.cshtml file so it contains this code:

```
<!DOCTYPE html>
<html>
<head>
    <meta name="viewport"
          content="width=device-width, initial-scale=1.0" />
    <title>@ViewData["Title"]</title>
    <link rel="stylesheet" type="text/css"
          href="~/lib/bootstrap/dist/css/bootstrap.min.css">
</head>
<body>
    <div class="container">
        <header class="p-4 mb-3 bg-light border">
            <h1>My Movies</h1>
        </header>
        @RenderBody()
    </div>
</body>
</html>
```

Make sure the href attribute specifies the correct path to the bootstrap.min.css file!

6. Remove all action methods from the HomeController except for the Index() method.

Code the classes for the model and the DB context

7. Add a Movie class to the Models folder and edit it so it contains the code shown in figure 4-4. Don't forget to add the using directive for data annotations.

8. Add a MovieContext class to the Models folder and edit it so it contains the code shown in figure 4-4. Don't forget to add the using directive for the EF Core namespace.

9. Modify the MovieContext class to contain the code for the OnModelCreating() method shown in figure 4-5.

10. Add the connection string to the appsettings.json file as shown in figure 4-6. However, to avoid database conflicts, specify a name of MoviesExercise for the database by editing the Database parameter like this:

    `Database=MoviesExercise`

    Make sure to enter the entire connection string on one line and to add a comma to the end of the previous line.

11. Modify the Program.cs file so it includes the code shown in figure 4-6. This enables dependency injection for DbContext objects. At the top of the file, make sure to include all of the necessary using directives, including the using directive for the Models namespace.

Create the Movies database

12. Using figure 4-7 as a guide, open the Package Manager Console. At the command prompt, enter the "Add-Migration Initial" command. This should add a Migrations folder and migration files to the Solution Explorer. If you get an error, troubleshoot the problem.

13. At the Package Manager Console command prompt, enter the "Update-Database" command. This should create the database. If you get an error, troubleshoot the problem.

14. View your database. To do that, display the SQL Server Object Explorer as described in figure 4-7. Then, expand the nodes until you can see the Movies-Exercise database that you just created.

15. View the seed data. To do that, expand the MoviesExercise node and the Tables node. Then, right-click on the dbo.Movies table and select View Data. This should show the data that's stored in the Movies table.

Modify the Home controller and its view

16. Modify the Home controller so it contains the code shown in figure 4-10.

17. Modify the Home/Index view so it contains the code shown in figure 4-10.

18. Run the app. It should display the list of movies in the default browser. However, clicking the Add, Edit, or Delete links should cause an error.

Add the Movie controller and its views

19. Add a new, empty controller named MovieController to the Controllers folder. Then, modify this controller so it contains the code shown in figure 4-11. Make sure to include the using directive for the Models namespace.

20. Add a folder named Movie under the Views folder.

21. Add a new view named Edit to the Views/Movie folder. Then, modify this view so it contains the code shown in figure 4-12.

22. Add a new view named Delete to the Views/Movie folder. Then, modify this view so it contains the code shown in in figure 4-13.

23. Run the app. It should display the list of movies. In addition, you should be able to add, edit, and delete movies.

Update the database to store genre data

24. Add a Genre class to the Models folder. Then, modify this class so it contains the code shown in figure 4-14.

25. Modify the code for the Movie class so it includes a Genre property and foreign key as shown in figure 4-14. Be sure to include the using directive for the Microsoft.AspNetCore.Mvc.ModelBinding.Validation namespace that contains the ValidateNever attribute.

26. Modify the MovieContext class to add the Genre model and seed it with initial data as shown in figure 4-15.

27. Open the Package Manager Console and enter the "Add-Migration Genre" command. This should add a migration file to the Solution Explorer.

28. At the Package Manager Console command prompt, enter the "Update-Database" command. This should add a Genre table and data to the database.

Update the controllers and views to work with genre data

29. Modify the Home controller's Index() method so it contains the code shown in figure 4-17.

30. Modify the Home/Index view so it contains the code shown in figure 4-17.

31. Modify the Movie controller's Add() and Edit() action methods so they contain the code shown in figure 4-18.

32. Modify the Movie/Edit view so it contains the code shown in figure 4-18.

33. Run the app. It should work with genre data.

Make the URLs more user friendly

34. Edit the Program.cs file as shown in figure 4-19 to make the URLs for the app lowercase and with a trailing slash.

35. Add a slug to the URLs for editing or deleting a movie as described in figure 4-20.

36. Run the app. Its URLs should now be lowercase and use slugs when editing or deleting a movie.

5

How to manually test and debug an ASP.NET Core web app

Testing and debugging are often the most difficult and time-consuming phase of web development. Fortunately, Visual Studio includes an integrated debugger that can help you locate and correct even the most obscure bugs. In this chapter, you'll learn how to use this debugging tool. In addition, you'll learn how to use your browser's developer tools to analyze the HTML and CSS for a page.

The tools presented in this chapter provide a way for you to manually test an app by running it, clicking on links, entering data, and so on. This approach is adequate when you're learning how to develop a simple web app. However, as you develop more complex web apps, you'll also want to automate the testing for your apps as described in chapter 14.

How to test an ASP.NET Core web app

When you *test* a web app, you try to make it fail. In other words, the goal of testing is to find all of the errors. When you *debug* an app, you determine the cause of any errors that you've found and fix them.

To test an ASP.NET Core web app, you typically start by running it from Visual Studio in the default browser. Then, you test the app with other web browsers to make sure it works right in all of them.

How to run a web app

Figure 5-1 begins by showing how to change the default browser. Then, it presents several ways you can run a web app in the default browser. The first three techniques run the app without the debugger. However, the next three techniques show how to run the app with the debugger.

So, when should you run the app with the debugger and when should you run it without the debugger? This is mostly a matter of personal preference. If you don't think you'll need to use the debugger, you can run the app without debugging. Since Visual Studio doesn't need to attach the debugger, this starts the app slightly faster than when you use the debugger. Then, if an error occurs, it displays the Internal Server Error page shown in figure 5-4. In most cases, you can use this page to determine the cause of the error and fix it.

However, if you need to take a closer look at an error, you can run the app with debugging. This allows you to use the debugger to find the cause of an error as described later in this chapter. Since it's common to need to fix errors when you're developing an app, some developers almost always run the app with debugging. This may cause the app to start slightly more slowly, but if the app encounters an error, the debugger can help you find and fix the error more quickly.

Once you've thoroughly tested a web app with your default browser, you typically want to test it for *browser incompatibilities*. To do that, you need to run your app in all of the browsers it supports to make sure it is formatted correctly in all of them. One way to do that is to use the last technique presented in this figure to run the app in multiple browsers at the same time. This runs the app without the debugger. In most cases, that's fine since you don't usually need the debugger to resolve browser incompatibilities. Instead, you typically use the browser's developer tools as shown in figure 5-3.

The Start drop-down menu and the Web Browser menu

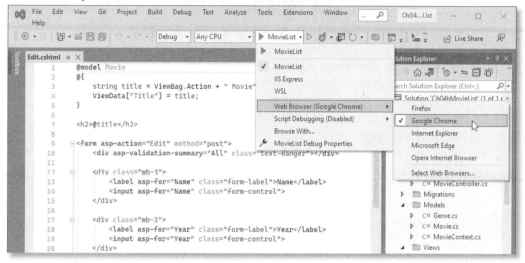

How to change the default browser

- Display the Start drop-down menu by clicking on its down arrow. Then, display the Web Browser menu and select a browser from it.

How to run an app without debugging

- Press Ctrl+F5.
- Click the Start Without Debugging button in the Standard toolbar.
- Select Debug→Start Without Debugging.

How to run an app with debugging

- Press F5.
- Click the Start button in the Standard toolbar.
- Select Debug→Start Debugging.

How to stop debugging

- Press Shift+F5.
- Click the Stop Debugging button in the Debug toolbar.
- Select Debug→Stop Debugging.

How to run an app in multiple browsers

- To run an app in two or more browsers, select Browse With from the Start drop-down menu. Then, in the resulting dialog, hold down the Ctrl key, select the browsers you want to use, and click the Browse button.
- When you run an app in two or more browsers, the app is run without debugging.

Figure 5-1   How to run a web app

How to use the Hot Reload feature

Visual Studio 2022 introduced the *Hot Reload* feature described in figure 5-2. This feature allows you to make changes to an app and apply them while the app is running. That saves you the time of having to restart an app every time you make changes.

The Hot Reload feature is based on the Edit and Continue feature that was available with earlier versions of Visual Studio. The Edit and Continue feature allows you to make changes to the C# code for an app while in break mode and then continue running the app. You'll learn more about working in break mode later in this chapter.

In contrast to the Edit and Continue feature, you can use Hot Reload at any time during the execution of an app by simply switching to Visual Studio. Then, you can make the code changes you want, save the changes, and click the Hot Reload Button. The type of change you make determines when the change goes into effect.

For example, suppose you click the Add Movie link from the Movie List page to display the Add page. Then, suppose you change the Add() method in the MovieController class as shown in the screen in this figure so it sorts the genre names in descending order. In this case, after saving the change and using Hot Reload, the change takes effect immediately since the genres are saved in the ViewBag. That means that the genre names in the drop-down list are displayed in descending order.

In other cases, you have to re-execute the code you changed for it to take effect. For example, if you display the Edit Movie page and then change the Slug property in the Movie model so the slug is formatted differently, the change won't take effect immediately. Instead, you have to return to the Movie List page by clicking the Save or Cancel button and then click the Edit Movie Link again.

Note that not all changes can be applied using Hot Reload. For example, you can't change a method declaration or a property attribute. If you try to do that, Visual Studio displays the dialog in this figure. Then, you can click the Rebuild and Apply Changes button to rebuild the app so the changes are applied. You can also select the "Always rebuild when updates can't be applied" option to prevent this dialog from being displayed in the future. Or, you can click the Continue Editing button to return to the Code Editor.

You also can't make changes to code that runs when an application starts. That includes C# code in the Program.cs file, and the _Layout.cshtml, _ViewImports.cshtml, and _ViewStart.cshtml files. To apply these changes, you have to restart the application. However, Visual Studio won't notify you if you try to apply these changes while an app is running.

In addition to changing the C# code for an app, you can use Hot Reload to apply changes you make to the CSS in a Razor view. For example, you can remove or add the classes that are applied to the table on the Movie List page. You can also make changes to the CSS in an external style sheet. In that case, though, Hot Reload isn't required because the browser is automatically refreshed.

How to use Hot Reload

The dialog that's displayed if a change can't be made

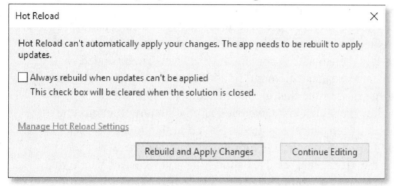

Types of code changes you can apply with Hot Reload

- Changes to most C# code in controllers, models, and Razor views
- Changes to CSS code

Description

- *Hot Reload* is a feature of Visual Studio 2022 that lets you apply changes to an app while it's running without restarting the app. To do that, you save the changes and then click the Hot Reload button in the Standard toolbar.

- You can use Hot Reload with most .NET 6 apps either with or without debugging. If you're using .NET 5 or earlier, you can only use Hot Reload with debugging.

- If Hot Reload can't apply the changes you've made while the app is running, the dialog shown above is displayed asking if you want to rebuild the app or continue editing.

- By default, you must save your changes before applying them with Hot Reload. To automatically apply your changes when you save them, display the drop-down list for the Hot Reload button, select the Settings item, and then select the "Apply Hot Reload on File Save" option.

Figure 5-2   How to use the Hot Reload feature

How to use the browser's developer tools

When you test your app and find that the pages aren't formatted correctly in all browsers, you need to change the HTML or CSS so the formatting is correct. In some cases, though, it's hard to figure out what HTML or CSS needs to be changed. To help you with that, most browsers provide *Developer Tools* that let you view the HTML elements and CSS styles that are rendered by the web server. Figure 5-3 presents the basic skills for working with the developer tools in three popular browsers.

To start, you can open or close the Developer Tools in Chrome and Edge by pressing F12. Because of that, these tools are sometimes called *F12 tools*. If you're using Safari, though, you have to use the other techniques described in this figure to open and close the Developer Tools.

The screen in this figure shows the Developer Tools in Chrome. To display the HTML and CSS for a page, you use the Elements tab as shown here. This tab displays the HTML in a hierarchical structure. Then, you can expand and collapse elements using the arrowheads to the left of the elements. In this case, a <div> element that uses the Bootstrap container class has been expanded so you can see that it contains a <header> element. In addition, the <header> element has been expanded so you can see that it contains an <h1> element.

If you want to view the styles that have been applied to any element, you just select that element. Then, the styles are displayed in the Styles tab that's displayed below the Elements tab. In this figure, for example, the Styles tab shows the styles for the <h1> element. This shows the styles for each style rule, and it shows what style sheet contains the style rule. In this example, all of the style sheets are part of the Bootstrap library.

When a line appears through a style, it means that the style has been overridden by another style. Knowing this can be helpful when you're trying to figure out why your styles aren't working the way you expect.

One of the best uses for the Developer Tools is to determine the cause of formatting issues. Another is to view the HTML that's generated by ASP.NET Core and returned to the browser. Yet another is to view the JavaScript that's generated for the validation controls.

Although this figure shows the Developer Tools for Chrome, the Developer Tools for the other browsers work similarly. The best way to learn how to use these tools is to experiment with them. You can also learn about all of the functionality provided by these tools by searching for more information online.

Chrome with the Elements tab of the developer tools open

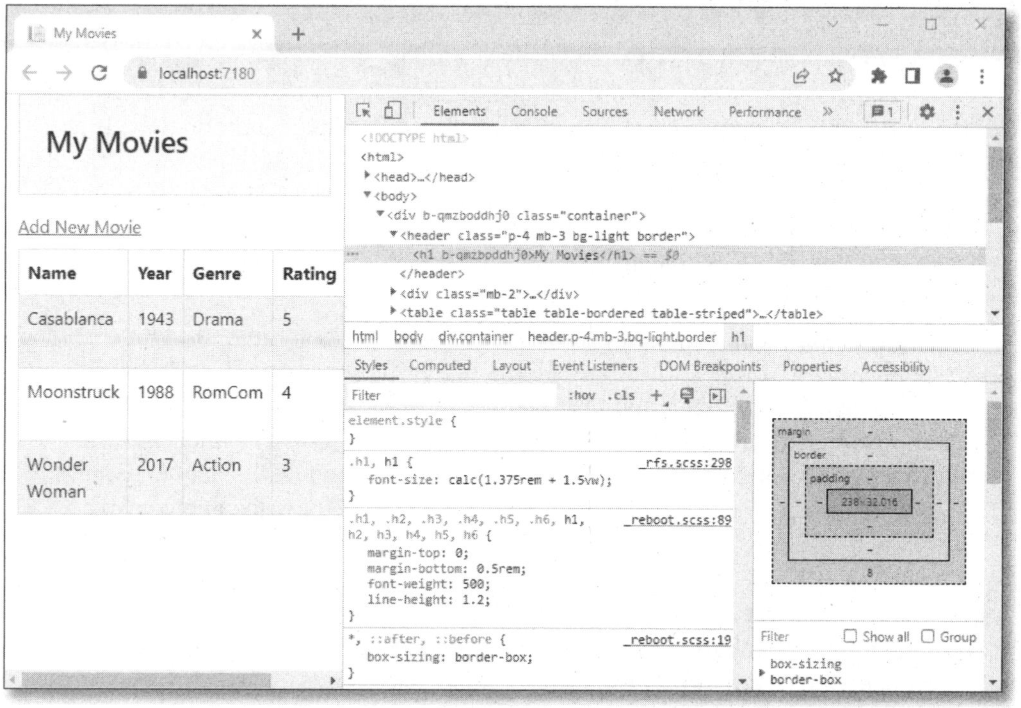

How to open and close the Developer Tools in Chrome and Edge

- To open, press F12. Or, right-click an element in the page and select Inspect.
- To close, press F12. Or, click the X in the upper right corner of the tools panel.

How to open and close the Developer Tools in Safari

- To open, right-click an element in the page and select Inspect Element.
- To close, click the X in the upper right corner of the tools panel.
- You must enable the developer tools before you can use them. To do that, select Preferences, click the Advanced tab, and select the "Show Develop menu" item.

How to view the rendered HTML and CSS styles

- Open the Elements panel by clicking on its tab.
- Expand the nodes to navigate to the element you want. Then, click that element.
- The HTML elements for a page are typically shown in the top of the panel, and the CSS styles for the selected element are typically shown below the HTML elements.

Description

- The *Developer Tools* of the major browsers provide some excellent debugging features, like viewing the HTML elements rendered by the web server and viewing the styles applied to those HTML elements.

Figure 5-3   How to use the browser's developer tools

How to use the Internal Server Error page

As you test an ASP.NET Core web app, you may encounter errors known as *exceptions* that prevent the app from executing. Often, you can write code that anticipates these exceptions, catches them, and handles them appropriately. If an exception isn't handled, however, the app can't continue.

If you are running an app without debugging, the app displays an Internal Server Error page like the one shown in figure 5-4. For example, this page is displayed if an exception occurs when the Movie List app attempts to add a new movie to the database.

This Internal Server Error page isn't user friendly. In other words, you wouldn't want to display it to the end users of your app because it contains technical details about your app that aren't helpful to end users. However, the Internal Server Error page often provides all the information a developer needs to determine the cause of an exception. As a result, you typically want to use this page when you're developing an app. Later, when you deploy the app, you can replace it with a user-friendly error page that you've designed for the end users of your app.

The Internal Server Error page begins by displaying the name and description of the unhandled exception that occurred. In this figure, for example, a SqlException occurred because the app attempted to insert a NULL value into a column in the database that doesn't allow NULL values. This information alone is often enough to give you a good idea of what's causing the exception.

After displaying the name and description of the exception, the Internal Server Error page displays a row of links that allow you to learn more about the exception. By default, the Stack link is selected. This link displays a *stack trace*, which is a list of the methods that were active when the exception occurred. If you scroll down through this list of methods, you can find the line of code in your app that caused the exception. That's important because determining the cause of the exception is the first step to fixing your code to prevent or handle the exception.

In addition, the Internal Server Error page includes links that allow you to display the query strings, cookies, and routing data for the current request. These links can be helpful for determining the cause of some types of errors, and the information that they display should make more sense to you as you progress through this book and learn more about query strings, cookies, and routing.

The Internal Server Error page

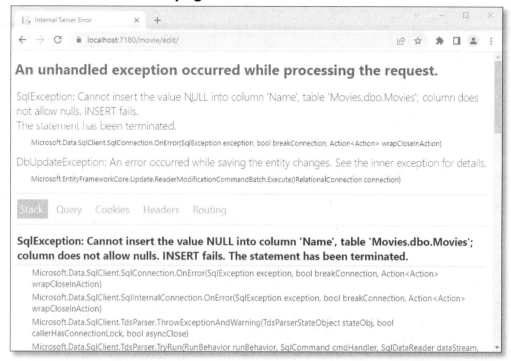

The Internal Server Error page can display…

- The name and description of the exception.
- A stack trace that you can use to find the line of code that caused the exception.
- Query strings, cookies, headers, and routing data for the current request.

Description

- An *exception* is an error that may occur when you run an app. If an exception occurs and isn't handled, the app can't continue.
- During development, if you run an app without debugging and an exception occurs, ASP.NET Core typically stops the app and sends an Internal Server Error page to the browser.
- By default, the Internal Server Error page selects the Stack link to display a *stack trace*, which is a list of the methods that were active when the exception occurred. However, you can also display information about the current request by clicking the Query, Cookies, Headers, and Routing links.

Figure 5-4   How to use the Internal Server Error page

How to use the Exception Helper

If you are running an app with debugging and you encounter an exception like the one described in the previous figure, the app enters break mode and displays an Exception Helper like the one in figure 5-5. This non-modal dialog box indicates the type of exception that occurred and points to the statement that caused the error.

In many cases, you can use this information to determine what caused the error and what should be done to correct it. For example, the Exception Helper dialog box in this figure indicates that EF can't add a movie to the database if the Name column of the Movie table is NULL. In addition, the Exception Helper shows that this exception was caused by this line of code in the MovieController class:

```
context.SaveChanges();
```

Based on that information, you can assume that your code must have set the name of the movie to NULL. This could happen, for example, if the app didn't include the Required attribute before the Name property of the Movie class, the Name property is nullable, and the user didn't enter a name for a new movie. This would cause an exception because the database requires this data, but the app isn't supplying it. As a result, the call to the SaveChanges() method causes an exception to occur. To fix this issue, you can start by checking to make sure that the Required attribute for the Name property is set properly and that the property isn't nullable.

When you are testing and debugging, you will encounter many exceptions that apply to general system operations such as arithmetic operations and the execution of methods. In addition, if your apps use databases, you will encounter EF and SQL exceptions.

In some cases, you won't be able to determine the cause of an exception just by analyzing the information displayed by the Exception Helper. Then, to get more information about the possible cause of the exception, you can use the links at the bottom of the Exception Helper to view the details of the exception, copy the details of the exception, or even start a Live Share session to collaborate with other developers. But first, you typically want to use the debugger to further analyze the problem as described in the next few figures.

The Exception Helper

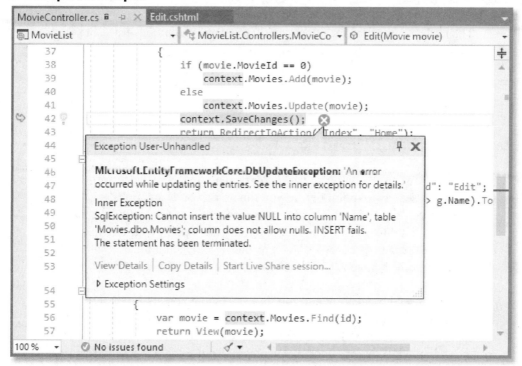

Description

- If you run an app with debugging and an exception occurs, the debugger stops on the line of code that caused the exception and displays the Exception Helper.

- The Exception Helper provides the name and description of the exception and points to the statement that caused the exception. It also includes links to view the details, copy the details, or start a Live Share session.

- The Exception Helper often provides all the information you need to determine the cause of an exception.

- Since the Exception Helper is a non-modal dialog box, you can edit code while it is open.

- If you want to close the Exception Helper, you can click the X in its upper right corner. Then, you can open it again by clicking on the exception icon (the red circle with an X in it). This icon is displayed to the right of the statement that caused the exception.

- If you continue program execution after an exception occurs by pressing F5 or clicking on the Continue button, ASP.NET Core terminates the app and sends an error page to the browser as described in the previous figure.

Figure 5-5   How to use the Exception Helper

How to use the debugger

The topics that follow introduce you to the basic techniques for using the Visual Studio *debugger* to debug an ASP.NET Core app. These techniques are almost identical to the techniques you use to debug any type of .NET app. As a result, if you have experience debugging other types of .NET apps, you should already be familiar with most of these techniques.

How to use breakpoints

Figure 5-6 shows how to use *breakpoints* in an ASP.NET Core app. To start, you can set a breakpoint before you run an app or as an app is executing. However, a web app ends after it generates a page. So, if you switch from the browser to Visual Studio to set a breakpoint, the breakpoint won't be taken until the next time the page is executed. As a result, if you want a breakpoint to be taken the first time a page is executed, you'll need to set the breakpoint before you run the app.

After you set a breakpoint and run the app, the app enters *break mode* before it executes the statement that contains the breakpoint. In this figure, for example, the app will enter break mode before it executes the statement that caused the exception in the last figure to occur. Then, you can use the debugging features to debug the app.

In some cases, you may want to set more than one breakpoint. You can do that either before you begin the execution of the app or while the app is in break mode. Then, when you run the app, it stops at the first breakpoint. And when you continue execution, the app executes up to the next breakpoint.

Once you set a breakpoint, it remains active until you remove it. In fact, it remains active even after you close the project. If you want to remove a breakpoint, you can use one of the techniques presented in this figure.

If you don't want to remove a breakpoint completely, but you don't want to stop on it, you can disable it using one of the techniques shown in this figure. Then, if you later want to stop on that breakpoint, you can enable it.

One easy way to enable and disable breakpoints is to use the Breakpoints window. This window lets you perform more advanced tasks like labeling groups of breakpoints, filtering breakpoints, and setting break conditions and hit counts.

The Movie controller with a breakpoint

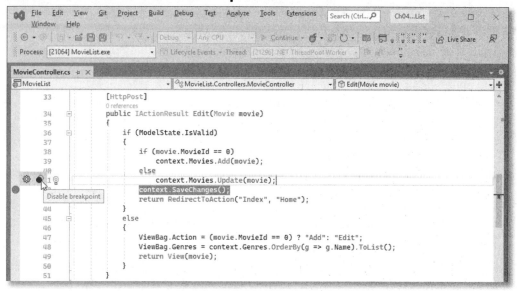

How to set and remove breakpoints

- To set a breakpoint, click in the margin indicator bar to the left of the line number for a statement. This highlights the statement and adds a breakpoint indicator (a red dot) in the margin.
- To remove a breakpoint, click the breakpoint indicator.
- To remove all breakpoints, select Debug→Delete All Breakpoints.

How to enable and disable breakpoints

- To enable or disable a breakpoint, point to the breakpoint indicator and select Enable/Disable Breakpoint from the resulting menu.
- To disable all breakpoints, select Debug→Disable All Breakpoints.
- To enable all breakpoints, select Debug→Enable All Breakpoints.
- To display the Breakpoints window, select Debug→Windows→Breakpoints. This window is most useful for enabling and disabling existing breakpoints.

Description

- When Visual Studio encounters a *breakpoint*, it enters *break mode* before it executes the statement on which the breakpoint is set.
- You can set and remove breakpoints before you run an app or while you're in break mode.
- You can only set a breakpoint on a line that contains an executable statement.

Figure 5-6   How to use breakpoints

How to work in break mode

Figure 5-7 shows the Movie controller of the Movie List app in break mode. In this mode, the next statement to be executed is highlighted. Then, you can use the debugging information that's available to try to determine the cause of an exception or a logical error.

One easy way to get information about what your code is doing is to use *data tips*. A data tip displays the current value of a variable or property when you hover the mouse pointer over it. You can also view the values of the members of an array, structure, or object by placing the mouse pointer over the arrowhead in a data tip.

In this figure, for example, the screen shows a data tip for a Movie object. This data tip displays its properties, including its Name property, whose value is null. You can view all this information just by pointing the mouse at variables and properties. When you move the mouse, the data tip disappears. However, you can keep the data tip open by clicking on the pin icon to the right of a data tip.

The debugging windows at the bottom of Visual Studio also display the values of variables and properties. In this figure, for example, the Locals window provides access to the same Movie object that's displayed in the data tip. In the next figure, you'll learn more about this window as well as some other debugging windows.

Once you're in break mode, you can use the commands summarized in this figure to control the execution of the app. Except for the Break All command, these commands are available from the Debug menu as well as the Debug toolbar. In addition, you can use shortcut keys to start these commands.

To execute the statements of an app one at a time, you use the Step Into command. Each time you use this command, the app executes the next statement and returns to break mode. That way, you can check the values of properties and variables and perform other debugging functions as you step through code one statement at a time. The Step Over command is similar to the Step Into command, but it executes the statements in called methods without interruption (they are "stepped over").

The Step Out command executes the remaining statements in a method without interruption. When the method finishes, the app enters break mode before the next statement in the calling method is executed.

If your app gets caught in a loop that keeps executing indefinitely without generating a page, you can force it into break mode by choosing the Debug→Break All command. This command lets you enter break mode any time during the execution of an app. You can also use the Stop Debugging command to end an app that's caught in a loop.

The Movie List app in break mode

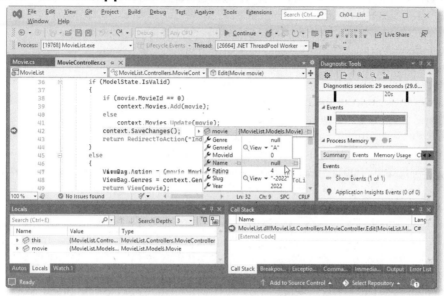

Commands in the Debug menu and toolbar

Command	Keyboard	Function
Start/Continue	F5	Start or continue execution of the app.
Break All	Ctrl+Alt+Break	Suspend execution of the app and enter break mode. (Toolbar only)
Stop Debugging	Shift+F5	Stop debugging and end execution of the app.
Restart	Ctrl+Shift+F5	Restart the entire app.
Step Into	F11	Execute one statement at a time.
Step Over	F10	Execute one statement at a time except for called methods.
Step Out	Shift+F11	Execute the remaining lines in the current method.

Description

- When you enter break mode, the debugger highlights the next statement to be executed. Then, you can use the debugging windows, the commands in the Debug menu, and the buttons in the Debug toolbar to control the execution of the program and determine the cause of an exception.

- To display the value of a variable or property in a *data tip,* position the mouse pointer over the variable or property in the Code Editor window. You can also use the pin icon to the right of a data tip to pin the data tip so it remains displayed.

- To display the members of an array, structure, or object in a data tip, position the mouse pointer over it to display its data tip, and then point to the arrow to the left of the data tip.

- You can use the Step Into, Step Over, and Step Out commands to execute one or more statements and return to break mode.

Figure 5-7   How to work in break mode

How to monitor variables and expressions

If you need to view the values of several app variables or expressions, you can do that using the Autos, Locals, or Watch windows. By default, these windows are displayed in the lower left corner of the IDE when an app enters break mode. If they're not displayed, you can display them by selecting the appropriate command from the Debug→Windows menu.

Figure 5-8 begins by displaying the Locals and Watch windows. The Locals window displays information about the variables within the scope of the current method. If the code in a controller is currently executing, this window also includes information about the controller and all of its properties such as its ViewBag property. The Autos window is similar to the Locals window, but it only displays information about the variables used in the current statement and the previous statement.

Unlike the Autos and Locals windows, a Watch window lets you choose the values that are displayed. For example, the Watch window in this figure displays the Name property of the movie object. You can also add properties of the page or of a business class to a Watch window as well as the values of expressions. In fact, an expression doesn't have to exist in the app for you to add it to a Watch window.

To add an item to a Watch window, you can type it directly into the Name column. Alternatively, if the item appears in the Code Editor window, you can highlight it in that window and then drag it to a Watch window. You can also highlight the item in the Code Editor or data tip, right-click it, and select the Add Watch command. This adds the item to the Watch window that's currently displayed. If necessary, you can display up to four Watch windows. However, you typically only need one Watch window.

The Immediate window is useful for displaying or changing the values of variables or properties. To display a value, you type a question mark followed by the name of a variable or an expression. In this figure, for example, the first line is a command that displays the Name property of the movie object on the second line. This shows that the Name property is null.

The third line is a command that assigns a name of "Wizard of Oz" to the Name property. This immediately changes the value of the Name property in the currently executing app and is reflected by the Locals window. In addition, the fifth line displays the Slug property of the movie object on the sixth line. This also shows that the currently executing app is now using the new Name property.

You can also use the Immediate window to test an expression. For example, the seventh line tests an expression that divides 5 by 100. Since this expression uses integer division, the result on the eighth line is 0. To use decimal division, you can adjust the expression so it casts one of the integer values to the double type as shown in the ninth line. This displays a result of 0.05.

In the Immediate window, you can execute a command that you've already entered by repeatedly pressing the Up or Down arrow key to scroll through the commands. Then, when the command you want is displayed, you can execute it by pressing Enter. Or, if you want to remove all commands from the Immediate window, you can right-click on the window and select Clear All.

The Locals and Watch windows

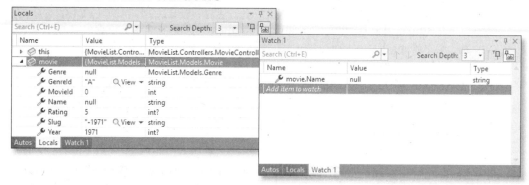

The Immediate window

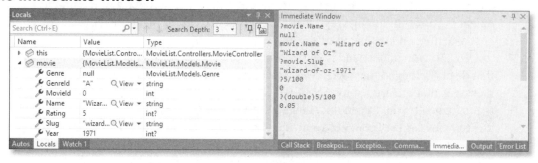

How to use the Locals, Autos, and Watch windows

- The Locals window displays information about the variables within the scope of the current method.
- The Autos window works like the Locals window, but it only displays information about variables used by the current statement and the previous statement.
- The Watch windows let you view the values of variables and expressions that you specify, called *watch expressions*. To add a watch expression, type a variable name or expression into the Name column. To delete a row from a Watch window, right-click the row and select Delete Watch.

How to use the Immediate window

- To display the current value of a variable or expression, type a question mark followed by a variable name or expression. Then, press Enter.
- To execute a statement, type the statement. Then, press Enter.
- To execute an existing command, press the Up or Down arrow until you have displayed the command. Then, press Enter.
- To remove all commands and output, right-click the window and select Clear All.

How to display these windows

- If the window's tab is visible, click the tab. Otherwise, select the window from the Debug→Windows menu.

Figure 5-8   How to monitor variables and expressions

How to use tracepoints

Visual Studio also provides a feature called *tracepoints*. A tracepoint is a special type of breakpoint that performs an action when it's encountered. For example, figure 5-9 begins by showing a tracepoint with its settings.

To set a tracepoint, you right-click a statement and select Breakpoint→Insert Tracepoint. Then, you use the Breakpoint Settings window to indicate what you want to do when the tracepoint is "hit." Typically, you want to log a message to the Output Window and continue execution.

The message you log can include variables and other expressions as well as special keywords. For example, the message shown here begins by using the $FUNCTION keyword to log the name of the method that's being executed. Then, the message uses braces to include the value of the Name property of the movie object. As a result, the message that's logged to the Output window includes the name of the method and the name of the movie.

To help you understand how this works, this figure shows the Output window that displays logged messages. Here, the Output window displays several debugging messages that are logged by ASP.NET Core. In addition, it displays the message that's logged by the tracepoint shown in this figure that says:

```
Inside MovieList.Controllers.MovieController.Edit(MovieList.Models.Movie)
getting ready to add movie null
```

This message shows that the code is inside the Edit() method of the Movie controller and that the movie's name is null. If the Output window isn't displayed on your system, you can open it by selecting View→Output.

By default, program execution continues after the tracepoint action is performed. If that's not what you want, you can remove the check mark from the Continue Code Execution option. Since this causes the app to enter break mode, it converts the tracepoint into a breakpoint and uses the standard breakpoint icon (a red circle) instead of a tracepoint icon (a red diamond). Conversely, you can convert a breakpoint to a tracepoint by displaying its Breakpoint Settings window and selecting the Continue Code Execution option.

Tracepoints are useful in situations where a standard breakpoint would be cumbersome, such as in the execution of a loop. For example, suppose you have a loop that performs 100 iterations, and an error is occurring somewhere in the middle of the loop. Imagine how tedious it would be to manually continue execution until you get to the iteration that caused the error. By contrast, you can use a tracepoint to quickly view the data for each iteration of the loop.

The Movie controller with a tracepoint that logs a message

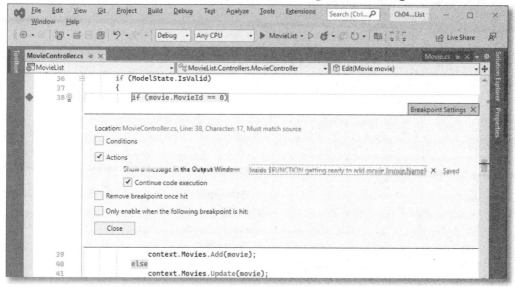

The Output window that displays the message

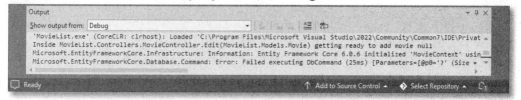

How to set a tracepoint

- To set a new tracepoint, right-click a statement and select Breakpoint→Insert Tracepoint. Then, complete the Breakpoint Settings window.

- To convert an existing breakpoint to a tracepoint, point to the breakpoint icon, click the Settings icon that looks like a gear, and complete the Breakpoint Settings window.

- For a tracepoint, the Breakpoint Settings window should have the Continue Code Execution option selected. That way, it doesn't enter break mode like a breakpoint.

- When logging a message to the Output window, you can include the value of a variable or other expression by placing the variable or expression inside braces, and you can include special keywords such as FUNCTION by coding a dollar sign ($) followed by the keyword.

Description

- A *tracepoint* is a special type of breakpoint that lets you perform an action and continue execution.

- You typically use tracepoints to log messages to the Output window. These messages can include text, variables, expressions, and special keywords.

- Visual Studio uses a red diamond icon to mark tracepoints.

Figure 5-9   How to use tracepoints

Perspective

Visual Studio provides a powerful set of tools for debugging ASP.NET Core MVC apps. For simple apps, you can usually find bugs by running the app and testing it manually. Then, you can use the techniques presented in this chapter to fix those bugs. For complex apps, though, it usually makes sense to also automate testing as described in chapter 14.

Terms

testing	stack trace
debugging	debugger
browser incompatibilities	breakpoint
Hot Reload	break mode
developer tools	data tip
F12 tools	watch expressions
exception	tracepoint

Summary

- When you *test* an app, you try to find all of its errors. When you *debug* an app, you find the causes of the errors and fix them.

- To test for *browser incompatibilities*, you run a web app in all of the most popular browsers to make sure they all display your app correctly.

- *Hot Reload* allows you to make changes to an app and apply them while the app is running. That saves you the time of having to restart an app every time you make changes.

- You can use the browser's *developer tools* to find problems in your HTML and CSS.

- *Exceptions* are errors that prevent the app from executing if they aren't handled.

- A *stack trace* is a list of methods that were active when an exception occurred.

- Visual Studio's *debugger* lets you set a *breakpoint*, step through the statements in an app when it is in *break mode*, and view the changes in the data after each statement is executed.

- *Data tips* provide an easy way to view the values of variables and expressions when an app is in break mode. You can also use the Autos, Locals, Watch, and Immediate windows to view the values of variables and expressions.

- *Tracepoints* are similar to breakpoints but they let you perform an action like printing a message to the Output window and then continue execution. They are often useful for debugging loops.

Exercise 5-1   Debug the Movie List app

In this exercise, you'll debug the Movie List app presented in chapter 4. To start, you'll open a version of the app that includes two bugs.

Use breakpoints, data tips, and the Locals window

1. Open the Ch05Ex1MovieList web app in the ex_starts directory.

2. Press Ctrl+F5 to run the app without debugging. The default browser should display a list of movies, but the genre for each movie should not be correct. Now, close the browser window to end the app.

3. Since the Index.cshtml file of the Views/Home folder displays the genre for each movie, open that file and view its code.

4. Set a breakpoint to the left of the table cell that displays the genre data.

5. Press F5 to run the app with debugging. This should cause the app to enter break mode just before the table cell that displays the genre data.

6. Hover the mouse pointer over @movie, expand the data tip for the Movie object and then the Genre object, and note that the Genre object has two properties (GenreId and Name) and that the Name property contains the genre data you want to display.

7. In the Locals window, expand the movie object, expand the Genre property, and note that it also displays the values of the GenreId and Name properties.

8. At this point, you could end the app, change the code so the genre is displayed correctly, and then run the app again. Instead, you'll do that using Hot Reload to see how that works.

Use Hot Reload

9. If you haven't already done so, use the Stop Debugging command to stop debugging and end the app.

10. Remove the breakpoint that you added to the Index.cshtml file.

11. Start the app again without debugging.

12. With the app still running, switch back to Visual Studio.

13. Change the code in the Index.cshtml file that displays the genre to @movie.Genre.Name, save the change, and click the Hot Reload button.

14. Switch back to the browser to see that the genre name is now displayed correctly.

Use the Internal Server Error page and the Exception Helper

15. With the app still running, attempt to add a new movie, but leave the Name field blank and enter appropriate values for all the other fields.

16. When you click the Save button, the app should display an Internal Server Error page that displays information about an exception that indicates that the database can't insert a NULL value into the Name column of the Movies table.

17. Close the browser, and then run the app with debugging. Again, attempt to add a new movie with a blank Name field but appropriate values for all the other fields.

18. When you click the Save button, Visual Studio should enter break mode even though you haven't set a breakpoint. In addition, Visual Studio should highlight the statement that caused the exception and use the Exception Helper to display much of the same information about the exception as in step 16.

19. To prevent this exception, modify your app to make sure that it doesn't allow the name of a movie to be null. To do that, open the Movie class in the Models folder and add the Required attribute above the Name property like this:

```
[Required(ErrorMessage = "Please enter a name.")]
```

In addition, remove the question mark from the data type for this property so it's non-nullable, and assign an initial value of string.Empty to it.

20. Run the app again and confirm that the error has been fixed. To do that, attempt to add a movie with a blank Name field. This time, the browser should display a user-friendly validation message on the Add Movie page.

Section 2

Master the essential skills

The eight chapters in this section review and expand upon the skills that you learned in section 1. To start, chapter 6 shows how to work with controllers and routing to provide user-friendly URLs that can improve search engine optimization. Chapter 7 shows how to use Razor views to display the user interface of an app. And chapter 8 shows how to transfer data from controllers to views and back.

After learning those essential skills for working with controllers and views, chapter 9 shows how to use session state and cookies to manage the state of an app. Chapter 10 shows how to work with model binding. Chapter 11 shows how to validate data that's stored in the model. And chapter 12 shows how to use EF Core to store the data for the model in a database.

Chapter 13 finishes this section by presenting the Bookstore app. This puts the skills presented in chapters 6 through 12 into the context of a complete app.

To a large extent, each of the chapters in this section is an independent unit. As a result, you don't have to read these chapters in sequence. If, for example, you want to know more about session state and cookies after you finish section 1, you can go directly to chapter 9. Eventually, though, you're going to want to read all eight chapters. So unless you have a compelling reason to skip around, we recommend reading the chapters in sequence.

6

How to work with controllers and routing

In chapter 4, you learned how to create an app that uses the default routing that's available from ASP.NET Core MVC. To start, this chapter describes how this default routing works in more detail. Then, it shows how to customize the routing so the URLs for your web app follow best practices. To finish, this chapter summarizes some best practices for creating URLs.

How to use the default route

This chapter begins by showing how to configure and use the default route for an ASP.NET Core MVC app. When you begin developing an app, it's common to start with this route.

How to configure the default route

Figure 6-1 shows a Program.cs file that configures the default route for an ASP.NET Core MVC app. To do that, it uses a routing system known as *endpoint routing* that was introduced in ASP.NET Core 3.0 and is recommended for any new development.

Before you can use endpoint routing, you need to add the necessary MVC services to the app. To do that, you can call one or more methods of the Services property of the WebApplicationBuilder object that's assigned to the builder variable. With ASP.NET Core 3.0 and later, you can call the AddControllersWithViews() method as shown in this figure.

Prior to ASP.NET Core 3.0, you had to use the AddMvc() method to add these services. However, this included the services for Razor Pages, which you don't need for an MVC app. As a result, unless you're developing an app that uses MVC and Razor Pages, it's better to use the AddControllersWithViews() method to add MVC services.

After you add the necessary services, you need to configure the routing. To do that, you can call the methods of the WebApplication object assigned to the app variable that are shown in this figure. First, you call the UseRouting() method to mark where the routing decisions are made. Then, you call the MapControllerRoute() method to configure the endpoints for each route.

Between the calls to the UseRouting() and MapControllerRoute() methods, you can add any services that you want to run after routing decisions have been made but before they have been executed. This typically includes the services for authenticating and authorizing users that are described later in this book.

The MapControllerRoute() method maps the endpoints for each controller. To do that, you can supply a pattern argument like the one shown in this figure. This pattern specifies the default route described in the next few figures.

Alternately, you can call the MapDefaultControllerRoute() method to map the default route for controllers. This approach has the advantage of being shorter and easier to code. However, using the MapControllerRoute() method has the advantage of allowing other programmers to easily view and modify the pattern.

The methods for adding the MVC service

Method	Description
AddControllersWithViews()	Adds the services necessary to support an MVC app. Available with ASP.NET Core 3.0 and later.
AddMvc()	Adds the services necessary to support an MVC app as well as the services that support Razor Pages. Available with all versions of ASP.NET Core.

Two methods for configuring the routes

Method	Description
UseRouting()	Selects the endpoint for the route if one is found.
MapControllerRoute()	Adds endpoints for controller actions and specifies a route.

Code in the Program.cs file that configures the default route

```
var builder = WebApplication.CreateBuilder(args);

// Add services to the container.
builder.Services.AddControllersWithViews();    // add MVC services

// add other services here

var app = builder.Build();

// Configure the HTTP request pipeline.
if (!app.Environment.IsDevelopment())
{
    app.UseExceptionHandler("/Home/Error");
    app.UseHsts();
}

app.UseHttpsRedirection();
app.UseStaticFiles();

app.UseRouting();

app.UseAuthorization();

app.MapControllerRoute(
    name: "default",
    pattern: "{controller=Home}/{action=Index}/{id?}");

app.Run();
```

Another way to map a controller to the default route

```
app.MapDefaultControllerRoute();
```

Description

- ASP.NET Core 3.0 introduced a new approach to routing known as *endpoint routing*. It's generally considered a best practice to use endpoint routing for all new development.
- Before you can use endpoint routing, you need to add the necessary MVC services to the app. Then, you need to mark where the routing decisions are made and configure the endpoints for each route.

Figure 6-1   How to configure the default route

How the default route works

Figure 6-2 begins by showing a URL that has a domain name and three *segments*. Here, the first segment is "Home", the second segment is "Index", and the third segment is "Joel".

The pattern for the *default route* specifies how to handle three segments like these. Here, the first segment specifies the controller, the second segment specifies the action method within the controller, and the third segment specifies an argument for the id parameter of the action method.

The pattern for the default route sets the Home controller as the default for the first segment, it sets the Index() action as the default for the second segment, and it uses a question mark (?) to specify that the third segment is optional. As a result, all three of these segments are optional. However, if you want to specify a later segment, you must also supply values for the earlier segments.

The table of request URLs shows how this works. Here, the first URL doesn't specify any of the three segments. As a result, the app routes the request to the Index() method of the Home controller and it doesn't pass an argument to the id parameter of this method.

Later in the table, the seventh URL specifies all three segments. As a result, the app routes the request to the List() method of the Product controller and passes an argument of "Guitars" to the id parameter of this method.

This table assumes that the List() method defines the id parameter as a string and doesn't provide a default value for this parameter. As a result, if the URL doesn't specify a third segment for the List() method, it sets the id parameter to null. Similarly, this table assumes that the Detail() method defines the id parameter as an int and doesn't provide a default value for this parameter. As a result, if the URL doesn't specify a third segment for the Detail() method, it sets the id parameter to the default int value of 0.

A URL that has three segments

```
https://localhost:7098/Home/Index/Joel
```
First segment   Second segment   Third segment

The pattern for the default route

```
{controller=Home}/{action=Index}/{id?}
```

How the default route works

- The first segment specifies the controller. Since the pattern sets the Home controller as the default controller, this segment is optional.
- The second segment specifies the action method within the controller. Since the pattern sets the Index() method as the default action, this segment is optional.
- The third segment specifies an argument for the id parameter of the action method. The pattern uses a question mark (?) to specify that this segment is optional.

How request URLs map to controller classes and their action methods

Request URL	Controller	Action	Id
http://localhost	Home	Index	null
http://localhost/Home	Home	Index	null
http://localhost/Home/Index	Home	Index	null
http://localhost/Home/About	Home	About	null
http://localhost/Product	Product	Index	null
http://localhost/Product/List	Product	List	null
http://localhost/Product/List/Guitars	Product	List	Guitars
http://localhost/Product/Detail	Product	Detail	0
http://localhost/Product/Detail/3	Product	Detail	3

Description

- The *default route* maps a request to an action method within a controller and can optionally pass an argument to that action method.
- All three segments of the default route are optional. However, if you want to specify a value for a later segment, you must supply values for the earlier segments as well.

Figure 6-2   How the default route works

How to code a simple controller and its actions

Figure 6-3 shows how to code a simple Home controller and two of its actions. To start, the class for an MVC controller typically inherits the Controller class from Microsoft's AspNetCore.Mvc namespace. In this figure, for example, the HomeController inherits the Controller class.

Within the class for a controller, an action method typically returns an object that implements the IActionResult interface, such as a ContentResult or ViewResult object. For example, in chapters 2 and 4, you saw how to use the View() method to return ViewResult objects.

Now, this chapter shows how to use the Content() method to return a ContentResult object. This allows you to return plain text directly to the browser without going through a view, which is a useful way to test the URLs of your app before you implement the views. For example, you can test the controller shown in this chapter by running the app and entering a URL in the browser's address bar as shown in this figure.

A method that a controller can use to return plain text to the browser

Method	Description
`Content(string)`	Creates a ContentResult object that contains the specified string.

The Home controller

```
using Microsoft.AspNetCore.Mvc;

namespace GuitarShop.Controllers
{
    public class HomeController : Controller
    {
        public IActionResult Index()
        {
            return Content("Home controller, Index action");
        }

        public IActionResult About()
        {
            return Content("Home controller, About action");
        }
    }
}
```

A browser after requesting the default page

A browser after requesting the Home/About page

Description

- The class for an MVC controller typically inherits the Controller class from Microsoft's AspNetCore.Mvc namespace.
- The action methods for a controller typically return an object that implements the IActionResult interface, such as a ContentResult or ViewResult object.
- To create a simple controller, you can begin by coding action methods that use the Content() method to return ContentResult objects that contain plain text.
- To test a controller, you can run the app and enter a URL in the browser's address bar.

Figure 6-3   How to code a simple controller and its actions

How to code a controller that uses the id segment

Figure 6-4 shows how to code a controller named ProductController that uses the id segment of the default route. Here, the Product controller begins much like the Home controller from the previous figure. However, both of its action methods provide a parameter named id that maps to the id segment of the default route.

The List() method uses the string type for the id parameter and provides a default value of "All". As a result, if a URL doesn't specify the id segment for this action, this method sets the id parameter to "All" as shown by the first browser window.

On the other hand, the Detail() method uses the int type for the id parameter and does not provide a default value. As a result, if a URL specifies the id segment for this action, this method sets the id parameter to the segment value as shown by the second browser window. Otherwise, this method sets the id parameter to the default int value of 0 as shown by the third browser window.

Note that if the URL specifies a value for the id segment that isn't numeric, the Detail() action method can't convert that value to an int. When that happens, the method sets the id parameter to the default int value of 0. In other words, it treats the URL the same as if it didn't specify a value for the id segment. So, for instance, the id parameter for a URL of /Product/Detail/Three would be 0.

The Product controller

```
using Microsoft.AspNetCore.Mvc;

namespace GuitarShop.Controllers
{
    public class ProductController : Controller
    {
        public IActionResult List(string id = "All")
        {
            return Content("Product controller, List action, id: " + id);
        }

        public IActionResult Detail(int id)
        {
            return Content("Product controller, Detail action, id: " + id);
        }
    }
}
```

A browser after requesting the Product/List action with no id segment

A browser after requesting the Product/Detail action with an id segment

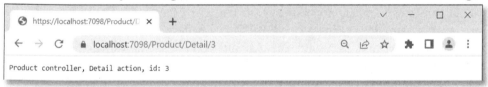

A browser after requesting the Product/Detail action with no id segment

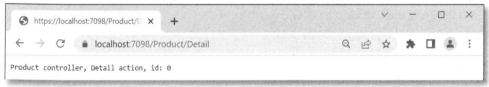

Description

- The List() method uses the string type for the id parameter and provides a default value of "All".
- The Detail() method uses the int type for the id parameter and does not provide a default value.

Figure 6-4   How to code a controller that uses the id segment

How to create custom routes

Now that you understand how the default route works, you're ready to learn how to create custom routes. One way to do that is to add static content to a route.

How to include static content in a route

All of the segments in the default pattern are dynamic. In other words, they specify content that can change with each URL. However, to make a URL easier to read, you may want to include static content as part of a segment. To do that, you can use a string literal as shown in the first example in figure 6-5. Here, the fourth segment of the pattern includes a string literal of "Page" just before it uses {num} to specify the name of the parameter. As a result, a segment of "Page4" passes an argument of "4" to the parameter named num.

In the pattern for the first example, none of the segments are optional or provide default values. As a result, you must supply all four segments. For the first two segments, you must specify the controller and action method. For the third segment, you must supply an id. And for the fourth segment, you must supply the static content of "Page" followed by the number for the page.

If you specify all four segments, the action method that's matched to the request URL can use its parameters to get the data from the third and fourth segments. For example, the List() method in this figure displays the data that's available from its id and num parameters. If you don't specify all four segments, the routing system doesn't match the URL to that pattern.

If you don't want to mix static and dynamic content in a segment, you can achieve a similar result by coding a routing pattern that specifies a completely static segment followed by a completely dynamic segment. In this figure, for example, the second routing pattern uses this approach. Here, the fourth segment is completely static and the fifth segment is completely dynamic. This works similarly to the first routing pattern. However, it uses five segments instead of four.

A pattern that mixes static and dynamic data for a segment

```
{controller}/{action}/{id}/Page{num}          // 4 segments
```

Example URLs

Request URL	Controller	Action	Parameters
/Product/List/All/Page1	Product	List	id=All, num=1
/Product/List/All/Page2	Product	List	id=All, num=2

The List() method of the Product controller

```
public IActionResult List(string id, int num)
{
    return Content("Product controller, List action, " +
        "Category " + id + ", Page " + num);
}
```

A URL that requests the Product/List action for page 1 of all categories

A pattern that supplies one segment that's completely static

```
{controller}/{action}/{id}/Page/{num}          // 5 segments
```

Example URLs

Request URL	Controller	Action	Parameters
/Product/List/All/Page/1	Product	List	id=All, num=1
/Product/List/All/Page/2	Product	List	id=All, num=2

A URL that requests the Product/List action for page 1 of all categories

Description

- To include static content as part of a segment, you can use a string literal to provide the static part of the segment and use braces to identify the dynamic part of the segment.
- To include a static segment, you can code a string literal for the entire segment.

Figure 6-5   How to include static content in a route

How to work with multiple routing patterns

When you create custom routes, it's common to use them in addition to the default route and other custom routes. When you map multiple routing patterns, you must code the most specific pattern first and the most general pattern last. Otherwise, the most general pattern will process all URLs.

The example in figure 6-6 shows how this works. To start, the first routing pattern is the most specific because it specifies five required segments where the fourth and fifth segments include static content for paging and sorting. As a result, a URL only matches this pattern if it includes five segments and matches the static content for paging and sorting.

The second routing pattern works like the first routing pattern, except that it doesn't specify the fifth segment for sorting. In other words, it only provides a fourth segment for paging. As a result, a URL only matches this pattern if it includes four segments and matches the static content for paging.

The third routing pattern is the least specific because it specifies the third segment as being optional and provides default values for the first two segments. As a result, a URL matches this pattern if it contains zero, one, two, or three segments.

The List() method shown in this figure shows how you can access the arguments in the URL segments. Here, the first parameter is named id so it can access the id argument specified by the third segment. The second parameter is named page so it can access the page argument specified by the fourth segment. And the third parameter is named sortby so it can access the sortby argument specified by the fifth segment. The tables at the bottom of this figure show how this works.

Code in Program.cs that maps three routing patterns

```
// most specific route - 5 required segments
app.MapControllerRoute(
    name: "paging_and_sorting",
    pattern: "{controller}/{action}/{id}/page{num}/sort-by-{sortby}");

// less specific route - 4 required segments
app.MapControllerRoute(
    name: "paging",
    pattern: "{controller}/{action}/{id}/page{num}");

// least specific route - 0 required segments
app.MapControllerRoute(
    name: "default",
    pattern: "{controller=Home}/{action=Index}/{id?}");
```

The List() method of the Product controller

```
public IActionResult List(string id = "All", int num = 1,
    string sortby = "Price")
{
    return Content("id=" + id + ", page=" + num + ", sortby=" + sortby);
}
```

Examples that use the default route

Request URL	Controller/Action	Parameters
/	Home/Index	id=null
/Home/About	Home/About	id=null
/Product/Detail/4	Product/Detail	id=4
/Product/List/Guitars	Product/List	id=Guitars

Examples that use the paging route

Request URL	Parameters
/Product/List/All/Page3	id=All, page=3
/Product/List/Guitars/Page2	id=Guitars, page=2
/Product/List/Guitars/Pg2	Not found because "Pg" doesn't match static "Page".

Examples that use the paging_and_sorting route

Request URL	Parameters
/Product/List/Guitars/Page2/Sort-By-Name	id=Guitars, page=2, sortby=Name
/Product/List/Guitars/Page2/By-Name	Not found because "By-" doesn't match "Sort-By-".

Description

- When you map multiple routing patterns, you must code the most specific ones first and the most general one last. If you code the most general pattern first, it will process all URLs.

Figure 6-6   How to work with multiple routing patterns

How to use attribute routing

So far, this chapter has shown how to use the Program.cs file to specify the routing patterns for an app. However, you can override this routing by decorating the action methods of a controller or the class for the controller with Route attributes. This is known as *attribute routing*.

How to change the routing for an action

Figure 6-7 starts by showing the class for the Home controller after attribute routing has been applied to its Index() and About() actions. To change the routing for the Index() action, this code *decorates* it with a Route attribute. That is, it places a Route attribute directly above the Index() method and specifies a route of "/". This maps the Index() action to a URL that requests the root folder of the app. Similarly, this code decorates the About() method with a Route attribute that maps the About() action to a request URL of "About".

These Route attributes specify static routes, not patterns. In addition, they override any routing patterns that are specified by the Program.cs file. As a result, if you add these attributes, you can't use a route of /Home, /Home/Index, or /Home/About. In other words, to access the Home/Index action, you must use a request URL of /. Similarly, to access the Home/About action, you must use a request URL of /About. Since that leads to shorter URLs, that's often what you want.

When you specify a static URL such as "About" for a route, the route doesn't change if you change the name of the About() action method later. That may be what you want. However, it's common to want the route to match the name of the action. To make this possible, you can use the [action] token in the Route attribute instead of hard coding the name in the route. Then, if you change the name of the action method, the route changes to match that name, which is often what you want. Since this makes your code more flexible, it's generally considered a best practice.

The [controller] token works much like the [action] token. Although this figure doesn't present an example of the [controller] token, the next two figures do.

With ASP.NET Core 3.0 or later, attribute routing is typically enabled by default. As a result, you typically don't need to add any code to the Program.cs file to enable it. However, if you find that attribute routing isn't working correctly on your system, you may need to enable it by calling the MapControllers() method as shown in the last example. Here, the MapControllers() method is coded before the pattern for the default route. That way, any attribute routing overrides the default routing pattern.

The Home controller with attribute routing for both actions

```
public class HomeController : Controller
{
    [Route("/")]
    public IActionResult Index()
    {
        return Content("Home controller, Index action");
    }

    [Route("About")]
    public IActionResult About()
    {
        return Content("Home controller, About action");
    }
}
```

How request URLs map to controller classes and their action methods

Request URL	Description
/	This maps to the Home/Index action.
/About	This maps to the Home/About action.

Two default routes that are overridden by the attribute routing

```
/Home/Index
/Home/About
```

Two tokens you can use to insert variable data into a route

Token	Description
[controller]	The name of the current controller.
[action]	The name of the current action.

A more flexible way to code the attribute for the Home/About action

```
[Route("[action]")]
```

How to map all controllers that use attribute routing

```
// map controllers that use attribute routing - often not necessary
app.MapControllers();

// map pattern for default route
app.MapControllerRoute(
    name: "default",
    pattern: "{controller=Home}/{action=Index}/{id?}");
```

Description

- To change the routing for an action, you can *decorate* the action method with a Route attribute. Then, the route specified by the attribute overrides the route that's specified in the Program.cs file. This is known as *attribute routing*.

- To specify a static route, you can code a string literal within the Route attribute.

- To insert the name of the current controller or action into a route, you can use the [controller] or [action] tokens.

Figure 6-7   How to use attributes to change the routing for an action

More skills for changing the routing for an action

Figure 6-8 begins by showing the class for the Product controller after attribute routing has been applied to its List() and Detail() actions. To do that, these methods are decorated with the Route attribute.

In addition, this class contains a helper method named GetSlug(). To indicate that this method is not an action method, it is decorated with the NonAction attribute. This prevents a URL from using the default routing to call the GetSlug() method. Since there's no reason to allow that, this is considered a best practice.

For the List() action, the Route attribute specifies a URL where the first segment is "Products" and the second segment is an optional argument named id. As a result, a request that specifies /Products calls this action without passing an argument, and a URL that specifies /Products/Guitars calls this action and passes an argument of "Guitars". The advantage of this approach over the default routing pattern is that it makes the URLs for accessing this action slightly shorter (/Products vs. /Product/List).

For the Detail() action, the Route attribute specifies a URL where the first segment is "Product" and the second segment is a required argument named id. As a result, a request that specifies /Product doesn't map to this action because it doesn't pass the required id argument. Instead, it maps to the Product/Index action. However, a request of /Product/3 calls this action and passes an id argument of 3. Again, the advantage of this approach over the default routing pattern is that it makes the URLs for accessing this action slightly shorter (/Product vs. /Product/Detail).

The last two examples in this figure show that you can make the attribute routing more flexible by using the [controller] token. For example, you can code the [controller] token followed by an s for the first segment of the List() action. This adds the s to the end of the controller name (Product) to make the segment Products. And you can code the [controller] token by itself for the first segment of the Detail() action. This makes the segment Product.

As you review this figure, note that you can use many of the same skills in the Route attributes that you used in the URL patterns in the Program.cs file. For example, you can use a question mark (?) to identify an optional argument. Similarly, you can add static content to a segment by entering a string literal for the static content.

The Product controller with attribute routing that specifies segments

```
public class ProductController : Controller
{
    public IActionResult Index()
    {
        return Content("Product controller, Index action");
    }

    [Route("Products/{id?}")]
    public IActionResult List(string id = "All")
    {
        return Content("Product controller, List action, Category: " + id);
    }

    [Route("Product/{id}")]
    public IActionResult Detail(int id)
    {
        return Content("Product controller, Detail action, ID: " + id);
    }

    [NonAction]
    public string GetSlug(string s) => s.Replace(' ', '-').ToLower();
}
```

How request URLs map to controller classes and their action methods

Request URL	Description
/Products	This maps to the Product/List action and uses the default parameter value of "All".
/Products/Guitars	This maps to the Product/List action and passes an argument of "Guitars".
/Product/3	This maps to the Product/Detail action and supplies a valid int argument of 3.
/Product	This maps to the Product/Index action, not the Product/Detail action. That's because it doesn't supply the required id segment.

Two default routes that are overridden by the attribute routing

```
/Product/List
/Product/Detail
```

A more flexible way to code the attribute for the Product/List action

```
[Route("[controller]s/{id?}")]
```

A more flexible way to code the attribute for the Product/Detail action

```
[Route("[controller]/{id}")]
```

Description

- To insert other segments into a route, you can use all of the skills for coding segments such as the ones described earlier in this chapter.

- If a controller contains methods that aren't action methods, you can decorate them with the NonAction attribute to prevent them from being mapped to a URL.

Figure 6-8   More skills for using attributes to change the routing for an action

How to change the routing for a controller

In the last two figures, you learned how to use attribute routing to override the routing for a single action in a controller. However, it's also possible to use attribute routing to override the routing for all actions within a controller. To do that, you can decorate the declaration for the controller's class with a Route attribute as shown in figure 6-9.

Here, the Route attribute that decorates the class declaration specifies four segments. The first segment is a static segment of "Retail", the second segment is the name of the controller, the third segment is the name of the action, and the fourth segment is an optional argument named id. As a result, you can use the URLs shown in the table to call the action methods of this controller and to pass arguments to them.

As with actions, the attribute routing for a controller overrides the default routing. As a result, when you use attribute routing for the controller, you can no longer use the default routing to request the actions of the controller. In this figure, for example, you can't use /Product/List to request the Product/List action. Instead, you must use /Retail/Product/List.

The code for the Product controller

```
[Route("Retail/[controller]/[action]/{id?}")]
public class ProductController : Controller
{
    public IActionResult List(string id = "All")
    {
        return Content("Product controller, List action, Category: " + id);
    }

    public IActionResult Detail(int id)
    {
        return Content("Product controller, Detail action, ID: " + id);
    }
}
```

How request URLs map to controller classes and their action methods

Request URL	Description
`/Retail/Product/List`	This maps to the Product/List action and uses the default parameter value of "All".
`/Retail/Product/List/Guitars`	This maps to the Product/List action and passes an argument of "Guitars".
`/Retail/Product/Detail`	This maps to the Product/Detail action and uses the default int value of 0.
`/Retail/Product/Detail/3`	This maps to the Product/Detail action and passes a valid int argument of 3.

Two default routes that are overridden by the attribute routing

```
/Product/List
/Product/Detail
```

Description

- To change the routing for all actions in a controller, you can decorate the controller's class with a Route attribute.

Figure 6-9   How to use attributes to change the routing for a controller

Best practices for creating URLs

As you design the URLs for your app, you should realize that they specify the interface for your app. As a result, once a website goes into production, you shouldn't change its URLs. If you do, you should redirect the old URLs to the new ones that provide the same functionality.

It's important to put some effort into designing the URLs of an app. Figure 6-10 lists some best practices for URLs. You'll want to follow these practices for a couple of reasons.

First, well-designed URLs can improve the usability of your app for both developers and end users. For example, if you want to cut and paste a URL to share with others, a well-designed URL is easier to read and gives others confidence that it leads to the content that they want. Also, if you need to type a URL or read it to someone over the phone, it's easier to do with a well-designed URL that's short and uses hyphens than it is with a long URL that uses long identifier values.

Second, well-designed URLs can improve the search engine optimization (SEO) for your app. These days, search engines don't rely on the URL for SEO as much as they used to. Still, you can improve your SEO by including keywords that describe the content of the page in your URL.

The first three examples show three ways to identify a product. The first example uses a number of 1307 to identify the product. The second example uses a *slug*, which is a descriptive string, to identify a product. Between these two, using a slug is more user-friendly, but it usually makes database queries less efficient. As a result, it often makes sense to use a number and a slug as shown by the third example. That way, you can use the number to query the database, but the slug still makes the URL user-friendly.

The last three examples compare bad practices to best practices. To start, the fourth example shows four URLs that use query strings to pass data to the controller. This isn't recommended because query strings use the ? and & characters, which make them more difficult to read than URLs that use segments to pass data to the controller, as shown so far in this chapter. In addition, these URLs use inconsistent capitalization, they use numbers to identify the products, and they don't use keywords.

The fifth example fixes most of these issues by following best practices. It uses segments to pass the same data. It uses all lowercase letters, which are easier to type than uppercase letters. It uses keywords such as "product" and "page". And it uses hyphens to separate words such as "page-1" and "fender-stratocaster". Using hyphens to separate words like this is known as *kebab case* because the hyphens look like the skewer in a shish kebob, and the letters look like the meat that's on the skewer.

The sixth example works much like the fifth example, but its URLs are even shorter. That's because this example uses /products instead of /product/list, which is four characters shorter. Similarly, it uses /product instead of /product/detail, which is six characters shorter. That might not seem like a big deal, but if a website is being used by millions of people, it's important to make the URLs as short and easy to use as possible.

Best practices for URLs

- Keep the URL as short as possible while still being descriptive and user-friendly.
- Use keywords to describe the content of a page, not implementation details.
- Make your URLs easy for humans to understand and type.
- Use hyphens to separate words, not other characters, especially spaces.
- Prefer names as identifiers over numbers.
- Create an intuitive hierarchy.
- Be consistent.
- Avoid the use of query string parameters if possible.

A URL that identifies a product...

With a number

```
https://www.domain.com/product/1307
```

With a name

```
https://www.domain.com/product/fender-special-edition-standard-stratocaster
```

With a number and name (to keep it descriptive but short)

```
https://www.domain.com/product/1307/fender-special
```

Four URLs that use query strings to pass data (not recommended)

```
https://www.murach.com/p/List?
   "       "     "    "  /p/List?catId=1
   "       "     "    "  /p/List?catId=1&pg=1
   "       "     "    "  /p/Detail?id=1307
```

Four URLs that follow best practices

```
https://www.murach.com/product/list
   "       "     "    "  /product/list/guitars
   "       "     "    "  /product/list/guitars/page-1
   "       "     "    "  /product/detail/1307/fender-stratocaster
```

Four URLs that follow best practices but are even shorter

```
https://www.murach.com/products
   "       "     "    "  /products/guitars
   "       "     "    "  /products/guitars/page-1
   "       "     "    "  /product/1307/fender-stratocaster
```

Description

- Well-designed URLs can improve the usability of your app for both developers and end users.
- Well-designed URLs can improve the search engine optimization (SEO) for your app.
- A *slug* is a string that describes the content of a page. Using a slug can make your URLs more user-friendly.
- Using hyphens to separate words is known as *kebab case*.

Figure 6-10   Best practices for URLs

How to work with areas

An ASP.NET Core MVC app can have multiple *areas*. Each area can have its own controllers, models, and views. This can help you organize the folders and files of an app. For example, you may want to create one area that allows administrators to perform tasks such as adding and updating the products that are stored in a database. Then, you can use another area to allow customers to browse through the products and add them to a cart.

How to set up areas

Figure 6-11 shows how to set up areas. By convention, you can create an area by adding a folder named Areas to the root folder for the app. Then, within the Areas folder, you can add a folder for the area. In this figure, for example, the folders and files for the Guitar Shop app include an area named Admin.

Within the folder for the area, you can add the necessary subfolders such as the Controllers, Models, Views, and so on. In this figure, for example, the Admin folder includes the Controllers and Views folders. Since this area is separate from the main area, it can use the same names for the controller and view files. For example, this area has a Home controller and a Home/Index view as well as a Product controller and a Product/List view. However, the Product/List view in the Admin area allows admin users to add, update, and delete products, but the Product/List view in the default area only allows customers to view products and add them to their carts.

To get the views for the Admin area to work correctly, it includes a layout named _AdminLayout that's shared by all of the views in this area. Then, it uses a _ViewImports file to import the same models as the default area. That way, the views can use the same Product and Category models defined in the default area. Finally, this area uses a _ViewStart file to specify _AdminLayout as the default layout. When you're setting up the folders and files for an Admin area, that's usually what you want. But don't worry if you don't understand the details of how these view files work. You'll learn more about them in the next chapter.

Once you've set up the folders and files for an area, you need to configure the routes for the app so they include the area. To do that, you can use the MapAreaControllerRoute() method. This method works much like the MapControllerRoute() method. However, you must use the second argument to specify a name for the area. In addition, you can use the third argument to specify a pattern for the route. In this figure, for example, the pattern uses a static segment of "Admin" to specify the first segment of the route for the Admin area. After that, the route works like the default route.

The starting folders for a Guitar Shop app that includes an Admin area

```
GuitarShop
    /Areas
        /Admin
            /Controllers
                /HomeController.cs
                /ProductController.cs
            /Views
                /Home
                    /Index.cshthml
                /Product
                    /AddUpdate.cshthml
                    /Delete.cshthml
                    /Index.cshtml
                    /List.cshthml
                /Shared
                    /_AdminLayout.cshtml
                _ViewImports.cshtml
                _ViewStart.cshtml
    /Controllers
        /HomeController.cs
        /ProductController.cs
    /Models
        /Category.cs
        /Product.cs
    /Views
        /Home
            /About.cshthml
            /Index.cshthml
        /Product
            /Detail.cshthml
            /Index.cshtml
            /List.cshthml
        /Shared
            /_Layout.cshtml
        _ViewImports.cshtml
        _ViewStart.cshtml
    Program.cs
```

A route in the Program.cs file that works with an area

```
app.MapAreaControllerRoute(
    name: "admin",
    areaName: "Admin",
    pattern: "Admin/{controller=Home}/{action=Index}/{id?}");

app.MapControllerRoute(
    name: "default",
    pattern: "{controller=Home}/{action=Index}/{id?}");
```

Description

- An ASP.NET Core MVC app can have multiple *areas*. Each area can have its own controllers, models, and views. This can help you organize the folders and files of an app.

- To configure the route for an area, you can use the MapAreaControllerRoute() method to add a route that specifies the name of the area and its routing pattern.

Figure 6-11   How to set up areas

How to associate controllers with areas

Before you can use a controller with an area, you must use the Area attribute to associate it with an area. To do that, you can decorate the controller with the Area attribute as shown in figure 6-12. The value specified in this Area attribute must match the areaName argument specified for the area route in the Program.cs file. In this figure, for example, the area name of "Admin" specified by the controller matches the areaName value of "Admin" specified by the Program.cs file.

After you add the Area attribute to the controller, you can use the [area] token to specify attribute routing for the actions of the controller. In this figure, for instance, the second example uses the [area] token to apply attribute routing to the List() action of the Product controller. This attribute routing specifies the name of the area as the first segment, the name of the controller plus an s as the second segment, and an optional id parameter as the third segment. As a result, you can't use the area routing of /Admin/Product/List to call the Product/List action. Instead, you must use the attribute routing of /Admin/Products.

To help you visualize how this works, this figure presents a table of URLs and describes how they work. Here, the first two URLs use the attribute routing to map to the Product/List action of the Admin area. As a result, they use two or three segments to call this action and pass it an argument. However, the next two elements use the routing specified in the Program.cs file to map to other actions in the Product controller of the Admin area. As a result, they use three or four segments to call an action and pass it an argument.

The Home controller for the Admin area

```
namespace GuitarShop.Areas.Admin.Controllers
{
    [Area("Admin")]
    public class HomeController : Controller
    {
        public IActionResult Index()
        {
            return View();  // maps to /Areas/Admin/Views/Home/Index.cshtml
        }
    }
}
```

A token you can use to insert the area into a route

Token	Description
[area]	The name of the current area.

The Product controller for the Admin area

```
namespace GuitarShop.Areas.Admin.Controllers
{
    [Area("Admin")]
    public class ProductController : Controller
    {
        public IActionResult Index() {...};

        [Route("[area]/[controller]s/{id?}")]
        public IActionResult List(string id = "All") {...};

        public IActionResult Add() {...};
        public IActionResult Update(int id) {...};
        public IActionResult Delete(int id) {...};
    }
}
```

How request URLs map to controller classes and their action methods

Request URL	Description
/Admin/Products	This maps to the Product/List action and uses the default parameter value of "All".
/Admin/Products/Guitars	This maps to the Product/List action and passes an argument of "Guitars".
/Admin/Product/Add	This maps to the Product/Add action.
/Admin/Product/Update/3	This maps to the Product/Update action and passes an id argument of 3.

Description

- Before you can use a controller with an area, you must use the Area attribute to associate it with an area.
- After you add the Area attribute to the controller, you can use the [area] token to specify attribute routing for the actions of the controller.

Figure 6-12   How to associate controllers with areas

Perspective

Now that you've read this chapter, you should have a general understanding of how to set up the controllers and routing of an MVC app. In addition, you should have a good idea of how to follow best practices to create well-designed URLs for a web app. With that as background, you're ready to learn more about developing the views for an MVC app. That's why the next chapter presents some of the most useful skills for working with views. As you'll see, many of these skills are interrelated with the skills for working with controllers and routing.

Of course, there's more to controllers and routing than what's presented in this chapter. For example, you may want to constrain a segment so it only matches certain data types. You may want to map legacy URLs to the new routing system. Or, you may want to specify a pattern that supports a variable number of segments. When you're first getting started, you typically don't need these more advanced routing skills. If you find that you do need them, you should have the foundation you need to learn more about them. To do that, you can begin by searching the web.

Terms

endpoint routing

URL path segment

default route

attribute routing

slug

kebab case

areas of an app

Summary

- ASP.NET Core 3.0 introduced a new approach to routing known as *endpoint routing*. It's generally considered a best practice to use endpoint routing for any new development.

- The path for a URL consists of zero or more *segments* where each segment is separated by a slash (/).

- The *default route* maps a request to an action method within a controller and can optionally pass an argument to that action method.

- The use of the Route attribute to specify the routing for a controller or its actions is known as *attribute routing*. Attribute routing overrides any routing patterns specified in the Program.cs file.

- A *slug* is a string that describes the content of a page.

- The use of hyphens to separate words is known as *kebab case*.

- An ASP.NET Core MVC app can have multiple *areas*. Each area can have its own controllers, models, and views.

Exercise 6-1   Practice routing

In this exercise, you'll review the essential skills for working with routing.

View and test the default route for the app

1. Open the Ch06Ex1RoutingPractice web app in the ex_starts directory.

2. Open the Program.cs file and view its code. Note that it includes the default route:

    ```
    {controller=Home}/{action=Index}/{id?}
    ```

3. Open the HomeController class in the Controllers folder and view its code. Note that the Index() action method displays text that says "Home" and the Privacy() action method displays text that says "Privacy".

4. Run the app. This should start your browser and automatically call this URL:

    ```
    https://localhost:<port_number>
    ```

    This should display text that says, "Home".

5. Enter URLs in the browser to display the text returned by the Index() and Privacy() methods. For example, try these URLs:

    ```
    https://localhost:<port_number>/home
    https://localhost:<port_number>/home/privacy
    ```

6. In the HomeController class, view the code for the Display() action method. Note that this method accepts a string parameter named id. Review the code that works with this parameter.

7. Run the app and and test the Display() method by entering these URLs:

    ```
    /home/display
    /home/display/123abc
    ```

    The first URL should display a message that indicates that the id hasn't been supplied, and the second URL should display a message that says, "ID: 123abc".

Add an action method that uses the default route

8. In the HomeController class, add the following action method. When you do, make sure to declare a parameter of the int type with a name of id and a default value of 0 like this:

    ```
    public IActionResult Countdown(int id = 0)
    {
        string contentString = "Counting down:\n";
        for(int i = id; i >= 0; i--)
        {
            contentString += i + "\n";
        }
        return Content(contentString);
    }
    ```

9. Run the app and enter a URL that calls the Countdown() method like this:

    ```
    /home/countdown
    ```

    This should display "Counting down:" followed by a 0 on the next line. That's because the URL omits the optional third segment of the default route. As a result, the method uses the default value of 0 for the id parameter.

10. Run the app and enter a URL that calls the Countdown() method like this:

```
/home/countdown/10
```

This should display a countdown that starts at 10 and counts down to 0 with each integer on its own line. That's because the URL included a value of 10 for the third segment.

Use attribute routing to customize the route for an action method

11. Add a Route attribute immediately above the Countdown() method like this:

```
[Route("[action]/{id?}")]
public IActionResult Countdown(int id = 0) {...}
```

12. Run the app and enter a URL that calls the Countdown() method like this:

```
/countdown/10
```

Note that you only have to type the name of the action (countdown) and the value of the id segment (10) in this URL, not the name of the controller (home).

13. Run the app and enter the previous URL that uses the default route to call the Countdown() method like this:

```
home/countdown/10
```

Now you should get an error message that the page you requested can't be found. That's because the routing attribute for the Countdown() method overrides the default route.

14. In the Countdown() method, change the name of the parameter from id to num. However, in the Route attribute, continue to use id as the name of the second segment.

15. Run the app and test the Countdown() method without an id segment. It should work correctly.

16. Test the Countdown() method with an id segment of 10 as before. This should only display the default value of 0. That's because the segment name in the Route attribute must match the parameter name in the method.

17. In the Route attribute, change the second segment from {id?} to {num?}.

18. Run the app and test the CountDown() method with a second segment of 10. This should display a countdown from 10 to 0.

Add more segments to a route

19. Edit the Countdown() method so it includes three parameters, and edit the Route attribute for this method so the segment names match the parameter names like this:

```
[Route("[action]/{start}/{end?}/{message?}")]
public IActionResult Countdown(int start, int end = 0,
    string message = "")
```

Note that the first two segments are required but the third and fourth are optional.

20. Modify the code for the Countdown() method so it starts counting down at the start parameter, ends at the end parameter, and displays the message parameter when the countdown is done.

21. Run the app and enter a URL that calls the Countdown() method like this:

    ```
    /countdown/3/1/Liftoff!
    ```

    This should display a countdown like this:

    ```
    Counting down:
    3
    2
    1
    Liftoff!
    ```

22. Enter a URL that calls the Countdown() method like this:

    ```
    /countdown
    ```

    The browser should not be able to find the web page. That's because the second segment is now required. As a result, you must specify the start segment when you enter this URL.

23. Enter a URL that calls the Countdown() method like this:

    ```
    /countdown/5
    ```

    This should use the default parameters of the Countdown() method to display a countdown from 5 to 0 with no message.

7

How to work with Razor views

In chapters 2 and 4, you learned the basic skills for using Razor views and layouts. Now, this chapter reviews some of those skills and expands upon them. When you're done, you should have the skills you need to work with Razor views and layouts, including how to bind them to a model.

How to use Razor syntax

This chapter begins by reviewing the essential skills for using Razor syntax to mix C# code with HTML. This allows you to use most types of C# statements and expressions with HTML.

How to work with code blocks and inline expressions

Figure 7-1 begins by showing the syntax for a Razor *code block* that contains one or more C# statements and for an *inline expression*. After the syntax, the first example shows a controller action method that sets up the data for the view in the second example by storing a value of "John" in the CustomerName property of the ViewBag property.

The second example begins with a Razor code block. Within this block, the first statement declares a string variable named message and sets it equal to a value of "Welcome!". Then, this block uses a C# if statement to check whether the CustomerName property of the ViewBag has been set. If so, it sets the message variable to a value of "Welcome back!".

After the code block, the rest of the example mostly contains the static HTML for a web page. However, within this HTML, three inline expressions insert dynamic data. The first inline expression displays the value of the message variable created by the code block at the top of the example. The second inline expression displays the value stored in the CustomerName property of the ViewBag. And the third inline expression displays the result of adding 2 plus 2.

Of these three inline expressions, parentheses aren't necessary for the first two. That's because the first expression just displays the value of a variable, and the second expression just displays a value stored in a property of the ViewBag. However, the third expression requires parentheses because it displays the result of an arithmetic expression.

In general, it's considered a best practice to perform arithmetic calculations like this one in the controller or model and pass the result of the calculation to the view. Then, the view can use an inline expression to display the result of the calculation. However, if necessary, you can use an inline expression to perform a calculation or to do other types of processing.

The syntax for a Razor code block

```
@{
    // one or more C# statements
}
```

The syntax for an inline expression

```
@(csharp_expression)
```

The Index() action method of the Home controller

```
public IActionResult Index()
{
    ViewBag.CustomerName = "John";
    return View();              // returns Views/Home/Index.cshtml
}
```

The Views/Home/Index.cshtml file

```
@{
    string message = "Welcome!";
    if (ViewBag.CustomerName != null)
    {
        message = "Welcome back!";
    }
}
<!DOCTYPE html>
<html>
<head>
    <meta name="viewport" content="width=device-width, initial-scale=1.0" />
    <title>Home</title>
</head>
<body>
    <h1>@message</h1>
    <p>Customer Name: @ViewBag.CustomerName</p>
    <p>2 + 2 = @(2 + 2)</p>
</body>
</html>
```

The view displayed in a browser

Description

- To execute one or more C# statements, you can declare a Razor *code block* by coding the @ sign followed by a pair of braces (`{ }`). Within the braces, you can code one or more C# statements.

- To evaluate a C# expression and display its result, you can code an *inline expression* by coding the @ sign and then coding the expression within a pair of parentheses. For many expressions, the parentheses are optional.

Figure 7-1   How to work with code blocks and inline expressions

How to code inline loops

Figure 7-2 shows how to code an *inline loop* within a view. Within these loops, you can use HTML tags to send HTML to the view.

In the first example, for instance, an inline loop displays the numbers 1 through 12 as the options that are available from a drop-down list. To do that, a for loop declares a month variable that begins at 1, ends at 12, and is incremented by 1. Within the loop, an HTML <option> element uses inline expressions to set its value and content to the current value of the month variable. This displays a drop-down list that lets the user select a number for the month.

The second example sets up the controller to provide the data that's used by the view in the third example. To do that, it creates a list of musical instrument categories and stores that list in the Categories property of the ViewBag.

In the third example, an inline loop displays one link for each category stored in the ViewBag. To do that, a foreach loop declares a category variable that's set to each of the categories stored in the Categories property of the ViewBag. Within the loop, an HTML <div> element contains an <a> element that uses inline expressions to set the URL and content for the link to the value of the category variable. This displays a list of categories as links.

To keep these examples simple, this figure doesn't use Bootstrap CSS classes or tag helpers. However, you would typically use Bootstrap classes to format a drop-down list like the one shown in the first example. In addition, you would typically use tag helpers to specify the URL for the link in the third example. Later in this chapter, the examples use Bootstrap CSS classes and tag helpers to improve the formatting and function of the HTML elements.

A for loop that displays a drop-down list of month numbers

```
<label for="month">Month:</label>
<select name="month" id="month">
    @for (int month = 1; month <= 12; month++)
    {
        <option value="@month">@month</option>
    }
</select>
```

The result displayed in a browser

Code in a controller that creates a list of strings

```
public IActionResult Index()
{
    ViewBag.Categories = new List<string>
    {
        "Guitars", "Basses", "Drums"
    };
    return View();
}
```

A foreach loop that displays a list of links

```
@foreach (string category in ViewBag.Categories)
{
    <div>
        <a href="/Product/List/@category/">@category</a>
    </div>
}
```

The result displayed in a browser

Description

- You can code *inline loops* within a view. Within these loops, you can use HTML tags to send HTML to the view.

Figure 7-2   How to code inline loops

How to code inline conditional statements

Figure 7-3 shows how to code *inline conditional statements* such as if/else and switch statements within a view. Like inline loops, these statements can use HTML tags to send HTML to the view.

The first example uses a C# if-else statement to check the ProductID property of the ViewBag. Then, it displays a <p> tag whose content depends on the value stored in this property. This should give you a good idea of how you can use if-else statements within a view to display or not display content.

The second example works like the first example. However, it uses a C# switch statement instead of an if-else statement.

The third example uses a C# if statement to check whether the SelectedCategoryName property of the ViewBag is equal to a string of "All". If so, it adds a Bootstrap CSS class named active to the class attribute of the <a> element. Since this <a> element is an item in a Bootstrap CSS list group, this marks the element as the active item. To make this work, the example uses the <text> tag to send the active class as plain text.

The fourth example converts the simple if statement in the third example so it uses an *inline conditional expression* instead of a statement. This has the benefit of making the code shorter. To do that, this code uses C#'s conditional operator (? :) to separate three arguments. The first argument checks the same condition as the previous example, the second argument specifies the value to return if the condition is true, and the third value specifies the value to return if the condition is false. As a result, if the condition is true, this expression returns a string of "active". Otherwise, it returns an empty string. Like the arithmetic expression from figure 7-1, this inline expression requires parentheses.

Although the fourth example uses an inline conditional expression to send plain text to the view, it could also send HTML tags. For example, the true value could be one <div> element and the false value could be another <div> element. However, it's more common to use conditional expressions to set attribute values.

An if-else statement in a view

```
@if (ViewBag.ProductID == 1)
{
    <p>Fender Stratocaster</p>
}
else if (ViewBag.ProductID == 2)
{
    <p>Gibson Les Paul</p>
}
else
{
    <p>Product Not Found</p>
}
```

A switch statement in a view

```
@switch (ViewBag.ProductID)
{
    case 1:
        <p>Fender Stratocaster</p>
        break;
    case 2:
        <p>Gibson Les Paul</p>
        break;
    default:
        <p>Product Not Found</p>
        break;
}
```

An if statement that adds a Bootstrap CSS class if true

```
<a asp-controller="Product" asp-action="List" asp-route-id="All"
    class="list-group-item
    @if (ViewBag.SelectedCategoryName == "All") {
        <text>active</text>
    }">
    All
</a>
```

A conditional expression that adds a Bootstrap CSS class if true

```
<a asp-controller="Product" asp-action="List" asp-route-id="All"
    class="list-group-item
    @(ViewBag.SelectedCategoryName == "All" ? "active" : "")">
    All
</a>
```

Description

- You can code *inline conditional statements* such as if-else and switch statements within a view. These statements can use HTML tags to send HTML to the view.

- To send plain text to a view, you can use the <text> tag. This is useful for sending part of an HTML tag such as an HTML attribute or its value.

- You can code an *inline conditional expression* by using C#'s conditional operator (? :) to send HTML tags or plain text to the view. This works like other complex inline expressions that require parentheses.

Figure 7-3   How to work with inline conditional statements and expressions

Essential skills for Razor views

Now that you understand the basics for using Razor syntax, you're ready to learn some essential skills for working with views. To start, you're ready to learn how to set up the starting folders and files for an app.

The starting folders and files for an app

Figure 7-4 shows the starting folders and files for a website named Guitar Shop that sells musical instruments. These folders and files follow the ASP.NET conventions for storing the models, views, controllers, and static files for an MVC app. By now, you should be familiar with this structure, but let's review it with a focus on how it impacts views.

To start, this folder and file structure maps the actions of each controller to the appropriate view. For example, the List() action method of the Product controller maps to the Views/Product/List.cshtml file. Similarly, the About() action method of the Home controller maps to the Views/Home/About.cshtml file.

Within the Views folder, the Shared folder stores any layouts that can be shared by the views. In this figure, there is only one layout named _Layout. cshtml. However, you can add additional layouts if necessary, as described later in this chapter.

The Views folder also stores the _ViewImports.cshtml and _ViewStart. cshtml files. These files make it easier to work with views by importing models and tag helpers and by specifying the default layout.

The wwwroot folder stores the CSS and JavaScript files that can be used by the views. In this figure, the lib folder contains the CSS file for Bootstrap and the css folder contains a custom CSS file that can be used to provide CSS formatting that overrides the Bootstrap CSS whenever that's necessary.

The root folder for the app stores the Program.cs file, which sets up and runs the app. As part of the setup, it contains code that configures the middleware for the app, including the routing that specifies how controllers and their action methods are mapped to URLs. In this figure, the controller uses the default routing to map the first segment of the URL to a controller, the second segment to the controller's action method, and the third segment to an optional argument named id.

The starting folders and files for the Guitar Shop app

```
GuitarShop
    /Controllers
        /HomeController.cs
        /ProductController.cs
    /Models
        /Category.cs
        /Product.cs
        /Shopcontext.cs
    /Views
        /Home
            /Index.cshtml     -- the view for the Home/Index action
            /About.cshtml     -- the view for the Home/About action
        /Product
            /List.cshtml      -- the view for the Product/List action
            /Details.cshtml   -- the view for the Product/Details action
            /Update.cshtml    -- the view for the Product/Update action
        /Shared
            /_Layout.cshtml   -- a layout that can be shared by views
        _ViewImports.cshtml   -- imports models and tag helpers for views
        _ViewStart.cshtml     -- specifies the default layout for views
    /wwwroot
        /css
            /site.css
        /lib
            /bootstrap/dist/css/bootstrap.min.css
    Program.cs                -- configures middleware that may impact views
```

The routing that's specified in the Program.cs file

```
app.UseRouting();
...
app.MapControllerRoute(
    name: "default",
    pattern: "{controller=Home}/{action=Index}/{id?}");
```

Description

- By convention, you store the views for an MVC app in a series of folders and files whose names correspond to the controllers and action methods that return the views.

- The Program.cs file typically contains code that configures the middleware for the app including the routing that specifies how controllers and their action methods are mapped to URLs.

Figure 7-4   The starting folders and files for an app

How to code controllers that return views

Figure 7-5 shows how to code controllers that return views. To do that, the action methods of the controllers typically use the View() method to create ViewResult objects. Then, they return this object.

By default, the View() method creates a ViewResult object from the view file that corresponds to the current controller and action method. In this figure, for example, the Index() action method of the Home controller uses the View() method to create a ViewResult object from the view file that's in the Home/Index.cshtml file.

However, if you don't want to use this default behavior, you can specify the name of the view as an argument of the View() method. In this figure, for example, the Index() action method of the Product controller names the List view in the View() method. This creates a ViewResult object from the Product/List.cshtml view file instead of the Product/Index.cshtml view file that would have been used had the view name been omitted. Note that the Product/List.cshtml view is also used by the List() action method of the Product controller. In other words, this provides a way for two actions to use the same view file, which is sometimes useful.

In this figure, the List() and Details() action methods of the Product controller store the id argument in the ViewBag property so it can be accessed by the view. To do that, you can just use Razor syntax as described earlier in this chapter.

All the action methods in this figure specify a return type of the IActionResult interface even though these action methods all return ViewResult objects. This is possible because the ViewResult object implements the IActionResult interface. Similarly, the ContentResult object described in the previous chapter also implements this interface. This shows that coding the IActionResult interface as the return type makes your action methods flexible by allowing them to return different object types.

A method that a controller can use to return a view result to the browser

Method	Description
`View()`	Creates a ViewResult object that corresponds to the name of the current controller and action method.
`View(name)`	Creates a ViewResult object that corresponds to the current controller and the specified view name.

The Home controller

```
public class HomeController : Controller
{
    public IActionResult Index()
    {
        return View();              // Views/Home/Index.cshtml
    }
}
```

The Product controller

```
public class ProductController : Controller
{
    public IActionResult Index()
    {
        return View("List");        // Views/Product/List.cshtml
    }

    public IActionResult List(string id = "All")
    {
        ViewBag.Category = id;
        return View();              // Views/Product/List.cshtml
    }

    public IActionResult Details(string id)
    {
        ViewBag.ProductSlug = id;
        return View();              // Views/Product/Details.cshtml
    }
}
```

Description

- A controller typically contains action methods that are mapped to the view files in the Views folder.

Figure 7-5   How to code controllers that return views

How to create a default layout and enable tag helpers

Figure 7-6 shows the code that's necessary to create a default layout and enable tag helpers. This makes it possible to share code between multiple view files.

To start, you can add a Razor layout to your project as described in chapter 2. A Razor layout typically specifies code that's shared between multiple views such as the <html>, <head>, and <body> elements for a view. In addition, it often imports the CSS and JavaScript files for a view. In this figure, for example, the Razor layout named _Layout specifies all of these HTML elements and imports the CSS file for the Bootstrap library as well as a custom CSS file.

Within a Razor layout, the ViewData or ViewBag property is often used to display a title that's set in the view. In this figure, for example, the <title> element uses an inline Razor expression to display the Title property of the ViewBag. In the next chapter you'll learn more about the ViewData and ViewBag properties, including how they're similar and how they're different.

Within a Razor layout, the RenderBody() method renders the body of the view. In other words, this method inserts the HTML elements and Razor code defined by a view into the layout.

In a typical web app, most of the views share the same layout. As a result, it usually makes sense to specify a default layout for all views. To do that, you can add a _ViewStart file to the project and set the Layout property to the name of the Razor layout. In this figure, for example, the _ViewStart file sets the default layout to the layout named _Layout. That way, when you code a view, you only needs to specify a layout if you want to override this default as shown later in this chapter.

When you work with views, it's common to use the tag helpers that are available from ASP.NET Core in most views. As a result, it typically makes sense to enable tag helpers for all views. The easiest way to do that is to add a _ViewImports file to your project like the one shown in this figure.

The _Layout.cshtml file in the Views/Shared folder

```
<!DOCTYPE html>
<html>
<head>
    <title>@ViewBag.Title</title>
    <link rel="stylesheet"
          href="~/lib/bootstrap/dist/css/bootstrap.min.css" />
    <link rel="stylesheet" href="~/css/site.css" />
</head>
<body class="container-fluid">
    @RenderBody()
</body>
</html>
```

A _ViewStart.cshtml file that sets the default layout

```
@{
    Layout = "_Layout";
}
```

A _ViewImports.cshtml file that enables all ASP.NET Core tag helpers

```
@addTagHelper *, Microsoft.AspNetCore.Mvc.TagHelpers
```

How to add a Razor layout, view start, or view imports file

1. Right-click on the folder where you want to add the file and select the Add→New Item item.
2. In the resulting dialog, select the ASP.NET Core→Web category.
3. Select the Razor item you want to add and respond to the resulting dialog boxes.

Description

- To specify code that can be shared between multiple view files, add a Razor layout to the Views/Shared folder of your project.
- Within a Razor layout, the ViewBag or ViewData property is often used to display a title that's set in the view.
- Within a Razor layout, the RenderBody() method renders the body of the view.
- To specify a default layout for all views, add a _ViewStart file to the Views folder of your project and set the Layout property to the name of the Razor layout.
- To enable all ASP.NET Core tag helpers for all views, add a _ViewImports file to the Views folder of your project that contains the code shown above.

Figure 7-6   How to create a default layout and enable tag helpers

How to use tag helpers to generate URLs for links

When you code an <a> element for a link, you can use the href attribute to hardcode its URL. However, in general, it's considered a best practice to use tag helpers to generate the URL for a link.

In figure 7-7, the first example shows two ways to code a link to the same URL. Here, the first approach uses the href attribute and a hard-coded string value, and the second approach uses tag helpers to specify the controller, action method, and id argument for the route.

Between these approaches, the first approach is short and easy to read, but the second approach is recommended because it's more flexible. For example, if you change the routing for the app so the List() action method of the Product controller maps to /Products instead of /Product/List, the second approach adjusts automatically. The first approach, by contrast, would break and need to be fixed manually.

The second example shows that you don't need to code the asp-controller tag helper when you're coding a link to another action method in the same controller. Here, the example assumes that the link is coded in the Index view that's displayed by the Home controller. As a result, it displays the About view of the Home controller. Of course, if you want to display a view that's in another controller, you can just add the asp-controller tag helper to the link as shown in the third example.

The fourth example shows what happens if you use the asp-route tag helper to specify a value for a parameter name that exists in one of the app's routes. Here, the asp-route tag helper specifies a value for the id parameter that's the third segment of the default route. As a result, the app uses the parameter value as the third segment of the generated URL.

The fifth example shows what happens if you use the asp-route tag helper to specify a value for a parameter name that doesn't exist in the app's route. Here, the asp-route tag helper specifies values for the parameters named page and sort_by. However, these parameters don't exist in the default route. As a result, the app adds the parameter names and values to the end of the URL as part of the URL's query string.

As you learned in the last chapter, using query strings in a URL makes the URL difficult to read. As a result, it's considered a best practice to avoid using them whenever possible. To do that for this example, you could add a route to the app for the List() action method of the Product controller that includes the page and sort_by parameters.

Three tag helpers that you can use to generate URLs

Tag helper	Description
`asp-controller`	Specifies the controller. This is only necessary if you want to specify a URL for an action method from another controller.
`asp-action`	Specifies the action method.
`asp-route-`param_name	Specifies a route parameter where param_name is the name of the parameter. If you specify a parameter name that exists in one of the app's routes, the app uses the parameter value as a segment of the URL. Otherwise, it adds the parameter name and value to the end of the URL as part of the URL's query string.

Two ways to code a link

Use HTML to hardcode the URL in the href attribute

```
<a href="/Product/List/Guitars">View guitars</a>
```

Use ASP.NET tag helpers to generate the URL

```
<a asp-controller="Product" asp-action="List"
   asp-route-id="Guitars">View guitars</a>
```

The URL for both links

```
/Product/List/Guitars
```

How to code a link to an action method in the same controller

```
<a asp-action="About">About Us</a>
```

The URL that's generated

```
/Home/About
```

How to code a link to an action method in a different controller

```
<a asp-controller="Product" asp-action="List">View all products</a>
```

The URL that's generated

```
/Product/List
```

How to code a link that includes a parameter that's in a route

```
<a asp-controller="Product" asp-action="List"
   asp-route-id="Guitars">View guitars</a>
```

The URL that's generated

```
/Product/List/Guitars
```

A link that specifies route parameters that don't exist

```
<a asp-controller="Product" asp-action="List"
   asp-route-page="1" asp-route-sort_by="price">Products - Page 1</a>
```

The URL that's generated

```
/Product/List?page=1&sort_by=price
```

Description

- In general, it's considered a best practice to use tag helpers to generate the URL for a link.

Figure 7-7   How to use tag helpers to generate URLs for links

Three views that use the default layout and tag helpers

To put the previous figures into a larger context, figure 7-8 shows the code for three views that use the default layout. Here, the Razor code block at the top of each view stores a title for the page in the ViewData property. That way, the layout for the view can display the title in the <title> element.

However, this Razor code block doesn't set the Layout property to override the default layout. As a result, these views use the default layout file (_Layout) that's specified by the _ViewStart file. Both of these files are shown earlier in this chapter.

After the Razor code block, the Home/Index view specifies the level-1 heading for the page followed by a <div> element that uses a Bootstrap class to identify its content as a list group. This is possible because the layout for the view includes a link to the library for the Bootstrap CSS classes.

Within this <div> element are three links. Here, the first link uses tag helpers to specify the Product controller and the List() action method. The second link uses tag helpers to specify the Product controller, the List() action method, and a route id parameter of "Guitars". And the third link uses tag helpers to specify the Product controller, the Details() action method, and a route id parameter of "Fender-Stratocaster".

The Product/List view works much like the Home/Index view. However, within the <div> element, it displays the Category property of the ViewBag that was set by the List() action method. In addition, this view's first link doesn't use a tag helper to specify a controller since that link is to an action that's also in the Product controller.

The Product/Details view works much like the Product/List view. However, within the <div> element, it displays the ProductSlug property of the ViewBag that was set by the Details() action method.

The Home/Index view

```
@{
    ViewData["Title"] = "Home";
}
<h1>Home</h1>
<div class="list-group">
    <a asp-controller="Product" asp-action="List">View all products</a>

    <a asp-controller="Product" asp-action="List"
        asp-route-id="Guitars">View guitars</a>

    <a asp-controller="Product" asp-action="Details"
        asp-route-id="Fender-Stratocaster">View Fender Stratocaster</a>
</div>
```

The Product/List view

```
@{
    ViewData["Title"] = "Product List";
}
<h1>Product List</h1>
<div class="list-group">
    <p>Category: @ViewBag.Category</p>

    <a asp-action="Details"
        asp-route-id="Fender-Stratocaster">View Fender Stratocaster</a>

    <a asp-controller="Home" asp-action="Index">Home</a>
</div>
```

The Product/Details view

```
@{
    ViewData["Title"] = "Product Details";
}
<h1>Product Details</h1>
<div class="list-group">
    <p>Slug: @ViewBag.ProductSlug</p>

    <a asp-controller="Home" asp-action="Index">Home</a>
</div>
```

Description

- Since the Razor code block at the top of the page doesn't set the Layout property, these views use the layout (_Layout) that's specified by the _ViewStart file.
- These views use tag helpers to specify the controller class, action method, and route id parameter for <a> elements.

Figure 7-8   Three views that use the default layout and tag helpers

The three views displayed in a browser

To make it easier to visualize the three views presented in the previous figure, figure 7-9 shows them after they are displayed in a browser. Here, the tab at the top of the browser window displays the title for the page. The address bar shows the URL for each page. And the rest of the browser displays the web page that's generated by the Razor view and its layout.

The Home page displays a level-1 heading for the page followed by three links. Here, the first two links lead to the Product List page and the third link leads to the Product Details page.

The Product List page works much like the Home page. However, after the heading, it displays the category that's set by the List() action method of the Product controller. In this figure, it displays a category of "Guitars" since the user clicked on the "View guitars" link. However, if the user clicks on the "View all products" link, it would display a category of "All".

The Product Details page works like the Product List page. However, after the heading, it displays the product slug that's set by the Details() action method of the Product controller. In this figure, it displays a slug of "Fender-Stratocaster" since the user clicked on the "View Fender Stratocaster" link.

Although these pages might not seem useful, they show you the basics of how you can use controllers, views, and layouts to create pages. Later in this chapter, you'll learn how to display a list of products that matches the category. Similarly, you'll learn how to display the details of a product when the user clicks on it. That allows you to use web pages to display useful information to your users.

A browser displaying the Home page

A browser after clicking the View Guitars link

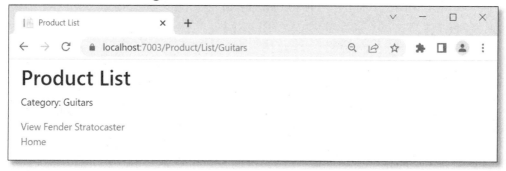

A browser after clicking the View Fender Stratocaster link

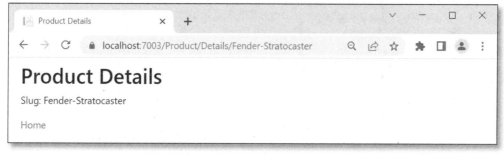

Figure 7-9   The three views displayed in a browser

More skills for Razor views

Now that you know some essential skills for working with Razor views, you're ready to learn some more skills for working with views.

More tag helpers for generating URLs for links

Earlier in this chapter, you learned how to use three tag helpers to generate URLs for links. When coding links, these are the tag helpers that you'll use most of the time. However, in some cases, you may need to use the tag helpers described in figure 7-10 to generate URLs for links.

To start, if you organize your app into multiple routing areas as described in chapter 6, you may need to use the asp-area tag as shown in the first example in this figure. Here, the asp-area tag helper specifies an area of "Admin". This accesses an area that allows admin users to manage the list of products that's available from the website. This area is different from the area that allows regular end users such as customers to view products and add them to their carts.

Second, if you have a long page, you may want to use a URL *fragment* to allow the user to jump to a specified placeholder on the page as shown by the second example. Here, the <h2> element includes an id attribute that marks a placeholder named "Fender" on the page. Then, the link uses the asp-fragment tag helper to identify the placeholder it should jump to. If the user clicks on this link, it causes the browser to scroll up or down until it displays the part of the page that contains the placeholder. In a URL, a fragment is preceded by the hash mark (#) as shown by both the second and third examples.

When coding a link for a website, it's common to use a *relative URL*, which is a URL that's relative to the app's root directory. So far, this book has only shown how to code relative URLs. However, if you need to code a link to a different domain, you may need to code an *absolute URL* that specifies the name of the host. In the third example, for instance, the link uses the asp-protocol and asp-host tag helpers to specify the HTTP protocol and host for the link. As a result, no matter what host your app is running on, this link jumps to the https://murach.com domain.

Relative URLs are more flexible than absolute URLs because they allow your app to work on multiple domains. For example, if you use relative URLs, your web app runs equally well on localhost or murach.com. That way, you can develop and test the app on localhost and deploy it to murach.com when it's ready for production. However, if you use absolute URLs, your web app only runs on the specified host. As a result, you should only use an absolute URL when you want to code a link to a domain outside your web app.

In addition to specifying the protocol and host for the link, the third example specifies a controller, action method, route parameter, and fragment. This shows that you can use tag helpers to generate all parts of a URL.

More tag helpers for generating URLs

Tag helper	Description
asp-area	Specifies the area for the URL. For info about setting up areas, see chapter 6.
asp-fragment	Specifies the placeholder that you want to jump to.
asp-protocol	Specifies the protocol. By default, it is set to HTTP. However, it's common for apps to automatically redirect to HTTPS, even if you specify HTTP.
asp-host	Specifies the name of the server.

How to code a link to an area

```
<a asp-area="Admin" asp-controller="Product"
    asp-action="List">Admin - Product Manager</a>
```

The URL that's generated

```
/Admin/Product/List
```

How to work with placeholders

How to code an HTML placeholder

```
<h2 id="Fender">Fender Guitars</h2>
```

How to code a URL that jumps to an HTML placeholder on the same page

```
<a asp-fragment="Fender">View Fender Guitars</a>
```

The URL that's generated

```
/#Fender
```

How to code an absolute URL

```
<a asp-protocol="https"
    asp-host="murach.com"
    asp-controller="Shop"
    asp-action="Details"
    asp-route-id="html-and-css"
    asp-fragment="reviews">Murach's HTML and CSS - Reviews</a>
```

The URL that's generated

```
https://www.murach.com/Shop/Details/html-and-css#reviews
```

Description

- A URL *fragment* allows you to jump to a specified placeholder on a web page. A placeholder is identified by an id attribute, and a fragment is preceded by the hash mark (#) in a URL.

- A *relative URL* is a URL that's relative to the app's root directory.

- An *absolute URL* is a URL that specifies the host.

- Relative URLs are more flexible than absolute URLs because they allow your app to work on multiple hosts. As a result, you should only use an absolute URL when coding a link to a specific host outside your app.

Figure 7-10   More skills for using tag helpers to generate URLs for links

How to format numbers in a view

In general, it's considered a best practice for a controller to be responsible for providing the data for a view. For example, a view shouldn't retrieve data from a database because that's the job of the controllers.

Similarly, a view shouldn't calculate a value to be displayed because that's the job of the model. However, once the model calculates the value, and the controller gets that value and passes it to the view, the view can format the value. That's because formatting and displaying data is the job of the view.

Figure 7-11 shows how to format numbers so they can be displayed to the user. In particular, the examples show how to apply currency, number, and percent formatting.

In a Razor expression, you can use C#'s format specifiers to specify a format and the number of decimal places for a number. By default, these specifiers return two decimal places, but you can also specify the number you want returned. In other words, both C and C2 return two decimal places. Some programmers prefer to use C2 because it's clear that it returns two decimal places. Others prefer to use C because it's shorter.

If necessary, the format specifiers round the number to the nearest decimal place. In most cases, that's what you want. If it isn't, you can apply rounding before you display the view. For example, you can apply rounding in the model.

This figure presents three of the most common format specifiers, but many others exist. So, if you need to apply formatting that goes beyond the formatting specified in this figure, you can search the internet for more information.

Format specifiers you can use to format numbers

Specifier	Name	Description
C	Currency	Formats a number as a currency value for the current locale.
N	Number	Formats a number using a separator for the thousandths places.
P	Percent	Formats a number as a percentage.

Code in a controller that stores numbers in the ViewBag property

```
ViewBag.Price = 12345.67;
ViewBag.DiscountPercent = .045;
ViewBag.Quantity = 1234;
```

Razor expressions that format and display the numbers

Expression	Result
@ViewBag.Price.ToString("C")	$12,345.67
@ViewBag.Price.ToString("C1")	$12,345.7
@ViewBag.Price.ToString("C0")	$12,346
@ViewBag.Price.ToString("N")	12,345.67
@ViewBag.Price.ToString("N1")	12,345.7
@ViewBag.Price.ToString("N0")	12,346
@ViewBag.DiscountPercent.ToString("P")	4.50%
@ViewBag.DiscountPercent.ToString("P1")	4.5%
@ViewBag.DiscountPercent.ToString("P0")	5%

Code in a view that displays the numbers

```
<div>Price: @ViewBag.Price.ToString("C")</div>
<div>Discount Percent: @ViewBag.DiscountPercent.ToString("P1")</div>
<div>Quantity: @ViewBag.Quantity.ToString("N0")</div>
```

The view displayed in a browser

Description

- In a Razor expression, you can use C#'s format specifiers to format a number with thousandths separators, as currency, or as a percent. One way to do that is to call the ToString() method from the numeric data type and pass it the format specifier.

- By default, the format specifiers return two decimal places, but you can specify a different number.

- If necessary, the format specifiers round numbers to the nearest decimal place.

- This figure presents three of the most common format specifiers, but many others exist. For more information, you can search the internet.

Figure 7-11   How to format numbers in a view

How to work with a model

So far, this chapter has shown how to work with views that aren't bound to a model. However, when using the MVC pattern, the controller typically stores the data for the view in a model and binds that model to the view. This makes it easier to pass the data back and forth between the controller and the view.

How to pass a model to a view

Figure 7-12 begins by showing a C# class that defines a Product object that can be used as a *model*. This class defines properties to store the product ID, category ID, code, name, and price for the product. In addition, it defines a read-only property that creates a slug for the product by replacing any spaces in the product's name with dashes. This property is read-only because it uses a lambda expression to specify a return value but doesn't specify a way to set that value.

This figure continues by showing a class that defines a Category object that can be used as a model. In this figure, you can use the Category property of the Product object to store the model for a category within a product. In this way, you can define a model of the data that's available to a view.

After you define the model, you can create an object from the model and fill that model with data. To do that, you often begin by reading the data for the model from the database. In the third example, for instance, the Product/Details() action method begins by reading a Product object that corresponds to the id parameter from the database, along with its related Category object. To do that, this example uses the context variable to access the DbContext object that provides the data for the app. This uses EF and LINQ to get the Product and Category objects as described in chapter 4.

Note here that if a product with the specified ID isn't found, a new Product object is created. If this code wasn't included and the product wasn't found, the FirstOrDefault() method would return null, which isn't what you want.

After you fill the model with data, you can pass it to the view. To do that, you can use the View() method that's available to all controllers as shown in the third example. This creates a ViewResult object that can be returned by the action method.

Most of the time, you can use the first overload of the View() method shown in this figure to pass the model to the view. This passes the model to the view that corresponds to the name of the action method. However, in some cases, you may want to use the second overload of the View() method to pass the model to the view specified by the first argument. For instance, you may want the Product/Add() action method to pass a new Product model to the Update view as shown in the fourth example. To do that, this code specifies the name of the Update view as the first argument of the View() method. That way, the Update view can

The Product model

```
namespace GuitarShop.Models
{
    public class Product
    {
        public int ProductID { get; set; }
        public int CategoryID { get; set; }
        public string Code { get; set; } = string.Empty;
        public string Name { get; set; } = string.Empty;
        public decimal Price { get; set; }
        public string Slug => Name.Replace(' ', '-');
        public Category Category { get; set; } = null!;
    }
}
```

The Category model

```
namespace GuitarShop.Models
{
    public class Category
    {
        public int CategoryID { get; set; }
        public string Name { get; set; } = string.Empty;
    }
}
```

A method that a controller can use to pass a model to a view

Method	Description
View(model)	Passes the specified model to the corresponding view and creates a ViewResult object.
View(name, model)	Passes the specified model to the view with the specified name and creates a ViewResult object.

The Product/Details() action method that passes a model to a view

```
public IActionResult Details(int id)
{
    Product product = context.Products.Where(p => p.ProductID == id)
                                      .Include(p => p.Category)
                                      .FirstOrDefault() ?? new Product();
    return View(product);
}
```

A Product/Add() action method that passes a model to the specified view

```
[HttpGet]
public IActionResult Add()
{
    return View("Update", new Product());
}
```

Description

- A *model* is a regular C# class that defines an object.
- In a controller, you can use the View() method to pass a model object to a view. Then, an action method can return the ViewResult object.
- In this figure, the context variable refers to a DbContext object that provides access to the data for the app as described in chapter 4.

Figure 7-12   How to pass a model to a view

display the empty fields that need to be entered for a new product. Similarly, you may want the Product/Update() action method to pass a Product model to the Update view. That way, the Update view can display the data for an existing product that can be updated.

How to display model properties in a view

Figure 7-13 shows how to display model properties in a view. To start, you can add an @using directive to the _ViewImports file that specifies the namespace for the model classes. That way, it's easy to access these classes in your views as shown in this figure. If you don't add an @using directive, you can still access a model, but you must fully qualify the name of its class.

At the beginning of a view, you can use the @model directive to identify the class for the model. In this figure, for instance, the view begins by identifying the Product class as its model class. This binds the Product model to the view.

After that, you can use the built-in Model property of the view to access the model object. In this figure, for instance, the first use of @Model displays the ProductID property of the Product object. The second use of @Model displays the Name property of the Product object. The third use of @Model displays the Name property of the Category object that's nested in the Product object. And the fourth use of @Model displays the Price property of the Product object.

Before this example displays the product's price, it uses the ToString() method to convert the price from a number to a string. As it does this, it uses C#'s format specifiers to format it as currency with two decimal places as described earlier in this chapter.

To help you remember the correct capitalization, remember that a property typically begins with an uppercase letter. For example, you use @Model to access the built-in Model property, and you use @ViewData to access the built-in ViewData property. On the other hand, a directive like @model or @using typically begins with a lowercase letter.

A directive and a property you can use to display model properties in a view

Razor syntax	Description
@model	A directive that specifies the data type (class) for the model and binds the model to the view.
@Model	Accesses the built-in Model property that accesses the model object that's bound to the view.

A _ViewImports file that imports the Models namespace for all views

```
@addTagHelper *, Microsoft.AspNetCore.Mvc.TagHelpers
@using GuitarShop.Models
```

The code for the Product/Details view

```
@model Product
@{
    ViewData["Title"] = "Product Details";
}
<h1>Product Details</h1>
<div>ID: @Model.ProductID</div>
<div>Name: @Model.Name</div>
<div>Category: @Model.Category.Name</div>
<div>Price: @Model.Price.ToString("C2")</div>
<a asp-controller="Home" asp-action="Index">Home</a>
```

The view displayed in a browser

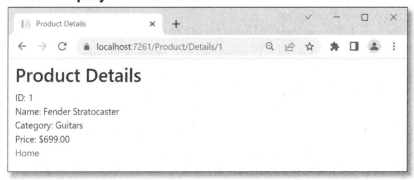

Description

- In a view, you can use the @model directive to bind a model to a view. After that, you can use the Model property to access the properties and methods of the model object.

Figure 7-13   How to display model properties in a view

How to bind model properties to HTML elements

When you code a form within a view, you typically use the asp-for tag helper to bind model properties to HTML elements as shown in figure 7-14. This makes it easier to write and maintain the code for the views.

The first example in this figure shows how this works. Here, the view begins by using the @model directive to specify that it uses a Product model. Then, within the <form> element, this view binds the first <label> and <input> elements to the Name property of the model. This displays the name of the product in the first text box. Next, this view binds the second <label> and <input> elements to the Price property of the model. This displays the price of the product in the second text box. Finally, this view binds the third and fourth <input> elements to the ProductID and Category.Name properties of the model. Since these <input> elements are hidden, this data isn't displayed to the user. However, it is passed to the controller.

The second example shows the HTML that's generated for the Price property of the Product model. This shows that the asp-for tag helpers generate the HTML attributes necessary for client-side and server-side code to access these elements. In other words, it generates the for, id, and name attributes.

The asp-for tag helper for the <label> element also generates the content for the label if it isn't specified. The content is the name of the bound property, in this case, Price. You can also specify the name to be displayed by coding a [Display] attribute for the property as shown in chapter 11. To be sure that the name is displayed correctly, most of the examples in this book include the name as the content for the <label> element.

The asp-for tag helper for the <input> element also generates the value attribute necessary to display the product's price, as well as the type attribute that identifies the type of field to be displayed. If you compare the <input> element that uses the tag helper to the <input> element that's generated by the tag helper, you can see that the tag helper makes the <input> element shorter and it has less code duplication. As a result, it makes your code easier to write and maintain.

Note that the value of the type attribute is determined by the data type of the property that the <input> element is bound to. In this example, the Price property has a data type of decimal, so the type attribute is set to "text" so a normal text field is displayed. If you want to change the type of field that's displayed, you can code the type attribute with the value you want on the <input> element. For example, if an <input> element is bound to a property with a data type of DateTime, the type attribute will be set to "datetime-local" and a control that allows the user to enter both a date and a time will be displayed. If you just want the user to enter a date, though, you can set the type attribute to "text" to display a normal text box or to "date" to display a control that allows the user to enter just a date.

A tag helper you can use to bind HTML elements to model properties

Tag helper	Description
`asp-for`	Specifies the model property for the HTML element.

The code for a view

```
@model Product
@{
    ViewData["Title"] = "Update Product";
}
<h1>Update Product</h1>
<form asp-action="Update" method="post">
    <div class="mb-3">
        <label asp-for="Name" class="form-label"></label>
        <input asp-for="Name" class="form-control">
    </div>
    <div class="mb-3">
        <label asp-for="Price" class="form-label"></label>
        <input asp-for="Price" class="form-control">
    </div>

    <input type="hidden" asp-for="ProductID" />
    <input type="hidden" asp-for="Category.Name" />

    <button type="submit" class="btn btn-primary">Update</button>
    <a asp-action="List" class="btn btn-primary">Cancel</a>
</form>
```

The view displayed in a browser

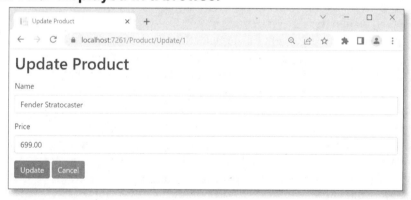

The HTML that's generated for the Price <label> and <input> elements

```
<label class="form-label" for="Price">Price</label>
<input class="form-control" type="text"
       id="Price" name="Price" value="699.00">
```

Description

- In a form, you typically use the asp-for tag helper to bind model properties to HTML elements such as the <label> and <input> elements.

Figure 7-14   How to bind model properties to HTML elements

How to bind a list of items to a <select> element

If you need to code a drop-down list in a form, you can use the asp-items tag helper to bind items to a <select> element as shown in figure 7-15. This creates the <option> elements for the <select> element. This is usually easier and less error-prone than using an inline foreach loop to manually create the <option> elements.

The first example in this figure shows an action method named Update() that creates the model and passes it to the view. To start, the first statement uses the DbContext object to get a list of Category objects and stores it in the ViewBag property so it's available to the view. Then, the second statement uses the DbContext object to find the Product object that corresponds to the specified id argument. Or, if a product with that id isn't found, a new Product object is created. After that, the third statement uses the View() method to pass the Product object to the view.

The second example shows the code that binds the list of Category objects to a <select> element. To start, the <label> and <select> elements use the asp-for tag helper to bind the CategoryID property of the model to the view as described in the previous figure. Then, this example uses the asp-items tag helper to bind the list of Category objects to the <select> element.

To bind the list of Category objects, this code uses a Razor expression to create a new SelectList object. To do that, it passes three arguments to the SelectList() constructor. The first argument specifies the list of Category objects that are stored in the ViewBag property. The second argument specifies the CategoryID property as the data value. And the third argument specifies the Name property as the display text.

In this example, the fourth argument of the SelectList() constructor that specifies the selected value isn't needed. That's because the <select> element is bound to the CategoryId property with the asp-for tag helper. This tag helper marks the option that matches the CategoryId property as selected. As a result, when the user displays this view, the drop-down list selects the correct category for the product that's being updated.

When you call the SelectList() constructor, the first argument is the only required argument. As a result, for some simple drop-down lists, you might not need to code the other three arguments. In most cases, though, you'll need to code more than one argument.

The third example shows the HTML that's generated for the <select> element. This shows that the asp-items tag helper generates the <option> elements necessary to display the three Category objects. Here, the value attribute uses the CategoryID property to get its value, the Name property is used as the display text, and the selected attribute is set for the first option. As a result, when the view displays the drop-down list, the Guitars category is selected.

A tag helper you can use to add options to a <select> element

Tag helper	Description
`asp-items`	Specifies the items for a <select> element.

The constructor of the SelectList class

Constructor	Description
`SelectList(list, value, text, selectedValue)`	Specifies the enumerable collection that contains the objects for each item, an optional property name that specifies the data value for the item, an optional property name that specifies the display text for the item, and an optional value that specifies the value of the selected item.

An action method that gets model data and passes it to the view

```
public IActionResult Update(int id)
{
    ViewBag.Categories = context.Categories.ToList();
    Product product = context.Products.Find(id) ?? new Product();
    return View(product);
}
```

The code that binds items to a <select> element

```
<div class="mb-3">
    <label asp-for="CategoryID" class="form-label">Category</label>
    <select asp-for="CategoryID"
            asp-items="@(new SelectList(ViewBag.Categories,
                         "CategoryID", "Name"))"
            class="form-select"></select>
</div>
```

The <select> element and its label displayed in a browser

The HTML that's generated for the <select> element

```
<select class="form-select" id="CategoryID" name="CategoryID">
    <option selected="selected" value="1">Guitars</option>
    <option value="2">Basses</option>
    <option value="3">Drums</option>
</select>
```

Description

- You can use the asp-items tag helper to bind items to a <select> element. This creates the <option> elements for the <select> element.
- In this figure, the context variable refers to a DbContext object that provides access to the data for the app as described in chapter 4.

Figure 7-15   How to bind a list of items to a <select> element

How to display a list of model objects

If you need to display a list of model objects, you can display them in a table. For example, figure 7-16 shows how to display a list of Product objects in a table.

The first example in this figure shows a controller action method named List() that creates the model and passes it to the view. To start, the first statement gets a list of Category objects and stores it in the ViewBag property so this list is available to the view. Then, the second statement stores the id parameter in the ViewBag property so the selected category is available to the view.

Next, the action method code uses the id parameter to get the list of Product objects for the selected category. It uses an if statement to determine whether to get all the products or to filter them by category. After that, the last statement uses the View() method to pass the list of Product objects to the view.

The second example shows the code for a view that displays the list of Product objects in a table. To start, this example uses the @model directive to bind the list of Product objects to the view. Next, this example uses an inline if statement to check whether the Categories property of the ViewBag has been set. If so, it uses an inline foreach statement to display each category as a series of links just below the Product List heading. These links use tag helpers to pass the category to the Product/List() action method as its id parameter. Similarly, the link that follows the foreach loop also uses these tag helpers to pass a category of "All" to the Product/List() action method as its id parameter.

After displaying links below the Product List heading, this code displays the name of the selected category as a heading. To do that, it uses an inline @if statement to check whether the SelectedCategory property of the ViewBag has been set to a value of "All". If so, it displays the All Products heading. Otherwise, it displays a heading that corresponds to the name of the selected category.

An action method that creates the model and passes it to the view

```
public IActionResult List(string id = "All")
{
    ViewBag.Categories = context.Categories.ToList();
    ViewBag.SelectedCategory = id;

    // initialize the model
    List<Product> products = null!;

    // populate the model based on id value
    if (id == "All")
    {
        products = context.Products.ToList();
    }
    else
    {
        products = context.Products
                    .Where(p => p.Category.Name == id)
                    .ToList();
    }

    // pass the model to the view
    return View(products);
}
```

The code for the view

```
@model List<Product>
@{
    ViewData["Title"] = "Product List";
}

<h1>Product List</h1>
@if (ViewBag.Categories != null)
{
    foreach (Category c in ViewBag.Categories)
    {
        <a asp-controller="Product" asp-action="List"
            asp-route-id="@c.Name">@c.Name</a><text> | </text>
    }
}
<a asp-controller="Product" asp-action="List"
    asp-route-id="All">All</a>
<hr />

@if (@ViewBag.SelectedCategory == "All")
{
    <h2>All Products</h2>
}
else
{
    <h2>@ViewBag.SelectedCategory</h2>
}
```

Figure 7-16   How to display a list of model objects (part 1)

Part 2 of this figure shows the <table> element that displays the list of Product objects. To start, the <table> element uses its class attribute to specify some Bootstrap CSS classes to format the table. Then, it uses the <thead> element to identify the header row for the table. Within this element, the <tr> and <th> elements define a header row that contains four columns: a Name heading, a Price heading, and two blank headings.

After the <thead> element, the <tbody> element identifies the body for the table. Within this element, an inline foreach loop displays all Product objects in the model. In other words, it displays all products in the current category.

Within the foreach loop, the <tr> and <td> elements define a row that contains four columns. The first column displays the Name property of the Product object. The second column displays the Price property of the Product object after currency formatting has been applied to it. The third column displays a View link that provides a way to view details about the product. And the fourth column displays an Update link that provides a way to update the data for the product.

The third and fourth columns use tag helpers to specify the action method for the link. For example, the third column specifies that clicking the View link calls the Product/Details() action method. In addition, both of these columns use the asp-route-id tag helper to specify the id argument for the action method.

This figure finishes by showing the view after it has been displayed in a browser. Here, the URL displays the product category as the third segment of the URL. In this case, the view displays all products in the Guitars category. However, if the user clicks on the Basses link at the top of the page, it would display all products in the Basses category. And so on.

The code for the view (continued)

```
<table class="table table-bordered table-striped">
    <thead>
        <tr>
            <th>Name</th>
            <th>Price</th>
            <th></th>
            <th></th>
        </tr>
    </thead>
    <tbody>
        @foreach (var product in @Model)
        {
            <tr>
                <td>@product.Name</td>
                <td>@product.Price.ToString("C")</td>
                <td>
                    <a asp-controller="Product" asp-action="Details"
                        asp-route-id="@product.ProductID">View</a>
                </td>
                <td>
                    <a asp-controller="Product" asp-action="Update"
                        asp-route-id="@product.ProductID">Update</a>
                </td>
            </tr>
        }
    </tbody>
</table>
```

The view displayed in a browser

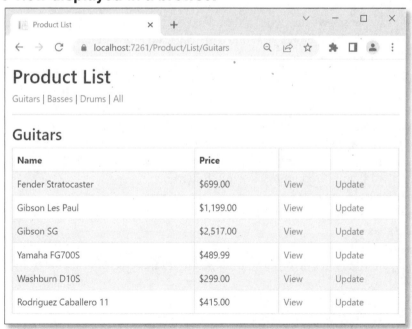

Figure 7-16   How to display a list of model objects (part 2)

How to work with Razor layouts

So far in this book, you've learned how to create web apps that use a single Razor layout, and you've been setting this layout as the default. As a result, all views in the app use this layout. However, as your web app becomes more complex, you may need to create additional Razor layouts. That way, different views can use different layouts.

How to create and apply a layout

In chapter 2, you learned how to use Visual Studio to add a Razor layout to your web app. In particular, you learned how to add a layout like the _Layout file presented earlier in this chapter in figure 7-6. Now, figure 7-17 shows the code for a layout file named _MainLayout. Like the _Layout file, this file is stored in the Views/Shared folder. That makes sense as both of these files are shared by multiple views.

The code for the _MainLayout file works much like the code for the _Layout file. However, within the <body> element, it includes <header> and <footer> elements that define a header and footer for the page. Here, the header contains three links (Home, Products, and About) and an <hr> element that displays a horizontal rule. The footer also uses an <hr> element to display a horizontal rule, along with copyright info for the website. This info consists of the HTML entity for the copyright symbol (©), a Razor expression that gets the current year, and the name of the website.

The second example shows the code in the _ViewStart file that sets the Layout property to the layout named _Layout. This causes the layout named _Layout to be the default layout for all views.

The third example shows how to override this default for a specific view. To do that, you can use the Razor code block at the beginning of the view to set the Layout property to another layout. In this example, the Home/Index view sets the Layout property to the _MainLayout file shown at the top of this figure. That's why the Home page shown in the browser includes the header and footer.

When you set the Layout property as shown here, the framework will look for the specified layout file in the following folders:

1. `/Areas/<area-name>/Views/<controller-name>`
2. `/Areas/<area-name>/Views/Shared`
3. `/Views/Shared`
4. `/Pages/Shared`

As long as the layout file is in one of these folders, the framework will be able to discover it.

You can also set the Layout property with a full file path, like so:

```
Layout = "~/Views/Shared/_Layout.cshtml";
```

This is useful when your layout is in a different folder than those listed above, or when you want to make it clear which layout is being used.

The Views/Shared/_MainLayout.cshtml file

```
<!DOCTYPE html>
<html>
<head>
    <title>@ViewBag.Title</title>
    <link rel="stylesheet"
        href="~/lib/bootstrap/dist/css/bootstrap.min.css" />
    <link rel="stylesheet" href="~/css/site.css" />
</head>
<body class="container-fluid">
    <header>
        <a asp-controller="Home" asp-action="Index">Home</a> |
        <a asp-controller="Product" asp-action="List">Products</a> |
        <a asp-controller="Home" asp-action="About">About</a>
        <hr />
    </header>

    <main>
        @RenderBody()
    </main>

    <footer>
        <hr />
        <p>&copy; @DateTime.Now.Year - Guitar Shop</p>
    </footer>
</body>
</html>
```

The code for a _ViewStart.cshtml file that sets the default layout

```
@{
    Layout = "_Layout";
}
```

The code for a Home/Index view that explicitly specifies a layout

```
@{
    Layout = "_MainLayout";
    ViewBag.Title = "Home";
}
<p>Welcome to the Guitar Shop!</p>
```

The Home page

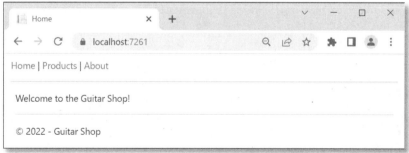

Description

- A project can contain multiple Razor layouts. That way, different views can use different layouts.

Figure 7-17   How to create and apply a layout

How to nest layouts

If you compare the layout named _Layout in figure 7-6 with the layout named _MainLayout in figure 7-17, you'll see that these two layouts contain some duplicate code. For example, they both use the same <head> element. In some cases, this duplication is fine. In general, though, it's considered a good practice to avoid code duplication because it usually makes your code easier to maintain.

When working with layouts, you can avoid code duplication by nesting one layout within another as shown in figure 7-18. To illustrate how this works, this figure shows the code for three layouts. To start, the layout named _Layout specifies the <html>, <head>, and <body> elements that can be used by a simple view and by other layouts.

The layout named _MainLayout sets its Layout property to the layout named _Layout, which causes it to be nested within this layout. As a result, the <header>, <main>, and <footer> elements specified by _MainLayout are rendered within the <body> element of the layout named _Layout.

Similarly, the layout named _ProductLayout is nested within the layout named _MainLayout. As a result, the <h1> element, the series of links, and the <hr> element specified by _ProductLayout are rendered within the <main> element of _MainLayout.

The _Layout file

```
<!DOCTYPE html>
<html>
<head>
    <title>@ViewBag.Title</title>
    <link rel="stylesheet"
        href="~/lib/bootstrap/dist/css/bootstrap.min.css" />
    <link rel="stylesheet" href="~/css/site.css" />
</head>
<body class="container-fluid">
    @RenderBody()
</body>
</html>
```

The _MainLayout file

```
@{
    Layout = "_Layout";
}
<header>
    <a asp-controller="Home" asp-action="Index">Home</a> |
    <a asp-controller="Product" asp-action="List"
        asp-route-id="All">Products</a> |
    <a asp-controller="Home" asp-action="About">About</a>
    <hr />
</header>

<main>
    @RenderBody()
</main>

<footer>
    <hr />
    <p>&copy; @DateTime.Now.Year - Guitar Shop</p>
</footer>
```

The _ProductLayout file

```
@{
    Layout = "_MainLayout";
}

<h1>Product List</h1>
@if (ViewBag.Categories != null)
{
    foreach (Category c in ViewBag.Categories)
    {
        <a asp-controller="Product" asp-action="List"
            asp-route-id="@c.Name">@c.Name</a><text> | </text>
    }
    <a asp-controller="Product" asp-action="List"
        asp-route-id="All">All</a>
}
<hr />

@RenderBody()
```

Description

- To avoid code duplication, you can build layouts by nesting one layout within another.

Figure 7-18   How to nest layouts (part 1)

To help you visualize how this works, part 2 begins by showing the code for a Product List view that uses _ProductLayout. Here, the code for _MainLayout displays the header that includes the Home, Products, and About links as well as the footer that displays the copyright info. Then, the code for _ProductLayout displays the Product List heading and the links for the product categories.

As you review this figure, take a moment to consider how you might use these three layouts for the pages of your web app. You can use _Layout for any custom views that need to link to the CSS files but don't need the standard header and footer for the web app. You can use _MainLayout to provide the standard header and footer for most pages of the web app. And you can use _ProductLayout to provide the Product List heading and category links for any pages that are used to view and update products.

The code for a view that uses the _ProductLayout view

```
@model List<Product>
@{
    Layout = "_ProductLayout";
    ViewBag.Title = "Product List";
}

@if (@ViewBag.SelectedCategory == "All")
{
    <h2>All Products</h2>
}
else
{
    <h2>@ViewBag.SelectedCategory</h2>
}

<!-- The rest of the code is the same as the <table> element
     in part 2 of figure 7-16 -->
```

The view displayed in a browser

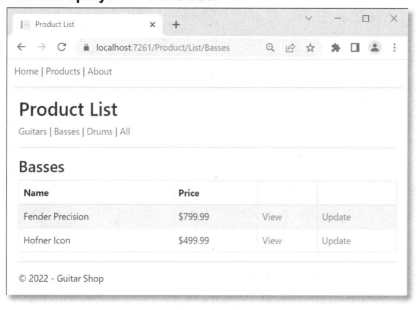

Figure 7-18   How to nest layouts (part 2)

How to use view context

The ViewContext property is available to all views and layouts. A layout can use this property to get data about the context of the current view, such as its route. Then, the layout can use this data to perform formatting tasks such as setting the active navigation link.

To show how this works, figure 7-19 presents a modified version of the _MainLayout that was presented earlier in this chapter. To start, the Razor code block for this layout uses the ViewContext property to get the current controller and action. Then, it uses a navbar to display the Home, Products, and About links using Bootstrap skills described in chapter 3. For each link, this layout uses an inline conditional expression to display the active attribute for the current controller and action.

For example, if the current controller is the Product controller and the current action is the List() action, this code sets the active attribute for the Products link. This displays the Products link as the active link. Otherwise, this code doesn't set the active attribute for the Products link. This displays the Products link as an inactive link.

To help you visualize how this works, this figure finishes by showing this layout after it has been displayed in a browser. Here, a navbar is displayed across the top of the screen. Within the navbar, the About link is displayed in a brighter color to indicate that it's the active link, and the Home and Products links are displayed in a more muted color to show that they are inactive links.

The _MainLayout file after it has been modified to use view context

```
@{
    Layout = "_Layout";
    string c = ViewContext.RouteData.Values["controller"]?.ToString() ?? "";
    string a = ViewContext.RouteData.Values["action"]?.ToString() ?? "";
}
<header>
    <nav class="navbar navbar-expand-md navbar-dark bg-primary fixed-top">
        <div class="container-fluid">
            <a class="navbar-brand" href="/">My Guitar Shop</a>
            <!-- toggle button same as figure 3-20 -->
            <nav class="collapse navbar-collapse"
                id="navbarSupportedContent">
                <div class="navbar-nav me-auto">
                    <a class="nav-item nav-link
                    @(c == "Home" && a == "Index" ? "active" : "")"
                    asp-controller="Home" asp-action="Index">Home</a>
                    <a class="nav-item nav-link
                    @(c == "Product" ? "active" : "")"
                    asp-controller="Product" asp-action="List">Products</a>
                    <a class="nav-item nav-link
                    @(c == "Home" && a == "About" ? "active" : "")"
                    asp-controller="Home" asp-action="About">About</a>
                </div>
            </nav>
        </div>
    </nav>
</header>

<main>
    @RenderBody()
</main>

<footer>
    <hr />
    <p>&copy; @DateTime.Now.Year - Guitar Shop</p>
</footer>
```

A view that uses this layout

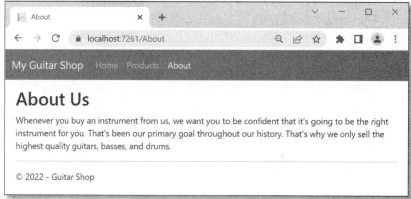

Description

- A layout can use the ViewContext property to get data about the route of the current view. Then, it can use this data to perform tasks such as setting the active navigation link.

Figure 7-19   How to use view context in a layout

How to use sections

The table at the top of figure 7-20 presents the RenderSection() method. This method is similar to the RenderBody() method, except that you use it to insert the content of a named *section* in a view into a layout. Then, only the content outside the sections is inserted by the RenderBody() method.

As you'll see in a moment, you use the Razor @section declaration to specify a section and its content.

The first parameter of the RenderSection() method is the name of the section to insert. The second parameter is a Boolean value that indicates whether the section is required. If it is, then all views that use the layout that contains the RenderSection() method must provide a section with the name specified in the first parameter. Otherwise, the section is optional.

To give you an idea of how this works, the examples in this figure show how to insert optional <script> elements into a layout. The first example presents a layout file that calls the RenderSection() method at the end of the <body> element. The parameters indicate that the content of a section named scripts will be inserted and that this section is optional. That is, a view that uses this layout can insert additional <script> elements if it needs to, but it doesn't have to.

The second example presents a view file that contains the section named scripts. To specify this section, the view file uses a Razor @section declaration. This section contains two <script> elements that import the jQuery libraries that perform client-side data validation. This inserts these two <script> elements at the location of the RenderSection() method in the layout file.

The last example in this figure shows how to use sections with nested layouts. For instance, the application that you'll see next has a layout file named _Layout that's similar to the layout file shown here. It also has a nested layout file named _AdminLayout that's the default layout for the views in the Admin area. Because the views that add and update data need the jQuery validation libraries, you can make them available by coding a section with the same name within the nested layout. Then, within that section, you can code a RenderSection() method that inserts the section into the layout. That way, because _AdminLayout is nested within _Layout, the jQuery files are also available to any views that use _Layout.

The examples in this figure illustrate a common use of optional sections, which is to allow views that need additional JavaScript libraries to load them. Then, if a view doesn't need the libraries, it can omit the section so the view will load more quickly. By contrast, a common use of required sections is for providing content that can vary. For example, although every view that uses a specific layout may require a sidebar, the content of that sidebar may vary for each view.

A method that can insert content from a section into a layout

Method	Description
`RenderSection(name, required)`	Inserts the content from the section with the specified name into the layout. If the section is required, all views must include a section with the specified name or attempting to view the page will result in an error.

A layout file that inserts the content from an optional section named scripts

```
<!DOCTYPE html>
<html>
<head>
    <title>@ViewBag.Title</title>
    <link rel="stylesheet" href="~/lib/bootstrap/css/bootstrap.min.css" />
    <link rel="stylesheet" href="~/css/site.css" />
</head>
<body class="container-fluid">
    @RenderBody()

    <script src="~/lib/popper.js/popper.min.js"></script>
    <script src="~/lib/bootstrap/js/bootstrap.min.js"></script>
    <script src="~/lib/jquery/jquery.min.js"></script>
    @RenderSection("scripts", required:false)
</body>
</html>
```

A view file with a section named scripts

```
@model Product
@{
    ViewData["Title"] = "Update Product";
}

@section scripts {
    <script src="~/lib/jquery-validate/jquery.validate.min.js"></script>
    <script src="~/lib/jquery-validation-unobtrusive/
                      jquery.validate.unobtrusive.min.js"></script>
}

<h2>Update</h2>
// the HTML elements for the rest of the view body go here
```

A nested layout with a section that inserts content from a section

```
@section scripts{
    @RenderSection("scripts", required:false)
}
```

Description

- Within a layout, you can use the RenderSection() method to specify where content from a section can be inserted into the layout. A *section* is a block of content that has a name.

- Within a view, you can use the Razor @section declaration to specify a section that will be inserted into the designated location in the layout.

- You can also code an @section declaration that contains a RenderSection() method in a nested layout. Then, the code in that section is available to any layout that uses the nested layout and that also includes a RenderSection() method for the section.

Figure 7-20   How to use sections in a layout

The Guitar Shop website

To show how the skills described in chapters 6 and 7 fit together within a semi-realistic website, this chapter ends by showing the user interface for the Guitar Shop website that's included with the download for this book. If you study this user interface, you might be able to guess how it uses some of the skills presented in chapters 6 and 7.

But really, the best way to study this web app is to open it in Visual Studio, run it to see how it works, and study the code files. To help you understand the code, these files have more comments than would typically be included in a web app. In addition, the exercise at the end of this chapter guides you through the process of reviewing this code and modifying it to make improvements to the website.

The user interface for customers

Figure 7-21 shows two pages of the user interface that's available to end users, or customers, of the Guitar Shop website. Both of these pages display the same navigation bar at the top of the page and the same footer at the bottom. That's because the views for these pages use the same layout.

The Product List page includes a column of categories on the left side of the page that customers can use to select a category of products. Then, if customers want to learn more about a product, they can click the View Details link to display the Product Details page. This page displays details about the product, including an image. On both pages, the customer can add the product to the cart, though this feature hasn't been implemented yet by this website.

If users click the Admin link on the right side of the navigation bar, the website displays the Admin pages shown in figure 7-22. Typically, a website would require admin users, or administrators, to log in to make sure the user is authorized to view the Admin pages. However, this feature hasn't been implemented yet by this website.

The user interface for administrators

Figure 7-22 shows four pages of the user interface for administrators. Like the pages for end users, the views for these pages use the same layout. However, this layout is different from the one that's displayed for end users. That's because the Admin pages provide different functionality. But this layout and the one the end user pages use are nested within the same layout.

The Product Manager page looks much like the Product List page for end users. However, it provides links that let admin users update or delete a product. In addition, it provides a button that lets admin users add a new product. To perform these tasks, admin users can use the Add Product, Update Product, and Delete Product pages shown in this figure.

The Product List page for customers

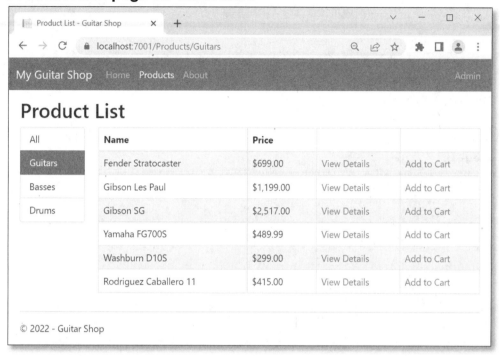

The Product Details page

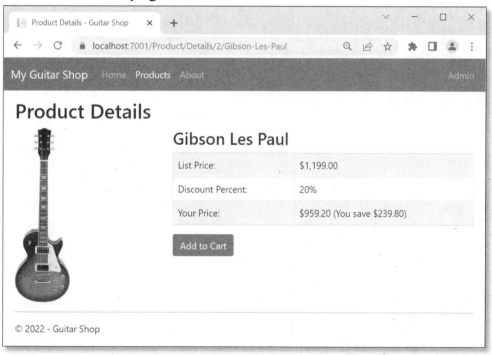

Figure 7-21   The Guitar Shop user interface for customers

The Product Manager page for administrators

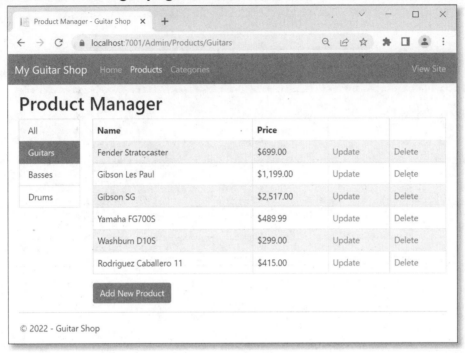

The Update Product page

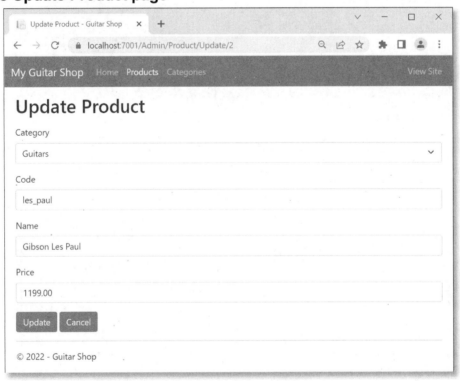

Figure 7-22 The Guitar Shop user interface for administrators (part 1)

The Add Product page

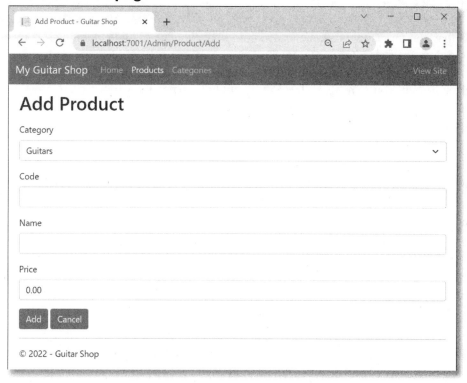

The Delete Product page

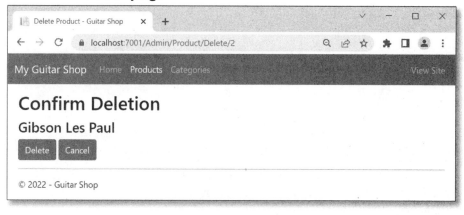

Figure 7-22   The Guitar Shop user interface for administrators (part 2)

Perspective

Now that you've read this chapter, you should have a general understanding of how to set up the Razor views and layouts of an MVC app. In addition, you should have a good idea of how to create a model and bind it to a view. With that as background, you're ready to learn more about transferring data between controllers and views as described in the next chapter.

Terms

code block	fragment
inline expression	relative URL
inline loop	absolute URL
inline conditional statement	model
inline conditional expression	section

Summary

- Within a view, you can use a Razor *code block* to execute one or more C# statements.

- Within a view, you can code an *inline expression* to evaluate a C# expression and display its result.

- Within a view, you can code *inline loops*. Within these loops, you can use HTML tags to send HTML to the view.

- Within a view, you can code *inline conditional statements* such as if/else and switch statements. Within these statements, you can use HTML tags to send HTML to the view.

- Within a view, you can code an *inline conditional expression* by using C#'s conditional operator (**?:**) to send HTML tags or plain text to the view. This works like other complex inline expressions that require parentheses.

- A URL *fragment* allows you to jump to a specified placeholder on a web page. A placeholder is identified by an id attribute, and a fragment is preceded by the hash mark (#) in a URL.

- A *relative URL* is a URL that's relative to the app's root directory.

- An *absolute URL* is a URL that specifies the name of the host.

- A *model* is a regular C# class that defines an object that stores and processes the data for an app.

- Within a view, you can use the Razor @section declaration to specify a *section*, which is a block of content that has a name. Then, you can use the RenderSection() method to insert the section into a layout.

Exercise 7-1   Modify the Guitar Shop website

In this exercise, you'll review the folders and files that are used by the Guitar Shop website. Then, you'll modify some of these files to see how those changes affect the app.

Open the Guitar Shop website and review its files

1. Open the Ch07Ex1GuitarShop website in the ex_starts folder.

2. Run the app. It should display the Home page in your browser.

3. Click the "About" link in the navigation bar. It should display some information about the guitar shop.

4. Click the "Products" link. It should display the Product List page. If you get an error message that says, "Cannot open database", create the database by running the Update-Database command as described in chapter 4.

5. The left column of the Product List page should display product categories of All, Guitars, Basses, and Drums. Click on each of these categories and note both the items listed for each category and the URL for each category.

6. Open the HomeController class and the corresponding Home/About.cshtml view file. Make sure to open the controller file in the main area, not in the Admin area.

7. In the HomeController class, note that the About() method has a Route attribute that allows it to be called with a URL of "/About", not "/Home/About".

8. In the About.cshtml view file, view the code and note that no model is declared.

9. Open the ProductController class and the corresponding Product/List.cshtml view file. Make sure to open the files in the main area, not in the Admin area.

10. In the ProductController class, note that the List() method has a Route attribute that allows it to be called with a URL of "/Products", not "/Product/List". Note also that the id parameter of this method has a default value of "All".

11. In the List.cshtml file, view the code and note that the @model directive at the top of the code specifies a list of Product objects as the model.

12. In the ProductController class, note that the List() method declares and populates the list of Product objects and passes it to the view as the model. To do that, it uses an if statement to check the id parameter. Then, it uses LINQ method syntax to populate the list with products from the correct category.

13. In the List.cshtml file, note that the foreach loop iterates through the Model property (which contains the list of products) and displays the appropriately formatted data related to each product.

Add a Contact Us action method and view

14. In the HomeController class, add an action method named ContactUs() that calls the View() method. Use a Route attribute so a URL of "/ContactUs" calls the action. (You can use the About() action method as a guide.)

15. In the Views/Home folder, add a view file named ContactUs.cshtml. In the view file, set the Title property of the ViewData object and the content of an <h1> tag to "Contact Us". Then, add a <p> tag whose value is "Here's how you can reach us:" and save your changes.

16. In the Views/Shared folder, open the _MainLayout.cshtml file. Note how it uses the ViewContext property to get the current controller and action.

17. Use tag helpers to add a navigation link for the Contact Us page, and use the current controller and action to mark the link active or not. (You can use one of the other navigation links in the layout as a guide.)

18. Run the app and navigate to the Contact Us page. It should display just the contents of the <h1> and <p> tags that you added in step 15.

Add a model to the Contact Us action method and use it in the view

19. Update the ContactUs() action method so it creates a dictionary with string keys and values that holds contact data, like this:

```
var contact = new Dictionary<string, string> {
    { "Phone", "555-123-4567" },
    { "Email", "info@myguitarshop.com" }
};
```

Add any additional ways of contacting the company that you want.

20. Pass the dictionary as the model to the view.

21. Update the ContactUs.cshtml view so it's bound to a dictionary with string keys and values.

22. Add an HTML table below the <p> tag that uses a foreach loop to iterate through the Model property and display its values, like this:

```
@foreach (var item in @Model)
{
    <tr>
        <td>@item.Key</td>
        <td>@item.Value</td>
    </tr>
}
```

23. Run the app and navigate to the Contact Us page. This time, a table with the contact information should be displayed in addition to the <h1> and <p> tags.

Review the layout files

24. In the Views/Shared folder, open the _Layout.cshtml file. Notice that it calls the RenderBody() and RenderSection() methods.

25. Open the _MainLayout.cshtml file in the same folder. Notice that it's nested within the _Layout.cshtml file and that it calls the RenderBody() method.

26. In the Areas/Admin/Views/Shared folder, open the _AdminLayout.cshtml file. Notice that it's also nested within the _Layout.cshtml file and that the framework is able to find it even though it's in a different shared folder. Also notice that it calls the RenderBody() method, and it has a section named scripts that calls the RenderSection() method.

27. Run the app and click on the Admin link. Notice how the nav bar changes but the footer stays the same. Now, click on the View Site link to return to the home page.

Update the Category/AddUpdate view to include data validation JavaScript files

28. In the Admin area, open the Product/AddUpdate.cshtml view file. Notice that it has a section named scripts that contains <script> elements for two JavaScript files for data validation.

29. In the Admin area, open the Category/AddUpdate.cshtml view file. Add a section named scripts that contains <script> elements for two JavaScript files for data validation. (You can use the Product/AddUpdate.cshtml file as a guide.)

30. Run the app and display the Admin page. Click on Categories and then Add New Category.

31. Right click the page in the browser and select View page source. In the source file, scroll to the bottom to see that the <script> tags for the JavaScript data validation files have been added.

8

How to transfer data from controllers

So far, this book has focused on using the action methods of a controller to get data from the model layer and then transfer that data to a view. Now, this chapter presents more details about how that works. In addition, it presents several new ways to transfer data from a controller to a view or to another controller.

How to use ActionResult objects

The apps you've seen so far in this book have transferred data from a controller to a view by passing a model object to the View() method. This method returns a ViewResult object, which is a subtype of the ActionResult class. Now, this topic presents more details about how you can use the ActionResult class to transfer data from a controller to a view.

An introduction to ActionResult subtypes

The ActionResult type provides information to MVC about the type of HTTP response an action method should return. The response can be content, like HTML or JSON, or it can be an HTTP status code such as 404 Not Found.

Figure 8-1 begins by presenting the hierarchy of the ActionResult class. Here, the abstract ActionResult class implements the IActionResult interface. Then, several subtypes inherit and extend the ActionResult class.

The table in this figure lists some of the most common subtypes of the ActionResult type. Each subtype has a specific purpose. For instance, the ViewResult class renders a view and sends the resulting HTML to the browser. The JsonResult class sends JSON to the browser. The FileResult class sends a file to the browser. The RedirectToActionResult class uses HTTP to instruct the browser to redirect to a URL that corresponds to the specified action method. And so on.

This table is not an exhaustive list. If you'd like to learn more about all the subtypes of the ActionResult class, the Microsoft documentation provides a full list, and you can find it at the URL shown in this figure.

The ActionResult hierarchy

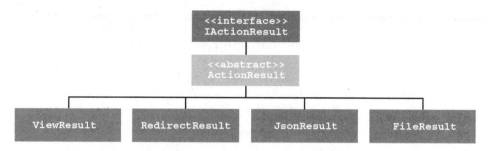

Common ActionResult subtypes

Class	Description
`ViewResult`	Renders a specified view as HTML and sends it to the browser.
`RedirectResult`	Performs an HTTP redirection to the specified URL.
`RedirectToActionResult`	Performs an HTTP redirection to a URL that's created by the routing system using specified controller and action data.
`JsonResult`	Serializes an object to JSON and sends the JSON to the browser.
`FileResult`	Returns a file to the browser.
`StatusCodeResult`	Sends an HTTP response with a status code to the browser.
`ContentResult`	Returns plain text to the browser.
`EmptyResult`	Returns an empty response to the browser.

A URL that provides a full list of the ActionResult subtypes

https://docs.microsoft.com/en-us/dotnet/api/
microsoft.aspnetcore.mvc.actionresult

Description

- Within a controller, an action method can return any type of ActionResult object. The ActionResult class is an abstract class that implements the IActionResult interface.

- Since the ActionResult class has many subtypes, an action method can return many different types of result objects.

Figure 8-1   An introduction to the ActionResult subtypes

How to return ActionResult objects

The ActionResult object that's returned by an action method tells MVC the type of response that should be sent to the browser. The Controller class provides several methods that create an ActionResult object. To create an appropriate result object, you can call these methods. Then, you can return the result object.

The first table in figure 8-2 presents some of methods of the Controller class that return an ActionResult object. The names of these methods correspond to the ActionResult subtype they return. For instance, the View() method creates a ViewResult object, the RedirectToAction() method creates a RedirectToActionResult object, and so on.

Most of these methods have several overloads. The second table illustrates this by reviewing some of the overloads of the View() method. The first overload accepts no arguments and renders the default view for the current controller and action method. For instance, if an Index() method in the Home controller calls the View() method with no arguments, MVC renders the HTML for the Home/ Index view.

The second overload accepts a model object that's used by the default view. For instance, if an Index() action method in the Home controller passes an object to the View() method, MVC transfers that object to the Home/Index view. Then, the view uses that object to render its HTML.

The third overload accepts a string that tells MVC which view file to use. MVC starts by looking for this file in the folder for the current controller. Then, it looks in the Shared folder. For instance, if an Index() action method in the Home controller passes the string "Error" to the View() method, MVC looks for the Error.cshtml file in the Views/Home folder. Then, it looks in the Views/ Shared folder.

The fourth overload accepts a string and a model object. Thus, if an Index() action method in the Movie controller passes the string "Edit" and an object to the View() method, MVC passes the specified object to the Edit.cshtml file in the Views/Movie folder.

When Visual Studio generates action methods, it uses a return type of IActionResult. If the action method might return different ActionResult subtypes, this approach works well, as shown by the third example in this figure. However, if your action method is only going to return one type of ActionResult subtype, it's considered a good practice to use a more specific subtype as the return type as shown by the first two examples. This can improve performance, and it makes your code more clear.

A problem can arise if you want to use a string as a model object. In that case, MVC might interpret the string as the name of a view file to look for, not as the model object. To fix this problem, you can cast the string to the object type before passing it to the View() method as shown by the third code example.

Some methods of the Controller class that return an ActionResult object

Method	Returns a...
`View()`	ViewResult object
`Redirect()`	RedirectResult object
`RedirectToAction()`	RedirectToActionResult object
`File()`	FileResult object
`Json()`	JsonResult object

Some of the overloads of the View() method

Method	Description
`View()`	Renders the default view for that controller and action method.
`View(model)`	Transfers a model object to the default view and renders that view.
`View(name)`	Renders the specified view. This method starts by searching for the specified view in the view folder for the current controller. Then, it searches in the Views/Shared folder.
`View(name, model)`	Transfers a model object to the specified view and renders that view.

An action method that returns a ViewResult object

```
public ViewResult List() {
    var names = new List<string> { "Grace", "Ada", "Charles" };
    return View(names);
}
```

An action method that returns a RedirectToActionResult object

```
public RedirectToActionResult Index() => RedirectToAction("List");
```

An action method that may return different types of result objects

```
[HttpPost]
public IActionResult Edit(string id) {
    if (ModelState.IsValid)
        return RedirectToAction("List");
    else
        return View((object)id);    // cast string model to object
}
```

Description

- The Controller class provides several methods that create objects of ActionResult subtypes. Most of these methods include several overloads that allow you to customize the ActionResult object that's created.

- When Visual Studio generates action methods, it uses IActionResult as the return type.

- If an action method only returns one type of ActionResult object, it's a good practice to specify that subtype as the return type.

- If an action method may return multiple types of ActionResult objects, you can specify the ActionResult abstract class or the IActionResult interface as the return type.

- If you want to use a string as a model, you must cast it to an object first.

Figure 8-2   How to return ActionResult objects from controller action methods

How to use the ViewData and ViewBag properties

In earlier chapters, you've seen how to use the ViewBag and ViewData properties of the Controller class to transfer data from an action method to a view. Now, this topic reviews those properties and explains them in more detail.

How to use the ViewData property

The ViewData property of the Controller class has a data type of ViewDataDictionary. This means that the property is a collection of key/value pairs. For this dictionary type, the key is a string and the value is an object.

The first code example in figure 8-3 shows how to add data to the ViewData property. Here, a string value and a double value are added to the dictionary, each with a unique string key.

The ViewData property is shared with the associated view, including the view's layout. As a result, any data stored in the ViewData dictionary is available to the view and its layout.

The ViewDataDictionary class also has some properties that a view can use. The table in this figure summarizes some of these properties. Then, the second code example shows how a view can use these properties to display the data in the ViewData dictionary to the user. To do that, the code uses the Count property to display the number of items, and it uses a KeyValuePair object to get each item and display its key and value.

If you just want to display a ViewData value in the browser, you don't need to do anything special to it. That's because Razor automatically calls the ToString() method of an object in the dictionary so it can be displayed. However, if you want to work with a value in the ViewData dictionary in code, you must first cast it to the appropriate data type. For instance, the third code example shows how to display the value of the Price item with currency formatting. To do that, you must first cast the Price item to the double type and then call the ToString() method to format it.

Before you call a method from a value, you should check to make sure the value isn't null. One way to do that is to use the *null-conditional operator* (?). Then, if the value is null, the method isn't executed. That can prevent your app from throwing null reference exceptions. However, the null-conditional operator only works with nullable types. So, if the value you're checking is non-nullable, you'll need to cast it to a nullable type for this to work.

For instance, the first statement in the fourth code example shows how to check if the Price value is null. To do that, it casts the value to a nullable double type (double?). Then, before calling the ToString() method, it uses the null-conditional operator to check that the value is not null. That way, if the value is null, the Razor expression returns null.

Controller code that adds two items to the ViewData property

```
public ViewResult Index() {
    ViewData["Book"] = "Alice in Wonderland";
    ViewData["Price"] = 9.99;
    return View();
}
```

Some of the properties of the ViewDataDictionary class

Property	Description
Count	Returns the number of key/value pairs in the dictionary.
Keys	Returns a collection of strings containing the keys in the dictionary.
Values	Returns a collection of objects containing the values in the dictionary.

Razor code that displays all the items in the ViewData object

```
<h2>@ViewData.Count items in ViewData</h2>
@foreach (KeyValuePair<string, object?> item in ViewData) {
    <div>@item.Key - @item.Value</div>
}
```

The view in the browser

2 items in ViewData

Book - Alice in Wonderland
Price - 9.99

Razor code that casts a ViewData object to the double type

```
<h4>Price: @(((double)ViewData["Price"]).ToString("c"))</h4>
```

The view in the browser

Price: $9.99

Razor code that uses the null conditional operator to check for null

Cast a value type (double) to a nullable type

```
<h4>Price: @(((double?)ViewData["Price"])?.ToString("c"))</h4>
```

Cast a reference type (string) to a nullable type

```
<h4>Book: @ViewData["Book"]?.ToString().ToUpper()</h4>
```

Description

- The Controller class has a ViewData property that lets you transfer data to a view.
- The ViewData property is of the ViewDataDictionary type, which is a collection of key/value pairs where the key is a string and the value is an object.
- When you display a ViewData value in a view, Razor automatically calls the object's ToString() method.
- If you want to work with a ViewData value in code, you must cast the value to its data type. When you work with a ViewData value like this, you should check that the value isn't null.

Figure 8-3   How to use the ViewData property

The second statement is similar except it gets the Book value. And, instead of casting the Book value to a nullable type like this:

```
<h4>Book: @(((string?)ViewData["Book"])?.ToUpper())</h4>
```

it uses the ToString() method to do that. Then, it uses the ToUpper() method to convert the string to uppercase. Here again, if you didn't need to work with the value in code, you wouldn't need to call the ToString() method explicitly.

How to use the ViewBag property

The ViewBag property of the Controller class uses C#'s *dynamic type*. As a result, you can add properties to the ViewBag, and .NET determines the type of those properties at runtime.

The first code example at the top of figure 8-4 shows how to add data to the ViewBag property. Here, as in the previous figure, this example adds a string property and a double property.

Like the ViewData property, the ViewBag property is shared with the associated view, including its layout. As a result, any data stored in the ViewBag is available to the view and its layout.

Under the hood, the ViewBag property stores its data in the ViewData dictionary. Thus, you can use the ViewData property to get values that were added to the ViewBag. For instance, the second code example uses ViewData to display the values that the first example added to the ViewBag. Because the ViewBag uses the ViewData dictionary like this, it's often thought of as an *alias* for the ViewData dictionary.

Since the ViewBag is dynamically typed, you don't need to explicitly cast property values to work with the data that they contain. This is illustrated by the third example. However, it's still a good idea to check that a value isn't null before calling a method of that value. This is illustrated by the fourth example. As you can see, these tasks are easier to do with the ViewBag.

In general, the ViewBag is easier to work with than the ViewData dictionary. As a result, you should use it in most scenarios. However, there are a few scenarios where it makes sense to use ViewData. For example, you can use ViewData if you need to use names for your keys that aren't valid in C# or if you need to be able to access the properties of the ViewDataDictionary class. In addition, if you use Visual Studio to generate code, it may use the ViewData dictionary. In that case, it may be easier to leave the generated code than to change it to use the ViewBag.

One disadvantage of both the ViewBag and ViewData properties is that Visual Studio doesn't provide compile-time checking or IntelliSense for them. This is true for both the controller and the view. Because of this, some programmers avoid using either of these properties and use view models instead. You'll learn about view models later in this chapter.

Controller code that adds two dynamic properties to the ViewBag property

```
public ViewResult Index() {
    ViewBag.Book = "Alice in Wonderland";
    ViewBag.Price = 9.99;
    return View();
}
```

Razor code that uses ViewData to display ViewBag properties

```
<h2>@ViewData.Count ViewBag properties</h2>
@foreach (KeyValuePair<string, object?> item in ViewData) {
    <div>@item.Key - @item.Value</div>
}
```

The view in the browser

2 ViewBag properties

Book - Alice in Wonderland
Price - 9.99

Razor code that works with a ViewBag property without casting

```
<h4>Price: @ViewBag.Price.ToString("c")</h4>
```

The view in the browser

Price: $9.99

Razor code that checks ViewBag properties for null

Value type (double)

```
<h4>Price: @ViewBag.Price?.ToString("c")</h4>
```

Reference type (string)

```
<h4>Book: @ViewBag.Book?.ToUpper()</h4>
```

Use ViewData instead of ViewBag when you need to...

- Use a key name that isn't valid in C#, such as one that contains spaces.
- Call properties and methods of the ViewDataDictionary class, such as its Count property or its Clear() method.
- Loop through all the items in the ViewData dictionary.

Description

- The Controller class has a ViewBag property that lets you transfer data to a view.
- The ViewBag uses the C# *dynamic type* to let you add properties. Later, .NET determines the type of those properties at runtime.
- Under the hood, the ViewBag uses the ViewData dictionary to store its dynamic properties. Thus, you can think of the ViewBag property as an *alias* for ViewData.
- In most scenarios, ViewBag is easier to use. However, there are a few scenarios where it makes more sense to use ViewData.

Figure 8-4   How to use the ViewBag property

The NFL Teams 1.0 app

The next few figures present the NFL Teams app. This simple app illustrates some of the skills presented so far in this chapter.

The user interface

To understand the NFL Teams app, you need to know a little about the conferences and divisions of the National Football League (NFL). This information is presented at the top of figure 8-5. Then, this figure presents the user interface of this app.

The first page shows how the NFL Teams app looks when it first loads. In this case, logos for all the NFL teams are displayed in alphabetical order. When users move the mouse over a team logo, that team's name, conference, and division are displayed in a tool tip. For example, on the first page, the user's mouse is over the first logo. This logo is for the Arizona Cardinals, whose conference is the NFC and whose division is West.

The left side of the page displays two sections with links the user can click to filter the teams by conference or division. Each section also includes an "All" option that allows the user to display all the teams in a conference or division. These are the options that are selected by default when the app first loads.

The second page shows the app after the user selected the AFC option in the Conference section and the East option in the Division section. As a result, the app only displays the logos of the teams in the East division of the AFC conference, or the AFC East for short.

How the teams of the National Football League (NFL) are organized

- There are two conferences, the NFC and the AFC.
- Each conference contains four divisions named North, South, East, and West.
- Each division contains four teams.

The NFL Teams app on first load

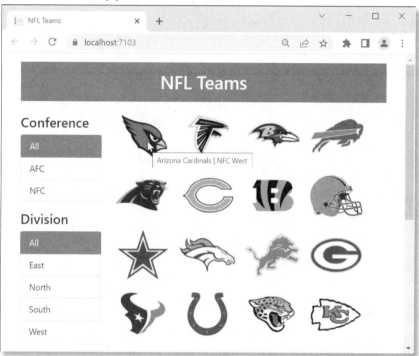

The NFL Teams app after a conference and division are selected

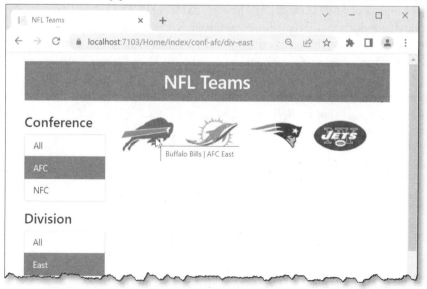

Figure 8-5   The user interface of the NFL Teams 1.0 app

The model layer

Figure 8-6 presents the code for the model layer of the NFL Teams app. This code is stored in the Models folder.

Before moving on, remember that nullable reference types are enabled by default when you create a new MVC app. As you know, this means that reference types can't contain null values. Because of this, each of the properties of the classes in the model layer are assigned either a default value or a null value with the null-forgiving operator (!) to suppress compiler warnings.

The Conference class is an entity class that represents a conference. It has two string properties, one for an ID value and the other for the name of the conference.

The Division class is an entity class that represents a division. Like the Conference class, it has two string properties, one for an ID value and the other for the name of the division.

The Team class is an entity class that represents a team. It has string properties for an ID value, the team name, and the filename for the logo image. In addition, it has two properties of the Conference and Division types to hold information about the conference and division for the team. Since the app only needs to read and display data, though, the Team class doesn't have foreign key properties for the related conference and division.

The TeamContext class is a DB context class like the MovieContext class you learned about in chapter 4. The NFL Teams app uses this class to communicate with a database named NFLTeams. This database holds the information about the NFL teams. While not shown here, this app also has an appsettings.json file and a Program.cs file configured for database access. You can refer to chapter 4 to review how these files work.

The TeamContext class inherits and extends the DbContext class. It has three DbSet properties named Teams, Conferences, and Divisions.

The TeamContext class also overrides the OnModelCreating() method of the DbContext class to seed initial data for the conferences, divisions, and teams. Note, however, that the code that seeds the team data doesn't use Team objects to do the seeding. That's because the Team object doesn't have foreign key properties for the conference ID and division ID values, but you want to include these values in the database table. To do that, the code that seeds the team data uses an anonymous object that includes the conference ID and division ID values. This is a common work-around for data seeding issues like this.

The Conference class

```
public class Conference
{
    public string ConferenceID { get; set; } = string.Empty;
    public string Name { get; set; } = string.Empty;
}
```

The Division class

```
public class Division
{
    public string DivisionID { get; set; } = string.Empty;
    public string Name { get; set; } = string.Empty;
}
```

The Team class

```
public class Team
{
    public string TeamID { get; set; } = string.Empty;
    public string Name { get; set; } = string.Empty;
    public Conference Conference { get; set; } = null!;
    public Division Division { get; set; } = null!;
    public string LogoImage { get; set; } = string.Empty;
}
```

The TeamContext class

```
public class TeamContext : DbContext
{
    public TeamContext(DbContextOptions<TeamContext> options)
        : base(options) { }

    public DbSet<Team> Teams { get; set; } = null!;
    public DbSet<Conference> Conferences { get; set; } = null!;
    public DbSet<Division> Divisions { get; set; } = null!;

    protected override void OnModelCreating(ModelBuilder modelBuilder) {
        base.OnModelCreating(modelBuilder);

        modelBuilder.Entity<Conference>().HasData(
            new Conference { ConferenceID = "afc", Name = "AFC"},
            ...
        );

        modelBuilder.Entity<Division>().HasData(
            new Division { DivisionID = "north", Name = "North" },
            ...
        );

        modelBuilder.Entity<Team>().HasData(
            new {TeamID = "ari", Name = "Arizona Cardinals",
                ConferenceID = "nfc", DivisionID = "west",
                LogoImage = "ARI.png"},
            ...
        );
    }
}
```

Figure 8-6   The model layer

The Home controller

Figure 8-7 presents the code for the Home controller of the NFL Teams app. This controller starts by defining a private TeamContext property named context. Then, it defines a constructor that accepts a TeamContext object. When the app starts, MVC automatically creates a TeamContext object and passes it to the constructor. Then, the constructor stores the TeamContext object in the private context property.

The Home controller has a single action method named Index(). This action method returns a ViewResult object, not any other type of ActionResult object. To make that clear, this code specifies ViewResult as the return type, not ActionResult or IActionResult. As an added benefit, the compiler doesn't need to determine the type of object to return at runtime, which can improve performance.

The Index() action method has two string parameters named activeConf and activeDiv. These parameters are the IDs of the currently selected conference and division. Each has a default value of "all". So, if the user doesn't select a conference or division, this action returns all teams.

Since this action accepts two parameters, it doesn't work well with the default route, which is designed to work with a single parameter. To fix this, this app adds the custom route shown at the bottom of this figure. This route uses two static literal values of "conf-" and "div-", as well as two required parameters named activeConf and activeDiv. Since this route is more specific than the default route, it must be coded before the default route.

Within the Index() action method, the code starts by creating two ViewBag properties named ActiveConf and ActiveDiv. Then, it stores the activeConf and activeDiv parameters in these properties. This is how the controller transfers the selected conference and division IDs to the view.

After storing the selected IDs, the code retrieves all the conferences and divisions from the database and stores these two lists in two more ViewBag properties named Conferences and Divisions. This is how the controller transfers these lists to the view.

After storing the conferences and divisions, the code gets the teams from the database. It starts by building a query expression that returns all teams, sorted in alphabetical order by team name. Then, if the active conference is not "all", it adds a where clause to get the teams in the selected conference. After that, if the active division is not "all", it adds a where clause to get the teams in the selected division.

After building the query, the code calls ToList() to execute the query and retrieve a list of Team objects. Then, it passes the list of Team objects to the View() method and returns a ViewResult object. This is how the controller transfers the list of Team objects to the view.

The Home controller

```
public class HomeController : Controller
{
    private TeamContext context;

    public HomeController(TeamContext ctx)
    {
        context = ctx;
    }

    public ViewResult Index(string activeConf = "all",
                            string activeDiv = "all")
    {
        // store selected conference and division IDs in view bag
        ViewBag.ActiveConf = activeConf;
        ViewBag.ActiveDiv = activeDiv;

        // store conferences and divisions from database in view bag
        ViewBag.Conferences = context.Conferences.ToList();
        ViewBag.Divisions = context.Divisions.ToList();

        // get teams - filter by conference and division
        IQueryable<Team> query = context.Teams.OrderBy(t => t.Name);
        if (activeConf != "all")
            query = query.Where(
                t => t.Conference.ConferenceID.ToLower() ==
                    activeConf.ToLower());
        if (activeDiv != "all")
            query = query.Where(
                t => t.Division.DivisionID.ToLower() ==
                    activeDiv.ToLower());

        // pass list of teams to view as model
        var teams = query.ToList();
        return View(teams);
    }
}
```

The custom route in the Program.cs file

```
app.MapControllerRoute(
    name: "custom",
    pattern: "{controller}/{action}/conf-{activeConf}/div-{activeDiv}");

app.MapControllerRoute(
    name: "default",
    pattern: "{controller=Home}/{action=Index}/{id?}");
```

Figure 8-7   The Home controller and endpoints in the Program.cs file

The layout

Figure 8-8 presents the code for the layout of the NFL Teams app. This layout is similar to other layouts that you've seen in earlier chapters.

To start, this layout uses Razor code to get the Title property from the ViewBag. It's possible to use the ViewData dictionary instead of the ViewBag to get the same data. However, since using the ViewBag yields code that's shorter and cleaner, this layout uses ViewBag, not ViewData.

Within the <body> element, the view uses Bootstrap classes to style the header that appears at the top of every page. This creates a header that says "NFL Teams" and is centered with white text, a blue background, some extra margin on top, and some extra padding on all four sides.

The layout

```
<!DOCTYPE html>

<html>
<head>
    <meta name="viewport" content="width=device-width, initial-scale=1.0" />
    <link href=
        "~/lib/bootstrap/dist/css/bootstrap.min.css" rel="stylesheet" />
    <link href="~/css/site.css" rel="stylesheet" />
    <title>@ViewBag.Title</title>
</head>
<body>
    <div class="container">
        <header class="text-center text-white">
            <h1 class="bg-primary mt-3 p-3">NFL Teams</h1>
        </header>
        <main>
            @RenderBody()
        </main>
    </div>
</body>
</html>
```

Figure 8-8   The layout

The Home/Index view

Figure 8-9 presents the code for the Home/Index view of the NFL Teams app. This view begins with a directive indicating that the model for this view is a collection of Team objects. This works because when the Index() action method calls the View() method, it passes a collection of Team objects to this view.

The Razor code block starts with a statement that assigns the value "NFL Teams" to the ViewData dictionary with a key of "Title". This is the same value that the view's layout retrieves from the ViewBag for the <title> element. This shows that you can use the ViewData and ViewBag properties interchangeably.

The Razor code block continues by defining a helper method named Active() that returns a string. This method accepts two strings and compares them. If they match, the method returns the string "active". Otherwise, it returns an empty string.

The HTML in this view contains a Bootstrap row with two columns. The first column displays the Conference and Division sections on the left side of the page.

The Conference section starts with an <h3> element that displays the title of the section. Then, it has a <div> element styled as a Bootstrap list group. Within the <div> element, an <a> element builds a link for the "All" option, with the asp-route-activeConf value set to "all" and the asp-route-activeDiv value set to the active division from the ViewBag.

After that, a Razor foreach statement loops through all the Conference objects in the ViewBag and builds a link for each one. Here, the asp-route-activeConf value changes for each Conference object, while, once again, the asp-route-activeDiv value is set to the active division from the ViewBag.

In addition, each link determines whether it is the active link by calling the Active() method and passing it the ID of the current Conference object and the active conference ID from the ViewBag. If the current conference ID matches the active conference ID, this code adds the active class. Otherwise, it doesn't add any classes.

The Division section works much like the Conference section. This time, of course, it loops through the Division objects in the ViewBag. However, it also uses the IDs of the active division and conference to build the links and determine the active division.

The second column contains the team logos in a <ul> element. This element uses the Bootstrap list-inline class so the logos display side by side. Within the <ul> element, a Razor foreach statement loops through all the Team objects in the model and builds an <li> element that contains an <img> element for each one. This works because the images folder of the wwwroot folder contains image files that correspond to the filename stored in the LogoImage property of the Team object.

The Home/Index view

```
@model IEnumerable<Team>
@{
    ViewData["Title"] = "NFL Teams";
    string Active(string filter, string selected) {
        return (filter.ToLower() == selected.ToLower()) ? "active" : "";
    }
}
<div class="row">
    <div class="col-md-3">
        <h3 class="mt-3">Conference</h3>
        <div class="list-group">
            <a asp-action="Index"
                asp-route-activeConf="all"
                asp-route-activeDiv="@ViewBag.ActiveDiv"
                class="list-group-item @Active("all", ViewBag.ActiveConf)">
                All</a>

            @foreach (Conference conf in ViewBag.Conferences) {
                <a asp-action="Index"
                    asp-route-activeConf="@conf.ConferenceID"
                    asp-route-activeDiv="@ViewBag.ActiveDiv"
                    class="list-group-item @Active(conf.ConferenceID,
                                        ViewBag.ActiveConf)">
                    @conf.Name</a>
            }
        </div>
        <h3 class="mt-3">Division</h3>
        <div class="list-group">
            <a asp-action="Index"
                asp-route-activeConf="@ViewBag.ActiveConf"
                asp-route-activeDiv="all"
                class="list-group-item @Active("all", ViewBag.ActiveDiv)">
                All</a>

            @foreach (Division div in ViewBag.Divisions) {
                <a asp-action="Index"
                    asp-route-activeConf="@ViewBag.ActiveConf"
                    asp-route-activeDiv="@div.DivisionID"
                    class="list-group-item @Active(div.DivisionID,
                                        ViewBag.ActiveDiv)">
                    @div.Name</a>
            }
        </div>
    </div>
    <div class="col-md-9">
        <ul class="list-inline">
            @foreach (Team team in Model) {
                <li class="list-inline-item">
                    <img src="~/images/@team.LogoImage" alt="@team.Name"
                        title="@team.Name |
                            @team.Conference.Name @team.Division.Name" />
                </li>
            }
        </ul>
    </div>
</div>
```

Figure 8-9   The Home/Index view

How to work with view models

The applications you've seen so far have used the View() method to transfer a single entity object or a collection of entity objects to a view. Sometimes, however, the data needed by a view doesn't match the data in an entity model.

For example, the model object for the Index view of the NFL Teams app is a collection of Team objects. However, that view also needs a collection of Conference objects and a collection of Division objects to build the links to filter by conference and division. In addition, it needs the IDs of the active conference and division.

In the NFL Teams 1.0 app, the controller used the ViewBag to transfer this other data to the view. Unfortunately, IntelliSense doesn't work for data in the ViewBag or the ViewData dictionary, and the compiler doesn't warn you of problems in your code. Instead, you have to wait until runtime to discover these problems. That's why many developers prefer to use a view model to transfer data to a view.

How to create a view model

A *view model* is a regular C# class that holds all of the data that a specific view requires. By convention, this kind of class ends with the suffix "ViewModel", but that isn't required.

The code example in figure 8-10 presents the TeamsViewModel class. The first two properties are the ID values of the active conference and division, which are set to default values of "all". The next property is the collection of Team objects that the view needs. And the last two properties are the collections of Conference and Division objects that the view needs.

Typically, view models are lightweight classes that contain only data. However, they can also contain simple helper methods for the view. For instance, the TeamsViewModel class provides two methods named CheckActiveConf() and CheckActiveDiv() that the view can use to determine the active link in the conference and division sections. That's acceptable because this logic only impacts how the view is displayed. However, a view model shouldn't have logic that impacts other parts of the app such as the entity model or controller.

A view model for the NFL Teams app

```
public class TeamsViewModel
{
    public string ActiveConf { get; set; } = "all";
    public string ActiveDiv { get; set; } = "all";

    public List<Team> Teams { get; set; } = new List<Team>();
    public List<Conference> Conferences { get; set; } =
        new List<Conference>();
    public List<Division> Divisions { get; set; } =
        new List<Division>();

    // methods to help view determine active link
    public string CheckActiveConf(string c) =>
        c.ToLower() == ActiveConf.ToLower() ? "active" : "";

    public string CheckActiveDiv(string d) =>
        d.ToLower() == ActiveDiv.ToLower() ? "active" : "";
}
```

Description

- A *view model* is a regular C# class that defines a model of the data that's needed by a view.

- By convention, the name of a view model class ends with a suffix of "ViewModel", but this isn't required.

- Most view models only provide data. However, a view model can also contain simple methods that help the view display that data.

Figure 8-10   How to create a view model

The updated Index() action method

Now that you have a view model, you can update the NFL Teams app to use it. The first code example in figure 8-11 shows the updated Index() action method of the Home controller. Here, the two parameters shown in figure 8-7 have been replaced with a parameter of type TeamsViewModel. Then, MVC uses model binding to assign the values of any route segments that are passed to the method properties of this object.

You'll learn more about model binding in chapter 10. For now, you just need to know that if the activeConf and activeDiv segments shown in figure 8-7 are passed to the Index() action method, they're assigned to the ActiveConf and ActiveDiv properties of the view model.

The code within the Index() action is similar to the code shown in figure 8-7. Instead of storing the conference and division data that's retrieved from the database in the ViewBag, though, it stores this data in the Conferences and Divisions properties of the view model. And instead of using the activeConf and activeDiv parameters in the if statements, it uses the ActiveConf and ActiveDiv properties of the view model. Then, it executes the query, stores the results in the Teams property of the view model, and returns the model to the view.

The updated Home/Index view

The second code example in this figure presents the updated code for the Home/Index view. The statement at the top of the Index view now indicates that the model for this view is a TeamsViewModel object.

In this view, the Razor code block only contains the ViewData code that sets the <title> element in the layout. In other words, this version doesn't need the Active() helper function that you saw earlier in the chapter.

The HTML in this updated view works much like it did in the previous version. The main difference is that you use the properties of the view model rather than the properties of the ViewBag. This may not seem like much, but using a view model like this means you have IntelliSense and compile-time error checking. As a result, the IDE warns you of problems before you run the app. With the ViewBag, you won't discover typos or other errors until you actually run the app.

Another difference is that this view uses the CheckActiveConf() and CheckActiveDiv() helper methods of the TeamsViewModel class to mark the correct link as the active link. This code is shorter and cleaner than the code presented earlier in this chapter.

Finally, the Razor foreach statement that loops through the list of Team objects transferred from the controller now gets those objects from the Teams property of the view model. However, the HTML and Razor code that builds the logo images is the same as in figure 8-9.

The updated Index() action method of the Home controller

```
public ViewResult Index(TeamsViewModel model)
{
    model.Conferences = context.Conferences.ToList();
    model.Divisions = context.Divisions.ToList();

    IQueryable<Team> query = context.Teams.OrderBy(t => t.Name);
    if (model.ActiveConf != "all")
        query = query.Where(t =>
            t.Conference.ConferenceID.ToLower() ==
                model.ActiveConf.ToLower());
    if (model.ActiveDiv != "all")
        query = query.Where(t =>
            t.Division.DivisionID.ToLower() ==
                model.ActiveDiv.ToLower());
    model.Teams = query.ToList();
    return View(model);
}
```

The updated Home/Index view

```
@model TeamsViewModel
@{
    ViewData["Title"] = "NFL Teams"; // helper function no longer needed
}
<div class="row">
    <div class="col-md-3">
        <h3 class="mt-3">Conference</h3>
        <div class="list-group">
            <a asp-action="Index"
                asp-route-activeConf="all"
                asp-route-activeDiv="@Model.ActiveDiv"
                class="list-group-item @Model.CheckActiveConf("all")">
                All</a>

            @foreach (Conference conf in Model.Conferences) {
                <a asp-action="Index"
                    asp-route-activeConf="@conf.ConferenceID"
                    asp-route-activeDiv="@Model.ActiveDiv"
                    class="list-group-item
                        @Model.CheckActiveConf(conf.ConferenceID)">
                     @conf.Name</a>
            }
        </div>
        <h3 class="mt-3">Division</h3>
        ...
    </div>
    <div class="col-md-9">
        <ul class="list-inline">
            @foreach (Team team in Model.Teams)
                ...
            }
        </ul>
    </div>
</div>
```

Figure 8-11   The updated Index() action method and Home/Index view

How to redirect a request

In addition to using a view to send a web page to the browser, you can use some of the subtypes of the ActionResult class to redirect an HTTP request to another URL. You'll learn how to do that in the topics that follow.

How to use the ActionResult classes for redirection

When a browser makes a request to a server, the server returns an HTTP status code along with the response. For instance, when a server returns HTML, it also returns a 200 OK status code. Or, when a browser requests a URL that doesn't exist, the server returns a 404 Not Found status code.

The first table in figure 8-12 presents two of the HTTP status codes for redirection. Both the 302 Found and the 301 Moved Permanently status codes direct the browser to make a GET request to another URL. The difference is that the 301 Moved Permanently status code tells the browser that this move is permanent and all future requests should be directed to the other URL. Most browsers cache this response and never request the original URL again.

The second table presents the ActionResult subtypes you can use for redirection. The Controller class provides 302 Found and 301 Moved Permanently versions of methods that return these subtypes. Both versions perform the redirection, but the permanent version returns a 301 status code. Typically, you use the 301 status code to support old URLs in your app.

The third table provides guidance on when to use each subtype. To navigate within your app, it's common to use RedirectToActionResult. That's because this method builds the specified URL based on your app routes. To navigate based on route names, you can use RedirectToRouteResult. However, this is less common, and some developers consider it a bad practice.

You can use LocalRedirectResult to pass a URL that the user should return to later. For example, a user might return to the URL after they log in. This ActionResult subtype makes sure that the return URL is part of your app. Thus, it prevents *open redirection attacks* that attempt to redirect to a malicious external site.

Most of the methods that return ActionResult objects for redirection have several overloads. The fourth table illustrates this by presenting some of the overloads for the RedirectToAction() method. These overloads require you to specify the action method you want to redirect to, and they allow you to optionally specify the controller and any route parameters.

The code below the last table shows examples of the overloads of the RedirectToAction() method. To pass a route parameter to a method, you can code an anonymous object with a property that specifies the name and value of a route segment as shown in the third example. If the parameter name in the method matches the route segment name, you can use a shortcut as shown in the fourth example. Or, if you prefer, you can use a dictionary with a string key and value to pass route parameters as shown in the last example.

Two of the HTTP status codes for redirection

Code	Description
`302 Found`	Directs the browser to make a GET request to another URL.
`301 Moved Permanently`	Directs the browser to make a GET request to another URL for this and all future requests.

The ActionResult subtypes for redirection

Subtype	302 Found method	301 Moved Permanently method
`RedirectResult`	`Redirect()`	`RedirectPermanent()`
`LocalRedirectResult`	`LocalRedirect()`	`LocalRedirectPermanent()`
`RedirectToActionResult`	`RedirectToAction()`	`RedirectToActionPermanent()`
`RedirectToRouteResult`	`RedirectToRoute()`	`RedirectToRoutePermanent()`

How to know which subtype to use for redirection

Subtype	Use when...
`RedirectResult`	Redirecting to an external URL, such as https://google.com.
`LocalRedirectResult`	Making sure you redirect to a URL within the current app.
`RedirectToActionResult`	Redirecting to an action method within the current app.
`RedirectToRouteResult`	Redirecting within the current app by using a named route.

Some of the overloads available for the RedirectToAction() method

Arguments	Redirect to...
`(a)`	The specified action method in the current controller.
`(a, c)`	The specified action method in the specified controller.
`(a, routes)`	The specified action method in the current controller with route parameters.
`(a, c, routes)`	The specified action method in the specified controller with route parameters.

Code that redirects to another action method

Redirect to the List() action method in the current controller

```
public RedirectToActionResult Index() => RedirectToAction("List");
```

Redirect to the List() action method in the Team controller

```
public RedirectToActionResult Index() => RedirectToAction("List", "Team");
```

Redirect to the Details() action method in the current controller with a parameter

```
public RedirectToActionResult Index(string id) =>
    RedirectToAction("Details", new { ID = id });
```

Use a shortcut when variable name and route segment name match

```
public RedirectToActionResult Index(string id) =>
    RedirectToAction("Details", new { id });
```

Use a string-string dictionary to supply parameters

```
public RedirectToActionResult Index(string id) =>
    RedirectToAction("Details",
        new Dictionary<string, string>(){ { "ID", id } } );
```

Figure 8-12   How to use the ActionResult classes for redirection

How to use the Post-Redirect-Get pattern

GET requests are designed to retrieve data but be *idempotent*, which means that they make no changes on the server. Because of that, a user can resubmit a GET request multiple times by clicking the browser's Refresh button, and it doesn't affect any data on the server.

POST requests, by contrast, are designed to post, or write, data to the server. Typically, you don't want your users to resubmit a POST request. For example, if a POST request submits an order to the server, you don't want the user to accidentally resubmit that order by clicking the browser's Refresh button.

To help prevent that, most browsers display a message like the one shown in figure 8-13 if a user resubmits a POST request. However, if the user chooses to continue despite the browser warning, the user can submit the POST request again, which may not be what you want.

To prevent resubmission of a POST request, it's common to use the *Post-Redirect-Get (PRG) pattern* when you're making changes on the server. This figure presents an example of code that implements the PRG pattern.

Here, the Add() action method handles the POST request that updates the server with the team data it receives. The last statement in this action uses the RedirectToAction() method to return a 302 Found status code to the browser. This tells the browser to issue a GET request for the Index() action method of the Home controller

The Index() action method of the Home controller handles the GET request that the browser makes in response to the 302 Found status code it receives. This action reads the updated data from the server and passes it to the view for display to the user. As a result, if the user clicks the Refresh button, it requests the data from the database again, and displays it again. But, crucially, the Index() action shown here doesn't change any data on the server. In other words, it's an idempotent request.

The downside of the PRG pattern is that the redirection requires a second roundtrip to the server. However, the upside of avoiding problems caused by resubmitting a form typically outweighs this downside.

If you have a POST action method that makes changes on the server and then returns a view, you should consider using the PRG pattern to split that action into two action methods. That way, you can use a POST action method to make changes to the data on the server. Then, you can redirect to a GET action method to display a view. When you do that, the GET action method is idempotent and can be run one or more times without affecting the data that's stored on the server.

A browser message that's displayed when you refresh a page that's displayed by a POST request

Confirm Form Resubmission

The page that you're looking for used information that you entered. Returning to that page might cause any action you took to be repeated. Do you want to continue?

Continue   Cancel

Code that uses the Post-Redirect-Get (PRG) pattern

An action method that handles a POST request

```
[HttpPost]                                              // Post
public RedirectToActionResult Add(Team team)
{
    // code that updates the server with the new team data
    return RedirectToAction("Index", "Home");           // Redirect
}
```

The action method that the POST action method redirects to

```
[HttpGet]                                               // Get
public ViewResult Index(TeamsViewModel model)
{
    // code that reads the updated data from the server
    return View(model);
}
```

Description

- To prevent resubmission of POST data, you can use the *Post-Redirect-Get* (*PRG*) *pattern*. With this pattern, a POST action writes data to the server and then redirects to a GET action to read data from the server.

Figure 8-13   How to use the Post-Redirect-Get (PRG) pattern

How to use the TempData property

So far, this chapter has shown how to transfer data from a controller to a view. Sometimes, though, you need to transfer data from a controller to another controller. To do that, you can use the built-in TempData property that's available from controllers and views.

How to get started with TempData

The TempData property of the Controller class works much like the ViewData property described earlier in this chapter. To start, it uses a dictionary to store a collection of key/value pairs where the key is a string and the value is an object. As a result, if you want to work with a value in the TempData dictionary, you must cast it to the appropriate data type. But first, you should check to make sure the value exists.

The TempData property differs from the ViewData property in how long its data persists. With ViewData, the data persists only for the life of the current request. That is, once the server sends its response to the browser, all the data in the ViewData (and ViewBag) property is lost. With TempData, on the other hand, the data persists across multiple requests. In fact, this data persists until it is read. Once a TempData item is read, it's marked as read. Then, at the end of each request, every item that's marked as read is removed from the TempData dictionary.

Because the items in TempData persist beyond the current request, TempData is often used in conjunction with the PRG pattern. The code in figure 8-14 illustrates how this works. Here, an action method handles a POST request and redirects to another action method that handles a GET request, just like the example in the last figure.

Now, though, the POST action wants to notify the user of the result of the action. But it can't use the ViewData property to transfer the message to the GET action of the PRG pattern. So, it stores a message that's created using an interpolated string in the TempData property. This works because the data in the TempData property persists after the POST request and is available to the subsequent GET request.

The Index() action method shown here gets the message for the user from TempData and sends it to the view in the ViewBag. However, it's common to display messages like this in the layout for the application. That way, you don't end up with repetitive code in the actions and views.

The layout view shown in this figure uses a Razor if statement to check whether the TempData property contains an item with a key of "message". To do that, it uses the Keys property of the TempData dictionary and the Contains() method of the collection of keys. If the item exists, the view uses an <h4> element to display its value. This element is styled with Bootstrap CSS classes so it appears as shown in this figure.

By default, TempData can only store data that can be serialized, such as primitive types like int or string. However, the next chapter presents a technique that allows you to store complex data types in TempData.

Code that uses TempData with the PRG pattern

An action method for a POST request that stores a string in TempData

```
[HttpPost]
public RedirectToActionResult Add(Team team)
{
    // code that updates the server with the new team data
    TempData["message"] = $"{team.Name} added to your favorites";
    return RedirectToAction("Index", "Home");
}
```

An action method for a GET request that retrieves a string from TempData

```
[HttpGet]
public ViewResult Index(TeamsViewModel model)
{
    // code that reads the updated data from the server
    ViewBag.Message = TempData["message"];
    return View(model);
}
```

A Layout view that checks for a TempData value and displays it if it exists

```
...
@if (TempData.Keys.Contains("message"))
{
    <h4 class="bg-success p-2">@TempData["message"]</h4>
}
...
```

How it looks in a browser when a TempData value exists

Description

- The Controller class has a property named TempData that lets you transfer data to another controller or view.

- Data in TempData persists across multiple requests until it is read. By contrast, data in ViewData and ViewBag only persists until the end of the current request.

- TempData is often used with the PRG pattern because that pattern takes place across two requests (the POST request and the subsequent GET request).

- TempData can only store data that can be serialized, such as primitive types.

- Because TempData is a dictionary, it has normal dictionary properties like Keys and Values, which in turn have a Contains() method you can use to check for values.

- By default, ASP.NET Core 3.0 and later automatically enable TempData when you call the AddControllersWithViews() method in the Program.cs file.

Figure 8-14   How to get started with TempData

How to use methods of the TempData dictionary

When you read an item from TempData as described in the last figure, it's marked as read. Then, at the end of the current request, any items marked as read are removed. Sometimes, though, you may want an item to persist even after you've read it. In these cases, you can use the Keep() and Peek() methods of the TempDataDictionary class as described in figure 8-15.

The Keep() method has two overloads. If you call it with no arguments, it marks all the items in TempData as unread, even if they have been read. As a result, none of the items are removed at the end of the request. If you pass a key to this method, it marks the value for that key as unread, even if it has been read. Again, this means that the value won't be removed at the end of the request.

The Peek() method accepts a key and returns the value for that key. However, it doesn't mark that item as read. Thus, the item remains in the TempData dictionary.

Generally, you use the Peek() method when you know that you don't want to mark the value as read. However, if you might want to mark the value as read, you can read the value normally. Then, you can call the Keep() method if a condition for keeping that value is met.

In the code example shown here, the methods use a view model named TeamsViewModel. This class is the same as the one you saw in figure 8-10, except it also has a Team property to store the Team object for the selected team.

The POST request for the Details() action method assumes that the TeamsViewModel parameter includes all of the data needed to view the details for the specified team (the active conference and division IDs and the specified team ID). To start, the POST action method calls a static method from a class named Utility to write the team's ID to the server. Because of that, you don't want this request to be posted more than once. So, this action method needs to redirect and pass its data to the GET request for the Details() method. To do that, it stores the active division and conference IDs in the TempData property. Then, it uses the RedirectToAction() method to pass the ID for the team to the GET request.

The GET request then re-constructs the TeamsViewModel object. To do that, it uses the team ID to get the correct Team object from the database and set the Team property. Then, it uses the TempData property to get the active division and conference IDs and set the ActiveConf and ActiveDiv properties. As it does this, it uses the Peek() method to read the ActiveConf and ActiveDiv keys of the TempData property without marking them as read. That way, these properties are available to the view, even if the user resubmits the GET request one or more times.

If you find that you often need to keep TempData items after you've read them, you should probably use session state instead. The items in session state are kept until the user closes the browser, and it's described in the next chapter.

Two methods of the TempDataDictionary class

Method	Description
`Keep()`	Marks all the values in the dictionary as unread, even if they've been read.
`Keep(key)`	Marks the value associated with the specified key as unread, even if it has been read.
`Peek(key)`	Reads the value associated with the specified key but does not mark it as read.

The overloaded Details() action method of the Home controller

```
[HttpPost]
public RedirectToActionResult Details(TeamsViewModel model)
{
    Utility.LogTeamClick(model.Team.TeamID);
    TempData["ActiveConf"] = model.ActiveConf;
    TempData["ActiveDiv"] = model.ActiveDiv;
    return RedirectToAction("Details", new { ID = model.Team.TeamID });
}


[HttpGet]
public ViewResult Details(string id)
{
    var model = new TeamsViewModel {
        Team = context.Teams
            .Include(t => t.Conference)
            .Include(t => t.Division)
            .FirstOrDefault(t => t.TeamID == id),
        ActiveConf = TempData.Peek("ActiveConf").ToString(),
        ActiveDiv = TempData.Peek("ActiveDiv").ToString()
    };
    return View(model);
}
```

When to use the Keep() and Peek() methods

- Use Peek() when you know you want the value to stay marked as unread.
- Use a normal read and Keep() when you want to use a condition to determine whether to mark the value as unread.

Description

- With a normal read, an item from TempData is marked as read and deleted at the end of the current request. However, the TempDataDictionary class provides some methods to keep an item in TempData even after it has been read.
- If you consistently need to keep items in the TempData dictionary, you should consider storing the item in session state instead as described in the next chapter.
- When you redirect an HTTP request, MVC automatically calls the Keep() method under the hood.

Figure 8-15   How to use methods of the TempData dictionary

The NFL Teams 2.0 app

The next few figures present an updated version of the NFL Teams app. This version of the app illustrates some of the skills for working with redirection, the PRG pattern, and TempData.

The user interface

The first screen in figure 8-16 shows the updated NFL Teams app when it first loads. This is similar to the version you saw in figure 8-5. However, in this version of the app, the team logo is a clickable image link rather than just an image. You can tell that it's a link because the cursor is a hand rather than an arrow. And, when you hover over the image, the URL for the link shows in the lower left corner.

After the user clicks on a team logo, a Details page like the one in the second screen is displayed. This page includes an Add to Favorites button that the user can click to add the selected team to a list of their favorite teams.

The Home page with image links for the team logos

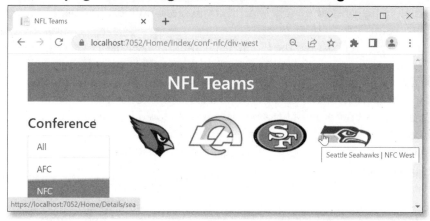

The Details page for a team after a team logo is clicked

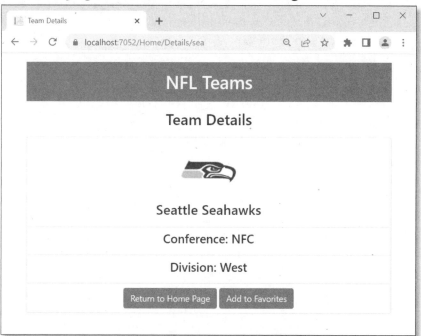

Description

- In this version of the NFL Teams app, the team logos are image links that the user can click to see a details page for the selected team.
- The details page has an Add to Favorites button that the user can click to add the selected team to their favorites.

Figure 8-16   The user interface of the NFL Teams 2.0 app (part 1)

The first screen in part 2 of figure 8-16 shows the Home page after the user has added a team to their list of favorites. As you can see, a notification message is displayed just below the header.

Then, the second screen shows the Home page after the user has clicked the browser's refresh button. You should notice two things about this second screen. First, there's no resubmission warning. That's because this version of the NFL Teams app uses the PRG pattern to add a team to favorites. Second, the notification message is now gone. That's because it was stored in TempData, so it was removed after it was read when the page first loaded.

You should know that, for now, the NFL Teams app doesn't actually store the user's favorite teams anywhere. Rather, it just displays the notification message you see here and redirects as needed. In addition, it doesn't "remember" the user's previous conference and division selections. Rather, it displays all the teams when it returns to the main page after the user clicks the Add to Favorites button.

However, in the next chapter you'll learn how to store the user's conference and division selections in session state. And, you'll learn how to store the user's favorite teams in session state and in cookies.

The Home page after adding a team to favorites

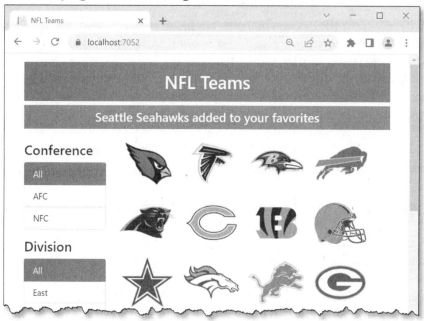

The Home page after clicking the browser's refresh button

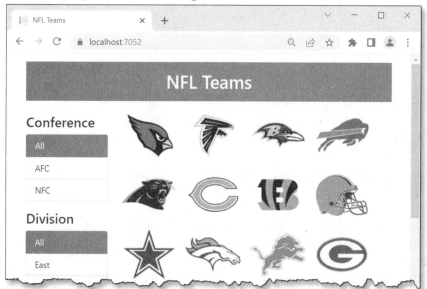

Description

- This version of the NFL Teams app uses the PRG pattern to add a team to favorites, and TempData to provide a notification message to the user.

Figure 8-16   The user interface of the NFL Teams 2.0 app (part 2)

The Home/Index view

Figure 8-17 shows the Razor code in the Home/Index view that displays the team logos. Like the Razor code in figure 8-9, it uses a Razor foreach statement within a <ul> element (not shown) to loop through all the Team objects in the model and build an <li> element for each one. In this case, though, each <img> element is coded within an <a> element to create an image link. The <a> element uses tag helpers to assign the action method and ID route segment. Since there's no controller assigned, it will use the current controller. That means these links will send GET requests to the Details() action method of the Home controller, and they will include the team ID in the URL.

The Details() action method of the Home controller

Figure 8-17 also shows the Details() action method of the Home controller. This method handles the GET requests that the image links send to the server.

The Details() action method starts by creating a Team object for the current team. To do that, it uses the FirstOrDefault() method to execute a query that gets the team with the ID that's passed to the method. This query also uses the Include() method to load information about the team's conference and division. Then, it passes the Team object to the Home/Details view.

The Home/Details view

Finally, figure 8-17 shows the code for the Home/Details view of the updated NFL Teams app. The model object for this view is a Team object. Remember, that's what the Details() action method for GET requests sends to the view.

Most of this code is similar to what you've seen in other views. That is, it uses Razor statements embedded in HTML to display the team's data to the user. The main thing to notice is the <form> element in the last <li> element. This form posts to the Add() action method of the Favorites controller, and it contains a Return to Home Page link, an Add to Favorites submit button, and two hidden fields.

The link is styled as a button, and it's coded within the form so it aligns with the button. But it doesn't need to be within the form to work properly. The submit button, by contrast, does need to be inside the form to work properly. In addition, the team name and ID are coded in hidden fields within the form. That way, this data is posted to the Add() action method.

The Razor loop in the Home/Index view that displays the team logos

```
@foreach (Team team in Model.Teams)
{
    <li class="list-inline-item">
        <a asp-action="Details" asp-route-id="@team.TeamID">
            <img src="~/images/@team.LogoImage" alt="@team.Name"
                title="@team.Name |
                @team.Conference.Name @team.Division.Name" />
        </a>
    </li>
}
```

The Details() action method of the Home controller

```
public IActionResult Details(string id)
{
    var team = context.Teams
                .Include(t => t.Conference)
                .Include(t => t.Division)
                .FirstOrDefault(t => t.TeamID == id) ?? new Team();
    return View(team);
}
```

The Home/Details view

```
@model Team
@{
    ViewData["Title"] = "Team Details";
}

<h2 class="text-center p-2">Team Details</h2>

<div class="row">
    <div class="col">
        <ul class="list-group text-center">
            <li class="list-group-item">
                <img src="~/images/@Model.LogoImage" alt="" />
                <h3>@Model.Name</h3></li>
            <li class="list-group-item">
                <h4>Conference: @Model.Conference.Name</h4></li>
            <li class="list-group-item">
                <h4>Division: @Model.Division.Name</h4></li>
            <li class="list-group-item">
                <form method="post" asp-action="Add"
                    asp-controller="Favorites">
                    <a asp-action="Index" class="btn btn-primary">
                        Return to Home Page</a>
                    <button type="submit" class="btn btn-primary">
                        Add to Favorites</button>
                    <input type="hidden" asp-for="@Model.TeamID" />
                    <input type="hidden" asp-for="@Model.Name" />
                </form>
            </li>
        </ul>
    </div>
</div>
```

Figure 8-17   The Home/Index view and the Home/Details action method and view

The Add() action method of the Favorites controller

Figure 8-18 shows the Add() action method of the Favorites controller. This method receives a Team object when the user clicks the Add to Favorites button in the Home/Details view. However, the Add() action method doesn't do anything with this object in this version of the NFL Teams app. In chapter 9, however, you'll learn how to store this data in session state and in cookies.

When the Add() action method receives the team name and ID from the hidden fields in the Home/Details view, MVC creates a new Team object and assigns the values of those fields to the TeamID and Name properties. You'll learn more about how that works in chapter 10. Then, this method simply adds a message to TempData that includes the team name and redirects to the Index() action of the Home controller. In other words, it uses the PRG pattern to avoid resubmission errors, and it uses TempData to preserve data across more than one request.

The layout view

Figure 8-18 also shows the layout view for the updated NFL Teams app. In most ways, it's similar to the layout you saw in figure 8-8. However, this version of the layout has a Razor if statement that checks whether the TempData dictionary has a "message" key. If it does, the layout reads the item associated with the key and displays it in an <h4> element. Then, after the item is read, it's marked for deletion. That's why the "added to favorites" message disappears when the user makes a subsequent request like refreshing the browser or selecting a new conference or division.

The Add() action method of the Favorites controller

```
[HttpPost]
public RedirectToActionResult Add(Team team)
{
    // code to store favorite team in session goes here - see chapter 9

    TempData["message"] = $"{team.Name} added to your favorites";

    return RedirectToAction("Index", "Home");
}
```

The Layout view

```
<!DOCTYPE html>

<html>
<head>
    <meta name="viewport" content="width=device-width" />
    <link href=
        "~/lib/bootstrap/dist/css/bootstrap.min.css" rel="stylesheet" />
    <link href="~/css/site.css" rel="stylesheet" />
    <title>@ViewBag.Title</title>
</head>
<body>
    <div class="container">
        <header class="text-center text-white">
            <h1 class="bg-primary mt-3 p-3">NFL Teams</h1>

            @* show any message in TempData *@
            @if (TempData.Keys.Contains("message"))
            {
                <h4 class="bg-success p-2">@TempData["message"]</h4>
            }
        </header>
        <main>
            @RenderBody()
        </main>
    </div>
</body>
</html>
```

Description

- The Add() action method of the Favorites controller uses the Post-Redirect-Get (PRG) pattern. After it updates the server with the data it receives, it redirects to the Index() action method of the Home controller rather than sending a view to the browser. This prevents form re-submission problems.

- The Add() action method stores a notification message for the user in TempData.

- The Layout view checks TempData for a notification message, and displays it to the user if it exists.

Figure 8-18   The Favorites/Add action method and the layout view

Perspective

The goal of this chapter is to show how to transfer data from a controller to a view or to another controller. To do that, this chapter reviewed some skills that were presented in chapter 2 such as using the ViewBag and ViewData properties. In addition, it presented several new ways to transfer data from a controller to a view including using ViewBag, ViewData, or a view model. Finally, it showed how to transfer data to another controller by using the TempData property.

The skills presented in this chapter should provide a solid foundation for transferring data from a controller. However, there are other ways to transfer data within your app, and the next two chapters present the most useful techniques. To start, the next chapter shows how to use session state and cookies to maintain state in an app.

Terms

dynamic type
alias
view model
idempotent
Post-Redirect-Get (PRG) pattern
open redirection attack

Summary

- ViewBag properties use C#'s *dynamic type*. As a result, the data type of each property is set at runtime.

- Under the hood, the ViewBag property uses the ViewData dictionary to store its dynamic properties. Thus, you can think of the ViewBag property as an *alias* for the ViewData dictionary.

- A *view model* is a regular C# class that holds all of the data that's needed by a view.

- An *idempotent* request has the same effect on the server whether it's made once or multiple times.

- To prevent resubmission of POST data, you can use the *Post-Redirect-Get (PRG) pattern*. With this pattern, a POST action writes data to the server and then redirects to a GET action to read data from the server.

- *Open redirection attacks* attempt to redirect to a malicious external site.

Exercise 8-1   Update the Guitar Shop app to use a view model and TempData

In this exercise, you'll update the Guitar Shop app presented in chapter 7 so it uses a view model and TempData.

Run the app and add a view model for the products pages

1. Open the Ch08Ex1GuitarShop web app in the ex_starts directory.

2. Run the app and test it. Make sure to test the Product List page in the default area as well as the Product List page in the Admin area.

3. In the Models folder, create a new C# class named ProductsViewModel and enter this code:

```
public class ProductsViewModel
{
    public List<Category> Categories { get; set; } = null!;
    public List<Product> Products { get; set; } = null!;
    public string SelectedCategory { get; set; } = string.Empty;
    public string CheckActiveCategory(string category) =>
        category == SelectedCategory ? "active" : "";
}
```

Review and update the Product List controller in the default area

4. In the Controllers folder, open the ProductController class and review the List() action method. Notice that it has a parameter named id that matches the id segment of the default route. Because the view model doesn't have a property with the same name as the id route segment, you can't use it as the parameter for this method. As a result, you'll need to manually create and populate the view model object.

5. In the List() action method, delete the statements that use the ViewBag.

6. Before the return statement, create and populate the view model object like this:

```
var model = new ProductsViewModel
{
    Categories = categories,
    Products = products,
    SelectedCategory = id
};
```

7. Modify the return statement so it passes the view model to the View() method.

Update the Product/List view in the default area

8. Open the Product/List view and change its model from List<Product> to ProductsViewModel.

9. Before the first foreach loop, modify the code that sets the active class for the All category so it uses the CheckActiveCategory() method of the view model.

10. Modify the first loop so it gets its categories from the view model, not the ViewBag.

11. Within the first loop, modify the code that sets the active class for each category so it uses the CheckActiveCategory() method of the view model.

12. Modify the second loop so it gets its products from the Products property of the view model.

13. Run the app and test the Product List page in the default area. It should work the same as before.

Update the Product List controller and view in the Admin area

14. Open the ProductController class in the Admin area.

15. In the List() action method, delete the code that uses the ViewBag and add code that creates and populates a Products view model as described earlier in this exercise. Then, modify the return statement to pass the model to the view.

16. Still in the Admin area, open the Product/List view and change its view model from List<Product> to ProductsViewModel.

17. Before the first loop, modify the code that sets the active class for the All category so it uses the CheckActiveCategory() method of the view model.

18. Modify the first loop so it gets its categories from the view model, not the ViewBag.

19. Within the first loop, use the CheckActiveCategory() method of the view model to determine whether to set the active class for the category.

20. Modify the second loop so it gets its products from the Products property of the view model.

21. Run the app and test the Product List page for the Admin area. It should work like it did before.

Use TempData to display messages to the user

22. In the default area, open the _Layout.cshtml file in the Shared folder. Within the body element, before the call to @RenderBody(), add a Razor if statement that checks for a TempData item with the key "message" and displays it in an <h4> element. Use Bootstrap to style the <h4> element the way you want.

23. In the Admin area, open the Product and Category controllers. Modify the code to store an appropriate message in TempData when a product or category is added, updated, or deleted. When you do that, use a key of "message".

24. Run the app and test that it displays a message after you add, update, or delete a product or category.

25. Update the Cart controller so it uses a TempData item with a key of "message" to display a message in the Product/List rather than in the Cart/Add view when a product is added to the cart. To do that, you can delete the statement in the Add() action that sets the ProductSlug property of the ViewBag and then update the return statement so it redirects to the List action of the Product controller.

26. Run the app one more time to be sure a message is displayed on the Product List page when a product is added to the cart.

9

How to work with session state and cookies

In the previous chapter, you learned some ways to transfer data from a controller to a view or to another controller across one or more requests. However, you sometimes need data to persist for as long as the browser is open or even longer. In this chapter, you'll learn how to do that.

How ASP.NET MVC handles state

The data that a web app maintains for a user, such as variables, is the *state* of that app. However, HTTP is a *stateless* protocol. This means that HTTP doesn't keep track of an app's state between round trips. Rather, once a browser makes a request and receives a response, the app terminates and its state is lost.

Six ways to maintain state

Figure 9-1 presents two tables that describe some of the ways that you can maintain state in a web app between HTTP requests. The first table presents four features for maintaining state that are common to all web apps (hidden fields, query strings, session state, and cookies). And the second table presents two features for maintaining state that are specific to ASP.NET Core (routes and TempData).

This book has already shown how to use most of the features in these tables. For example, chapter 6 showed how to use route segments and query strings, and chapter 8 showed how to use TempData. In addition, many of the apps presented so far in this book use hidden fields to post data to the server. Now, this chapter shows how to use session state and cookies to maintain state.

An introduction to session state

To understand how session state works, you need to know a little about cookies. A *cookie* is a key/value pair that's created on the server and passed to the user's browser in an HTTP response. Then, the browser passes the cookie back to the server with each subsequent HTTP request.

When you use *session state*, the data for a user session is stored in key/value pairs on the server. This data persists across all the HTTP requests that a user makes until the app removes the data or the session ends. A session can end in one of two ways. First, the user can end the session by closing the browser. Second, the session can end when the browser is open but the app is inactive for a specified period of time.

To make it possible for session state to work, the server creates a session ID to identify the user's session. Then, it sends this session ID to the user's browser in a cookie. With each subsequent request, the user's browser sends the cookie that contains the session ID back to the server, and the server uses that ID to retrieve the session data associated with that user.

Common web programming features for maintaining state

Feature	Description
Hidden field	Uses an <input> element to store data in a page that posts back to the server.
Query string	Uses the URL to store data and pass it between requests. See chapter 6.
Cookie	Uses a cookie object to store data in the user's browser or on hard disk. Then, the browser passes that data to the server with every subsequent request.
Session state	Uses a session state object to store data throughout the user's session.

Two ASP.NET Core MVC features for maintaining state

Feature	Description
Routes	Uses the URL to store data and pass it between requests. See chapter 6.
TempData	Uses a session state object to store data until it is read. See chapter 8.

How ASP.NET Core MVC keeps track of a session

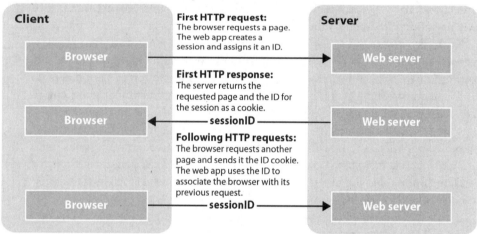

Description

- *State* refers to the current status of the properties, variables, and other data maintained by an app for a single user.

- HTTP is a *stateless protocol*. That means that it doesn't keep track of state between round trips. Once a browser makes a request and receives a response, the app terminates and its state is lost.

- ASP.NET Core MVC provides several ways to maintain the state of a web app.

- A *cookie* is a key/value pair that's passed to the user in an HTTP response and passed back to the server with each subsequent HTTP request.

- *Session state* works by having the server store the session data for a user and by using a cookie to associate the user's web browser with the correct session data.

Figure 9-1   How ASP.NET MVC handles state

How to work with session state

Session state allows you to store data that you want to persist across multiple HTTP requests. This feature is extremely useful and commonly used by many types of web apps such as those that maintain a shopping cart.

How to configure an app to use session state

By default, ASP.NET Core MVC doesn't enable session state. Because of that, you need to configure the middleware pipeline for your app so it includes all of the services needed for session state. To do that, open the Program.cs file and add the statements in the first example in figure 9-2.

First, session state needs to be added to the services for the app. To do that, this code calls the AddMemoryCache() and AddSession() methods that are available from the Services property of the WebApplicationBuilder object named builder. For this to work, these methods must be called before the AddControllersWithViews() method.

Next, the service to use for session state needs to be identified. To do that, this code calls the UseSession() method from the WebApplication object named app. For this to work, this method must be called before any routes are mapped.

If you configure your app as shown in the first example in this figure, you're ready to begin working with session state using its default settings. In some cases, however, you may want to change these defaults settings. For instance, you may want to change how long a session can be inactive before it times out.

The last code example shows how to change some of the default settings for a session. To do that, you can pass a SessionOptions object to the AddSession() method of the Services property.

In this example, the first statement uses the IdleTimeout property to change the timeout from 20 minutes to 5 minutes. Reducing the idle timeout can be useful in development when you're testing.

The next two statements use the Cookie property to change how the session cookie works. To start, the second statement sets the HttpOnly property to false. This allows client-side scripts to access the cookie. By default, this isn't allowed to protect from certain scripting attacks.

The third statement sets the IsEssential property to true to indicate that the session cookie is required for the app to function properly. This allows session state to work even if your web app requires users to consent to your cookie policy before the app can use non-essential cookies as specified by the General Data Protection Regulation (GDPR) requirements developed by the European Union (EU). That's because the session cookie is non-essential by default. Similarly, the TempData cookie is non-essential by default, but you can change it to essential if necessary.

How to configure an app to use session state

The Program.cs file

```
...
var builder = WebApplication.CreateBuilder(args);

// must be called before AddControllersWithViews()
builder.Services.AddMemoryCache();
builder.Services.AddSession();

builder.Services.AddControllersWithViews();
...

var app = builder.Build();

// Configure the HTTP request pipeline.
...

app.UseRouting();

// must be called before routes are mapped
app.UseSession();
...

app.MapControllerRoute(
    name: "default",
    pattern: "{controller=Home}/{action=Index}/{id?}");

app.Run();
```

How to change the default session state settings

```
builder.Services.AddSession(options =>
{
    // change idle timeout to 5 minutes - default is 20 minutes
    options.IdleTimeout = TimeSpan.FromSeconds(60 * 5);
    options.Cookie.HttpOnly = false;     // default is true
    options.Cookie.IsEssential = true;   // default is false
});
```

Description

- By default, session state is not enabled. To enable it, you can add code to the Program.cs file that calls the AddMemoryCache(), AddSession(), and UseSession() methods in the correct sequence.

- To change the default settings for session state, you can use a lambda expression to pass a SessionOptions object to the AddSession() method.

Figure 9-2   How to configure an app to use session state

How to work with session state items in a controller

The ISession interface provides methods that allow you to set, get, and remove items from session state. The table in figure 9-3 presents some of these methods. Here, the two set methods allow you to store an int or a string in session state, the two get methods allow you to retrieve an int or a string from session state, and the remove method allows you to remove an item from session state.

All of the methods in this figure accept a key as the first argument. This key is a string that uniquely identifies a key/value pair in session state. The set methods also accept an int or string value as the second argument. This value is stored as the value part of the key/value pair in session state.

Both of the get methods return nullable types. In other words, they return a string or a nullable int. As a result, if no value in session state is associated with the specified key, these methods return null.

The Controller class includes a property named HttpContext that's of the HttpContext type. This class contains information about the current HTTP request. One of its properties, Session, is an implementation of the ISession interface. As a result, you can use this property to work with the items in session state.

The first code example in this figure shows how you can use the Session object. Here, the first statement uses the GetInt32() method of the Session property to retrieve an int value. The second statement increments that value. And the third statement uses the SetInt32() method of the Session property to store the updated int value in session state.

How to get session state values in a view

A view provides a property named Context that's of the HttpContext type. So, you can use its Session property to work with the items in session state.

The last two code examples in figure 9-3 show how to use the Context property of the view to work with session state. The first example presents a Razor code block that uses the GetInt32() method of the Session property to retrieve the int value from session state. The second code example also retrieves the int value from session state, but it uses an inline Razor expression within a <div> element. As a result, the <div> element displays the int value on the web page.

Methods of the ISession interface that set, get, and remove items

Method	Description
`SetInt32(key, value)`	Stores the int value in the session object and associates it with the specified key.
`SetString(key, value)`	Stores the string value in the session object and associates it with the specified key.
`GetInt32(key)`	Returns the int value associated with the specified key, or null if there is no value.
`GetString(key)`	Returns the string value associated with the specified key, or null if there is no value.
`Remove(key)`	Removes the value associated with the specified key if the key is found.

An action method that gets and sets a session state value

```
public ViewResult Index() {
    int num = HttpContext.Session.GetInt32("num");
    num += 1;
    HttpContext.Session.SetInt32("num", num);
    return View();
}
```

A Razor code block that gets a session state value

```
@{
    int num = Context.Session.GetInt32("num");
}
```

A Razor expression that gets a session state value

```
<div>@Context.Session.GetInt32("num")</div>
```

Description

- The HttpContext class has a property named Session that implements the ISession interface, which provides methods for setting, getting, and removing items in session state.
- A controller has an HttpContext property that has a data type of HttpContext.
- A view has a Context property that has a data type of HttpContext.
- In ASP.NET Core MVC, session state can only store int and string values. However, you can extend session state so it can store more complex types as shown in the next figure.

Figure 9-3   How to work with session state items in controllers and views

How to use JSON to store objects in session state

The ISession interface provides methods for storing string and int values but doesn't provide methods for storing more complex data types. To get around this limitation, you can *serialize* an object of a complex type by converting it to a string and storing that string in session state. Later, you can *deserialize* the object by converting its string back into an object.

JSON (JavaScript Object Notation) is a data format that's often used for serialization. Historically, .NET programmers have relied on third-party libraries such as Newtonsoft Json.NET to work with JSON. However, .NET Core 3.0 and later provide a native JSON library that you can use to work with JSON. The easiest way to use this library is to include a using directive for the namespace that contains it, as shown in the first code example in figure 9-4.

To serialize and deserialize objects, you use the two static methods of the JsonSerializer class shown in the table in this figure. Here, the Serialize() method accepts an object of any data type and returns a JSON string, and the Deserialize<T>() method accepts a JSON string and returns an object of the specified type.

The first code example below the table shows how to store a Team object in session state as a JSON string. Here, the first statement creates a Team object with values for its TeamID and Name properties. Then, the second statement uses the Serialize() method to convert the Team object to a JSON string and store it in a string variable named json. At this point, the json variable contains the following string:

```
{"TeamID":"sea","Name":"Seattle Seahawks","Conference":null,
"Division":null,"LogoImage":""}
```

Finally, the third statement stores the string in session state by passing the json variable to the SetString() method of the Session property.

The next code example shows how to retrieve a JSON string from session state and convert it back to a Team object. Here, the first statement calls the GetString() method of the ISession interface to retrieve the JSON string from session state and store it in a variable named json. Then, the second statement calls the Deserialize<Team>() method to convert the JSON string to a Team object.

When you call the Serialize() method, you don't need to explicitly specify the data type. That's because Serialize() can infer the type based on the type of the argument it receives. However, when you call the Deserialize<T>() method, you must specify the data type. That's because this method can't infer the data type from the string argument it receives.

Sometimes, you may not want to serialize all the properties of a class. For instance, a property might contain sensitive data or be based on values that are already serialized. In these cases, you can mark the property that you don't want to serialize with the JsonIgnore attribute, as shown in the last code example.

A using directive that imports the JSON library

```
using System.Text.Json;
```

Two static methods of the JsonSerializer class

Method	Description
`Serialize(object)`	Converts an object to a JSON string.
`Deserialize<T>(string)`	Converts a JSON string to an object of type T.

Code in an action method that sets a Team object in session state

```
Team team = new Team { TeamID = "sea", Name = "Seattle Seahawks" };
string json = JsonSerializer.Serialize(team);
HttpContext.Session.SetString("team", json);
```

Code in an action method that gets a Team object from session state

```
string json = HttpContext.Session.GetString("team");
Team team = JsonSerializer.Deserialize<Team>(json);
```

How to mark a class property so it's not included in the serialization

```
using System.Text.Json.Serialization;
...
public class User
{
    public string FirstName { get; set; } = string.Empty;
    public string LastName { get; set; } = string.Empty;
    [JsonIgnore]
    public string FullName => FirstName + " " + LastName;
}
```

Description

- *JSON* (*JavaScript Object Notation*) is a data format that facilitates the transfer of data.

- To *serialize* .NET objects to JSON strings and back again, you can use C#'s native JSON library, which is in the System.Text namespace.

- You can use the JsonIgnore attribute to mark properties in a class that you don't want to serialize. This attribute is in the System.Text.Json.Serialization namespace.

Figure 9-4   How to use JSON to store objects in session state

How to encapsulate session values

So far, this chapter has shown some low-level techniques for working with session state that are effective but lead to unwieldy code that can be hard to read. That's because you have to include using directives, and the method calls for both the HttpContext class and the JsonSerializer class are long. In addition, these techniques require that you use keys to access your session state items. These keys can be hard to remember from one file to the next and are prone to typos that you don't discover until runtime.

That's why the next two figures present two techniques that you can use to make it easier to work with session state. Both of these techniques *encapsulate* the using directives, method calls, and string keys in one place. As a result, these statements aren't scattered throughout your app. In addition, you can use techniques like these with TempData and cookies.

How to extend the ISession interface

Figure 9-5 shows how to add extension methods to the ISession interface. Here, the first code example presents a static class with two generic extension methods named SetObject<T>() and GetObject<T>(). The file that contains this class starts with a using directive for the JSON library. Note that the figure uses an ellipsis (…) to indicate that the namespace statement for this class isn't shown.

Within the class, the set method uses the Serialize() method of the JsonSerializer class to store an object of type T in session state, and the get method uses the Deserialize<T>() method to retrieve an object of type T from session state. Note that if an item isn't found in session state with the key that's passed to the get method, the default value of the type is returned. Because that value may be null, the return type for the method is nullable.

The second code example shows how to use these extension methods in a controller or a view. In the controller, the first statement uses a key of "team" to get a Team object from session state. If no Team object exists for this key, the code creates a new Team object. Then, the second statement changes the name that's stored in the Team object, and the third statement sets the Team object in session state with a key of "team".

In the view, the statement in the Razor code block gets the Team object that's stored with a key of "team". This works similarly to the controller code, except that it uses the Context property of the view to access the Session property, not the HttpContext property of the controller.

The third code example also shows how to use these extension methods in a controller or a view, but it works with a list of Team objects instead of a single Team object. The main difference here is that the second statement in the controller adds a new Team object to the list instead of changing the name for a team object.

When working with the extensions, the call to the SetObject<T>() method doesn't explicitly specify the data type. That's because the compiler can infer

Two extension methods for the ISession interface

```
using System.Text.Json;
...
public static class SessionExtensions
{
    public static void SetObject<T>(this ISession session,
                                    string key, T value)
    {
        session.SetString(key, JsonSerializer.Serialize(value));
    }

    public static T? GetObject<T>(this ISession session, string key)
    {
        var json = session.GetString(key);
        if (string.IsNullOrEmpty(json))
        {
            return default(T);
        }
        else
        {
            return JsonSerializer.Deserialize<T>(json);
        }
    }
}
```

Code that uses the extension methods to work with a single team

In a controller

```
var team = HttpContext.Session.GetObject<Team>("team") ?? new Team();
team.Name = "Seattle Seahawks";
HttpContext.Session.SetObject("team", team);
```

In a view

```
@{
    var team = Context.Session.GetObject<Team>("team") ?? new Team();
}
```

Code that uses the extension methods to work with a list of teams

In a controller

```
var teams = HttpContext.Session.GetObject<List<Team>>("teams") ??
            new List<Team>();
teams.Add(new Team { TeamID = "gb", Name = "Green Bay Packers" });
HttpContext.Session.SetObject("teams", teams);
```

In a view

```
@{
    var teams = Context .Session.GetObject<List<Team>>("teams") ??
            new List<Team>();
}
```

Description

- To make it easier to store objects in session state, you can add extension methods to the ISession interface.

Figure 9-5   How to extend the ISession interface

it based on the type of the second argument. However, the compiler can't infer the type for the GetObject<T>() method because it always receives a string argument.

How to use a wrapper class

Although the code in the previous figure was an improvement over the code in figure 9-4, it's still unwieldy. That's why figure 9-6 shows how to create a wrapper class for all the session state code for your app. A *wrapper class* is any class that "wraps up" or encapsulates the functionality of another class or component. For example, the MySession class encapsulates the method calls and string keys necessary to work with an ISession object and its extension methods. As a result, these statements aren't scattered throughout your app. In addition, you can use a similar technique to work with TempData and cookies.

The first code example presents the wrapper class named MySession. To start, this class defines a constant value for the "teams" key. Next, it defines a constructor that receives an ISession argument and stores it in a private property named session. Finally, it defines two methods named GetTeams() and SetTeams() that use the ISession extension methods from the last figure to store and retrieve a list of Team objects in session state.

The second code example shows how to use the MySession class in a controller or a view. In the controller, this code starts by passing the Session property of the HttpContext property to the constructor to create a MySession object. After that, it calls the GetTeams() method to get a list of Team objects from session state, adds a new Team object to the list, and calls the SetTeams() method to store the new list in session state. This code is a significant improvement over the third example of the last figure.

In the view, the first statement in the Razor code block creates the MySession object. This works similarly to the controller code except that it uses the Context property of the view, not the HttpContext property of the controller. Then, the second statement calls the GetTeams() method of the MySession object to get a list of Team objects.

A wrapper class that encapsulates the code for working with session state

```
public class MySession
{
    private const string TeamsKey = "teams";

    private ISession session { get; set; }
    public MySession(ISession sess) => session = sess;

    public List<Team> GetTeams() =>
        session.GetObject<List<Team>>(TeamsKey) ?? new List<Team>();

    public void SetTeams(List<Team> teams) =>
        session.SetObject(TeamsKey, teams);
}
```

Code that uses the wrapper class to work with a list of teams

In a controller

```
var session = new MySession(HttpContext.Session);
var teams = session.GetTeams();
teams.Add(new Team { TeamID = "gb", Name = "Green Bay Packers" });
session.SetTeams(teams);
```

In a view

```
@{
    var session = new MySession(Context.Session);
    var teams = session.GetTeams();
}
```

Description

- To make it easier to work with session state in your app, you can create a wrapper class that encapsulates the using directives, method calls, and string keys in one place.

- A wrapper class can call extension methods from the ISession interface like the ones shown in the previous figure.

Figure 9-6   How to use a wrapper class

The NFL Teams 3.0 app

The next few topics present a version of the NFL Teams app that keeps track of a user's favorite teams in session state. Since this app updates the NFL Teams app that was presented in chapter 8, this chapter only presents code that is new or changed. If you haven't read chapter 8 yet, you should at least review that chapter before you continue.

The user interface

The first screen in figure 9-7 shows the Home page after a user has clicked the "Add to Favorites" button from the Details page for the Green Bay Packers to add that team to their list of favorites.

As you recall from chapter 8, the message that indicates a new team has been added to favorites only displays immediately after the team is added. If the user takes any other action on the Home page, such as selecting a new conference, this message disappears. That's because this message is transferred via TempData, so it's automatically removed after it's read.

There are two new things to notice about this Home page. First, the Home page displays a "My Favorite Teams" link that the user can click to view the teams that have been added to their favorites. To the right of this link, a Bootstrap badge displays a count of the user's favorite teams. This badge is displayed until the user closes the browser, the session times out, or the user clears their favorites. That's because the user's favorite teams are stored in session state in this version of the NFL Teams app.

Second, if the user returns to the Home page after displaying a team page or the Favorites page, the Home page displays the same conference and division that were selected the last time this page was displayed. That's because the IDs of the selected conference and division are also stored in session state in this version of the NFL Teams app.

The second screen in this figure shows the Favorites page after two teams have been added to favorites. This page is displayed when the user clicks on the "My Favorite Teams" link on the Home page. This page retrieves the user's favorite teams from session state and displays them. It also includes a button to return to the Home page, and a button to clear all the teams from the Favorites page. When the user clicks this second button, all the Team objects are removed from session state.

The Home page after a team has been added to favorites

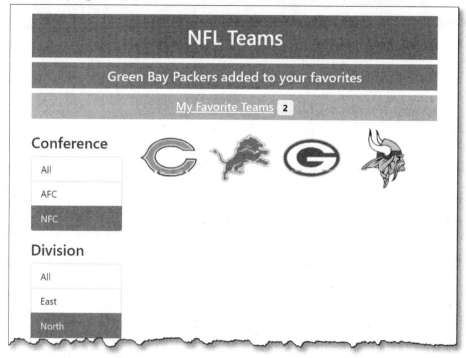

The Favorites page

Description

- This version of the NFL Teams app stores the conference and division the user has selected, as well as any teams the user has added to their favorites, in session state.

Figure 9-7   The user interface of the NFL Teams 3.0 app

The session classes

Figure 9-8 presents two classes that have been added to the model layer for this version of the NFL Teams app. The SessionExtensions class starts with a using directive for the JSON library. Then, this class defines two generic extension methods for the ISession interface. This code is similar to the code presented earlier in this chapter, but it uses a conditional operator instead of an if statement in the GetObject<T>() method.

The NFLSession class encapsulates all the session state calls that the NFL Teams app needs to make. To start, it defines four private constants for key names. The use of constants like this decreases the chance of typos and errors when working with session state keys. It also lets you use IntelliSense when you're typing keys.

After defining the constants, this class defines a constructor that accepts an argument of the ISession type. Then, it stores the value it receives in a private property named session.

After the constructor, this class defines several methods that store and retrieve session state items. Note that all of the getter methods either include a default value or use the (?) operator to define a nullable type. This helps avoid null reference errors, as well as null reference warnings from Visual Studio.

The SetMyTeams() method accepts a list of Team objects. Then, it uses the SetObject() extension method of the SessionExtensions class to store the list of teams in session state. In addition, it uses the SetInt32() method of the ISession interface to store a count of the teams in session state. This class stores the count of teams separately so the app doesn't have to retrieve and deserialize the entire list when it only needs a count of the teams.

The GetMyTeams() method and GetMyTeamCount() method retrieve the data stored by the SetMyTeams() method. Here, GetMyTeams() gets a list of the teams, and GetMyTeamCount() retrieves the count of teams. The GetMyTeams() methods return a default value if there's no value in session state. By contrast, the GetMyTeamCount() method returns a nullable int, which is what the GetInt32() method of the ISession interface returns. That means that the GetMyTeamsCount() method will return null if there's no count value in session.

The SetActiveConf() method uses the SetString() method of the ISession interface to store a string in session state, and the GetActiveConf() method uses the GetString() method to retrieve it. The SetActiveDiv() and GetActiveDiv() methods work similarly.

Finally, the RemoveMyTeams() method uses the Remove() method of the ISession interface to remove all data about favorite teams from session state. To do that, it removes both the list and count of the favorite teams.

The SessionExtensions class

```
using System.Text.Json;
...
public static class SessionExtensions
{
    public static void SetObject<T>(this ISession session,
        string key, T value)
    {
        session.SetString(key, JsonSerializer.Serialize(value));
    }

    public static T? GetObject<T>(this ISession session, string key)
    {
        var json = session.GetString(key);
        return (string.IsNullOrEmpty(json)) ? default(T) :
            JsonSerializer.Deserialize<T>(json);
    }
}
```

The NFLSession class

```
public class NFLSession
{
    private const string TeamsKey = "myteams";
    private const string CountKey = "teamcount";
    private const string ConfKey = "conf";
    private const string DivKey = "div";

    private ISession session { get; set; }
    public NFLSession(ISession session) => this.session = session;

    public void SetMyTeams(List<Team> teams) {
        session.SetObject(TeamsKey, teams);
        session.SetInt32(CountKey, teams.Count);
    }
    public List<Team> GetMyTeams() =>
        session.GetObject<List<Team>>(TeamsKey) ?? new List<Team>();
    public int? GetMyTeamCount() => session.GetInt32(CountKey);

    public void SetActiveConf(string activeConf) =>
        session.SetString(ConfKey, activeConf);
    public string GetActiveConf() =>
        session.GetString(ConfKey) ?? string.Empty;

    public void SetActiveDiv(string activeDiv) =>
        session.SetString(DivKey, activeDiv);
    public string GetActiveDiv() =>
        session.GetString(DivKey) ?? string.Empty;

    public void RemoveMyTeams() {
        session.Remove(TeamsKey);
        session.Remove(CountKey);
    }
}
```

Figure 9-8   The session classes

The view model

Figure 9-9 presents the TeamsViewModel class, which has been updated to include a property of type Team that stores a single Team object. As you'll see in a minute, this allows the Details() action method of the Home controller to return a view model that includes a Team object, as well as IDs for the active conference and division, to the view that displays the details for a team.

The rest of this class is the same as you saw in chapter 8. To review, it has properties that hold the IDs of the active conference and division, properties that hold collections of Team, Conference, and Division objects, and helper methods that the view can use to mark the selected conference and division as active.

The Home controller

Figure 9-9 also presents the Home controller for this version of the app. Here, the Home controller uses session state to store and retrieve the active conference and division IDs.

The Index() action method starts by creating an NFLSession object. To do that, it passes the Session property of the controller's HttpContext property to the constructor of the NFLSession class. Then, the code calls methods of the NFLSession class to store the IDs of the active conference and division in session state. The rest of the code is the same as in figure 8-11. To review, it populates the TeamsViewModel object with data from the database and transfers the view model to the view.

The Details() action method also starts by creating an NFLSession object. Then, it creates a view model object, populates it with team data from the database and the active conference and division IDs from session state, and passes the view model to the view.

The view model

```
public class TeamsViewModel
{
    // add a property to store a single team
    public Team Team { get; set; } = new Team();

    // rest of code same as figure 8-10
}
```

The Home controller

```
public class HomeController : Controller
{
    private TeamContext context;
    public HomeController(TeamContext ctx) => context = ctx;

    public ViewResult Index(TeamsViewModel model)
    {
        // store selected conference and division in session
        var session = new NFLSession(HttpContext.Session);
        session.SetActiveConf(model.ActiveConf);
        session.SetActiveDiv(model.ActiveDiv);

        // populate TeamsViewModel as in figure 8-11

        return View(model);
    }

    public ViewResult Details(string id)
    {
        // get selected conference and division from session
        // and pass them to the view in the view model
        var session = new NFLSession(HttpContext.Session);
        var model = new TeamsViewModel
        {
            Team = context.Teams
                .Include(t => t.Conference)
                .Include(t => t.Division)
                .FirstOrDefault(t => t.TeamID == id) ?? new Team(),
            ActiveConf = session.GetActiveConf(),
            ActiveDiv = session.GetActiveDiv()
        };
        return View(model);
    }
}
```

Description

- The TeamsViewModel class is updated to include a property for a single Team object.

- The Index() action method of the Home controller is updated to store the selected conference and division in session state.

- The Details() action method of the Home controller is updated to return a view model object to the view. The view model object contains a Team object for the selected team and the active conference and division from session state.

Figure 9-9   The TeamsViewModel class and the Home controller

The layout

Figure 9-10 presents the code for the Razor layout for this new version of the NFL Teams app. This view works much like the layout presented in the previous chapter, but it displays a link to the Favorites page and the number of teams that have been added to favorites. However, it doesn't display this link and team count if the app is already displaying the Favorites page. To determine which page is currently displayed, the layout uses the ViewContext property described in chapter 7 to get the name of the current controller.

If the current controller isn't the Favorites controller, the Razor code block starts by creating a new NFLSession object and passing it the Session property of the Context property. Then, the code uses the GetMyTeamCount() method of the NFLSession object to get the number of teams in session state and stores it in a nullable int variable named count. This variable must be nullable because the GetMyTeamCount() method returns null if session state doesn't contain a team count.

Next, the layout uses a Razor if statement to see if the nullable count variable has a value. If it does, the view constructs an <h5> element that contains an <a> element and a <span> element. The <a> element redirects to the Index action method of the Favorites controller. The <span> element displays the number of favorite teams and is styled as a Bootstrap badge.

The layout

```
@{
    string controller =
        ViewContext.RouteData.Values["controller"]?.ToString() ?? "";
}
<!DOCTYPE html>
<html>
<head>
    <meta name="viewport" content="width=device-width, initial-scale=1.0" />
    <link href=
        "~/lib/bootstrap/dist/css/bootstrap.min.css" rel="stylesheet" />
    <link href="~/css/site.css" rel="stylesheet" />
    <title>@ViewBag.Title</title>
</head>
<body>
    <div class="container">
        <header class="text-center text-white">
            <h1 class="bg-primary mt-3 p-3">NFL Teams</h1>

            @* show any message in TempData *@
            @if (TempData.Keys.Contains("message"))
            {
                <h4 class="bg-success p--2">@TempData["message"]</h4>
            }

            @* show link to Favorites page unless on Favorites page *@
            @if (controller != "Favorites")
            {
                var session = new NFLSession(Context.Session);
                int? count = session.GetMyTeamCount();

                @* if there are fave teams in session, display faves link *@
                @if (count.HasValue)
                {
                    <h5 class="bg-info p-2">
                        <a asp-controller="Favorites" asp-action="Index"
                            class="text-white">My Favorite Teams</a>
                        <span class="badge bg-light text-black">@count</span>
                    </h5>
                }
            }
        </header>
        <main>
            @RenderBody()
        </main>
    </div>
</body>
</html>
```

Description

- The layout checks whether the current page is the Favorites page. If not and there are favorites in session state, it displays a link to the Favorites page along with the number of favorite teams in a Bootstrap badge.

Figure 9-10   The layout

The Home/Details view

Figure 9-11 presents the code for the Home/Details view. In this version of the NFL Teams app, the model for the Details view is a TeamsViewModel object rather than a Team object. Remember from figure 9-9 that the controller populates the view model with team data from the database, and with the active conference and division IDs from session state.

The rest of the Details view is the same as in chapter 8, with one difference. Now, the Razor code that builds the "Return to Home Page" link can use the ActiveConf and ActiveDiv properties of the view model to add route segments for the active conference and division. Then, when the user clicks this link, the Home page displays the conference and division the user previously selected.

The Home/Details view

```
@model TeamsViewModel
@{
    ViewData["Title"] = "Team Details";
}

<h2 class="text-center p-2">Team Details</h2>

<div class="row">
    <div class="col">
        <ul class="list-group text-center">
            <li class="list-group-item">
                <img src="~/images/@Model.Team.LogoImage" alt="" />
                <h3>@Model.Team.Name</h3>
            </li>
            <li class="list-group-item">
                <h4>Conference: @Model.Team.Conference.Name</h4>
            </li>
            <li class="list-group-item">
                <h4>Division: @Model.Team.Division.Name</h4>
            </li>
            <li class="list-group-item">
                <form asp-action="Add" asp-controller="Favorites"
                    method="post">
                    <a asp-action="Index" class="btn btn-primary"
                        asp-route-activeConf="@Model.ActiveConf"
                        asp-route-activeDiv="@Model.ActiveDiv">
                        Return to Home Page
                    </a>
                    <button type="submit" class="btn btn-primary">
                        Add to Favorites
                    </button>
                    <input type="hidden" asp-for="Team.TeamID" />
                </form>
            </li>
        </ul>
    </div>
</div>
```

Description

- The Details view is updated to bind to a TeamsViewModel object, which is passed from the controller.

- This view model contains the active conference and division that the controller retrieved from session state.

- The Details view adds route segments for the active conference and division to the Return to Home Page link so that page can display the previously selected conference and division.

Figure 9-11   The Home/Details view

The Favorites controller

Figure 9-12 presents the Favorites controller of the NFL Teams app. This controller has an Index() action method that handles GET requests and Add() and Delete() action methods that handle POST requests.

The app calls the Index() action method when the user clicks on the "My Favorite Teams" link. This action method starts by creating a new NFLSession object and passing it the Session property of the controller's HttpContext property. Then, it creates a new TeamsViewModel object and uses the NFLSession object to load it with data from session state. Specifically, it gets the active conference and division IDs and the list of favorite teams. Finally, it transfers this view model to the view.

The app calls the Add() action method when the user clicks on the "Add to Favorites" button on the Details page. This method receives the TeamID that's posted by the form and stores it in the TeamID property of the Team object that's the parameter of this method. Then, the code for this method starts by using the TeamID property to get the rest of the data for the selected team from the database.

After getting data from the database, this code creates a new NFLSession object. Then, it calls the GetMyTeams() method of that object to retrieve the list of favorite teams from session state, it adds the selected team to the list, and it calls the SetMyTeams() method to store the updated list in session state and update the team count in session state.

After updating session state, the code stores a message in TempData about the team that was just added to favorites. The layout displays this message as shown in figure 9-10. Then, after the layout reads the message, the message doesn't persist in TempData. This shows how TempData is ideal for storing temporary data that you don't want to store in session state.

Finally, the code redirects the user back to the Index() action of the Home controller. To do that, it gets the ID values of the active conference and division from session state. Then, it builds an anonymous object to pass those IDs to the activeConf and activeDiv route parameters of the URL.

The app calls the Delete() action method when the user clicks on the "Clear Favorites" button on the Favorites page. Because it doesn't need any data from the page to do its work, this action method doesn't accept any parameters.

The Delete() action method starts by creating a new NFLSession object and passing it the Session property of the controller's HttpContext property. Then, it calls the RemoveMyTeams() method of the NFLSession object. This causes both the list of favorite teams and the team count to be removed from session state.

After removing this data from session state, the code stores a message in TempData that tells the user that their favorite teams have been cleared. Finally, the code redirects the user back to the Index() action of the Home controller using the same code as the Add() action method.

The Favorites controller

```
public class FavoritesController : Controller
{
    private TeamContext context;
    public FavoritesController(TeamContext ctx) => context = ctx;

    [HttpGet]
    public ViewResult Index()
    {
        var session = new NFLSession(HttpContext.Session);
        var model = new TeamsViewModel
        {
            ActiveConf = session.GetActiveConf(),
            ActiveDiv = session.GetActiveDiv(),
            Teams = session.GetMyTeams()
        };
        return View(model);
    }

    [HttpPost]
    public RedirectToActionResult Add(Team team)
    {
        team = context.Teams
                .Include(t => t.Conference)
                .Include(t => t.Division)
                .Where(t => t.TeamID == team.TeamID)
                .FirstOrDefault() ?? new Team();

        var session = new NFLSession(HttpContext.Session);
        var teams = session.GetMyTeams();
        teams.Add(team);
        session.SetMyTeams(teams);

        // notify user and redirect to home page
        TempData["message"] = $"{team.Name} added to your favorites";
        return RedirectToAction("Index", "Home",
            new {
                ActiveConf = session.GetActiveConf(),
                ActiveDiv = session.GetActiveDiv()
            });
    }

    [HttpPost]
    public RedirectToActionResult Delete()
    {
        var session = new NFLSession(HttpContext.Session);
        session.RemoveMyTeams();

        // notify user and redirect to home page
        TempData["message"] = "Favorite teams cleared";
        return RedirectToAction("Index", "Home",
            new {
                ActiveConf = session.GetActiveConf(),
                ActiveDiv = session.GetActiveDiv()
            });
    }
}
```

Figure 9-12   The Favorites controller

The Favorites/Index view

Figure 9-13 presents the code for the Favorites/Index view for this version of the NFL Teams app. The model object for this view is a TeamsViewModel object. As you may recall, that's what the Index() action method of the Favorites controller transfers to it.

In this view, the HTML consists of two <div> elements. The first uses the Bootstrap text-center class to center the <h2>, <a>, and <button> elements within the <div> element. It also includes a <form> element that posts to the Delete() action method of the current controller, which is the Favorites controller. Since the <a> and <button> elements are both within the <form> element, they display side-by-side.

In the first <div> element, the <a> element uses Bootstrap classes to style the link like a button. In addition, it links back to the Home page. To do that, it uses the properties of the model object to add the route parameters for the active conference and division IDs.

The submit button in this <div> element starts a POST request to the Delete() action method. This code doesn't include a hidden field or any other element with data that posts to the server. For this app, that isn't necessary because the Delete() action method doesn't need any data from the page.

The second <div> element uses Bootstrap classes to create a row with one indented column. The column displays the favorite teams in a <ul> element styled as a Bootstrap list-group. Within the <ul> element, a Razor foreach statement loops through all the Team objects in the Teams property of the model. For each team, it adds an item to the list group where each item displays that team's logo, name, conference, and division.

The Favorites/Index view

```
@model TeamsViewModel
@{
    ViewData["Title"] = "Favorites";
}

<div class="text-center mb-4">
    <h2>My Favorites</h2>
    <form asp-action="Delete" method="post">
        <a asp-action="Index" asp-controller="Home" class="btn btn-primary"
            asp-route-activeConf ="@Model.ActiveConf"
            asp-route-activeDiv="@Model.ActiveDiv">
            Back to Home Page
        </a>
        <button type="submit" class="btn btn-primary">
            Clear Favorites
        </button>
    </form>
</div>

<div class="row">
    <div class="col-8 offset-2">
        <ul class="list-group">
            @foreach (Team team in Model.Teams)
            {
                <li class="list-group-item">
                    <div class="row">
                        <div class="col-sm-4">
                            <img src="~/images/@team.LogoImage" alt="" />
                        </div>
                        <div class="col-sm-4">
                            @team.Name
                        </div>
                        <div class="col-sm-4">
                            @team.Conference.Name @team.Division.Name
                        </div>
                    </div>
                </li>
            }
        </ul>
    </div>
</div>
```

Description

- Like the Home/Details view, the Favorites/Index view gets a TeamsViewModel object from the controller and adds route segments for the currently selected conference and division to the link that navigates back to the Home page.

Figure 9-13   The Favorites/Index view

How to work with cookies

A *cookie* is a key/value pair that's stored in the user's browser or on the user's disk. A web app sends a cookie to a browser via an HTTP response. Then, each time the browser sends an HTTP request to the server, it sends that cookie back.

A *session cookie* is stored in the browser's memory and exists only for the duration of the browser session. A *persistent cookie*, on the other hand, is stored on the user's disk and is retained until the cookie's expiration date, or until the user clears the cookie.

How to work with session cookies

The first table in figure 9-14 presents two properties of the Controller class that you can use to work with cookies. The Request property represents the current HTTP request sent from the browser to the server, and the Response property represents the current HTTP response sent from the server to the browser. Each of these properties has a Cookies collection.

Below the table, the first two code examples show how to use the Response property to set and delete a cookie. The first example sets a cookie by calling the Append() method of the Cookies property and passing it two string values. The first string specifies the unique key, and the second string specifies the value to be stored.

The second example deletes a cookie by calling the Delete() method of the Cookies property and passing it a single string value. This string value specifies the key of the cookie to delete.

The third example shows how to use the Request property to retrieve, or get, a cookie. This code retrieves a value from the Cookies collection by specifying the associated key for the value. To do that, it uses brackets to specify the key. In other words, it doesn't use parentheses because it isn't calling a method.

How to work with persistent cookies

The second table presents some of the properties of the CookieOptions class. This class allows you to change some of the settings of a cookie.

To set a persistent cookie, you need to set the Expires property of the CookieOptions class. To do that, you create a CookieOptions object, set its Expires property to a DateTime value in the future, and include the CookieOptions object when you create a cookie. This is shown by the last example in figure 9-14. To start, it creates a new CookieOptions object with an Expires property of 30 days from the current date and time. Then, it passes that object to the Append() method as the third argument.

Two properties of the Controller class

Property	Description
Request	Represents the HTTP request sent from the browser to the server.
Response	Represents the HTTP response sent from the server to the browser.

Code that sets a session cookie

```
Response.Cookies.Append("username", "Grace");
```

Code that deletes a cookie

```
Response.Cookies.Delete("username");
```

Code that gets a cookie

```
string value = Request.Cookies["username"];  // brackets, not parentheses
```

Some of the properties of the CookieOptions class

Property	Description
Domain	The domain to associate the cookie with. The default value is null.
Expires	The cookie's expiration date and time. The default value is null.
Path	The cookie's path. The default path is "/".
MaxAge	The maximum age for the cookie. The default value is null.
SameSite	The value for the cookie's SameSite attribute. The values can be Lax or Strict. The default value is Lax.
Secure	Indicates whether the cookie can be transmitted over HTTPS only. The default value is false.

Code that sets a persistent cookie

```
var options = new CookieOptions { Expires = DateTime.Now.AddDays(30) };
Response.Cookies.Append("username", "Grace", options);
```

Description

- A *cookie* is a key/value pair that's stored in the user's browser or on the user's disk.
- A web app sends a cookie to a browser via an HTTP response. Then, each time the browser sends an HTTP request to the server, it sends that cookie back.
- A *session cookie* is stored in the browser's memory and exists only for the duration of the browser session.
- A *persistent cookie* is stored on the user's disk and is retained until the cookie's expiration date or until the user clears the cookie.
- To set or delete a cookie, use the Cookies property of the controller's Response property.
- To get a cookie, use the Cookies property of the controller's Request property.
- To set a persistent cookie, use a CookieOptions object that expires in the future.

Figure 9-14   How to work with cookies

The NFL Teams 4.0 app

Now that you know how to work with cookies, you're ready to see a version of the NFL Teams app after it has been updated to store the IDs of the user's favorite teams in a persistent cookie. That way, the app "remembers" its users' favorite teams, even when they close their browsers and return to this app later.

The cookies class

Figure 9-15 presents the NFLCookies class. This class encapsulates the code that the NFL Teams app uses to work with cookies. It starts by declaring two private constants. The first stores the key for accessing the team IDs, and the second stores the delimiter value (in this case, a dash) that's used to separate the team IDs.

The NFLCookies class has two constructors. The first accepts an object of the IRequestCookieCollection type and stores it in the private property named requestCookies. The second accepts an object of the IResponseCookies type and stores it in a private property named responseCookies. As a result, to create an NFLCookies object, you can pass it the cookie collection from a Request or Response object.

After the constructors, this class defines three methods. The first one sets a persistent cookie, the second one gets that cookie, and the third one removes the cookie from the user's browser.

The SetMyTeamIds() method accepts a list of Team objects. Then, it uses the LINQ Select() method to get a list of team ID values from that list of Team objects. Next, it uses the Delimiter constant to join the list of strings into a single string where each string is separated by a dash. After that, the code initializes a CookieOptions object with an Expires property that's set to 30 days in the future. Finally, it deletes any previous cookie and stores the new one.

The GetMyTeamIds() method retrieves the persistent cookie that was set by the SetMyTeamIds() method and assigns it to a string variable. Then, it checks if that string is null or empty. If so, it returns an empty string array. Otherwise, it uses the Delimiter constant to split the string variable and return a string array of team ID values.

The RemoveMyTeamIds() method uses the Delete() method of the collection of response cookies to remove the persistent cookie. To do that, this method uses the responseCookies private object.

The NFLCookies class

```
public class NFLCookies
{
    private const string TeamsKey = "myteams";
    private const string Delimiter = "-";

    private IRequestCookieCollection requestCookies { get; set; } = null!;
    private IResponseCookies responseCookies { get; set; } = null!;

    public NFLCookies(IRequestCookieCollection cookies)
    {
        requestCookies = cookies;
    }
    public NFLCookies(IResponseCookies cookies)
    {
        responseCookies = cookies;
    }

    public void SetMyTeamIds(List<Team> myteams)
    {
        List<string> ids = myteams.Select(t => t.TeamID).ToList();
        string idsString = String.Join(Delimiter, ids);
        CookieOptions options = new CookieOptions {
            Expires = DateTime.Now.AddDays(30)
        };
        RemoveMyTeamIds();       // delete old cookie first
        responseCookies.Append(TeamsKey, idsString, options);
    }

    public string[] GetMyTeamsIds()
    {
        string cookie = requestCookies[MyTeams] ?? String.Empty;
        if (string.IsNullOrEmpty(cookie))
            return Array.Empty<string>();   // empty string array
        else
            return cookie.Split(Delimiter);
    }

    public void RemoveMyTeamIds()
    {
        responseCookies.Delete(TeamsKey);
    }
}
```

Description

- This app stores the IDs of the user's favorite teams in a persistent cookie.
- The NFLCookies class has an overloaded constructor that accepts the Cookies collection from the Request object or from the Response object.

Figure 9-15   The cookies class

The Home controller

Figure 9-16 shows the Index() action method of the Home controller that's been updated to work with cookies. This action method now retrieves the IDs of the user's saved favorite teams from a persistent cookie.

The updated Index() action method starts as it did in figure 9-9. That is, it creates a new NFLSession object and stores the IDs of the active conference and division in session state.

After that, it calls the GetMyTeamCount() method of the NFLSession object and assigns its return value to a nullable int variable named count. Then, the code checks whether the count variable has a value. If it doesn't, it means that session state doesn't contain any favorites data. This is the case, for example, when the web browser is loading the app for the first time or the user hasn't selected any favorites.

If there is no team count in session state, the code creates a new NFLCookies object and passes it the Cookies collection of the controller's Request object. Next, it calls the GetMyTeamIds() method to get a string that contains the team IDs from the persistent cookie and converts that string to a string array of team IDs. Then, it checks the length of the string array. If the string array contains one or more team IDs, this code uses a LINQ query to get data about the user's favorite teams from the database. To do that, the Where() method uses the LINQ Contains() method to determine what team IDs are contained in the string array. Finally, this code stores the list of Team objects in session state.

The rest of the Index() action method is the same as in figure 8-11. To review, this code populates the TeamsViewModel object with conference, division, and team data from the database and then transfers the view model to the view.

The Index() action method of the Home controller

```
public ViewResult Index(TeamsViewModel model)
{
    var session = new NFLSession(HttpContext.Session);
    session.SetActiveConf(model.ActiveConf);
    session.SetActiveDiv(model.ActiveDiv);

    // if no count in session, get cookie and restore fave teams in session
    int? count = session.GetMyTeamCount();
    if (!count.HasValue)
    {
        var cookies = new NFLCookies(Request.Cookies);
        string[] ids = cookies.GetMyTeamIds();

        if (ids.Length > 0)
        {
            var myteams = context.Teams
                .Include(t => t.Conference)
                .Include(t => t.Division)
                .Where(t => ids.Contains(t.TeamID))
                .ToList();
            session.SetMyTeams(myteams);
        }
    }

    // populate TeamsViewModel as in figure 8-11

    return View(model);
}
```

Description

- This app stores the IDs of the user's favorite teams in a persistent cookie.
- The Index() action method of the Home controller uses the cookie collection of the Request object to get the IDs of the user's favorite teams from a persistent cookie and stores the data for the teams in session state.

Figure 9-16　The Home controller

The Favorites controller

Figure 9-17 shows the Add() and Delete() action methods of the Favorites controller that have been updated to work with cookies. These action methods work much like the ones in figure 9-12. This time, though, the Add() action method updates the favorite team data in the persistent cookie after it updates session state, and the Delete() action method removes the persistent cookie after it removes teams from session state.

To update the persistent cookie, the code for the Add() action method creates a new NFLCookies object by passing it the Cookies collection of the controller's Response object. Then, this code calls the SetMyTeamIds() method of the NFLCookies object and passes it the updated list of Team objects.

To remove the persistent cookie, the code for the Delete() action method creates a new NFLCookies object and passes it the Cookies collection of the controller's Response object. Then, this code calls the RemoveMyTeamIds() method of the NFLCookies object.

The Add() action method of the Favorites controller

```
[HttpPost]
public RedirectToActionResult Add(Team team)
{
    team = context.Teams
        .Include(t => t.Conference)
        .Include(t => t.Division)
        .Where(t => t.TeamID == team.TeamID)
        .FirstOrDefault() ?? new Team();

    var session = new NFLSession(HttpContext.Session);
    var cookies = new NFLCookies(Response.Cookies);

    var teams = session.GetMyTeams();
    teams.Add(team);
    session.SetMyTeams(teams);
    cookies.SetMyTeamIds(teams);

    TempData["message"] = $"{team.Name} added to your favorites";

    return RedirectToAction("Index", "Home",
        new {
            ActiveConf = session.GetActiveConf(),
            ActiveDiv = session.GetActiveDiv()
        });
}
```

The Delete() action method of the Favorites controller

```
[HttpPost]
public RedirectToActionResult Delete()
{
    var session = new NFLSession(HttpContext.Session);
    var cookies = new NFLCookies(Response.Cookies);

    session.RemoveMyTeams();
    cookies.RemoveMyTeamIds();

    TempData["message"] = "Favorite teams cleared";

    return RedirectToAction("Index", "Home",
        new {
            ActiveConf = session.GetActiveConf(),
            ActiveDiv = session.GetActiveDiv()
        }
    );
}
```

Description

- The Add() action method uses the cookie collection of the Response object to update the data in the persistent cookie. But first, it updates session state.
- The Delete() action method uses the cookie collection of the Response object to remove the persistent cookie that stores the IDs of the favorite teams. But first, it removes the favorite teams from session state.

Figure 9-17   The Favorites controller

Perspective

The goal of this chapter is to show you how to use ASP.NET Core MVC to work with session state and cookies. If you understand the NFL Teams apps presented in this chapter, you're ready to develop web apps that use session state and cookies. In addition, you should have a solid understanding of when to use TempData, which was presented in the previous chapter, and when to use session state or cookies.

If you develop a production website, it's a good idea to meet the General Data Protection Regulation (GDPR) requirements developed by the European Union (EU). To do that, the users of your website need to consent to your privacy and cookie policy before your website can send non-essential cookies to the browser. Typically, a website gets consent from a user by providing an alert that allows the user to click on an Accept button.

Fortunately, ASP.NET Core provides APIs and templates to help you meet the EU's GDPR requirements. The official documentation for ASP.NET Core explains this in detail and provides sample code that you can use.

Terms

state	wrapper class
stateless protocol	serialize
cookie	deserialize
session state	session cookie
JSON (JavaScript Object Notation)	persistent cookie

Summary

- *State* refers to the current status of the properties, variables, and other data maintained by an app for a single user.

- HTTP is a *stateless protocol*. That means that it doesn't keep track of state between round trips. Once a browser makes a request and receives a response, the app terminates and its state is lost.

- A *cookie* is a key/value pair that's passed to the browser in an HTTP response and stored in the browser or on disk. Then, the cookie is passed back to the server with each subsequent HTTP request.

- *Session state* works by having the server store the session data for a user and by using a cookie to associate the user's browser with the correct session data.

- *JSON (JavaScript Object Notation)* is a data format that facilitates the transfer of data.

- To *serialize* a .NET object to a JSON string, you can use C#'s native JSON library. Later, you can *deserialize* the object by using this library to convert its JSON string back into a .NET object.

- A *session cookie* is stored in the browser's memory and exists only for the duration of the browser session.

- A *persistent cookie* is stored on the user's disk and is retained until the cookie's expiration date or until the user clears the cookie.

Exercise 9-1   Store the user's name in session state

In this exercise, you'll review the NFLTeams app presented in this chapter and update it so it can store the user's name in session state.

Review the NFLTeams app
1. Open the Ch09Ex1NFLTeams web app in the ex_starts directory.
2. Run the app and make sure that you can add and clear favorites, that all pages except the Favorites page display a link to the Favorites page with the number of favorites in the badge if there are favorites, and that the app remembers the conference and division that you select.

Update the models and add a controller
3. In the Models folder, open the NFLSession class and add methods that can get and set the user's name. The method that sets the user's name should remove the user's name from session state if the value it receives is null or an empty string.
4. Open the TeamsViewModel class and update it so it includes a UserName property that can get and set the user's name.
5. Open the Favorites controller. In the Index() action method, add the user's name to the values that the action gets from session and sends to the view.
6. In the Controllers folder, add a new controller class named NameController.
7. In the Name controller, add an Index() action method for GET requests that displays the Name/Index view. This action method should retrieve from session state and pass to the view the same data as the Index() action method of the Favorites controller.
8. In the Name controller, add a Change() action method for POST requests that accepts a TeamsViewModel object. The Change() action method should get the user's name from the view model, set that name in session state, and redirect to the Home page. You can use the Delete() action method of the Favorites controller as a guide, but don't add anything to TempData.

Create the Name/Index view

9.   In the Views folder, create a Name folder.

10.   In the Name folder, create a view named Index that defines a page that can change a user's name. This view should use a TeamsViewModel object as its model, and it should include a form that calls the Change() action method of the Name controller like this:

```
<form asp-action="Change" method="post">
    <input asp-for="UserName" placeholder="Type name here"
        class="mb-3" /><br />
    <!-- you can code a link to the Home page here -->
    <button type="submit" class="btn btn-primary">
        Change Name
    </button>
</form>
```

11.   Note that the asp-for tag helper binds the UserName property to the view model. This makes it easy for the Change() action method to get the user's name from the model.

Update the Favorites/Index view

12.   Open the Favorites/Index view. Before the Clear Favorites button, add this code to display a link that calls the Index() action of the Name controller:

```
<a asp-action="Index" asp-controller="Name" class="btn btn-primary">
    Change Name
</a>
```

13.   Modify the <h2> element so it displays "My Favorites" if the UserName property of the model is null, or "Mary's Favorites" if a name of Mary is stored in the property. To do that, you can use a Razor expression within the <h2> element like this:

```
<h2>@(String.IsNullOrEmpty(Model.UserName)
    ? "My" : Model.UserName + "'s") Favorites</h2>
```

Update the layout view

14.   Open the layout for this app (Views/Shared/_Layout). Note that an NFLSession object is already used to create the "My Favorite Teams" link in an <h5> element.

15.   Modify the <h5> element so it displays "My Favorite Teams" if a name is stored in session state or "Mary's Favorites Teams" if a name of Mary is stored in session state. This should look like the code in step 13, but use the NFLSession object to get the value from session state.

16.   Run the app and add a favorite team. When the Home page is displayed again, the second heading should say "My Favorite Teams".

17.   Navigate to the Favorites page and use the Change Name button to change the user's name to John. When you do, you should be redirected to the Home page and the second heading should say "John's Favorite Teams". In addition, if you navigate back to the Favorites page, its heading should say "John's Favorites".

18.   Navigate to the Favorites page and use the Change Name button again. This time, clear the Name text box to remove the name. Now, the second heading should say "My Favorite Teams". And if you navigate back to the Favorites page, its heading should say "My Favorites".

10

How to work with model binding

In chapter 2, you learned that if you post a strongly-typed view to an action method with a parameter of the same type, MVC automatically populates the parameter object with values from the view. This is known as *model binding*, and this chapter describes how it works in more detail.

An introduction to MVC model binding

In a web app, you often need to retrieve values that have been sent by the browser to the server in either a GET or a POST request. To start, you'll learn how to do that manually by using some of the properties of the Controller class. Then, you'll learn how to use model binding to do the same thing. This leads to simpler code that's easier to maintain. Finally, you'll learn how to use model binding with complex types.

How to use controller properties to retrieve GET and POST data

The first table in figure 10-1 presents two properties of the Controller class. The Request property represents the HTTP request that's been sent from the browser to the server, and the RouteData property represents the MVC route for the current request.

The second table presents two properties of the Request property. The Query property is a dictionary that holds all the values in the URL's query string. The Form property is a dictionary that holds all the values in the body of a POST request.

The third table presents one of the properties of the RouteData property. The Values property is a dictionary that holds all the route data for the current request. The first two values in this dictionary are the name of the current controller and the name of the current action method. After that, it contains any named route parameters.

Below these tables, the code examples show how to use these properties to retrieve data. The first example shows a URL that has a query string parameter with a name of page and a value of 2.

The second example shows an action method that uses the Query property of the Request property to retrieve that value from the query string parameter. Here, the name of the parameter (page) is the key that's used to get the associated value from the dictionary.

The third example shows form data from a POST request that has a parameter with a name of firstname and a value of "Grace". This is similar to query string data, but it's in the body of the HTTP request, not the URL.

The fourth example has an action method that uses the Form property of the Request property to retrieve that value from the form data. Once again, the name of the parameter (firstname) is the key that's used to get the associated value from the dictionary.

The fifth example shows a URL that has a third segment with a value of "all". For the default route, this segment is a route parameter with a name of id.

The sixth example has an action method that uses the Values property of the RouteData property to retrieve the value from that route parameter. Once again, the code uses the name of the route parameter (id) as the key to get the associated value from the dictionary.

Two properties of the Controller class

Property	Description
Request	Represents the HTTP request sent from the browser to the server.
RouteData	Represents the MVC route for the current request.

Two properties of the Request property

Property	Description
Query	A dictionary that holds the query string parameters in the URL.
Form	A dictionary that holds the form values in the body of a POST request.

One property of the RouteData property

Property	Description
Values	A dictionary that holds the route data for the current request, including the current controller, action method, and named route parameters.

A URL with a query string parameter

```
https://localhost:7078/Home/Index?page=2
```

An action method that retrieves the value of the query string parameter

```
public IActionResult Index() {
    ViewBag.Page = Request.Query["page"];
    return View();
}
```

Form data in the body of a POST request

```
firstname=Grace
```

An action method that retrieves the form data

```
public IActionResult Index() {
    ViewBag.FirstName = Request.Form["firstname"];
    return View();
}
```

A URL with a value for the id parameter of the default route

```
https://localhost:7078/Home/Index/all
```

An action method that retrieves the value of the route parameter named id

```
public IActionResult Index() {
    ViewBag.Id = RouteData.Values["id"];
    return View();
}
```

Description

- An HTTP request can pass data from the browser to the server in the query string of the URL or in the body of a POST request.

- MVC can pass data from the browser to the server in the route segments of the URL.

- The Controller class provides several properties that allow you to access this data.

Figure 10-1   How to use controller properties to retrieve GET and POST data

How to use model binding to retrieve GET and POST data

Although you can access form, route, and query string data directly as shown in the previous figure, there are many drawbacks to this approach. First, the references to the Request and RouteData properties can get repetitive. Second, you have to manually type case-sensitive key names that aren't checked by IntelliSense or the compiler and that must match the parameter and route names. As a result, they are prone to typos that you won't discover until runtime.

Third, the values from the form, route, or query string are strings. As a result, you must cast them to the type that's needed by the action method. Fourth, you need to know where you're getting your values from, and if that changes, you need to change your code. For example, if you change from a query string parameter to a route parameter, you need to update the code in the action method that retrieves that value.

Fortunately, MVC *model binding* fixes these problems. Model binding works by automatically mapping named request and route parameters to the names of an action method's parameters. As a result, you don't need to explicitly retrieve the data. This is shown by the first example in figure 10-2.

In addition, you don't need to specify whether the data is in the form, route, or query string. That's because MVC checks all three by default. So, if you change how you pass data to an action method, you don't have to change your code. For example, you can update your application to use a route parameter instead of a query string parameter.

When using model binding, MVC looks for a parameter name that matches the name of an action method parameter in a specific order. First, it looks in the body of the POST request. If it isn't there, it looks in the route values provided by MVC routing. If it isn't there, it looks in the URL's query string. When it finds the name it's looking for, it binds the associated value to the action method parameter and skips any remaining checks.

MVC model binding is case insensitive. This means that an action method parameter named ID or Id matches a route parameter named id.

If MVC doesn't find a name that matches the parameter name, it sets the value of the action method parameter to the default value for its data type. For instance, it sets a string parameter to null and an int parameter to 0.

A final benefit is that MVC automatically casts a value to the type of the action method parameter. Sometimes, though, the value can't be cast. For instance, MVC can't cast the value "three" to an int. When this happens, MVC doesn't throw an exception. Instead, it adds an error message to the ModelStateDictionary property of the Controller class. As a result, you can check the IsValid property of the controller's ModelState property to make sure the model binding completed successfully. You'll learn more about that in the next chapter.

An action method that uses model binding to get a string value

```
public IActionResult Index(string id)
{
    ViewBag.Id = id;
    return View();
}
```

Three types of data this action method can retrieve

A form parameter in the body of a POST request
```
id=2
```

A route parameter
```
https://localhost:7078/Home/Index/2
```

A query string parameter
```
https://localhost:7078/Home/Index?id=2
```

The order in which MVC looks for data to bind to a parameter

1. The body of the POST request.
2. The route values in the URL.
3. The query string parameters in the URL.

The benefits of model binding

- You don't have to write repetitive code to retrieve values.
- You don't have to work with string literal keys, which are prone to errors.
- MVC automatically casts the value to match the data type of the action method parameter.
- Model binding is not case sensitive.
- You can change how you pass data to an action without having to change its code.

Description

- *Model binding* in MVC automatically maps data in the HTTP request to an action method's parameters by name.
- MVC looks for parameter names in the order listed above. When it finds a name, it binds its associated value and moves on to the next parameter, if any. In other words, it doesn't continue looking once it finds a value that matches a parameter name.
- If there's no request parameter name that matches the name of an action method parameter, MVC binds the default value of the data type.
- If a value can't be cast to the correct type, MVC doesn't throw an error. Instead, it adds an error message to the ModelState property of the Controller class as described in chapter 11.

Figure 10-2   How to use model binding to retrieve GET and POST data

How to use model binding with complex types

The last figure showed how to use model binding with a single primitive type, a string parameter named id. Often, that's all you need to do. For example, it's common to have an action method parameter named id bind to the default route parameter named id and for this parameter to be a primitive type like a string or an int.

However, an action method can also accept a complex type like the ToDo class shown in the first example in figure 10-3, and you can use that type for model binding. To help illustrate why it makes sense to bind complex types, the second example in this figure shows how to use model binding with two primitive types that are used to create a complex type. Here, the action method receives a string parameter that contains a description and a DateTime parameter that contains a due date. Then, this action method creates a ToDo object and uses the values it receives to initialize that object.

This code is an improvement over accessing the Form property of the controller's Request property directly. However, you must be sure that the names of the action method parameters match the names posted by the view. Because model binding isn't case sensitive, though, these values don't need to match exactly. For example, the <input> element with a name attribute of duedate in the view in this example is successfully bound to the action method parameter named dueDate.

Also, this action method needs to explicitly initialize the ToDo object. In this case, that's not a big problem since the code only initializes two properties of this object. However, if your complex object has dozens of properties that need to be initialized, doing that manually would be tedious and lead to code that's unwieldy and difficult to maintain.

Fortunately, MVC allows you to bind to complex types as shown by the third example. Here, the action method has a single parameter of the ToDo type. As a result, this method no longer needs to create and initialize a ToDo object. That's because MVC automatically initializes the object when you bind to a complex type. To do that, it looks for request or route parameters with the same names as the properties of the object.

For a complex type to work with model binding, it must have a default constructor, and the properties to be bound must be public and writeable. The ToDo class shown in this figure meets these criteria. Although this class doesn't explicitly code a default constructor, which is a constructor without any parameters, the C# compiler will generate one for you if a class doesn't include any constructors.

In the third example, the view is strongly typed and uses the asp-for tag helper with the <input> elements to specify the property names of the model object. This provides for IntelliSense and compiler checking, which makes it easier and less error-prone to enter these property names.

Note here that the type="text" attribute is included on the <input> element for the DueDate property. That way, a normal text field will be displayed rather than a more specialized field for a date and time.

The class for a complex type

```
public class ToDo
{
    public int Id { get; set; }
    public string Description { get; set; } = string.Empty;
    public DateTime? DueDate { get; set; }
}
```

An action method and view that bind to primitive types

The action method

```
[HttpPost]
public IActionResult Add(string description, DateTime duedate){
    ToDo task = new ToDo {
        Description = description,
        DueDate = duedate
    };
    // rest of code
}
```

The view

```
<form asp-action="Add" method="post">
    <label for="description">Description:</label>
        <input type="text" name="description">
    <label for="duedate">Due Date:</label>
        <input type="text" name="duedate">
    <button type="submit">Add</button>
</form>
```

An action method and view that bind to a complex type

The action method

```
[HttpPost]
public IActionResult Add(ToDo task){
    // rest of code
}
```

The view

```
@model ToDo
...
<form asp-action="Add" method="post">
    <label asp-for="Description">Description:</label>
        <input asp-for="Description">
    <label asp-for="DueDate">Due Date:</label>
        <input asp-for="DueDate" type="text">
    <button type="submit">Add</button>
</form>
```

Description

- MVC allows you to bind complex types.
- You can use the asp-for tag helper to set the name attribute of an HTML element.
- MVC automatically initializes an action method parameter that's a complex type. To do that, it looks for values with the same names as the property names of the parameter.

Figure 10-3   How to use model binding with complex types

How to use model binding with nested complex types

The last figure showed how to use model binding with complex types. However, it's common to have complex types nested within other complex types. For instance, the first example in figure 10-4 shows a view model class named TeamsViewModel that has a property named Team that's of type Team. In other words, the complex type Team is nested within the complex type TeamsViewModel. Then, in the second example, the action method has a single parameter of the TeamsViewModel type.

As you just learned, MVC initializes the object when you bind to a complex type. That includes properties that are complex types. Here, for instance, MVC will initialize a TeamsViewModel object for the model parameter, and it will initialize a Team object for the Teams property of the model object.

Once it has initialized the complex object and any nested complex objects, MVC looks for request or route parameters with the same names as the object properties. However, to bind to the property of the nested complex type, the name must include the name of the property as well as the name of the complex type that contains it. To do that, you use dot notation as shown in the view in the third example. Here, the first input element has a name attribute of "team.teamid". So, MVC will bind the value in this element to the TeamID property of the Team property of the TeamsViewModel object.

In the next example, the view is strongly typed and uses the asp-for tag helper in the <input> elements to specify the property names of the model object. This provides for IntelliSense and compiler checking, which makes it easier and less error-prone to enter these property names. Once again, you use dot notation to identify both the name of the complex type and the name of the property of that complex type.

The class for a complex type with a nested complex type

```
public class TeamsViewModel
{
    public string ActiveConf { get; set; } = "all";
    public string ActiveDiv { get; set; } = "all";
    public Team Team { get; set; } = new Team();    // nested complex type
}
```

An action method that binds to the complex type

```
[HttpPost]
public IActionResult Add(TeamsViewModel model){
    // rest of code
}
```

An untyped view that posts to the action method

```
<form asp-action="Add" method="post">
    <label for="team.teamid">Team ID:</label>
        <input type="text" name="team.teamid">
    <label for="team.name">Team Name:</label>
        <input type="text" name="team.name">
    <button type="submit">Add</button>
</form>
```

A strongly typed view that posts to the action method

```
@model TeamsViewModel
...
<form asp-action="Add" method="post">
    <label asp-for="Team.TeamID">Team ID:</label>
        <input asp-for="Team.TeamID">
    <label asp-for="Team.Name">Team Name:</label>
        <input asp-for="Team.Name">
    <button type="submit">Add</button>
</form>
```

Description

- MVC allows you to bind complex types nested within other complex types.

- You can use the asp-for tag helper to set the name attribute of an HTML element. To bind to a property of the nested complex type, use dot notation to identify the property.

- If you don't use the asp-for tag helper, you need to use dot notation to identify the name of the nested complex type and the property to bind to.

Figure 10-4   How to use model binding with nested complex types

More skills for binding data

So far, you've learned the basics of model binding in MVC. Now, you'll learn more skills for working with model binding.

How to use a submit button to post a value

In addition to using HTML text boxes, drop-down lists, and hidden fields to post data to the server, you can use submit buttons to post data to the server. Figure 10-5 shows how this works.

The first example shows an action method named Add() that has a parameter of the Team type. Then, the second example shows a model directive for a strongly-typed view like those in the following examples. Each of these views contains a <form> element that posts to the Add() action method.

The <form> element in the third example includes a hidden field and a submit button like you've seen previously. Because the hidden field includes an asp-for tag with a value of "TeamID", the value of the team ID is bound to the TeamID property of the Team parameter that's defined by the Add() action method when the submit button is clicked.

Although it's common to use hidden fields like this to post values to the server, this may not always work the way you want. For instance, if you needed to display a submit button for more than one team, each hidden field and button would need to be in a separate form. That's because, for model binding to work, each hidden field would need to be named TeamID. But, if a single form contains multiple hidden fields with the same name, their values will all post to the server in an array, which isn't what you want.

Instead of coding each hidden field and submit button within a separate form, you can omit the hidden fields and code all the submit buttons within a single form. For this to work, you need to set the name attribute of each button to TeamID and the value attribute to the team ID. That way, when a submit button is clicked, it posts the team ID to the server and binds it to the TeamID property of the Team parameter of the action method. You can do this using either <input> or <button> elements.

If you use an <input> element as shown in the fourth example, you can use the asp-for tag helper to set the name attribute to "TeamID" and the value attribute to the team ID. You saw how this works in figure 7-14 of chapter 7. Although the asp-for tag helper simplifies the code, it causes the value attribute to be displayed as the text of the button, which may not be what you want. Here, for example, the button displays the team ID.

If you use a <button> element instead of an <input> element, you can display whatever content you want. In the last example, for instance, the team name is displayed. However, you can't use the asp-for tag helper with <button> elements. As a result, you have to set the name and value attributes manually. When you do that, you need to make sure that the value of the name attribute matches the name of the action method parameter or parameter property so the value is bound properly.

An action method that accepts a Team object

```
[HttpPost]
public IActionResult Add(Team team) { // action method code }
```

The model directive in the view for the following examples

```
@model Team;
```

How to use a hidden field to post a value to the action method

```
<form asp-action="Add" method="post">
    <input type="hidden" asp-for="TeamID" />
    <button type="submit" class="btn btn-primary">@Model.Name</button>
</form>
```

How the button looks in the browser

Seattle Seahawks

How to use an <input> submit button to post a value to the action method

```
<form asp-action="Add" method="post">
    <input type="submit" asp-for="TeamID" class="btn btn-primary" />
</form>
```

How the button looks in the browser

sea

How to use a <button> submit button to post a value to the action method

```
<form asp-action="Add" method="post">
    <button type="submit" name="TeamID" value="@Model.TeamID"
        class="btn btn-primary">@Model.Name</button>
</form>
```

How the button looks in the browser

Seattle Seahawks

The <input> element...

- Allows you to use the asp-for tag helper to generate the name and value attributes.
- Automatically displays the value attribute as the text for the button.

The <button> element...

- Gives you control over the text (or image) that's displayed for the button.
- Can't use the asp-for tag helper. You must explicitly code the name and value attributes, making sure the value in the name attribute matches the name of the action method parameter or property to bind to.

Description

- You can use the name and value attributes of a submit button to POST a value to an action method.
- You can use an <input> or <button> element to create a submit button.

Figure 10-5   How to use a submit button to post a value to an action method

How to post an array to an action method

The last topic mentioned that when elements in a form have the same name, the values of the elements post to the server as an array. One scenario where this is useful is when you want to filter data by multiple criteria.

The first example in figure 10-6 shows an action method named Filter() that handles POST requests. It has a parameter named filter that's an array of strings.

Below the action method is a view with a form that posts to the Filter() action method. This form contains two <select> elements. The first contains several price options, and the second contains several color options.

Crucially, both of these <select> elements have the same name, and that name matches the name of the parameter of the action method. As a result, when this form is posted, MVC collects the selected value of each <select> element in a string array and binds it to the parameter of the action method.

Below the view, an image shows the string array that the Filter() action method receives when the user selects the "Under $10" and "Blue" options and clicks the Filter button. Again, for this to work, the names of the <select> elements need to match the name of a parameter for the action method or one of the properties of the parameter. In addition, the action method parameter or property needs to be of the IEnumerable type, such as an array or a List<T> type.

An action method that accepts a string array

```
[HttpPost]
public IActionResult Filter(string[] filter)
{
    // code that does the filtering
}
```

A view that posts a string array to the action method

```
<h3>Filter By:</h3>
<form asp-action="Filter" method="post">
    <!-- make sure each select element has the same name and that it
    matches the action method parameter name -->
    <label>Price</label>
    <select name="filter">
        <option value="all">All</option>
        <option value="lt10">Under $10</option>
        <option value="10to50">$10 to $50</option>
        <option value="gt50">Over $50</option>
    </select>
    <label>Color</label>
    <select name="filter">
        <option>All</option>
        <option>Red</option>
        <option>Blue</option>
        <option>Yellow</option>
        <option>Green</option>
        <option>Purple</option>
    </select>
    <button type="submit">Filter</button>
</form>
```

An example of a string array received by the action method

Description

- You can pass an array to an action method by coding multiple HTML elements that have the same name within a form.

- The name of the HTML elements must match the name of the action method parameter or property to bind to.

- The action method parameter or property must be of the IEnumerable type, such as an array or a List<T> type.

Figure 10-6   How to post an array to an action method

How to control the source of bound values

As you learned earlier, MVC model binding automatically checks for names in multiple places and in a specific sequence. To start, it checks posted data, then route data, and then query string data. However, in some situations you might want more control over this sequence. For example, you might want MVC to look only in the route. Or, you might want to bind to data that's sent in other ways, such the headers of the HTTP request or via dependency injection.

You can use the From attributes presented in the table in figure 10-7 to control where MVC looks for the values an action method binds to. The first three attributes direct MVC to look in one of the three places it already looks. However, if you use one of these attributes, MVC only looks in that one place and doesn't check the others. For example, if you use the FromRoute attribute, MVC doesn't check the posted data first.

The FromBody attribute is typically used when a client-side script, such as JavaScript, posts JSON data to an action method of a controller. This is common in Web API apps. When you use this attribute, you can only decorate one parameter per action method. However, when you use the other From attributes, you can decorate as many parameters per action method as you like.

Below the table, the figure presents some examples of working with the From attributes. In the first example, an action method tells MVC to get the value for the id parameter from the URL's route segments, and it tells MVC to get the value for the pagenum parameter from the URL's query string.

In the second example, an action method tells MVC to get the value for the agent parameter from the headers of the HTTP request. However, since an HTTP request doesn't include a header that matches the name of the parameter, this attribute includes a Name argument that specifies that MVC should bind to the request header named User-Agent.

The third example shows that you can apply From attributes to class properties as well as action method parameters. Here, a class named Browser has a property named UserAgent. This property is decorated with a FromHeader attribute that uses a Name argument to specify that the header has a name of User-Agent. As a result, when you use model binding with the Browser class, MVC always looks in the User-Agent request header for the value for this property, and it doesn't look anywhere else.

Some of the attributes that specify the source of the value to be bound

Attribute	Tells MVC to retrieve the value...
[FromForm]	from the form parameters in the body of a POST request.
[FromRoute]	from the route parameters of the URL.
[FromQuery]	from the query string parameters of the URL.
[FromHeader]	from the HTTP request header.
[FromServices]	from services that are injected into the app as described in section 3.
[FromBody]	from the body of the HTTP request. This is often used when a client-side script sends JSON data to an action method. This attribute can only decorate one parameter per action method.

An action method that specifies the source of its parameters

```
public IActionResult Index([FromRoute] string id, [FromQuery] int pagenum)
{
    ViewBag.Id = id;
    ViewBag.Page = pagenum;
    return View();
}
```

An action method that passes an argument to an attribute

```
public IActionResult Index([FromHeader(Name = "User-Agent")] string agent)
{
    ViewBag.UserAgent = agent;
    return View();
}
```

A class that applies an attribute to a property

```
using Microsoft.AspNetCore.Mvc;
...
public class Browser
{
    [FromHeader(Name = "User-Agent")]
    public string UserAgent { get; set; }
    ...
}
```

Description

- You can use attributes to control how binding works.
- You can apply attributes to parameters of action methods in a controller or to properties of model classes.
- You can pass arguments to an attribute to further refine its behavior.
- If you specify a From attribute, MVC only looks for the specified value from that source and doesn't check other sources.
- The From attributes are in the Microsoft.AspNetCore.Mvc namespace.

Figure 10-7   How to control the source of bound values

How to control which values are bound

In the previous figure, you learned how to the control *where* MVC looks when it binds values to the parameters in an action method. In this figure, you'll learn how to control *which* properties of a complex type are bound. To do that, you can use the Bind and BindNever attributes presented in the first table in figure 10-8. Curiously, these attributes are stored in different namespaces as shown by the second table.

The Bind attribute accepts a list of strings. This list tells MVC the names of the properties that can be set during model binding. MVC doesn't bind any properties that aren't in this list, even if values for them are sent to the server. When you code a Bind attribute, you can apply it to a parameter of an action method or to the model itself.

By contrast, the BindNever attribute tells MVC that a property can't be set during model binding. As a result, MVC doesn't bind the specified property, even if a value for it has been sent to the server. When you code a BindNever attribute, you can only apply it to a property of a model, not to a parameter of an action method.

An important thing to know about both of these attributes is that they only prevent MVC model binding from setting the value of a property. You can still write code that manually sets the property.

When you control which properties are set during model binding, you protect against *mass assignment attacks*, also called *over posting attacks*. In this kind of attack, a malicious user manipulates the data that's sent to the server to set properties that the app isn't expecting. For example, the Employee model shown in the first example has an IsManager property that the app might use to decide which pages users can view or what actions they can take. If a user manages to set that property to true, the security of your web app could be compromised.

The code below the Employee model presents three ways that you can use the Bind and BindNever attributes to make sure that a malicious user can't set the value of the IsManager property. First, you can decorate the employee parameter in the action method with a Bind attribute. Here, only the Name and JobTitle properties of the Employee object can be set during model binding. However, the IsManager property can still be set in code.

Second, you can decorate the Employee class itself with the Bind attribute. Again, only the Name and JobTitle properties of the Employee object can be set during model binding. If you're sure you never want the unlisted properties to be bound, this technique is optimal. However, if you may want the unlisted properties to be bound occasionally, you're better off using the Bind attribute to decorate the parameter in the action method.

Third, you can decorate the IsManager property itself with the BindNever attribute. This technique is optimal when your model has many properties, and you only want to prevent a few of them from being bound. In that case, listing all the properties in the Bind attribute would be tedious.

Two attributes that determine which values are bound

Attribute	Description
`[Bind(names)]`	Allows you to list the names of the properties that can be set during model binding. This attribute can be applied to a class or to a parameter of an action method.
`[BindNever]`	Indicates that a property should never be set during model binding. This attribute can only be applied to a property of a class.

The namespaces of the two attributes

Attribute	Namespace
`[Bind]`	`Microsoft.AspNetCore.MVC`
`[BindNever]`	`Microsoft.AspNetCore.MVC.ModelBinding`

The Employee class

```
public class Employee {
    public string Name { get; set; }
    public string JobTitle { get; set; }
    public bool IsManager { get; set; }
}
```

Three ways to make sure the IsManager property is not bound

With the Bind attribute in the parameter list of an action method

```
[HttpPost]
public IActionResult Index([Bind("Name", "JobTitle")] Employee employee) {
    if (ModelState.IsValid) {
        if (employee.JobTitle == "Boss")
            employee.IsManager = true;       // can be set in code
    }
    return View(employee);
}
```

With the Bind attribute on the class

```
[Bind("Name", "JobTitle")]
public class Employee {
    public string Name { get; set; }
    public string JobTitle { get; set; }
    public bool IsManager { get; set; }
}
```

With the BindNever attribute on the IsManager property

```
public class Employee {
    public string Name { get; set; }
    public string JobTitle { get; set; }

    [BindNever]
    public bool IsManager { get; set; }
}
```

Description

- You can use attributes to tell MVC which properties to set during model binding.

Figure 10-8   How to control which values are bound

The ToDo List app

To put some of the model binding skills you just learned into context, this chapter finishes by presenting a ToDo List app. This app allows users to store a list of tasks in a database. If you haven't already done so, you'll need to run the Update-Database command from the Package Manager Console to create the database before running this app.

The user interface

The ToDo List app consists of the two pages shown in figure 10-9. Here, the first two screens show the Home page, and the third screen shows the Add page.

On first load, the Home page displays all the tasks in the database, ordered by due date. In addition, it highlights any task that's past due and open.

The left column of the Home page provides three drop-down lists that allow users to filter the tasks by category, by due date, and by status. All of the drop-down lists that provide filtering default to the value "All" as shown in the first screen. However, if the user selects one or more filter options and clicks the Filter button, the app only displays the filtered tasks as shown in the second screen. Here, the app filters the tasks to display only those with a category of "Work" and a status of "Open".

The ToDo List app uses the default id route parameter to pass the filter values. To do that, it uses a dash-separated value for the id parameter. For instance, the URL for the second screen is:

```
/home/index/work-all-open/
```

This provides filter values of "work" for category, "all" for due date, and "open" for status. Note that this app makes its URL lowercase with a trailing slash by setting the routing options in the Program.cs file as described in chapter 4.

The Home page provides a Mark Completed button for each task that hasn't been completed. This button allows a user to change the status of a task from open to completed. Below the list of tasks, the Home page provides an Add new task button that takes the user to the Add page. It also provides a Delete completed tasks button that deletes all the tasks marked as completed.

The Add page allows a user to add a new task to the database. In this figure, this page displays a validation message that says, "The value 'tomorrow' is not valid for DueDate". That's because the user entered a string value of "tomorrow" for the due date, which can't be converted to the DateTime type that the app expects. When you review the code for this app, you'll see that it doesn't explicitly add data validation for this. Instead, MVC adds this message to the validation messages when it tries to cast the due date value during model binding.

The Home page with no filtering

The Home page after it has been filtered to show open work tasks

The Add page with a validation message

Figure 10-9   The user interface

The entity classes

Figure 10-10 presents the code for the entity classes of the ToDo List app. Here, the Category class stores data about the category for a task, and the Status class stores data about the status for a task. These classes are used for the Category and Status filters.

The ToDo class holds data about the task the user wants to add, update, or delete. By the way, this class is called ToDo rather than Task to avoid conflicts with the Task class in the System.Threading.Tasks namespace.

The ToDo class defines several properties. The first property it defines is an Id property that's set by the database. The last property it defines is a read-only property named Overdue that indicates whether a task is overdue.

Between these properties, this class defines four public properties that hold data entered by a user. Each of these properties also has a data validation attribute indicating that the field is required. As a result, if the user doesn't enter data for one of these properties, the app displays a validation message.

In addition, this class defines two navigation properties that make it easy to get the Category and Status objects that correspond to the current task. To avoid unexpected data validation results, these properties are decorated with the ValidateNever attribute you learned about in chapter 4. This attribute is in the Microsoft.AspNetCore.Mvc.ModelBinding.Validation namespace.

Note that there's no validation attribute for the DueDate property that specifies that it must be a valid date that can be converted to the DateTime type. That's because MVC model binding handles that for you.

Unlike the Category and Status filters, there's no entity class for the Due filter. Instead, the code for the Filters class defines a dictionary with the values that will be displayed in the Due list. You'll see this class in the next figure.

As you recall, properties that are reference types can produce null reference errors and warnings. To avoid that, the classes in this figure and the next that let you set the value of a property provide default values. Specifically, string.Empty is assigned to string properties, and null with the null-forgiving operator (!) is assigned to other reference types. For properties that are value types, like the DateTime type for the DueDate property, this isn't necessary. However, as you learned in chapter 2, value types must be nullable for the Required attribute to work properly.

The Category class

```
public class Category
{
    public string CategoryId { get; set; } = string.Empty;
    public string Name { get; set; } = string.Empty;
}
```

The Status class

```
public class Status
{
    public string StatusId { get; set; } = string.Empty;
    public string Name { get; set; } = string.Empty;
}
```

The ToDo class

```
using System.ComponentModel.DataAnnotations;
using Microsoft.AspNetCore.Mvc.ModelBinding.Validation;
...
public class ToDo
{
    public int Id { get; set; }

    [Required(ErrorMessage = "Please enter a description.")]
    public string Description { get; set; } = string.Empty;

    [Required(ErrorMessage = "Please enter a due date.")]
    public DateTime? DueDate { get; set; }

    [Required(ErrorMessage = "Please select a category.")]
    public string CategoryId { get; set; } = string.Empty;
    [ValidateNever]
    public Category Category { get; set; } = null!;

    [Required(ErrorMessage = "Please select a status.")]
    public string StatusId { get; set; } = string.Empty;
    [ValidateNever]
    public Status Status { get; set; } = null!;

    public bool Overdue =>
        StatusId == "open" && DueDate < DateTime.Today;
}
```

Figure 10-10   The entity classes

The database context class

Figure 10-11 presents the context class that the ToDo List app uses to communicate with the database. This class provides the DbSet properties for working with the ToDo, Category, and Status objects. In addition, its OnModelCreating() method provides the initial values for the Category and Status tables. In short, this context class works similarly to the one presented in chapter 4 for the Movie List app. As a result, you shouldn't have much trouble understanding how it works.

Although it isn't shown here, this app also stores its database connection string in an appsettings.json file. In addition, it uses the Program.cs file to configure the database context for the app. Again, this works similarly to the Movie List app presented in chapter 4, so you shouldn't have much trouble understanding how it works.

A utility class for filtering

Figure 10-11 also presents a utility class named Filters. The app uses this class to help filter tasks by category, due date, and status.

The constructor for the Filters class accepts a dash-separated string that contains the values for the three filters. To start, the constructor stores this value in a property named FilterString. However, if the string is null or empty, the constructor stores a default value that displays all the tasks in the database. Next, the constructor splits the string at the dashes and loads the values of the resulting array into the CategoryId, Due, and StatusId properties. All of these properties are read-only. As a result, they can only be set in the constructor.

After these four properties, the Filters class defines three read-only Has properties that indicate whether the user has selected one of the filter criteria. These properties work by checking whether a filter value is "all". If not, the user has selected a value to filter by, and the property is set to true. Otherwise, it's set to false.

After the three Has properties, the Filters class provides four more properties to handle filtering by due date. To start, the static DueFilterValues property defines a dictionary whose keys and values are strings. This dictionary holds the values that appear in the Due drop-down list. This code defines this property as a dictionary instead of a list because it provides an easy way to capitalize values for display to the user, and use lowercase for the filter value that MVC retrieves from the id route parameter. That's why the keys here are lowercase and the values are uppercase.

After the DueFilterValues property, the three read-only Is properties indicate whether the user wants to filter by due dates in the past, the future, or today. These properties work by checking the value in the Due property.

The ToDoContext class

```
public class ToDoContext : DbContext
{
    public ToDoContext(DbContextOptions<ToDoContext> options)
        : base(options) { }

    public DbSet<ToDo> ToDos { get; set; } = null!;
    public DbSet<Category> Categories { get; set; } = null!;
    public DbSet<Status> Statuses { get; set; } = null!;

    protected override void OnModelCreating(ModelBuilder modelBuilder)
    {
        modelBuilder.Entity<Category>().HasData(
            new Category { CategoryId = "work", Name = "Work" },
            new Category { CategoryId = "home", Name = "Home" },
            new Category { CategoryId = "ex", Name = "Exercise" },
            new Category { CategoryId = "shop", Name = "Shopping" },
            new Category { CategoryId = "call", Name = "Contact" }
        );
        modelBuilder.Entity<Status>().HasData(
            new Status { StatusId = "open", Name = "Open" },
            new Status { StatusId = "closed", Name = "Completed" }
        );
    }
}
```

The Filters class

```
public class Filters
{
    public Filters(string filterstring)
    {
        FilterString = filterstring ?? "all-all-all";
        string[] filters = FilterString.Split('-');
        CategoryId = filters[0];
        Due = filters[1];
        StatusId = filters[2];
    }
    public string FilterString { get; }
    public string CategoryId { get; }
    public string Due { get; }
    public string StatusId { get; }

    public bool HasCategory => CategoryId.ToLower() != "all";
    public bool HasDue => Due.ToLower() != "all";
    public bool HasStatus => StatusId.ToLower() != "all";

    public static Dictionary<string, string> DueFilterValues =>
        new Dictionary<string, string> {
            { "future", "Future" },
            { "past", "Past" },
            { "today", "Today" }
        };
    public bool IsPast => Due.ToLower() == "past";
    public bool IsFuture => Due.ToLower() == "future";
    public bool IsToday => Due.ToLower() == "today";
}
```

Figure 10-11   The database context class and a utility class for filtering

The Home controller

Figure 10-12 presents the Home controller. To start, part 1 presents the private variable for the database context, the constructor, and the first three action methods.

The Index() action method has a single parameter named id of the string type. As you know, MVC can bind this parameter to a POST request parameter named id, to a route parameter named id, or to a query string parameter named id. In practice, though, this action method always binds to the id parameter of the default route that's defined in the Program.cs file.

To start, the Index() action method creates a new Filters object and passes the id parameter to its constructor. Next, it gets lists of Category and Status objects from the database and the due date filter dictionary from the Filters object. The view uses these lists to create drop-down lists for filtering. To keep things simple, this action method uses the ViewBag to pass the lists to the view.

After storing data in the ViewBag, the Index() action method retrieves the tasks to display from the database. To start, it builds a query for ToDo objects and their related Category and Status objects. Then, it uses the Has properties of the Filters object to add WHERE clauses to the query if the user has selected filter criteria. For the due date filtering, it also uses the Is properties to add the correct WHERE clause for the due date filter. Next, the code completes the query by sorting the results by due date and calling the ToList() method. Finally, it passes the collection of tasks to the view.

The first Add() action method handles GET requests. To do that, it gets lists of Category and Status objects from the database and assigns these collections to the ViewBag. That way, the view can use these collections to create the drop-down lists the user needs to add a new task to the database. This action method also creates a new ToDo object and sets its StatusId property to "open". That way, when the Add view is displayed, the Open status will be selected by default.

The second Add() action method handles POST requests. This method has a single parameter of the ToDo type named task. Since MVC model binding starts by searching the body of a POST request, and since this action method handles POST requests, the values for this task argument are always posted from the Add page. As a result, the names of the elements in the view for the Add page must match the names of the properties of the ToDo object.

To start, this Add() action method makes sure there aren't any validation errors, either from the validation attributes in the ToDo class or from MVC's model binding. To do that, it checks the IsValid property of the ModelState property of the Controller class.

If there aren't any validation errors, the code adds the new ToDo object to the ToDos context collection and calls the SaveChanges() method to update the database. Then, it redirects the user back to the Home page, where the new task now displays in the list of tasks.

The Home controller

```
public class HomeController : Controller
{
    private ToDoContext context;
    public HomeController(ToDoContext ctx) => context = ctx;

    public IActionResult Index(string id)
    {
        var filters = new Filters(id);
        ViewBag.Filters = filters;
        ViewBag.Categories = context.Categories.ToList();
        ViewBag.Statuses = context.Statuses.ToList();
        ViewBag.DueFilters = Filters.DueFilterValues();

        IQueryable<ToDo> query = context.ToDos
            .Include(t => t.Category).Include(t => t.Status);
        if (filters.HasCategory) {
            query = query.Where(t => t.CategoryId == filters.CategoryId);
        }
        if (filters.HasStatus) {
            query = query.Where(t => t.StatusId == filters.StatusId);
        }
        if (filters.HasDue) {
            var today = DateTime.Today;
            if (filters.IsPast)
                query = query.Where(t => t.DueDate < today);
            else if (filters.IsFuture)
                query = query.Where(t => t.DueDate > today);
            else if (filters.IsToday)
                query = query.Where(t => t.DueDate == today);
        }
        var tasks = query.OrderBy(t => t.DueDate).ToList();
        return View(tasks);
    }


    [HttpGet]
    public IActionResult Add()
    {
        ViewBag.Categories = context.Categories.ToList();
        ViewBag.Statuses = context.Statuses.ToList();
        var task = new ToDo { StatusId = "open" };
        return View(task);
    }


    [HttpPost]
    public IActionResult Add(ToDo task)
    {
        if (ModelState.IsValid) {
            context.ToDos.Add(task);
            context.SaveChanges();
            return RedirectToAction("Index");
        }
        else {
            ViewBag.Categories = context.Categories.ToList();
            ViewBag.Statuses = context.Statuses.ToList();
            return View(task);
        }
    }
}
```

Figure 10-12   The Home controller (part 1)

If there are validation errors, the code sets the collections for the drop-down lists in the ViewBag and sends the task to the view. This causes the view to display the data the user entered again with validation messages for the invalid entries.

Part 2 of figure 10-12 presents the last three action methods of the Home controller. All of these methods handle POST requests.

The Filter() action method has a parameter named filter that's an array of strings. MVC binds this parameter to an array of strings that it gets from the POST request. The next figure shows that this array comes from three <select> elements that have a name of filter. The action method takes this array and converts it into a single dash-separated string. Then, it redirects to the Index() action method and passes the dash-separated string as the value for the id parameter of the default route.

The MarkComplete() action method has a string parameter named id and a ToDo parameter named selected. Here, the id parameter includes the FromRoute attribute that tells MVC to look for its value in a route parameter. This attribute is necessary because the ToDo class also has a property named Id that's sent to the server in the POST request. Without the FromRoute attribute, MVC would look first in the POST request, find a parameter named Id, bind its value to this parameter, and skip any further checks. With this attribute, though, MVC skips the POST request and looks for the value in the route parameter named id. By contrast, the ToDo parameter doesn't need a FromForm attribute because MVC looks for the property values in the POST request first by default.

The form posts to this action method when the user clicks the Mark Completed button for a task. When the form posts, the URL it posts to has a route parameter named id that contains the filter string that's bound to the id parameter. It also posts a submit button named Id that contains the task ID value that's bound to the Id property of the ToDo object.

In the body of the action method, the code marks the task as completed. To do that, it queries the database to get the ToDo object for the specified ToDo ID. After that, it sets the StatusId value to "closed" and calls the SaveChanges() method to update the task in the database. Then, it redirects back to the Index() action method, passing the id parameter of the action method to the id parameter of the route. This preserves any filtering the user did before clicking the Mark Completed button.

Like the MarkComplete() action method, the DeleteComplete() action method has a string parameter named id whose value comes from the route parameter named id. Unlike the parameter of the MarkComplete() action method, though, it isn't necessary to include the FromRoute attribute on the parameter of the DeleteComplete() action method. That's because the POST request doesn't include an ID value, so MVC will automatically bind the value in the route parameter named id to the id parameter of the method.

The app posts to this action method when the user clicks the Delete completed tasks button. When the form posts, it sends a route parameter named id that contains the filter string that's bound to the id parameter.

The code in the action method starts by querying the database for all the tasks with a status of "closed". Then, it loops through the tasks, passing each

The Home controller (continued)

```
[HttpPost]
public IActionResult Filter(string[] filter)
{
    string id = string.Join('-', filter);
    return RedirectToAction("Index", new { ID = id });
}

[HttpPost]
public IActionResult MarkComplete([FromRoute]string id, ToDo selected)
{
    selected = context.ToDos.Find(selected.Id)!;
    if (selected != null)
    {
        selected.StatusId = "closed";
        context.SaveChanges();
    }

    return RedirectToAction("Index", new { ID = id });
}

[HttpPost]
public IActionResult DeleteComplete(string id)
{
    var toDelete = context.ToDos
        .Where(t => t.StatusId == "closed").ToList();

    foreach(var task in toDelete)
    {
        context.ToDos.Remove(task);
    }
    context.SaveChanges();

    return RedirectToAction("Index", new { ID = id });
}
}
```

Figure 10-12   The Home controller (part 2)

one to the Remove() method. When the loop completes, the code calls the SaveChanges() method to delete the tasks in the database. Finally, it redirects back to the Index() action method, passing the id parameter of the action method to the id parameter of the route to preserve any filtering.

The layout

Figure 10-13 presents the code for the Razor layout of the ToDo List app. This layout works much like other layouts presented in this book. As a result, you shouldn't have much trouble understanding how it works.

The Home/Index view

Figure 10-13 also presents the code for the Home/Index view. To start, part 1 shows the @model directive that binds the view to a collection of ToDo objects. Then, it shows a Bootstrap column with the three drop-down lists that let a user filter by category, due date, and status.

This Bootstrap column contains a form that posts to the Filter() action method presented in part 2 of figure 10-12. The form contains three <select> elements that all share the same name, filter. This name is also the name of the parameter in the Filter() action method. As a result, this form posts the values of these three <select> elements to the Filter() action method as an array of strings.

The Razor code for each <select> element passes four arguments to the constructor of the SelectList class described in chapter 7. The first argument is the collection that the controller transferred in the ViewBag. The SelectList class uses the items in this collection to create the <option> elements for the drop-down list.

The second argument is the name of the property to bind to the value attribute of the option tag, and the third is the name of the property to display to the user. For the <select> element for the due date, these names are "Key" and "Value". That's because that <select> element is bound to a dictionary of key/value pairs, not a list of objects.

The fourth argument comes from the Filters object that the controller transferred in the ViewBag, and it identifies the currently selected option. This is how the <select> elements "remember" what filters the user selected.

After the Razor code that generates <option> elements is a final <option> element that displays the "All" item. Although this element is coded after the Razor code, the option will be displayed at the top of the list. That's the case with any hardcoded <option> elements.

The Bootstrap column ends with two buttons. The Filter button submits the values of the drop-down lists to the server as an array. The Clear button resets the drop-down lists by reloading the Home page with no id route parameter. This causes the default values of "all" to load in the Filters object, which resets the drop-down lists to "All".

The layout

```
<!DOCTYPE html>
<html>
<head>
    <meta name="viewport" content="width=device-width, initial-scale=1.0" />
    <link href="~/lib/bootstrap/dist/css/bootstrap.min.css" rel="stylesheet" />
    <title>My Tasks</title>
</head>
<body>
    <div class="container">
        <header class="bg-primary text-white text-center">
            <h1 class="m-3 p-3">My Tasks</h1>
        </header>
        <main>
            @RenderBody()
        </main>
    </div>
</body>
</html>
```

The Home/Index view

```
@model IEnumerable<ToDo>

<div class="row">
    <div class="col-md-2">
        <form asp-action="Filter" method="post">
            <div class="mb-3">
                <label class="form-label">Category:</label>
                <select name="filter" class="form-select"
                    asp-items="@(new SelectList(ViewBag.Categories,
                        "CategoryId", "Name", ViewBag.Filters.CategoryId))">
                    <option value="all">All</option>
                </select></div>
            <div class="mb-3">
                <label class="form-label">Due:</label>
                <select name="filter" class="form-select"
                    asp-items="@(new SelectList(ViewBag.DueFilters,
                        "Key", "Value", ViewBag.Filters.Due))">
                    <option value="all">All</option>
                </select></div>
            <div class="mb-3">
                <label class="form-label">Status:</label>
                <select name="filter" class="form-select"
                    asp-items="@(new SelectList(ViewBag.Statuses,
                        "StatusId", "Name", ViewBag.Filters.StatusId))">
                    <option value="all">All</option>
                </select></div>
            <button type="submit" class="btn btn-primary">Filter</button>
            <a asp-action="Index" asp-route-id="" class="btn btn-primary">
                Clear
            </a>
        </form>
    </div>
```

Figure 10-13   The layout and the Home/Index view (part 1)

Part 2 of figure 10-13 presents the code for the rest of the Home/Index view. Specifically, it shows a Bootstrap column that contains two forms. The first form posts to the MarkComplete() action method that you saw in part 2 of figure 10-12. This form uses a tag helper to set the route parameter named id to the FilterString property of the Filters object that's stored in the ViewBag. This property contains the dash-separated string that holds the filter values. As a result, this string is sent to the MarkComplete() action method as a route parameter named id.

Within this form is a table that displays information about the tasks. The body of this table uses a Razor foreach statement to loop through the collection of ToDo objects that is the model for this view. Then, it builds one row for each ToDo object. To start, it checks the Overdue property of the current ToDo object and stores the result in a string variable named overdue. If the Overdue property returns true, the name of a Bootstrap class for displaying the background for a warning is assigned to the variable. Otherwise, an empty string is assigned to the variable.

After setting the overdue variable, the code creates a row with five data columns. The first four columns display information about the tasks such as the description, category, due date, and status. Here, the third and fourth columns use the overdue variable to assign a Bootstrap class if the task is overdue.

The fifth column displays the MarkCompleted buttons for any tasks that haven't already been completed. Within that column, the code creates a <button> element that's a submit button and sets its name and value attributes to the name and value of the Id property of the current ToDo object. To reduce the chances of error, the code uses the C# nameof operator to set the name attribute.

In this case, all of the Mark Completed buttons have a name attribute of Id. In addition, a single form contains all of the buttons. But when the user clicks one of these buttons, only the value of the Id property of the task that corresponds to that button is posted to the server. Then, that value is bound to the Id property of the ToDo object of the MarkComplete() action method.

After this form is a second form that posts to the DeleteComplete() action method that you saw in part 2 of figure 10-12. This form also uses a tag helper to set the route parameter named id to the FilterString property of the Filters object that's stored in the ViewBag. Again, this causes the dash-separated string that holds the filter values to be sent to the DeleteComplete() action method as a route parameter named id.

The second form contains a link styled like a button that displays the Add page. It also contains a Delete completed tasks button that posts to the DeleteComplete() action method. Unlike the Mark Complete buttons, this delete button doesn't need to post values to the server. So, its name and value attributes aren't set.

The Home/Index view (continued)

```
<div class="col-md-10">

    <form asp-action="MarkComplete" method="post"
        asp-route-id="@ViewBag.Filters.FilterString">

        <table class="table table-bordered table-striped mt-2">
            <thead>
                <tr>
                    <th>Description</th>
                    <th>Category</th>
                    <th>Due Date</th>
                    <th>Status</th>
                    <th class="w-25"></th>
                </tr>
            </thead>
            <tbody>
            @foreach (ToDo task in Model)
            {
                string overdue = task.Overdue ? "bg-warning" : "";
                <tr>
                    <td>@task.Description</td>
                    <td>@task.Category.Name</td>
                    <td class="@overdue">
                        @task.DueDate?.ToShortDateString()</td>
                    <td class="@overdue">@task.Status.Name</td>
                    <td>
                    @if (@task.StatusId == "open")
                    {
                            <button type="submit"
                                class="btn btn-primary btn-sm"
                                name="@nameof(ToDo.Id)"
                                value="@task.Id">
                                Mark Completed
                            </button>
                    }
                    </td>
                </tr>
            }
            </tbody>
        </table>
    </form>

    <form asp-action="DeleteComplete" method="post"
        asp-route-id="@ViewBag.Filters.FilterString">

        <a asp-action="Add" class="btn btn-primary">
            Add new task</a>
        <button type="submit" class="btn btn-primary">
            Delete completed tasks</button>
    </form>
</div>
</div>
```

Figure 10-13   The layout and the Home/Index view (part 2)

The Home/Add view

Figure 10-14 presents the code for the Home/Add view. It starts with the @model directive that indicates this view is strongly typed and bound to a ToDo object. After displaying a heading for the view, the code uses a <div> element with a tag helper to display a summary of any validation errors it receives from the controller.

After the summary of validation errors, this view includes a form that posts to the Add() action method presented in part 1 of figure 10-12. This form contains two <input> elements for text boxes and two <select> elements for drop-down lists that the user can use to enter the data for a task.

All four of these elements use the asp-for tag helper to bind the element to a property of the model. This accomplishes two goals. First, it makes sure that the name attributes of the tags match the property names of the Add() action method parameter. Second, if there's a validation error, it redisplays the values the user entered.

In this view, the Razor code for the <select> elements only pass three arguments to the constructor of the SelectList class. The fourth argument that identifies the currently selected option isn't necessary here because that's handled by the asp-for tag helper. In other words, because the value attribute that this tag helper generates is bound to a property of the ToDo object, its value determines the option that's selected.

Like the <select> elements in the Home/Index view, the <select> element in this view that lists the categories ends with a hardcoded <option> element. In this case, though, the value of this element is an empty string and the element doesn't contain any content. Since this element appears first in the drop-down list, that means the user will need to select a different option before adding a task.

By contrast, the <select> element that lists the statuses doesn't end with a hardcoded <option> element. That's because the value of the StatusId is set in the Add() action method for a GET request, so that value determines the option that's selected. In this case, that is the Open option.

This view ends by displaying two buttons. The Add button submits the values of the <input> and <select> elements to the server. And the Cancel button, which is a link styled as a button, returns the user to the Home page without adding the task.

The Home/Add view

```
@model ToDo

<h2>New Task</h2>

<div asp-validation-summary="All" class="text-danger"></div>

<form asp-action="Add" method="post">
    <div class="mb-3">
        <label asp-for="Description" class="form-label">Description:</label>
        <input asp-for="Description" class="form-control">
    </div>

    <div class="mb-3">
        <label asp-for="CategoryId" class="form-label">Category:</label>
        <select asp-for="CategoryId" class="form-select"
            asp-items="@(new SelectList(ViewBag.Categories,
                "CategoryId", "Name"))">
            <option value=""></option>
        </select>
    </div>

    <div class="mb-3">
        <label asp-for="DueDate" class="form-label">Due Date:</label>
        <input asp-for="DueDate" class="form-control" type="text">
    </div>

    <div class="mb-3">
        <label asp-for="StatusId" class="form-label">Status:</label>
        <select asp-for="StatusId" class="form-select"
            asp-items="@(new SelectList(ViewBag.Statuses,
                "StatusId", "Name"))">
        </select>
    </div>

    <button type="submit" class="btn btn-primary">Add</button>
    <a asp-action="Index" class="btn btn-primary">Cancel</a>
</form>
```

Figure 10-14   The Home/Add view

Perspective

The goal of this chapter is to teach you the details of model binding so you can benefit from it in your ASP.NET Core MVC apps. Now, if this chapter has succeeded, you should be able to benefit from model binding and control how it works when you need to. As usual, there's always more to learn. Still, this chapter should give you a good foundation for working with model binding.

Terms

model binding
mass assignment attack
over posting attack

Summary

- *Model binding* in ASP.NET Core MVC automatically maps data in the HTTP request to an action method's parameters.

- In a *mass assignment attack*, also known as an *over posting attack*, a malicious user manipulates the data sent to the server to set properties that the app isn't expecting. You can protect against these attacks by controlling which properties are set during model binding.

Exercise 10-1   Update the model binding for the ToDo List app

In this exercise, you'll update the ToDo List app presented in this chapter so it binds its views to a view model instead of binding them to entity models.

Create a view model

1. Open the Ch10Ex1ToDoList app in the ex_starts directory.

2. In Visual Studio, run the app and review how it works. Make sure to add one or more tasks.

3. In the Models directory, create a new class named ToDoViewModel with the following code:

```
public class ToDoViewModel
{
    public Filters Filters { get; set; } = null!;
    public List<Status> Statuses { get; set; } = null!;
    public List<Category> Categories { get; set; } = null!;
    public Dictionary<string, string> DueFilters { get; set; }
        = null!;
    public List<ToDo> Tasks { get; set; } = null!;
    public ToDo CurrentTask { get; set; } = null!;  // used for Add
}
```

4. Note that the view model provides all the properties necessary to store the data that the app currently stores in the ViewBag.

Modify the Home/Index() action method so it uses a view model

5. Open the HomeController class.

6. In the Index() action method, create a ToDoViewModel object. Then, modify the code that stores data in the ViewBag so it stores that data in this view model object.

7. Modify the return statement so it passes the view model to the view.

Bind the view model to the Home/Index view

8. Open the Home/Index view.

9. At the top of the file, change its model from an IEnumerable<ToDo> object to a ToDoViewModel object.

10. Modify the code so it uses the new view model instead of the ViewBag. For example, you can change all instances of ViewBag.Categories to Model.Categories.

11. Modify the code so it uses the new view model instead of the old view model. For example, in the loop, make sure that the tasks come from the Tasks property of the new view model like this:

```
@foreach (ToDo task in Model.Tasks)
```

12. Run the app and make sure that the Home page works as it did before.

Modify the Home/Add() action methods so they work with a view model

13. Open the HomeController class.

14. In the Add() action method that doesn't accept any arguments, add a statement that creates a ToDoViewModel object.

15. Modify the code that stores data in the ViewBag so it stores that same data in the ToDoViewModel object.

16. Modify the statement that creates a new ToDo object so that object is stored in the CurrentTask property of the ToDoViewModel object.

17. Modify the return statement so it passes the view model to the view.

18. In the Add() action method that accepts a ToDo parameter, change the parameter so it uses the ToDoViewModel type and has a name of model.

19. In the if block, modify the code that adds the task so it uses the CurrentTask property of the view model parameter like this:

    ```
    context.ToDos.Add(model.CurrentTask);
    ```

20. In the else block, modify the code that stores data in the ViewBag so it stores data in the view model parameter.

21. Modify the return statement so it passes the view model to the view.

Bind the view model to the Home/Add view

22. Open the Home/Add view.

23. At the top of the file, change its view model from a ToDo object to a ToDoViewModel object.

24. Modify the code so it uses properties of the ToDoViewModel object instead of the old ToDo model. For example, you can change

    ```
    <label asp-for="Description">
    ```

    to

    ```
    <label asp-for="CurrentTask.Description">
    ```

25. Modify the code so it uses properties of the ToDoViewModel object instead of the ViewBag. For example, you can change all instances of ViewBag.Categories to Model.Categories.

26. Run the app and test the Add page. If you receive unexpected data validation messages, add ValidateNever attributes to the properties of the ToDoViewModel as needed.

27. Test the Add page again to make sure it works as it did before.

11

How to validate data

In chapter 2, you learned how to validate data for simple scenarios like making sure a user has entered a value for a field and making sure the value falls within a specified range. Now, this chapter reviews those skills and presents some more advanced skills for validating data, including how to create custom data attributes, and how to make custom validation work on both the client and the server.

How data validation works in MVC

The next few figures review some of the skills for working with data validation that were presented in earlier chapters. In addition, they present some new skills for using attributes for data validation.

The default data validation provided by model binding

Figure 11-1 begins by presenting a model class for a Movie object, a strongly-typed view that's bound to this model, and the action method that this view posts to. The view includes <input> tags that use the asp-for tag helper to bind them to properties of the model. In addition, it includes a <div> tag that uses the asp-validation-summary tag helper to display validation messages. This <div> tag is assigned to Bootstrap's text-danger class so the validation messages appear in red.

The action method accepts a Movie object named movie. When the view posts to this method, MVC binds the values it receives from the view to the Movie object. If MVC can't bind a value, it adds a validation message to the ModelState property of the Controller class. That's why this action method starts by checking whether the ModelState is valid. If it is, no errors occurred during model binding. In this case, the action method adds the movie to the database and redirects to the page that lists the movies.

Otherwise, if errors occurred during model binding, the action method returns the original view. In addition, it passes the Movie object it receives back to the view. As a result, the view can redisplay the values the user entered. Also, since the ModelState property contains validation messages, the validation summary <div> tag displays those messages in red.

In this figure, the Movie class doesn't decorate its properties with any data attributes. However, as described in the previous chapter, when MVC performs model binding, it casts the data posted by the view to the parameter type specified by the action method. If this data conversion fails, MVC adds a message to the ModelState property. As a result, this code notifies the user about data conversions that fail, even though there are no data attributes in the model.

For example, the screen in this figure shows the view after the user enters a string of "four" in the Rating field. Since MVC can't cast that string to the int type, the data conversion fails and MVC adds a message to the ModelState property and sets its IsValid property to false. Then, when the action method checks the IsValid property, its value is false. This causes the view to display a validation message along with the values the user entered.

You can also avoid this error by removing the type="text" attribute from the <input> element. Then, the asp-for tag helper will generate a number field instead of a text field since the Rating property has a data type of int. The text attribute was included here to show what a default validation message looks like.

The Movie class

```
public class Movie
{
    public string Name { get; set; } = string.Empty;
    public int Rating { get; set; }
}
```

A strongly-typed view that posts a Movie object to an action method

```
@model Movie
...
<div asp-validation-summary="All" class="text-danger"></div>

<form asp-action="Add" method="post">
    <div class="row">
        <div class="col-1">
            <label asp-for="Name" class="form-label">Name:</label>
        </div>
        <div class="col-4">
            <input asp-for="Name" class="form-control" />
        </div>
        <div class="col-2">
            <label asp-for="Rating" class="form-label">Rating (1-5):</label>
        </div>
        <div class="col-2">
            <input asp-for="Rating" class="form-control" type="text" />
        </div>
        <div class="col">
            <button type="submit" class="btn btn-primary">Submit</button>
        </div>
    </div>
</form>
```

An action method that receives a Movie object from the view

```
[HttpPost]
public IActionResult Add(Movie movie)
{
    if (ModelState.IsValid) {
        // code that adds movie to database
        return RedirectToAction("List");
    }
    else {
        return View(movie);
    }
}
```

How it looks in the browser when the rating can't be cast to an int

> • The value 'four' is not valid for Rating.
>
> Name: [   ]   Rating (1-5): [four]   Submit

Description

- When MVC can't cast a value to the data type specified by the action method parameter, it adds an error message to the ModelState property of the Controller class.

Figure 11-1   The default data validation provided by model binding

How to use data attributes for validation

Chapter 2 showed how to validate user data by decorating model properties with *data attributes*. This is called *property-level validation*. Now, figure 11-2 reviews these data validation skills and presents some new ones. To start, the first table presents some of the most common data attributes that are stored in the System.ComponentModel.DataAnnotations namespace.

The Required attribute checks that the value of a property is not null, an empty string, or whitespace. To work properly, the property that this attribute decorates must be nullable. As a result, for numeric values, the property must use a nullable type like int? or double?.

The Range attribute checks that the value of a property is within a specified range. The property that this attribute decorates must implement the IComparable interface. Fortunately, most C# types (int, double, decimal, string, DateTime, etc.) implement this interface.

The two-argument Range attribute accepts int or double values that specify the minimum and maximum values of the range. However, the three-argument Range attribute also accepts a type argument that indicates the type of the values to compare. For example, the next figure shows how to use this type argument to compare DateTime values. When you use the type argument, the minimum and maximum values must be strings.

The StringLength attribute checks that the value of a string property doesn't exceed a specified number of characters. This attribute accepts an int value that specifies the maximum number of characters.

The RegularExpression attribute checks that the value of a property matches a regular expression (regex) pattern. It accepts a string value that's the pattern to match. Regular expression patterns are beyond the scope of this book, but you can find many good resources and regex libraries online.

The Compare attribute checks that the value of the property matches the value of another property in the model. It accepts a string value that contains the name of the other property.

The Display attribute doesn't check any values. Instead, it specifies how the name of the property should be displayed to the user. That includes not only how it's displayed in a validation message, but how it's displayed in a label that's bound to the property.

The first code example shows the properties of the Movie class decorated with some data attributes. Below that, the screen shows the validation messages that these attributes produce in the browser. This works because each attribute has a default validation message as shown in the second table.

However, sometimes the default message isn't user friendly. For instance, here's an example of a default message for the RegularExpression attribute: 'The field Username must match the regular expression "^[a-zA-Z0-9]+$ "', which is not user friendly. Fortunately, to create user-friendly messages, you can use the ErrorMessage property to add your own validation message to a data attribute as shown by the second code example.

Common data attributes for validation

Attribute	Description
`Required`	Makes sure the property value is not null, an empty string, or whitespace. Numeric data types like int should be nullable.
`Range(min, max)`	Makes sure the property value is within the specified range of values. The property must implement the IComparable interface.
`Range(type, min, max)`	Makes sure a value of a type other than int or double is within a range of values. The min and max arguments must be strings.
`StringLength(length)`	Makes sure the string property value doesn't exceed a specific length.
`RegularExpression(ex)`	Makes sure a property value matches a regex pattern.
`Compare(other)`	Makes sure the property has the same value as another property.
`Display(Name = "n")`	Specifies how the field name should be displayed to the user.

The Movie entity class decorated with data attributes

```
using System.ComponentModel.DataAnnotations;
...
public class Movie
{
    [Required]
    [StringLength(30)]
    public string Name { get; set; }

    [Range(1, 5)]
    public int Rating { get; set; }
}
```

The view after the user submits invalid data

- The field Name must be a string with a maximum length of 30.
- The field Rating must be between 1 and 5.

Name: Eternal Sunshine of the Spo   Rating (1-5): -1   Submit

The default validation messages

Attribute	Message
`Required`	The field [Name] is required.
`Range`	The field [Name] must be between [minimum] and [maximum].
`StringLength`	The field [Name] must be a string with a maximum length of [length].
`RegularExpression`	The field [Name] must match the regular expression '[pattern]'.
`Compare`	'[Name]' and '[OtherName]' do not match.

How to replace the default message with a custom message

```
[Required(ErrorMessage = "Please enter a name")]
[StringLength(30, ErrorMessage = "Name must be 30 characters or less.")]
public string Name { get; set; }

[Range(1, 5, ErrorMessage = "Please enter a rating between 1 and 5.")]
public int Rating { get; set; }
```

Figure 11-2   How to use data attributes for validation

A Registration page with data validation

Figure 11-3 shows how to code a Registration page that validates user input in a variety of ways. The first code example presents the model class for a Customer object that has four properties. This class decorates all four properties with a Required attribute that specifies a custom error message.

The Username property also has a RegularExpression attribute with a regex pattern that only allows uppercase letters, lowercase letters, and numbers. This attribute includes a user-friendly validation message that describes the requirements of the regex pattern.

The DOB property also has a Range attribute that includes a type argument to indicate that the range is of the DateTime type. Then, it passes two string arguments that indicate the minimum and maximum dates for the range. This code sets the maximum value to a date that's in the distant future to make sure the current date is always before the maximum value. Later, this chapter presents some techniques for using code to compare a date to the current date.

Note that the DOB property is of the DateTime? type, not the DateTime type. This is necessary for the Required attribute to work properly.

The Password property also has StringLength and Compare attributes. The StringLength attribute only allows string values of 25 characters or less. This attribute doesn't include a custom validation message because the default message is adequate. In addition, text fields and password fields often prevent the error message from being displayed by not allowing the user to enter more than the specified number of characters.

The Compare attribute tells MVC to check that the value of this property matches the value of the ConfirmPassword property. This attribute doesn't include a custom validation message. That's because the default message for the Compare attribute is adequate here.

The ConfirmPassword property also has a Display attribute that adds a space to the property name. As a result, this property displays as "Confirm Password in the default validation message of the Compare attribute that decorates the Password property.

The second code example presents the validation <div> and <input> tags in a strongly-typed view that posts a Customer object to an action method. Here, the <input> tags for the passwords are of the password type. This displays bullets for the characters. And, the <input> tag for the DOB is of the text type, so a standard text box is rendered in the browser.

The last code example presents the action method that receives the Customer object from the view. To start, this action method checks the IsValid property of the controller's ModelState property. If it's false, the code passes the Customer object to the view. That way, the view can redisplay the data to the user as well as the validation messages as shown by the screen at the bottom of this figure. Note, however, that the view doesn't redisplay the values in the two password fields even if the values of those fields are valid. In this case, for example, the user entered a value for the Password field but not for the Confirm Password field.

The Customer class

```
public class Customer {
    [Required(ErrorMessage = "Please enter a username.")]
    [RegularExpression("^[a-zA-Z0-9]+$",
        ErrorMessage = "Username may not contain special characters.")]
    public string Username { get; set; } = string.Empty;

    [Required(ErrorMessage = "Please enter a date of birth.")]
    [Range(typeof(DateTime), "1/1/1900", "12/31/9999",
        ErrorMessage = "Date of birth must be after 1/1/1900.")]
    public DateTime? DOB { get; set; }

    [Required(ErrorMessage = "Please enter a password.")]
    [StringLength(25)]
    [Compare("ConfirmPassword")]
    public string Password { get; set; } = string.Empty;

    [Required(ErrorMessage = "Please confirm your password.")]
    [Display(Name = "Confirm Password")]
    public string ConfirmPassword { get; set; } = string.Empty;
}
```

A validation tag in a strongly-typed view that posts a Customer object

```
<div asp-validation-summary="All" class="text-danger"></div>
<input asp-for="Username" class="form-control" />
<input asp-for="DOB" class="form-control" type="text" />
<input asp-for="Password" class="form-control" type="password" />
<input asp-for="ConfirmPassword" class="form-control" type="password" />
```

An action method that receives a Customer object from the view

```
public IActionResult Add(Customer customer) {
    if (ModelState.IsValid) {
        // code that adds customer to database
        return RedirectToAction("Welcome");
    } else {
        return View(customer);
    }
}
```

The view after the user submits invalid data

- Username may not contain special characters.
- Date of birth must be after 1/1/1900.
- 'Password' and 'Confirm Password' do not match.
- Please confirm your password.

Username	Mary D!
DOB	1/1/1872
Password	
Confirm Password	Submit

Figure 11-3   A Registration page with data validation

How to control the user experience

So far, you've learned how to use Bootstrap CSS classes to make messages in a validation summary <div> tag display in red. In addition, you've learned how to add your own validation messages to a data attribute. In the next few figures, you'll learn more skills for controlling how MVC displays validation messages to the user.

How to format validation messages with CSS

When you use data attributes and model binding as described in the previous two figures, MVC automatically adds data-* attributes to the <input> tags. These data-* attributes are an HTML feature that allows you to embed data that's specific to an app in your HTML.

The first example in figure 11-4 shows the HTML that MVC emits for an <input> tag that's bound to the Username property. This HTML includes a data-val attribute with a value of "true". In addition, it includes several data-val-* attributes that contain information MVC emits for the Required and RegularExpression attributes that decorate the Username property. When data validation fails, MVC also assigns a CSS class named input-validation-error to the <input> tag as shown in the second example.

The <div> tags that use the asp-validation-summary tag helper work similarly. For instance, the third example shows that MVC adds a data-valmsg-summary attribute to the <div> tag. In addition, if validation succeeds, it assigns the <div> tag to a CSS class named validation-summary-valid. However, if validation fails, MVC assigns the <div> tag to a CSS class named validation-summary-errors as shown by the fourth example.

You can define style rules for these CSS classes to control how these tags appear to the user. For instance, the last example presents style rules for all three CSS classes. For <input> tags that have failed validation, the CSS adds a border that's the same color as the Bootstrap text-danger CSS class. In addition, it adds a background color. The screen at the bottom of this figure shows how such an <input> tag appears on the page.

The last two style rules are for validation summary <div> tags. When validation succeeds (or when the page first loads), the first style rule sets the display to none. This hides the <div> tag and prevents it from taking up any space on the page. Then, if you want, you can include a generic message like this and it won't be displayed unless validation fails:

```
<div asp-validation-summary="All" class="text-danger">
    <h4>Please correct the following errors:</h4>
</div>
```

When validation fails, the last style rule removes the bullets from the unordered list items. The screen at the bottom of the figure shows how such a <div> tag appears on a page.

The HTML that MVC emits for an <input> tag bound to the Username property

```
<input class="form-control" type="text"
    data-val="true"
    data-val-regex="User name may not contain special characters."
    data-val-regex-pattern="^[a-zA-Z0-9]&#x2B;$"
    data-val-required="Please enter a user name."
    id="Username" name="Username" value="" />
```

The HTML that MVC emits for the <input> tag when data validation fails

```
<input class="form-control input-validation-error" type="text"
    data-val="true"
    data-val-regex="User name may not contain special characters."
    data-val-regex-pattern="^[a-zA-Z0-9]&#x2B;$"
    data-val-required="Please enter a user name."
    id="Username" name="Username" value="" />
```

The HTML that MVC emits for a summary of valid data

```
<div class="text-danger validation-summary-valid"
    data-valmsg-summary="true">
    <ul><li style="display:none"></li></ul>
</div>
```

The HTML that MVC emits for a summary of invalid data

```
<div class="text-danger validation-summary-errors"
    data-valmsg-summary="true">
    <ul>
        <li>Please enter a user name.</li>
        <li>Please enter a date of birth.</li>
    </ul>
</div>
```

Some CSS styles in the site.css file

```
.input-validation-error {
    border: 2px solid #dc3545;      /* same red as text-danger */
    background-color: #faebd7;      /* antique white */
}

.validation-summary-valid { display: none; }

.validation-summary-errors ul { list-style: none; }
```

The view after the user submits invalid data

Description

- When performing validation, MVC emits HTML that has CSS classes that you can style to control the appearance of the validation.

Figure 11-4   How to format validation messages with CSS

How to check validation state and use code to set validation messages

The ModelState property of the Controller class has a data type of ModelStateDictionary. This dictionary stores the data that a form posts to the controller. It stores this data as key/value pairs. It also stores any validation messages produced during model binding.

The first table in figure 11-5 shows some of the properties of the ModelStateDictionary class. The Count property returns the number of key/value pairs sent to the server, and the ErrorCount property returns the number of validation messages. For instance, if a form posts three values and one of them produces a validation message, the Count property is 3 and the ErrorCount property is 1.

The IsValid property returns false if there are any validation messages. The Keys property is a collection that contains the names of the form data parameters that were posted. And the Values property is a collection that contains the values of those parameters.

The second table in this figure shows two of the methods of the ModelStateDictionary class. The AddModelError() method adds a validation message. It accepts two string values. The first argument specifies the name of the property that's associated with the validation message. However, if you want to associate the message with the overall model, you can pass an empty string to this argument. The second argument specifies the validation message itself.

The GetValidationState() method returns the validation state of the specified property. It accepts a string value that's the name of the property to check and returns a value of the ModelValidationState enum.

Below the tables, the code example uses these properties and methods to check the DOB property against the current date. Here, the action method accepts a Customer object and starts by checking whether the DOB value passed MVC validation during model binding.

To perform this check, the code uses the nameof operator to get the name of the DOB property and store it in a variable named key. This is less error prone than coding a string literal of "DOB". Then, the code calls the GetValidationState() method, passes it the variable that contains the name of the DOB property, and compares its return value to the Valid value of the ModelValidationState enum. If they match, the DOB value passed MVC validation and is a date that's later than 1/1/1900 and before 12/31/9999.

If the DOB value passes MVC validation, the code checks if the date is a future date. If so, the code calls the AddModelError() method and adds an error message for the DOB field to the ModelState property. Finally, the code checks the IsValid property and proceeds based on the value of that property.

Some of the properties of the ModelStateDictionary class

Property	Description
Count	The number of key/value pairs sent to the server and stored in the dictionary.
ErrorCount	The number of validation messages stored in the dictionary.
IsValid	A Boolean value indicating whether any of the key/value pairs are invalid or not validated.
Keys	A collection of the keys of the form data parameters.
Values	A collection of the values of the form data parameters.

Two of the methods of the ModelStateDictionary class

Method	Description
AddModelError(key, msg)	Adds a validation message to the dictionary and associates it with the property that matches the specified key. To associate a validation message with the overall model rather than a specific property, specify an empty string as the key.
GetValidationState(key)	Gets the ModelValidationState enum value for the specified property name. Possible values are Valid, Invalid, Unvalidated, and Skipped.

Code that adds a validation message to the ModelState property

```
using Microsoft.AspNetCore.Mvc.ModelBinding;
...
[HttpPost]
public IActionResult Add(Customer customer)
{
    string key = nameof(Customer.DOB);

    if (ModelState.GetValidationState(key) == ModelValidationState.Valid) {
        if (customer.DOB > DateTime.Today) {
            ModelState.AddModelError(
                key, "Date of birth must not be a future date.");
        }
    }

    if (ModelState.IsValid) {
        // code that adds customer to database
        return RedirectToAction("Welcome");
    }
    else {
        return View(customer);
    }
}
```

Description

- The Controller class has a property named ModelState of the ModelStateDictionary type. This dictionary stores key/value pairs that represent the form parameters sent to the server and the validation messages associated with those parameters.

- The ModelValidationState enum is in the Microsoft.AspNetCore.Mvc.Model-Binding namespace.

Figure 11-5   How to check validation state and use code to set validation messages

How to display model-level and property-level validation messages

In the last figure, you learned how to associate a validation message with either a specific property or the overall domain model. But what difference does that make? Well, MVC has features that let you display validation messages differently based on this association.

The first table in figure 11-6 shows two MVC tag helpers that you can use with data validation. So far, the examples in this book have used the asp-validation-summary helper. This helper targets the <div> tag and displays one or more validation messages for one or more properties in an unordered list (a <ul> tag). It accepts a value of the ValidateSummary enum that's described in the second table.

The asp-validation-for tag helper, by contrast, targets the <span> tag and displays a single validation message for a specific property. If there's more than one validation message for a property, it displays the first one. It accepts a string value that's the name of the property.

The second table presents the values of the ValidateSummary enum. So far, the examples in this book have used the All value. This value tells MVC to display all the validation messages in the ModelState dictionary. By contrast, the ModelOnly value tells MVC to display only those messages that are associated with the model. That is, it tells MVC to display only messages that have a key value of an empty string, not any messages that have a key value of a property name.

The code below the tables shows how to display model-level messages in one place and property-level messages in another. This action method accepts a Customer object as an argument. As usual, it uses the controller's ModelState property to check whether validation has succeeded. If not, the code adds another message and associates it with the model.

The view has a <div> tag that uses the asp-validation-summary tag helper. This time, though, the code sets the tag helper to "ModelOnly" rather than "All". This means that the <div> tag only displays model-level messages like the one added by the action method in this figure.

Below the <div> tag, the view includes the <input> tags for the form. Here, each <input> tag is followed by a <span> tag that uses the asp-validation-for tag helper. This HTML sets the value of each tag helper to the same property name that's bound to the corresponding <input> tag. This means that each <span> tag displays the first property-level message for the specified property.

The screen at the bottom of the figure shows what the browser displays when validation fails. Here, above the form, the page displays the model-level message that notifies the user that the form contains errors. Then, the property-level messages for each entry display to the right of each text box.

Two tag helpers used with data validation

Tag Helper	Description
`asp-validation-summary`	Displays the validation messages in the ModelState property. Accepts a value of the ValidateSummary enum to determine which messages to display. Targets the <div> tag.
`asp-validation-for`	Displays the first validation message in the ModelState property for the specified property. Targets the <span> tag.

The values of the ValidateSummary enum

Value	Description
`All`	Displays all the validation messages in the ModelState property.
`ModelOnly`	Displays messages in the ModelState property that are associated with the model. In other words, only displays messages whose key is an empty string.
`None`	Displays no messages.

An action method that adds a model-level validation message

```
[HttpPost]
public IActionResult Add(Customer customer) {
    if (ModelState.IsValid) {
        // code that adds customer to database
        return RedirectToAction("Welcome");
    } else {
        ModelState.AddModelError("", "There are errors in the form.");
        return View(customer);
    }
}
```

Part of a view that displays both model-level and property-level messages

```
<div asp-validation-summary="ModelOnly" class="text-danger"></div>

<form asp-action="Add" method="post">
    <div class="row mb-2">
        <div class="col-md-2">
            <label asp-for="Username" class="form-label"></label>
        </div>
        <div class="col-md-4">
            <input asp-for="Username" class="form-control" />
        </div>
        <div class="col-md-6">
            <span asp-validation-for="Userame" class="text-danger"></span>
        </div>
    </div>
    ...
```

The form in the browser after validation fails

Figure 11-6   How to display model-level and property-level validation messages

How to enable client-side validation

So far, this book has shown how to validate data by posting it to the server, checking it on the server, and returning validation results to the client. However, it's generally considered a good practice to validate data on the client before sending it to the server. This can improve the responsiveness of your app significantly since it prevents a round trip to the server.

Fortunately, it's easy to enable client-side validation in an MVC app. All you need to do is to add the jQuery libraries shown in figure 11-7 as described in chapter 3. These libraries use data-val-* attributes to perform data validation without making a round trip to the server. This works well with MVC since it automatically emits data-val-* attributes when you use server-side validation as described in this chapter.

After you add these libraries, you can include them with your view using <script> tags. When you code these tags, you must code them in the order shown in this figure. This example adds these <script> tags to the end of the <head> tag. However, many programmers prefer to add the jQuery libraries at the end of the <body> tag as shown later in this chapter.

There are some caveats to using client-side validation in your MVC app. First, client-side validation only works correctly with property-level validation, not with model-level validation. That's because there's no round trip to the server with client-side validation, so the ModelState dictionary doesn't contain any model-level validation messages. As a result, if the user doesn't enter valid data, the form doesn't submit and the app doesn't display any model-level messages explaining why the form didn't submit. This leaves the user wondering why the form didn't submit. Because of that, it's best to use property-level validation with client-side validation.

Second, if there's custom validation on the server, such as the DOB check shown in figure 11-5, validation can run twice. In other words, after the client-side validation passes, the form posts to the server, and the server-side validation runs. This can lead to a process where the user gets validation messages in two different steps, which some users might not like. Whenever possible, it's best to let your users know in one step everything they need to do to fix their data entry.

Third, not all of the MVC data attributes work properly with the jQuery validation libraries. In particular, the Range attribute doesn't work well with dates. For example, in the screen at the bottom of this figure, the user has entered a date of 1/1/1971, which is after 1/1/1900, but the client-side validation is telling the user otherwise. In a case like this, you need to use custom validation as shown later in this chapter.

When working with validation, keep in mind that client-side validation *is not* a substitute for server-side validation. That's because a user's browser might have JavaScript turned off, or a malicious user might tamper with the JavaScript. As a result, you should think of client-side validation as a convenience for your users. You should always validate user input on the server as well.

The jQuery libraries that download by default with the MVC template

The jQuery libraries in the head section of a Layout view

```
<head>
    <meta name="viewport" content="width=device-width" />
    <link href="~/lib/bootstrap/dist/css/bootstrap.min.css"
        rel="stylesheet" />
    <link href="~/css/site.css" rel="stylesheet" />
    <script src="~/lib/jquery/dist/jquery.min.js"></script>
    <script src="~/lib/jquery-validation/dist/jquery.validate.min.js">
    </script>
    <script src="~/lib/jquery-validation-unobtrusive/
                                jquery.validate.unobtrusive.min.js">
    </script>
    <title>@ViewBag.Title</title>
</head>
```

Some caveats to client-side validation

- It only works correctly with property-level validation, not model-level validation.
- Any server-side validation doesn't run until all client-side validation passes. This can lead to a 2-step process that may annoy some users.
- Not all data annotations work properly on the client. In the example below, for instance, the Range annotation for the DOB field isn't working as it should.

The form in the browser after validation fails

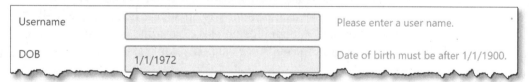

Description

- To enable client-side validation, add the jQuery, jQuery validation, and jQuery unobtrusive validation libraries to your app in the order shown above.
- Client-side validation is optional and should be thought of as a convenience for the user. For security reasons, you should always perform server-side validation too.

Figure 11-7   How to enable client-side validation

How to customize server-side validation

The built-in data attributes that MVC provides are often all you need to validate the data for an app. However, you may occasionally need to create custom validation for an app as shown in the next few figures.

How to create a custom data attribute

One way to customize validation is to create a custom data attribute. Then, you can use it just like the built-in data attributes.

The first table in figure 11-8 presents three of the classes that you use to create a custom data attribute. The ValidationAttribute class is the base class for data attributes. The ValidationContext class provides information about the context in which the validation takes place, including information about the property being validated. And the ValidationResult class contains information about the result of the validation.

The second table presents the virtual IsValid() method of the ValidationAttribute class. This method accepts two arguments. The first is an object that's the value to check, and the second is a ValidationContext object. This method returns a ValidationResult object.

The third table presents a constructor and a static field of the ValidationResult object. The constructor accepts a string value that specifies the validation message to associate with the property being checked. The static Success field is used to indicate success.

To create a custom data attribute, you code a class that inherits the ValidationAttribute class and overrides its IsValid() method as shown by the PastDateAttribute class presented in this figure. It's a convention to include a suffix of *Attribute* at the end of the class name. However, you don't include that suffix when you decorate a model property.

The IsValid() method of the PastDateAttribute class starts by checking whether the value it receives is a date. If so, it casts that value to a DateTime value. Then, it checks whether the date is in the past. If so, the IsValid() method returns the Success field of the ValidationResult class. Note that because the Success field can contain a null, the null-forgiving operator (!) is used to suppress compiler warnings.

If the date isn't in the past, the IsValid() method returns a new ValidationResult object that contains an error message. But first, it builds the message to pass to the constructor of the ValidationResult object. To do that, it checks the ErrorMessage property of the base class. If it's null, no custom validation message has been set. In that case, the code creates a default validation message. To do that, the code uses the ValidationContext parameter to get the display name of the property being checked.

The last two code examples in this figure show how to use the PastDate data attribute with a default or custom validation message. This works just like the built-in data attributes that you learned about earlier in this chapter.

Three classes used to create a custom data attribute

Class	Description
ValidationAttribute	The base class for a custom data attribute.
ValidationContext	Describes the context for the validation.
ValidationResult	Contains data that represents the validation results.

A virtual method of the ValidationAttribute class

Virtual method	Description
IsValid(object?, context)	Checks whether a value is valid. Accepts the value to check and a ValidationContext object. Returns a ValidationResult object.

A constructor and a field of the ValidationResult class

Constructor	Description
ValidationResult(string)	Creates an object with the validation message.

Static field	Description
Success	Indicates that validation was successful.

A custom data attribute that checks if a date is in the past

```
using System.ComponentModel.DataAnnotations;
...
public class PastDateAttribute : ValidationAttribute
{
    protected override ValidationResult IsValid(object? value,
    ValidationContext ctx)
    {
        if (value is DateTime) {
            DateTime dateToCheck = (DateTime)value;
            if (dateToCheck < DateTime.Today) {
                return ValidationResult.Success!;
            }
        }

        string msg = base.ErrorMessage ??
            $"{ctx.DisplayName} must be a valid past date.";
        return new ValidationResult(msg);
    }
}
```

Code that uses the PastDate attribute with the default validation message

```
[PastDate]
public DateTime? DOB { get; set; }
```

How it looks in the browser

DOB	1/1/2050	DOB must be a valid past date.

Code that uses the PastDate attribute with a custom validation message

```
[PastDate(ErrorMessage = "Please enter a date of birth in the past.")]
public DateTime? DOB { get; set; }
```

Figure 11-8   How to create a custom data attribute

How to pass values to a custom data attribute

Sometimes a data attribute needs additional information to validate the value of a property. For instance, the Compare attribute needs the name of the property to compare, and the Range attribute needs the minimum and maximum values in the range. To enable this in your own custom data attribute class, you can use the class constructor and public properties.

Figure 11-9 presents a class for a custom data attribute named YearsFromNow. This attribute checks that the value of a property is a valid past or future date within a specified number of years from the current date.

Like the class in the last figure, the YearsFromNowAttribute class inherits the ValidationAttribute base class and overrides its IsValid() method. However, it also has a constructor that accepts an int value and assigns it to a private variable named numYears. In addition, it has a property named IsPast that has a default value of false. This property accepts a Boolean value and determines whether a valid date is in the past or the future.

The IsValid() method in this figure starts by making sure that the value it receives is a date. If so, it casts it to a DateTime value. After that, it assigns the current date to a DateTime variable named now and declares another DateTime variable named limit. These variables define the range of valid dates.

The code then uses the IsPast property to calculate the limit variable. If the date is in the past, the code creates a new DateTime value for January 1 of the current year and assigns it to the limit variable. Then, this code subtracts the number of years in the numYears variable. So, if the current year is 2025 and the value in numYears is 25, the limit date would be 1/1/2000.

Conversely, if the date is in the future, the code creates a new DateTime value for December 31 of the current year and assigns it to the limit variable. Then, this code adds the number of years in the numYears variable. So, if the current year is 2025 and the value in numYears is 25, the limit date will be 12/31/2050.

Once the limit date is calculated, the code checks whether the date is valid. For a past date, the code checks if the parameter value is greater than or equal to the limit date and less than the current date. Conversely, for a future date, the code checks if the parameter value is greater than the current date and less than or equal to the limit date. If the validation succeeds, the code returns the Success field of the ValidationResult class. Otherwise, the code gets either the custom validation message or the default validation message, passes it to the constructor of a new ValidationResult object, and returns that object.

The second code example shows how to use the YearsFromNow attribute. This shows that you can pass the values of parameters defined by the constructor, as well as the values of properties defined by the class. When you do that, you should code the parameter values first, followed by the named property values.

A custom attribute that accepts values via a constructor and a property

```
public class YearsFromNowAttribute : ValidationAttribute
{
    private int numYears;
    public YearsFromNowAttribute(int years) {    // constructor
        numYears = years;
    }
    public bool IsPast { get; set; } = false;    // property with default

    protected override ValidationResult IsValid(object? value,
    ValidationContext ctx)
    {
        if (value is DateTime) {
            // cast value to DateTime
            DateTime dateToCheck = (DateTime)value;

            // calculate date range
            DateTime now = DateTime.Today;
            DateTime limit;

            if (IsPast) {
                limit = new DateTime(now.Year, 1, 1);
                limit = limit.AddYears(-numYears);
            }
            else {
                limit = new DateTime(now.Year, 12, 31);
                limit = limit.AddYears(numYears);
            }

            // check date
            if (IsPast) {
                if (dateToCheck >= limit && dateToCheck < now) {
                    return ValidationResult.Success!;
                }
            }
            else {
                if (dateToCheck > now && dateToCheck <= limit) {
                    return ValidationResult.Success!;
                }
            }
        }
        string msg = base.ErrorMessage ??
            ctx.DisplayName + " must be a " + (IsPast ? "past" : "future") +
            " date within " + numYears + " years of now.";
        return new ValidationResult(msg);
    }
}
```

A DOB property that requires a past date no more than 100 years ago

```
[YearsFromNow(100, IsPast = true)]    // constructor parameter first
public DateTime? DOB { get; set; }
```

Description

- You can use the class constructor and named properties to accept data for a data attribute.
- When you use an attribute, you must code the values for the constructor parameters first, followed by the values for the properties.

Figure 11-9   How to pass values to a custom data attribute

How to check multiple properties

The two custom data attributes you've seen so far only check the value of the property they decorate. However, it's possible to create a data attribute that checks more than one property in the model object. For instance, the RequiredContactInfo data attribute at the top of figure 11-10 checks that a user has entered either a phone number or an email address.

To do that, the code in the IsValid() method uses the ObjectInstance property of the ValidationContext class to return the object that contains the properties being checked. However, it returns it as the object type, so you need to cast it to the correct type. In this example, the code casts the object to the Customer type. To use an attribute like this, you only need to decorate one of the properties it validates with the attribute.

Because this custom data attribute class only works with the Customer model class, it may be hard to reuse. As a result, it sometimes can make more sense to simply validate the class rather than create several data attributes that you may not be able to use anywhere else. This is called *class-level validation*, and the rest of this figure shows how it works.

To start, the two tables present the IValidatableObject interface and its Validate() method. To code a class that can validate itself, you need to implement this interface and method. Like the IsValid() method, the Validate() method accepts a ValidationContext object. However, the Validate() method returns a collection of ValidationResult objects rather than a single ValidationResult object. MVC calls the Validate() method during model binding.

The third table presents another constructor for the ValidationResult class. Like the constructor presented in figure 11-8, this constructor accepts a string value for the validation message. However, it also accepts a list of strings for the properties associated with the validation message.

Below the tables, the example shows some of the code in a Customer class that's been updated to validate itself. This class implements the IValidatableObject interface and its Validate() method. Within the Validate() method, the code returns a validation error if the DOB value is in the future. Similarly, it returns a validation error if there isn't a value for either the phone number or the email address.

When you use class-level validation, you can still use regular data attributes to perform property-level validation. In this example, for instance, the class decorates the DOB property with the Required attribute. However, class-level validation only runs if all the property-level validation has passed. This can create a 2-step validation process that users might not like.

One way to address this issue is to only use class-level validation. To do that, you avoid data attributes and manually code all validation in the Validate() method. Of course, this isn't as convenient as using data attributes. And, depending on how much validation there is, this can result in unwieldy code. So, whether you code a class that validates itself or individual data attributes that are specific to that class depends on your needs and preferences.

A custom attribute that checks more than one property in a class

```
public class RequiredContactInfoAttribute : ValidationAttribute
{
    protected override ValidationResult IsValid(object? v,
                                                ValidationContext c){
        var cust = (Customer)c.ObjectInstance;
        if (string.IsNullOrEmpty(cust.PhoneNumber) &&
            string.IsNullOrEmpty(cust.EmailAddress))
        {
            string msg = base.ErrorMessage ?? "Enter phone number or email.";
            return new ValidationResult(msg);
        }
        else {
            return ValidationResult.Success!;
        }
    }
}
```

The single method of the IValidatableObject interface

Method	Description
Validate(context)	Checks whether an object is valid. Accepts a ValidationContext object. Returns an IEnumerable of ValidationResult objects.

A constructor of the ValidationResult class

Constructor	Description
ValidationResult(string, list)	Creates an object with the validation message and list of properties.

A custom validation class that checks more than one field

```
public class Customer : IValidatableObject {
    ...
    [Required(ErrorMessage = "Please enter a date of birth.")]
    public DateTime? DOB { get; set; }

    public string? PhoneNumber { get; set; }
    public string? EmailAddress { get; set; }

    public IEnumerable<ValidationResult> Validate(ValidationContext ctx) {
        if (DOB > DateTime.Now)
        {
            yield return new ValidationResult(
                "Date of birth can't be in the future.",
                new[] { nameof(DOB) });
        }
        if (string.IsNullOrEmpty(PhoneNumber) &&
            string.IsNullOrEmpty(EmailAddress))
        {
            yield return new ValidationResult(
                "Please enter a phone number or email address.",
                new[] { nameof(PhoneNumber), nameof(EmailAddress) });
        }
    }
}
```

Figure 11-10   How to check multiple properties

How to customize client-side validation

The previous figures have shown how to add custom server-side data validation to an app. Now, the next few figures show how to add custom client-side data validation to an app.

How to add data attributes to the generated HTML

When you create a custom data attribute, it's a good practice to enable it to perform validation on the client too. That way, the attribute can participate in client-side validation as described in figure 11-7.

To add client-side validation, you can start by updating your data attribute class to emit the data-val-* attributes that the jQuery validation libraries use as shown in figure 11-11. Then, you can add jQuery code to do the actual validation as shown in the next figure.

To specify the HTML that MVC emits for the tag that's being validated, a data attribute must implement the IClientModelValidator interface and its AddValidation() method shown in the table at the top of this figure. This is illustrated by the PastDate attribute in the first code example. This version accepts an optional constructor argument that allows you to limit valid past dates to a given time span.

This code starts by including the namespace that contains the IClientModelValidator interface. Then, the class includes a constructor that accepts an int value and assigns it to the numYears variable. If there's no value, it assigns a default of -1.

The IsValid() method contains the validation that runs on the server. For instance, if the user has JavaScript disabled, MVC runs this code. This method is similar to the method presented in figure 11-8. However, this version checks if the number of years in the past is limited.

The AddValidation() method accepts a ClientModelValidationContext object that describes the context in which the validation is taking place. Here, the code uses the Attributes property of this object to add data-val-* attributes to the generated HTML. To start, it checks whether the data-val attribute exists before adding it. That's necessary because an error can occur if another custom data attribute has already added a data-val attribute and your code attempts to add it again. Then, it adds the attributes that store the number of years limit and the validation message.

To get the validation message, this code calls the GetMsg() method and passes it the DisplayName attribute for the property if it has one, the Name attribute if it doesn't, or a string value if both attributes are null. To get these attributes, it uses the ModelMetadata property, which allows you to access data about the model property. Then, it uses a conditional operator to determine if a max number of years in the past is included in the message.

The second code example shows the DOB property decorated with the PastDate attribute. This example passes a value of 100 to the constructor. As a result, this validation fails if the date of birth is in the future or more than 100 years in the past.

A method of the IClientModelValidator interface

Method	Description
`AddValidation(context)`	Adds data-val-* attributes to the generated HTML.

The updated PastDate attribute with client-side validation

```
using Microsoft.AspNetCore.Mvc.ModelBinding.Validation;
...
public class PastDateAttribute : ValidationAttribute, IClientModelValidator
{
    private int numYears;
    public PastDateAttribute(int years = -1) => numYears = years;

    protected override ValidationResult IsValid(object? value,
        ValidationContext ctx)
    {
        if (value is DateTime) {
            DateTime dateToCheck = (DateTime)value;
            if (numYears == -1) {      // no limit on past date
                if (dateToCheck < DateTime.Today)
                    return ValidationResult.Success!;
            } else {
                DateTime minDate = DateTime.Today.AddYears(-numYears);
                if (dateToCheck >= minDate && dateToCheck < DateTime.Today)
                    return ValidationResult.Success!;
            }
        }
        return new ValidationResult(GetMsg(ctx.DisplayName ?? "Value"));
    }

    public void AddValidation(ClientModelValidationContext c)
    {
        if (!c.Attributes.ContainsKey("data-val"))
            c.Attributes.Add("data-val", "true");
        c.Attributes.Add("data-val-pastdate-numyears", numYears.ToString());
        c.Attributes.Add("data-val-pastdate", GetMsg(
            c.ModelMetadata.DisplayName ?? c.ModelMetadata.Name ?? "Value"));
    }

    private string GetMsg(string name) =>
        base.ErrorMessage ?? name + " must be a valid past date" +
        (numYears == -1 ? "." : " (max " + numYears + " years ago).");
}
```

A model property decorated with the PastDate attribute

```
[PastDate(100)]
public DateTime? DOB { get; set; }
```

The HTML that the PastDate attribute emits

```
<input type="text" class="form-control" data-val="true"
    data-val-pastdate="DOB must be a valid past date (max 100 years ago)."
    data-val-pastdate-numyears="100" id="DOB" name="DOB" value="" />
```

Description

- To add the data-val-* attributes jQuery uses for validation to an HTML element, implement the IClientModelValidator interface and its AddValidation() method.

Figure 11-11   How to add data attributes to the generated HTML

The last example in figure 11-11 shows the HTML that MVC generates for an <input> tag that's bound to this DOB property. This HTML includes a data-val attribute set to true, a data-val-pastdate attribute set to the default error message for 100 years, and a data-val-pastdate-numyears attribute set to 100.

How to add a validation method to the jQuery validation library

In the previous figure, you learned how to update your custom data attribute to generate data-val-* attributes. Now, figure 11-12 shows how to tell the jQuery validation libraries to use these attributes. To do that, you need to add a JavaScript function that performs the validation to the jQuery validation library. In addition, you need to add the name of the validation function and its parameters to the adapters collection of the jQuery unobtrusive validation library.

This figure begins by presenting a JavaScript file named pastdate.js. This file starts by calling the addMethod() function of the jQuery validation library. The two arguments of this function specify the name of the function you're adding and the code for the function.

The anonymous function that's passed to the addMethod() function defines three parameters. The first parameter specifies the value of the HTML element that's being validated. By default, this parameter is a string, but you can cast it to another type if necessary. The second parameter specifies the HTML element. You can use this parameter to get information about the HTML element such as the values of its attributes. And the third parameter specifies any other parameters the function needs to do its work. In this figure, it's mapped to the numyears parameter.

The body of the anonymous function starts by checking whether the user entered a value. If so, it checks whether the value is a valid date. If either of these checks fail, the function returns false.

After those preliminary checks, the code converts the third parameter to a number and stores it in the numYears variable. This variable stores the number of years that's passed to the constructor of the PastDate attribute. Or, if the code didn't pass any years, it stores the default value of -1.

Next, the code gets the current date, and it checks the date entered by the user. If the numYears variable is -1, there's no limit to how far in the past the date can be. In that case, the code just checks whether the date is before the current date. However, if the numYears variable stores a positive value, the code calculates the minimum date and checks whether the date is after the minimum date and in the past.

The last statement in this file adds the name of the validation function to the adapters collection of the jQuery unobtrusive validation library. To do that, it uses the addSingleVal() function because the pastdate() function accepts a single parameter value named numyears. If a validation function doesn't accept any parameters, you can use the addBool() function to add it to the adapters collection. Or, if a validation function accepts multiple parameters, you can use

The pastdate.js file

```
jQuery.validator.addMethod("pastdate", function (value, element, param) {
    // get date entered by user, confirm it's a date
    if (value === '') return false;
    var dateToCheck = new Date(value);
    if (dateToCheck === "Invalid Date") return false;

    // get number of years
    var numYears = Number(param);

    // get current date
    var now = new Date();

    // check date
    if (numYears == -1) {
        if (dateToCheck < now) return true;
    } else {
        // calculate limit
        var minDate = new Date();
        var minYear = now.getFullYear() - numYears;
        minDate.setFullYear(minYear);

        if (dateToCheck >= minDate && dateToCheck < now) return true;
    }
    return false;
});

jQuery.validator.unobtrusive.adapters.addSingleVal("pastdate", "numyears");
```

The header section of the layout

```
<head>
    <meta name="viewport" content="width=device-width" />
    <link href="~/lib/bootstrap/dist/css/bootstrap.min.css" rel="stylesheet" />

    <script src="~/lib/jquery/jquery.min.js"></script>
    <script src="~/lib/jquery-validation/jquery.validate.min.js"></script>
    <script src="~/lib/jquery-validation-unobtrusive/
                jquery.validate.unobtrusive.min.js"></script>
    <script src="~/js/pastdate.js"></script>
    <title>@ViewBag.Title</title>
</head>
```

Description

- To implement client-side validation, you need to use the addMethod() function to add a JavaScript function that performs the validation to the jQuery validation library.

- To map a JavaScript validation function to its HTML data-val-* attributes, you need to use a JavaScript function to add the validation function to the adapters collection of the jQuery unobtrusive validation library.

- To map a JavaScript validation function that accepts one argument, you can use the addSingleVal() function. For validation functions that accept zero arguments, you can use the addBool() function. And for validation functions that accept multiple arguments, you can use the add() function.

Figure 11-12   How to add a validation function to the jQuery validation library

the add() function. However, the details of using these functions are beyond the scope of this book.

To use the code in the pastdate.js file, you need to include a <script> element for that file in addition to the required jQuery libraries. When you do that, be sure to code your custom file after the jQuery libraries.

How to work with remote validation

In addition to enabling custom attributes so the validation runs on the client, you can write code on the server that's called by the client without reloading the page. This is called *remote validation*, and you can use it when you need to perform a task on the server like accessing a file or a database.

To enable remote validation, you can use the Remote attribute that's in the Microsoft.AspNetCore.Mvc namespace. The table at the top of figure 11-13 presents two constructors of the RemoteAttribute class. Both accept arguments that tell MVC where to find the server-side code to run.

Below the table, the first code example shows how to use the Remote attribute. To do that, you decorate a property in your model with this attribute and provide the appropriate constructor arguments. Here, the Remote attribute specifies "CheckEmail" as the name of the action method and "Validation" as the name of the controller.

When you code the action method for the Remote attribute, the method must have a return type of JsonResult and it must accept a parameter with the same name as the property that the Remote attribute decorates. Usually, it's best to code this parameter as a string. Then, you can convert the value to another type in the body of the method if necessary.

In the second example, the CheckEmail() action method checks whether the specified email already exists. To do that, it starts by calling the CheckEmail() method of a static data access class named DB. Then, if the email does exist, the action method returns a validation message. Otherwise, it returns true. Either way, this code returns the data as a JsonResult object by calling the Json() method that's provided by the controller.

The second table presents the AdditionalFields property of the RemoteAttribute class. This property lets you identify additional values that the action method should retrieve from the POST request.

The code below this table shows how to use the AdditionalFields property. This code shows how you can pass additional parameters to an action method if necessary. In this figure, the code passes a username that's bound to the model as well as a region that's included in a hidden field.

There are three important things to understand about remote validation. First, it doesn't run if the field is left blank. So, you may want to code a Required attribute before your remote attribute. Second, it requires the jQuery validation libraries. Third, even though the code for the Remote attribute is in a controller on the server, it's only called by the client. As a result, if a user has JavaScript disabled in their browser, the remote validation doesn't run. So, you should always code your app so the validation runs on the server too as shown later in this chapter.

Two constructors of the RemoteAttribute class

Constructor	Description
`RemoteAttribute(act, ctl)`	Identifies the action method and controller to be called by the client.
`RemoteAttribute(act, ctl, area)`	Identifies the action method, controller, and area to be called by the client.

A model property with a Remote attribute

```
using Microsoft.AspNetCore.Mvc;
...
[Remote("CheckEmail", "Validation")]
public string Email { get; set; } = string.Empty;
```

The CheckEmail() action method in the Validation controller

```
public JsonResult CheckEmail(string email) {
    bool hasEmail = DB.CheckEmail(email);      // checks database
    if (hasEmail)
        return Json($"Email address {email} is already registered.");
    else
        return Json(true);
}
```

One property of the RemoteAttribute class

Property	Description
`AdditionalFields`	A comma-separated list of any additional values to be sent to the specified action method.

Remote validation that gets data from additional fields

The model

```
[Remote("CheckEmail", "Validation", AdditionalFields = "Username, Region")]
public string Email { get; set; } = string.Empty;
public string Username { get; set; } = string.Empty;
```

The view

```
<input asp-for="EmailAddress" class="form-control" />
<input asp-for="Username" class="form-control" />
<input type="hidden" name="Region" value="West" />
```

The CheckEmail() action method in the Validation controller

```
public JsonResult CheckEmail (string email, string username, string region){
    // validation code
}
```

Description

- *Remote validation* allows you to write code on the server that's called by the client without reloading the whole page. It requires the jQuery validation libraries.

- The AdditionalFields property of the Remote attribute lets you identify other HTTP values that the action method should retrieve from the POST request.

- The code in the controller is only called by the client. You should always make sure there's a server-side version, too.

Figure 11-13   How to work with remote validation

The Registration app

The rest of this chapter presents the Registration page of the Registration app. This page uses many of the validation techniques presented so far in this chapter. If you haven't already done so, you'll need to run the Update-Database command from the Package Manager Console to create the database before running this app.

The user interface and CSS

Figure 11-14 shows the user interface for the Registration page after the user has entered invalid data and clicked the Register button. This shows that the app uses the CSS presented at the bottom of this figure to style the text boxes with validation messages.

Most of the validation on this page is handled by the built-in data attributes that are provided by MVC. For instance, all of the fields use the Required attribute. In addition, the Username field uses the RegularExpression attribute to make sure the user doesn't enter special characters. Similarly, the Password field uses the Compare attribute to make sure the Password and Confirm Password fields match, and it uses the StringLength attribute to make sure the password is less than a maximum number of characters.

However, this page also uses two custom validation techniques. First, the Email Address field uses the Remote attribute to access the server to check that the email address entered by the user isn't already in use. As a convenience to the user, client-side code performs this check. For security reasons, server-side code also performs this check.

Second, the DOB field uses a custom data attribute to check that the user is at least 13 years old. Again, this check is performed by client-side code to keep the page responsive and by server-side code to keep the page secure.

The Registration app with invalid data

The CSS for the validation class

```
.input-validation-error {
    border: 2px solid #dc3545;    /* same red as text-danger */
    background-color: #faebd7;    /* antique white */
}
```

Description

- The Registration page uses data validation to make sure all the fields have a value, the username doesn't have special characters, the email address isn't already in use, the user is at least 13 years old, the password is less than 25 characters, and the confirm password matches the password.

- The Registration page validates data on the client as a convenience to users but performs the same validation on the server.

- The Registration page uses CSS to highlight the text boxes associated with a validation message.

Figure 11-14   The user interface and CSS for the Registration page

The Customer and RegistrationContext classes

Figure 11-15 presents the Customer model class and the RegistrationContext database context class. The Customer class decorates its properties with several of the standard data attributes. Most of these attributes include custom validation messages, though the Compare attribute on the Password property uses the default validation message.

The EmailAddress property is decorated with a Remote attribute. The values passed to the constructor of this attribute tell it to use code in the CheckEmail() action method of the Validation controller to validate the email address. The code for this action method is shown later in this chapter.

The EmailAddress property is also decorated with the DisplayName attribute. This provides MVC with a friendly name to display in validation messages that refer to this property, and in <label> elements that are bound to this property.

The DOB property is decorated with a custom data attribute named MinimumAge. This attribute includes a constructor with an argument that specifies the minimum age as well as a property value that specifies a custom validation message. This custom data attribute class and the code that allows it to work on the client as well as the server is presented in the next figure.

The ConfirmPassword property is decorated with the DisplayName attribute. Again, this provides MVC with a friendly name to display in validation messages and labels. This property is also decorated with the NotMapped attribute. This attribute isn't used for data validation. Instead, it's used to prevent EF Core from creating a ConfirmPassword column in the Customers table that's created from this Customer class.

The Customer class

```
using System.ComponentModel.DataAnnotations;
using System.ComponentModel.DataAnnotations.Schema; // for NotMapped attribute
using Microsoft.AspNetCore.Mvc;                      // for Remote attribute
...
public class Customer
{
    public int ID { get; set; }  // automatically generated by database

    [Required(ErrorMessage = "Please enter a username.")]
    [RegularExpression("^[a-zA-Z0-9 ]+$",
        ErrorMessage = "Username may not contain special characters.")]
    public string Username { get; set; } = string.Empty;

    [Required(ErrorMessage = "Please enter an email address.")]
    [Remote("CheckEmail", "Validation")]
    [Display(Name = "Email Address")]
    public string EmailAddress { get; set; } = string.Empty;

    [Required(ErrorMessage = "Please enter a date of birth.")]
    [MinimumAge(13, ErrorMessage = "You must be at least 13 years old.")]
    public DateTime? DOB { get; set; }

    [Required(ErrorMessage = "Please enter a password.")]
    [Compare("ConfirmPassword")]
    [StringLength(25,
        ErrorMessage = "Please limit your password to 25 characters.")]
    public string Password { get; set; } = string.Empty;

    [Required(ErrorMessage = "Please confirm your password.")]
    [Display(Name = "Confirm Password")]
    [NotMapped]
    public string ConfirmPassword { get; set; } = string.Empty;
}
```

The RegistrationContext class

```
public class RegistrationContext : DbContext
{
    public RegistrationContext(DbContextOptions<RegistrationContext> options)
        : base(options) { }

    public DbSet<Customer> Customers { get; set; } = null!;
}
```

Description

- The Customer class provides data validation by decorating its properties with attributes from the System.ComponentModel.DataAnnotations namespace.

- The Customer class uses the Remote attribute to use server-side code to check if the email address entered by the user is already in the database.

- The Customer class uses a custom MinimumAge attribute to check if the user is at least 13 years old.

- The RegistrationContext class communicates with the database. To configure it, you must modify the Program.cs and appsettings.json files as described in chapter 4.

Figure 11-15   The Customer and RegistrationContext classes

The MinimumAgeAttribute class

Figure 11-16 presents the MinimumAgeAttribute class. The code for this class imports the namespace that contains the ValidationAttribute class that provides the basic functionality of a data attribute. Then, the MinimumAgeAttribute class inherits the ValidationAttribute class.

In addition, the MinimumAgeAttribute class imports the namespace that contains the IClientModelValidator interface. Then, this class implements the AddValidation() method of that interface so it can generate data-val-* attributes in the HTML. That way, the custom JavaScript function that's added to the jQuery validation libraries can use these attributes.

The MinimumAgeAttribute class has a constructor that accepts an int value and assigns it to a private variable named minYears. This is the value that determines the minimum age that's checked by the validation.

The IsValid() method overrides the virtual IsValid() method of the ValidationAttribute base class. First, it checks whether the value entered by the user is a date. If so, the code casts it to a DateTime value and calls the AddYears() method of the DateTime class to add the number of years in the minYears variable to the date to check.

After adding the years to the date, the code checks whether the date is less than or equal to today's date. If it is, the user is older than the minimum number of years. As a result, the code returns the Success field of the ValidationResult class. Otherwise, it returns a new ValidationResult object. To get the validation message for this object, it calls the GetMsg() method at the end of this class and passes it the DisplayName property of the ValidationContext parameter or a default value.

The AddValidation() method uses the context object parameter to add data-val-* attributes to the HMTL element. This code only adds the data-val attribute if it doesn't exist. In addition, it calls the GetMsg() method to get the validation message to embed in the HTML.

The minimum-age JavaScript file

Figure 11-16 shows a JavaScript file named minimum-age.js that calls the addMethod() function of the jQuery validation library and passes it an anonymous function. This anonymous function starts by checking if the user entered a value and if that value is a valid date. If not, it returns false. Otherwise, it uses the parameter named param to get the value from the data-val-minimumage-years attribute and uses it to calculate the date to check. Then, the code returns a Boolean value that indicates whether the date to check is valid (less than or equal to the current date). Finally, the last line of code adds the name of the new validation function and its parameters to the adapters collection of the jQuery unobtrusive validation library.

The MinimumAgeAttribute class

```
using System.ComponentModel.DataAnnotations;
using Microsoft.AspNetCore.Mvc.ModelBinding.Validation;
...
public class MinimumAgeAttribute : ValidationAttribute, IClientModelValidator
{
    private int minYears;
    public MinimumAgeAttribute(int years) {
        minYears = years;
    }

    // overrides IsValid() method of ValidationAttribute base class
    protected override ValidationResult IsValid(object? value,
    ValidationContext ctx) {
        if (value is DateTime) {
            DateTime dateToCheck = (DateTime)value;
            dateToCheck = dateToCheck.AddYears(minYears);
            if (dateToCheck <= DateTime.Today) {
                return ValidationResult.Success!;
            }
        }
        return new ValidationResult(GetMsg(ctx.DisplayName ?? "Date"));
    }

    // implements AddValidation() method of IClientModelValidator interface
    public void AddValidation(ClientModelValidationContext ctx) {
        if (!ctx.Attributes.ContainsKey("data-val"))
            ctx.Attributes.Add("data-val", "true");
        ctx.Attributes.Add("data-val-minimumage-years",
            minYears.ToString());
        ctx.Attributes.Add("data-val-minimumage",
            GetMsg(ctx.ModelMetadata.DisplayName ??
                    ctx.ModelMetadata.Name ?? "Date"));
    }

    private string GetMsg(string name) =>
        base.ErrorMessage ?? $"{name} must be at least {minYears} years ago.";
}
```

The minumim-age JavaScript file

```
jQuery.validator.addMethod("minimumage", function(value, element, param) {
    if (value === '') return false;

    var dateToCheck = new Date(value);
    if (dateToCheck === "Invalid Date") return false;

    var minYears = Number(param);

    dateToCheck.setFullYear(dateToCheck.getFullYear() + minYears);

    var today = new Date();
    return (dateToCheck <= today);
});

jQuery.validator.unobtrusive.adapters.addSingleVal("minimumage", "years");
```

Figure 11-16   The MinimumAgeAttribute class and JavaScript file

The Validation and Register controllers

The Registration page uses remote validation to enable the client to check whether the email address is already in the database. However, if the user has JavaScript disabled, this check doesn't occur on the client. In that case, the Registration page also checks the email address on the server. To reduce duplication, both client-side and server-side code call the same method to perform the check.

The first code example in figure 11-17 shows the Validation controller. It starts with a constructor that accepts a database context object and assigns it to a private variable named context. Then, it defines an action method named CheckEmail() that accepts an email address. The client-side code calls this action method when it performs remote validation.

The CheckEmail() action method starts by passing the context object and email address to the static EmailExists() method of the static Check class that's shown in the third example. This method returns a validation message if the email address is already in the database or an empty string if it isn't.

The CheckEmail() action method continues by checking whether the message returned by the EmailExists() method is empty or null. If it is, the email address is OK, and the code stores a true value in TempData that the server-side check can use later. Otherwise, the code returns the validation message. Either way, the code calls the Json() method of the controller to convert the value that's sent to the client to JSON format.

The second example shows the Register controller. This controller also starts with a constructor that accepts a database context object and assigns it to a private variable named context. Then, it defines an overloaded action method named Index(). The overload that handles GET requests simply returns a view. The overload that handles POST requests, on the other hand, accepts a Customer object from the form and processes it.

To start, the Index() action method for POST requests uses TempData to determine whether it needs to perform a server-side check of the email address. If there's a value in TempData, the client-side check has succeeded, so the server-side check can be skipped. Also, reading the TempData value clears it, so you don't need to remove it manually.

If TempData returns a null value, that means the client-side check didn't run. So, the Index() action method needs to check the email. To do that, it passes the context object and the EmailAddress value to the static EmailExists() method shown in the third example. This time, if that method returns a validation message, the code adds it to the ModelState property of the controller with the EmailAddress property name as the dictionary key.

After the Index() action method adds any necessary messages to its ModelState property, it checks the IsValid property of the ModelState property and updates the database only if all validation has passed. This includes the validation check for the email address as well as the validation checks for all of the other data attributes that decorate the properties of the Customer class.

The Validation controller

```
public class ValidationController : Controller
{
    private RegistrationContext context;
    public RegisterController(RegistrationContext ctx) => context = ctx;

    public JsonResult CheckEmail(string emailAddress)
    {
        string msg = Check.EmailExists(context, emailAddress);
        if (string.IsNullOrEmpty(msg)) {
            TempData["okEmail"] = true;
            return Json(true);
        }
        else return Json(msg);
    }
}
```

The Register controller

```
public class RegisterController : Controller
{
    private RegistrationContext context;
    public RegisterController(RegistrationContext ctx) => context = ctx;

    public IActionResult Index() => View();

    [HttpPost]
    public IActionResult Index(Customer customer)
    {
        if (TempData["okEmail"] == null) {
            string msg = Check.EmailExists(context, customer.EmailAddress);
            if (!String.IsNullOrEmpty(msg)) {
                ModelState.AddModelError(nameof(Customer.EmailAddress), msg);
            }
        }
        if (ModelState.IsValid) {
            context.Customers.Add(customer);
            context.SaveChanges();
            return RedirectToAction("Welcome");
        }
        else return View(customer);
    }
}
```

The static Check class

```
public static class Check
{
    public static string EmailExists(RegistrationContext ctx, string email) {
        string msg = string.Empty;
        if (!string.IsNullOrEmpty(email)) {
            var customer = ctx.Customers.FirstOrDefault(
                c => c.EmailAddress.ToLower() == email.ToLower());
            if (customer != null)
                msg = $"Email address {email} already in use.";
        }
        return msg;
    }
}
```

Figure 11-17   The Validation and Register controllers

The layout

Figure 11-18 shows the Razor layout for the Registration app. It includes the main jQuery library because that library might be used by many pages of an app. For this app, the layout places the <script> tag for the jQuery library at the end of the <body> tag, which is what many programmers prefer. As you know, however, you can also include the jQuery library in the <head> tag.

After the <script> tag that includes the jQuery library, the layout calls the RenderSection() method that's available to layouts and views. The first argument to that method specifies the name of the section to render ("scripts"), and the second specifies a Boolean value indicating whether a view is required to have a section named "scripts". This Razor method allows individual views to optionally include additional JavaScript files. Since it comes *after* the tag that includes the jQuery library, any JavaScript files added by a view will have access to this library.

In summary, this layout loads the main jQuery library for every page in the Registration app. In addition, it provides a way for the other pages to load additional JavaScript files. This makes it possible for pages that need to validate user input to load the jQuery validation libraries as well as any custom JavaScript files for client-side validation as shown in the next figure. Since this approach only loads the JavaScript validation files when they're needed, it can decrease the amount of time that it takes to load a page.

The layout

```
<!DOCTYPE html>
<html>
<head>
    <meta name="viewport" content="width=device-width, initial-scale=1.0" />
    <title>@ViewData["Title"]</title>
    <link rel="stylesheet" type="text/css"
        href="~/lib/bootstrap/dist/css/bootstrap.min.css">
    <link rel="stylesheet" href="~/css/site.css" />
</head>
<body>
    <div class="container">
        <header class="bg-primary text-white text-center">
            <h1 class="m-3 p-3">Registration</h1>
        </header>
        <main>
            @RenderBody()
        </main>
    </div>
    <script src="~/lib/jquery/dist/jquery.min.js"></script>
    @RenderSection("scripts", required: false)
</body>
</html>
```

Description

- The layout includes the jQuery library at the end of the <body> tag, though you can include it in the <head> tag instead if you prefer.

- The layout calls the RenderSection() method. This allows individual views to add additional JavaScript files. It places this statement *after* the <script> tag that includes the jQuery library.

Figure 11-18   The layout

The Register/Index view

Figure 11-19 presents the Index view for the Registration page. It's a strongly-typed view with a Customer object as its model.

The Index view has a Razor section named scripts. This is the section that the layout in the previous figure renders after it includes the main jQuery library. In this view, the scripts section contains three <script> tags. The first two include the jQuery validation libraries that provide for client-side validation. The third includes the JavasScript file named minimum-age.js that's stored in the js folder. This is the JavaScript file that adds client-side validation to the custom MinimumAge attribute.

When you include JavaScript files, you need to make sure to include them in the correct order. For this app, the layout includes the main jQuery library that you need first. Then, within a view, you can include the jQuery validation library, followed by the jQuery unobtrusive validation library, followed by any custom validation files.

The Index view contains a <form> tag that posts to the Index() action method of the current controller, which is the Register controller. Within this tag, the view has several <div> tags that are formatted as a Bootstrap row. Each of these <div> tags contains a <label> and <input> tag that's bound to a property of the Customer model object. And after each <input> tag is a <span> tag that uses the asp-validation-for tag helper to display validation messages for that property.

Due to space constraints, this figure doesn't show the <div> tags for the email address and confirm password fields. However, they look similar to the other <div> tags, except that the <input> tag for the confirm password field specifies a type of "password". If you'd like to view these tags, you can open the file for the Register/Index view that's in the downloadable app for this chapter.

The Register/Index view

```
@model Customer

@{
    ViewData["Title"] = "Registration";
}

@section scripts {
    <script src="~/lib/jquery-validation/dist/jquery.validate.min.js"></script>
    <script src="~/lib/jquery-validation-unobtrusive/
                      jquery.validate.unobtrusive.min.js"></script>
    <script src="~/js/minimum-age.js"></script>
}

<form asp-action="Index" method="post">
    <div class="row mb-2">
        <div class="col-md-2">
            <label asp-for="Username" class="form-label"></label></div>
        <div class="col-md-4">
            <input asp-for="Username" class="form-control" /></div>
        <div class="col">
            <span asp-validation-for="Username" class="text-danger"></span>
        </div>
    </div>
    <!-- Email address field not shown -->
    <div class="row mb-2">
        <div class="col-md-2">
            <label asp-for="DOB" class="form-label"></label></div>
        <div class="col-md-4">
            <input asp-for="DOB" class="form-control" type="text" /></div>
        <div class="col">
            <span asp-validation-for="DOB" class="text-danger"></span>
        </div>
    </div>
    <div class="row mb-2">
        <div class="col-md-2">
            <label asp-for="Password" class="form-label"></label></div>
        <div class="col-md-4">
            <input asp-for="Password" class="form-control" type="password" />
        </div>
        <div class="col">
            <span asp-validation-for="Password" class="text-danger"></span>
        </div>
    </div>
    <!-- ConfirmPassword field not shown -->
    <div class="row">
        <div class="offset-md-2 col">
            <button type="submit" class="btn btn-primary">Register</button>
        </div>
    </div>
</form>
```

Description

- The Register/Index view has a Razor section that includes the jQuery validation libraries and the minimum-age.js file. That way, these files are only loaded for the Registration page, not for other pages of the app that don't need them.

Figure 11-19   The Register/Index view

Perspective

The goal of this chapter is to teach you how to validate the data that a user inputs into an ASP.NET MVC app. Now, if this chapter has worked, you should be able to use client-side and server-side code to validate data. This includes using the data attributes that are provided by MVC, as well as creating your own custom data attributes. As usual, there's always more to learn. Still, this chapter should give you a good foundation for working with data validation.

Terms

data attribute
property-level validation
class-level validation
remote validation

Summary

- You specify the validation to be applied to a model class by decorating its properties with *data attributes*.

- Code that validates a property of a class is called *property-level validation*. Code that validates the entire class instead of individual properties is called *class-level validation*. Class-level validation only runs if all the property-level validation has passed.

- *Remote validation* allows you to write code on the server that's called by the client without reloading the whole page.

Exercise 11-1   Add data validation to an app

In this exercise, you'll review the default data validation provided by model binding and add some custom data validation to an app.

View the domain model and test the default data validation

1. Open the Ch11Ex1TempManager web app in the ex_starts directory.

2. Open the Package Manager Console and enter the Update-Database command to create the database for this web app.

3. In the Models folder, open the Temp class and view its code. Note that none of the properties have any data validation attributes.

4. Run the app and click the Add a Temp button. Enter a date, a low temperature, and a high temperature. Then, click the Add button.

5. Click the Add Temp button again. This time, click the Add button without entering any data. Note that the page doesn't display validation messages. Instead, it displays blank data. Use the Delete button to delete the blank data.

6. Click the Add Temp button again. This time, enter "tomorrow" for the date and "four" for the low temperature. Click the Add button and review the validation messages that MVC displays because it can't convert the data you entered to the correct types.

Add data validation to the Temp domain model

7. In the Temp class, add a using statement for the data annotations namespace.

8. Add the following data annotations to the Temp class:

   • The Date, Low, and High fields are required.

   • The Low and High fields must be within a range of -200 to 200.

9. Run the app and enter some incorrect Temp data. The app should display appropriate validation messages, so the user can correct the data.

Display model-level and property-level validation messages

10. In the Controllers folder, open the HomeController class and find the Add() action method for POST requests.

11. In the else block that runs when the model state is not valid, add a model-level error with a message of "Please correct all errors" to the ModelState property.

12. In the Views folder, open the Home/Add view and modify the validation summary <div> tag so it only displays model-level validation messages.

13. Add a <span> tag after each <input> tag to display a property-level validation message.

14. Run and test the app. When you enter invalid data, it should display one model-level validation message plus one or more property-level messages.

Make your data validation run on the client

15. In the Add view, add a Razor @section block named scripts. Within this block, add <script> tags for the jQuery validation library and the jQuery unobtrusive validation library.

16. Run and test the app. When you enter invalid data, the model-level validation message should not display. That's because the validation is failing on the client, so the data isn't being sent to the server for validation there.

Add remote validation that checks for a duplicate date in the database

17. In the Controllers folder, add a new class named ValidationController.

18. Add a using statement for the TempManager.Models namespace.

19. Code a constructor that accepts a TempManagerContext object and stores it in a private property.

20. Code an action method named CheckDate(). This method should return a JsonResult object and define a string parameter named date.

21. In the method, convert the string parameter named date to a DateTime object and query the database for a Temp object with that date.

22. Use the Json() method to return true if that query returns null. Otherwise, return an error message.

23. In the Models folder, open the Temp class.

24. Add a using statement for the Mvc namespace and update the Date property to use the Remote attribute with the CheckDate() action method of the Validation controller.

25. Run the app and enter new Temp data with a duplicate date. This should display a validation message indicating that the date is already in the database.

Add a server-side check for the remote validation

26. Turn off JavaScript in your browser. To do that with Chrome, click the Chrome menu in the top right corner, select Settings, select "Privacy and security", click Site Settings, click Javascript, and change "Sites can use Javascript" to "Don't allow sites to use Javascript".

27. Run the app and test it. It should allow you to enter Temp data with a duplicate date. When you're done, delete the Temp data that has the duplicate date.

28. In the HomeController class, add code to the Add() action method for POST requests that checks if the date is duplicate. If so, this code should add a property-level validation message to the ModelState property.

29. Run the app and enter new Temp data with a duplicate date. This should display a property-level validation message.

30. Make sure to turn Javascript back on in your browser!

12

How to use EF Core

In this chapter, you'll learn how to use Entity Framework (EF) Core to work with a database. This includes how to create a new database from code (Code First development), how to create code from an existing database (Database First development), and how to create a data access class.

How to create a database from code

Entity Framework (EF) Core is an *object-relational mapping* (*ORM*) framework that allows you to map your entity classes to the tables of a database. The most common way to work with EF Core is to code your entity classes and a database context class first. Then, you can use EF to create a new database from these classes. This is called *Code First* development, and it's the approach that you'll learn about now.

How to code entity and DB context classes

Entity classes represent the data structure for an app. For example, a bookstore has entities like books, authors, and genres. As a result, a Bookstore app needs entity classes to store data for those entities.

To illustrate, figure 12-1 begins with two examples that show the Book and Author entity classes. You can create objects from these classes to store the data that's needed by your app.

After you create your entity classes, you need to code a *database* (*DB*) *context class* that can communicate with a database. This class inherits the DbContext base class. To illustrate, the third example shows a context class named BookstoreContext that inherits the DbContext class. In addition, it has a constructor that accepts a DbContextOptions object and passes it to the constructor of the DbContext class. These options are usually configured by the Program.cs class as described in figure 4-6 of chapter 4.

To enable your context class to work with collections of your entity classes, you need to add DbSet<*Entity*> properties. For instance, the BookstoreContext class has a Books property of the DbSet<Book> type and an Authors property of the DbSet<Author> type. When you create a database, these properties generate its tables with the specified names. Then, you can use LINQ to query these properties.

The DbContext class has two virtual methods named OnConfiguring() and OnModelCreating(). You can override these methods to configure your context class and its DbSet properties. In this figure, the BookstoreContext class overrides both of these methods.

The OnConfiguring() method configures the context itself. For example, you can specify the connection string here. However, that's usually done in the appsettings.json file as shown by figure 4-6. You can also configure other features such as change tracking and logging, though that's beyond the scope of this book.

The OnModelCreating() method configures your entity classes. This, in turn, configures the database tables that are created from these entities. You'll learn more about how this works as you progress through this chapter.

Before going on, you should notice that the properties in the Book and Author entity classes of the string type are initialized with empty strings. In addition, the DbSet<> properties of the BookstoreContext class are initialized

A Book entity class

```
public class Book
{
    public int BookId { get; set; }
    public string Title { get; set; } = string.Empty;
    public double Price { get; set; };
}
```

An Author entity class

```
public class Author
{
    public int AuthorId { get; set; }
    public string FirstName { get; set; } = string.Empty;
    public string LastName { get; set; } = string.Empty;
}
```

A BookstoreContext class

```
using Microsoft.EntityFrameworkCore;
...
public class BookstoreContext : DbContext
{
    public BookstoreContext(DbContextOptions<BookstoreContext> options)
        : base(options) { }

    public DbSet<Book> Books { get; set; } = null!;
    public DbSet<Author> Authors { get; set; } = null!;

    protected override void OnConfiguring(
        DbContextOptionsBuilder optionsBuilder)
    {
        // code that configures the DbContext goes here
        base.OnConfiguring(optionsBuilder);
    }

    protected override void OnModelCreating(ModelBuilder modelBuilder)
    {
        // code that configures the DbSet entities goes here
        base.OnModelCreating(modelBuilder);
    }
}
```

Description

- *Entity classes* define the data structure for the app and map to tables in a relational database. A *database* (*DB*) *context class* inherits the DbContext class and includes entity classes as DbSet properties.

- In the DB context class, the OnConfiguring() method allows you to configure the context, such as providing the connection string. Usually, though, you do this in the Program.cs file.

- In the DB context class, the OnModelCreating() method allows you to configure the entity classes, such as providing initial seed data.

- To work with EF, you need to configure the database context. To do that, you can modify your appsettings.json and Program.cs files as described in figure 4-6 of chapter 4.

Figure 12-1   How to code entity classes and a database context class

with null followed by the null-forgiving operator (!). This prevents Visual Studio from displaying warnings when your code may refer to an object that is null, and it is particularly important when working with EF Core.

How to configure the database

You can configure your entity classes so they create the database tables you want in three ways. First, you can configure them by convention. Second, you can configure them with data attributes. And third, you can configure them by using code.

When you configure by convention, you code your classes following established conventions, and EF takes it from there. Figure 12-2 starts by presenting some of these conventions. For example, if you code a property named Id (or ID) or join the name of the entity and Id (or ID), EF treats that property as the primary key of the database table. Additionally, if this property is of the int type, EF makes the primary key an identity column. Then, the database generates the key's value when a new row is inserted.

Other conventions are that string properties create columns of the nvarchar(max) type, and those columns allow null values. Value types like int and double, by contrast, create columns that don't allow null values.

The first code example in this figure shows how to create an identity column that serves as the primary key by convention. Here, the Book class has an int property named BookId. Since this is so easy, you should configure your classes by convention whenever possible.

Sometimes, though, the EF conventions may not yield the results you want. For instance, you may not want a string property to allow null. You may want a string property to be smaller than nvarchar(max). Or, you may not want the database to generate values for a primary key.

In these cases, you can use attributes like those presented in the first table in this figure. These attributes are stored in the DataAnnotations and DataAnnotations.Schema namespaces shown in the second example. Some of the data attributes in the DataAnnotations namespace can also be used for configuration. For example, you can use the Required and StringLength attributes to change the default configuration of a string property.

The second code example in this figure shows the Book entity class with some attributes for configuration. For instance, the Key attribute configures the ISBN property so it's the primary key even though it wouldn't be configured as the primary key by convention.

Sometimes, you might not want to configure by convention or by attributes. This could be because you have complex requirements, or because you want to keep configuration information out of your entity classes. In these cases, you can use the methods of the *Fluent API* to write code that configures your classes.

The second table in this figure shows several of the Fluent API methods for configuration. Then, the code example below the table shows how you can use some of them. Here, the OnModelCreating() method shown in the previous

Some of the conventions for configuration in EF Core

- A property named Id or *ClassName*Id is the primary key. If the property is of the int type, the key is an identity column and its value is generated automatically by the database.

- A string property has a database type of nvarchar(max) and is nullable.

- An int or double property is not nullable.

How to set an identity primary key by convention

```
public class Book {
    public int BookId { get; set; }
}
```

Some of the data attributes for configuration

Attribute	Description
Key	The database column that's the primary key.
NotMapped	Indicates that a property or table shouldn't be mapped to the database.
DatabaseGenerated	Specifies how the database generates a value. Uses the Computed, Identity, and None values of the DatabaseGeneratedOptions enum.

How to use attributes to adjust the default configuration

```
using System.ComponentModel.DataAnnotations
using System.ComponentModel.DataAnnotations.Schema
...
public class Book {
    [Key]
    public string ISBN { get; set; }  // make primary key

    [Required]
    [StringLength(200)]
    public string Title { get; set; } // make string column not nullable
}
```

Some of the Fluent API methods for configuration

Method	Description
Entity<T>()	Registers an entity for configuration.
Property(lambda)	Registers a property for configuration.
HasKey(lambda)	Configures the primary key or keys for the entity.
HasData(entityList)	Allows you to seed data for the entity when the database is created.
ToTable(string)	Identifies the table that an entity maps to.
IsRequired()	Configures a database column to be not nullable.
HasMaxLength(size)	Configures the size of a database column.

How to chain Fluent API method calls to configure a property

```
protected override void OnModelCreating(ModelBuilder modelBuilder)
{
    modelBuilder.Entity<Book>()
        .Property(b => b.Title).IsRequired().HasMaxLength(200);
}
```

Figure 12-2 How to configure the database

figure contains some configuration code. This code uses the ModelBuilder parameter to configure the Title property of the Book entity. To do that, it chains together four methods of the Fluent API. This produces the same result as coding the Required and StringLength(200) attributes above the Title property.

How to manage configuration files

The first code example in figure 12-3 shows the OnModelCreating() method of a context class with several statements that configure a Book entity. The first statement sets the ISBN property as the primary key. This is necessary because that property doesn't follow the naming convention for a primary key. The second statement makes the Title property not allow null and to have a maximum length of 200 characters. And the third statement uses the HasData() method to provide seed data when the table is created.

The statements in this example are for a single entity that has two properties. However, imagine how this code will grow as you add more properties to this entity and as you add other entities to the app. This is especially true if you decide to do all your configuration with the Fluent API. And the longer the code gets, the harder it becomes to read and maintain.

To keep this code manageable, you can store your configuration code in separate files, where each file stores a configuration class for each entity. Then, each class can implement the interface named IEntityTypeConfiguration<T> and override its Configure() method.

The second example shows a configuration class named BookConfig that configures the Book entity. This class implements the IEntityTypeConfiguration<Book> interface and overrides its Configure() method. This method accepts an EntityTypeBuilder<Book> object that represents the entity being configured. In this case, that entity is the Book entity. Then, this method uses that object to perform the same configuration shown in the first example.

For this to work, the class must include a using directive for the Microsoft.EntityFrameworkCore namespace, which contains the IEntityTypeConfiguration<T> interface. It must also include a using directive for the Microsoft.EntityFrameworkCore.Metadata.Builders namespace, which contains the EntityTypeBuilder<TEntity> class.

Once you've coded a separate configuration file, you apply it in the OnModelCreating() method of the context class. To do that, you create a new instance of the configuration class and pass it to the ApplyConfiguration() method of the ModelBuilder object as shown by the last example. This reduces the six lines of code in the first example to one line of code. As you can imagine, this goes a long way toward keeping the code in the OnModelCreating() method manageable, especially when an app contains many complex entities.

Code that configures the Book entity in the OnModelCreating() method

```
protected override void OnModelCreating(ModelBuilder modelBuilder)
{
    modelBuilder.Entity<Book>().HasKey(b => b.ISBN);

    modelBuilder.Entity<Book>().Property(b => b.Title)
        .IsRequired().HasMaxLength(200);

    modelBuilder.Entity<Book>().HasData(
        new Book { ISBN = "1548547298", Title = "The Hobbit" },
        new Book { ISBN = "0312283709", Title = "Running With Scissors" }
    );
}
```

Code that uses a separate configuration class for the Book entity

A configuration class for the Book entity

```
using Microsoft.EntityFrameworkCore;
using Microsoft.EntityFrameworkCore.Metadata.Builders;

internal class BookConfig : IEntityTypeConfiguration<Book>
{
    public void Configure(EntityTypeBuilder<Book> entity)
    {
        entity.HasKey(b => b.ISBN);

        entity.Property(b => b.Title).IsRequired().HasMaxLength(200);

        entity.HasData(
            new Book { ISBN = "1548547298", Title = "The Hobbit" },
            new Book { ISBN = "0312283709", Title = "Running With Scissors" }
        );
    }
}
```

Code that applies the configuration class in the OnModelCreating() method

```
protected override void OnModelCreating(ModelBuilder modelBuilder)
{
    modelBuilder.ApplyConfiguration(new BookConfig());
}
```

Description

- If you have a lot of Fluent API configuration code in the OnModelCreating() method of your context class, it can become difficult to understand and maintain. In that case, it's considered a best practice to divide this code into one configuration file per entity.

- To create a configuration file, you code a class that implements the IEntityTypeConfiguration<T> interface and its Configure() method.

- The Configure() method accepts an EntityTypeBuilder<T> object that represents the entity being configured.

- To apply the configuration code, you pass a new instance of the configuration class to the ApplyConfiguration() method of the ModelBuilder object that's passed to the OnModelCreating() method of the context class.

Figure 12-3   How to manage configuration files

EF commands for working with a database

In chapter 4, you learned how to use the NuGet Package Manager Console (PMC) to execute PowerShell commands such as Add-Migration and Update-Database to create a database from DB context and entity classes. Figure 12-4 starts by reviewing how you open the PMC window. Then, it summarizes the Add-Migration and Update-Database commands, as well as some additional commands for working with a database. For any of these commands to work, your app needs to be configured to access a database as shown in figure 4-6.

The first command, Add-Migration, generates a migration file based on your context and entity classes. By default, this command creates the file with the name you specify in the Migrations folder. If that folder doesn't exist, this command creates it. If you want, you can use the -OutputDir parameter to specify another folder, as you'll see shortly.

The second command, Remove-Migration, removes the last migration file from the Migrations folder. This only works, though, if the migration file hasn't yet been applied to the database. If it has, you need to use the Update-Database command to revert the migration to a previous migration before you can remove the migration file. You'll see an example of this in the next figure.

The third command, Update-Database, applies any migration files that haven't yet been applied to the database. You can also use the Update-Database command to revert migrations as shown in the next figure.

The fourth command, Drop-Database, deletes the database. If this command doesn't work correctly, you can use SQL Server Object Explorer or another comparable tool to delete the database.

The fifth command, Script-Migration, generates a SQL script based on one or more migration files. Due to space limitations, this book doesn't show any examples of using this command. However, if you need to use it, you can find many examples online.

The sixth command, Scaffold-DbContext, generates DB context and entity classes from an existing database. Since you use this command with Database First development, it's described later in this chapter.

The next three tables in this figure show some of the parameters you can use with the Add-Migration, Update-Database, and Script-Migration commands to change their default behavior. The -Name parameter is required for the Add-Migration command. However, the rest of these parameters are optional. As a result, if you execute these commands without parameters, they use their default values.

The first time you run the Add-Migration command, EF creates a file named *DbContextName*ModelSnapshot.cs and stores it in the same folder as the migration files. For instance, a context class named BookstoreContext generates a file named BookstoreContextModelSnapshot.cs. This file contains a "snapshot" in code of the current database schema, or structure. When you add or remove migrations with the Add-Migration and Remove-Migration commands, EF updates this file.

How to open the NuGet Package Manager Console (PMC) window

- Select Tools→NuGet Package Manager→Package Manager Console.

Some of the PowerShell EF commands

Command	Description
`Add-Migration`	Adds a named migration file to the Migrations folder. If this folder doesn't exist yet, it creates the folder.
`Remove-Migration`	Removes the last migration file from the Migrations folder. Only works with migrations that have not yet been applied with the Update-Database command.
`Update-Database`	Updates the database to the last migration or reverts the database to the migration specified by the optional -Name parameter.
`Drop-Database`	Deletes the database.
`Script-Migration`	Generates a SQL script based on the migration file or files.
`Scaffold-DbContext`	Generates DB context and entity classes from an existing database. See figure 12-14.

Parameters for the Add-Migration command

Parameter	Description
`-Name`	The name of the migration file. This is a required parameter.
`-OutputDir`	The folder where the file will be created. The default is "Migrations".

Parameter for the Update-Database command

Parameter	Description
`-Name`	The name of the migration file. The default is the last migration.

Parameters for the Script-Migration command

Parameter	Description
`-From`	The starting migration file. The default is the first one.
`-To`	The ending migration file. The default is the last one.
`-Output`	The file to write to. Defaults to a generated name in the solution folder.
`-Idempotent`	Generates checks to make sure SQL commands aren't repeated.

Description

- The PMC executes PowerShell commands to create, apply, and revert migration files.
- A migration file contains C# code for creating or updating database objects. Specifically, each migration file has an Up() method with code that runs when a migration is applied, and a Down() method with code that runs when a migration is reverted.
- The first time you run the Add-Migration command, EF creates a file named *DbContextName*ModelSnapshot.cs. This file contains a "snapshot" of the current database schema. When you add or remove subsequent migrations, that file is updated.

Figure 12-4   EF commands for working with a database

How to use EF migration commands

Figure 12-5 presents some examples that use EF commands in the Package Manager Console (PMC) to work with the Bookstore database. The first scenario in this figure shows how to create and then update the database. Step 1 creates a migration file named Initial.cs in the Migrations folder. Then, step 2 updates the database. This applies the Initial migration and creates the database.

Although it's not required, you can include the -Name flag with the Add-Migration command like this:

```
PM> Add-Migration -Name Initial
```

If you want to change the name of the migrations folder, you can include the optional -OutputDir parameter like this:

```
PM> Add-Migration Initial -OutputDir MyMigrations
```

Finally, if you want to specify a path for the migrations folder, you can do that like this:

```
PM> Add-Migration Initial -OutputDir Models/DataLayer/Migrations
```

Here, the path is relative to the project folder.

Step 3 adds a new property named Discount to the Book entity. Then, step 4 generates a new migration file that includes this new column.

Steps 5 through 7 describe what to do if you realize that you made a mistake in adding your new property in steps 3 and 4. For example, suppose you forgot to indicate that the Discount property is nullable. To fix that, you can change the data type for this property in the Book class so it is nullable. Then, you can run the Add-Migration command again to create another migration file to correct the one that adds the Discount property. At this point, you have two migration files ready to be applied. So, when you update the database in step 8, both migration files are applied.

The next two scenarios show how to revert migrations that have been applied to the database. To do this, you use the Update-Database command and include the name of the migration you want to revert to. The first of these scenarios, for example, reverts to the AddDiscount migration, which means that the Discount property is no longer nullable. Then, you can use the Remove_Migration command to remove the migration file that made this property nullable.

The second of these scenarios shows how to revert all migrations. To do that, you enter 0 for the migration name. Then, you can use the Remove-Migration command to delete the unused migration files. Or, you can delete them manually. When manually deleting all migration files, you also need to delete the snapshot file.

You can also use the Remove-Migration command to remove a migration that hasn't been applied yet. You might want to do that if you notice a problem with a migration file before you apply it. Then, you can adjust your code and run the Add-Migration command again to correct the problem.

How to create and then update a database

1. Create a migration file named Initial based on the context and entity classes presented earlier in this chapter by entering this command:
   ```
   PM> Add-Migration Initial
   ```
2. Create a database based on the migration file by entering this command:
   ```
   PM> Update-Database
   ```
3. Add a property named Discount of the double type to the Book class.
4. Create a migration file named AddDiscount by entering this command:
   ```
   PM> Add-Migration AddDiscount
   ```
5. Review the migration file and note that the Discount property doesn't accept nulls.
6. Change the Discount property in the Book class to the data type of double?.
7. Generate another migration file by entering this command:
   ```
   PM> Add-Migration MakeDiscountNullable
   ```
8. Apply the migration files to the database by entering this command:
   ```
   PM> Update-Database
   ```

The Migrations folder after completing these steps

```
▲   📁 Migrations
    ▷   C# 20190328233004_Initial.cs
    ▷   C# 20190329000840_AddDiscount.cs
    ▷   C# 20190329000934_MakeDiscountNullable.cs
```

How to revert one or more migrations

1. To revert changes to the database by running the Down() method in every migration file that comes after the AddDiscount file, enter this command:
   ```
   PM> Update-Database AddDiscount
   ```
2. To remove the unapplied MakeDiscountNullable migration file that was reverted in step 1 from the Migrations folder, enter this command:
   ```
   PM> Remove-Migration
   ```

How to revert all the migrations

1. To revert all changes that have been applied to the database by running the Down() method in all the migration files, enter this command:
   ```
   PM> Update-Database 0
   ```
2. To remove all migration files from the Migrations folder, enter the Remove-Migration command repeatedly. Or, manually delete all the migration files from the Migrations folder, including the snapshot file.

Note

- When you run one of these commands, you might see a warning to update your tools. To do that, you can run an Install-Package command like this:
  ```
  PM> Install-Package Microsoft.EntityFrameworkCore.Tools -Version 6.0.7
  ```
  However, you should use the version number that's included in the warning message.

Figure 12-5   How to use EF migration commands

How to work with relationships

So far, you have learned how to code entity classes and use those classes to create database tables. However, entities are typically related to other entities. Similarly, the corresponding database tables are typically related to other tables. For example, a genre might have many books. An author might have a detailed bio. A book might have several authors. And an author might have several books. That's why the next few figures show how to configure relationships between entities and their corresponding tables.

How entities are related

Entities can be related to other entities by values in specific properties. The two entities at the top of figure 12-6 illustrate this concept. Here, the Genre entity is related to the Book entity because they share a property, GenreId. Note that it's common for the properties that establish relationships to have that same name, but it's not required, as you'll see in a moment.

Typically, relationships exist between the primary key in one entity and the foreign key in another entity. A *primary key* (*PK*) uniquely identifies an instance of an entity. A *foreign key* (*FK*) refers to a primary key in another entity. In this figure, the diagram shows that the GenreId property in the Genre entity is a primary key, and the GenreId property in the Book entity is a foreign key. In other words, the foreign key in the Book entity refers to the primary key of the Genre entity.

The most common relationship between entities is a *one-to-many relationship*. This is the relationship shown in the diagram. It's a one-to-many relationship because a Book entity can only have one GenreId value that relates it to one Genre entity (the *one* side). However, a Genre entity can be related to several Book entities (the *many* side). Entities can also have a *one-to-one* or *many-to-many relationship* as described in the first table in this figure.

You can configure relationships by convention, with data attributes, and by using the Fluent API. In the next three figures, you'll learn how to configure the three types of relationships described here. First, though, this figure presents some of the attributes and methods used to configure relationships in EF Core.

The second table presents two attributes used to configure relationships. The ForeignKey attribute specifies the property that's the foreign key, and the InverseProperty attribute specifies the navigation property on the other end of a relationship. These attributes are in the System.ComponentModel. DataAnnotations.Schema namespace.

The third table presents some methods of the Fluent API for configuring relationships. This API uses the Has/With pattern to configure relationships. Here, methods that begin with Has represent the starting point of a relationship, and the methods that begin with With represent the ending point.

Two entities that have a one-to-many relationship

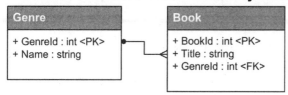

Three types of relationships between entities

Relationship	Example
One to many	Each book can be related to only one genre, but each genre can be related to one or more books.
One to one	Each author is related to only one author bio, and each author bio is related to only one author.
Many to many	Each book is related to one or more authors, and each author is related to one or more books.

Two attributes that can be used to configure relationships

Attribute	Description
`ForeignKey`	Specifies the property that's the foreign key in a relationship.
`InverseProperty`	Specifies the navigation property on the other end of a relationship.

The Has/With configuration pattern in the Fluent API

- *Has* represents the side of the relationship where the configuration starts.
- *With* represents the side of the relationship where the configuration ends.

Fluent API methods used to configure relationships in EF Core

Methods	Description
`HasOne(lambda)` `WithOne(lambda)`	Configures the *one* side of a one-to-many or one-to-one relationship.
`HasMany(lambda)` `WithMany(lambda)`	Configures the *many* side of a one-to-many or many-to-many relationship.
`HasForeignKey<T>(lambda)`	Specifies which property is the foreign key in a relationship.
`UsingEntity(lambda)`	Configures the linking entity for a many-to-many relationship. See figures 12-9 and 12-10.
`OnDelete(behavior)`	Specifies how the database deals with related rows when a row is deleted. See figure 12-11.

Description

- Relationships are defined with a *primary key* (*PK*) that uniquely identifies an entity and a *foreign key* (*FK*) that relates rows in another table to the primary key.
- Relationships in EF Core can be configured by convention, with data attributes, or by using the Fluent API.

Figure 12-6   How entities are related

How to configure a one-to-many relationship

The first code example in figure 12-7 shows the simplest way to configure a one-to-many relationship by convention. Here, the relationship is created by nesting a Genre entity as a property of the Book entity.

This is a common way of creating a one-to-many relationship. However, this approach has some drawbacks. For example, you need to specifically include the nested entity and all of its data even if all you need is the ID value. In addition, you can run into problems if the nested entity has data validation requirements.

As a result, it's typically a better practice to fully define the relationship by explicitly coding the foreign key property. The second example in this figure shows how this works. Here, the Book entity explicitly includes the foreign key property, GenreId. This Book entity also includes the Genre entity, but now it's clear that this property is a *navigation property*. In other words, it's a way to navigate to the values of the related entity from the primary entity.

When you fully define a relationship, it's a good practice to include a navigation property at each end of the relationship. To illustrate, the second example includes a Genre navigation property in the Book entity (the one side) and a Book collection property in the Genre entity (the many side). This collection is initialized in the constructor to a new HashSet<Book> collection to prevent null-reference warnings. Although you could use another type of collection such as List, it's best to use HashSet because it doesn't allow duplicates.

Here, the example still configures the relationship by convention. However, fully defining the foreign key and navigation properties makes the code easier to work with. In addition, it makes the relationship between the two entities more clear.

Most one-to-many relationships can be configured by convention. As a result, the main reason to use data attributes is if your naming doesn't follow conventions. For instance, the third example in this figure uses a name of Category for the Genre property and a name of CategoryId for the foreign key property of the Genre entity. Because of that, it uses the ForeignKey and InverseProperty attributes to define the relationship.

The last example shows how to use the Fluent API to configure a one-to-many relationship between the Book and Genre entities. This statement starts at the Book end of the relationship. However, you could also start at the Genre end. Then, the statement would look like this:

```
modelBuilder.Entity<Genre>()
    .HasMany(g => g.Books)
    .WithOne(b => b.Genre);
```

For this to work, you need to fully define the foreign key and navigation properties in your entities.

Most of the time, you only use the Fluent API to configure a one-to-many relationship if you also need to provide configuration that can't be provided by convention or with data attributes. For example, if you need to configure how the database handles deletions, you can use the Fluent API to configure a one-to-many relationship as shown in figure 12-11.

How to configure a one-to-many relationship by convention

```
public class Book {
    public int BookId { get; set; }

    public Genre Genre { get; set; } = null!;
}

public class Genre {
    public int GenreId { get; set; }
    public string Name { get; set; } = string.Empty;
}
```

How to fully define the one-to-many relationship by convention (recommended)

```
public class Book {
    public int BookId { get; set; }

    public int GenreId { get; set; }                    // foreign key property
    public Genre Genre { get; set; } = null!;           // navigation property
}

public class Genre {
    // initialize navigation property collection in constructor
    public Genre() => Books = new HashSet<Book>();

    public int GenreId { get; set; }
    public string Name { get; set; } = string.Empty;

    public ICollection<Book> Books { get; set; }        // navigation property
}
```

How to configure a one-to-many relationship with attributes

```
public class Book {
    public int BookId { get; set; }
    public int CategoryId { get; set; }

    [ForeignKey("CategoryId")]              // FK property in Book class
    [InverseProperty("Books")]              // nav property in Genre class
    public Genre Category { get; set; } = null!;
}

public class Genre {
    public int GenreId { get; set; }
    public string Name { get; set; } = string.Empty;

    [InverseProperty("Category")]           // nav property in Book class
    public ICollection<Book> Books { get; set; }
}
```

How to configure a one-to-many relationship with the Fluent API

```
protected override void OnModelCreating(ModelBuilder modelBuilder)
{
    modelBuilder.Entity<Book>()
        .HasOne(b => b.Genre)              // nav property in Book class
        .WithMany(g => g.Books);          // nav property in Genre class
}
```

Figure 12-7   How to configure a one-to-many relationship

How to configure a one-to-one relationship

If an entity has a one-to-one relationship with another entity, the data in the two entities could be stored in one entity, and the data in the two underlying database tables could be stored in one table. This is useful when you need to store large objects such as images, sound, and videos. Then, you can store those objects in a separate entity and underlying table and only join them when you need to retrieve the large object.

A one-to-one relationship can also be useful when an entity has data that is frequently null. For example, suppose that in most cases, the only data you need to store for an author is the name. In a few cases, though, suppose you want to store bio data in addition to the name. Then, instead of storing null values for all of the authors that don't have this data, you can store the values for authors that do have bio data in a separate table and only retrieve it when you need it.

The first example in figure 12-8 shows how to configure a fully defined one-to-one relationship by convention. This example works similarly to the second example in the previous figure. To start, each entity configures its primary key by convention and defines a navigation property. In addition, the AuthorBio entity configures its foreign key property by giving it the same name as the primary key of the Author entity.

Most one-to-one relationships can be configured by convention. However, if your naming doesn't follow conventions, you can use data attributes. For instance, you might not want to follow the EF conventions because you want to use the same name for the primary key in both entities. The second example shows how to do this. Here, the Author entity is unchanged, but the AuthorBio entity now uses its AuthorId property as its primary key and its foreign key.

The third example shows how to use the Fluent API to configure a one-to-one relationship. Typically, you only need to use this API if you also need to perform other tasks in addition to configuring the relationship. For example, you may need to split a table as shown by the fourth example.

Table splitting allows you to use two entities to represent the data that's stored in a single table. This can be useful when the table in the database contains a lot of columns, but you don't always want to retrieve all those columns. In this example, the author and author bio data is stored in a single table. However, this table is configured so its data is split between two entities, one that contains the data for authors and one that contains the data for author bios.

How to configure a one-to-one relationship by convention

```
public class Author {
    public int AuthorId { get; set; }                // primary key property
    public string Name { get; set; } = string.Empty;

    public AuthorBio Bio { get; set; } = null!;     // navigation property
}

public class AuthorBio {
    public int AuthorBioId { get; set; }             // primary key property
    public int AuthorId { get; set; }                // foreign key property
    public DateTime? DOB { get; set; }

    public Author Author { get; set; } = null!;     // navigation property
}
```

How to configure a one-to-one relationship with attributes

```
public class Author {
    // same as above
}

public class AuthorBio {
    [Key]
    public int AuthorId { get; set; }                // PK and FK property
    public DateTime? DOB { get; set; }

    [ForeignKey("AuthorId")]                         // FK property
    public Author Author { get; set; } = null!;     // navigation property
}
```

How to configure a one-to-one relationship with the Fluent API

```
protected override void OnModelCreating(ModelBuilder modelBuilder)
{
    modelBuilder.Entity<Author>()
        .HasOne(a => a.Bio)            // nav property in Author class
        .WithOne(ab => ab.Author)      // nav property in AuthorBio class
        .HasForeignKey<AuthorBio>(ab => ab.AuthorId);  // FK property
}
```

How to configure a one-to-one relationship within a single table

```
protected override void OnModelCreating(ModelBuilder modelBuilder)
{
    modelBuilder.Entity<Author>()
        .HasOne(a => a.Bio)
        .WithOne(ab => ab.Author)
        .HasForeignKey<AuthorBio>(ab => ab.AuthorId);

    modelBuilder.Entity<Author>().ToTable("Authors");
    modelBuilder.Entity<AuthorBio>().ToTable("Authors");
}
```

Figure 12-8   How to configure a one-to-one relationship

How to configure a many-to-many relationship

In a database, a many-to-many relationship uses an intermediate table called a *join table* or a *linking table*. Then, the linking table has a one-to-many relationship with the two tables in the many-to-many relationship. In other words, a many-to-many relationship is broken down into two one-to-many relationships.

Prior to EF Core 5.0, a many-to-many relationship could only be configured with the Fluent API. That's because you had to code an entity for the linking table, code each one-to-many relationship, and code the composite primary key that linking tables typically use. Now, with EF Core 5.0 and later, you can configure a many-to-many relationship by convention, and you no longer need to worry about the linking table.

The first example in figure 12-9 shows how this works. Here, a many-to-many relationship is configured between the Book entity and the Author entity by adding a navigation property to each entity. So, the Book entity has a navigation property that's a collection of Author objects, and the Author entity has a navigation property that's a collection of Book objects.

Then, based on these navigation properties, EF Core creates a linking table in the database like the one shown here. The AuthorsAuthorId column of the generated AuthorBook table is related to the primary key (AuthorId) of the Author entity. Similarly, the BooksBookId column of the AuthorBook table is related to the primary key (BookId) of the Books entity.

Crucially, though, your code doesn't need to know anything about this linking table. Instead, you can use the navigation properties to skip right over the linking table and get the collection of objects on the other side of the relationship. Because of this, the navigation properties for a many-to-many relationship are sometimes called *skip navigation properties*.

When you configure a many-to-many relationship by convention, EF Core names the linking table and its columns based on the names of the entities being linked. Often, that's fine. However, if you want more control over the column names, you can use data attributes as shown in the second example. Here, the ForeignKey attribute is used to specify the names of the foreign key columns. Then, EF Core will use these names when it generates the linking table. In this example, for instance, the column names will be 'BookId' and 'AuthorId' rather than 'BooksBookId' and 'AuthorsAuthorId'.

The third example shows how to use the Fluent API to configure the many-to-many relationship between the Book and Author entities. When you do that, you can set the name of the linking table as well as the column names.

This code starts at the Book end of the relationship and uses the HasMany() and WithMany() methods to identify the skip navigation properties at either end of the relationship. Then, it calls the UsingEntity() method, passing it the name of the linking table followed by lambda expressions that set the foreign key columns. Note that EF Core currently uses the type Dictionary<string, object> to represent the linking entity, but the EF Core documentation says that may change in the future.

How to configure a many-to-many relationship by convention

```
public class Book {
    public Book() => Authors = new HashSet<Author>();

    public int BookId { get; set; }
    public string Title { get; set; } = string.Empty;

    public ICollection<Author> Authors { get; set; }  // skip nav property
}

public class Author {
    public Author() => Books = new HashSet<Book>();

    public int AuthorId { get; set; }
    public string Name { get; set; }

    public ICollection<Book Books { get; set; }          // skip nav property
}
```

The linking table that EF Core creates in the database

How to configure a many-to-many relationship with attributes

```
public class Book {
    // same as above

    [ForeignKey("BookId")]        // foreign key column in linking table
    public ICollection<Author> Authors { get; set; }
}

public class Author {
    // same as above

    [ForeignKey("AuthorId")]      // foreign key column in linking table
    public ICollection<Book> Books { get; set; }
}
```

How to configure a many-to-many relationship with the Fluent API

```
protected override void OnModelCreating(ModelBuilder modelBuilder)
{
    modelBuilder.Entity<Book>()
        .HasMany(b => b.Authors)
        .WithMany(a => a.Books)
        .UsingEntity<Dictionary<string, object>>(
            "BookAuthors",                  // name linking table
            ba => ba.HasOne<Author>()       // set Author foreign key column
                .WithMany()
                .HasForeignKey("AuthorId"),
            ba => ba.HasOne<Book>()         // set Book foreign key column
                .WithMany()
                .HasForeignKey("BookId")
    );
}
```

Figure 12-9   How to configure a many-to-many relationship

How to seed data in the linking table of a many-to-many relationship

In figure 12-3 you saw how to use the HasData() method to seed initial data in a database table that EF Core creates based on an entity class. You can also seed data in a linking table for a many-to-many relationship. To do that, you need to call HasData() as part of a lambda expression sent to the UsingEntity() method.

Figure 12-10 presents two ways to seed data in the linking table for a many-to-many relationship. Both of these examples use the Fluent API in the OnModelCreating() method. And both start by identifying the skip navigation properties at either end of the relationship and then calling the UsingEntity() method.

When the many-to-many relationship is configured by convention or with data attributes, all you need to do is pass a lambda expression that calls HasData() to the UsingEntity() method, as shown in the first example. In this case, the UsingEntity() method doesn't need to specify the data type of the linking entity.

As you learned in figure 12-3, when you call HasData(), you pass it one or more instances of the entity that you're seeding. However, if there's no entity for the linking table, you must use anonymous objects, as shown here. When you do that, you must make sure that the property names of the anonymous object match the column names that EF Core generates. For instance, this example shows seed data for a many-to-many relationship that's configured by convention, so the property names match the column names in the linking table shown in the last figure. If you set the column names using the ForeignKey attribute, the property names must match those names.

When the many-to-many relationship is configured with the Fluent API as shown in the last figure, you update the configuration code to include a lambda expression that calls the HasData() method, as shown in the second example. In this case, you use the foreign key names set in the HasForeignKey() methods as the property names for the anonymous objects.

How to seed data in the linking table for a many-to-many relationship

When the relationship is configured by convention or with attributes

```
protected override void OnModelCreating(ModelBuilder modelBuilder)
{
    modelBuilder.Entity<Book>()
        .HasMany(b => b.Authors)
        .WithMany(a => a.Books)
        .UsingEntity(
            ba => ba.HasData(
                new { BooksBookId = 1, AuthorsAuthorId = 18 },
                new { BooksBookId = 2, AuthorsAuthorId = 20 },
                ...
                new { BooksBookId = 29, AuthorsAuthorId = 25 }
    ));
}
```

When all the configuration is done with the Fluent API

```
protected override void OnModelCreating(ModelBuilder modelBuilder)
{
    modelBuilder.Entity<Book>()
        .HasMany(b => b.Authors)
        .WithMany(a => a.Books)
        .UsingEntity<Dictionary<string, object>>(
            "BookAuthors",
            ba => ba.HasOne<Author>()
                .WithMany()
                .HasForeignKey("AuthorId"),
            ba => ba.HasOne<Book>()
                .WithMany()
                .HasForeignKey("BookId"),
            ba => ba.HasData(
                new { BookId = 1, AuthorId = 18 },
                new { BookId = 2, AuthorId = 20 },
                ...
                new { BookId = 29, AuthorId = 25 }
    ));
}
```

Description

- You can use the HasData() method within the lambda expression for the UsingEntity() method to seed initial data in a linking table.

Figure 12-10   How to seed data in the linking table of a many-to-many relationship

How to control delete behavior

When an app deletes a row from a database, related rows that are dependent on that row can become corrupted. For example, if an app deletes the genre "Novel" from the Genre table, all the rows in the Books table whose genre is "Novel" have invalid data.

To prevent this, most databases throw an exception when you try to delete a row that has dependent, or child, rows. However, most databases also allow you to configure foreign keys with cascading deletes. A *cascading delete* causes all child rows to be automatically deleted when a parent row is deleted.

By default, Code First development configures a foreign key with cascading deletes if the foreign key is not nullable. This is true whether you define the relationship by convention, with data attributes, or using the Fluent API.

Sometimes, cascading deletes are what you want. For example, when you delete a Book, you also want to delete related rows in the linking table that relates it to Authors. Similarly, when you delete an Author, you also want to delete the related row in the AuthorBios table.

Other times, though, cascading deletes are *not* what you want. For example, when you delete the "Novel" genre, you *don't* want to delete all books that are novels from the Books table. In this case, it's better for the database to throw an exception. This helps to prevent you from accidentally deleting data that you don't want to delete.

You can use the OnDelete() method of the Fluent API to configure how dependent rows are handled when a parent row is deleted. This method accepts a value of the DeleteBehavior enum as an argument. The table at the top of figure 12-11 shows the values of this enum.

The Cascade value configures the foreign key so all dependent rows are deleted. Again, this is the default behavior in Code First development for foreign keys that are not nullable.

The SetNull value configures the foreign key so that when a parent row is deleted, the foreign key value of any dependent rows is set to null. This only works if the foreign key is nullable, and it isn't usually what you want.

The Restrict value configures the foreign key so nothing happens to dependent rows when the parent row is marked for deletion. In other words, it "turns off" the cascading delete. If a property remains in this state when SaveChanges() is called, EF throws an exception, which is often what you want.

The code example below the table in this figure shows how to use the OnDelete() method. Here, the GenreId foreign key property in the Book entity is configured so it doesn't have a cascading delete. As a result, if you try to delete a genre that has related books, EF throws an exception.

The values of the DeleteBehavior enum

Value	Description
Cascade	Deletes dependent rows automatically. This is EF Core's default behavior for foreign keys that are not nullable.
SetNull	Sets the value of the foreign key in the dependent row to null. This is only possible when the foreign key is nullable. If the foreign key is not nullable, this causes an exception to be thrown.
Restrict	Prevents deletion of dependent rows. If a property remains in this state when SaveChanges() is called, this causes an exception to be thrown. This is EF Core's default behavior for foreign keys that are nullable.

How to configure an entity to throw an error when attempting to delete a dependent row

```
protected override void OnModelCreating(ModelBuilder modelBuilder)
{
    modelBuilder.Entity<Book>()
        .HasOne(b => b.Genre)
        .WithMany(g => g.Books)
        .OnDelete(DeleteBehavior.Restrict);
}
```

Description

- When a row is deleted from a database, related rows that are dependent on that row can become corrupted. To prevent this, most databases throw an exception when you try to delete a row that has dependent rows.

- Most databases also allow you to configure *cascading deletes*, which cause dependent rows to be automatically deleted.

- You can use the OnDelete() method of the Fluent API to configure how dependent rows are handled when a parent row is deleted.

Figure 12-11   How to control delete behavior

The Bookstore database classes

Now that you know how to code entity classes that are related to each other, you're ready to see the entity, context, and configuration classes for the Bookstore website that's presented in the next chapter.

The entity classes

Figure 12-12 shows the classes for the Author, Book, and Genre entities that are used by the Bookstore website. For the most part, these entities are configured by convention. For example, the Author, Book, and Genre classes configure their primary keys and foreign keys by convention and include navigation properties to make it easy to work with related entities. This includes the skip navigation properties that configure the many-to-many relationship between the Author and Book classes.

The Bookstore website also decorates the properties of the entity classes with data attributes for validation. These attributes are applied to the database when you create it too, which is usually what you want. For example, the Required attribute causes the corresponding database column to not allow null values. Similarly, the StringLength attribute specifies the maximum number of characters that can be stored for a string column.

The Book class also decorates its Genre property with the ValidateNever attribute, which does not affect the database. Instead, this attribute causes MVC to ignore the Genre property when it validates a Book object. That can prevent model binding errors if this property is set to null.

The context and configuration classes

Figure 12-13 shows the context class for the Bookstore website. This class begins by defining the DbSet properties for the Author, Book, and Genre entities presented in figure 12-12.

After defining the DbSet properties, the OnModelCreating() method applies the code that's stored in the configuration classes that follow. You can apply these classes in any sequence, regardless of how the entities are related to each other.

All of these configuration classes use the Fluent API to seed initial data. In addition, the ConfigureBooks class turns off cascading deletes. That way, if the user attempts to delete a genre that is related to one or more books, EF won't delete the genre. Instead, it will throw an exception.

The ConfigureBookAuthors() class seeds the initial data for the linking table that EF Core creates for the many-to-many relationship between Book and Author entities. Because these entities configure this relationship by convention, the code that seeds the data for the linking table must use property names that match the column names that EF Core generates for the linking table. In this case, those names are BooksBookId and AuthorsAuthorId.

The Author class

```
using System.ComponentModel.DataAnnotations;
using Microsoft.AspNetCore.Mvc;                            // for Remote

namespace Bookstore.Models
{
    public class Author
    {
        public Author() => Books = new HashSet<Book>();

        public int AuthorId { get; set; }

        [Required(ErrorMessage = "Please enter a first name.")]
        [MaxLength(200)]
        public string FirstName { get; set; } = string.Empty;

        [Required(ErrorMessage = "Please enter a last name.")]
        [MaxLength(200)]
        [Remote("CheckAuthor", "Validation", "Admin",
            AdditionalFields = "FirstName, Operation")]
        public string LastName { get; set; } = string.Empty;

        public string FullName => $"{FirstName} {LastName}";    // read-only

        public ICollection<Book> Books { get; set; }       // skip nav property
    }
}
```

The Book class

```
using System.ComponentModel.DataAnnotations;
using Microsoft.AspNetCore.Mvc.ModelBinding.Validation;    // for ValidateNever

namespace Bookstore.Models
{
    public class Book
    {
        public Book() => Authors = new HashSet<Author>();

        public int BookId { get; set; }

        [Required(ErrorMessage = "Please enter a title.")]
        [MaxLength(200)]
        public string Title { get; set; } = string.Empty;

        [Range(0.0, 1000000.0, ErrorMessage = "Price must be 1 or more.")]
        public double Price { get; set; }

        [Required(ErrorMessage = "Please select a genre.")]
        public string GenreId { get; set; } = string.Empty;

        [ValidateNever]
        public Genre Genre { get; set; } = null!;

        public ICollection<Author> Authors { get; set; } // skip nav property
    }
}
```

Figure 12-12   The entity classes for the Bookstore database (part 1)

The Genre class

```
using System.ComponentModel.DataAnnotation;
using Microsoft.AspNetCore.Mvc;                              // for Remote

namespace Bookstore.Models
{
    public class Genre
    {
        public Genre() => Books = new HashSet<Book>();

        [MaxLength(10)]
        [Required(ErrorMessage = "Please enter a genre id.")]
        [Remote("CheckGenre", "Validation", "Admin")]
        public string GenreId { get; set; } = string.Empty;

        [StringLength(25)]
        [Required(ErrorMessage = "Please enter a genre name.")]
        public string Name { get; set; } = string.Empty;

        public ICollection<Book> Books { get; set; }   // nav property
    }
}
```

Figure 12-12   The entity classes for the Bookstore database (part 2)

The BookstoreContext class

```
using Microsoft.EntityFrameworkCore;

namespace Bookstore.Models
{
    public class BookstoreContext : DbContext
    {
        public BookstoreContext(DbContextOptions<BookstoreContext> options)
            : base(options)
        { }

        public DbSet<Genre> Genres { get; set; } = null!;
        public DbSet<Book> Books { get; set; } = null!;
        public DbSet<Author> Authors { get; set; } = null!;

        protected override void OnModelCreating(ModelBuilder modelBuilder)
        {
            modelBuilder.ApplyConfiguration(new ConfigureGenres());
            modelBuilder.ApplyConfiguration(new ConfigureBooks());
            modelBuilder.ApplyConfiguration(new ConfigureAuthors());
            modelBuilder.ApplyConfiguration(new ConfigureBookAuthors());
        }
    }
}
```

The ConfigureAuthors class

```
using Microsoft.EntityFrameworkCore;
using Microsoft.EntityFrameworkCore.Metadata.Builders;

namespace Bookstore.Models
{
    internal class ConfigureAuthors : IEntityTypeConfiguration<Author>
    {
        public void Configure(EntityTypeBuilder<Author> entity)
        {
            // seed initial data
            entity.HasData(
                new Author { AuthorId = 1, FirstName = "Michelle",
                             LastName = "Alexander" },
                new Author { AuthorId = 2, FirstName = "Stephen E.",
                             LastName = "Ambrose" },
                ...
                new Author { AuthorId = 26, FirstName = "Seth",
                             LastName = "Grahame-Smith" }
            );
        }
    }
}
```

Figure 12-13   The DB context and configuration classes (part 1)

The ConfigureBooks class

```
using Microsoft.EntityFrameworkCore;
using Microsoft.EntityFrameworkCore.Metadata.Builders;

namespace Bookstore.Models
{
    internal class ConfigureBooks : IEntityTypeConfiguration<Book>
    {
        public void Configure(EntityTypeBuilder<Book> entity)
        {
            // remove cascading delete with Genre
            entity.HasOne(b => b.Genre)
                .WithMany(g => g.Books)
                .OnDelete(DeleteBehavior.Restrict);

            // seed initial data
            entity.HasData(
                new Book { BookId = 1, Title = "1776", GenreId = "history",
                        Price = 18.00 },
                new Book { BookId = 2, Title = "1984", GenreId = "scifi",
                        Price = 5.50 },
                ...
                new Book { BookId = 29,
                        Title = "Harry Potter and the Sorcerer's Stone",
                        GenreId = "novel", Price = 9.75 }
            );
        }
    }
}
```

The ConfigureGenres class

```
using Microsoft.EntityFrameworkCore;
using Microsoft.EntityFrameworkCore.Metadata.Builders;

namespace Bookstore.Models
{
    internal class ConfigureGenres : IEntityTypeConfiguration<Genre>
    {
        public void Configure(EntityTypeBuilder<Genre> entity)
        {
            // seed initial data
            entity.HasData(
                new { GenreId = "novel", Name = "Novel" },
                new { GenreId = "memoir", Name = "Memoir" },
                new { GenreId = "mystery", Name = "Mystery" },
                new { GenreId = "scifi", Name = "Science Fiction" },
                new { GenreId = "history", Name = "History" }
            );
        }
    }
}
```

Figure 12-13   The DB context and configuration classes (part 2)

The ConfigureBookAuthors class

```
using Microsoft.EntityFrameworkCore;
using Microsoft.EntityFrameworkCore.Metadata.Builders;

namespace Bookstore.Models
{
    internal class ConfigureBookAuthors : IEntityTypeConfiguration<Book>
    {
        public void Configure(EntityTypeBuilder<Book> entity)
        {
            entity
                .HasMany(b => b.Authors)   // many to many relationship
                .WithMany(a => a.Books)
                .UsingEntity(
                    ba => ba.HasData(      // seed initial data
                        new { BooksBookId = 1, AuthorsAuthorId = 18 },
                        new { BooksBookId = 2, AuthorsAuthorId = 20 },
                        ...
                        new { BooksBookId = 28, AuthorsAuthorId = 4 },
                        new { BooksBookId = 28, AuthorsAuthorId = 26 },
                        new { BooksBookId = 29, AuthorsAuthorId = 25 }
            ));
        }
    }

}
```

Figure 12-13   The DB context and configuration classes (part 3)

How to create code from a database

So far in this book, you have learned how to use Code First development to create a database from your context and entity classes. Sometimes, though, you already have a database. In that case, you need to create context and entity classes from your database. This approach is called *Database First* development.

How to generate DB context and entity classes

To get started with Database First development, you can use the Scaffold-DbContext command to generate the code for the context and entity classes. The table at the top of figure 12-14 presents some of the parameters that are available for this command. The first two parameters, Connection and Provider, are required. The rest of the parameters are optional.

It's a best practice to store the connection string in the appsettings.json file. Then, you can use the name of the connection string setting as the value of this parameter. However, if that doesn't work, you can specify a string literal for the connection string as shown by the fourth example in this figure.

The DataAnnotations parameter indicates whether you want to perform configuration by adding data attributes to your entity classes. If you include this parameter, EF uses data attributes to perform configuration as much as possible. However, EF may still use the Fluent API for some of the configuration. That's because it's often not possible to do all configuration with attributes.

The Force parameter indicates whether you want to overwrite existing files. This is useful when you want to regenerate your code files after making changes to the database. If you don't include this flag and the files already exist, the PMC displays an error message.

The first example in this figure shows a connection string named BookstoreContext that's stored in the appsettings.json file. Due to space limitations, this string is displayed on two lines here. For it to work correctly, though, it must be stored on one line in the file.

The second and third examples show how to generate class files from a SQL Server database, output these files to the Models\DataLayer folder, and overwrite any existing files. Here, the second example includes the flags for the two required parameters, and the third omits them. If you omit the flags, you need to specify the parameters in the sequence shown here.

This figure finishes by showing the generated files in the Models\DataLayer folder. The code for these files includes a namespace based on the folder path. So, if these files are in a project named Bookstore, the generated classes are in the Bookstore.Models.DataLayer namespace. Note that EF Core singularizes the names of entity classes even if the names of the database tables are plural. This behavior is new with EF Core 5.0.

Parameters for the Scaffold-DbContext command

Parameter	Description
-Connection	The connection string. You can use name=*ConnectionStringName* to specify the name of a connection string that's stored in the appsettings.json file. This parameter is required.
-Provider	The provider, often a NuGet package name. This parameter is required.
-OutputDir	The folder to store the generated files. The default is the root folder for the project.
-DataAnnotations	Adds data attributes to entity classes where possible. Otherwise, EF uses the Fluent API in the DB context class to perform all configuration.
-Force	Overwrites existing files. Otherwise, EF doesn't overwrite existing files.

A connection string that's stored in the appsettings.json file

```
"ConnectionStrings": {
  "BookstoreContext": "Server=(localdb)\\mssqllocaldb;
  Database=Bookstore;Trusted_Connection=True;MultipleActiveResultSets=true"
}
```

An EF command that generates entity classes from a Sql Server database

```
PM> Scaffold-DbContext -Connection name=BookstoreContext
-Provider Microsoft.EntityFrameworkCore.SqlServer
-OutputDir Models\DataLayer -DataAnnotations -Force
```

The same command with the flags for the required parameters omitted

```
PM> Scaffold-DbContext name=BookstoreContext
Microsoft.EntityFrameworkCore.SqlServer
-OutputDir Models\DataLayer -DataAnnotations -Force
```

A -Connection parameter with a string literal for the connection string

```
-Connection "Server=(localdb)\mssqllocaldb;Database=Bookstore;
Trusted_Connection=True;MultipleActiveResultSets=true"
```

The generated files in the Models\DataLayer folder

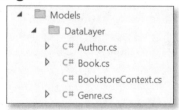

Description

- You can use the Scaffold-Database command to generate context and entity classes based on an existing database.
- You can omit the flag for required parameters.
- When specifying the connection string, it's considered a best practice to use a connection string that's stored in the appsettings.json file.

Figure 12-14   How to generate DB context and entity classes

How to configure a generated DB context class

When you use the Scaffold-DbContext command to generate context and entity classes, the OnConfiguring() method of the context class contains the connection string and provider information. Usually, though, you need to make some adjustments before your project is ready to run.

The first code example in figure 12-15 shows the OnConfiguring() method that's generated by a Scaffold-DbContext command like the one shown in the previous figure. Here, the UseSqlServer() method specifies that the provider is a SQL Server database. And the argument that's passed to this method specifies the name of the connection string that's stored in the appsettings.json file as shown in the previous figure.

However, your app won't run until you configure it to use dependency injection with your generated DB context. To do that, you can modify the Program.cs file as shown in the second code example in this figure. This works like the Code First example presented in figure 4-6.

Since the OnConfiguring() method sets the provider (SQL Server) and the name of the connection string, it duplicates configuration options that are now stored in the Program.cs file. If you want, you can leave the OnConfiguring() method as shown in the first example in this figure. That's because the OnConfiguring() method uses an if statement to only configure database options if they have not already been configured in the Program.cs file. However, if you prefer, you can remove the if statement from the OnConfiguring() method and then just call the OnConfiguring() method of the base class, as shown in the third example.

The OnConfiguring() method in the generated context class

```
protected override void OnConfiguring(
    DbContextOptionsBuilder optionsBuilder)
{
    if (!optionsBuilder.IsConfigured)
    {
        optionsBuilder.UseSqlServer("name=BookstoreContext");
    }
}
```

The Program.cs file configuration for injection of the DB context

```
using Microsoft.EntityFrameworkCore;
using Bookstore.Models.DataLayer;

var builder = WebApplication.CreateBuilder(args);

builder.Services.AddControllersWithViews();

builder.Services.AddDbContext<BookstoreContext>(
    options => options.UseSqlServer(
        builder.Configuration.GetConnectionString("BookstoreContext")));
...
```

The OnConfiguring() method after it has been cleaned up

```
protected override void OnConfiguring(
    DbContextOptionsBuilder optionsBuilder)
{
    base.OnConfiguring(optionsBuilder);
}
```

Description

- When you use the Scaffold-DbContext command to create DB context and entity classes, it adds configuration code to the OnConfiguring() method of the context class.

- To get the DB context to work, you need to add configuration to the Program.cs file that enables the DB context to be injected into the controllers of the app.

- For this Program.cs code to work, the appsettings.json file must store the specified connection string. If it doesn't, you can edit that file so it contains the specified connection string.

Figure 12-15   How to configure a generated DB context class

How to modify a generated entity class

When you work with Database First development, it's common to enhance the entity classes that it generates. For instance, you may want to add data validation attributes. Or, you may want to add more properties such as read-only properties that indicate the state of the entity.

However, if you make changes to the database, it's common to need to regenerate the entity classes. When this happens, though, you lose any additions you've made to those classes. Fortunately, you can use partial classes to avoid this problem.

The first example in figure 12-16 presents an entity class named Books that was generated by EF Core. You should notice two important things about this class. First, it's a partial class. Second, EF generated it in a namespace that corresponds to the folder structure for the class.

The second example presents another partial class named Book that adds to the generated partial class of the same name. This works because C# compiles these two partial classes into a single class named Book.

You should notice two important things about this second partial class. First, it's in the same namespace as the generated class. However, because the class file has the same name as the generated Books class file, it must be stored in a different folder than this file. Or, you could give the file a different name.

Second, it adds a read-only property named HasTitle. This property returns a Boolean value that indicates whether the Title property has a value. Because this custom property is not in the generated file, it won't be lost if the Book class is regenerated from the database.

The third example in this figure presents a class named BookMetadata. This class contains the data validation attributes for the generated Book entity class. Again, since these attributes are in a separate class file, they won't be lost if the Book class needs to be regenerated. Also, this class is in the same namespace as both of the partial Book classes. That's because all three of these classes need to be in the same namespace for this technique to work.

Finally, the fourth example shows how to apply the data attributes in the BookMetadata class to the Book entity class. To do that, you decorate the Book class with the ModelMetadataType attribute. This attribute uses the typeof operator to pass the type of a class that contains the attributes, or metadata, that should be applied to the generated entity class. In this case, of course, the attributes in the BookMetadata class are applied.

At this point, you might be wondering why you can't just include the data validation attributes in the Book partial class that adds the HasTitle property to the generated partial class. The reason is that, to add data validation attributes, you need to code the property you want to validate. For instance, you would need to code a Price property if you wanted to decorate it with data validation attributes. But, because the Price property is already coded in the generated Book partial class, the compiler won't let you code it a second time in another partial class.

The Book class generated by EF Database First

```
namespace Bookstore.Models.DataLayer
{
    public partial class Book
    {
        ...
    }
}
```

How to add a custom property in a separate partial Book class

```
namespace Bookstore.Models.DataLayer
{
    public partial class Book
    {
        public bool HasTitle => !string.IsNullOrEmpty(Title);
    }
}
```

A metadata class that adds validation for a Book property

```
using System.ComponentModel.DataAnnotations;

namespace Bookstore.Models.DataLayer
{
    public class BookMetadata
    {
        [Range(0.0, 1000000.0,
            ErrorMessage = "Price must be greater than zero.")]
        public double Price { get; set; }
    }
}
```

How to associate the metadata class with the Book class

```
using Microsoft.AspNetCore.Mvc;

namespace Bookstore.Models.DataLayer
{
    [ModelMetadataType(typeof(BookMetadata))]
    public partial class Books
    {
        public bool HasTitle => !string.IsNullOrEmpty(Title);
    }
}
```

Description

- When EF Core generates entity classes, it creates partial classes.

- If you add data validation attributes or custom properties directly to a generated entity class, those additions are lost if you regenerate the classes when the database changes.

- To prevent that, you can write your own partial classes that contain custom properties, and metadata classes that contain data validation attributes.

- To associate a metadata class with an entity class, decorate the entity class with the [ModelMetadataType] attribute of the Microsoft.AspNetCore.Mvc namespace. It's best to decorate a separate partial class so it's not lost when you regenerate the classes.

Figure 12-16   How to modify a generated entity class

How to work with data in a database

Chapter 4 introduced some basic skills for working with the data in a database. Now, you'll review those skills and learn some new ones.

How to query data

You can use *LINQ to Entities* to query the DbSet properties of a context class. The first code example in figure 12-17 shows a context property named context that's used by subsequent examples. This context has DbSet properties named Books and Authors.

The second set of examples shows how to create and execute a query. When you do that using two statements, you create a query variable of the IQueryable<T> type that holds a query, not data. Then, when you execute the query, the data is retrieved from the database and stored in an object of the IEnumerable<T> type. When you do that using one statement, you can use the var keyword to declare the variable where the results are stored so the compiler will automatically determine the type. In this case, it uses the List<Book> type, which is usually what you want.

The third set of examples shows how to sort the results of a query. The first statement uses the OrderBy() method to sort the results in ascending order by title, and the second uses the OrderByDescending() method to sort the results in descending order by title.

The fourth set of examples shows how to filter a query to limit the number of rows it returns. Most of these examples use the Where() method to specify the criteria to filter by. However, the second statement uses the Find() method to get a book by its ID. This is a shortcut for the first statement that uses the Where() method. In these statements, the Find() and FirstOrDefault() methods execute the query and return the requested data.

The fourth set of examples finishes by showing how to conditionally filter the results by multiple criteria. First, this code declares an initial query that returns all books. This code doesn't use the var keyword to implicitly type the query variable because the compiler would infer the DbSet<T> type instead of the IQueryable<T> type. Then, this code uses if statements to build the where clause. If none of these conditions are true, this code executes the initial query to retrieve all books.

The fifth example shows how to get a subset of results using the Skip() and Take() methods. This is common in scenarios where you want to allow the user to be able to scroll through pages of results.

The sixth example shows how to disable change tracking. Normally, the DbContext object tracks all changes that are made to the data it retrieves. In read-only scenarios, though, this isn't necessary. As a result, you can use the AsNoTracking() method to disable it.

The last example shows how to get a random book. To do that, the OrderBy() method sorts books randomly by assigning a new globally unique identifier (GUID) to each book and sorting on that value. Then, this example gets the first book from the newly sorted list of books.

The context class used in the following examples

```
private BookstoreContext context { get; set; }
```

Code that creates and executes a query

In two statements

```
IQueryable<Book> query = context.Books;          // create the query
IEnumerable<Book> books = query.ToList();         // execute the query
```

In one statement

```
var books = context.Books.ToList();              // implicit typing is common
```

Code that sorts the results

Sort by Title in ascending order (A to Z)

```
var books = context.Books.OrderBy(b => b.Title).ToList();
```

Sort by Title in descending order (Z to A)

```
var books = context.Books.OrderByDescending(b => b.Title).ToList();
```

Code that filters the results

Get a single book by ID

```
var book = context.Books.Where(b => b.BookId == 1).FirstOrDefault();
var book = context.Books.Find(1);     // shortcut for above
```

Get a list of books by genre

```
var books = context.Books.Where(b => b.Genre.Name == "Mystery").ToList();
```

Get a list of books in a price range

```
var books = context.Books.Where(b => b.Price > 10 && b.Price < 20).ToList();
```

Conditionally filter by multiple criteria

```
// build the query (can't use implicit typing here)
IQueryable<Book> query = context.Books;
if (selectedMaxPrice != null)
    query = query.Where(b => b.Price < selectedMaxPrice);
if (selectedGenre != null)
    query = query.Where(b => b.Genre.Name == selectedGenre);

// execute the query
var books = query.ToList();
```

Code that gets a subset of results

```
int pageNumber = 2, booksPerPage = 4;
var books = context.Books.Skip((pageNumber - 1) * booksPerPage)
                    .Take(booksPerPage)
                    .ToList();
```

Code for a read-only query that disables change tracking

```
var books = context.Books.AsNoTracking().ToList();
```

Code that gets a random book

```
var randBook = context.Books.OrderBy(r => Guid.NewGuid()).FirstOrDefault();
```

Figure 12-17   How to query data

How to work with projections and related entities

When you query data as described in the last figure, the query retrieves all of the properties in an entity, whether you need them or not. Usually, this is fine. Sometimes, though, you may have entities with so many properties that it's inefficient to retrieve all of them. Or, you may have properties with sensitive data, like passwords, that you don't want to retrieve.

One way to limit the number of properties returned is to use table splitting as mentioned earlier in this chapter. Another way to do that is to use projections. A *projection* uses the LINQ Select() method to retrieve only some of an entity's properties.

One way to create a projection is to use an anonymous type like the one shown in the first example in figure 12-18. This type consists of the AuthorId property of the Authors entity and a property that's a combination of the FirstName and LastName properties. Because the second property doesn't match an entity property, it must be explicitly named as shown here.

Anonymous types are convenient and quick, but they can be hard to work with in an MVC app. That's because they're hard to pass to views, as the error message below the first example shows.

A better way to work with projections in MVC is to use a simple *data transfer object (DTO)* that's designed to transfer data from one place to another. For example, the DTO in the second set of examples provides the value and text for a drop-down list. This allows the Select() method to create a new instance of the DTO rather than creating an instance of an anonymous type. Then, it can pass the DTO to a view.

In addition to limiting the properties that are returned, you may sometimes need to include the data for related entities in your query. To do this, you use the Include() and ThenInclude() methods of the Microsoft.EntityFrameworkCore namespace as shown by the last set of examples.

Both statements in the first example use chained Include() methods to include all the books and their related genres and authors. In the first statement, the Include() methods accept lambda expressions that specify the entity to include. By contrast, the Include() methods in the second statement accept string literals that specify the entity.

The second example shows how to retrieve related entities that are nested more than one layer deep. Here, the first statement uses an Include() method to get the genres and their related books. Then, the ThenInclude() method gets the authors related to the books. Both of these methods use lambda expressions. The second statement shows how to retrieve the same data using a single Include() method and a literal string. With this technique, the nested entities are represented with dot notation.

The advantage of using lambda expressions is that they're checked at compile time. As a result, they're less error-prone because the IDE alerts you right away if you make a typo or the entity doesn't exist. By contrast, strings aren't checked until runtime. However, the string option can give you more flexibility as described later in this chapter.

How to create a projection with an anonymous type

```
var authors = context.Authors
    .Select(a => new {
        a.AuthorId,                            // can infer property name
        Name = a.FirstName + ' ' + a.LastName  // must specify property name
    })
    .ToList();
```

Error when you pass the projection to a view that expects a list of Authors

```
InvalidOperationException: The model item passed into the ViewDataDictionary
is of type 'System.Collections.Generic.List`1[<>f_AnonymousType0`2
[System.Int32,System.String]]', but this ViewDataDictionary instance
requires a model item of type 'System.Collections.Generic.IEnumberable`1
[BookList.Models.Author]'.
```

How to create a projection with a concrete type

The concrete type

```
public class DropdownDTO
{
    public string Value { get; set; } = string.Empty;
    public string Text { get; set; } = string.Empty;
}
```

The projection

```
var authors = context.Authors
    .Select(a => new DropdownDTO {
        Value = a.AuthorId.ToString(),
        Text = a.FirstName + ' ' + a.LastName
    })
    .ToList();
```

Code that includes related entities

Two techniques for getting all books and their related genres and authors

```
var books = context.Books.Include(b => b.Genre).Include(b => b.Authors)
    .ToList();
var books = context.Books.Include("Genre").Include("Authors").ToList();
```

Two techniques for getting all genres and their related books and authors

```
var books = context.Genres.Include(g => g.Books)
    .ThenInclude(b => b.Authors).ToList();
var books = context.Genres.Include("Books.Authors").ToList();
```

Description

- A *projection* allows you to retrieve a subset of the properties of an entity.

- To create a projection, you can use an anonymous type or a concrete type. However, anonymous types can be hard to use in views.

- You can use the Include() and ThenInclude() methods to include related entities in a query. These methods accept lambda expressions to identify the entities to include.

- The Include() method also accepts a string literal to identify the entities to include.

Figure 12-18   How to work with projections and include related entities

How to insert, update, and delete data

In addition to querying data, you need to know how to insert, update, and delete data. Fortunately, the methods of the DbSet and DbContext classes make that easy to do. You learned about these methods in chapter 4, but now figure 12-19 reviews them and explains them in more detail.

The Add(), Update(), and Remove() methods of the DbSet class only affect the DbSet. The Add() method adds a new entity to the DbSet and marks it as Added, and the Update() and Remove() methods mark an existing entity as Modified or Deleted. To mark an entity, EF uses the EntityState enum. In most cases, you can let EF mark these changes for you automatically. However, you can also set the state of an entity manually, if necessary.

In contrast to the Add(), Update(), and Remove() methods, the SaveChanges() method of the DbContext class affects the underlying database. When you call this method, all the Added, Modified, and Deleted actions pending in the DbSet properties are executed against the database.

The code examples show how to use these methods. The first example adds a new entity, the second and third examples update an existing entity, and the fourth example deletes an existing entity. While this code is easy to follow, you should notice a few things.

First, although these examples all perform a single action and then call SaveChanges(), that's not a requirement. You can make several calls to Add(), Update(), or Remove() before you call SaveChanges(). In fact, in some scenarios, it can improve efficiency to only call SaveChanges() once after all your modifications are done.

Second, when it comes to updates, the second example shows how to work with a *disconnected scenario* because it's commonly used with web apps. In this scenario, the Edit() action method gets the Book entity from an HTTP POST request. As a result, the code in this figure must use Update() to update the state of the entity before calling SaveChanges().

With desktop apps, it's more common to use a *connected scenario*. However, a connected scenario can also occur in web apps as shown by the third example. Here, the first statement of the Edit() action method uses the Find() method to retrieve the Book entity from the database. This causes the context to track the state of this entity. As a result, you don't need to call the Update() method. Instead, this code just sets the new price for the book and calls the SaveChanges() method. This generates SQL that's slightly more efficient than calling Update(). However, if you wanted to make the code easier to read and understand, you could add a statement that calls Update() before calling SaveChanges().

Finally, when you delete a parent entity in EF Core, it's common for all of the related child entities to be automatically deleted too. That's because EF Core enables cascading deletes by default for foreign keys that are not nullable. However, if you disable cascading deletes as described earlier in this chapter, you'll need to delete all the child entities before you can delete the parent entity.

Three methods of the DbSet class

Method	Description
Add(entity)	Sets the state of the specified entity to Added and adds it to the DbSet.
Update(entity)	Sets the state of the specified entity to Modified.
Remove(entity)	Sets the state of the specified entity to Deleted.

One method of the DbContext class

Method	Description
SaveChanges()	Saves all changes to the underlying database.

Code that adds a new entity

```
[HttpPost]
public IActionResult Add(Book book)
{
    context.Books.Add(book);
    context.SaveChanges();
    return RedirectToAction("List", "Book");
}
```

Code that updates an existing entity in a disconnected scenario

```
[HttpPost]
public IActionResult Edit(Book book)      // Book object is disconnected
{
    context.Books.Update(book);           // call to Update() required
    context.SaveChanges();
    return RedirectToAction("List", "Book");
}
```

Code that updates an existing entity in a connected scenario

```
[HttpPost]
public IActionResult Edit(int id, double price)
{
    Book book = context.Books.Find(id); // Book object is connected
    book.Price = price;                  // call to Update() not required
    context.SaveChanges();
    return RedirectToAction("List", "Book");
}
```

Code that deletes an entity

```
[HttpPost]
public IActionResult Delete(Book book)
{
    context.Books.Remove(book);
    context.SaveChanges();    // related data deleted if cascade delete on
    return RedirectToAction("List", "Book");
}
```

Figure 12-19   How to insert, update, and delete data

How to handle concurrency conflicts

Concurrency allows two or more users to work with a database at the same time. However, if two users retrieve and then attempt to update the same entity (row in a table), their updates may conflict with each other, and you need to handle this *concurrency conflict*.

In EF Core, you have two options for concurrency control. The default option is called "*last in wins*". This option doesn't perform any checking. Instead, the last update overwrites any previous changes. In some cases, this option is adequate, but it can lead to corrupted data.

The other option is called *optimistic concurrency*. It checks whether a row has been changed since it was retrieved. If so, EF refuses the update or deletion and throws an exception. Then, the app can handle this exception. You can use data attributes or the Fluent API to configure your apps to use optimistic concurrency.

How to check for concurrency conflicts

One common way to enable optimistic concurrency is to check an entire entity for changes. To do that, you add and configure a *rowversion* property as shown in the first and second examples of figure 12-20. The first example decorates a property named RowVersion with the Timestamp attribute, and the second example uses the IsRowVersion() method of the Fluent API to configure the same property. For a rowversion property to work, it must be declared as a byte[] type.

After you've added and configured a rowversion property and updated the database, every query retrieves the value of this property. In addition, EF automatically updates its value whenever any column in an entity's underlying table row is modified. That way, when your app attempts to update or delete a row, EF compares the rowversion value that was retrieved with the initial query to its current value. If they don't match, EF refuses the action and throws an exception. For this to work, you need to make sure the original value of the rowversion is stored in the view and posted with the update or delete. Usually, you do this with a hidden field.

When you're testing your app to make sure it handles concurrency conflicts the way you want it to, you may need to simulate a situation in which a row is modified after it's retrieved but before it's updated or deleted. To do that, you can use the ExecuteSqlRaw() method to execute a standard SQL statement like the one shown in the third example of this figure.

Another way to enable optimistic concurrency is to check an individual property for changes. To do that, you can configure an individual property with a *concurrency token*. However, it doesn't usually make sense to check individual properties with an MVC app that uses a disconnected environment. That's because it can be hard to track the original values of the checked properties, especially if there are a lot of them.

How to configure a rowversion property with attributes

```
public class Book {
    public int BookId { get; set; }
    public string Title { get; set; } = string.Empty;
    public double Price { get; set; }

    [Timestamp]
    public byte[] RowVersion { get; set; } = null!;
}
```

How to configure a rowversion property with the Fluent API

```
protected override void OnModelCreating(ModelBuilder modelBuilder)
{
    modelBuilder.Entity<Book>()
        .Property(b => b.RowVersion)
        .IsRowVersion();
}
```

How to simulate a concurrency conflict

```
var book = context.Books.Find(1);          // get a book from the database
book.Price = 14.99;                          // change price in memory

context.Database.ExecuteSqlRaw(              // change price in the database
    "UPDATE dbo.Books SET Price = Price + 1 WHERE BookId = 1");

context.SaveChanges();
```

Description

- A *concurrency conflict* is when data is modified after it's retrieved for editing or deletion.

- A *rowversion property* lets you check all the properties in an entity for conflicts and must be an array of bytes.

- The DbContext class has a Database property whose ExecuteSqlRaw() method can be used to simulate concurrency conflicts.

- A *concurrency token* lets you check an individual property for conflicts.

Figure 12-20   How to check for concurrency conflicts

How handle a concurrency exception

If you've enabled optimistic concurrency and an update or delete operation fails because of a concurrency problem, EF throws a concurrency exception. To handle this exception, you call the SaveChanges() method within the try block of a try-catch statement, and you include a catch block that catches the exception.

Figure 12-21 shows a controller action method named Edit() that handles a concurrency exception. Here, within the catch block, this code uses the Entries property of the concurrency exception to get the current values of the entity being updated. The Entries property is a collection of DbEntityEntry objects, but it only has one entry here. As a result, the code uses the LINQ Single() method to retrieve the entry. If you want to be more cautious, you can use the SingleOrDefault() method and check for null.

The DbEntityEntry class has properties named CurrentValues and OriginalValues, but those properties typically aren't useful in a disconnected scenario. Instead, this example uses the GetDatabaseValues() method to retrieve the current values of the entity from the database.

After calling the GetDatabaseValues() method, the code checks whether the return value is null. If it is, the entity has been deleted and is no longer in the database. As a result, the code adds a class-level error to the ModelState object notifying the user that the row no longer exists.

If the object returned by the GetDatabaseValues() method is not null, the entity has been updated. As a result, the code adds a class-level error to the ModelState object notifying the user that the data has changed. After that, it casts the object holding the current database values to a Book object. Then, it compares each database value to the value passed in for editing. Whenever it finds a mismatch, it adds a property-level error to the ModelState object that notifies the user of the new value in the database.

In either case, this code displays the view with the values that were originally passed to this method. That way, any data that was entered is not lost, and your users can decide what they want to do next.

The last example shows a snippet of the Edit view that posts to this action method. Here, the form uses hidden fields to store both the book's primary key value and its rowversion value. As a result, these values are posted to the action method of the controller.

A controller action method that handles a concurrency conflict

```
[HttpPost]
public IActionResult Edit(Book book)
{
    if (ModelState.IsValid) {
        context.Books.Update(book);

        // simulate the row being changed after retrieval and before save
        // to test a concurrency conflict

        try {
            context.SaveChanges();
            return RedirectToAction("Index");
        }
        catch (DbUpdateConcurrencyException ex) {
            var entry = ex.Entries.Single();
            var dbValues = entry.GetDatabaseValues();
            if (dbValues == null) {
                ModelState.AddModelError("", "Unable to save - "
                    + "this book was deleted by another user.");
            }
            else {
                ModelState.AddModelError("", "Unable to save - "
                    + "this book was modified by another user. "
                    + "The current database values are displayed "
                    + "below. Please edit as needed and click Save, "
                    + "or click Cancel.");

                var dbBook = (Book)dbValues.ToObject();

                if (dbBook.Title != book.Title)
                    ModelState.AddModelError("Title",
                        $"Current db value: {dbBook.Title}");

                // check rest of properties for equality
            }
            return View(book);
        }
    }
    else {
        return View(book);
    }
}
```

Some of the code in the Edit view

```
@* both primary key and row version value needed for edit *@
<input type="hidden" asp-for="BookId" />
<input type="hidden" asp-for="RowVersion" />
<button type="submit" class="btn">Submit</button>
```

Description

- The DbUpdateConcurrencyException is thrown when there's a concurrency conflict.
- The DbUpdateConcurrencyException has an Entries property that provides a way to get the new database values for the row that's being saved.

Figure 12-21   How to handle a concurrency exception

How to encapsulate your EF code

So far, the EF Core code you've seen has been in the action methods of controllers. Usually, though, this code should be in its own data layer. This makes your code easier to test. In addition, it allows you to store your data access code in a separate project. Finally, it makes it possible to change from EF Core to another ORM framework without affecting the rest of your code.

How to code a data access class

The first set of examples in figure 12-22 shows the code for creating and using a simple data access class. Here, the first example presents a class named BookData that encapsulates two data access methods. The first method, Get(), returns the data associated with a book ID in a Book object. And the second method, List(), returns the data for all the books in the database in a IEnumerable collection of Book objects.

Instead of returning the data that results from executing a query, a method can return the query itself in an IQueryable object. The advantage of doing that is that a calling method can modify the query before executing it. The disadvantage of returning an IQueryable object is that it mixes data access code with other layers of the app, which reduces the benefits of having a data layer. On the other hand, if a method returns a single object or an IEnumerable object, the data access code can be kept in the data layer. In most cases, then, you'll want to return the actual data.

Once you create a data access class, you can create a new object from the class by passing a context object to its constructor. For instance, the second code example creates a new BookData object by passing a BookstoreContext object to its constructor. Then, the third code example calls the List() method to retrieve all the books in the database.

To make the methods of a data access class more flexible, you can code them so they accept LINQ expressions as arguments. To do that, you use the Expression class of the System.Linq.Expressions namespace to represent a lambda expression. The last set of examples illustrates how this works.

In the first example, the overloaded List() method has a lambda expression for a where parameter and a lambda expression for an orderby parameter. Within the method, the code uses these lambdas as the arguments for the Where() and OrderBy() methods.

The second and third examples show two ways to call the List() method that accepts LINQ expressions. The first way is shorter, but the second way uses named parameters to make the code easier to read and understand. Either way, this code returns all books with a price that's less than 10, and it sorts those books by title.

A simple data access class for Book objects

```
public class BookData
{
    private BookstoreContext context { get; set; }
    public BookData(BookstoreContext ctx) => context = ctx;

    public Book Get(int bookId)
    {
        return context.Books.Find(bookId) ?? new Book();
    }

    public IEnumerable<Book> List()
    {
        return context.Books.ToList();
    }
}
```

Code that creates a BookData object

```
var data = new BookData(context);
```

Code that uses the BookData object to retrieve all the books in the database

```
var books = data.List();
```

How to use LINQ expressions to make a data access class more flexible

```
using System.Linq.Expressions;
...
public class BookData {
    public Book Get(int bookId) {...}
    public IEnumerable<Book> List(){...}

    // overloaded List() method that accepts LINQ expressions
    public IEnumerable<Book> List(Expression<Func<Book, bool>> where,
                                  Expression<Func<Book, Object>> orderby)
    {
        return context.Books
            .Where(where)
            .OrderBy(orderby)
            .ToList();
    }
}
```

Code that uses the BookData object to retrieve books under $10 sorted by title

```
var books = data.List(b => b.Price < 10, b => b.Title);
```

Code that uses named arguments to make the method call easier to understand

```
var books = data.List(where: b => b.Price < 10, orderby: b => b.Title);
```

Description

- It's a good practice to encapsulate the code that works with data. To do that, you can code data access classes.
- To make your data access classes more flexible, you can code them with methods that accept LINQ expressions as arguments.

Figure 12-22   How to code a data access class and use LINQ expressions

How to use a generic query options class

In the previous figure, you learned how to code LINQ functions as parameters on the methods of a data access class to provide for sorting and filtering. Now, you'll learn how to build upon that by coding a generic query options class that provides for those functions as well as others.

Figure 12-23 presents a generic class named QueryOptions. It begins by defining public LINQ expression properties for sorting and filtering and int properties for paging. Then, it defines a private array for storing strings that specify the related entities the query should include. This private field is initialized to an empty string array. The Includes property is a write-only property that accepts a comma-separated string, removes any spaces, splits the string at the commas, and stores the resulting string array in the private field. And the GetIncludes() method returns the value of the private field.

Finally, the QueryOptions class defines three read-only Boolean properties. These properties indicate whether the filtering, sorting, and paging properties have values.

Next, this figure shows how to add an extension method to the IQueryable<T> interface. You might want to do this for operations that you perform frequently, like paging. An *extension method* is similar to a regular method except that it's defined outside the data type that it's used with.

In this example, a generic extension method named PageBy<T>() is added to the IQueryable<T> interface, as indicated by the first parameter for this method. This method also accepts the number and size values needed for paging. Then, it uses the Skip() and Take() methods to modify the query so the requested pages will be retrieved, and it returns the IQueryable object. This allows your extension method to be chained with other LINQ methods.

The third example shows the List() method of the BookData class from the previous figure after it has been updated to use the QueryOptions class and the PageBy() extension method. This code starts with a query that returns all the books in the table. Then, it uses the properties of the QueryOptions class to refine that query.

First, the code loops through the strings returned by the GetIncludes() method and passes them to the Include() method of the query object. Next, the code uses the HasWhere, HasOrderBy, and HasPaging properties to check whether the arguments for filtering, sorting, and paging have been set. If so, it passes the appropriate query option argument to the appropriate query method. Finally, the code calls the ToList() method to execute the query and return the resulting collection of Book objects.

The last example calls the List() method and passes it a QueryOptions object. This example doesn't specify a query option for filtering, but it does include query options to retrieve related author and genre data, to sort the results by book title, and to provide for paging.

A QueryOptions class makes your data layer more flexible and easier to use. For example, code that calls the List() method only includes values for the QueryOptions properties it needs. In addition, you can easily add other query functionality to the QueryOptions class.

A generic query options class

```
using System.Linq.Expressions;
...
public class QueryOptions<T>
{
    public Expression<Func<T, Object>> OrderBy { get; set; } = null!;
    public Expression<Func<T, bool>> Where { get; set; } = null!;
    public int PageNumber { get; set; }
    public int PageSize { get; set; }

    private string[] includes = Array.Empty<string>();
    public string Includes {
        set => includes = value.Replace(" ", "").Split(',');
    }
    public string[] GetIncludes() => includes;

    public bool HasOrderBy => OrderBy != null;
    public bool HasWhere => Where != null;
    public bool HasPaging => PageNumber > 0 && PageSize > 0;
}
```

A class that adds an extension method to the IQueryable<T> interface

```
public static class QueryExtensions
{
    public static IQueryable<T> PageBy<T>(this IQueryable<T> query,
        int pageNumber, int pageSize)
    {
        return query
            .Skip((pageNumber - 1) * pageSize)
            .Take(pageSize);
    }
}
```

A method that uses the options class

```
public IEnumerable<Book> List(QueryOptions<Book> options) {
    IQueryable<Book> query = context.Books;
    foreach (string include in options.GetIncludes()) {
        query = query.Include(include);
    }
    if (options.HasWhere)
        query = query.Where(options.Where);
    if (options.HasOrderBy)
        query = query.OrderBy(options.OrderBy);
    if (options.HasPaging)
        query = query.PageBy(options.PageNumber, options.PageSize);
    return query.ToList();
}
```

Code that uses the method

```
var books = data.List(new QueryOptions<Book> {
    Includes = "Authors, Genre",
    OrderBy = b => b.Title,
    PageNumber = 2,
    PageSize = 4
});
```

Figure 12-23   How to use a generic query options class

How to use the repository pattern

One popular way to implement a data layer is to use the *repository pattern*. This pattern encapsulates data code within a data access layer and also uses interfaces to provide a layer of abstraction. One benefit of this pattern is that it makes it easier to automate testing as shown in chapter 14.

The first example in figure 12-24 presents a simple generic interface named IRepository that you can create to work with a repository. This interface has six methods. The first two query data, the next three modify data, and the last one saves changes to the data.

When using the repository pattern, you should use one repository per entity. For example, a Bookstore app shouldn't use one big Bookstore repository. Instead, it should use a Book repository, an Author repository, a Genre repository, and so on.

One way to do that is to have each repository implement the IRepository interface. For example, you could have a BookRepository class, an AuthorRepository class, and so on. However, there are some problems with this approach. First, if you later change your interface, say to add a Count() method, you'll need to update all your repositories. Second, you'll have to implement all the methods of the interface for every repository, even if you're not going to use all of them for an entity. Third, this will lead to code duplication among repositories.

A better approach is to implement a generic Repository class like the one in the second example in this figure. This class uses a generic DbSet object. Then, its constructor calls the Set<T>() method of the context object to get a DbSet object for the specified type. Next, it uses that DbSet object to implement all the methods of the IRepository interface.

You can use this generic repository class to create various entity collections. For example, this code creates an Author repository:

```
var data = new Repository<Author>(ctx);
```

Often a generic Repository class like this is all you need for basic *CRUD (Create, Read, Update, Delete)* operations for each entity.

The third example shows some code from a controller that uses the generic Repository class. Here, the Author controller begins by defining a private property of the Repository<Author> type named data. Then, the constructor initializes this private property. Next, the Index() action method uses the repository to get a list of Author objects sorted by the author's first name.

If you need more specialized operations than the generic Repository class provides, you can inherit that class and override one or more of its methods. For example, if you need to insert a new author into the Author table but you don't want to add a new row to the AuthorBio table if all properties in the AuthorBio entity are null, you can code an AuthorRepository class that inherits the generic Repository class. Then, you can override its Insert() method to create an Insert() method that works the way you want.

The generic IRepository interface

```
public interface IRepository<T> where T : class {
    IEnumerable<T> List(QueryOptions<T> options);
    T? Get(int id);
    void Insert(T entity);
    void Update(T entity);
    void Delete(T entity);
    void Save();
}
```

A generic Repository class that implements IRepository

```
public class Repository<T> : IRepository<T> where T : class
{
    protected BookstoreContext context { get; set; }
    private DbSet<T> dbset { get; set; }

    public Repository(BookstoreContext ctx) {
        context = ctx;
        dbset = context.Set<T>();
    }

    public virtual IEnumerable<T> List(QueryOptions<T> options) {
        IQueryable<T> query = dbset;
        foreach (string include in options.GetIncludes()) {
            query = query.Include(include);
        }
        if (options.HasWhere)
            query = query.Where(options.Where);
        if (options.HasOrderBy)
            query = query.OrderBy(options.OrderBy);
        if (options.HasPaging)
            query = query.PageBy(options.PageNumber, options.PageSize);
        return query.ToList();
    }
    public virtual T? Get(int id) => dbset.Find(id);
    public virtual void Insert(T entity) => dbset.Add(entity);
    public virtual void Update(T entity) => dbset.Update(entity);
    public virtual void Delete(T entity) => dbset.Remove(entity);
    public virtual void Save() => context.SaveChanges();
}
```

A controller that uses the generic Repository class

```
public class AuthorController : Controller
{
    private Repository<Author> data { get; set; }

    public AuthorController(BookstoreContext ctx) =>
        data = new Repository<Author>(ctx);

    public ViewResult Index() {
        var authors = data.List(new QueryOptions<Author> {
            OrderBy = a => a.FirstName
        });
        return View(authors);
    }
}
```

Figure 12-24   How to use the repository pattern

Perspective

This chapter showed how to use EF Core to work with data in a database, including how to encapsulate your EF code in a data layer. This presents the most important classes of the data layer that are used by the Bookstore website presented in the next chapter. As a result, studying that app is a great way to get started with EF Core.

Terms

entity class	linking table
database (DB) context class	cascading delete
Entity Framework (EF) Core	LINQ to Entities
object relational mapping (ORM)	projection
Code First development	data transfer object (DTO)
Database First development	disconnected scenario
Fluent API	connected scenario
primary key (PK)	concurrency
foreign key (FK)	concurrency conflict
one-to-many relationship	optimistic concurrency
many-to-many relationship	rowversion property
one-to-one relationship	concurrency token
table splitting	extension method
navigation property	repository pattern
skip navigation property	CRUD (Create, Read, Update, Delete)
join table	

Summary

- *Entity classes* define the data structure for an app and map to the tables in a relational database.

- A *database (DB) context class* inherits the DbContext class and includes one DbSet property for each entity class.

- *Entity Framework (EF) Core* is an *object relational mapping (ORM)* framework that allows you to map your entity classes to the tables of a database.

- With *Code First* development, you code your entity classes and a context class first. Then, you use EF to create a database from these classes.

- With *Database First* development, you create your database tables first. Then, you generate the context and entity classes from your database.

- You can configure your database by convention, by adding data attributes to your entity classes, or by writing code that uses the *Fluent API*.

- Relationships are defined with a primary key and a foreign key. The *primary key (PK)* uniquely identifies an entity, and the *foreign key (FK)* identifies related entities.

- A *one-to-many relationship* relates one entity to many entities. A *many-to-many relationship* relates many entities to many other entities. And a *one-to-one relationship* relates one entity to one other entity.

- A *navigation property* provides a way to navigate to a related entity from the primary entity.

- *Table splitting* allows you to use two entities to represent the data that's stored in a single table.

- A many-to-many relationship uses an intermediate table in the database called a *join table* or *linking table*.

- A *skip navigation property* lets you skip over the linking table for a many-to-many relationship to get the collection on the other side of the relationship.

- A *cascading delete* causes all dependent child rows to be automatically deleted when a parent row is deleted.

- You can use *LINQ to Entities* to query the DbSet properties of a context class.

- A *projection* allows you to retrieve a subset of the properties of an entity.

- A *data transfer object* (*DTO*) is a simple object that's designed to store data that's being transferred from one place to another.

- With the *disconnected scenario*, an action method gets an entity from an HTTP POST request. Then, the method must call the Update() method to update the state of the entity before calling the SaveChanges() method.

- With the *connected scenario*, an action method retrieves an entity from the database so the context can track the state of the entity. Then, you don't need to call the Update() method. Instead, you just change the entity and call the SaveChanges() method.

- *Concurrency* allows two or more users to work with a database at the same time.

- A *concurrency conflict* occurs when data is modified by one user after it's retrieved for editing or deletion by another user.

- *Optimistic concurrency* checks whether a row has been changed since it was retrieved. If so, it refuses the update or deletion and throws an exception.

- A *rowversion property* lets you check all properties of an entity for concurrency conflicts.

- A *concurrency token* lets you check an individual property of an entity for concurrency conflicts.

- An *extension method* is similar to a regular method except that it's defined outside the data type that it's used with. You can use extension methods to extend the IQueryable interface so you can encapsulate your data access code.

- With the *repository pattern*, you create one repository per entity, and each repository has its own DB context.

- You can use a generic repository class that implements a repository interface to provide for basic *CRUD (Create, Read, Update, Delete)* operations for each entity in a DB context.

Exercise 12-1   Review the data layer of an app and improve it

In this exercise, you'll review domain model and configuration code as well as the migration file EF Code First creates from that code. Then, you'll modify this code to improve it.

Review the domain model and configuration files

1. Open the Ch12Ex1ClassSchedule web app in the ex_starts directory.

2. Open the Models/DomainModels folder and review the code in the three class files it contains.

3. Open the Models/Configuration folder and review the code in the three configuration files it contains.

Review the migration file

4. Open the Migrations folder and review the code in the Initial migration file.

5. Note how the migration file determines the primary and foreign keys based on how the properties in the domain model are coded (configuration by convention).

Create the database

6. Open the Package Manager Console and enter the Update-Database command to run the migration and create the database.

7. Take a moment to review the SQL code in the console after the command runs.

8. Run the app and review the data it displays for classes and teachers.

Test the cascading delete behavior of the Teacher object

9. Run the app and navigate to the Show All Teachers page. Click the Add Teacher link and add your name as a teacher.

10. Navigate to the Show All Classes page. Click the Add Class link and add a new class with yourself as the teacher.

11. Review the updated class list to make sure it displays the class you just added.

12. Navigate back to the Show All Teachers page and delete your name.

13. Navigate back to the Show All Classes page, and note that the class you previously added has also been deleted.

Restrict the cascading delete behavior of the Teacher object

14. In the Models/Configuration folder, open the ClassConfig configuration file.

15. Add code to change the delete behavior for the Teacher foreign key to Restrict.

16. Open the Package Manager Console and use the Add-Migration command to create a new migration file. When you do that, use a descriptive name for the migration file.

17. Review the code in the migration file that's generated.

18. Enter the Update-Database command to apply the migration to the database.

19. Repeat steps 9 through 13 to test the cascading delete behavior. When you attempt to delete your name from the teacher list, the application should throw an exception.

20. Run the app again, find the class you added, click on Edit, and change the teacher to another teacher.

21. Navigate to the Show All Teachers page and delete your name from the teacher list. This time, the app should let you.

Change how the list of classes is ordered

22. Open the Home controller and review the code in its Index() action method. Note that the classes are ordered by day on first load and ordered by time when filtering by day.

23. Run the app. When it displays all classes, note that it doesn't display the classes for Monday in ascending order by time. Then, click on the filter link for Monday and note that now it *does* display the classes in ascending order by time.

24. In the Models/DataLayer folder, open the QueryOptions class. Note that this version is shorter than the QueryOptions class presented in the chapter. That's because it doesn't provide for paging.

25. Add a new property named ThenOrderBy that works like the OrderBy property.

26. Add a new read-only property named HasThenOrderBy that works like the HasOrderBy property.

27. Open the Repository class and find the List() method. Update the code that handles ordering so it uses the ThenOrderBy property like this:

```
if (options.HasOrderBy) {
  if (options.HasThenOrderBy) {
    query = query.OrderBy(options.OrderBy).ThenBy(options.ThenOrderBy);
  }
  else {
    query = query.OrderBy(options.OrderBy);
  }
}
```

28. In the Home controller, update the Index() action method to use the new property to sort by time as well as day on first load.

29. Repeat step 23. The class times should be in ascending order on both pages.

Add an overload for the Get() method in the Repository class

30. Open the Class controller and review the private helper method named GetClass(). Note that it uses the List() method of the Repository<Class> class to get an IEnumerable<Class> with one Class item. Then, it uses the LINQ FirstOrDefault() method to retrieve that item.

31. In the Models/DataLayer folder, open the IRepository<T> interface and add a second Get() method that accepts a QueryOptions<T> object.

32. Open the Repository<T> class and implement the new Get() method. To do that, you can copy the code from the repository's List() method that builds a query, leaving out the code for ordering the list. Then, you can return the single object by calling the FirstOrDefault() method instead of the List() method.

33. In the Class controller, update the GetClass() method to use the new Get() method.

34. Run the app and test it. It should work the same as it did before.

13

The Bookstore website

The Bookstore website presented in this chapter is a realistic website that uses the skills presented so far in this book. Due to space limitations, this chapter doesn't present every line of code for this website. However, the complete code for this website is available in the download for this book. So, as you read this chapter, you can run the website to see how it works, and you can review its code. That's a great way to learn!

The user interface and folder structure

This chapter begins by presenting some of the pages of the Bookstore website. Then, it shows how the folders and files for this website are structured. This should give you a good idea of how this website works.

The end user pages

Like all the pages of the Bookstore website, the pages shown in figure 13-1 use a layout that begins with a Bootstrap navbar followed by a header that displays text and a logo. This app uses custom CSS to format the header.

Each link in the Bootstrap navbar also has a Font Awesome icon. For example, the Home link has an icon of a house, and the Books link has an icon of an open book. Also, the app marks the link and icon for the current page as active by displaying them in white rather than gray. The navbar also contains a Bootstrap badge that indicates how many books are currently in the user's shopping cart. If there are no books in the cart, the app doesn't display this badge.

The Home page uses EF Core to access a database like the one described in chapter 12 that contains data about books, authors, and genres. It selects a random book and displays it as the staff pick. The title of the book is a link to the details page for the book. That link contains the book ID and a title slug. For instance, the URL for the link shown here is:

```
/book/details/4/band-of-brothers
```

The Book Catalog page uses EF Core to query the database for a list of books, and it displays those books in a table styled with Bootstrap. For each book, it displays the title, author(s), genre, and price, as well as a button to add the book to the shopping cart. The title and authors displayed for each book are also links that take the user to a details page.

The Book Catalog page doesn't display all the books in the database. Rather, it displays a page of no more than four books at a time. It also lets the user know how many of these pages exist by presenting links the user can click to navigate through the pages and view the rest of the books.

In addition to paging, the Book Catalog page allows the user to sort the list of books by title, genre, or price in ascending or descending order. To do that, it makes the headers for these columns links that the user can click to change the sort order.

The Home page

The Book Catalog page

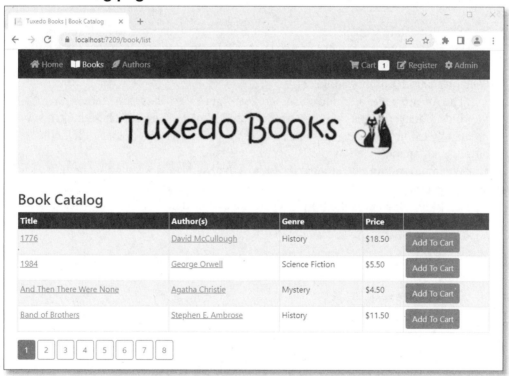

Figure 13-1   The end user and admin user pages (part 1)

The Author Catalog page, shown in part 2 of figure 13-1, uses EF Core to query the database for a list of authors. Then, it displays those authors in a table styled with Bootstrap. For each author, the table displays the author's first name, last name, and the book or books written by that author.

The first and last names for the author are also links to a details page for the author. These links include the author ID and a name slug. For instance, the URL for the link for both the first name and last name of the first author shown here is:

```
/author/details/7/agatha-christie
```

Similarly, each book title is a link that takes the user to a details page for the book as described in the previous figure.

Like the Book Catalog page, the Author Catalog page provides links for paging through the data that's retrieved from the database. In addition, it provides for sorting by first or last name. However, this page doesn't provide for sorting by the Book(s) column.

The admin user pages

The Bookstore website has an Admin area that you can use to add, edit, or delete a book, author, or genre in the database. Right now, this Admin area can be accessed by any user. However, you'll learn how to limit access to authorized users in section 3 of this book.

The Admin page, also shown in part 2 of figure 13-1, has three tabs with the titles Manage Books, Manage Authors, and Manage Genres. These tabs are created by using Bootstrap classes, and they allow the user to manage the books, authors, and genres used by the Bookstore website.

When the Admin page loads, it displays the Manage Books tab by default. This page contains a link you can click to add a book and a drop-down list you can use to locate an existing book so you can edit or delete it.

The Author Catalog page

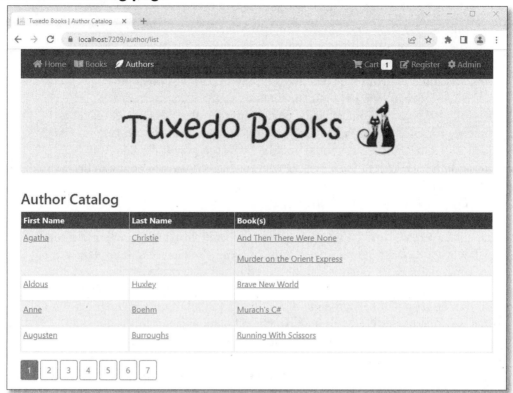

The Manage Books tab of the Admin page

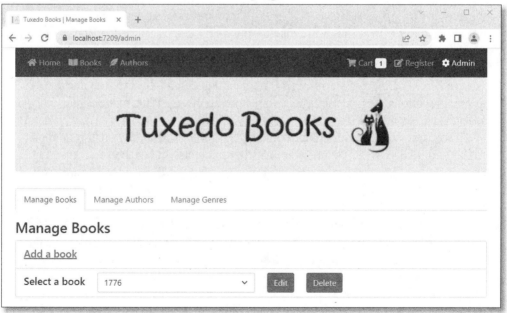

Figure 13-1   The end user and admin user pages (part 2)

The folders and files

Figure 13-2 shows the Controllers and Models folders of the Bookstore website. The Controllers folder contains a controller file for the first four navigation links: Home, Books, Authors, and Cart. The controllers for the Admin link are stored in their own area, as you'll see in part 2 of this figure.

The Models folder, by contrast, contains a much larger assortment of files, as well as several subfolders. This makes sense because it's considered a best practice for an MVC app to have a "fat" model and "skinny" controllers. The idea is that the controllers should only be in charge of getting data from the model and passing it to the views. However, the model should contain the data itself as well as the business logic for working with that data.

Of course, a "fat" model might lead to its own problems if you try to store all of the code in just one or two class files. That's why it's considered a good practice to create a model like the one shown here, with the business logic and data files broken down into several smaller files. It's also common in larger apps for different parts of the model to be stored in separate projects, though that's beyond the scope of this book. Still, the same concept applies. Namely, the bulk of your code should be stored in your model, and you should organize this model in a way that makes it easy to understand and maintain.

In this figure, the Models folder has several subfolders. The DataLayer folder contains the DB context class, the QueryOptions class, the IQueryable extension methods class, and two more subfolders. These subfolders store the repository classes and interfaces, and the configuration files used by the DB context class.

The DomainModels folder contains the classes that describe the entities that the application works with, such as books, authors, and cart items. Some, but not all, of these entity classes are also used by EF Core to create the Bookstore database. The DTOs subfolder contains data transfer object (DTO) classes used to transfer data. Unlike a view model class, which is used specifically with a view, a DTO is a more general-purpose object that can be used to transfer data to other locations. For example, the Bookstore app uses DTOs to store data in session state or in cookies.

The ExtensionMethods folder contains class files that add extension methods to the String class, to a custom list of CartItem objects, and to the session and cookie objects. The Grid folder contains classes that the Bookstore website uses to create the tables, or grids, of data on the Author Catalog and Book Catalog pages.

The ViewModels folder contains classes that hold data needed by views. In this folder, the Nav class doesn't have the conventional ViewModel suffix. That's because it isn't really a view model. Rather, it's a static class that the layouts use to mark the navigation link for the current page as active. In other words, it's more of a utility class. However, since it's only used with views, it makes sense to store it with the view models.

The Controllers folder

The Models folder and its subfolders

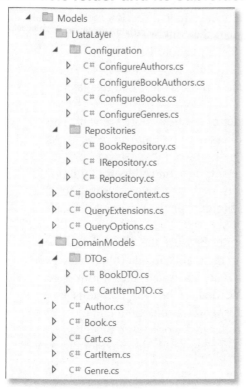

Figure 13-2   The folders and files (part 1)

Part 2 of figure 13-2 shows the Views and Admin folders of the Bookstore website. The Views folder contains subfolders that correspond to the controllers for the end user pages: Home, Book, Author, and Cart. In addition, it contains the standard Shared folder that contains the layout for the views, as well as the _ViewImports.cshtml and _ViewStart.cshtml files.

The Home and Cart folders each contain a default Index view. In addition, the Cart folder contains an Edit view to edit a cart item and a Checkout view. The Author and Book folders, by contrast, don't have a default Index view. That's because the Book and Author controllers have Index() action methods that redirect to the List view in each folder. That way, the Author Catalog and Book Catalog pages have URL segments of author/list and book/list, respectively. Since these URLs describe the pages more accurately, they're more user friendly. The Book and Author folders also each contain a Details view that displays details about an individual book or author.

The Areas folder contains the Admin folder of the Bookstore website. This folder contains the models, views, and controllers used by the Admin page. As shown in part 2 of figure 13-1, the Admin page has three tabs: Manage Books, Manage Authors, and Manage Genres. As a result, the Controllers folder has Book, Author, and Genre controllers that correspond to those tabs. Similarly, the Views folder has Book, Author, and Genre subfolders that correspond to those tabs.

The Models folder doesn't contain many files because the Admin page does most of its work using the classes contained in the main Models folder. However, the Models folder does contain two classes that are specific to the Admin page. The BookViewModel class holds data that's needed by the view that adds and edits book data. The Validate class provides for remote validation, and the Controllers folder contains a Validation controller that works with this class. Since these files work like the ones described in chapter 11, this chapter doesn't show how they work.

The Views folder

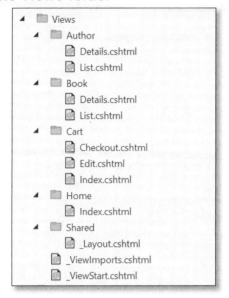

The Admin area folder and its subfolders

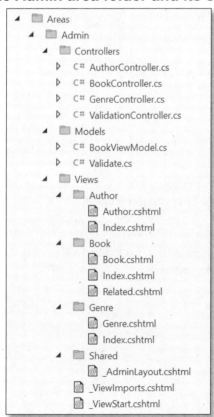

Figure 13-2   The folders and files (part 2)

Some general-purpose code

In the next few topics, you'll review some of the general-purpose code that the Bookstore website uses. This code consists of extension methods for strings as well as updated versions of the generic QueryOptions and Repository classes presented in chapter 12.

Extension methods for strings

The first example in figure 13-3 adds several extension methods to the String class. The first, Slug(), creates a dash-separated string. To do that, this method begins by removing all punctuation in the string except for the dash character (-). That way, dashes that are a part of a book's or author's name aren't removed from the string. Then, it replaces spaces with dashes and converts the characters to lowercase.

The EqualsNoCase() method uses the string's ToLower() method to perform a case-insensitive comparison. Unfortunately, this method doesn't work with EF Core queries. For those, you must use a standard equality operator and the ToLower() method if you want the comparison to be case-insensitive.

The ToInt() method uses the static TryParse() method of the int type to convert a string to an int. If the string can't be converted, this method returns the default value of an int, which is zero.

The Capitalize() method makes the first character of the string uppercase and all the remaining characters lowercase. To do this, it uses the string's Substring() method.

The generic QueryOptions class

The second example in figure 13-3 presents an updated version of the QueryOptions class that you saw in chapter 12. This version adds an OrderByDirection property of the string type that a repository class can use with the OrderBy property to sort items in ascending or descending order. This property has a default value of "asc", which means that if its value isn't explicitly set, the query sorts the items in ascending order.

Extension methods for the String class

```
public static class StringExtensions
{
    public static string Slug(this string str) {
        var sb = new StringBuilder();
        foreach (char c in str) {
            if (!char.IsPunctuation(c) || c == '-') {
                sb.Append(c);
            }
        }
        return sb.ToString().Replace(' ', '-').ToLower();
    }

    public static bool EqualsNoCase(this string str, string tocompare) =>
        str?.ToLower() == tocompare?.ToLower();

    public static int ToInt(this string str) {
        int.TryParse(str, out int value);
        return value;
    }

    public static string Capitalize(this string str) =>
        str?.Substring(0, 1)?.ToUpper() + str?.Substring(1).ToLower();
}
```

The generic QueryOptions class

```
public class QueryOptions<T>
{
    public Expression<Func<T, Object>> OrderBy { get; set; } = null!;
    public Expression<Func<T, bool>> Where { get; set; } = null!;
    public string OrderByDirection { get; set; } = "asc";  // default
    public int PageNumber { get; set; }
    public int PageSize { get; set; }

    private string[] includes = Array.Empty<string>();
    public string Includes {
        set => includes = value.Replace(" ", "").Split(',');
    }
    public string[] GetIncludes() => includes;

    // read-only properties
    public bool HasWhere => Where != null;
    public bool HasOrderBy => OrderBy != null;
    public bool HasPaging => PageNumber > 0 && PageSize > 0;
}
```

Description

- These extension methods for strings make it easier to perform tasks like creating slugs, comparing strings in a case-insensitive way, casting a string value to an int, and capitalizing strings.
- This version of the generic QueryOptions class adds an OrderByDirection property that allows you to sort in ascending or descending order. The default value for this property is "asc" for ascending.

Figure 13-3   Extension methods for strings and the generic QueryOptions class

The generic Repository class

Chapter 12 showed how to build a generic Repository class that you can use to encapsulate code that interacts with the database. Now, figure 13-4 presents a version of a Repository class that's similar to the one you saw in that chapter. However, this Repository class adds a few more features.

First, it adds a public read-only Count property of the int type that returns the value returned by the Count() method of the private DbSet<T> property. This Count property is used to determine the number of paging links a view should provide.

Second, it adds an overload for the Get() method that has a string parameter. This overload, like the one that has an int parameter, calls the Find() method of the DbSet<T> class and passes it the argument it receives.

Third, it has a private BuildQuery() method that accepts a QueryOptions object and uses it to build a query expression. This private method is used by both the public List() method and one of the the public Get() methods. In fact, the only difference between those two methods is that the List() method calls the ToList() method to execute the query and return a list of entities, while the Get() method calls the FirstOrDefault() method to execute the query and return a single entity or null.

Fourth, the query expression built by the BuildQuery() method has more options for sorting than the one presented in chapter 12. Now, the if statement that checks for an order by clause contains another if statement that checks the OrderByDirection property. If it's "asc", the code uses the OrderBy() method to build a query that sorts in ascending order. Otherwise, it uses the OrderByDescending() method to build a query that sorts in descending order.

In chapter 12, the Repository class implemented the IRepository interface. That's true of this Repository class as well. While not shown here, the IRepository interface that this class implements also has the read-only Count property and the third overload of the Get() method.

The generic Repository class

```
using Microsoft.EntityFrameworkCore;
...
public class Repository<T> : IRepository<T> where T : class
{
    protected BookstoreContext context { get; set; }
    private DbSet<T> dbset { get; set; }

    public Repository(BookstoreContext ctx) {
        context = ctx;
        dbset = context.Set<T>();
    }

    public int Count => dbset.Count();

    public virtual IEnumerable<T> List(QueryOptions<T> options) =>
        BuildQuery(options).ToList();

    public virtual T? Get(int id) => dbset.Find(id);
    public virtual T? Get(string id) => dbset.Find(id);
    public virtual T? Get(QueryOptions<T> options) =>
        BuildQuery(options).FirstOrDefault();

    public virtual void Insert(T entity) => dbset.Add(entity);
    public virtual void Update(T entity) => dbset.Update(entity);
    public virtual void Delete(T entity) => dbset.Remove(entity);
    public virtual void Save() => context.SaveChanges();

    // private helper method to build query expression
    private IQueryable<T> BuildQuery(QueryOptions<T> options)
    {
        IQueryable<T> query = dbset;
        foreach (string include in options.GetIncludes()) {
            query = query.Include(include);
        }
        if (options.HasWhere) {
            query = query.Where(options.Where);
        }
        if (options.HasOrderBy) {
            if (options.OrderByDirection == "asc")
                query = query.OrderBy(options.OrderBy);
            else
                query = query.OrderByDescending(options.OrderBy);
        }
        if (options.HasPaging) {
            query = query.PageBy(options.PageNumber, options.PageSize);
        }
        return query;
    }
}
```

Description

- The private BuildQuery() method builds the query expression for the public List() and Get() methods. Then, those methods call the ToList() and FirstOrDefault() methods, respectively, of the IQueryable object that BuildQuery() returns.

Figure 13-4   The generic Repository class

The paging and sorting of the Author Catalog

With ASP.NET Web Forms, a table that provides for paging and sorting is available out of the box via the GridView server control. With ASP.NET Core MVC, however, you must "roll your own" grid for paging and sorting. The next few figures present the code that the Bookstore website uses for the grid that provides for paging and sorting the data that's displayed on the Author Catalog page.

The user interface and custom route

The first two columns of the table in the Author Catalog page has column headers that are links you can click to sort the data for the page. When you first click a link, the sort order is ascending. On subsequent clicks of the same link, the order toggles between descending and ascending. Below the table, you can click the paging links to navigate through the pages of authors.

Figure 13-5 shows the Author Catalog page after a user has sorted the authors by last name in descending order and navigated to the third page of authors. The URL that produces this page is shown below the screen.

For this to work, you need to add a custom route to the Program.cs file as shown below the URL. This custom route specifies static segments of "page", "size", and "sort" that make the route more user friendly. In addition, it specifies four route parameters named pagenumber, pagesize, sortfield, and sortdirection. Since this route is more specific than the default route, it must be coded before that route.

Page 3 of the Author Catalog sorted by last name in descending order

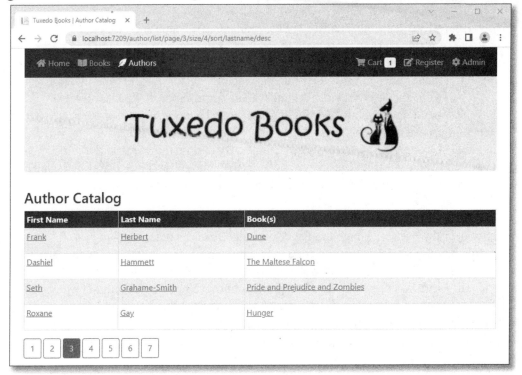

The URL for the above page

```
https://localhost:7079/author/list/page/3/size/4/sort/lastname/desc
```

The custom route in the Program.cs file

```
app.MapControllerRoute(
    name: "page_sort",
    pattern: "{controller}/{action}/page/{pagenumber}/size/{pagesize}/
                                sort/{sortfield}/{sortdirection}");
```

Description

- The Author Catalog page displays four authors at a time and provides links styled as buttons that allow the user to page through the authors.
- In the grid, the first two column headers are links that allow the user to sort the authors by first name or last name in ascending or descending order.
- The Bookstore website adds a custom route for paging and sorting.

Figure 13-5   The Author Catalog page and its custom route

The abstract GridData class

Figure 13-6 presents an abstract class named GridData. The Bookstore website uses this class to work with the values of the custom route you saw in the previous figure. For MVC model binding to work, the names of the properties in this class match the names of the route parameters, except for the capitalization.

The GridData class provides default values for three of its four properties: PageNumber, PageSize, and SortDirection. That's because these properties are general purpose and make sense in any app. As a result, if no values are provided in the URL route, the app uses these defaults. By contrast, there's no default provided for the SortField property because the name of the field to sort by is app specific. In a moment, you'll see how classes that inherit this abstract class set this value.

Because of space considerations, the Bookstore website doesn't provide a way for the user to change the PageSize value from its default value of 4. It would be easy to allow users to change the number of items that display in a grid, however, and many real-world web apps provide this functionality.

The GridData class also has four general purpose public methods. The GetTotalPages() method accepts a count value and uses that value and the PageSize property to determine the total number of pages for a grid. This arithmetic expression works because both the count and page size are integers, so the result is an integer.

The SetSortAndDirection() method determines the sort order of the items. To do that, it compares the value of the new sort field to the SortField value of the current route. If they are the same, the user has clicked on the header for the column that was previously clicked for sorting. In that case, the method toggles between ascending and descending order. If the values are different, the user has clicked on the header of a different column. In that case, the items are sorted by that column in ascending order.

The Clone() method uses the MemberwiseClone() method to return a copy of the current object. Because the MemberwiseClone() method returns type Object, the code casts the return value to a GridData object. As you'll see later, this method is called from the Author/List and Book/List views so that view has two copies of the GridData class.

The ToDictionary() method returns the values of the four properties as a string-string dictionary. As you learned in chapter 8, you can use a string-string dictionary to build links with the correct route segment values. So, this method is used by views to build links, as you'll see later in this chapter.

The AuthorGridData subclass

Figure 13-6 also presents a subclass named AuthorGridData that inherits the abstract GridData class. The Bookstore website uses the AuthorGridData subclass to work with the values of the custom route you saw in the last figure. In its constructor, it sets the default value of the SortField property to the FirstName property of the Author object.

The abstract GridData class

```
public abstract class GridData
{
    // public properties for model binding the route segments
    public int PageNumber { get; set; } = 1;
    public int PageSize { get; set; } = 4;
    public string SortDirection { get; set; } = "asc";
    public string SortField { get; set; } = string.Empty;

    public int GetTotalPages(int count) => (count + PageSize - 1) / PageSize;

    public void SetSortAndDirection(string newSortField, GridData current)
    {
        SortField = newSortField;

        if (current.SortField.EqualsNoCase(newSortField) &&
            current.SortDirection == "asc")
            SortDirection = "desc";
        else
            SortDirection = "asc";
    }

    // make copy of self
    public GridData Clone() => (GridData)MemberwiseClone();

    public virtual Dictionary<string, string> ToDictionary() =>
        new Dictionary<string, string> {
            { nameof(PageNumber), PageNumber.ToString() },
            { nameof(PageSize), PageSize.ToString() },
            { nameof(SortField), SortField },
            { nameof(SortDirection), SortDirection },
        };
}
```

The AuthorGridData subclass

```
using System.Text.Json.Serialization;
...
public class AuthorGridData : GridData
{
    // set initial sort field in constructor
    public AuthorGridData() => SortField = nameof(Author.FirstName);

    [JsonIgnore]
    public bool IsSortByFirstName =>
        SortField.EqualsNoCase(nameof(Author.FirstName));
}
```

Description

- The abstract GridData class has public properties for the paging and sorting route segments, and general purpose methods for working with sorting and paging. It also uses the MemberwiseClone() method to make a copy of itself.

- The AuthorGridData class inherits the GridData class and sets the initial sort field in its constructor. The read-only IsSortByFirstName property determines whether the authors are sorted by first name. This property is decorated with the JsonIgnore attribute so it isn't included when the object is serialized to JSON.

Figure 13-6   The abstract GridData class and the AuthorGridData subclass

Then, the read-only IsSortByFirstName property determines whether the authors are currently sorted by first name. Because the value of this property can always be determined by the value of the FirstName property of the Author object, it isn't necessary to include this property when the AuthorGridData object is serialized to JSON. Because of that, it's decorated with the JsonIgnore attribute.

The Author/List view model
and the Author controller

Figure 13-7 presents the AuthorListViewModel class. This class uses its three properties to store the data a view needs to display a grid of authors with paging and sorting. The Authors property contains a collection of the Author objects to display. The CurrentRoute property contains an AuthorGridData object with the paging and sorting route segment values from the current URL. And the TotalPages property contains an int indicating how many paging links to display.

This figure also presents the Author controller. This controller has a constructor that creates an Author repository and assigns it to a private property named data. In addition, it has a default Index() action method that redirects to the List() action method.

The List() action method accepts an AuthorGridData object. Remember, the base class for this object, GridData, has properties that match the custom route for paging and sorting. And all four of those properties have default values: three of them are set in the GridData base class and one in the constructor of the AuthorGridData subclass. As a result, after model binding, this object contains the parameter values in the URL if they exist or the default values if the route parameter values don't exist.

The List() action method starts by creating a new object of type QueryOptions<Author>. Then, it uses the AuthorGridData object to set the query options. For the OrderBy property, the code checks the value of the Boolean IsSortByFirstName property. If it's true, the expression sorts the authors by first name. Otherwise, it sorts by last name.

Once the QueryOptions object is complete, the code initializes a view model object and loads it with data from the database and the AuthorGridData object. Then, it passes the view model to the view.

The Author controller also has a Details() action method that accepts an ID. This method builds a new QueryOptions<Author> object and passes it to the Get() method of the Author repository. Then, if the author is found, that author and any related books is stored in the author variable. Otherwise, a new Author object is stored in this variable. To do that, this code uses the null-coalescing operator (??). In either case, the Author object is passed to the view.

The Author/List view model

```
public class AuthorListViewModel
{
    public IEnumerable<Author> Authors { get; set; } = new List<Author>();
    public AuthorGridData CurrentRoute { get; set; } = new AuthorGridData();
    public int TotalPages { get; set; }
}
```

The Author controller

```
public class AuthorController : Controller
{
    private Repository<Author> data { get; set; }
    public AuthorController(BookstoreContext ctx) =>
        data = new Repository<Author>(ctx);

    public IActionResult Index() => RedirectToAction("List");

    public ViewResult List(AuthorGridData values)
    {
        var options = new QueryOptions<Author> {
            Includes = "Books",
            PageNumber = values.PageNumber,
            PageSize = values.PageSize,
            OrderByDirection = values.SortDirection,
        };
        if (values.IsSortByFirstName)
            options.OrderBy = a => a.FirstName;
        else
            options.OrderBy = a => a.LastName;

        var vm = new AuthorListViewModel {
            Authors = data.List(options),
            CurrentRoute = values,
            TotalPages = values.GetTotalPages(data.Count)
        };
        return View(vm);
    }

    public IActionResult Details(int id)
    {
        var author = data.Get(new QueryOptions<Author> {
            Where = a => a.AuthorId == id,
            Includes = "Books"
        }) ?? new Author();
        return View(author);
    }
}
```

Description

- The List() action method of the Author controller accepts an AuthorGridData object and uses its paging and sorting values to create a query options object and retrieve the specified authors from the database.
- The List() action method creates a view model with the author, route, and paging data the view needs to create an author grid with sorting and paging.
- The Details() action method gets an Author object passes it to the Details view.

Figure 13-7   The Author/List view model and the Author controller

The Author/List view

Figure 13-8 presents the Author/List view. This is a strongly-typed view whose model object is an instance of the AuthorListViewModel class.

The Razor code in the block at the top of the view creates an AuthorGridData variable named current and a GridData variable named routes. The current variable holds the CurrentRoute property of the view model and functions as an alias. This makes code that works with the CurrentRoute property shorter and easier to read.

The routes variable, by contrast, holds a *copy* of the CurrentRoute property. This allows the view to create URLs for the sorting and paging links without losing the values of the current URL. In other words, to do its work, this view needs a GridData object that holds the current route values, and another GridData object with values it can change.

In the view, an HTML table styled with Bootstrap displays the author data. In the <thead> element, the column headers for the first two columns are links that the user can click to sort the author data by that field.

To create these sorting links, the view has a Razor code block before the HTML for each column header. Within each block, the code calls the SetSortAndDirection() method of the routes object and passes it the name of the current column header and the AuthorGridData object for the current URL. After the method completes, the routes object holds the correct sort field and direction for the column header. Then, the header link calls the ToDictionary() method of the routes object to assign a string-string dictionary to the asp-all-route-data tag helper. This creates a URL for the link that has the correct routing segments.

In the <tbody> element, a Razor foreach statement loops through the Author collection of the view model and displays each author's first name, last name, and the books associated with them. This displays each author name and book title as a link to a details page with a value for the ID and slug route parameters. As you saw in the last figure, the Details() action method of the Authors controller only accepts an ID parameter. As a result, the slug route segment isn't used by the controller. However, it makes the URL more user friendly. The Book Details page works the same way.

Below the HTML table, a Razor code block builds the paging links. This code starts by re-assigning a copy of the CurrentRoute property of the view model to the routes variable. This resets that variable to hold the segment values of the current URL. In other words, it clears the changes made while creating the sorting URLs.

Then, it defines a for loop that starts with an index of 1 and runs until the index equals the value in the TotalPages property of the view model. Within this loop, the code uses the index value to set both the PageNumber property of the routes object and the text of the link. And, the code calls the static Nav. Active() method to check whether the paging link matches the current page. If so, this method returns "active", which is added to the list of classes in the class attribute. This is a Bootstrap class that marks the paging link as the active link.

The Author/List view

```
@model AuthorListViewModel
@{
    ViewData["Title"] = " | Author Catalog";

    AuthorGridData current = Model.CurrentRoute;
    GridData routes = Model.CurrentRoute.Clone();
}
<h1>Author Catalog</h1>
<table class="table table-bordered table-striped table-sm">
    <thead class="bg-dark text-white">
      <tr>
        <th>
          @{ routes.SetSortAndDirection(nameof(Author.FirstName), current); }
              <a asp-action="List"
                 asp-all-route-data="@routes.ToDictionary()"
                 class="text-white">First Name</a></th>
        <th>
          @{ routes.SetSortAndDirection(nameof(Author.LastName), current); }
              <a asp-action="List"
                 asp-all-route-data="@routes.ToDictionary()"
                 class="text-white">Last Name</a></th>
        <th>Books(s)</th>
      </tr>
    </thead>
    <tbody>
      @foreach (Author author in Model.Authors) {
      <tr>
        <td>
          <a asp-action="Details" asp-route-id="@author.AuthorId"
             asp-route-slug="@author.FullName.Slug()">@author.FirstName</a>
        </td>
        <td>
          <a asp-action="Details" asp-route-id="@author.AuthorId"
             asp-route-slug="@author.FullName.Slug()">@author.LastName</a>
        </td>
        <td>
          @foreach (var ba in author.BookAuthors) {
            <p>
              <a asp-action="Details" asp-controller="Book"
                 asp-route-id="@ba.BookId"
                 asp-route-slug="@ba.Book.Title.Slug()">@ba.Book.Title</a></p>
          }
        </td>
      </tr>
      }
    </tbody>
</table>
@{
    routes = current.Clone();          // reset to current route values
    for (int i = 1; i <= Model.TotalPages; i++) {
        routes.PageNumber = i;
        string active = @Nav.Active(i, current.PageNumber);
        <a asp-action="List" asp-all-route-data="@routes.ToDictionary()"
           class="btn btn-outline-primary @active">@i</a>
    }
}
```

Figure 13-8   The Author/List view

The paging and sorting of the Book Catalog

Like the Author Catalog page, the Book Catalog page provides for paging and sorting. However, the Book Catalog uses different columns for sorting, and it sorts on three columns rather than two. The next few figures present the code the Bookstore website uses to page and sort a grid of books.

The user interface and custom route

Figure 13-9 shows the Book Catalog page after a user has sorted the books by price in ascending order and navigated to the second page. The URL fragment below the screen shows the route segments that produce this page.

This URL uses the same custom route that the Author Catalog uses. Again, you need to add this custom route to the Program.cs file. The code below the URL presents the custom route as a refresher.

Page 2 of the Book Catalog sorted by price in ascending order

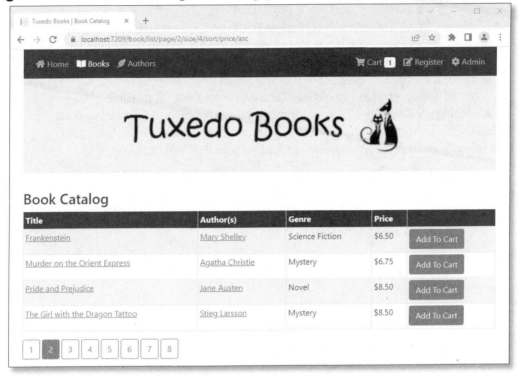

The URL for the above page

```
https://localhost:7079/book/list/page/2/size/4/sort/price/asc
```

The custom route in the Program.cs file

```
app.MapControllerRoute(
    name: "page_sort",
    pattern: "{controller}/{action}/page/{pagenumber}/size/{pagesize}/
                              sort/{sortfield}/{sortdirection}");
```

Description

- The Book Catalog page displays four books at a time and provides links styled as buttons that allow the user to page through the books.
- In the grid, the user can sort the books in ascending or descending order by title, genre, or price.
- The Book Catalog page uses the same custom route as the Author Catalog page.

Figure 13-9   The Book Catalog page and its custom route

The BookGridData subclass

Figure 13-10 presents a class named BookGridData, which the Bookstore website uses to work with the values of the custom route you saw in the last figure. This class inherits the abstract GridData class and has many similarities to the AuthorGridData class.

In its constructor, the BookGrid Data class sets the default value of the SortField property to the Title property of the Book object. Then, because the books can be sorted by three columns instead of two, this class includes two read-only Boolean properties that determine how the books are sorted.

The BookGridData subclass

```
using System.Text.Json.Serialization;
...
public class BookGridData : GridData
{
    // set initial sort field in constructor
    public BookGridData() => SortField = nameof(Book.Title);

    // sort flags
    [JsonIgnore]
    public bool IsSortByGenre =>
        SortField.EqualsNoCase(nameof(Genre));

    [JsonIgnore]
    public bool IsSortByPrice =>
        SortField.EqualsNoCase(nameof(Book.Price));
}
```

Description

- The BookGridData class inherits the abstract GridData class and sets the initial sort field in its constructor.

- This class has two read-only Boolean properties that determine if the books are sorted by genre or price. These properties are decorated with the JsonIgnore attribute so they aren't included when the object is serialized to JSON.

Figure 13-10   The BookGridData subclass

The Book/List view model and the Book controller

Figure 13-11 presents the BookListViewModel class. This view model is similar to the AuthorListViewModel class. It includes a collection of Book objects to display, a BookGridData object that holds the values for the current URL, and an int that stores the number of paging links to display.

Below the view model, this figure presents the Book controller. This controller has a constructor that creates a BookRepository object and assigns it to a private property named data. In addition, it has a default Index() action method that redirects to the List() action method.

The List() action method accepts a BookGridData object. After model binding, this object, like an AuthorGridData object, contains the route segments for paging and sorting. Or, if there aren't any, it contains the default values set in the BookGridData class and the base GridData class.

The List() action method starts by creating a new object of type QueryOptions<Book>. Then, it uses the BookGridData object to set the query options. For the OrderBy property, the code first checks the value of the Boolean IsSortByGenre property. If it's true, the expression sorts the books by genre. Otherwise, if checks the IsSortByPrice property. If it's true, it sorts the books by price. If neither of the Boolean properties is true, the expression sorts the books by title.

Once the QueryOptions object is complete, the code initializes a view model object and loads it with data from the database and the BookGridData object. Then, it passes the view model to the view.

The Book controller also has a Details() action method that accepts an ID. This method builds a QueryOptions object and passes it to the Get() method of the Book repository. Like the Details() action method in the Author controller, this method passes the Book object from the database to the view if it's found or a new Book object otherwise.

The Book/List view model

```
public class BookListViewModel
{
    public IEnumerable<Book> Books { get; set; } = new List<Book>();
    public BookGridData CurrentRoute { get; set; } = new BookGridData();
    public int TotalPages { get; set; }
}
```

The Book controller

```
public class BookController : Controller
{
    Repository<Book> data { get; set; }
    public BookController(BookstoreContext ctx) =>
        data = new Repository<Book>(ctx);

    public RedirectToActionResult Index() => RedirectToAction("List");

    public ViewResult List(BookGridData values)
    {
        var options = new QueryOptions<Book> {
            Includes = "Authors, Genre",
            OrderByDirection = values.SortDirection,
            PageNumber = values.PageNumber,
            PageSize = values.PageSize
        };
        if (values.IsSortByGenre)
            options.OrderBy = b => b.GenreId;
        else if (values.IsSortByPrice)
            options.OrderBy = b => b.Price;
        else
            options.OrderBy = b => b.Title;

        var vm = new BookListViewModel {
            Books = data.List(options),
            CurrentRoute = values,
            TotalPages = values.GetTotalPages(data.Count)
        };
        return View(vm);
    }

    public ViewResult Details(int id)
    {
        var book = data.Get(new QueryOptions<Book> {
            Where = b => b.BookId == id,
            Includes = "Authors, Genre"
        }) ?? new Book();
        return View(book);
    }
}
```

Description

- The List() action method of the Book controller accepts a BookGridData object and uses it to create a query options object and retrieve the specified books from the database.
- The List() action method creates a view model with the book, route, and paging data the view needs to create a book grid with sorting and paging.
- The Details() action method gets a Book object and passes it to the Details view.

Figure 13-11   The Book/List view model and the Book controller

The Book/List view

Figure 13-12 presents the Book/List view. This is a strongly-typed view whose model object is an instance of the BookListViewModel class.

The Razor code in the block at the top of the view creates a BookGridData variable named current and a GridData variable named routes. The current variable holds the CurrentRoute property of the view model, and the routes variable holds a copy of this property. As with the Author/List view, this first variable stays the same to preserve the current URL values, and the second changes as the code creates the URLs for the sorting and paging links.

Like the Author/List view, this view contains an HTML table styled with Bootstrap to display the book data. However, unlike the Author/List view, this HTML table is coded within a <form> tag that posts to the Add action method of the Cart controller. That's because each book has an Add To Cart button that lets users add a book to the cart.

In the HTML table, the column headers for the first, third, and fourth columns are links that the user can click to sort the books by that field. To do that, this code uses the SetSortAndDirection() method of the routes object and passes it the name of the current column header and the BookGridData object for the current URL. Then, it assigns the return value of the ToDictionary() method of the routes object to the asp-all-route-data tag helper to create a URL for the link that has the correct routing segments.

The Book/List view

```
@model BookListViewModel

@{
    ViewData["Title"] = " | Book Catalog";

    BookGridData current = Model.CurrentRoute;
    GridData routes = Model.CurrentRoute.Clone();
}

<h1>Book Catalog</h1>

@* add to cart form *@
<form asp-action="Add" asp-controller="Cart" method="post">
    <table class="table table-bordered table-striped table-sm">
        <thead class="bg-dark text-white">
            <tr>
                <th>
                    @{ routes.SetSortAndDirection(
                        nameof(Book.Title), current); }
                    <a asp-action="List"
                        asp-all-route-data="@routes.ToDictionary()"
                        class="text-white">Title</a>
                </th>
                <th>Author(s)</th>
                <th>
                    @{ routes.SetSortAndDirection(
                        nameof(Genre), current); }
                    <a asp-action="List"
                        asp-all-route-data="@routes.ToDictionary()"
                        class="text-white">Genre</a>
                </th>
                <th>
                    @{ routes.SetSortAndDirection(
                        nameof(Book.Price), current); }
                    <a asp-action="List"
                        asp-all-route-data="@routes.ToDictionary()"
                        class="text-white">Price</a>
                </th>
                <th></th>
            </tr>
        </thead>
```

Figure 13-12   The Book/List view (part 1)

In the <tbody> element in part 2, a Razor foreach statement loops through the Book collection of the view model and displays each book's title, author or authors, genre, and price. This displays each author name and book title as a link to a details page with a value for the ID and slug route parameters.

The last column in each table row contains an Add To Cart button. This is a submit button with a name attribute of "id" and a value attribute that specifies the ID of the book. When the user clicks this button, the form is submitted and the ID of the specified book is posted to the Add() action method of the Cart controller, which you'll see later in this chapter.

Below the HTML table, a Razor code block builds the paging links. This works the same as the code presented in figure 13-8.

The Book/List view (continued)

```
        <tbody>
            @foreach (Book book in Model.Books)
            {
                <tr>
                    <td>
                        <a asp-action="Details" asp-route-id="@book.BookId"
                            asp-route-slug="@book.Title.Slug()">
                            @book.Title
                        </a>
                    </td>
                    <td>
                        @foreach (var a in book.Authors)
                        {
                            <p>
                                <a asp-action="Details"
                                    asp-controller="Author"
                                    asp-route-id="@a.AuthorId"
                                    asp-route-slug="@a.FullName.Slug()">
                                    @a.FullName
                                </a>
                            </p>
                        }
                    </td>
                    <td>@book.Genre.Name</td>
                    <td>@book.Price.ToString("c")</td>
                    <td>
                        <button type="submit" name="id" value="@book.BookId"
                                class="btn btn-primary">
                            Add To Cart
                        </button>
                    </td>
                </tr>
            }
        </tbody>
    </table>
</form>

@* paging links *@
@{
    routes = current.Clone();    // reset to current route values

    for (int i = 1; i <= Model.TotalPages; i++)
    {
        routes.PageNumber = i;
        string active = @Nav.Active(i, current.PageNumber);
        <a asp-action="List" asp-all-route-data="@routes.ToDictionary()"
            class="btn btn-outline-primary @active">@i</a>
    }
}
```

Figure 13-12   The Book/List view (part 2)

The Cart page

The Bookstore website has a shopping cart that keeps track of books that a user has selected by clicking on the "Add To Cart" button. The app uses session state to store these books during the user's session. In addition, the app stores cart data in a persistent cookie. That way, the Bookstore website "remembers" a user's books between sessions.

Extension methods for session and cookies

The Bookstore website uses extension methods to make it easier to work with complex objects in session and cookies. Figure 13-13 shows these extension methods.

The first example adds two extension methods to the ISession interface. The SetObject<T>() method serializes an object of type T to a JSON string and then stores that string in session state. The GetObject<T>() method deserializes a JSON string stored in session state back to an object of type T.

The second example adds three extension methods each to the IRequestCookieCollection and IResponseCookies interfaces. Like the extension methods for session state, these methods make it easier to work with complex objects. In addition, they make it easier to store integers and strings by adding methods like the ones for working with session state.

The extension methods that get values are added to the request cookie collection. Each get method accepts a string key and gets the cookie value associated with that key. The GetString() method simply returns that value or an empty string.

The GetInt32() method uses the TryParse() method of the int class to convert the cookie value to an int value. If the TryParse() method returns true, the cookie value was successfully converted to an int. As a result, the code returns that int value. Otherwise, the method returns null. To do that, though, it needs to cast null to match the return type of the method.

The GetObject<T>() method checks the cookie value for null. If it's null, the method returns the default value of type T. Otherwise, the method uses a static method of the JsonConvert class to convert the string value to an object of type T.

The extension methods that set values are added to the response cookie collection. Each set method accepts a key, a value, and an optional days argument with a default value of 30. As a result, by default, these methods create a persistent cookie that expires after 30 days. If you want to create a session cookie, you can pass a value of 0 for the days argument.

The SetString() method deletes any existing cookie for the specified key. Then, it creates and stores a session or persistent cookie based on the value of days. The SetInt32() converts the value it receives to a string by calling its ToString() method, and then passes the key and value to the SetString() method. The SetObject<T>() method works similarly. However, it converts the object value it receives to a JSON string by calling the static SerializeObject<T>() method of the JsonConvert class.

Extension methods for the ISession interface

```
using System.Text.Json;
...
public static class SessionExtensions
{
    public static void SetObject<T>(this ISession session, string key,
    T value) =>
        session.SetString(key, JsonSerializer.Serialize(value));

    public static T? GetObject<T>(this ISession session, string key) {
        var value = session.GetString(key);
        return (value == null) ? default(T) :
            JsonSerializer.Deserialize<T>(value);
    }
}
```

Extension methods for cookies

```
using System.Text.Json;
...
public static class CookieExtensions
{
    public static string GetString(this IRequestCookieCollection cookies,
    string key) => cookies[key] ?? string.Empty;

    public static int? GetInt32(this IRequestCookieCollection cookies,
    string key) {
        var value = cookies.GetString(key);
        return int.TryParse(value, out int i) ? i : (int?)null;
    }

    public static T? GetObject<T>(this IRequestCookieCollection cookies,
    string key) {
        var value = cookies.GetString(key);
        return value == null ? default(T) :
            JsonSerializer.Deserialize<T>(value);
    }

    public static void SetString(this IResponseCookies cookies, string key,
    string value, int days = 30) {
        cookies.Delete(key);     // delete old value first
        if (days == 0) {         // session cookie
          cookies.Append(key, value);
        } else {                 // persistent cookie
          CookieOptions options = new CookieOptions {
              Expires = DateTime.Now.AddDays(days)
          };
          cookies.Append(key, value, options);
        }
    }

    public static void SetInt32(this IResponseCookies cookies, string key,
    int value, int days = 30) =>
        cookies.SetString(key, value.ToString(), days);

    public static void SetObject<T>(this IResponseCookies cookies, string key,
    T value, int days = 30) =>
        cookies.SetString(key, JsonSerializer.Serialize(value), days);
}
```

Figure 13-13   Extension methods for session and cookies

The user interface

Figure 13-14 begins by showing the user interface for the Cart page. This page displays all the books in a user's shopping cart, as well as a subtotal of the cost for each book. The Cart page has buttons and links that allow the user to go to a checkout page, clear the cart, or continue shopping. In addition, each cart item has two buttons, one that allows the user to edit the item and another that removes the item from the cart.

To add a book to the cart, the user can click the "Add To Cart" button on either the Book Catalog page or the Book Details page. When a book is first added to the cart, it has a default quantity of 1. Then, to change that quantity, the user can edit the cart item by clicking on the Edit button. The edit page isn't shown in this chapter because it's similar to edit pages you've seen in previous chapters. However, you can view it by running the Bookstore website that's included in the download for this book.

The Cart page uses session state to store the books in the cart between requests. That's how the app can display the number of items in the cart in the badge that's displayed at the top of each page. In addition, the Cart page stores data about the cart items in a persistent cookie. As a result, if you add books to the shopping cart and close your browser, the next time you use that browser to view the Bookstore website it "remembers" those books.

The model classes

Figure 13-14 also presents the CartItem class. The Bookstore website uses this class to store the selected book and quantity in session state. The CartItem class also has a read-only Subtotal property that calculates the subtotal for an item by multiplying the book price by the quantity.

The CartItem class is designed to be serialized to JSON and stored in session state. You should be aware of two parts of this design. First, the Subtotal property is decorated with the JsonIgnore attribute. That's because this is a calculated value, so there's no reason to store it in session state.

Second, the Book property is of the BookDTO type rather than the Book type. That's because the JSON serializer doesn't always work correctly with EF domain models like the Book class. One common issue is that the serializer ends up with circular references when it tries to follow all the navigation properties of a domain model. To fix this issue, the CartItem class uses the BookDTO class that's presented in the next figure.

Another good reason to use a DTO class for serialization is that sometimes, the domain model retrieves more data from the database than you want to store. Of course, you can always decorate any properties you don't want to store with the JsonIgnore attribute. But, if there are a lot of them, that can get tedious. In addition, even if you mark the properties to avoid serialization, you're still retrieving data from the database that you don't need. In a case like this, a DTO is a better option than a domain model.

The Cart page

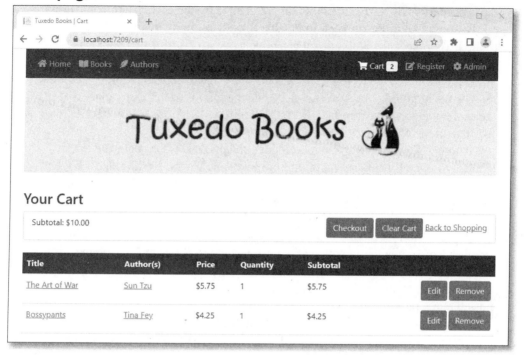

The CartItem class

```
using System.Text.Json.Serialization;
...
public class CartItem
{
    public BookDTO Book { get; set; } = new BookDTO();
    public int Quantity { get; set; }

    [JsonIgnore]
    public double Subtotal => Book.Price * Quantity;
}
```

Description

- The Cart uses a data transfer object named BookDTO to store book data in session. That's because trying to store a Book entity object in session can cause circular references when the JSON serializer tries to follow all the navigation properties.

- Another way to deal with this is to decorate the navigation properties of the Book entity class with the [JsonIgnore] attribute.

- You'll see the BookDTO class in the next figure.

Figure 13-14   The user interface for the Cart page and the CartItem class

Figure 13-15 begins by presenting the BookDTO class. This class holds only those properties of the Book class that are needed by the cart. When you use a DTO class like this, you need to be able to convert the domain model object to the DTO object. To do this, you can code a constructor for the BookDTO class that accepts a Book object and assigns the required data. Or, you can add a Load() or Init() method to the BookDTO class that accepts a Book object and assigns the required data. You can also code a method for the Book class that creates, populates, and returns a BookDTO object. The BookDTO class in this figure uses the constructor approach.

Another way to convert domain model objects to DTO objects and back again is to use a third-party mapping tool like AutoMapper. While that's beyond the scope of this book, this is the method that many developers prefer. If you want to learn more, many good resources are available online.

If you wanted to, you could use the SetObject<T>() and GetObject<T>() cookie extension methods to store and retrieve CartItem objects in cookies. In other words, you could have the data stored in the persistent cookie exactly match the data stored in session state.

However, many programmers prefer to store the minimum amount of data possible in a persistent cookie. Then, when the user returns to the web app and starts a new session, the app uses the data in the cookie to query a data store and restore the data in session state. That's the approach used by the Bookstore website.

The minimum data needed to restore a CartItem object is the ID of the book and the quantity value. To hold that data, the Bookstore website uses the CartItemDTO class presented in this figure.

To facilitate converting CartItem objects to CartItemDTO objects, the Bookstore website adds an extension method to a list of CartItem objects as shown in this figure. Within this method, the code calls the LINQ Select() method for the list of CartItems and passes it a lambda expression. This lambda expression creates and populates a new CartItemDTO object. Then, it calls the ToList() method to create and return the list of CartItemDTO objects.

This figure also presents the CartViewModel class that's used to pass data to the Cart view. This view model contains a collection of CartItem objects for display and a Subtotal property that provides a subtotal for all the books in the cart.

The BookDTO class

```
public class BookDTO
{
    public int BookId { get; set; }
    public string Title { get; set; } = string.Empty;
    public double Price { get; set; }
    public Dictionary<int, string> Authors { get; set; } =
        new Dictionary<int, string>();

    // default constructor (required for model binding)
    public BookDTO() { }

    // overloaded constructor accepts a Book object
    public BookDTO(Book book)
    {
        BookId = book.BookId;
        Title = book.Title;
        Price = book.Price;
        if (book.Authors?.Count > 0) {
            foreach (Author a in book.Authors) {
                Authors.Add(a.AuthorId, a.FullName);
            }
        }
    }
}
```

The CartItemDTO class

```
public class CartItemDTO
{
    public int BookId { get; set; }
    public int Quantity { get; set; }
}
```

An extension method for a list of CartItem objects

```
public static class CartItemListExtensions
{
    public static List<CartItemDTO> ToDTO(this List<CartItem> list) =>
        list.Select(ci => new CartItemDTO {
            BookId = ci.Book.BookId,
            Quantity = ci.Quantity
        }).ToList();
}
```

The CartViewModel class

```
public class CartViewModel
{
    public IEnumerable<CartItem> List { get; set; } = new List<CartItem>();
    public double Subtotal { get; set; }
}
```

Description

- These DTO classes and extension methods make it easier to get book and cart information in and out of session and cookies.

Figure 13-15   The DTO classes and the CartViewModel class

Figure 13-16 presents the Cart class. The Bookstore website uses this class to store and retrieve cart data in session state and in a persistent cookie.

The Cart class starts by declaring two private string constants. It uses these constants as keys for the cart itself and for the number of items in the cart. Notice that this class stores the count value separately. That's so the layout page doesn't need to retrieve and deserialize the entire cart in order to display the item count in the navbar badge for the cart.

After the constants, the Cart class declares several private properties. The first two store a list of CartItem objects and a list of CartItemDTO objects, respectively. The next three store objects to work with session state and cookies.

After the private properties, the Cart class contains a constructor that accepts an HttpContext object. It uses this object to initialize the three session and cookie private properties.

After the constructor, the Cart class contains a method named Load() that accepts a repository object for books. To start, the Load() method uses the session and cookie extension methods to get data stored in session state and in a persistent cookie. If either method returns null, that means there's no data in session state or the cookie. In that case, the code initializes the private collection to an empty list in order to avoid null reference errors.

Next, the code checks whether the cart items need to be restored to session state. To do that, it compares the count of the cookie items collection, which is retrieved from the cookie, to the count of the items collection, which is retrieved from session state. If there are more items in the cookie items collection, session state needs to be reloaded.

To load items into session state, the code first clears the session collection to make sure any previous values are removed. Then, it loops through the CartItemDTO objects in the cookie items collection. For each DTO object, it uses the BookId property to retrieve a Book object from the database. Then, it checks whether that Book object is null. If so, the book was deleted after the cookie was stored. In that case, the code doesn't do anything.

However, if the Book object isn't null, the code creates a new CartItem object with book and quantity data. For the book data, it creates a new BookDTO object and passes the Book object to the DTO's constructor. Then, the code adds the new CartItem object to the items collection. After the loop finishes, the code calls the Save() method to save the new cart to session state and to the persistent cookie.

The Cart class has three read-only properties. The Subtotal property uses the Sum() method of the items collection to add the values of the Subtotal property for every CartItem object in the collection. The Count property returns the number of items in the cart. It gets this count from session state if possible. But if there's no count value in session state, it gets the count from the persistent cookie. And the List property returns the CartItem objects in the private items collection.

The Cart class

```
public class Cart
{
    private const string CartKey = "mycart";
    private const string CountKey = "mycount";

    private List<CartItem> items { get; set; } = null!;
    private List<CartItemDTO> cookieItems { get; set; } = null!;

    private ISession session { get; set; }
    private IRequestCookieCollection requestCookies { get; set; }
    private IResponseCookies responseCookies { get; set; }

    public Cart(HttpContext ctx)
    {
        session = ctx.Session;
        requestCookies = ctx.Request.Cookies;
        responseCookies = ctx.Response.Cookies;
    }

    public void Load(Repository<Book> data)
    {
        // get cart items from session and cookie
        items = session.GetObject<List<CartItem>>(CartKey)
            ?? new List<CartItem>();
        cookieItems = requestCookies.GetObject<List<CartItemDTO>>(CartKey)
            ?? new List<CartItemDTO>();

        // if more items in cookie than session, restore from database
        if (cookieItems.Count > items.Count) {
            items.Clear(); // clear any previous session data

            foreach (CartItemDTO storedItem in cookieItems) {
                var book = data.Get(new QueryOptions<Book> {
                    Where = b => b.BookId == storedItem.BookId,
                    Includes = "Authors, Genre"
                });
                // skip if book is null - it's no longer in database
                if (book != null) {
                    CartItem item = new CartItem {
                        Book = new BookDTO(book),
                        Quantity = storedItem.Quantity
                    };
                    items.Add(item);
                }
            }
            Save();
        }
    }

    public double Subtotal => items.Sum(i => i.Subtotal);

    public int? Count => session.GetInt32(CountKey) ??
        requestCookies.GetInt32(CountKey);

    public IEnumerable<CartItem> List => items;
```

Figure 13-16   The Cart class (part 1)

The GetById() method uses the FirstOrDefault() method of the items collection to get the CartItem object whose Book property has a BookId value that matches the value in the ID argument. If there's no Book object with that ID, this method returns null.

The Add() and Edit() methods each accept a CartItem object and use it to update the items collection. They both start by calling the GetById() method to check if the CartItem object is already in the collection. They differ, however, in how they treat a CartItem object that already exists.

When the Add() method receives a CartItem object that's already in the items collection, it increments the value of the Quantity property by one. Otherwise, it calls the Add() method of the items collection to add the new object. By contrast, when the Edit() method receives a CartItem object that's already in the items collection, it replaces the previous value of the Quantity property with the new value.

The Remove() and Clear() methods both remove CartItem objects from the items collection. The difference is that the Remove() method accepts and removes a specific CartItem object, and the Clear() method removes all the CartItem objects in the collection.

The Save() method starts by checking how many CartItem objects are in the items collection. If there are none, the code removes all the cart items from session state and cookies. This way, when there aren't any items in the cart, the badge in the navbar doesn't display. If the code didn't do this, the badge in the navbar would display with a value of zero.

If there are CartItem objects in the items collection, the code stores the items collection and a separate count value in session state. In addition, the code stores a collection of CartItemDTO objects and a separate count value in persistent cookies. To do that, it gets the collection of CartItemDTO objects by calling the ToDTO() method of the items collection. This way, the number of items in the cart and the BookId value and Quantity value for each item are retained between sessions.

The Cart class (continued)

```
public CartItem? GetById(int? id) {
    if (items == null || id == null) {
        return null;
    } else {
        return items.FirstOrDefault(ci => ci.Book?.BookId == id);
    }
}

public void Add(CartItem item) {
    var itemInCart = GetById(item.Book.BookId);
    if (itemInCart == null) {   // if new, add
        items.Add(item);
    }
    else {                           // otherwise, increase quantity by 1
        itemInCart.Quantity += 1;
    }
}

public void Edit(CartItem item) {
    var itemInCart = GetById(item.Book.BookId);
    if (itemInCart != null) {
        itemInCart.Quantity = item.Quantity;
    }
}

public void Remove(CartItem item) => items.Remove(item);

public void Clear() => items.Clear();

public void Save() {
    if (items.Count == 0) {
        session.Remove(CartKey);
        session.Remove(CountKey);
        responseCookies.Delete(CartKey);
        responseCookies.Delete(CountKey);
    }
    else {
        session.SetObject<List<CartItem>>(CartKey, items);
        session.SetInt32(CountKey, items.Count);
        responseCookies.SetObject<List<CartItemDTO>>(
            CartKey, items.ToDTO());
        responseCookies.SetInt32(CountKey, items.Count);
    }
}
}
```

Description

- The Cart class stores and retrieves the books a user places in their cart. Since it uses persistent cookies as well as session state to do this, it remembers a user's cart between sessions.

Figure 13-16   The Cart class (part 2)

The Cart controller

Figure 13-17 presents the Cart controller. To start, the constructor accepts a BookstoreContext object. It uses that object to initialize a Repository<Book> object that it stores in a private property named data.

The private GetCart() helper method gets a Cart object and loads any cart items from session state or from a persistent cookie. To do that, this code creates a Cart object by passing the controller's HttpContext property to the Cart() constructor. Then, it calls the Load() method of the Cart object to load the cart items. Finally, it returns the loaded Cart object.

The Index() action method runs when a user navigates to the Cart page. To start, it uses the GetCart() method to get a loaded Cart object. Then, it creates a new CartViewModel object with the data needed by the Index view. Specifically, this is a list of cart items and a subtotal amount for the cart.

The Add() action method handles POST requests when a user clicks an Add to Cart button on the Book Catalog or Book Details page. It accepts an int argument and uses it to get the selected book from the database. If that book isn't in the database, it notifies the user.

Otherwise, if the book is in the database, the code creates a new CartItem object and initializes it with book data and a default quantity amount of 1. To load the book data, it creates a new BookDTO object and passes the Book object to its constructor.

Next, the code gets a Cart object, passes the CartItem object to its Add() method, and calls its Save() method. This stores the updated cart information in session state and in a persistent cookie. Finally, the code stores a message in TempData to notify the user that the book was added to the cart.

The Cart controller

```
public class CartController : Controller
{
    private Repository<Book> data { get; set; }
    public CartController(BookstoreContext ctx) =>
        new Repository<Book>(ctx);

    private Cart GetCart()
    {
        var cart = new Cart(HttpContext);
        cart.Load(data);
        return cart;
    }

    public ViewResult Index()
    {
        Cart cart = GetCart();

        var vm = new CartViewModel
        {
            List = cart.List,
            Subtotal = cart.Subtotal
        };

        return View(vm);
    }

    [HttpPost]
    public RedirectToActionResult Add(int id)
    {
        // get the book the user chose from the database
        var book = data.Get(new QueryOptions<Book> {
            Where = b => b.BookId == id,
            Includes = "Authors, Genre"
        });
        if (book == null){   // book not in database
            TempData["message"] = "Unable to add book to cart.";
        }
        else {
            // create a new CartItem object with a default quantity of one.
            CartItem item = new CartItem {
                Book = new BookDTO(book),
                Quantity = 1   // default value
            };

            // add new item to cart and save to session state
            Cart cart = GetCart();
            cart.Add(item);
            cart.Save();

            TempData["message"] = $"{book.Title} added to cart";
        }

        return RedirectToAction("List", "Book");
    }
```

Figure 13-17   The Cart controller (part 1)

The Remove() action method handles POST requests when the user clicks a Delete button for a cart item. It starts by creating a Cart object. Then, it gets the item with the specified ID from the cart. If it's not null, the code removes that item from the cart, calls the cart's Save() method to update session state and the persistent cookie, and stores a notification message in TempData. Finally, it redirects to the main Cart page.

The Clear() action method handles POST requests when the user clicks the Clear Cart button, and it works similarly to the Remove() action method. The main difference is that the Clear() method removes all the items from the cart.

The Edit() action method for GET requests creates a Cart object and then uses it to get the specified item from the cart. If there's no such item in session, the code adds a notification message to TempData and then reloads to the cart page. Otherwise, the action method passes the selected cart item to the Edit view.

The Edit() action methods for POST requests accepts a CartItem object, creates a new Cart object, passes the CartItem object to the Edit() method of the Cart object, and calls the Save() method of the Cart object to save the updated Cart data to session state and to the persistent cookie. Then it adds a notification message to TempData and reloads the cart page.

Finally, The Checkout() action methods handles requests when the user clicks the checkout button. Since checkout functionality hasn't been implemented for the Bookstore application, all this action method does is render a view. If you review the code in the download, you'll see that this view cautions against coding your own checkout functionality for security reasons. It also provides some links to third-party services you can explore for implementing checkout functionality.

The Cart controller (continued)

```
[HttpPost]
public RedirectToActionResult Remove(int id)
{
    Cart cart = GetCart();
    CartItem? item = cart.GetById(id);
    if (item != null)
    {
        cart.Remove(item);
        cart.Save();
        TempData["message"] = $"{item.Book.Title} removed from cart.";
    }
    return RedirectToAction("Index");
}

[HttpPost]
public RedirectToActionResult Clear()
{
    Cart cart = GetCart();
    cart.Clear();
    cart.Save();

    TempData["message"] = "Cart cleared.";
    return RedirectToAction("Index");
}

[HttpGet]
public IActionResult Edit(int id)
{
    // get selected cart item from session and pass it to the view
    Cart cart = GetCart();
    CartItem? item = cart.GetById(id);
    if (item == null) {
        TempData["message"] = "Unable to locate cart item";
        return RedirectToAction("Index");
    }
    else {
        return View(item);
    }
}

[HttpPost]
public RedirectToActionResult Edit(CartItem item)
{
    Cart cart = GetCart();
    cart.Edit(item);
    cart.Save();

    TempData["message"] = $"{item.Book.Title} updated";
    return RedirectToAction("Index");
}

public ViewResult Checkout() => View();
}
```

Figure 13-17   The Cart controller (part 2)

The Cart/Index view

Figure 13-18 presents the Cart/Index view. This is a strongly-typed view whose model object is an instance of the CartViewModel class.

The HTML for the <ul> tag at the top of the view file is coded within a <form> tag that posts to the Clear() action method of the Cart controller. In this form, the submit button posts to the server. However, this form doesn't post any data to the server when the user clicks on the submit button. That's because the Clear() action method doesn't have any parameters. As a result, it doesn't need any data from the view.

This form also contains a link to the Checkout() action method of the Cart controller and another to the List() action method of the Book controller. In addition, it uses the Subtotal property of the view model to display a subtotal value for all the items in the cart to the user.

The second <form> tag posts to the Remove() action method of the Cart controller. This form contains an HTML table that displays the cart items in the List property of the view model. The last table cell for each cart item contains an Edit link and a Delete button, though the Edit link is styled so it looks the same as the button.

The Edit link redirects to the Edit() action method in the Cart controller that handles GET requests. To do that, it uses the BookId and Title properties of the Book property of the current CartItem object to add the values for the ID and slug route parameters.

The Remove button posts the form to the server and sends the ID of the book to remove by assigning a value of "id" to its name attribute and by assigning the BookId value to its value attribute. This passes the ID of the current book as the ID parameter of the Remove() action method.

The Cart/Index view

```
@model CartViewModel
...
<h1>Your Cart</h1>
<form asp-action="Clear" method="post">
    <ul class="list-group mb-4">
        <li class="list-group-item">
            <div class="row">
                <div class="col">Subtotal: @Model.Subtotal.ToString("c")</div>
                <div class="col">
                    <div class="float-end">
                        <a asp-action="Checkout" class="btn btn-primary">Checkout</a>
                        <button type="submit" class="btn btn-primary">
                            Clear Cart</button>
                        <a asp-action="List" asp-controller="Book">
                            Back to Shopping</a>
                    </div>
                </div>
            </div>
        </li>
    </ul>
</form>
<form asp-action="Remove" method="post">
    <table class="table">
        <thead class="bg-dark text-white">
            <tr><th>Title</th><th>Author(s)</th><th>Price</th><th>Quantity</th>
                <th>Subtotal</th><th></th></tr>
        </thead>
        <tbody>
            @foreach (CartItem item in Model.List)  {
                <tr>
                    <td>
                        <a asp-action="Details" asp-controller="Book"
                            asp-route-id="@item.Book.BookId"
                            asp-route-slug="@item.Book.Title.Slug()">@item.Book.Title
                        </a></td>
                    <td>
                        @foreach (var pair in item.Book.Authors) {
                            <p><a asp-action="Details" asp-controller="Author"
                                asp-route-id="@pair.Key"
                                asp-route-slug="@pair.Value.Slug()">
                                @pair.Value</a></p>
                        }
                    </td>
                    <!-- cells that display book price, quantity, and subtotal -->
                    <td>
                        <div class="float-end">
                            <a asp-action="Edit" asp-controller="Cart"
                                asp-route-id="@item.Book.BookId"
                                asp-route-slug="@item.Book.Title.Slug()"
                                class="btn btn-primary">Edit</a>
                            <button type="submit" name="id" value="@item.Book.BookId"
                                class="btn btn-primary">Remove</button></div></td>
                </tr>
            }
        </tbody>
    </table>
</form>
```

Figure 13-18   The Cart/Index view

The Admin area

The Admin pages are in their own Admin area, and they allow you to add, edit, or delete books, authors, or genres. Most of this code is similar to what you've seen in earlier chapters, so it isn't presented here. However, the Admin area has two features that are different in the Bookstore website. First, it has a specialized repository class for books. Second, it doesn't allow users to delete authors or genres that are related to books.

The BookRepository subclass

Most of the time, the generic Repository class you saw in the last chapter is all you need for basic CRUD operations. Sometimes, though, it makes sense to extend that class to add more functionality. For example, figure 13-19 shows how you can extend this class to work with Book objects.

This figure starts by presenting an IBookRepository interface that inherits the IRepository<Book> interface and adds a method named AddUpdateAuthors(). This method accepts a Book object, an array of author IDs, and a repository object for working with author data.

Next, this figure presents the BookRepository class, which inherits the Repository<Book> class and implements the IBookRepository interface. The constructor of this class accepts a BookstoreContext object. Then, it passes that context object to the constructor of its base class, which is the Repository<Book> class.

The AddUpdateAuthors() method encapsulates the code for setting the authors related to a book, which is a bit complex due to the many-to-many relationship between books and authors. This method is called when a new book is added to the DbContext object as well as when an existing book is edited.

To start, the AddUpdateAuthors() method loops through the Book object's Authors property and passes each Author object to the Remove() method of the Authors property. This marks any existing authors in the linking table for deletion. If a new book is being added, of course, there are no existing authors in the linking table.

Then, the method loops through the array of author IDs it receives. Within the loop, it passes each ID value to the Get() method of the IRepository<Author> object to get the author data from the database. If the author is found, this method passes the returned Author object to the Add() method of the Book object's Authors property. This adds the Author object to the DbContext object and marks it for insertion into the linking table.

It's important to understand that the AddUpdateAuthors() method doesn't make any changes at the database. Rather, it marks Author objects as Deleted or Added. Then, when the SaveChanges() method is called by other code, these changes will be made in the linking table at the database. But this method does need to access the database to retrieve author data, which is why it accepts an IRepository<Author> object.

The IBookRepository interface

```
public interface IBookRepository : IRepository<Book>
{
    void AddUpdateAuthors(Book book, int[] authorids,
        IRepository<Author> authorData);
}
```

The BookRepository class

```
public class BookRepository : Repository<Book>, IBookRepository
{
    public BookRepository(BookstoreContext ctx) : base(ctx) { }

    public void AddUpdateAuthors(Book book, int[] authorids,
        IRepository<Author> authorData)
    {
        // first remove any current authors
        foreach (Author author in book.Authors)
        {
            book.Authors.Remove(author);
        }

        // then add new authors
        foreach (int id in authorids)
        {
            Author? author = authorData.Get(id);
            if (author != null)
                book.Authors.Add(author);
        }
    }
}
```

Description

- The IBookRepository interface inherits the IRepository<Book> interface and adds a method for working with related author data.
- The BookRepository class inherits the Repository<Book> class and implements the IBookRepository interface.
- The BookRepository subclass must pass the BookstoreContext object it receives in its constructor to the constructor of the Repository<Book> base class.

Figure 13-19   A Repository subclass

The Related Books page

The Bookstore app warns users when they try to delete an author or genre that is related to one or more books. The first screen in figure 13-20 shows the Related Books view after a user tries to delete the author Agatha Christie. Since this author is related to two books in the database, the Bookstore app doesn't allow the deletion. Instead, it notifies the user, displays the related books, and gives the user the option of deleting the books. Or, the user can click on one of the Manage tabs to return to the desired Admin page.

The second screen shows the Related Books view after a user tries to delete the genre History. Again, since this genre is related to books in the database, the Bookstore app prevents the deletion and displays the related books. As you review these screens, you'll see that the only difference between them is the message that's displayed and the final route segment in the URL.

The view when a user tries to delete an author that has books

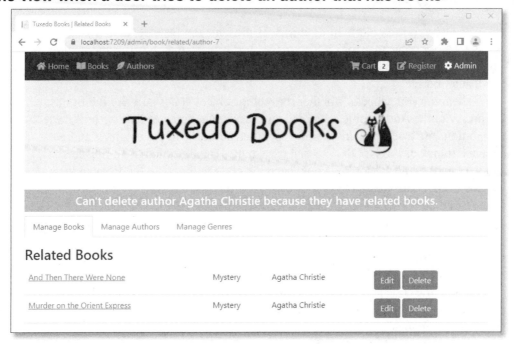

The view when a user tries to delete a genre that has books

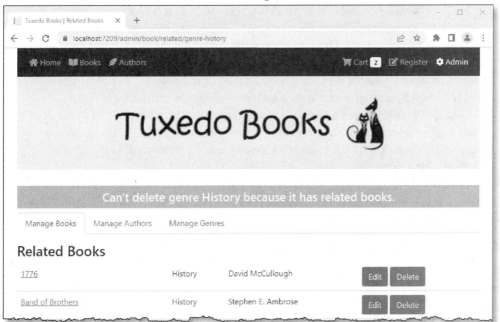

Description

- The Admin area has add, edit, and delete forms for books, authors, and genres. If a user tries to delete an author or genre with related books, the Related Books view is displayed.

Figure 13-20   The related book user interface for the Admin page

The Delete() and Related() action methods

The first code example in figure 13-21 presents the Delete() action method of the Author controller for GET requests. It receives an author ID, and it starts by querying the database for the author with that ID, including all books related to that author.

Then, the code checks whether the Author object is not null and the Books property of the Author object has a Count value that's greater than zero. If these conditions are true, it means that the specified author is in the database and is related to one or more books. In that case, a message is added to TempData indicating that the author has books, and the code redirects to the Related view of the Book controller. Note that the value for the id route of the URL has a prefix of "author-".

The second code example in this figure presents the Delete() action method of the Genre controller for GET requests. It is similar to the Delete() action method for the Author controller, except it receives a genre ID. Then, it gets the specified genre and its related books from the database. If the genre exists and has books, the code adds a message to TempData and redirects to the Related view of the Book controller. This time, the value for the id route of the URL has a prefix of "genre-".

The last code example in this figure presents the Related() action method of the Book controller. It starts by splitting the id string it receives from the route on the "-" character. Remember that this route contains a prefix that was set in the Delete() action method of the Author or Genre controller, along with the ID of the author or genre. Then, it assigns the first element of the array that's returned, which contains the prefix, to a string variable named type. And it assigns the second element of the array, which contains the ID of the author or genre, to the id parameter of the method so it no longer contains the prefix.

Next, the code creates a QueryOptions object for the book that includes the related authors and genre data, and it orders the books by title. Then, it adds a where clause based on the type of deletion the user attempted. If the type is "author", the where clause uses the LINQ Any() method to select any author in the Authors collection whose author ID matches the value of the id parameter. That is, it gets all books that are related to the specified author ID. Conversely, if the type is "genre", it gets all books that have the specified genre ID. Finally, the code passes the QueryOptions object to the List() method of the book repository, and then passes the resulting list of books to the view.

The Delete() action method of the Author controller for GET requests

```
[HttpGet]
public IActionResult Delete(int id)
{
    var author = data.Get(new QueryOptions<Author> {
        Where = a => a.AuthorId == id,
        Includes = "Books"
    });

    if (author != null && author.Books.Count > 0) {
        TempData["message"] = $"Can't delete author {author.FullName} " +
                              "because they have related books.";
        return RedirectToAction("Related", "Book",
            new { id = "author-" + id });
    }
    else { return View("Author", author); }
}
```

The Delete() action method of the Genre controller for GET requests

```
[HttpGet]
public IActionResult Delete(string id)
{
    var genre = data.Get(new QueryOptions<Genre> {
        Where = g => g.GenreId == id,
        Includes = "Books"
    });

    if (genre != null && genre.Books.Count > 0) {
        TempData["message"] = $"Can't delete genre {genre.Name} " +
                              "because it has related books.";
        return RedirectToAction("Related", "Book",
            new { id = "genre-" + id });
    }
    else { return View("Genre", genre); }
}
```

The Related() action method of the Book controller

```
public ViewResult Related(string id)
{
    var parts = id.Split('-');
    string type = parts[0];
    id = parts[1];

    var options = new QueryOptions<Book> {
        OrderBy = b => b.Title,
        Includes = "Authors, Genre"
    };
    if (type.EqualsNoCase("author"))
        options.Where = b => b.Authors.Any(ba => ba.AuthorId == id.ToInt());
    else if (type.EqualsNoCase("genre"))
        options.Where = b => b.GenreId.ToLower() == id;

    return View(bookData.List(options));
}
```

Figure 13-21   The Delete() and Related() action methods

Perspective

The Bookstore website presented in this chapter uses professional coding techniques that are somewhat abstract and may be difficult to understand at first. If you don't understand all of the code presented in this chapter right away, don't be discouraged. At first, it's okay if you only get the general idea of how this website works.

To help you understand this website, you can start by running it to see how it works. As you do this, you can study the source code that makes it work the way it does. At times, you may need to refer to earlier chapters to refresh your memory about how something works. But that's how you learn.

As you study this website, you will probably see some ways in which it can be improved. If you do, you should try to make some of those improvements. That gives you a chance to modify or enhance someone else's code, which is a common practice in the real world. In addition, it demonstrates the value of a logical folder structure and the use of the MVC pattern. And that's a great way to learn.

Exercise 13-1   Run and test the Bookstore web app

In this exercise, you'll run the Bookstore web app and test it to see how it works. Then, you'll add the ability to change the number of books that display per page.

Run the Bookstore web app and test it

1. Open the Ch13Ex1Bookstore app in the ex_starts directory.

2. If you haven't already created the database for the Bookstore app, open the Package Manager Console and enter the Update-Database command.

3. Run the app. When the Home page loads, it should display a "Staff Selection" book title. Refresh the page or click the Home nav link once or twice and note that the "Staff Selection" changes.

4. Click on each of the nav links. With the exception of the Register link, which isn't implemented yet, the app should mark the current link as active.

5. Navigate to the Author Catalog page and click on the Last Name column header to sort the authors by last name. Click that header again to reverse the sort order. Then, click the paging links to page through the authors.

6. Click on an author's first or last name to go to the author details page. From there, click on a book name to go to the book details page.

7. Navigate to the Book Catalog page and experiment with sorting and paging there too.

8. Add two or more books to the cart. Note that adding a book displays a notification message on the Book Catalog page. Then, click on a sorting or paging link and note that the notification message disappears.

9. Navigate to the Cart page and review your cart. Click on the Edit button for a book and increase its quantity. Then, delete that book. Finally, click the Clear Cart button to clear the cart.

10. Navigate to the Admin area. In the Manage Books tab, select a book, click Edit, change the price, and click Save.

11. In the Manage Genres tab, attempt to delete the Novel genre. Note that you can't delete this genre because it contains books.

12. Continue experimenting in the Admin area by adding, editing, and deleting a book, an author, and a genre.

Use the URL to change the number of books per page

13. Navigate to the Book Catalog page and click on Page 2 of the paging links.

14. In the browser, review the URL and find the size route segment. Then, change its value from 4 to 10 and press the Enter key. This should display 10 books per page.

Add a drop-down list for changing the number of books per page

15. In the Models/ViewModels folder, open the BookListViewModel class. Add a read-only property named PageSizes that returns an int array that contains the values 1 through 10.

16. In the Controllers folder, open the BookController class and add an action method for POST requests named PageSize() that accepts a BookGridData object named currentRoute and returns a RedirectToActionResult. Since the name of the parameter matches the name of the CurrentRoute property of the BookListViewModel class, it will be bound to the CurrentRoute property.

17. In the PageSize() action method, code a RedirectToAction() method that redirects to the List() action method with the current route values. To do this, use the return value of the ToDictionary() method of the BookGridData object as the second argument of the RedirectToAction() method.

18. In the Views folder, open the Book/List view and add a <form> element that posts to the PageSize() action method before the existing <form> element.

19. Within the <form> element, add a <div> element that's formatted as a row. The <div> element should contain a <label> element, another <div> element with a <select> element, three hidden fields, and a <div> element with a submit button. To get the label, drop-down list, and button to be sized properly, you can use the col-auto class instead of specifying exact column widths.

20. Use the asp-for tag helper to bind the <select> element to the PageSize property of the CurrentRoute property of the view model. Similarly, use the asp-for tag helper to bind the hidden fields to the PageNumber, SortField, and SortDirection properties of the CurrentRoute property of the view model.

21. Use the asp-items tag helper to add the options available from the PageSizes array of the view model to the <select> element. When you're done, the <select> element should look like this:

    ```
    <select asp-for="CurrentRoute.PageSize" class="form-select"
        asp-items="@(new SelectList(Model.PageSizes))">
    </select>
    ```

22. Run the app and use the new drop-down list to change the page size. Then change the page size in the URL as described in step 14 and note that the drop-down list reflects the change.

Section 3

Add more skills as you need them

Sections 1 and 2 of this book presented the ASP.NET Core MVC skills that you need to build a complex database-driven website such as the Bookstore website presented in chapter 13. Now, this section presents more ASP.NET Core MVC skills that are commonly needed for real-world websites. To make it easy to learn these skills as you need them, each chapter in this section is written as an independent training module. As a result, you can read them in whatever sequence you prefer.

To start, chapter 14 shows how to use dependency injection (DI) to make your code more flexible and easier to test. In addition, it shows how to automate the testing of an app with unit testing.

Chapter 15 shows how to create and use custom tag helpers, partial views, and view components. These features provide a way to reduce code duplication in your views, which makes them more flexible and easier to maintain.

Chapter 16 shows how to restrict access to parts of a website such as the Admin area of a website. Then, it shows how to authenticate users and allow authorized users with the appropriate privileges to access restricted parts of the website.

Chapter 17 shows how to use Visual Studio's Publish wizard to create publish profiles that you can use to deploy your apps. Specifically, it shows how to create publish profiles for deploying apps to a folder and to Microsoft's Azure.

To finish, chapter 18 shows how to use Visual Studio Code. This source code editor is a popular alternative to the Visual Studio IDE that has been presented so far in this book.

14

How to use dependency injection and unit testing

Dependency injection (DI) is a design pattern that can make your code more flexible and easier to change. In addition, DI makes it possible to automate testing of a web app with unit testing. However, dependency injection also increases the complexity of an app. Because of that, it's less useful if you don't use unit testing or if your app is small and unlikely to change much.

In this chapter, you'll learn how to use DI to improve the Bookstore website presented in the previous chapter. This includes how to use unit testing to automate testing of that website.

How to use dependency injection (DI)

Often, an object depends on another object to do its work. For example, a controller that works with a database depends on a DbContext object. You can code that other object, known as a *dependency*, within the containing object. However, if you do that and the dependency changes, you need to modify the containing object.

A better way to do this is to use a design pattern called *dependency injection* (*DI*). With DI, you code the containing object with a constructor that accepts an interface. Then, you can *inject* the dependency by passing an object that implements the interface to the constructor. That way, you can easily change the dependency by passing a different object to the constructor. This will work as long as the object implements the correct interface. And, as you'll see later in this chapter, coding an object this way also makes it easier to test.

How to configure your app for DI

To use DI with MVC, you must register, or *map*, your dependencies. In other words, you must tell MVC what object to inject for an interface parameter. To do that, you use the WebApplicationBuilder object in the Program.cs file.

The WebApplicationBuilder object has a property named Services that's of the IServiceCollection type. The table in figure 14-1 presents three methods of this property that you can use to map dependencies.

When you map a dependency, you must choose a *life cycle* for the object that MVC will create. With the transient life cycle, MVC creates a new object every time it needs to inject a dependency.

With the scoped life cycle, MVC creates a new object the first time it needs to inject a dependency. Then, for the rest of the current scope, MVC reuses that object for each subsequent injection. In a web app, the current scope is usually the current HTTP request.

With the singleton life cycle, MVC creates a new object the first time it needs to inject a dependency. Then, MVC reuses that object for each subsequent injection.

Most of the time, you'll use the transient lifecycle. If you use the longer life cycles, you should make sure that the object being injected can handle concurrency.

The first code example in this figure shows how to map a dependency for a class that doesn't use generics. Here, the AddTransient() method tells MVC to create and inject an instance of the BookRepository class every time it encounters an IBookRepository parameter. To do that, this example specifies the interface and class types within the angle brackets of the method call, not within the parentheses.

The second code example shows how to map a dependency for a generic class. Here, the AddTransient() method tells MVC to create and inject an instance of the Repository<T> class every time it encounters an IRepository<T> parameter. This time, the interface and class types are passed within the parentheses of the method call, not within the angle brackets.

Three methods of the IServiceCollection object that map dependencies

Method	Description
AddTransient<interface, class>()	Transient life cycle. MVC creates a new instance of the class every time it needs to inject a dependency.
AddScoped<interface, class>()	Scoped life cycle. MVC creates a new instance of the class the first time it needs to inject a dependency and reuses that instance for all subsequent injections in the scope. Usually, a scope is an HTTP request.
AddSingleton<interface, class>()	Singleton life cycle. MVC creates a new instance of the class the first time it needs to inject a dependency and reuses that instance for all subsequent injections.

How to configure DI for a class that doesn't use generics

```
var builder = WebApplication.CreateBuilder(args);
...
builder.Services.AddTransient<IBookRepository, BookRepository>();
...
```

How to configure DI for a generic class

```
builder.Services.AddTransient(typeof(IRepository<>), typeof(Repository<>));
```

How to configure DI for the HTTP context accessor

Manually

```
builder.Services.AddSingleton<IHttpContextAccessor, HttpContextAccessor>();
```

With a method of the IServiceCollection object

```
builder.Services.AddHttpContextAccessor();
```

Description

- *Dependency injection (DI)* is a design pattern in which the *dependencies* needed by an object are passed as parameters rather than being coded as part of the object.

- To use DI, you code the constructor of the object so it accepts an interface. Then, you can *inject* the dependency by passing any object that implements the interface to the constructor.

- DI makes code easier to change and facilitates unit testing.

- To use DI with MVC, you must register, or *map*, your dependencies in the Program.cs file.

- The Services property of the WebApplicationBuilder object is of the IServiceCollection type. It has methods you can use to map dependencies.

- When you map dependencies, you must decide which *dependency life cycle* to use.

- You can map a dependency for the HttpContextAccessor class manually or with the AddHttpContextAccessor() method of the IServiceCollection interface.

Figure 14-1   How to configure your app for DI

The third code example shows how to map a dependency for the HTTP context accessor. This allows you to use DI to work with objects like session state or cookies. To do that, you can manually map the IHttpContextAccessor interface and the HttpContextAccessor class as a singleton dependency. Or, you can call the AddHttpContextAccessor() method of the IServiceCollection interface.

How to use DI with controllers

Once you've mapped your dependencies, you can request instances of the mapped classes throughout your app. The code in figure 14-2 shows how this works. In particular, this code shows how DI makes controllers like the ones in the Bookstore app from the previous chapter more flexible. Later, this chapter shows how DI also makes controllers easy to test.

The first code example shows a controller that receives a DbContext object via DI. More specifically, it shows the Author controller from the previous chapter that accepts a BookstoreContext object. MVC uses DI to pass an instance of the BookstoreContext class to this controller.

This makes it easy to use classes that inherit the DbContext class of EF Core in controllers. However, it also makes those controllers *tightly coupled* with EF Core. As a result, if you ever wanted to change your data access to something other than EF Core, you'd need to change your Repository class, *and* you'd need to change every controller that receives a DbContext class. In a large app, that could be quite an undertaking!

The second code example shows the controller from the first example after it has been modified to receive a Repository object via DI. To do that, MVC uses the IRepository<T>/Repository<T> mapping shown in the previous figure. Then, when MVC encounters the IRepository<Author> parameter, it injects an instance of the Repository<Author> class. For this to work, the data type of the private data property must also be IRepository<Author>, not Repository<Author>. In addition, the Repository<T> class must implement the IRepository<T> interface, and it must accept a DbContext object in its constructor as shown in chapter 12.

Since the controller in the second example only accesses the IRepository interface, there's no tight coupling with the DbContext class of EF. In other words, it's now *loosely coupled* with EF. As a result, you can change data access from EF to another framework without affecting this controller.

So, in this second example, how does the Repository<Author> class get the BookstoreContext class it needs? Well, when MVC creates an object to inject, it inspects the constructors of that class, and it injects objects according to its mappings. This is called *dependency chaining*.

An Author controller that injects a DbContext object

```
public class AuthorController : Controller
{
    private Repository<Author> data { get; set; }

    public AuthorController(BookstoreContext ctx) =>
        data = new Repository<Author>(ctx);
    ...
}
```

An Author controller that injects a repository object

```
public class AuthorController : Controller
{
    private IRepository<Author> data { get; set; }

    public AuthorController(IRepository<Author> rep) =>
        data = rep;
    ...
}
```

Description

- Controllers that receive DbContext objects via dependency injection are *tightly coupled* with EF Core because they must specify a class derived from the DbContext base class.

- Controllers that receive repository objects via dependency injection are *loosely coupled* with EF Core because they only need to specify the appropriate interface, which may or may not use EF Core.

- When MVC creates an object to inject, it inspects the constructors of the class and injects objects according to the mappings in the Program.cs file. This is called *dependency chaining*.

Figure 14-2   How to use DI with controllers

How to create an interface for an existing class

When you use dependency injection with your application from the start, you'll create classes that implement interfaces, because that's the best way to work with DI. Sometimes, though, you'll want to add dependency injection to an existing application that wasn't built with DI in mind. To do that, you'll need to update any class you want to inject so it implements an interface.

The easiest way to generate an interface for an existing class is to use Visual Studio's refactoring feature, as described in figure 14-3. This feature generates an interface for a class, and it adds code to the class declaration so it implements the new interface.

The first example in this figure shows the ICart interface that Visual Studio generates based on the Cart class from the Bookstore app of the previous chapter. The second example shows the declaration of the Cart class after Visual Studio has updated it to implement the new ICart interface. The rest of the Cart class is the same as it was before.

After you create an interface and update a class to implement it, you need to map that dependency in the Program.cs file as you learned in figure 14-1. This is shown in the last example. Now, you're ready to use the ICart interface with DI.

How to use Visual Studio to generate an interface for a class

- Open the C# file that contains the class and right-click the class name.

- In the context menu, select the Quick Actions and Refactoring item, then select the Extract Interface item.

- In the Extract Interface dialog, enter a name, a destination, select the public members of the interface, and click OK.

- Visual Studio will generate the interface and update the class to implement the interface.

The ICart interface generated by Visual Studio from the Cart class

```
public interface ICart
{
    int? Count { get; }
    IEnumerable<CartItem> List { get; }
    double Subtotal { get; }

    void Add(CartItem item);
    void Clear();
    void Edit(CartItem item);
    CartItem? GetById(int? id);
    void Load(IRepository<Book> data);
    void Remove(CartItem item);
    void Save();
}
```

The Cart class updated by Visual Studio to implement the interface

```
public class Cart : ICart {
    ...
}
```

The DI mapping in the Program.cs file

```
// other DI mappings
builder.Services.AddTransient<ICart, Cart>();
```

Description

- When you update an existing application to use dependency injection, it's common to need to create interfaces for existing classes.

- The easiest way to create an interface for an existing class is to use Visual Studio's refactoring feature to generate it for you.

- Once you have an interface for the existing class, you can add DI mappings for it in the Program.cs file.

Figure 14-3   How to generate an interface for an existing class

How to use DI with an HttpContextAccessor object

Earlier in this chapter, you learned how to map a dependency for the IHttpContextAccessor interface, which provides access to the HttpContextAccessor object for an app. Now, you'll learn how to use DI to work with an HttpContextAccessor object.

The Cart object in the Bookstore app in chapter 13 accepts an HttpContext object in its constructor to work with session state and cookies. Then, when the Cart controller creates a Cart object, it passes its HttpContext property to this constructor. Since several of the Cart controller action methods use a Cart object, it would make sense to create a Cart object in the constructor of the controller.

However, that doesn't work because the value of a controller's HttpContext property is null until after the controller's constructor completes its execution. As a result, each action method in the Cart controller that needs a Cart object has to create its own Cart object and call its Load() method. To reduce code duplication, the controller uses a private helper method named GetCart() that creates a new Cart object and calls its Load() method. Then, each action method that needs a Cart object calls this helper method. Still, this isn't optimal.

One way to fix this issue is to change the Cart class so its constructor accepts an HttpContextAccessor object via DI, and to change the Cart controller so its constructor accepts a Cart object via DI. Figure 14-4 shows how this works.

The first example shows a Cart class that accepts an IHttpContextAccessor object in its constructor. Within the constructor, the code initializes the private variables that hold session and cookie objects. To do that, it uses the HttpContext property of the HttpContextAccessor object. Note that this example uses the null-forgiving operator (!). That's because the HttpContext property can be null.

The second example shows a Cart controller that accepts two parameters in its constructor. The first parameter specifies the IRepository<Book> type, and the second specifies the ICart type. When this constructor is called, the DI provider consults its dependency mappings and passes a Repository<Book> object and a Cart object to this constructor.

Within the constructor, the first two statements assign the objects injected by DI to private properties. Then, the third statement calls the Load() method of the Cart object. For this to work, the Load() method of the Cart class has been updated to accept an IRepository<Books> argument, as you can see in the first example.

At this point, the Cart object is ready to be used by the action methods of the controller. Because of that, those action methods no longer need to create and load their own Cart objects. Instead, the action methods use the private Cart object, as shown in the Index() action method presented here.

This Cart controller as well as the Repository<Book> and Cart classes are good examples of dependency chaining. When the Bookstore app creates a CartController, for example, MVC inspects its constructor and determines that it needs Repository<Book> and Cart objects based on the mappings in the Program.cs file. In addition, when it inspects the constructors of the Repository<Book> and Cart objects, it determines that they need BookstoreContext and HttpContextAccessor objects, respectively.

A Cart class that injects an HttpContextAccessor object

```
public class Cart : ICart
{
    ...
    private ISession session { get; set; }
    private IRequestCookieCollection requestCookies { get; set; }
    private IResponseCookies responseCookies { get; set; }

    public Cart(IHttpContextAccessor ctx) {
        session = ctx.HttpContext!.Session;
        requestCookies = ctx.HttpContext!.Request.Cookies;
        responseCookies = ctx.HttpContext!.Response.Cookies;
    }

    public void Load(IRepository<Book> data) {
        // code that uses the repository and HttpContext to load cart items
    }
    ...
}
```

A Cart controller that injects a Cart object

```
public class CartController : Controller
{
    private IRepository<Book> data { get; set; }
    private Cart cart { get; set; }    // model-level Cart object

    public CartController(IRepository<Book> rep, ICart c)
    {
        data = rep;
        cart = c;                      // create model-level Cart object
        cart.Load(data);               // load cart items
    }

    public ViewResult Index()
    {
        // use model-level Cart object - method no longer needs
        // to create its own Cart object
        var vm = new CartViewModel {
            List = cart.List,
            Subtotal = cart.Subtotal
        };
        return View(vm);
    }

    // rest of Cart methods, which also use the model-level Cart object
}
```

Figure 14-4   How to use DI with an HttpContextAccessor object

How to use DI with action methods

When you work with DI, you typically want to use dependency injection with the constructor of a controller as shown in the previous examples in this chapter. Sometimes, though, it makes sense to inject a dependency directly into an action method. For example, you may want to do this when only one action method in a controller needs that dependency.

To illustrate, the first code example in figure 14-5 presents the Validation controller that the Bookstore app from the previous chapter uses to perform remote validation. This controller has two action methods that check whether a value is already in the database. To do that, these methods use Repository objects. However, each action method needs a different Repository object. The CheckGenre() action method needs a Repository<Genre> object, and the CheckAuthor() action method needs a Repository<Author> object.

To accomplish this, the ValidationController class has a private property for each Repository. Then, the constructor uses the BookstoreContext object it receives to create each of the Repository objects. However, each action method only needs one of these Repository objects. But each time one of these action methods runs, the other Repository object is created too, but never used. Obviously, this is not optimal.

You could update this controller to accept the two Repository objects via dependency injection, which would fix the problem of being tightly coupled with the BookstoreContext class. However, you'd still create two Repository objects when you only need one.

In a case like this, it's better to inject the required Repository object directly into the action method. To do that, you add an interface parameter to the action method and decorate it with the FromServices attribute. This tells MVC to use its DI mappings to get the value for this parameter.

The second code example in this figure shows how this works. Here, the Validation controller has been updated to use action method injection. This means it no longer needs a constructor or private properties for the repositories. Instead, each action method directly accepts the Repository<T> object it needs from MVC's DI provider, based on its DI mappings.

A controller whose constructor accepts a DbContext object

```
public class ValidationController : Controller
{
    // private repository properties
    private Repository<Author> authorData { get; set; }
    private Repository<Genre> genreData { get; set; }

    // constructor that accepts a DB context and initalizes repositories
    public ValidationController(BookstoreContext ctx) {
        authorData = new Repository<Author>(ctx);
        genreData = new Repository<Genre>(ctx);
    }

    public JsonResult CheckGenre(string genreId) {
        validate.CheckGenre(genreId, genreData);
        ...
    }

    public JsonResult CheckAuthor(string firstName, string lastname,
    string operation) {
        validate.CheckAuthor(firstName, lastName, operation, authorData);
        ...
    }
}
```

The same controller with DI in its action methods

```
public class ValidationController : Controller
{
    // private properties and constructor no longer needed

    public JsonResult CheckGenre(
    string genreId, [FromServices] IRepository<Genre> data) {
        validate.CheckGenre(genreId, data);
        ...
    }

    public JsonResult CheckAuthor(string firstName, string lastName,
    string operation, [FromServices] IRepository<Author> data) {
        validate.CheckAuthor(firstName, lastName, operation, data);
        ...
    }
}
```

Description

- To inject an object into an action method, you can use the FromServices attribute.
- For this to work, the CheckGenre() and CheckAuthor() methods define the repository parameter as an interface type, not a class type.

Figure 14-5   How to use DI with action methods

How to use DI with views

If necessary, you can use dependency injection with views. Most of the time, you don't want to do that because a view should get what it needs from the controller. However, when a layout view has a dependency, there's no controller to pass the required object to the layout. In that case, you may want to inject the object into the layout.

The first code example in figure 14-6 shows a navigation link in a layout view that uses a Cart object to get and display the number of items in the cart. Specifically, this code uses a Razor expression to call the Count property of the Cart object.

The second example shows how the layout view for the Bookstore app in the previous chapter gets that Cart object. Here, a Razor code block creates a new Cart object and passes it the Context property of the layout, which is of the HttpContext type. This works because the constructor of the Cart class described in the previous chapter accepts an HttpContext object, not an HttpContextAccessor object as described in this chapter.

A better approach is to use DI to get the layout view the Cart object it needs. To do that, you use the @inject directive to inject the Cart object into the layout as shown in the last example. This example uses the Cart object described in this chapter, which implements the ICart interface and accepts an HttpContextAccessor object in its constructor.

The @inject directive shown here specifies a variable named cart of the ICart type. When MVC encounters the @inject directive, it consults its mappings and injects an object created from the class that's mapped to the interface. In this case, the ICart interface is mapped to the Cart class, so MVC injects a Cart object. As before, MVC also uses dependency chaining to make sure it injects the HttpContextAccessor object that the Cart object needs.

As a result of these changes, you no longer need to create a Cart object in the Razor code block at the beginning of the layout. Instead, the navigation link can use the injected Cart object named cart.

A navigation link in a layout view that uses the Cart object

```
<a class="nav-link" asp-action="Index" asp-controller="Cart" asp-area="">
    <span class="fas fa-shopping-cart"></span> Cart
    <span class="badge badge-light">@cart.Count</span>
</a>
```

Code in a layout that creates a Cart object

```
@{
    var cart = new Cart(Context);
    ...
}
```

Code in a layout that injects a Cart object

```
@inject ICart cart

@{
    ...
}
```

Description

- You can use the @inject directive to inject an object into a view. To do that, the data type for the object is the interface type, not the class type.

Figure 14-6   How to use DI with views

How to get started with unit testing

So far, you've learned how to manually test a project by running it and entering valid and invalid input data to be sure that it works in every case. Although this works for simple apps, testing becomes more difficult and tedious as your apps become larger and more complex. One way to improve this process is to automate some of this testing with a process called unit testing. This helps you improve the quality of your apps and leads to many other benefits. As mentioned earlier, using dependency injection makes it easier to automate testing with unit tests.

How unit tests work

As figure 14-7 shows, *unit testing* provides a way of isolating individual units of code (usually methods) and verifying that they work as expected. Typically, you need to write a series of unit tests for each method to be tested so you can test every possible outcome of the method. Each unit test is a method that calls the method being tested and determines if the return value matches what you expect.

Many unit testing frameworks are available, and some of them integrate seamlessly with Visual Studio. This chapter presents the xUnit framework because it's included with Visual Studio, and it's one of the most popular unit testing frameworks for ASP.NET Core apps. However, other unit testing frameworks such as MSTest and NUnit work much the same way.

Each unit test is a method in a unit test project that you typically include in your Visual Studio solution. Typically, each Visual Studio solution has only one unit test project, but this project may contain one or more classes. Each class in the unit test project tests a different class elsewhere in the Visual Studio solution. You can write unit tests for model classes, utility classes, and controller classes.

Unit tests should be executed often. For example, you can execute them every time you make a change to your code. To do that, you can use the unit testing framework to automatically re-execute the unit tests. This allows you to quickly identify any defects that may be introduced in your code. In this way, unit testing helps you find problems earlier in the development cycle than would be possible by manually testing all your methods.

Unit testing can help you save development time. You save time on data entry because you don't need to load the app and manually enter data into your app every time you make a code change. Since the unit testing framework lets you know when a test fails, you also save time because only the most recent code changes need to be debugged.

The unit testing process

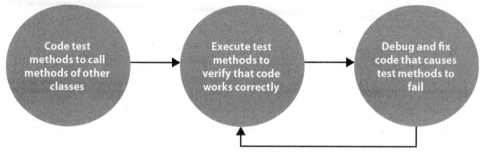

Advantages of unit testing

- It reduces the amount of time you have to spend manually testing an app by running it and entering data.

- It makes it easy to test an app after each significant code change. This helps you find problems earlier in the development cycle than you typically would when using manual testing.

- It makes debugging easier because you typically test an app after each significant code change. As a result, when a test fails, you only need to debug the most recent code changes.

Description

- *Unit testing* provides a way to write code that automatically tests individual methods, called *units*, to verify that they work properly in isolation.

- You code unit tests within a separate project that's part of the solution that contains the classes to be tested.

- Visual Studio provides several types of test projects for .NET Core apps. This chapter shows how to use xUnit.

Figure 14-7   How unit tests work

How to add an xUnit project to a solution

To get started with unit testing, you typically add a new xUnit project to the solution that contains the project with the methods you want to test. To do this, you can follow the steps presented in figure 14-8. In short, you display the Add a new project dialog and use it to select the xUnit Test Project template for C#. Then, you enter a name for your unit test project and specify a location where the files for the project will be stored.

Although you can give your unit test project any name you want, unit tests are usually created to mirror the code being tested. As a result, it's considered a best practice to give the unit test project a name that's related to the project it is testing. For example, if you are testing a project named Bookstore, you can name your unit test project Bookstore.Tests. It's also considered a best practice to store your unit test project in the same solution as the project that you're testing, although that isn't required.

After you create the unit test project, you must add a reference to the project that you're testing as described in this figure. Otherwise, the code in your unit test project won't be able to access the code in that project.

When you create an xUnit project, Visual Studio adds a single class named UnitTest1 by default. Because this isn't a very meaningful name, you'll want to change it to something that is more meaningful. For example, if the class will be used to test the methods in a class named Nav, you might rename this class to NavTests.

Later, when you need to add other classes to store your unit tests, you can add them by right-clicking on the unit test project and selecting the Add→ Class item. For example, you can add a class named AuthorControllerTests that contains the unit tests for the Author controller.

Note that the xUnit project that Visual Studio generates includes a file named Usings.cs that contains this line of code:

```
global using Xunit;
```

This is a *global using directive*, which is a feature that was added in C# 10. When you include a global using directive, the namespace is imported and available to all other files in the project. Unit test classes often require the same namespaces, such as Microsoft.AspNetCore.Mvc and the namespace that contains the model classes of the project being tested. Because of that, it makes sense to import those namespaces globally in the Using.cs file. This can help keep your unit test classes uncluttered. You'll see an example of a Usings.cs file later in the chapter.

The Add a new project dialog

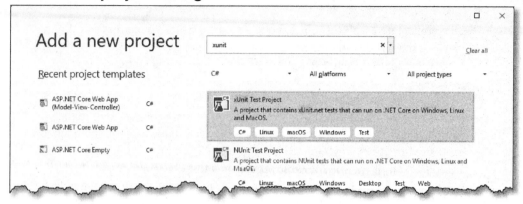

How to add a unit test project to a solution

1. Right-click the solution and select Add→New Project.
2. In the Add a new project dialog, select the xUnit Test Project template and click Next. To help find the template, you can search for "xunit".
3. Enter a name and location for the project and click Create.

The web app project and the unit test project in the Solution Explorer

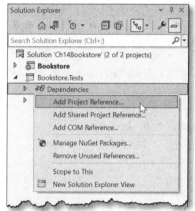

Description

- By convention, a unit test project is named after the web app project it's testing.
- For the unit test project to work correctly, it must include a reference to the web app project. To add a reference, right-click Dependencies and select Add Project Reference. In the resulting dialog, click Projects, select the web app project, and click OK.
- To add new classes to a unit test project, right-click the project and select Add→Class.

Figure 14-8   How to add an xUnit project to a solution

How to write a unit test

After you create a unit test class, you can start writing your unit tests. Figure 14-9 presents the basic skills for doing that.

To start, the first table in this figure presents some of the static methods of the Assert class that you can use to test various conditions. Then, the second table presents three attributes that you can use to decorate your test methods. The Assert class and the attributes that are used with unit tests are included in the Xunit namespace. As you learned in the last topic, this namespace is included as a global using directive, so you don't have to include it in each unit test.

The code example below the tables presents a test class named NavTests with two test methods. These methods test the Active() method in the Nav class of the Bookstore app. Although it's not shown here, you should know that this test class needs access to the namespace that contains the class that it's testing. You can provide that access by adding a using directive in the test class or by adding a global using directive to the Using.cs file.

When you code your test methods, it's good to use a consistent naming convention. In this case, both test method names consist of the name of the method to be tested, an underscore, and a description of the behavior the test expects. Names like these can help you keep your unit tests organized.

It's also common to use the *Arrange/Act/Assert (AAA) pattern* for each unit test you write. The code in the Arrange section initializes any arguments needed by the method being tested. Then, the code in the Act section calls the method being tested. Finally, the code in the Assert section checks whether the method being tested behaved as expected.

In this figure, the first test method is decorated with the Fact attribute. As a result, Visual Studio executes this test method when the unit tests run. In the Arrange section, the code creates two string variables. In the Act section, the code passes these variables to the static Active() method of the Nav class and assigns the return value to a variable name result. Finally, in the Assert section, the code uses the static IsType() method of the Assert class to check that the return value is of the string type. If so, the test passes.

The second test method is decorated with the Theory attribute. This tells Visual Studio that this test method has parameters. When you use a test method that has parameters, you must also use the InlineData attribute to provide the values for those parameters. Each InlineData attribute you code represents a separate test. So, this test method runs twice, once with the values "Home" and "Home", and once with the values "Books" and "Books". The Assert section of this test uses the Equal() method of the Assert class to test that it returns the string "active" when the values passed to the Active() method match.

When you write unit tests for a method, you should try to cover as many code paths as possible. For example, in addition to testing that the Active() method returns what you expect when the values match, you should add a test for when the values don't match. Although a unit test like this isn't presented in this figure, this unit test is included in the downloadable app for this chapter.

Some static methods of the Assert class

Method	Description
`Equal(expected, result)`	Tests whether the specified objects are equal.
`NotEqual(expected, result)`	Tests whether the specified objects are not equal.
`False(Boolean)`	Tests whether the specified condition is false.
`True(Boolean)`	Tests whether the specified condition is true.
`IsType<T>(result)`	Tests whether the specified object is of the specified type.
`IsNull(result)`	Tests whether the specified object is null.

Three attributes of the Xunit namespace

Attribute	Description
`Fact`	Identifies a test method.
`Theory`	Identifies a test method that has parameters.
`InlineData(p1, p2, ...)`	Provides parameter values to test.

A test class with two test methods

```
public class NavTests
{
    [Fact]
    public void ActiveMethod_ReturnsAString()
    {
        string s1 = "Home";                 // arrange
        string s2 = "Books";

        var result = Nav.Active(s1, s2);   // act

        Assert.IsType<string>(result);      // assert
    }

    [Theory]
    [InlineData("Home", "Home")]
    [InlineData("Books", "Books")]
    public void ActiveMethod_ReturnsValueActiveIfMatch(string s1,
    string s2)
    {
        string expected = "active";         // arrange

        var result = Nav.Active(s1, s2);   // act

        Assert.Equal(expected, result);    // assert
    }
}
```

Description

* Code in a unit test is often organized using the *Arrange/Act/Assert (AAA) pattern*.

Figure 14-9   How to write a unit test

How to run a unit test

After you have written your unit tests, you can use the Visual Studio Test Explorer shown in figure 14-10 to run them. To open this window, use one of the techniques described in this figure.

The Test Explorer displays the name of your test project, each test class within the project, and each test method within each test class. In addition, for parameterized test methods, it displays a line for each InlineData attribute. In other words, it shows you how many times the parameterized test method runs, and the data that's passed to it each time it runs. For example, the first screen shows that the ActiveMethod_ReturnsValueActiveIfMatch() method runs twice, once for each pair of string values.

If your tests don't appear in the Test Explorer, you need to build your test project. To do that, you can select the Build→Build Solution item from the menu system. Or, you can click the Run All Tests in View button in the Test Explorer toolbar, which is the first green triangle on the far left side of the toolbar.

The Test Explorer toolbar also displays the number of total tests in the project, how many have passed, how many have failed, and how many haven't run yet. The total tests are marked with a lab test bottle, the successful tests with a green check mark, the failed tests with a red X, and the un-run tests with a blue exclamation point.

To run your tests, click the Run All Tests in View button. After your tests run, the Test Explorer indicates how long it took for each unit test to complete. This can be useful because you may need to fix some code if the unit test is taking too long to run, even if the unit test passes. You can display more details for any group or individual unit test by clicking on it in the Test Explorer. This displays details about the item on the right side of the Test Explorer.

Another way to run your tests is to click the Run button, which is the second green triangle on the left side of the Test Explorer toolbar. You can click this button's down arrow to display the menu shown in the second screen. From this menu, you can run your tests in several different ways: you can run all the tests, only the selected tests, only the tests that have failed, or only the tests that haven't been run yet. You can also set a breakpoint in one or more unit tests and debug them just as you would debug a regular app. Stepping through your code with the Visual Studio debugger takes you seamlessly back and forth between the unit tests and the methods that you are testing.

If one or more unit tests fail, you know that there's either a problem in the method that you're testing or a problem with the unit test. In that case, you need to debug your code until you can get your unit tests to pass.

Once you have your unit tests set up, you should run them often. In fact, many programmers like to run their unit tests after every significant code change.

The Test Explorer in Visual Studio

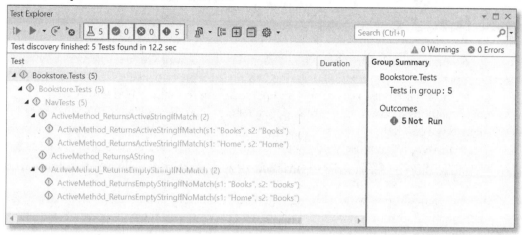

Some options to run tests in Test Explorer

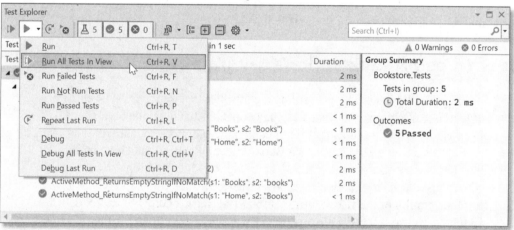

Two ways to open the Test Explorer

- From the menu system, select Test→Test Explorer.
- In the Solution Explorer, right-click on the test class and select Run Tests.

Description

- The Test Explorer shows whether or not tests have been run, as well as which tests passed or failed. It also shows how long it took to execute each unit test.
- The Test Explorer marks tests that succeed with a green check mark, tests that fail with a red X, and tests that have not run yet with a blue exclamation point.
- You have many options to run tests from the Test Explorer. You can also set breakpoints and debug unit tests the same way you would debug regular methods.

Figure 14-10   How to run a unit test

How to test methods that have dependencies

So far, you've learned how to test methods that accept simple arguments. For example, the Active() method described earlier accepts two strings. In that case, the test just hardcoded two strings and passed them to that method. However, many methods have more complex dependencies, and these dependencies themselves can fail.

For example, suppose you want to test an action method of a controller class whose constructor accepts an IRepository<Book> object. In that case, if you pass a Repository<Book> object to the constructor and the test fails, it may be difficult to determine why. Although it could be an error in the action method code, it could also be a problem with the database or with the network that communicates with the database.

To test just the code in an action method, you can use a fake, or *mock*, version of the dependency that doesn't communicate with the database. That makes it easier to pinpoint the problem if the test fails.

How to use a fake repository object

Figure 14-11 starts by presenting a controller that depends on a repository object. Specifically, it presents a Home controller that depends on an IRepository<Book> object that it stores in a private property named data. Then, its Index() action method returns a Book object by calling the Get() method of the IRepository<Book> interface and passing it a QueryOptions<Book> object.

To test the Index() action method of this controller, you can code a new implementation of the IRepository<Book> interface. Then, you can code its Get() method so it returns a Book object without accessing the database. That's what the FakeBookRepository class shown in the second example does.

An easy way to code an implementation of an interface is to use Visual Studio's code generation feature as described in this figure. This generates a stub for each property and method of the interface that throws a NotImplementedException object. Then, you implement the properties and methods used by the unit tests so they don't throw an exception. Here, the second example implements the Get() method so it returns a Book object. This is the only method needed by the unit test in the third example.

This test method creates an instance of the FakeBookRepository class and passes it to the constructor of the Home controller. Then, it calls the controller's Index() action method and tests that the return value of that action method is of the ViewResult type. If so, the test passes.

A controller that depends on a repository object

```
public class HomeController : Controller
{
    private IRepository<Book> data { get; set; }
    public HomeController(IRepository<Book> rep) => data = rep;

    public ViewResult Index() {
        var random = data.Get(new QueryOptions<Book> {
            OrderBy = b => Guid.NewGuid()
        });
        return View(random);
    }
}
```

A fake repository class that implements the Get() method

```
using Bookstore.Models;
...
public class FakeBookRepository : IRepository<Book>
{
    public int Count => throw new NotImplementedException();
    public void Delete(Book entity) => throw new NotImplementedException();
    public Book Get(QueryOptions<Book> options) => new Book();
    ...
}
```

A unit test that passes an instance of the fake repository to the controller

```
[Fact]
public void IndexActionMethod_ReturnsAViewResult() {
    // arrange
    var rep = new FakeBookRepository();
    var controller = new HomeController(rep);

    // act
    var result = controller.Index();

    // assert
    Assert.IsType<ViewResult>(result);
}
```

How to use Visual Studio to implement an interface

- Create a new class that implements the interface. Visual Studio will display a red squiggle that indicates that the interface hasn't been implemented.
- Hover the mouse pointer over the red squiggle, click the lightbulb icon, and select Implement Interface to generate stubs for each property and method of the interface.

Description

- To test a method that depends on a repository class, you can create a fake repository class that implements the interface for the repository class. Then, you can implement the method used by the method you're testing so it doesn't access the database.
- When you use a fake repository class to test a method, you can be sure that if the test fails, it isn't due to problems with the database or the network connection to the database.

Figure 14-11   How to use a fake repository object

How to use a fake TempData object

In the previous figure, you learned how to pass a fake version of an object to the constructor of a controller. This works because the controller uses dependency injection, and it uses interface parameters to specify the object it needs. As a result, it's easy to swap in any object that implements the correct interface.

However, controllers that use TempData don't receive a TempData object by dependency injection. Instead, they use the TempData property of the Controller class, as shown by the Edit() action method in the first example of figure 14-12. Fortunately, you can use a variation of the technique from the previous figure to handle this situation.

As before, you need to create a fake version of the object that the action method depends on. This time, though, you create a fake version of the TempData object by implementing the ITempDataDictionary interface. This interface has several properties and methods as well as an indexer. As before, if you use Visual Studio to generate a class for this interface, it generates stubs that throw exceptions. Then, you can write code for the members that the action method you're testing uses. In this figure, the Edit() action method only needs to add a value to TempData, so you only need to write code for the indexer.

The second example shows the FakeTempData class generated by Visual Studio after the indexer is implemented. This implementation doesn't actually do anything because the test only needs the Edit() action method to be able to set a TempData value without throwing an exception.

The Author controller that contains the Edit() action method accepts an IRepository<Author> object in its constructor. To test this method, you can use a FakeAuthorRepository class that works like the FakeBookRepository class from the previous figure. In this case, however, you need to implement the Update() and Save() methods of the FakeAuthorRepository class because the Edit() action method calls these methods.

When you implement a property or method that's used by a method being tested, you should do the most minimal implementation possible. This can be as simple as returning null as shown by the get accessor in the second example, or removing all the code from a method with a void return type as shown by the Update() and Save() methods in the third example.

The fourth example presents a method that tests the Edit() action method. As before, it creates a fake repository object and passes it to the constructor of the controller. This time, however, it also creates a fake TempData object and assigns it to the TempData property of the controller. Then, the test method calls the controller's Edit() action method and tests that its return value is of the RedirectToActionResult type. If so, the test passes.

An action method that accesses TempData

```
[HttpPost]
public IActionResult Edit(Author author)
{
    if (ModelState.IsValid) {
        data.Update(author);
        data.Save();
        TempData["message"] = $"{author.FullName} updated.";
        return RedirectToAction("Index");
    }
    else {
        return View("Author", author);
    }
}
```

The FakeTempData class with an indexer that does nothing

```
using Microsoft.AspNetCore.Mvc.ViewFeatures;      // for ITempDataDictionary
...
public class FakeTempData : ITempDataDictionary
{
    public object? this[string key] { get => null; set { } }
    public ICollection<string> Keys => throw new NotImplementedException();
    ...
}
```

Two methods of the FakeAuthorRepository class that do nothing

```
public void Update(Author entity) { }   // does nothing
public void Save() { }                   // does nothing
```

A test method that tests the action method that uses TempData

```
[Fact]
public void Edit_POST_ReturnsRedirectToActionResultIfModelStateIsValid() {
    // arrange
    var rep = new FakeAuthorRepository();
    var controller = new AuthorController(rep) {
        TempData = new FakeTempData()
    };

    // act
    var result = controller.Edit(new Author());

    // assert
    Assert.IsType<RedirectToActionResult>(result);
}
```

Description

- To test an action method that accesses TempData, you must create a fake TempData object. Otherwise, the test will fail due to a NullReferenceException.

- To create a fake TempData class, create a new class that implements the ITempDataDictionary interface from the Microsoft.AspNetCore.Mvc.ViewFeatures namespace.

Figure 14-12   How to use a fake TempData object

How to create fake objects with Moq

In the last two figures, you learned how to create mock objects to test a method. That way, your unit tests only test the code in the method being tested, not external code like code that accesses a database or works with TempData.

As you've seen, you can use the code generation features of Visual Studio to create the mock objects you need. However, that can lead to problems setting up your mock objects for each individual test. For instance, the test method in figure 14-11 needs the implementation of the Get() method of the FakeBookRepository class shown in that figure. If you had tests that needed different implementations of that method, though, you might need to generate different versions of that class. As you can imagine, that could get messy fast.

To solve this issue, many programmers prefer to use a third-party tool to create mock objects. That's why the next few figures show how to use a popular mocking tool called Moq.

How to work with mock objects

Before you can use the Moq framework, you need to add its NuGet package to your test project as described in figure 14-13. Then, you can use the Mock<T> and It classes to create mock objects. The two tables in this figure present some of the properties and methods of these classes, and the code examples below the tables show how to use them.

The first code example presents the using directive for the Moq namespace. Then, the second example shows how to create an object from the generic Mock<T> class. To do that, this example specifies the IRepository<Author> type as the data type to mock.

The third code example shows how to implement a method of the mock object. To do this, the code uses the Setup() method of the Mock<T> class. The argument passed to the Setup() method is a lambda expression that identifies the method to implement. In this case, the code implements the Get() method, but you can use the same technique for other methods.

If the method you're implementing accepts arguments, you configure the arguments with the static methods of the It class. Here, the Get() method is configured to accept any int. This means that your test method can pass any int value to the method that you're testing. You can also specify acceptable values as shown by the fourth example.

If the method you're implementing doesn't return any data, you don't need to do anything else. If, however, the method returns data, you need to tell the mock object what to return. To do this, you use the Returns() method of the Mock<T> class. In this figure, the code in the third and fourth examples returns a new Author object because the Get() method being mocked should return an Author object.

The fifth example shows how to pass a mock object to a controller. To do that, you just use the Object property of the Mock<T> class to access the mock object. Here, the code passes an IRepository<Author> object to the Author controller.

How to add the Moq framework to your test project

1. In the Solution Explorer, right-click the test project and select Manage NuGet Packages from the resulting menu.
2. In the NuGet Package Manager, click Browse, search for "moq", select the Moq package, and click Install.
3. In the resulting dialogs, click OK and I Accept.

Two methods and one property of the Mock<T> class

Method	Description
`Setup(lambda)`	Configures a mock object by specifying a lambda expression that identifies the method to mock.
`Returns(value)`	Identifies the return value of the method identified by Setup().
Property	**Description**
`Object`	Returns the instance of the fake object.

Two static methods of the It class

Method	Description
`IsAny<T>()`	Identifies an argument to be passed to the method under test.
`Is<T>(lambda)`	Identifies and further specifies an argument to be passed to the method under test.

The using directive for the Moq namespace

```
using Moq;
```

Code that creates a Mock<IRepository<Author>> object

```
var rep = new Mock<IRepository<Author>>();
```

Code that sets up Get() to accept any int and return an Author object

```
rep.Setup(m => m.Get(It.IsAny<int>())).Returns(new Author());
```

The same code statement adjusted to accept any int greater than zero

```
rep.Setup(m => m.Get(It.Is<int>(i => i > 0))).Returns(new Author());
```

Code that passes the mock object to a controller

```
var controller = new AuthorController(rep.Object);
```

Description

*   It can be time consuming to create your own fake objects. Because of that, many developers prefer to use a mocking tool instead. One popular mocking tool for .NET is the Moq framework.

Figure 14-13   How to work with mock objects

How to mock a repository object

Figure 14-11 showed how to code a fake repository class that you can use to test an action method that depends on a repository object. Now, the first example in figure 14-14 shows how to perform the same task using Moq.

Within the test method, the Arrange section starts by creating a Mock<IRepository<Book>> object. Then, it sets up the Get() method of the repository to accept any QueryOptions<Book> object and return a Book object. Finally, it passes the mock repository object to the constructor of the Home controller.

After the Arrange section, the Act section calls the Index() action method of the Home controller and stores the return value in a variable named result. Then, the Assert section checks whether the result is of the ViewResult type. If so, the test passes.

How to mock a TempData object

Figure 14-12 showed how to code a fake TempData class that you can use to test an action method that depends on a TempData object. Now, the second example in figure 14-14 shows how to perform the same task using Moq.

Just like the fake TempData class, the class that uses Moq includes a using directive for the Microsoft.AspNetCore.Mvc.ViewFeatures namespace that contains the ITempDataDictionary interface. Then, within the test method, the Arrange section begins by creating a Mock<IRepository<Author>> object and a Mock<ITempDataDictionary> object. Next, it creates an instance of the controller that contains the action method that's being tested. To do that, it passes the mock repository object to the controller's constructor and assigns the mock TempData object to the controller's TempData property.

With Moq, you don't need to explicitly set up the Update() and Save() methods of the repository. Similarly, you don't need to explicitly set up the TempData indexer. This is one of the benefits of using the Moq framework.

The Act section calls the Edit() action method and stores its result. Then, the Assert section checks whether the result is of the RedirectToActionResult type. If so, the test passes. This makes sure that the action method returns a RedirectToActionResult object when the controller's ModelState property is valid.

Of course, to test all code paths, you should also code a test method that makes sure that the action method returns a ViewResult object when the controller's ModelState property is invalid. A test method like this is shown later in this chapter. In addition, one is included in the downloadable app for this chapter. The key to this test method is that it includes a line of code that adds an error to the model like this:

```
controller.ModelState.AddModelError("", "Test error message.");
```

A test method that mocks a repository object

```
using Bookstore.Controllers;                    // for HomeController
...
[Fact]
public void IndexActionMethod_ReturnsViewResult()
{
    // arrange
    var rep = new Mock<IRepository<Book>>();
    rep.Setup(m => m.Get(It.IsAny<QueryOptions<Book>>()))
                .Returns(new Book());
    var controller = new HomeController(rep.Object);

    // act
    var result = controller.Index();

    // assert
    Assert.IsType<ViewResult>(result);
}
```

A test method that mocks a TempData object

```
using Bookstore.Areas.Admin.Controllers;       // for Admin.AuthorController
using Microsoft.AspNetCore.Mvc.ViewFeatures;    // for ITempDataDictionary
...
[Fact]
public void Edit_POST_ReturnsRedirectToActionResultIfModelStateIsValid()
{
    // arrange
    var rep = new Mock<IRepository<Author>>();
    var temp = new Mock<ITempDataDictionary>();
    var controller = new AuthorController(rep.Object)
    {
        TempData = temp.Object
    };

    // act
    var result = controller.Edit(new Author());

    // assert
    Assert.IsType<RedirectToActionResult>(result);
}
```

Description

- You can use the Moq framework to mock repository and TempData objects.

- To mock a TempData object, use the ITempDataDictionary interface from the Microsoft.AspNetCore.Mvc.ViewFeatures namespace as the type argument.

- When you use Moq, you don't need to explicitly set up indexers, properties, or most void methods.

Figure 14-14   How to mock repository and TempData objects

How to mock an HttpContextAccessor object

The past few figures have shown how to use Moq for a relatively simple setup. However, Moq can also help you with a more complex setup.

To illustrate a more complex setup, the first example in figure 14-15 shows a constructor for a Cart class that accepts an IHttpContextAccessor object. Then, in the body of the constructor, the first three statements use the HttpContext property of that interface to get objects needed to work with session state and cookies. As a result, to test the Cart class, you need to set up all these properties.

This constructor ends with a statement that initializes the private items variable with a list of CartItem objects. The web app project doesn't need this statement to run properly. However, the test project does need this statement. This shows that it's common to need to refactor code that wasn't built with testing in mind so you can test it. If you find a class or method hard to test, then, you may need to refactor it so it's easier to test.

The second example presents the Subtotal property of the Cart class that's tested by the test method shown in the third example. This Subtotal property uses the Sum() method that's available from LINQ to sum the values of the Subtotal property of every item in the cart.

The third example shows the test method that checks whether the Subtotal property returns a double value. The class that contains it includes a using directive for the Microsoft.AspNetCore.Http namespace that contains the IHttpContextAccessor interface.

Within the test method, the Arrange section starts by creating a new Mock<IHttpContextAccessor> object. Then, it creates a new DefaultHttpContext object. This object allows you to create an empty HttpContext object for testing.

Next, the Arrange section uses the DefaultHttpContext object and the Setup() method of the Mock<T> class to implement most of the properties that the Cart constructor needs. To implement the Session property, though, it needs to create a Mock<ISession> object and pass it to the Returns() method.

Finally, the Arrange section creates a new Cart object and passes the mock HttpContextAccessor object to its constructor. Then, it uses the Add() method of the Cart class to add an item to the cart. This is necessary because the Cart's items collection is private, so you can't populate it directly.

After the Arrange section, the Act section gets the value that's returned by the Subtotal property. Then, the Assert section checks that this value is of the double type. If so, the test passes.

The constructor of the Cart class

```
public Cart(IHttpContextAccessor ctx)
{
    // assign private variables
    session = ctx.HttpContext!.Session;
    requestCookies = ctx.HttpContext!.Request.Cookies;
    responseCookies = ctx.HttpContext!.Response.Cookies;
    items = new List<CartItem>(); // needed for test method to run
}
```

The Subtotal property of the Cart class

```
public double Subtotal => items.Sum(i => i.Subtotal);
```

A test method that tests the Subtotal property of the Cart with Moq

```
using Microsoft.AspNetCore.Http;       // for IHttpContextAccessor
...
[Fact]
public void SubtotalProperty_ReturnsADouble()
{
    // arrange
    var accessor = new Mock<IHttpContextAccessor>();
    var context = new DefaultHttpContext();

    accessor.Setup(m => m.HttpContext).Returns(context);
    accessor.Setup(m => m.HttpContext!.Request).Returns(context.Request);
    accessor.Setup(m => m.HttpContext!.Response).Returns(context.Response);
    accessor.Setup(m => m.HttpContext!.Request.Cookies)
        .Returns(context.Request.Cookies);
    accessor.Setup(m => m.HttpContext!.Response.Cookies)
        .Returns(context.Response.Cookies);

    var session = new Mock<ISession>();
    accessor.Setup(m => m.HttpContext!.Session).Returns(session.Object);

    Cart cart = new Cart(accessor.Object);
    cart.Add(new CartItem { Book = new BookDTO() });

    // act
    var result = cart.Subtotal;

    // assert
    Assert.IsType<double>(result);
}
```

Description

- You can use the Moq framework to mock an HttpContextAccessor object. To do that, use the IHttpContextAccessor interface of the Microsoft.AspNetCore.Http namespace as the type argument for the Mock constructor.
- The DefaultHttpContext class creates an empty instance of the HttpContext class that you can use to set up the HttpContextAccessor properties and methods you need.

Figure 14-15   How to mock an HttpContextAccessor object

The Bookstore.Tests project

The next few figures present some of the tests in the test project for the Bookstore app. These tests are similar to the ones you've already seen, although they build upon the concepts that have been presented so far.

The Test Explorer

Figure 14-16 shows the Test Explorer for the Bookstore.Tests project after all test methods have passed. These methods test a few of the Bookstore web app's models and controllers. A real-world project would probably have many more test methods than this, and those test methods would test more complex behaviors. However, these tests should give you a good idea of how to get started with unit testing.

The Test Explorer shows that the Bookstore.Tests project consists of six test classes. To name these test classes, this project adds a suffix of "Tests" to the name of the class being tested. For example, the CartTests and NavTests classes contain test methods for the Cart class and the Nav class, and the HomeControllerTests and BookControllerTests classes contain test methods for the Home and Book controllers. In addition, if a controller is in the Admin area, the project adds a prefix of "Admin". For example, the AdminAuthorControllerTests and AdminBookControllerTests classes contain test methods for the Author and Book controllers that are in the Admin area.

When you use the Test Explorer, it groups each test class so the test methods they contain display together in the window. This makes it easy to run just that group of tests if you want. For example, if you only want to run the tests for the CartTests class, you can select that class and click the Run button in the Test Explorer toolbar.

The Test Explorer also displays the number of test methods in each test class. For example, the HomeControllerTests class has only two tests.

In this project, the name of each test method identifies the method or property that's being tested and the expected results of the test. For example, the HomeControllerTests class has test methods named

```
IndexActionMethod_ModelIsABookObject()
```

and

```
IndexActionMethod_ReturnsViewResult()
```

This naming convention helps organize the tests and makes them self-documenting. When you use this convention, it leads to test method names that are unusually long. However, if these long method names help to organize and document the tests, it's usually worth the extra effort that it takes to create them.

The Test Explorer for the Bookstore.Tests project

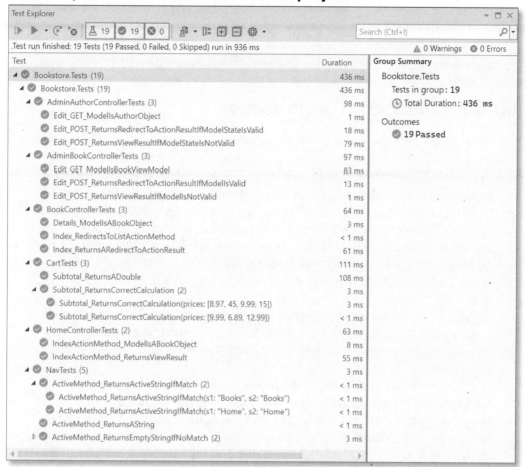

Description

- The Bookstore.Tests project tests some of the models and controllers of the Bookstore web app.

- The names of the test classes identify the model or controller that contains the methods being tested. If a controller is in an area, the name of the controller is prefixed with the name of the area.

- The names of the test methods identify the property or method being tested and the expected result of the test.

- The Test Explorer displays the test methods as children of a class. This makes it easy to run all tests for a class.

Figure 14-16   The Test Explorer for the Bookstore.Tests project

The Usings.cs file

Figure 14-17 presents the Usings.cs file, which provides global using directives for the namespaces that the unit test classes use most. This reduces repetitive code and helps keep the unit test classes less cluttered.

The BookControllerTests class

Figure 14-17 also presents the BookControllerTests class. To start, this class adds a using directive for the Controllers namespace of the Bookstore web app. This allows the unit test code to work with controller classes. This directive isn't included in the Usings.cs file because not all unit test classes test controllers.

Within the test class, the first method tests that the Index() action method returns a RedirectToActionResult object. To do that, the Arrange section creates a mock IRepository<Book> object. Then, it creates a new Book controller by passing the mock repository object to the controller's constructor. Since the Index() action method only redirects, the mock repository doesn't need any setup.

After the Arrange section, the Act section calls the controller's Index() action method and stores the result that's returned by the method. Then, the Assert section checks that the result is of the RedirectToActionResult type. If so, the test passes.

The second method tests that the Index() action method redirects to the List() action method. To do that, the Arrange section creates a mock IRepository<Book> object. Then, it creates a new Book controller object by passing the mock repository object to the controller's constructor. Again, since the Index() action method only redirects, the mock repository doesn't need any setup.

After the Arrange section, the Act section calls the controller's Index() action method and stores the object that's returned in a variable named result. Then, the Assert section checks if the result's ActionName property is equal to the expected value, which is "List". If it is, the test passes.

The third method tests that the Details() action method returns a ViewResult object with a Model property of the Book type. In other words, it checks that the object passed to the View() method in the Details() action method is of the Book type.

To do that, the Arrange section creates a mock IRepository<Book> object and sets up its Get() method to accept any QueryOptions<Book> object and to return a Book object. Then, it creates a new Book controller by passing this mock repository object to its constructor.

After the Arrange section, the Act section calls the Details() action method and passes it an int value. To get the model object, the code calls the Model property of the ViewData property of the ViewResult object that's returned by the Details() action method. Then, the Assert section checks that the model object is of the Book type. If so, the test passes.

The Usings.cs file

```
global using Xunit;
global using Microsoft.AspNetCore.Mvc;
global using Bookstore.Models;
global using Moq;
```

The BookControllerTests class

```
using Bookstore.Controllers;

namespace Bookstore.Tests
{
    public class BookControllerTests
    {
        [Fact]
        public void Index_ReturnsARedirectToActionResult() {
            // arrange
            var rep = new Mock<IRepository<Book>>();
            var controller = new BookController(rep.Object);

            // act
            var result = controller.Index();

            // assert
            Assert.IsType<RedirectToActionResult>(result);
        }

        [Fact]
        public void Index_RedirectsToListActionMethod() {
            // arrange
            var rep = new Mock<IRepository<Book>>();
            var controller = new BookController(rep.Object);

            // act
            var result = controller.Index();

            // assert
            Assert.Equal("List", result.ActionName);
        }

        [Fact]
        public void Details_ModelIsABookObject() {
            // arrange
            var rep = new Mock<IRepository<Book>>();
            rep.Setup(m => m.Get(It.IsAny<QueryOptions<Book>>()))
                .Returns(new Book());
            var controller = new BookController(rep.Object);

            // act
            var model = controller.Details(1).ViewData.Model;

            // assert
            Assert.IsType<Book>(model);
        }
    }
}
```

Figure 14-17   The Usings.cs file and the BookControllerTests class

The AdminBookControllerTests class

Figure 14-18 presents the AdminBookControllerTests class. This class includes two using directives. The Microsoft.AspNetCore.Mvc.ViewFeatures namespace makes it easy to create a mock TempData object. The using directive for the Controllers namespace in the Admin area makes it easy to work with the Book controller in that area.

Within the class, the first method is a helper method named GetBookController() that returns a BookController object. This method encapsulates the setup code necessary to mock a BookController object that accepts a Book repository, an Author repository, and a Genre repository. This helps to avoid duplicating the same setup code in multiple places in your test methods.

Within the GetBookController() method, the first group of statements creates a Book repository and sets up its Get() and List() methods. The second group of statements creates an Author repository and sets up its List() method. The third group of statements creates a Genre repository and sets up its List() method. Finally, the last statement creates a new BookController object, passes the mock Book, Author, and Genre repositories to its constructor, and returns the BookController object.

The first test method checks whether the Edit() action method for GET requests passes a model of the BookViewModel type to the view. To start, the Arrange section calls the helper method to get a BookController object.

After the Arrange section, the Act section calls the Edit() action method of the controller, passes it an int value, and gets an object for the view model. Then, the Assert section checks whether this view model is of the BookViewModel type. If so, the test passes.

The AdminBookControllerTests class

```
using Microsoft.AspNetCore.Mvc.ViewFeatures;      // for ITempDataDictionary
using Bookstore.Areas.Admin.Controllers;

namespace Bookstore.Tests
{
    public class AdminBookControllerTests
    {
        // helper method for unit test class - not a test
        public BookController GetBookController()
        {
            // mock book repository
            var bookRep = new Mock<IBookRepository>();
            bookRep.Setup(m => m.Get(It.IsAny<QueryOptions<Book>>()))
                .Returns(new Book());
            bookRep.Setup(m => m.List(It.IsAny<QueryOptions<Book>>()))
                .Returns(new List<Book>());

            // mock author repository
            var authorRep = new Mock<IRepository<Author>>();
            authorRep.Setup(m => m.List(It.IsAny<QueryOptions<Author>>()))
                .Returns(new List<Author>());

            // mock genre repository
            var genreRep = new Mock<IRepository<Genre>>();
            genreRep.Setup(m => m.List(It.IsAny<QueryOptions<Genre>>()))
                .Returns(new List<Genre>());

            // return controller
            return new BookController(
                bookRep.Object, authorRep.Object, genreRep.Object);
        }

        [Fact]
        public void Edit_GET_ModelIsBookObject()
        {
            // arrange
            var controller = GetBookController();

            // act
            var model = controller.Edit(1).ViewData.Model;

            // assert
            Assert.IsType<BookViewModel>(model);
        }
```

Figure 14-18   The AdminBookControllerTests class (part 1)

The second test method tests whether the Edit() action method for POST requests returns a ViewResult if the model state is not valid. Within this method, the Arrange section begins like the previous method. However, after creating the controller object, the Arrange section makes the model state invalid by adding an error to it. To do that, it calls the AddModelError() method of the controller's ModelState property. Then, the Arrange section finishes by creating the BookViewModel object that's required by the Edit() action method for POST requests.

After the Arrange section, the Act section calls the Edit() action method and passes it the BookViewModel object that it requires and stores the result. Then, the Assert section checks whether the result is of the ViewResult type. That makes sense because the Edit() action method displays the view again if the model state is not valid. If the result is of the ViewResult type, the test passes.

The third test method tests whether the Edit() action method for POST requests returns a RedirectToActionResult if the model state is valid. This works much like the second method. However, the Arrange section doesn't need to add an error to the model state. Instead, it needs to create a mock TempData object and assign it to the controller's TempData property. That's because the code path for a valid model state uses TempData to display a message that indicates that the book was successfully edited. Conversely, the code path for an invalid model state doesn't use TempData.

After the Arrange section, the Act section calls the Edit() action method, passes it a BookViewModel object, and stores the result. Then, the Assert section checks whether the result is of the RedirectToActionResult type. That makes sense because the Edit() action method redirects to the List() action method if the model state is valid. If the result is of the RedirectToActionResult type, the test passes.

The AdminBookControllerTests class (continued)

```
[Fact]
public void Edit_POST_ReturnsViewResultIfModelIsNotValid()
{
    // arrange
    var controller = GetBookController();
    controller.ModelState.AddModelError("", "Test error message.");
    BookViewModel vm = new BookViewModel();

    // act
    var result = controller.Edit(vm);

    // assert
    Assert.IsType<ViewResult>(result);
}

[Fact]
public void Edit_POST_ReturnsRedirectToActionResultIfModelIsValid()
{
    // arrange
    var controller = GetBookController();
    var temp = new Mock<ITempDataDictionary>();
    controller.TempData = temp.Object;
    BookViewModel vm = new BookViewModel { Book = new Book() };

    // act
    var result = controller.Edit(vm);

    // assert
    Assert.IsType<RedirectToActionResult>(result);
}
    }
}
```

Figure 14-18   The AdminBookControllerTests class (part 2)

The CartTests class

Figure 14-19 presents the CartTests class. To start, it includes a using directive for the Microsoft.AspNetCore.Http namespace so it can access HttpContext objects.

Within the class, the first method is a helper method named GetCart() that returns a Cart object. This method encapsulates the setup code presented in figure 14-15 to mock an HttpContextAccessor object. This helps to avoid duplicating the same setup code in multiple places in your test methods.

The first test method performs the same test as the method presented in figure 14-15. Now, though, it uses the GetCart() helper method to get a Cart object with a mock HttpContextAccessor object. This shortens the test code and makes it easier to read.

The CartTests class

```
using Microsoft.AspNetCore.Http;    // for IHttpContextAccessor

namespace Bookstore.Tests
{
    public class CartTests
    {
        private Cart GetCart()
        {
            // create HTTP context accessor
            var accessor = new Mock<IHttpContextAccessor>();

            // setup request and response cookies
            var context = new DefaultHttpContext();
            accessor.Setup(m => m.HttpContext)
                .Returns(context);
            accessor.Setup(m => m.HttpContext!.Request)
                .Returns(context.Request);
            accessor.Setup(m => m.HttpContext!.Response)
                .Returns(context.Response);
            accessor.Setup(m => m.HttpContext!.Request.Cookies)
                .Returns(context.Request.Cookies);
            accessor.Setup(m => m.HttpContext!.Response.Cookies)
                .Returns(context.Response.Cookies);

            // setup session state
            var session = new Mock<ISession>();
            accessor.Setup(m => m.HttpContext!.Session)
                .Returns(session.Object);

            return new Cart(accessor.Object);
        }

        [Fact]
        public void Subtotal_ReturnsADouble()
        {
            // arrange
            Cart cart = GetCart();
            cart.Add(new CartItem { Book = new BookDTO() });

            // act
            var result = cart.Subtotal;

            // assert
            Assert.IsType<double>(result);
        }
```

Figure 14-19   The CartTests class (part 1)

The second test method checks whether the Subtotal property of a Cart object returns the correct calculation. To do that, this test method accepts a double array of prices as its parameter. This parameter uses the params keyword so the array of prices can be passed in a comma-separated list. That way, the test method can work with the comma-separated lists of prices contained in the InlineData attributes. This also makes it possible to pass a variable number of prices to the test method.

Within the test method, the Arrange section calls the private GetCart() method to get a Cart object that has a mock HttpContextAccessor object. Then, it loops through the prices array and creates a cart item for each price. In addition, it specifies a quantity of 1 for each item. Next, it adds each item to the cart. Finally, the code calculates the expected value by calling the Sum() LINQ extension method from the array of prices.

After the Arrange section, the Act section stores the value of the Subtotal property of the Cart object in a variable named result. Then, the Assert section compares the expected value to this result value. To correct for any imprecision that can occur with double values, it uses the static Math.Round() method to round both the expected and result values to 2 decimal places.

The CartTests class (continued)

```
[Theory]
[InlineData(9.99, 6.89, 12.99)]
[InlineData(8.97, 45.00, 9.99, 15.00)]
public void Subtotal_ReturnsCorrectCalculation(
    params double[] prices)
{
    // arrange
    Cart cart = GetCart();
    for (int i = 0; i < prices.Length; i++)
    {
        var item = new CartItem
        {
            Book = new BookDTO { BookId = i, Price = prices[i] },
            Quantity = 1
        };
        cart.Add(item);
    }
    double expected = prices.Sum();

    // act
    var result = cart.Subtotal;

    // assert
    Assert.Equal(Math.Round(expected, 2), Math.Round(result, 2));
}
}
}
```

Figure 14-19   The CartTests class (part 2)

Perspective

This chapter shows how to use dependency injection (DI) to make your code more flexible. In addition, it shows how to automate the testing of a web app by using DI to make it possible to work with unit testing. This includes using the xUnit and Moq frameworks. These skills should provide a good foundation for working with DI and unit testing, even if you need to use another unit testing framework such as MSTest or NUnit.

Terms

dependency injection (DI)	dependency chaining
dependency	unit testing
inject a dependency	unit
dependency life cycle	Arrange/Act/Assert (AAA) pattern
tightly coupled	mock
loosely coupled	

Summary

- *Dependency injection* (*DI*) is a design pattern in which the *dependencies* needed by an object are passed as parameters rather than being coded as part of the object.

- To use DI, you code the constructor of the object so it accepts an interface. Then, you can *inject* the dependency by passing any object to the constructor that implements the interface.

- When you map dependencies, you must decide which *dependency life cycle* to use. Most of the time, you can use the transient life cycle, which is the shortest life cycle.

- Controllers that receive DbContext objects via dependency injection are *tightly coupled* with EF Core because they must specify a class that's derived from the DbContext base class.

- Controllers that receive repository objects via dependency injection are *loosely coupled* with EF Core because they only need to specify the appropriate interface, which may or may not use EF Core.

- When MVC creates an object to inject, it inspects the constructors of the class and injects dependencies according to the mappings in the Program.cs file. This is called *dependency chaining*.

- *Unit testing* provides a way to write code that automatically tests individual methods, called *units*, to verify that they work properly in isolation.

- Code in a unit test is often organized using the *Arrange/Act/Assert* (*AAA*) *pattern*.

- One way to test a method that has a dependency is to use a fake version, or *mock*, of the dependency.

Exercise 14-1   Add dependency injection and some unit tests

In this exercise, you'll modify a Class Schedule web app so it uses dependency injection. Then, you'll add a test project to the solution, write some unit tests with xUnit and Moq, and run the tests.

Run the app

1. Open the Ch14Ex1ClassSchedule web app in the ex_starts directory.

2. If you didn't do the exercises for chapter 12, open the Package Manager Console and enter the Update-Database command to create the database for this app.

3. Run the app and make sure it works correctly.

Add dependency injection for the data layer classes

4. In the Program.cs file, map dependencies for the following class:

   `Repository<T>`

5. Update each controller to use the IRepository<T> interface rather than the Repository<T> class, and update the constructor of each controller to use DI to get the repository class it needs.

6. Run the app and make sure it still works correctly.

Add a test project to the solution

7. Add an xUnit Test Project for C# to the solution. Name the test project ClassScheduleTests.

8. Add a reference to the project that contains the Class Schedule web app.

9. Open the Manage NuGet Packages for Solution window and add Moq to the test project.

10. Open the Usings.cs file and review the global using directive for Xunit.

Write a test

11. Rename the default file named UnitTest1.cs to TeacherControllerTests.cs. Then, rename the class it contains to TeacherControllerTests. (Visual Studio may offer to rename the class for you.)

12. Add using statements for the Moq, Microsoft.AspNetCore.Mvc, ClassSchedule.Models, and ClassSchedule.Controllers namespaces. You can use global using statements in the Usings.cs file, using statements in the unit test class file, or a combination of both.

13. Rename the default test method IndexActionMethod_ReturnsAViewResult().

14. Within the test method, write code that checks that the Index() action method of the TeacherController class returns a ViewResult object. Use Moq to create the repository object the controller depends on. This repository object shouldn't need any setup.

Open the Test Explorer and run your test

15. Open the Test Explorer. If you don't see your test there, build the solution. If you still don't see your test, make sure it's decorated with the Fact attribute.

16. Run your test. If it fails, debug your test method until it passes.

Write another test method and run it

17. Add another test method to the TeacherControllerTests class named IndexActionMethod_ModelIsAListOfTeacherObjects().

18. Within the test method, write code that checks that the Index() action method returns a ViewResult object with a Model property of the List<Teacher> type. For this test, set up the List() method to accept a QueryOptions<Teacher> object and return a List<Teacher> object.

19. Run both of your tests. If either test fails, debug your test methods until they both pass.

Write another test class and run it

20. Add a new class to the test project named HomeControllerTests. Make sure the class is public.

21. Add any necessary using statements listed earlier in step 12.

22. Add a test method named IndexActionMethod_ReturnsAViewResult().

23. Within that test method, write code that checks that the Index() action method of the HomeController class returns a ViewResult object. Use Moq to create the repository objects the controller depends on.

24. Run all of your tests. If any test fails, debug your test methods until they all pass.

15

How to work with tag helpers, partial views, and view components

So far, this book has shown how to use the built-in tag helpers provided by MVC. Now, this chapter reviews those tag helpers and shows how to create custom tag helpers. In addition, it shows how to create partial views and view components. You can use these features to reduce code duplication in your views, which makes your views more flexible and easier to maintain.

An introduction to tag helpers

MVC provides several built-in tag helpers to generate HTML that's sent to a browser. To start, this chapter reviews some of these built-in tag helpers and shows how to use and register them.

How to use tag helpers

The table in figure 15-1 presents some of the common tag helpers provided by MVC. Here, the first six tag helpers provide attributes for standard HTML elements like <form> and <input> tags. The last two, by contrast, provide non-standard HTML elements.

The built-in tag helpers that provide attributes have a prefix of "asp-". This makes it clear that the attributes are tag helpers and not standard HTML attributes. When you create custom tag helpers, it's generally considered a good practice to follow this convention of using a prefix. In this chapter, for instance, the examples use a prefix of "my-".

Below the table, the code examples show how to use some of the built-in tag helpers. The first example uses the asp-for tag helper to bind an <input> tag to a model property. This tag helper generates several attributes for the <input> tag, including the data attributes needed for the data validation in the model. Using this tag helper keeps your view markup clean and makes sure these attributes are generated correctly.

The second example uses the asp-action tag helper with a <form> tag to generate the URL the form should post to. Since there's no asp-controller tag helper, this tag helper uses the current controller and generates a relative URL. Using this tag helper makes the attribute more flexible and reduces the chances of coding an incorrect URL.

The third example uses the <environment> tag helper to send different CSS links to the browser for different hosting environments. For development, the view uses the regular Boostrap CSS file. But in other environments such as a production environment, the app uses the minified version of this CSS file. Unlike the previous examples, this tag helper is an element, not an attribute. That's why it doesn't use a prefix.

How to register tag helpers

Before you can use a tag helper in your app, you must register it. The easiest way to do that is to code one or more @addTagHelper directives in the _ViewImports.cshtml file, as shown by the last example in figure 15-1.

The first parameter for the @addTagHelper directive specifies the name of the tag helper to register. In this example, both directives use the wildcard symbol (*) to indicate that all tag helpers should be registered.

The second parameter is the name of the assembly that contains the tag helpers. For custom tag helpers, this is usually the name of your web app project as shown by the second directive.

Common built-in tag helpers

Tag helper	Description
`asp-action`	Attribute that indicates the action method in a route.
`asp-controller`	Attribute that indicates the controller in a route.
`asp-area`	Attribute that indicates the area in a route.
`asp-for`	Attribute that binds an element to a property of a model object. MVC will generate the appropriate attributes for the element.
`asp-validation-summary`	Attribute that controls the display of validation messages. Usually applied to a <div> tag.
`asp-validation-for`	Attribute that controls the display of a single validation message. Usually applied to a <span> tag.
`environment`	Element that uses include and exclude attributes to display HTML based on the current hosting environment.
`partial`	Element that renders a partial view. See figure 15-12.

A tag helper that generates attributes for an <input> tag

```
<input asp-for="FirstName" class="form-control" />
```

The HTML that's sent to the browser

```
<input class="form-control" type="text" data-val="true" data-val-
maxlength="The field FirstName must be a string or array type with a maximum
length of &#x27;200&#x27;." data-val-maxlength-max="200" data-val-
required="Please enter a first name." id="FirstName" maxlength="200"
name="FirstName" value="" />
```

A tag helper that generates a route-based URL in a <form> tag

```
<form asp-action="Add" method="post"></form>
```

The HTML that's sent to the browser

```
<form action="/author/add" method="post"></form>
```

Tag helpers that output a different CSS link based on hosting environment

```
<environment include="Development">
    <link rel="stylesheet" href="~/lib/bootstrap/css/bootstrap.css" />
</environment>
<environment exclude="Development">
    <link rel="stylesheet" href="~/lib/bootstrap/css/bootstrap.min.css" />
</environment>
```

A _ViewImports.cshtml file that registers all built-in and custom tag helpers

```
...
@addTagHelper *, Microsoft.AspNetCore.Mvc.TagHelpers
@addTagHelper *, Bookstore
```

Description

- To use tag helpers, you must register them with the @addTagHelper directive.

Figure 15-1   How to register and use tag helpers

How to create custom tag helpers

By now, you should understand how to use MVC's built-in tag helpers. However, it can be useful to create your own custom tag helpers for snippets of HTML that you use frequently.

How to create a custom tag helper

To create a custom tag helper, you need to code a class that inherits the TagHelper class of the TagHelpers namespace. The first code example in figure 15-2 shows the using directive for that namespace. This using directive also makes it easy to access other classes for working with tag helpers such as the TagHelperOutput and TagHelperAttributeList classes described in this figure.

When you create a tag helper class, it's common to store it in a folder named TagHelpers, but that isn't required. Similarly, it's common to add a suffix of TagHelper to the class name, but that's also not required.

If you name your tag helper class so it starts with the same name as an HTML element, MVC automatically applies your tag helper to that element. In this figure, for instance, the second example creates a tag helper named ButtonTagHelper. As a result, this tag helper targets the <button> element.

A tag helper class must inherit the TagHelper class, and it typically overrides the virtual Process() method of that class. The Process() method accepts TagHelperContext and TagHelperOutput arguments. This is illustrated by the ButtonTagHelper class shown here.

Within the Process() method, the code adds a class attribute that specifies two Bootstrap classes that style a button. To do that, it uses the Attributes property of the TagHelperOutput parameter to access a list of attributes for the <button> element. From this list of attributes, the code calls the SetAttribute() method to set the class attribute to "btn btn-primary". This overwrites any CSS classes that might already exist in the class attribute. Later, you'll see how to append rather than overwrite CSS classes.

The third code example shows two <button> elements in a view. Then, the fourth example shows the HTML that MVC sends to the browser. This shows that the tag helper makes sure that each <button> element has both of the Bootstrap classes for styling buttons.

Because the Process() method is a synchronous method, it can only call synchronous methods of the TagHelperOutput class. However, this class also contains an asynchronous method named GetChildContentAsync() that you may want to use from time to time. To call this method, you must override the ProcessAsync() method instead of the Process() method. The signature for the ProcessAsync() method looks like this:

```
public override async Task ProcessAsync(TagHelperContext
    context, TagHelperOutput output)
```

And the code that calls the asynchronous method looks like this:

```
var content = await output.GetChildContentAsync();
```

One virtual method of the TagHelper class

Method	Description
`Process(ctx, out)`	Manipulates and outputs an HTML element. Accepts a TagHelperContext object and a TagHelperOutput object. Also has an asynchronous version named ProcessAsync() that returns a Task object.

One property of the TagHelperOutput class

Property	Description
`Attributes`	A TagHelperAttributeList object that holds an element's attributes.

One method of the TagHelperAttributeList class

Property	Description
`SetAttribute(name, val)`	Sets the attribute in the attribute list with the specified name to the specified value. If the attribute doesn't exist, it's added to the end of the list.

The using directive for the TagHelpers namespace

```
using Microsoft.AspNetCore.Razor.TagHelpers;
```

A tag helper that applies to any standard HTML <button> element

```
public class ButtonTagHelper : TagHelper
{
    public override void Process(TagHelperContext context,
    TagHelperOutput output)
    {
        output.Attributes.SetAttribute("class", "btn btn-primary");
    }
}
```

Two button elements in a view

```
<button type="submit">Submit</button>
<button type="reset">Reset Form</button>
```

The HTML that MVC sends to the browser

```
<button type="submit" class="btn btn-primary">Submit</button>
<button type="reset" class="btn btn-primary">Reset Form</button>
```

Description

- To create a custom tag helper, you code a class that inherits the TagHelper class, and you typically override its virtual Process() method.
- A tag helper class automatically applies to the HTML element of the same name.
- By convention, tag helper classes have a suffix of TagHelper, but this is not required.
- The TagHelperContext class represents the current context of an HTML element.
- The TagHelperOutput class represents the state of the HTML element.

Figure 15-2   How to create a custom tag helper

How to create a tag helper
for a non-standard HTML element

In the last figure, you learned how to apply a custom tag helper to a standard HTML element such as a <button> element. However, it's also possible to apply a custom tag helper to a non-standard HTML element such as a <submit-button> element. For that to work, your tag helper needs to transform the non-standard HTML element into a standard HTML element.

The table at the top of figure 15-3 presents two more properties of the TagHelperOutput class that you can use to transform an HTML element. First, you can use the TagName property to replace the name within the element's start tag as well as its end tag, if the element has an end tag.

Second, you can use the TagMode property to specify the type of start and end tags the element should have. To do that, it uses the TagMode enumeration. As the table indicates, you can use this property to output an element with both start and end tags (<label></label>), a start tag only (<input>), or a self-closing tag (<input />).

The code below the table shows a tag helper class named SubmitButtonTagHelper. MVC automatically applies this tag helper to elements of the same name minus the TagHelper suffix. In addition, it automatically translates between the Pascal casing common to C# classes and the kebab casing common to HTML. So, a tag helper named SubmitButton or SubmitButtonTagHelper targets a non-standard HTML element named <submit-button>.

Within this class, the Process() method starts by assigning "button" to the TagName property. Then, it assigns the StartTagAndEndTag value to the TagMode property. As a result, the tag helper outputs a <button> element with start and end tags. Next, the code adds an attribute to make sure the button is of type submit.

After transforming the non-standard <submit-button> element into a standard <button> element, the code adds two Bootstrap button classes. Unlike the previous figure, though, this code appends the Bootstrap classes to any existing CSS classes. To do that, it uses the Attributes property to get the old CSS classes from the class attribute. Since the class attribute might not exist, this statement uses the ? operator to check for nulls. Then, the code appends the new classes to any old classes and sets the resulting classes as the class attribute.

The second code example shows a <submit-button> element in a view. Then, the third example shows the HTML that MVC sends to the browser for that element. This shows that the tag helper transforms the <submit-button> element to a <button> element, adds a type attribute whose value is "submit", and appends the "btn" and "btn-primary" class names to the existing class attribute.

Note that this tag helper doesn't change the inner HTML (the value between the start and end tags). This shows that a tag helper works with an existing element and only changes the specified parts of that element.

More properties of the TagHelperOutput class

Property	Description
TagName	Replaces the current start tag. Also replaces the end tag, if applicable.
TagMode	Uses the TagMode enumeration to indicate the type of tag. Options are SelfClosing, StartAndEndTag, and StartTagOnly.

A tag helper that applies to any non-standard <submit-button> element

```
public class SubmitButtonTagHelper : TagHelper
{
    public override void Process(TagHelperContext context,
    TagHelperOutput output)
    {
        // make it a button element with start and end tags
        output.TagName = "button";
        output.TagMode = TagMode.StartTagAndEndTag;

        // make it a submit button
        output.Attributes.SetAttribute("type", "submit");

        // append bootstrap button classes
        string newClasses = "btn btn-primary";
        string oldClasses =
            output.Attributes["class"]?.Value.ToString() ?? "";
        string classes = (string.IsNullOrEmpty(oldClasses)) ?
            newClasses : $"{oldClasses} {newClasses}";
        output.Attributes.SetAttribute("class", classes);
    }
}
```

A submit-button element in a view
```
<submit-button class="me-2">Submit</submit-button>
```

The HTML that MVC sends to the browser
```
<button type="submit" class="me-2 btn btn-primary">Submit</button>
```

Description

- MVC automatically translates between the Pascal casing of a C# class name such as SubmitButton and the kebab casing of the corresponding HTML element such as <submit-button>.

Figure 15-3   How to create a tag helper for a non-standard HTML element

How to use extension methods with tag helpers

The classes of the TagHelpers namespace are regular C# classes. As a result, you can add extension methods to them to encapsulate code that you use frequently. For instance, you might often need to append one or more CSS classes to a class attribute like the example in the previous figure. Or, you might often need to transform an element to a standard HTML element with start and end tags.

Figure 15-4 shows a static TagHelperExtensions class with three static extension methods. First, the AppendCssClass() method extends the TagHelperAttributeList class. This is the data type of the Attributes property of the TagHelperOutput class. As a result, you can call this method from the Attributes property of the TagHelperOutput parameter of the Process() method.

The AppendCssClass() method accepts a string of CSS classes. Then, rather than overwriting existing CSS classes, this code appends the new classes to any old CSS classes. To do that, it uses code that's similar to the code shown in the previous figure.

Second, the BuildTag() method extends the TagHelperOutput class. This method accepts string arguments that specify the name of a tag and the names of any CSS classes. The code assigns the value of the tagName parameter to the TagName property of the TagHelperOutput object, and it sets its TagMode property so the element has a start and end tag. Then, it calls the first extension method of the TagHelperExtensions class to append the value of the classNames parameter to the element's class attribute.

Note that the classNames parameter of the BuildTag() method is required. As a result, if you don't always want to add one or more CSS classes when you build a tag, you can change this parameter to be optional with a default value of an empty string.

Third, the BuildLink() method also extends the TagHelperOutput class. It accepts one string argument for a URL and another for a CSS class. Its code starts by calling the BuildTag() extension method. This transforms the targeted element to an <a> element with start and end tags and a class attribute. Then, it calls the SetAttribute() method to add an href attribute for the url argument.

After presenting the three extension methods, this figure presents the tag helpers shown in the previous two figures after they've been updated to use these extension methods. Now, the ButtonTagHelper class uses the AppendCssClass() method to add two Bootstrap classes to the element's class attribute. This improves this tag helper because it no longer overwrites any existing CSS classes like the example in figure 15-2 does.

Similarly, the SubmitButtonTagHelper class now uses the BuildTag() method to transform the <submit-button> element into a <button> element with start and end tags and two Bootstrap classes appended to the element's class attribute. The use of this extension method replaces six statements with one statement. Then, it calls the SetAttribute() method of the Attributes property to make the button a submit button.

Three extension methods for tag helpers

```
using Microsoft.AspNetCore.Razor.TagHelpers;
...
public static class TagHelperExtensions
{
    public static void AppendCssClass(this TagHelperAttributeList list,
    string newCssClasses)
    {
        string oldCssClasses = list["class"]?.Value.ToString() ?? "";
        string cssClasses = (string.IsNullOrEmpty(oldCssClasses)) ?
            newCssClasses : $"{oldCssClasses} {newCssClasses}";
        list.SetAttribute("class", cssClasses);
    }

    public static void BuildTag(this TagHelperOutput output,
    string tagName, string classNames)
    {
        output.TagName = tagName;
        output.TagMode = TagMode.StartTagAndEndTag;
        output.Attributes.AppendCssClass(classNames);
    }

    public static void BuildLink(this TagHelperOutput output,
    string url, string className)
    {
        output.BuildTag("a", className);
        output.Attributes.SetAttribute("href", url);
    }
}
```

Two tag helpers that use the extension methods

```
public class ButtonTagHelper : TagHelper
{
    public override void Process(TagHelperContext context,
    TagHelperOutput output)
    {
        output.Attributes.AppendCssClass("btn btn-primary");
    }
}

public class SubmitButtonTagHelper : TagHelper
{
    public override void Process(TagHelperContext context,
    TagHelperOutput output)
    {
        output.BuildTag("button", "btn btn-primary");
        output.Attributes.SetAttribute("type", "submit");
    }
}
```

Description

- You can use extension methods to add functionality to the classes of the TagHelpers namespace that you may use frequently.

Figure 15-4   How to use extension methods with tag helpers

How to control the scope of a tag helper

So far, you've learned how to apply a tag helper to a standard or non-standard HTML element by naming your tag helper class to match that element. However, what if you don't want your tag helper to apply to all instances of an HTML element? For instance, you might want the Button tag helper to only apply to submit buttons. Or, what if you want your tag helper to apply to more than one element? For instance, you might want the Button tag helper to apply to <button> elements and <input> elements of the submit type.

Fortunately, you can control the elements that your tag helper class targets by decorating it with the HtmlTargetElement attribute. With this attribute, you can narrow the scope of your tag helper so it only applies to an element under certain conditions. Or, you can widen the scope of your tag helper so it applies to more than one element. You can also use it to allow your class to use a different name than the element you want to match.

The HtmlTargetElement attribute accepts a constructor argument that specifies the name of the HTML element to target. It also accepts the two properties presented in the table at the top of figure 15-5. The Attributes property specifies the attributes an HTML element must have for the tag helper to be applied. If there's more than one attribute, they can be included in a comma-separated list. The ParentTag property specifies that the element must be a child of the listed element for the tag helper to be applied.

The examples below the table show how you can use the HtmlTargetElement attribute to control the scope of tag helpers. The first example presents a class named LabelTagHelper that doesn't use an HtmlTargetElement attribute. As a result, it applies to all <label> elements.

The second example uses the HtmlTargetElement attribute to specify that the class named MyLabelTagHelper applies to <label> elements. This allows the name of the class to be different from the element it targets.

The third example also applies to <label> elements. However, it uses the Attributes and ParentTag properties to narrow the scope of this tag helper so it only applies to <label> elements that have an asp-for attribute and are coded within a <form> element. Since the attribute specifies the element to target, this allows the name of the class to be more descriptive.

The fourth example shows that you can decorate your tag helper class with more than one HtmlTargetElement attribute. Here, the first attribute specifies that this tag helper applies to <input> elements within a <form> element. Then, the second attribute specifies that this tag helper also applies to <select> elements within a <form> element.

The last example shows another way to apply a tag helper to more than one element. Here, the first attribute skips the argument that specifies an HTML element and uses brackets to specify the name and value of the attribute. As a result, this tag helper applies to any element that has a type attribute with a value of "submit". Then, the second attribute applies this tag helper to <a> elements with a custom attribute named my-button.

Two properties of the HtmlTargetElement attribute

Property	Description
`Attributes`	The attributes an HTML element must have for the tag helper to be applied.
`ParentTag`	The parent tag that must contain an HTML element for the tag helper to be applied.

A tag helper that applies to any <label> element

```
public class LabelTagHelper : TagHelper {...}
```

Another tag helper that applies to any <label> element

```
[HtmlTargetElement("label")]
public class MyLabelTagHelper : TagHelper {...}
```

A tag helper that applies to bound <label> elements in a form

```
[HtmlTargetElement("label", Attributes = "asp-for", ParentTag = "form")]
public class FormLabelTagHelper : TagHelper {...}
```

A tag helper that applies to <input> or <select> elements in a form

```
[HtmlTargetElement("input", ParentTag = "form")]
[HtmlTargetElement("select", ParentTag = "form")]
public class FormTagHelper : TagHelper {...}
```

A tag helper that applies to any element of the submit type or any <a> element with a my-button attribute

```
[HtmlTargetElement(Attributes = "[type=submit]")]
[HtmlTargetElement("a", Attributes = "my-button")]
public class MyButtonTagHelper : TagHelper {...}
```

You can use the HTMLTargetElement attribute to...

- Allow a tag helper class to have a different name than the HTML element it targets.
- Narrow the scope of a tag helper so it only targets an element under certain conditions.
- Widen the scope of a tag helper so it targets multiple elements.

Description

- The HtmlTargetElement attribute specifies the target HTML element for a tag helper.
- You can apply multiple HtmlTargetElement attributes to a tag helper class.
- Within the HtmlTargetElement attribute, you can use brackets to specify the name and value of an attribute.

Figure 15-5   How to control the scope of a tag helper

How to use a tag helper to add elements

The first table in figure 15-6 shows that the TagHelperOutput class has properties named PreElement, Content, and PostElement. These properties are of the TagHelperContent type. This type provides many methods that you can use to get and set the HTML that's output to the browser. For example, it provides an AppendHtml() method that adds the HTML it receives to the output, and it provides a SetContent() method that replaces the text between the start and end tag of an element.

When you use these methods to set HTML, you could pass a string literal to the method like this:

```
output.PreElement.AppendHtml("<label>First Name</label>");
```

However, this approach tends to be error prone. As a result, it's generally considered a better practice to use the TagBuilder class to build the HTML.

The second table presents two properties of the TagBuilder class. The Attributes property is a dictionary that stores the attributes of the element being built. The InnerHtml property is a builder object that allows you to set the inner HTML of the element being built. In other words, it lets you set the HTML between the element's start and end tags.

Each of the properties in the second table has a method that's useful when building elements with the TagBuilder class. For example, the Add() method that's available from the Attributes property lets you add an attribute to the element, and the Append() method of the InnerHtml property lets you append HTML to the inner HTML of the element.

Below the tables, the first code example shows the using directive for the Rendering namespace that contains the TagBuilder class. Then, the second code example shows a tag helper that targets <input> elements that have an attribute named my-required.

Within its Process() method, the code starts by appending a Bootstrap CSS class named form-control to the <input> element. Then, it uses the TagBuilder class to create a <span> element, add a class attribute with two Bootstrap CSS classes to it, and set its inner HTML to an asterisk. To finish, this code uses the AppendHtml() method of the PostElement property to add the <span> element after the targeted <input> element.

The third example shows an <input> element that includes the my-required attribute. Then, the fourth example shows the HTML that MVC sends to the browser for that element. This shows that the required input tag helper adds a class attribute to the <input> element and a <span> element after it.

When you use the my-required attribute, you can code it without a value. That's because the value of the attribute isn't used anywhere. Rather, the attribute just needs to be present so MVC applies the tag helper. Also, note that MVC sends the attribute to the browser, but it isn't needed there since it isn't standard HTML. If you want, you can prevent it from being sent to the browser by coding a property in the tag helper with the same name as the attribute. You'll learn how to use properties with tag helpers in the next figure.

Three properties of the TagHelperOutput class

Property	Description
PreElement	The HTML before an element.
Content	The main content between the start and end tags of an element.
PostElement	The HTML after an element.

Two properties of the TagBuilder class

Property	Description
Attributes	A dictionary of an element's attributes. Can be used to add attributes to an element.
InnerHtml	A content builder that works with the inner HTML of an element.

The using directive for the Rendering namespace

```
using Microsoft.AspNetCore.Mvc.Rendering;      // for TagBuilder
```

A tag helper that adds a <span> element after the targeted element

```
[HtmlTargetElement("input", Attributes = "my-required")]
public class RequiredInputTagHelper : TagHelper
{
    public override void Process(TagHelperContext context,
    TagHelperOutput output)
    {
        // add CSS class to input element
        output.Attributes.AppendCssClass("form-control");

        // create a <span> element
        TagBuilder span = new TagBuilder("span");
        span.Attributes.Add("class","text-danger ms-2");
        span.InnerHtml.Append("*");

        // add span element after input element
        output.PostElement.AppendHtml(span);
    }
}
```

An <input> element that uses the tag helper

```
<input asp-for="Title" my-required />
```

The HTML that's sent to the browser

```
<input my-required type="text" id="Title" name="Title" value=""
       class="form-control" />
<span class="text-danger ms-2">*</span>
```

The elements displayed in a browser

Description

- The properties of the TagHelperOutput class return a type of TagHelperContent that provides methods for getting and setting the HTML that's output to the browser.

Figure 15-6   How to use a tag helper to add elements

More skills for custom tag helpers

So far, this chapter has presented some basic skills for creating and using custom tag helpers. Now, it shows how to take those skills to the next level.

How to use properties with a tag helper

A tag helper class is a normal C# class. As a result, you can code normal C# properties for it. In a tag helper class, the properties correspond to the attributes for the HTML element that the tag helper targets. Visual Studio even provides IntelliSense support for these attributes. In addition, MVC automatically translates between the Pascal casing of the C# property name and the kebab casing of the HTML attribute.

One reason to code a property in a tag helper class is to provide a way to prevent attributes that you need to apply a tag helper from being output to the browser. For example, if you added a Boolean MyRequired property to the tag helper in the previous figure, MVC wouldn't output the my-required attribute as part of the HTML for the targeted element. More often, though, you code properties in a tag helper class to get data that the tag helper needs.

Figure 15-7 presents a tag helper class with properties that get a minimum and a maximum number. This tag helper applies to <select> elements that have attributes named my-min-number and my-max-number. Here, the properties named Min and Max correspond to those attributes, as indicated by the HtmlAttributeName attribute that decorates each property. Without these attributes, the properties would have to be named MyMinNumber and MyMaxNumber, which would make them more difficult to refer to in the tag helper class.

Within the Process() method, the code uses a for loop that starts at the value of the Min property and runs until the counter reaches the value of the Max property. With each iteration of the loop, the code uses the TagBuilder class to create an <option> element and set its inner HTML to the number stored by the loop's counter variable. Then, the code appends the <option> element to the HTML content of the targeted <select> element.

The second example shows a <select> element in a view with attributes for the my-min-number and my-max-number attributes of the tag helper. Then, the third example shows the HTML that MVC sends to the browser for that element. This shows that the tag helper adds <option> elements for the numbers 1 through 10, as illustrated by the fourth example.

In the second example, the asp-for tag helper binds the <select> element to the Quantity property of the view's Model object. However, the tag helper doesn't mark the option that matches the current Quantity value as selected. To do that, you can use the technique described in the next figure.

A tag helper that generates numeric options for a \<select> element

```
[HtmlTargetElement("select", Attributes = "my-min-number, my-max-number")]
public class NumberDropDownTagHelper : TagHelper
{
    [HtmlAttributeName("my-min-number")]
    public int Min { get; set; }

    [HtmlAttributeName("my-max-number")]
    public int Max { get; set; }

    public override void Process(TagHelperContext context,
    TagHelperOutput output)
    {
        for (int i = Min; i <= Max; i++)
        {
            TagBuilder option = new TagBuilder("option");
            option.InnerHtml.Append(i.ToString());
            output.Content.AppendHtml(option);
        }
    }
}
```

A view that uses the tag helper

```
@model CartItem
...
<select asp-for="Quantity" class="form-select"
    my-min-number="1" my-max-number="10"></select>
```

The HTML that's sent to the browser

```
<select class="form-select" id="Quantity" name="Quantity">
    <option>1</option>
    <option>2</option>
    ...
    <option>10</option>
</select>
```

The \<select> element displayed in a browser

Description

- You can use properties in a tag helper class to get data from the view.
- You can use the HtmlAttributeName attribute to define the name of the HTML attribute if you want it to be different from the property name.

Figure 15-7   How to use properties with a tag helper

How to work with the model property that an element is bound to

As you've seen, the Process() method in a tag helper class accepts TagHelperContext and TagHelperOutput objects. So far, you've learned how to use the Attributes property of a TagHelperOutput object to work with the attributes of an element. Now, figure 15-8 shows how to use the AllAttributes property of the TagHelperContext class to work with the attributes of an element.

The difference is that the TagHelperContext class allows you to work with the attributes that are coded in the view, and TagHelperOutput class allows you to work with the attributes that are sent to the browser. As a result, if a view includes this HTML:

```
<input asp-for="FirstName" />
```

the TagHelperContext object stores one item for the asp-for attribute, but the TagHelperOutput object stores all attributes generated for the element including items for the type, id, name, and value attributes as well as any data validation attributes.

Since the AllAttributes property stores an item for the asp-for attribute, you can use it to get information about the property that the targeted element is bound to. To do that, you need to convert that item to the ModelExpression type that's available from the ViewFeatures namespace shown in the first code example.

The second table in this figure shows three of the properties of the ModelExpression class. The Name property stores the name of the bound property, and the Model property stores its value. However, the Model property is of the Object type. As a result, you may need to cast it to the actual data type of the property. Finally, the Metadata property contains other attributes of the bound property, including the value of any Display attribute.

The second code example shows the tag helper from the previous figure after it has been updated to use the TagHelperContext object to get the asp-for attribute. To do that, this code casts the value of the asp-for attribute that's available from the AllAttributes item to a ModelExpression type. Then, it casts the value of the Model property to the int type, which is the type of the Quantity property.

Within the loop, the code checks whether the value of the counter matches the value from the Model property. If so, the code adds a selected attribute to the <option> element. This marks the option that matches the current Quantity value as selected.

One property of the TagHelperContext class

Property	Description
AllAttributes	A list containing all attributes of the targeted element.

Three properties of the ModelExpression class

Property	Description
Name	The name of the bound property.
Model	The value of the bound property.
Metadata	Other attributes of the bound property including the display name.

The using statement for the ViewFeatures namespace

```
using Microsoft.AspNetCore.Mvc.ViewFeatures;    // for ModelExpression
```

The updated NumberDropDownTagHelper class

```
[HtmlTargetElement("select", Attributes = "my-min-number, my-max-number")]
public class NumberDropDownTagHelper : TagHelper
{
    // Min and Max properties same as before

    public override void Process(TagHelperContext context,
    TagHelperOutput output)
    {
        // get selected value from view's model
        ModelExpression aspfor =
            (ModelExpression) context.AllAttributes["asp-for"].Value;
        int modelValue = (int)aspfor.Model;

        for (int i = Min; i <= Max; i++)
        {
            TagBuilder option = new TagBuilder("option");
            option.InnerHtml.Append(i.ToString());

            // mark option as selected if matches model's value
            if (modelValue == i)
                option.Attributes["selected"] = "selected";

            output.Content.AppendHtml(option);
        }
    }
}
```

Description

- The ModelExpression class represents a model property that's bound to an element with the asp-for tag helper.
- You can use the AllAttributes property of the TagHelperContext class to retrieve a ModelExpression object for a bound element.

Figure 15-8   How to work with the model property that an element is bound to

How to use a ViewContext object with a tag helper

In some cases, a tag helper will need access to the ViewContext object. That way, it can work with the data for the view such as its route data, ViewData, session state, TempData, and so on. The first example in figure 15-9 shows the code for a tag helper class that gets the ViewContext.

The tag helper class in this example marks an <a> element in a Bootstrap navbar as active. To do that, it declares a public property of the ViewContext type. Then, it decorates that property with the ViewContext attribute. Interestingly, this data type and attribute are in different namespaces as shown by this example. This example also shows that the ViewContext property should be decorated with the HtmlAttributeNotBound attribute. This tells MVC that the value doesn't come from the HTML of the view.

Once you've coded a property with the ViewContext data type and attribute, MVC automatically sets this property to the view's ViewContext object. In other words, you don't need to do any further configuration for this to work.

In the Process() method, the code uses the ViewContext object to get the name of the current area and controller from the Values property of the RouteData property. Then, it uses the AllAttributes property of the TagHelperContext object to get the values of the "asp-area" and "asp-controller" tag helpers. Since there's always a controller value, the statements that get the controller values don't provide default values. Instead, they use the null-forgiving operator (!) to suppress any null reference warnings in Visual Studio.

Next, the code compares the current area and controller with the corresponding tag helper values. If they match, the tag helper appends the Bootstrap active class to the class attribute of the <a> element. This removes the need for the layout to use Razor code to set the active link, without adding any extra attributes to the Bootstrap navbar.

How to use dependency injection with a tag helper

Dependency injection (DI) provides a way to inject the objects that a class needs into the class without explicitly creating them within that class. If you've already read chapter 14, you shouldn't have any trouble understanding how to use DI with tag helpers. If you haven't read that chapter, you might want to skim it before continuing.

The second tag helper class in figure 15-9 has a constructor that accepts an ICart parameter. If you map a dependency for the Cart class as described in chapter 14, MVC automatically passes a Cart object to this constructor. Then, the constructor stores this object in the private cart variable. As a result, the Process() method can use the Count property of the Cart object to set the text of the targeted <span> element.

A tag helper that gets a ViewContext object

```
using Microsoft.AspNetCore.Mvc.ViewFeatures;    // ViewContext attribute
using Microsoft.AspNetCore.Mvc.Rendering;       // ViewContext data type
...
[HtmlTargetElement("a", Attributes = "[class=nav-link]", ParentTag = "li")]
public class ActiveNavbarTagHelper : TagHelper
{
    [ViewContext]
    [HtmlAttributeNotBound]
    public ViewContext ViewCtx { get; set; } = null!;

    public override void Process(TagHelperContext context,
    TagHelperOutput output)
    {
        string area = ViewCtx.RouteData.Values["area"]?.ToString() ?? "";
        string ctlr = ViewCtx.RouteData.Values["controller"]?.ToString()!;

        string aspArea = context.AllAttributes["asp-area"]?.Value?
            .ToString() ?? "";
        string aspCtlr = context.AllAttributes["asp-controller"]?.Value?
            .ToString()!;

        if (area == aspArea && ctlr == aspCtlr)
            output.Attributes.AppendCssClass("active");
    }
}
```

A tag helper that gets a Cart object via dependency injection

```
[HtmlTargetElement("span", Attributes = "my-cart-badge")]
public class CartBadgeTagHelper : TagHelper
{
    private ICart cart;
    public CartBadgeTagHelper(ICart c) => cart = c;

    public bool MyCartBadge { get; set; }

    public override void Process(TagHelperContext context,
    TagHelperOutput output)
    {
        output.Content.SetContent(cart.Count?.ToString());
    }
}
```

The tag helper in a layout

```
<span class="fas fa-shopping-cart"></span> Cart
<span class="badge bg-light text-dark" my-cart-badge></span>
```

Description

- If you create a property of the ViewContext type and decorate it with the ViewContext attribute, MVC automatically sets the value of that property to the value of the ViewContext object.

- The HtmlAttributeNotBound attribute tells MVC that a property isn't set in the HTML.

- You can use dependency injection to inject a custom object into a tag helper.

Figure 15-9   How to use ViewContext and dependency injection with a tag helper

This tag helper removes the need for the layout to use Razor code to display the count in the cart badge. However, it does require a my-cart-badge attribute like the one shown in the third example. Note that the Process() method for this tag helper doesn't use the corresponding MyCartBadge property. Instead, this property is included to prevent the my-cart-badge attribute that's coded in the layout from being sent to the browser.

How to create a conditional tag helper

Sometimes, you only want to display an HTML element under certain conditons. For instance, the first code example in figure 15-10 presents a layout that uses Razor code to only display an <h4> element if there's a message in TempData.

Then, the second code example shows how to use a tag helper to perform the same task. To do that, the tag helper can use the SuppressOutput() method that's summarized in the table. This method prevents MVC from sending any HTML for the targeted element to the browser.

In the second example, the tag helper class begins by getting the ViewContext object from the layout using the technique presented in the previous figure. Then, within the Process() method, the code uses the ViewContext object to get the TempData property and store it in a variable named td. Next, the code checks whether the key named message is in TempData.

If the key is in TempData, the code calls the BuildTag() extension method of the TagHelperOutput class and passes it a tag name of "h4" and a string that specifies several Bootstrap CSS classes. This transforms the non-standard my-temp-message element into a standard <h4> element and sets its class attribute. Next, it sets the content of the <h4> element to display the message from TempData.

However, if the key isn't in TempData, the code calls the SuppressOutput() method. This tells MVC to not send any HTML for the tag helper.

The third code example shows the layout after it's updated to use this tag helper. This shows that the code that uses the tag helper is more concise than the Razor code. In fact, no Razor code is needed to implement this functionality in the layout.

A layout that only displays an element if there's a value in TempData

```
<main>
    @if (TempData.ContainsKey("message"))
    {
        <h4 class="bg-info text-center text-white p-2">
            @TempData["message"]
        </h4>
    }
    @RenderBody()
</main>
```

A method of the TagHelperOutput class

Method	Description
SuppressOutput()	Prevents MVC from sending any HTML for the targeted element to the browser.

A tag helper that only outputs HTML if there's a value in TempData

```
using Microsoft.AspNetCore.Mvc.ViewFeatures;    // ViewContext attribute
using Microsoft.AspNetCore.Mvc.Rendering;       // ViewContext data type
...
[HtmlTargetElement("my-temp-message")]
public class TempMessageTagHelper : TagHelper
{
    [ViewContext]
    [HtmlAttributeNotBound]
    public ViewContext ViewCtx { get; set; } = null!;

    public override void Process(TagHelperContext context,
    TagHelperOutput output)
    {
        var td = ViewCtx.TempData;
        if (td.ContainsKey("message"))
        {
            output.BuildTag("h4", "bg-info text-center text-white p-2");
            output.Content.SetContent(td["message"].ToString());
        }
        else
        {
            output.SuppressOutput();
        }
    }
}
```

A layout that uses the conditional tag helper

```
<main>
    <my-temp-message />
    @RenderBody()
</main>
```

Description

- You can use the SuppressOutput() method of the TagHelperOutput class to create tag helpers that only send HTML to the browser under certain conditions.

Figure 15-10   How to create a conditional tag helper

How to generate URLs in a tag helper

Sometimes, you need your tag helper to generate a URL. In such a case, it's better to use the routing system to generate that URL rather than hardcoding the URL. MVC provides a LinkGenerator class that allows you to use the routing system to generate URLs.

Figure 15-11 presents a tag helper class that uses a LinkGenerator object to create a paging link. This class has a constructor that accepts a LinkGenerator object. When you code a constructor this way, MVC automatically injects the LinkGenerator object. You don't have to do any other configuration.

This tag helper class has a property named Number of the int type. This is how the tag helper gets the page number for the link it's creating. In addition, the tag helper has a property named Current of the GridData type like the one presented in chapter 13. This is how the tag helper gets the current route segments it needs to build the route-based URL.

Within the Process() method, the code calls the Clone() method of the GridData property to get a copy of the route segments. Then, it updates the PageNumber route segment to the value for this paging link.

Next, the code uses the ViewContext object to get the name of the current controller and action method. Then, it passes these values and a dictionary that contains the updated route segments to the GetPathByAction() method of the LinkGenerator class. This method returns a route-based URL, which the code stores in a variable named url.

After creating the URL for the paging link, the code builds the CSS for the paging link. First, it codes a string named linkClasses with two Bootstrap CSS classes. Then, it checks whether the value in the Number property matches the current page number. If it does, the code appends the active class to the linkClasses string.

Finally, the code calls the BuildLink() extension method of the TagHelperOutput class and passes it the route-based URL and the linkClasses string. This transforms the non-standard my-paging-link element to a standard <a> element and sets its href and class attributes. Then, it sets the content of the <a> element to display the value in the Number property.

The second example shows a view that uses this tag helper. This shows how the Number and Current properties in the class correspond to the number and current attributes in the view. The counter variable for the loop supplies the value for the number attribute, and the CurrentRoute property of the view's Model object supplies the value for the current attribute.

A tag helper that generates a paging link

```
using Microsoft.AspNetCore.Mvc.ViewFeatures;    // ViewContext attribute
using Microsoft.AspNetCore.Mvc.Rendering;       // ViewContext data type
using Bookstore.Models;                          // GridData
...
[HtmlTargetElement("my-paging-link")]
public class PagingLinkTagHelper : TagHelper
{
    private LinkGenerator linkBuilder;
    public PagingLinkTagHelper(LinkGenerator lg) => linkBuilder = lg;

    [ViewContext]
    [HtmlAttributeNotBound]
    public ViewContext ViewCtx { get; set; } = null!;

    public int Number { get; set; }
    public GridData Current { get; set; } = null!;

    public override void Process(TagHelperContext context,
    TagHelperOutput output)
    {
        // update routes for this paging link
        var routes = Current.Clone();
        routes.PageNumber = Number;

        // get controller and action method, create paging link URL
        string ctlr = ViewCtx.RouteData.
            Values["controller"]?.ToString() ?? "";
        string action = ViewCtx.RouteData.
            Values["action"]?.ToString() ?? "";
        string url = linkBuilder.GetPathByAction(
            action, ctlr, routes.ToDictionary()) ?? "";

        // build up CSS string
        string linkClasses = "btn btn-outline-primary";
        if (Number == Current.PageNumber)
            linkClasses += " active";

        output.BuildLink(url, linkClasses);
        output.Content.SetContent(Number.ToString());
    }
}
```

A view that uses the tag helper

```
@{
    for (int i = 1; i <= Model.TotalPages; i++) {
        <my-paging-link number="@i" current="@Model.CurrentRoute" />
    }
}
```

Description

- You can use the GetPathByAction() method of the LinkGenerator class to generate a route-based URL.

- If your tag helper has a constructor with a LinkGenerator parameter, MVC will inject it.

Figure 15-11   How to generate URLs in a tag helper

How to work with partial views

By now, you've learned that a tag helper is a powerful tool that provides many ways to reduce code duplication in a view. However, if you find yourself coding a tag helper that outputs a lot of HTML, it might be better to use a partial view.

How to create and use a partial view

A *partial view* can contain HTML, Razor code, or a combination of the two. Partial views are useful for blocks of HTML or Razor code that occur in multiple places in an app or in multiple apps.

To create a partial view, you start by following the same procedure for creating a normal view. Then, in the Add Razor View dialog, you check the "Create as a partial view" box as shown in figure 15-12. Since a partial view is just a view, it's OK if you forget to check this checkbox. In that case, you just need to delete the HTML that Visual Studio generates for a normal view.

When you create a partial view, you can name it whatever you want. Many developers prefer to add a prefix of an underscore and a suffix of Partial to the name of a partial view, and that's the approach this book uses. However, this isn't required.

Like other views, MVC expects partial views to be in the Views folder. MVC looks for a partial view in the folder for the current controller and in the Shared folder as shown by the first example.

When you create a new project for an ASP.NET Core web app with the MVC template, Visual Studio generates a partial view named _ValidationScriptsPartial in the Views/Shared folder. This partial view contains <script> tags for the jQuery validation libraries shown in the second example. Then, you can include this partial view in any page that requires validation.

To use a partial view, you need to tell MVC where in your view to insert the partial view. To do that, you can use the partial tag helper as shown by the third example. This renders the partial view asynchronously, which is usually what you want.

The fourth example shows a partial view named _NavbarMenuButtonPartial. This partial view contains the HTML for the menu button portion of a Bootstrap navbar. This is a good candidate for a partial view because it's needed in many apps, it doesn't usually change from one app to the next, and it's easy to type the HTML incorrectly.

The fifth example shows a layout that uses the partial tag helper to include the _NavbarMenuButtonPartial view as part of a Bootstrap navbar. This reduces several lines of HTML to a single line.

The Add Razor View dialog

How to add a partial view

- Right click the desired folder location and select Add→View.
- Use the Razor View template and check the Create as a partial view checkbox.

The paths that MVC searches for a partial view

```
/Views/ControllerName/PartialViewName
/Views/Shared/PartialViewName
```

A partial view that loads the jQuery validation libraries

```
<script src="~/lib/jquery-validation/dist/jquery.validate.min.js"></script>
<script src="~/lib/jquery-validation-unobtrusive/
              jquery.validate.unobtrusive.min.js"></script>
```

A tag helper that includes the partial view in a view

```
<partial name="_ValidationScriptsPartial" />
```

A partial view that contains the HTML for a Bootstrap navbar menu button

```
<button class="navbar-toggler" type="button" data-bs-toggle="collapse"
    data-bs-target="#menu" aria-controls="menu" aria-expanded="false"
    aria-label="Toggle navigation">
    <span class="navbar-toggler-icon"></span>
</button>
```

A layout that uses the partial view in a Bootstrap navbar

```
<nav class="navbar navbar-expand-md navbar-dark bg-dark">
    <partial name="_NavbarMenuButtonPartial" />
    <div class="collapse navbar-collapse" id="menu">
        <ul class="navbar-nav me-auto">...</ul>
    </div>
</nav>
```

Description

- A *partial view* can contain HTML and Razor code that can be used in multiple views.

Figure 15-12   How to create and use a partial view

How to pass data to a partial view

MVC treats a partial view as part of the view it's added to. As a result, the partial view can use the model object of the parent view. That means the model object for a partial view can change, depending on the parent view.

If that's not what you want, you can specify the model for a partial view. In that case, you can use the model attribute or the for attribute of the partial tag helper. These attributes are presented in the table in figure 15-13. Since these attributes are both used to set the model value, you can't use them together. In other words, if you set the model property, you can't set the for property.

A partial view also uses the same ViewData dictionary as the parent view. However, you can use the viewData attribute of the partial tag helper to change that too.

Below the table, the first example shows a partial view that creates a link to the details page for a book. To work properly, this partial view needs a Book object as its model object. Note here that a partial view can use built-in tag helpers like asp-action and asp-route-id in its HTML just like any other view.

If the parent view uses a Book object as its model object, you can use the partial tag helper as shown in the second example to include the _BookLinkPartial view. This works because the parent view uses a Book object as its model. As a result, there's no need to specify the model object.

However, if the parent view doesn't use a Book object as its model object, the partial tag helper needs to set the model for the partial view. In the third example, for instance, the parent view uses a BookListViewModel object as its model. As a result, the partial tag helper for the _BookLinkPartial view uses the model attribute to specify a Book object as its model. To do that, it uses a Razor expression to specify the name of the variable within the loop that contains a Book object.

Four attributes of the partial tag helper

Attribute	Description
name	The name of the partial view to render. This attribute is required.
model	The object for the partial view to use as its model. May not be used with the for attribute.
for	The object for the partial view to use as its model. May not be used with the model attribute.
viewData	The ViewDataDictionary object for the partial view to use as its ViewData.

The _BookLinkPartial partial view

```
@model Book

<a asp-action="Details" asp-controller="Book"
    asp-route-id="@Model.BookId"
    asp-route-slug="@Model.Title.Slug()">
    @Model.Title
</a>
```

The partial view included in a view that has the same model object

The Home/Index view

```
@model Book
...
<h5>
    <partial name="_BookLinkPartial" />
</h5>
...
```

The partial view included in a view that has a different model object

The Book/List view

```
@model BookListViewModel
...
@foreach (Book book in Model.Books) {
<tr>
    <td>
        <partial name="_BookLinkPartial" model="@book" />
    </td>
...
```

Description

- By default, the model object of a partial view is the model object of the parent view.

- By default, the ViewData dictionary of a partial view is the ViewData dictionary of the parent view.

- If you want the partial view to use a different model or ViewData dictionary, you can use the attributes of the partial tag helper to specify that model or dictionary.

Figure 15-13   How to pass data to a partial view

How to work with view components

Tag helpers and partial views provide many benefits, but they have downsides too. Tag helpers become unwieldy if they generate too much HTML, and partial views may behave differently from view to view. Both depend on the controller of the parent view for their data, and both are difficult to test. Luckily, view components solve most of these problems.

How to create and use a view component

A view component has two parts. First it has a class that functions as its controller. Second, it has a partial view that functions as its view. The class is a regular C# class that inherits the ViewComponent class, which is in the Microsoft.AspNetCore.Mvc namespace. Many developers store these classes in a separate folder named Components, but that isn't required.

Unlike the TagHelper class, the ViewComponent class doesn't have virtual methods to override. Instead, MVC typically expects a view component class to contain a method named Invoke(). This method is described in figure 15-14.

The first example shows that the view component class in the second example is stored in the Components folder. This class is named CartBadge, and it inherits the ViewComponent class. The ViewComponent class defines a synchronous Invoke() method. Like a controller class, the view component class has a constructor that accepts an ICart object via dependency injection.

Within the view component class, the Invoke() method functions like an action method. It passes the Count property of the Cart object to the view via the View() method. That makes it easy to test this view component using the techniques described in chapter 14. This is an improvement on the CartBadge tag helper presented earlier in this chapter because that tag helper would be hard to test.

The third example shows the partial view that's returned by the view component class. This partial view has a model object of a nullable int, which is the type that's returned by the Count property of the Cart object. Then, the partial view uses that object as the content of a <span> tag.

By default, MVC searches for the partial view that's associated with the view component class in the paths presented in the fourth example. However, you can override these default paths as shown in the next figure.

The last example shows how to use tag helper syntax to add a view component to a view. Here, the tag name consists of a prefix of "vc:" plus the name of the view component class. As with tag helpers, MVC translates between the Pascal case of the class name and the kebab case of the tag.

Although you'll typically code synchronous methods in your view components, you can also code asynchronous methods. To do that, you use the InvokeAsync() method instead of the Invoke() method. In that case, your method signature looks like this:

```
public async Task<IViewComponentResult> InvokeAsync()
```

A method MVC looks for in a ViewComponent class

Method	Description
`Invoke([params])`	Defines the logic of the view component and then calls a partial view.
	Is similar to an action method of a controller.
	Can have zero or more parameters.
	Returns an IViewComponentResult object.
	Has an asynchronous version named InvokeAsync() that returns a Task<IViewComponentResult> object.

The folder that stores the view component classes

```
/Components
```

A view component class that passes the Cart count to a partial view

```
using Microsoft.AspNetCore.Mvc;     // for view component classes
...
public class CartBadge : ViewComponent
{
    private ICart cart { get; set; }
    public CartBadge(ICart c) => cart = c;

    public IViewComponentResult Invoke() => View(cart.Count);
}
```

The Default.cshtml partial view

```
@model  int?
<span class="badge bg-light text-dark">@Model</span>
```

The paths that MVC searches for a view component's partial view

```
/Views/ControllerName/Components/ViewComponentName/ViewName
/Views/Shared/Components/ViewComponentName/ViewName
```

A layout that uses tag helper syntax to call the view component

```
<span class="fas fa-shopping-cart"></span> Cart
<vc:cart-badge></vc:cart-badge>
```

Description

- A *view component* is a class that sends data to a partial view. You can think of a view component as a controller for a partial view.
- To create a view component, you can create a new class file in the Components folder that inherits the ViewComponent class. Then, you typically code an Invoke() method as described above.
- The partial view for a view component is usually named Default.cshtml.
- You use tag helper syntax with a prefix of "vc:" to use a view component. For this to work, you must register the custom tag helpers for your app as described in figure 15-1.

Figure 15-14   How to create and use a view component

How to pass data to a view component

One way to pass data to a view component is via dependency injection as shown in the previous figure. Another way is to add one or more parameters to the Invoke() method. These parameters correspond to the attributes in the tag helper for the view component. Visual Studio even provides IntelliSense support for them. As you would expect, MVC automatically translates between the camel casing of the parameter name and the kebab casing of the tag helper attribute.

The first example in figure 15-15 presents a view component class named BookDetailsLink that creates a link to the Book/Details view. The partial view for this view component is the _BookLinkPartial partial view shown in the second example. This is the same partial view that you saw in figure 15-13. Its model is a Book object, and it uses this object to build an <a> element.

You can use the BookDetailsLink view component with views that need to link to the Book/Details page, but whose model object doesn't contain the Book object that the partial view expects. The Invoke() method of this view component accepts an int parameter named id and a string parameter named title. Then, it creates a new Book object and assigns the id parameter to the BookId property and the title parameter to the Title property.

The last statement in the Invoke() method calls the View() method and passes it two arguments. The first argument specifies a fully qualified path to the view file. This overrides the default search done by MVC. That means that, rather than looking for a view file named Default.cshtml in the default folders described in the previous figure, MVC looks for a view file named _BookLinkPartial.cshmtl in the Views/Shared folder. This is a useful technique when you want to reuse a partial view.

The second argument specifies the Book object created by the Invoke() method as the model for the partial view. This ensures that the partial view has the model it expects to create a link to the Book/Details view.

The third example shows how to use the BookDetailsLink view component in the Cart/Index view, which includes a link to the Book/Details view for each item in the cart. Here, a Razor loop gets a CartItem object from the List property of the view model. Then, it uses the Book property of that object to pass the BookId and Title values to the view component.

A view component with an Invoke() method that has parameters

```
public class BookDetailsLink : ViewComponent
{
    public IViewComponentResult Invoke(int id, string title)
    {
        Book book = new Book {
            BookId = id,
            Title = title
        };
        return View("~/Views/Shared/_BookLinkPartial.cshtml", book);
    }
}
```

The _BookLinkPartial partial view

```
@model Book

<a asp-action="Details" asp-controller="Book" asp-area=""
    asp-route-id="@Model.BookId"
    asp-route-slug="@Model.Title.Slug()">
    @Model.Title
</a>
```

A view that uses the view component

The Cart/Index view

```
@foreach (CartItem item in Model.List)  {
    @* use view component rather than partial view here bc CartItem
        Book property is type BookDTO, not Book *@
    <tr>
        <td>
            <vc:book-details-link id="@item.Book.BookId"
                title="@item.Book.Title"></vc:book-details-link>
        </td>
    ...
}
```

Description

- You can pass data to a view component by coding parameters in the Invoke() method. Then, you code the parameter value as an attribute in the tag helper for the view component.

- You can override the default search for the partial view by passing a fully qualified view name and path as the first argument of the View() method.

Figure 15-15   How to pass data to a view component

The Bookstore app

This chapter finishes by showing an updated version of the Bookstore app that uses many of the view components, partial views, and custom tag helpers you've seen in this chapter.

The Book Catalog page

Figure 15-16 presents the Book Catalog page of the Bookstore app. Although this page looks the same as the Book Catalog page from chapter 13, its code uses custom tag helpers, partial views, and view components as shown by the numbered callouts.

The first callout shows the links in the Bootstrap navbar, with the Books link marked as active. In chapter 13, the app marked active links by using Razor code to call a static method in the model. Now, this is handled by the ActiveNavbar tag helper shown in the next figure.

The second callout shows a Bootstrap badge with a value that indicates how many items are in the cart. In chapter 13, the app displayed the item count with Razor code that retrieved cart data from session state. In chapter 14, it handled this by injecting an ICart object into the layout. Now, the CartBadge view component retrieves its own Cart data so the layout doesn't have to.

The third callout shows an <h4> element that displays a message. In chapter 13, the app handled this by using Razor code to check for a TempData message and display the message if it existed. Now, it's handled by the TempMessage tag helper.

The fourth callout shows links for sorting books by title, genre, and price. In chapter 13, the view created these links using repetitive HTML and Razor code. Now, they're created by the SortingLink tag helper, which outputs links with the appropriate URLs and reduces code duplication. The SortingLink tag helper is similar to the PagingLink tag helper.

The fifth and sixth callouts show links to details pages for books and authors. In chapter 13, these links were coded with standard HTML and built-in tag helpers. However, because these links appear on several pages in this app, this caused code duplication. Now, these links are handled by partial views or by view components that re-use those partial views. This reduces code duplication.

The seventh callout shows <button> elements that are styled with Bootstrap CSS classes. Before, the app hardcoded the Bootstrap classes wherever a <button> or <a> element needed them. Now, the Button tag helper automatically applies the Bootstrap classes to specified elements. This reduces code duplication, and it also makes it easier to change the Bootstrap classes for all specified elements if you ever need to do that.

The eighth callout shows link buttons for paging through the books. In chapter 13, the view created these links using repetitive HTML and Razor code. Now, they're created by the PagingLink tag helper, which outputs links with the appropriate URLs and reduces code duplication.

The Book Catalog page

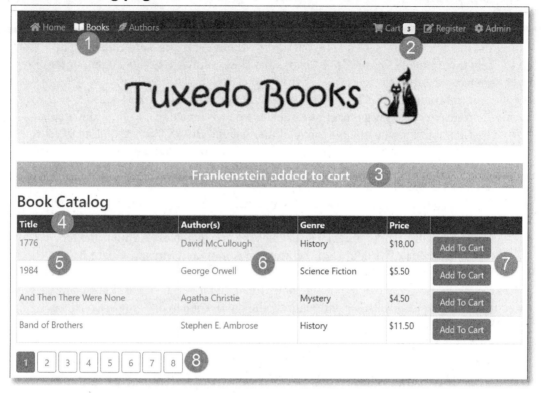

The custom tag helpers, partial views, and view components in this page

1. The ActiveNavbar tag helper from figure 15-9, updated as shown in the next figure.
2. The CartBadge view component from figure 15-14.
3. The TempMessage tag helper from figure 15-10.
4. A SortingLink tag helper that's similar to the PagingLink tag helper from figure 15-11.
5. The _BookLink partial view from figure 15-13.
6. An _AuthorLink partial view that works similarly to the _BookLink partial view.
7. The Button tag helper from figure 15-5.
8. The PagingLink tag helper from figure 15-11.

Description

- This version of the Bookstore app uses custom tag helpers, partial views, and view components to simplify code and reduce code duplication.

Figure 15-16   The Book Catalog page of the Bookstore app

The updated ActiveNavbar tag helper

The Bookstore app has two Bootstrap navbars. One is in the main layout and the other is in the nested layout in the Admin area. The ActiveNavbar tag helper presented in figure 15-17 marks the correct links as active in both of these navbars.

Unfortunately, this tag helper doesn't mark the Admin link as active for all the pages in the Admin area. For instance, when you navigate to the Admin area, the Admin link in the main layout and the Manage Books link are both marked as active. This is what you want. However, when you click on either the Manage Authors or Manage Genres links, the Admin link is greyed out like the rest of the nav links in the main layout. This is *not* what you want.

The ActiveNavbar tag helper behaves like this because it looks for a match for both the area and controller names. For the Admin link and the Manage Books link, this works because it matches the area value of "Admin" and the controller value of "Book". For the Manage Author and Manage Genre links, however, the controller value doesn't match.

To fix this, you can tell the tag helper that under certain conditions it should ignore the controller name and mark the link active when only the area values match. To do that, the tag helper class is updated to add a Boolean property named IsAreaOnly as shown in figure 15-18. Then, the Process() method adds an else if block to the if statement. Within this block, the code checks whether the IsAreaOnly value is true and the current area and the asp-area match. If so, the code marks the link as active.

Once the tag helper is updated like this, the app can include the my-mark-area-active attribute with the Admin link in the main layout. Then, this tag helper marks both the Admin link and the Manage link as active for every page in the Admin area. For instance, the screen in this figure shows the Manage Authors page with both the Admin link and the Manage Authors link marked as active.

The ActiveNavbar tag helper updated to account for the Admin area

```
[HtmlTargetElement("a", Attributes = "[class=nav-link]", ParentTag = "li")]
public class ActiveNavbarTagHelper : TagHelper
{
    [ViewContext]
    [HtmlAttributeNotBound]
    public ViewContext ViewCtx { get; set; }

    [HtmlAttributeName("my-mark-area-active")]
    public bool IsAreaOnly { get; set; }

    public override void Process(TagHelperContext context,
    TagHelperOutput output)
    {
        string area = ViewCtx.RouteData.Values["area"]?.ToString() ?? "";
        string ctlr = ViewCtx.RouteData.Values["controller"].ToString();

        string aspArea = context.AllAttributes["asp-area"]?.Value?
            .ToString() ?? "";
        string aspCtlr = context.AllAttributes["asp-controller"].Value
            .ToString();

        if (area == aspArea && ctlr == aspCtlr)
            output.Attributes.AppendCssClass("active");
        else if (IsAreaOnly && area == aspArea)
            output.Attributes.AppendCssClass("active");
    }
}
```

The two active navbar links on the Manage Authors page of the Admin area

Description

- The Bookstore app uses an updated version of the ActiveNavbar tag helper.
- This tag helper adds a Boolean property that allows you to identify navbar links that should be marked active when just the area names match.

Figure 15-17   The updated ActiveNavbar tag helper

The layout

Figure 15-18 shows the layout for the Bookstore app. This updated layout no longer uses any Razor code blocks. That's because it no longer needs to retrieve or manipulate any data, since that's now handled by the tag helpers and view components.

The body of the layout has a <nav> element that contains the HTML necessary for a Bootstrap navbar. It uses a partial view for the HTML for the navbar's menu button. This keeps the layout cleaner.

Within the navbar, the navigation links are <a> elements that have a class attribute with a value of "nav-link" and a parent tag that's an <li> element. That's exactly what the ActiveNavbar tag helper presented in this chapter targets. As a result, no additional attributes need to be added to most of the navigation links for the tag helper to work.

The only exception is the navigation link for the Admin area. This link needs to tell the tag helper to mark it active when only area names match. To do that, it includes the my-mark-area-active attribute. Since it's a Boolean value, the code only needs to include the attribute name. In other words, it's not necessary to specify a value for this attribute. However, it could also be coded with a true value like this:

```
my-mark-area-active="true"
```

Within the start and end tags for the navigation link for the cart, a <span> element displays an icon for the cart. Then, the code uses the Cart Badge view component to display a badge with the number of items in the cart. This creates another <span> element styled as a Bootstrap badge.

Within the main section of the body, the TempMessage tag helper displays any message that's stored in TempData. Since this is a conditional tag helper, this non-standard element is either transformed to a standard HTML <h4> element or suppressed and not output at all.

The layout

```html
<!DOCTYPE html>
<html lang="en">
<head>...</head>
<body>
    <div class="container">
        <nav class="navbar navbar-expand-md navbar-dark bg-dark ps-3 pe-3">
            <partial name="_NavbarMenuButtonPartial" />
            <div class="collapse navbar-collapse" id="menu">
                <ul class="navbar-nav me-auto">
                    <li class="nav-item">
                        <a class="nav-link" asp-action="Index"
                            asp-controller="Home" asp-area="">
                            <span class="fas fa-home"></span> Home
                        </a>
                    </li>
                    @* nav item links for Books and Authors go here *@
                </ul>
                <ul class="navbar-nav ms-auto">
                    <li class="nav-item">
                        <a class="nav-link" asp-action="Index"
                            asp-controller="Cart" asp-area="">
                            <span class="fas fa-shopping-cart"></span>
                             Cart
                            <vc:cart-badge></vc:cart-badge>
                        </a>
                    </li>
                    @* nav item link for Registration goes here *@
                    <li class="nav-item">
                        <a class="nav-link" asp-action="Index"
                            asp-controller="Book" asp-area="Admin"
                            my-mark-area-active>
                            <span class="fas fa-cog"></span> Admin
                        </a>
                    </li>
                </ul>
            </div>
        </nav>

        <header class="text-center">
            <a asp-action="Index" asp-controller="Home">
                <img src="~/images/logo.png" class="img-fluid center-block" />
            </a>
        </header>

        <main>
            <my-temp-message />
            @RenderBody()
        </main>
    </div>
    <script src="~/lib/jquery/dist/jquery.min.js"></script>
    <script src="~/lib/bootstrap/dist/js/bootstrap.bundle.min.js"></script>
    <script src="~/js/site.js" asp-append-version="true"></script>
    @RenderSection("Scripts", required: false)
</body>
</html>
```

Figure 15-18   The layout of the Bookstore app

The Book/List view

Figure 15-19 shows the Book/List view for the Bookstore app. It has a <form> element that posts to the Add() action method of the Cart controller when one of the Add to Cart buttons in the HTML table is clicked.

The add to cart form uses the SortingLink tag helper to create three links that allow the user to sort books by title, genre, and price. This tag helper accepts a value from the view that indicates what field each link should sort by. In addition, this tag helper accepts the value of the CurrentRoute property of the BookListViewModel model object, which the tag helper uses to build the appropriate URL for each link.

The add to cart form also includes partial views named _BookLinkPartial and _AuthorLinkPartial. Both of these partial views add links to a details page. The book partial view needs a Book object as a model, and the author partial view needs an Author object as a model. Since the model object for the view contains Book and Author objects, the code can use the model attribute to pass an appropriate model object to each partial view.

The Add to Cart buttons in the form have a type attribute of "submit". These buttons don't include any Bootstrap classes. However, the Button tag helper applies to any element that has a type attribute with a value of "submit", and it provides Bootstrap classes to style buttons. As a result, you can have <button> elements like this throughout your app, and the tag helper applies the styles. Because the styling for all of these buttons is stored in the same place, this makes it easy to change the styling of your buttons.

Below the add form, a Razor loop provides the links for paging through the books. To do that, it uses the PagingLink tag helper. This tag helper accepts the value of the loop counter as the page number for each link. And, like the SortingLink tag helper, this tag helper accepts the value of the CurrentRoute property of the BookListViewModel model object, which it uses to build the appropriate URL for each link.

The Book/List view

```
@model BookListViewModel
...
@* add to cart form *@
<form asp-action="Add" asp-controller="Cart" method="post">
    <table class="table table-bordered table-striped table-sm">
        <thead class="bg-dark text-white">
            <tr>
                <th>
                    <my-sorting-link sort-field="Title"
                    current="@Model.CurrentRoute">Title</my-sorting-link></th>
                <th>Author(s)</th>
                <th>
                    <my-sorting-link sort-field="Genre"
                    current="@Model.CurrentRoute">Genre</my-sorting-link></th>
                <th>
                    <my-sorting-link sort-field="Price"
                    current="@Model.CurrentRoute">Price</my-sorting-link></th>
                <th></th>
            </tr>
        </thead>
        <tbody>
            @foreach (Book book in Model.Books) {
            <tr>
                <td><partial name="_BookLinkPartial" model="@book" /></td>
                <td>
                    @foreach (var author in book.Authors) {
                        <p><partial name="_AuthorLinkPartial"
                            model="@author" /></p>
                    }
                </td>
                <td>@book.Genre?.Name</td>
                <td>@book.Price.ToString("c")</td>
                <td><button type="submit" name="id" value="@book.BookId">
                    Add To Cart</button></td>
            </tr>
            }
        </tbody>
    </table>
</form>

@{
    for (int i = 1; i <= Model.TotalPages; i++) {
        <my-paging-link number="@i" current="@Model.CurrentRoute" />
    }
}
```

Figure 15-19   The Book/List view of the Bookstore app

Perspective

This chapter has shown how to create and use custom tag helpers, partial views, and view components. You can use these features to reduce code duplication in your views, which makes your views more flexible and easier to maintain. In addition, you can use these features to simplify the code for your controllers and view models.

Terms

partial view
view component

Summary

- A *partial view* can contain HTML and Razor code that can be used in multiple views within an app or multiple apps.

- A *view component* is a class that sends data to a partial view. You can think of a view component as a controller for a partial view.

Exercise 15-1   Add some custom tag helpers and a view component

In this exercise, you'll add some custom tag helpers to the Class Schedule web app from the exercises for chapter 12. Then, you'll add a view component.

Run the app and review the HTML

1. Open the Ch15Ex1ClassSchedule app in the ex_starts directory.

2. If you didn't do the exercise for chapter 12 or 14, open the Package Manager Console and enter the Update-Database command to create the database for this app.

3. Run the app. On the first page, note that the links for the days aren't working. Also, note that the Edit and Delete links to the right of each class aren't working.

4. Click the Add Class link. On the Add Class page, note that the Cancel link doesn't work and the Add button doesn't have any styling.

5. In the Views folder, open the Home/Index view. Note that this code uses a <my-link-button> element for the day of the week links. This element is not standard HTML. In addition, note that the Edit and Delete links use the same non-standard <my-link-button> element.

6. Open the Class/AddEdit view. Note that the Save submit button doesn't specify Bootstrap CSS classes for styling, and the Cancel link uses a non-standard <my-link-button> element.

Add a tag helper to style submit buttons

7. Open the _ViewImports.cshtml file and add an @addTagHelper directive that registers all custom tag helpers for this web app.

8. Open the TagHelpers folder and review the code in the ExtensionMethods.cs file.

9. In the TagHelpers folder, add a class named SubmitButtonTagHelper that inherits the TagHelper class.

10. Decorate this class with an HtmlTargetElement attribute that applies this tag helper to all submit buttons.

11. Override the Process() method and add code that uses the AppendCssClass() extension method to apply the Bootstrap btn and btn-dark classes.

12. Run the app and view the Save buttons on the Add Class and Add Teacher pages. They should be styled correctly now.

Add a tag helper to transform the <my-link-button> element

13. In the TagHelpers folder, add a class named MyLinkButtonTagHelper that inherits the TagHelper class.

14. Within this class, add public string properties named Action, Controller, and Id.

15. Update the class to get a ViewContext object and to receive a LinkGenerator object via dependency injection.

16. In the Process() method, assign the value of the Action property to a string variable. Or, if the Action property is null, assign the value of the "action" item of the RouteData.Values collection.

17. Repeat the previous step for the Controller property.

18. Use the Id property to create an anonymous object for the id route segment, and assign it to a variable named id.

19. Use the action, controller, and id variables with the LinkGenerator object to create a URL, and assign this URL to a string variable.

20. Assign Bootstrap CSS classes to a string variable named css. If the value of the "id" item of the RouteData.Values collection of the ViewContext object matches the value of the Id proerty, assign the btn and btn-dark classes. Otherwise, assign the btn and btn-outline-dark classes.

21. Use the variables for the URL and the CSS classes with the BuildLink() extension method to transform a non-standard <my-link-button> element to a standard <a> element.

22. Run the app. Then, view the link buttons on the various pages. If you hover your mouse over a link button, the app should display the URL that the tag helper generated for it. And if you click on a link, it should work correctly.

Add a view component for the link buttons for the days of the week

23. Add a folder named Components.

24. In the Components folder, add a new class named DayFilter that inherits the ViewComponent class.

25. Update the class to receive an IRepository<Day> object via dependency injection. To do that, you can use the Teacher controller as a guide.

26. Add an Invoke() method that returns an IViewComponentResult object.

27. In the Invoke() method, add code that uses the IRepository<Day> object to get a collection of Day objects sorted by DayId. Use the View() method to pass this collection to the partial view.

28. Create a folder for the component's partial view. Make sure to create this folder in the location where MVC expects it.

29. In this folder, add a new partial view named Default.cshtml.

30. Declare the model of the partial view to be an IEnumerable<Day> object.

31. Move the Razor foreach loop from the Home/Index view to this partial view. Change the loop condition to loop through the Days collection that's stored in the model rather than the collection that's stored in the ViewBag.

32. Build the solution. Then, use tag helper syntax to add the view component to the Home/Index view where the foreach loop used to be. Note how this simplifies the view code.

33. Open the HomeController class and review its code. This controller no longer needs to send Day objects to the view. As a result, you can remove all of that code. Also, you can modify the constructor to only receive a Repository<Class> object. Note how this simplifies the controller code.

34. Run the app and make sure the day link buttons still work correctly.

16

How to authenticate and authorize users

The Bookstore app that you've seen in previous chapters allows any user to access any of its pages. Now, this chapter shows how to restrict access to some pages so only authorized users can access those pages. To provide this functionality, this chapter shows how to use ASP.NET Identity.

An introduction to authentication

If you want to limit access to all or part of your ASP.NET app to certain users, you can use *authentication* to verify each user's identity. Then, once you have authenticated the user, you can use *authorization* to check if the user has the appropriate privileges for accessing a page. That way, you can prevent unauthorized users from accessing pages that they shouldn't be able to access.

Three types of authentication

Figure 16-1 describes three types of authentication you can use in ASP.NET Core apps. The first, called *Windows-based authentication*, requires that you set up a Windows user account for each user. Then, you use standard Windows security features to restrict access to all or part of the app. When a user attempts to access the app, Windows displays a login dialog that asks the user to supply the username and password of the Windows account. This type of authentication is most appropriate for a local setting like a company intranet.

To use *individual user account authentication*, you have a login page that typically requires the user to enter a username and password. Then, ASP.NET displays this page automatically when it needs to authenticate a user who's trying to access the app. This type of authentication works well with web apps, and it's the type of authentication that's presented in this chapter.

In recent years, authentication services offered by third parties such as Google, Facebook, and others have also become popular. This type of authentication provides several advantages, but showing how to use these services is beyond the scope of this book.

Windows-based authentication

- Causes the browser to display a login dialog when the user attempts to access a restricted page.
- Is supported by most browsers.
- Is configured through the IIS management console.
- Uses Windows user accounts and directory rights to grant access to restricted pages.
- Is most appropriate for an intranet app.

Individual user account authentication

- Allows developers to code a login page that gets the username and password.
- Encrypts the username and password entered by the user if the login page uses a secure connection.
- Doesn't rely on Windows user accounts.

Third-party authentication services

- Is provided by third parties such as Google, Facebook, Twitter, and Microsoft using technologies like OpenID and OAuth.
- Allows users to use their existing logins and frees developers from having to worry about the secure storage of user credentials.
- Can issue identities or accept identities from other web apps and access user data on other services.

Description

- *Authentication* refers to the process of validating the identity of a user so the user can be granted access to an app. A user must typically supply a username and password to be authenticated.
- After a user is authenticated, the user must still be authorized to access the requested page. The process of granting user access to a page is called *authorization*.

Figure 16-1   Three types of authentication

How individual user account authentication works

To help you understand how individual user account authorization works, figure 16-2 shows a typical series of exchanges that occur between a web browser and a server when a user attempts to access a page that uses individual user accounts. The authentication process begins when a user requests the page. When the server receives the request, it checks whether the user has already been authenticated. To do that, it looks for an *authentication cookie* in the request for the page. If it doesn't find the cookie, it redirects the browser to the login page.

At the login page, the user enters a username and password and posts the login page back to the server. Then, if the server finds the username/password combination in the database, they are valid. In that case, the server creates an authentication cookie and redirects the browser back to the original page. As a result, when the browser requests the original page, it sends the cookie back to the server. This time, the server sees that the user has been authenticated, so it checks whether the user is authorized to view the protected page. If so, the server sends the requested page back to the browser. Otherwise, it sends a page that indicates that access was denied.

By default, the server sends the authentication cookie as a session cookie. In that case, the server only authenticates the user for the current session. However, the user can often specify that the cookie should be sent as a persistent cookie. Then, the browser automatically sends the authentication cookie for future sessions, until the cookie expires.

HTTP requests and responses with individual user account authentication

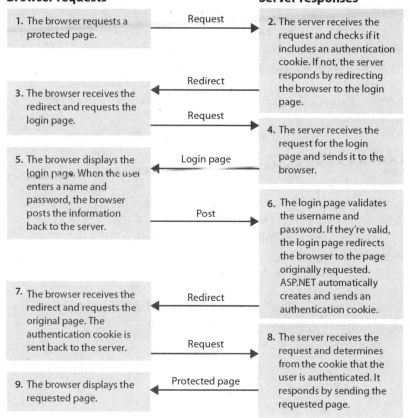

Browser requests

1. The browser requests a protected page.

3. The browser receives the redirect and requests the login page.

5. The browser displays the login page. When the user enters a name and password, the browser posts the information back to the server.

7. The browser receives the redirect and requests the original page. The authentication cookie is sent back to the server.

9. The browser displays the requested page.

Server responses

2. The server receives the request and checks if it includes an authentication cookie. If not, the server responds by redirecting the browser to the login page.

4. The server receives the request for the login page and sends it to the browser.

6. The login page validates the username and password. If they're valid, the login page redirects the browser to the page originally requested. ASP.NET automatically creates and sends an authentication cookie.

8. The server receives the request and determines from the cookie that the user is authenticated. It responds by sending the requested page.

Arrows: Request, Redirect, Request, Login page, Post, Redirect, Request, Protected page

Description

- When ASP.NET Core receives a request for a protected page from a user who has not been authenticated, the server redirects the user to the login page.

- To be authenticated, the user request must contain an *authentication cookie*. By default, this cookie is stored as a session cookie.

- ASP.NET Core automatically creates an authentication cookie when the app indicates that the user should be authenticated. ASP.NET Core checks for the presence of an authentication cookie any time it receives a request for a restricted page.

- The user can often specify that the authentication cookie should be made persistent. Then, the browser automatically sends the authentication cookie for future sessions, until the cookie expires.

Figure 16-2   How individual user account authentication works

An introduction to ASP.NET Identity

In versions of ASP.NET prior to 4.5.1, the Membership and Simple Membership systems provided authentication for ASP.NET apps. However, these systems were difficult to customize. In addition, it was hard or impossible to modify them to work with other data stores, devices, or third-party authentication providers. In response to these issues, Microsoft replaced these membership systems with the ASP.NET Identity system. Figure 16-3 describes some of the benefits of the Identity system.

To start, you can use it with all of the ASP.NET frameworks, including Web Forms and MVC. In addition, Identity is easier to customize, unit test, and update than the membership systems. It also supports claims-based authentication, which is a sophisticated form of authentication that can be more flexible than authorizing users based on roles as described later in this chapter.

Finally, it uses middleware called *OWIN*, or *Open Web Interface for .NET*. OWIN is an open-source project that defines a standard interface between .NET web servers and web apps. The goal of OWIN is to create lightweight components with as few dependencies on other frameworks as possible.

This figure also presents some of the main classes that ASP.NET Identity provides. These classes allow you to work with users and roles. A *role* lets you apply the same access rules to a group of users.

Some classes provided by ASP.NET Identity

Class	Description
IdentityDbContext	An Entity Framework DbContext object for working with the tables of the ASP.NET Identity system.
IdentityUser	Represents a user.
IdentityRole	Represents a role.
UserManager	Provides methods for working with users.
RoleManager	Provides methods for working with roles.
SignInManager	Provides methods for signing in users.
IdentityResult	Represents the result of an identity operation.

Some benefits of Identity

- It can be used with all ASP.NET frameworks, including MVC, Web Forms, Web API, and SignalR to build web, phone, Windows Store, or hybrid apps.

- You have control over the schema of the data store that holds user information, and you can change the storage system from the default of SQL Server.

- It's modular, so it's easier to unit test.

- It supports claims-based authentication, which can be more flexible than using simple roles.

- It supports third-party authentication providers like Google, Facebook, Twitter, and Microsoft.

- It's based on *OWIN (Open Web Interface for .NET)* middleware, which is an open-source project that defines a standard interface between .NET web servers and web apps.

- The classes that you need to work with it from code are available from ASP.NET Core.

Description

- The ASP.NET Identity system became available with ASP.NET 4.5.1. It replaces the ASP.NET Membership and Simple Membership systems and can be used with all ASP.NET frameworks.

- *Roles* let you apply the same access rules to a group of users.

Figure 16-3   An introduction to ASP.NET Identity

How to restrict access to controllers and actions

Figure 16-4 shows how to restrict access to the pages of a web app. To do that, you can apply the attributes in the Authorization namespace to an entire controller or to individual action methods. You can use the Authorization attributes to restrict access to your web pages before you use Identity to provide a way to let authorized users access those pages.

To restrict access to all action methods in a controller, you can decorate the class declaration with an authorization attribute. For instance, the first example decorates the CartController class with the Authorize attribute. This restricts access to all actions in the Cart controller to users who are logged in. However, the first example doesn't require the user to be a member of any role. By contrast, the second example uses the Roles parameter of the Authorize attribute to only grant access to users in the Admin role.

Although it's common to apply authorization attributes to the entire controller, you may sometimes need to apply authorization attributes to a specific action method. To do that, you decorate the declaration for the action method with the appropriate authorization attribute. For instance, the third example decorates the List() action method with the AllowAnonymous attribute. As a result, all users can access this method. This includes authenticated users who have logged in as well as anonymous users who haven't logged in.

In addition, this example decorates the Add() action method with the Authorize attribute. As a result, only users who are logged in can access this method. Similarly, this example decorates the Delete() action method with the Authorize attribute for users in the Admin role. As a result, only users who are logged in and belong to the Admin role can access this method.

The using directive for the Authorization namespace

```
using Microsoft.AspNetCore.Authorization;
```

Attributes for authorization

Attribute	Description
AllowAnonymous	Grants access to all users.
Authorize	Grants access only to logged in users.
Authorize(Roles = "r1, r2")	Grants access only to logged in users that belong to the specified roles.

Code that only allows logged in users to access an entire controller

```
[Authorize]
public class CartController : Controller {
    ...
}
```

Code that only allows logged in users in the Admin role to access an entire controller

```
[Authorize(Roles = "Admin")]
public class BookController : Controller {
    ...
}
```

Code that applies different attributes to different action methods

```
public class ProductController : Controller
{
    ...
    [AllowAnonymous]
    [HttpGet]
    public IActionResult List() {
        ...
    }

    [Authorize]
    [HttpGet]
    public IActionResult Add()
    {
        ...
    }

    [Authorize(Roles = "Admin")]
    [HttpGet]
    public IActionResult Delete(int id)
    {
        ...
    }
    ...
}
```

Description

- To restrict access to the pages of a web app, you can apply the attributes in the Authorization namespace to an entire controller or to individual action methods.

Figure 16-4   How to restrict access to controllers and actions

How to get started with Identity

Now that you've been introduced to some of the basic concepts of authentication and authorization, you're ready to get started with Identity. In particular, this topic shows how to get started with ASP.NET Core Identity.

How to add Identity classes to the DB context

To use ASP.NET Core Identity in your code, you include the using directive for the Microsoft.AspNetCore.Identity namespace as shown at the top of figure 16-5. Then, the table that follows shows some of the properties of the IdentityUser class in this namespace.

When you code a User entity class like the one shown in this figure, it must inherit the IdentityUser class. That way, it has access to the properties defined by this class. As a result, you don't need to code any additional properties if you only want to use properties of the IdentityUser class such as UserName, Email, Password, and ConfirmPassword.

If you want to use ASP.NET Core Identity with EF Core, you also need to add the NuGet package for Identity with EF Core to your project. This package provides classes for communicating with the database using Identity with EF Core. To add this package, you can use the same skills you use to add other NuGet packages. For example, chapter 4 showed how to install the NuGet package for EF Core. Now, figure 16-5 just shows the name of the NuGet package that you need to use ASP.NET Core Identity with EF Core.

Once you've installed the NuGet package for Identity, you can add the User entity class to the DB context class for the app. To do that, you must make sure that the DB context class inherits the IdentityDbContext<User> class, not the standard DbContext class. That way, EF knows to create all of the tables that are needed by Identity.

Finally, in the OnModelCreating() method, you must make sure to pass the ModelBuilder object to the same method of the base class. That's because the IdentityDbContext<T> class provides an implementation of this method that creates the Identity tables. If you don't call this method, you'll get errors when you attempt to update the database.

The using directive for the ASP.NET Core Identity namespace

```
using Microsoft.AspNetCore.Identity
```

Some properties of the IdentityUser class

Property	Description
UserName	The username for the user.
Password	The password for the user.
ConfirmPassword	Used to confirm that the password was entered correctly.
Email	The email address for the user.
EmailConfirmed	Used to confirm that the email was entered correctly.
PhoneNumber	The phone number for the user.
PhoneNumberConfirmed	Used to confirm that the phone number was entered correctly.

The User entity class

```
using Microsoft.AspNetCore.Identity;

namespace Bookstore.Models
{
    public class User : IdentityUser {
        // Inherits all IdentityUser properties
    }
}
```

The NuGet package for Identity with EF Core

```
Microsoft.AspNetCore.Identity.EntityFrameworkCore
```

The Bookstore context class

```
using Microsoft.EntityFrameworkCore;
using Microsoft.AspNetCore.Identity.EntityFrameworkCore;

namespace Bookstore.Models
{
    public class BookstoreContext : IdentityDbContext<User>
    {
        public BookstoreContext(DbContextOptions<BookstoreContext> options)
            : base(options) { }

        public DbSet<Author> Authors { get; set; } = null!;
        public DbSet<Book> Books { get; set; } = null!;
        public DbSet<Genre> Genres { get; set; } = null!;

        protected override void OnModelCreating(ModelBuilder modelBuilder)
        {
            base.OnModelCreating(modelBuilder);

            // configure entities
            modelBuilder.ApplyConfiguration(new ConfigureGenres());
            modelBuilder.ApplyConfiguration(new ConfigureBooks());
            modelBuilder.ApplyConfiguration(new ConfigureAuthors());
            modelBuilder.ApplyConfiguration(new ConfigureBookAuthors());
        }
    }
}
```

Figure 16-5   How to add Identity classes to the DB context

How to add Identity tables to the database

For Identity to work, you must create all the tables it needs in your database. These tables include the AspNetUsers table and the AspNetRoles table. To do that, you can follow the procedure at the top of figure 16-6. Here, the second step creates a migration file that contains the code for adding the tables. Then, the third step updates the database by executing the code in the migration file.

If you code the User entity and DB context classes correctly, the Add-Migration command should generate a migration that creates several tables. For instance, this figure shows the start of the Up() method of the generated migration class. This method begins by creating a table named AspNetRoles that stores the roles for the app. Then, it creates a table named AspNetUsers that stores the users for the app.

Both of these tables contain the basic columns (Id, Name, UserName, Password, and so on) that your app needs to work with simple authorization scenarios. In addition, they contain extra columns (TwoFactorEnabled, LockoutEnabled, and so on) that you may need later for more advanced authorization scenarios. To make sure the Update-Database command executed successfully, you can use the SQL Server Object Explorer or another comparable tool to view the tables for your database. If you can view the Identity tables (AspNetRoles, AspNetUsers, and so on) and their columns, the database has been updated successfully.

A procedure for adding Identity tables to the database

1. Start the Package Manager Console (PMC).
2. Add a migration that adds the tables by entering a command like this one:
   ```
   Add-Migration AddIdentityTables
   ```
3. Update the database by entering a command like this one:
   ```
   Update-Database
   ```

Some of the Up() method of the generated migration class

```
protected override void Up(MigrationBuilder migrationBuilder)
{
    migrationBuilder.CreateTable(
        name: "AspNetRoles",
        columns: table => new {
            Id = table.Column<string>(type: "nvarchar(450)", nullable: false),
            Name = table.Column<string>(type: "nvarchar(256)", maxLength: 256,
                nullable: true),
            NormalizedName = table.Column<string>(type: "nvarchar(256)",
                maxLength: 256, nullable: true),
            ConcurrencyStamp = table.Column<string>(type: "nvarchar(max)",
                nullable: true) },
        constraints: table => {
            table.PrimaryKey("PK_AspNetRoles", x => x.Id);
        });
    migrationBuilder.CreateTable(
        name: "AspNetUsers",
        columns: table => new {
            Id = table.Column<string>(type: "nvarchar(450)", nullable: false),
            UserName = table.Column<string>(type: "nvarchar(256)", maxLength:
                256, nullable: true),
            NormalizedUserName = table.Column<string>(type: "nvarchar(256)",
                maxLength: 256, nullable: true),
            Email = table.Column<string>(type: "nvarchar(256)", maxLength: 256,
                nullable: true),
            NormalizedEmail = table.Column<string>(type: "nvarchar(256)",
                maxLength: 256, nullable: true),
            EmailConfirmed = table.Column<bool>(type: "bit", nullable: false),
            PasswordHash = table.Column<string>(type: "nvarchar(max)", nullable:
                true),
            SecurityStamp = table.Column<string>(type: "nvarchar(max)", nullable:
                true),
            ConcurrencyStamp = table.Column<string>(type: "nvarchar(max)",
                nullable: true),
            PhoneNumber = table.Column<string>(type: "nvarchar(max)", nullable:
                true),
            PhoneNumberConfirmed = table.Column<bool>(type: "bit", nullable:
                false),
            TwoFactorEnabled = table.Column<bool>(type: "bit", nullable: false),
            LockoutEnd = table.Column<DateTimeOffset>(type: "datetimeoffset",
                nullable: true),
            LockoutEnabled = table.Column<bool>(type: "bit", nullable: false),
            AccessFailedCount = table.Column<int>(type: "int", nullable: false)},
        constraints: table => {
            table.PrimaryKey("PK_AspNetUsers", x => x.Id);
        });
    ...
```

Description

- For Identity to work, you must create all the tables it needs in your database. These tables include the AspNetUsers table and the AspNetRoles table.

Figure 16-6   How to add Identity tables to the database

How to configure the middleware for Identity

Figure 16-7 shows how to configure the middleware for Identity. To do that, you can add the code shown in this figure to the Program.cs class. To start, you can add a using directive for the Identity namespace as shown by the first example.

In the section of the Program.cs file that adds services to the container, you can add a statement that adds the Identity service as shown by the second example. This example adds an Identity service with a user defined by the User class shown earlier in this chapter and a role defined by the built-in IdentityRole class mentioned earlier in this chapter. In addition, it specifies the BookstoreContext class shown earlier in this chapter as the data store.

This example uses all of the default options for the Identity service. As a result, Identity requires that a password must be at least 8 characters long with at least one lowercase letter, one uppercase letter, one number, and one special character.

If you want to relax or further restrict the default password options, you can use a lambda expression to set password options as shown in the third example. Here, the password options have been relaxed to only require 6 characters with at least one lowercase and one uppercase letter. Since this allows users to create weak passwords, you probably wouldn't want to relax password requirements on a production system. However, allowing weak passwords can make it easier to test an app.

In the section of the Program.cs file that configures the HTTP request pipeline, you need to add statements that call the UseAuthentication() and UseAuthorization() methods. As you might expect, you need to code these statements in the correct sequence.

The using directive for the Identity namespace

```
using Microsoft.AspNetCore.Identity;
```

How to add the Identity service with default password options

```
...
var builder = WebApplication.CreateBuilder(args);

// other services

builder.Services.AddIdentity<User, IdentityRole>()
    .AddEntityFrameworkStores<BookstoreContext>()
    .AddDefaultTokenProviders();
...
```

Some properties of the PasswordOptions class

Property	Description
RequiredLength	Specifies the minimum length for the password. The default value is 8.
RequireLowercase	Specifies whether the password requires a lowercase letter.
RequireUppercase	Specifies whether the password requires an uppercase letter.
RequireDigit	Specifies whether the password requires a number.
RequireNonAlphanumeric	Specifies whether the password requires a special character.

How to set the password options

```
builder.Services.AddIdentity<User, IdentityRole>(options => {
    options.Password.RequiredLength = 6;
    options.Password.RequireNonAlphanumeric = false;
    options.Password.RequireDigit = false;
}).AddEntityFrameworkStores<BookstoreContext>()
    .AddDefaultTokenProviders();
```

How to configure your app to use authentication and authorization

```
...
var app = builder.Build();
...
app.UseRouting();

app.UseAuthentication();
app.UseAuthorization();

app.UseSession();
...
```

Description

- By default, a password must be at least 8 characters long with at least one lower-case letter, one uppercase letter, one number, and one special character.

Figure 16-7   How to configure the middleware for Identity

How to add Log In/Out buttons and links to the layout

Once you've configured the middleware for Identity, you can begin to add authentication to your app. To start, if your app has a layout that provides a Bootstrap navbar, you can add Log In/Out buttons to it. In addition, you can add a Register link.

In figure 16-8, for example, the first screen shows a navbar that includes a Register link and a Log In button. This is the navbar that's displayed when the user is not logged in. Then, the second screen shows a navbar that includes a Log Out button and a username of joel. This is the navbar that's displayed when the user is logged in.

To provide for a navbar that can change like this, the layout uses a Razor if statement to check whether the user is logged in. But first, it specifies a using directive for the Identity namespace, and it uses an inject directive to inject a SignInManager object named signInManager into the view. Then, the if statement checks whether the user is logged in. To do that, it passes the User property of the view to the IsSignedIn() method of the signInManager object.

If the user is logged in, the layout adds a form that posts to the LogOut() action method of the Account controller. This form contains a Log Out button that submits the form. In addition, it contains a <span> element that displays the username for the logged in user. To do that, it uses the User property of the view to access the authenticated user. Then, it uses the Identity and Name properties to get the username of that user.

If the user is not logged in, the layout displays a Register link that calls the Register() action method of the Account controller. The user can click this link to register a new account with the website. When the Register page is displayed, the register link should be the active link. To accomplish that, this code uses the ViewContext object to get the current action. Then, it uses the static Nav.Active() method to determine if the current action is "Register". If so, the Bootstrap active class is added to the class attribute, and the link is formatted as the active link.

In addition to the Register link, this view displays a Log In link that calls the LogIn() action method of the Account controller. A registered user can click this link to log in to the website. Notice that the Log In link is formatted as a button. That makes it look like the Log Out button.

If you read chapter 15, you should realize that you could also modify the tag helper that determines the active link for the navbar so it works correctly with these links. In addition, you should realize that you could use a view component or partial view for these Login buttons and links.

The Register link and the Log In button in the navbar

The Log Out button in the navbar

Some of the code for the navbar in the layout

```
<!-- Home, Books, Authors, and Cart links go here -->

@using Microsoft.AspNetCore.Identity
@inject SignInManager<User> signInManager
@if (signInManager.IsSignedIn(User))
{
    // signed-in user - Log Out button and username
    <li class="nav-item">
        <form method="post" asp-action="Logout" asp-controller="Account"
            asp-area="">
            <input type="submit" value="Log Out"
                class="btn btn-outline-light" />
            <span class="text-light">@User.Identity.Name</span>
        </form>
    </li>
}
else
{
    // get current action
    var action = ViewContext.RouteData.Values["action"]?.ToString();

    // anonymous user - Register link and Log In button
    <li class="nav-item @Nav.Active("Register", action)">
        <a asp-action="Register" asp-controller="Account" asp-area=""
            class="nav-link">
            <span class="fas fa-edit"></span> Register</a>
    </li>
    <li class="nav-item">
        <a asp-action="Login" asp-controller="Account" asp-area=""
            class="btn btn-outline-light">
            Log In</a>
    </li>
}

<!-- Admin link goes here -->
```

Description

- The layout for the Bookstore app includes a Bootstrap navbar that contains links that let anonymous users register or log in. If a user is already logged in, the navbar displays the user's name and a button that lets that user log out.

Figure 16-8   How to add Log In/Out buttons and links to the layout

How to start the Account controller

When a browser makes a request that doesn't pass authentication, ASP.NET Core MVC redirects to the /account/login URL by default. That's why it's common to use a controller named Account with a LogIn() action method to display the Login page. Figure 16-9 shows some starting code for a controller named Account.

When you code a controller that works with ASP.NET Core Identity, you can inject the UserManager<T>, SignInManager<T>, and RoleManager<T> objects into the controller. To do that, you can code private properties to store the objects. Then, you can code a constructor that accepts the UserManager<T>, SignInManager<T>, and RoleManager<T> objects and assigns them to the corresponding private properties. For instance, this figure defines private variables for UserManager<User> and SignInManager<User> objects, and it uses a constructor to initialize these objects. Once that's done, the rest of the methods in the controller can use these objects to work with Identity.

As you'll see throughout the rest of this chapter, the Manager<T> objects use asynchronous methods to work with the database. An *asynchronous method* can return control to the calling code before it finishes executing. This allows the calling code and the asynchronous method to execute simultaneously. Later, when the asynchronous method finishes executing, it returns its result. To make this possible, an asynchronous method typically runs in a different unit of processing, or *thread*, than the calling code.

By contrast, most of the code presented in this book uses synchronous methods. A *synchronous method* typically runs in the same thread as the calling code. As a result, it must finish executing before the calling code can continue. Synchronous methods are easier to understand and use than asynchronous methods. However, asynchronous methods can improve the responsiveness of an app, especially if the app needs to execute time-consuming tasks such as accessing a database.

At this point, your app has the infrastructure it needs for you to begin coding the view models, action methods, and views for registering and logging in the users of your app.

Some starting code for the Account controller

```
using Microsoft.AspNetCore.Mvc;
using Microsoft.AspNetCore.Identity;
using Bookstore.Models;

namespace Bookstore.Controllers
{
    public class AccountController : Controller
    {
        private UserManager<User> userManager;
        private SignInManager<User> signInManager;

        public AccountController(UserManager<User> userMngr,
            SignInManager<User> signInMngr)
        {
            userManager = userMngr;
            signInManager = signInMngr;
        }

        // The Register(), LogIn(), and LogOut()methods go here
    }
}
```

The URL that MVC redirects to for an unauthenticated request

```
/account/login
```

Description

- When you code a controller that works with ASP.NET Core Identity, you can inject the UserManager<T>, SignInManager<T>, and RoleManager<T> objects into the controller.

- The Manager<T> objects use asynchronous methods to work with the database.

- When you call an *asynchronous method*, it returns control to the calling code before it finishes executing. That way, the calling code and the asynchronous method can execute simultaneously. This is possible because an asynchronous method typically runs in a different *thread* than the calling code.

- In contrast to an asynchronous method, a *synchronous method* typically runs in the same thread as the calling code, and it must finish executing before the calling code can continue.

Figure 16-9   How to start the Account controller

How to register a user

To register a user, you can use a Register page like the one shown in figure 16-10. This page allows the user to register a new account with the website, and it logs that user in to the app. If the registration succeeds, the app redirects the user to the Home page. Otherwise, the app displays the Register page again with validation errors.

The Register view model

Before you code the Account/Register view, you need to code the view model for it. That view model should define all of the fields that your app requires for the user to register. For instance, the code example in this figure shows the class that defines the Register view model for the Bookstore website. This view model includes the Username and Password properties to require a user to supply a username and a password. To make sure the user enters the password correctly, this view model also includes the ConfirmPassword property.

To provide for data validation, this view model uses some of the data attributes described in chapter 11. For example, it uses the Required attribute to require the user to enter a value for all three fields. In addition, to allow the password fields to use the password options specified in the Program.cs file, this view model uses the DataType attribute to specify the Password data type. That way, you can easily change the validation that's required for the password by modifying the password options in the Program.cs file.

The Register page

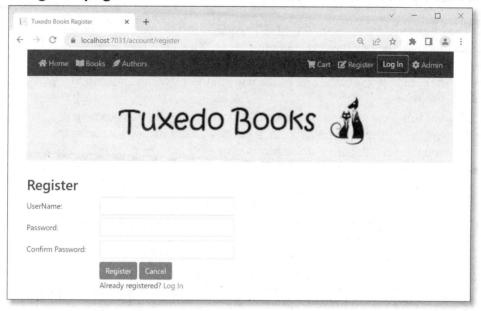

The Register view model

```
using System.ComponentModel.DataAnnotations;

namespace Bookstore.Models
{
    public class RegisterViewModel
    {
        [Required(ErrorMessage = "Please enter a username.")]
        [StringLength(255)]
        public string Username { get; set; } = string.Empty;

        [Required(ErrorMessage = "Please enter a password.")]
        [DataType(DataType.Password)]
        [Compare("ConfirmPassword")]
        public string Password { get; set; } = string.Empty;

        [Required(ErrorMessage = "Please confirm your password.")]
        [DataType(DataType.Password)]
        [Display(Name = "Confirm Password")]
        public string ConfirmPassword { get; set; } = string.Empty;
    }
}
```

Description
- The Register page creates a new user and signs in to the app as that user.
- If the registration succeeds, the app redirects the user to the Home page.
- If you want the password fields to use the password options specified in the Program.cs file, the view model must use the DataType attribute to specify the Password type.

Figure 16-10   The Register view model

The Account/Register view

The Register() action method for GET requests just displays the Account/ Register view defined by the code in figure 16-11. This view begins by specifying the RegisterViewModel class presented in the previous figure as its model. Then, the view sets the title of the page in the ViewBag and displays a heading for the page.

Most of this view consists of a form that posts to the Register() action of the Account controller. Before the form, a <div> element displays a summary for any model-level validation messages. Within the form, the code uses <div> elements to display five rows.

The first three rows use the asp-for and asp-validation-for tag helpers to bind to the Username, Password, and ConfirmPassword properties of the view model. That way, any property-level validation messages are displayed next to their corresponding <input> element.

The fourth row displays a Register button that submits the form to the Register() action method for POST requests that's shown in the next figure. If the user enters valid data, this action method registers the user and logs the user in. Otherwise, it displays the Account/Register view again with appropriate validation messages.

The fifth row displays a link to the LogIn() action method for GET requests. This action method displays the Login page shown later in this chapter. That way, a user who is already registered can click this link to jump directly to the Login page.

The Register() action method for GET requests

```
[HttpGet]
public IActionResult Register()
{
    return View();
}
```

The Account/Register view

```
@model RegisterViewModel
@{
    ViewBag.Title = "Register";
}

<h2>Register</h2>

<div asp-validation-summary="ModelOnly" class="text-danger"></div>
<form method="post" asp-action="Register">
    <div class="row mb-2">
        <label class="col-form-label col-md-2">UserName:</label>
        <div class="col-md-4">
            <input asp-for="Username" class="form-control" />
        </div>
        <div class="col">
            <span asp-validation-for="Username" class="text-danger"></span>
        </div>
    </div>
    <div class="row mb-2">
        <label class="col-form-label col-md-2">Password:</label>
        <div class="col-md-4">
            <input type="password" asp-for="Password"
                    class="form-control" />
        </div>
        <div class="col">
            <span asp-validation-for="Password" class="text-danger"></span>
        </div>
    </div>
    <div class="row mb-2">
        <label class="col-form-label col-md-2">Confirm Password:</label>
        <div class="col-md-4">
            <input type="password" asp-for="ConfirmPassword"
                    class="form-control" />
        </div>
    </div>
    <div class="row">
        <div class="col offset-md-2">
            <button type="submit" class="btn btn-primary">Register</button>
            <a asp-action="Index" asp-controller="Home"
                    class="btn btn-primary">Cancel</a>
        </div>
    </div>
    <div class="row">
        <div class="col offset-md-2">
            Already registered? <a asp-action="LogIn">Log In</a>
        </div>
    </div>
</form>
```

Figure 16-11   The Account/Register view

The Register() action method for POST requests

Figure 16-12 shows the Register() action method for POST requests in the Account controller. But first, it summarizes some of the methods and properties this action method uses. Here, all of the methods are asynchronous, which can improve the responsiveness of your web app when performing Identity operations. However, you work with asynchronous methods somewhat differently than you do synchronous methods.

The Register() action method shows how to work with asynchronous methods. To start, the declaration for this method includes the async keyword to indicate that it is also asynchronous. This is necessary since it makes calls to the CreateAsync() and SignInAsync() methods. In addition, the declaration for this method indicates that it returns an object of the Task<T> class that's available from the System.Threading.Tasks namespace.

Within the action method, the code starts by checking whether the model state is valid. If not, it passes the view model to the Account/Register view so it can display validation messages. However, if the model is valid, the code creates a User object and sets its Username property. Then, it attempts to create the user by passing the User object and the user's password to the CreateAsync() method of the private userManager property. For this asynchronous method call to work, it must be preceded by the await operator. This operator suspends execution of the Register() action method and returns control to the calling code. Then, when the CreateAsync() method finishes, the Register() action method resumes execution.

After calling the CreateAsync() method, the code uses the IdentityResult object that's returned to check whether the create operation succeeded. If so, it calls the SignInAsync() method of the private signInManager property to sign the user in using a session cookie. A session cookie makes sense here since you typically want to use a Remember Me check box to allow your users to choose whether they want to use a persistent cookie. Note that, as with the CreateAsync() method, the SignInAsync() method is preceded by the await operator. After signing the user in, this code ends the action method by redirecting to the Home page for the app.

If the create user operation fails, the code loops through the Errors collection of the IdentityResult object and adds each error to the ModelState property. It adds these errors as model-level errors, so the Account/Register view displays them above the form.

The LogOut() action method for POST requests

This figure also shows the LogOut() action method for POST requests in the Account controller, which is called when the user clicks the Log Out button in the navbar. Like the Register() method, its declaration includes the async keyword. The first statement in this method calls the SignOutAsync() method of the private signInManager property, preceded by the await operator, to sign the user out. Then, the second statement redirects the user to the Home page.

Three methods of the UserManager class

Method	Description
`CreateAsync(user)`	Creates a user and returns an IdentityResult object.
`UpdateAsync(user)`	Updates a user and returns an IdentityResult object.
`DeleteAsync(user)`	Deletes a user and returns an IdentityResult object.

Two methods of the SignInManager class

Method	Description
`SignInAsync(user, isPersistent)`	Logs in a user and returns an IdentityResult object. If the isPersistent argument is true, Identity uses a persistent cookie to keep the user logged in across multiple sessions. Otherwise, Identity uses a session cookie and the user is logged out when the current session ends.
`SignOutAsync()`	Logs out a user and returns an IdentityResult object.

Two properties of the IdentityResult class

Property	Description
`Succeeded`	A Boolean value that indicates whether the operation was successful.
`Errors`	A collection of errors for the operation.

The Register() action method for POST requests

```
[HttpPost]
public async Task<IActionResult> Register(RegisterViewModel model) {
    if (ModelState.IsValid) {
        var user = new User { UserName = model.Username };
        var result = await userManager.CreateAsync(user, model.Password);
        if (result.Succeeded) {
            await signInManager.SignInAsync(user, isPersistent: false);
            return RedirectToAction("Index", "Home");
        }
        else {
            foreach (var error in result.Errors) {
                ModelState.AddModelError("", error.Description);
            }
        }
    }
    return View(model);
}
```

The LogOut() action method for POST requests

```
[HttpPost]
public async Task<IActionResult> LogOut() {
    await signInManager.SignOutAsync();
    return RedirectToAction("Index", "Home");
}
```

Figure 16-12   The Register() and LogOut() action methods for POST requests

How to log in a user

To log in a user, you can use a Login page like the one shown in figure 16-13. This page allows a user who has already registered to log in to the website. If the login succeeds, the app redirects the user to the page specified by the ReturnURL parameter in the query string. In this figure, for example, the ReturnURL parameter has a value of admin.

In addition, if the user checks the Remember Me box, the app uses a persistent cookie to keep the user logged in across multiple sessions. Otherwise, the app uses a session cookie that expires at the end of each session.

The Login view model

Before you code the Account/Login view, you need to code the view model for it. That view model should define all of the fields needed by this page. For instance, this figure shows the class that defines the Login view model for the Bookstore website. Obviously, this view model needs to include the Username and Password properties that the user must enter to register.

In addition, the view model includes two more properties. First, the ReturnURL property stores the URL that the app should return to if the log in operation succeeds. Second, the RememberMe property stores a Boolean value that indicates whether to use a persistent cookie or a session cookie for authentication.

To provide for data validation, this view model uses some of the data attributes described in chapter 11. Note that it doesn't use the DataType attribute for the password field as described earlier in this chapter, though. That's because the password requirements were met when the username and password were added to the database on the Register page. So, the Login page doesn't need to display validation messages for a password that doesn't meet the minimum requirements. Instead, it only needs to display a message that indicates whether the username/password combination is valid or not.

The Login page

The Login view model

```
using System.ComponentModel.DataAnnotations;

namespace Bookstore.Models
{
    public class LoginViewModel
    {
        [Required(ErrorMessage = "Please enter a username.")]
        [StringLength(255)]
        public string Username { get; set; } = string.Empty;

        [Required(ErrorMessage = "Please enter a password.")]
        [StringLength(255)]
        public string Password { get; set; } = string.Empty;

        public string ReturnUrl { get; set; } = string.Empty;

        public bool RememberMe { get; set; }
    }
}
```

Description

- If the user logs in successfully, the app redirects the user to the page specified by the ReturnURL query string.
- If the user checks the Remember Me box, the app uses a persistent cookie to keep the user logged in across multiple sessions. Otherwise, the app uses a session cookie that expires at the end of the session.

Figure 16-13   The Login view model

The Account/Login view

The LogIn() action method for GET requests displays the Account/Login view defined by the code in figure 16-14. But first, it creates a LoginViewModel object and initializes its ReturnURL property to the returnURL parameter of the action method. This works because the name of this parameter matches the name of the query string parameter.

The Account/Login view begins by specifying the LoginViewModel class as its model. Then, the view sets the title of the page in the ViewBag, displays a heading for the page, and displays a summary of any model-level validation messages.

Most of the Account/Login view consists of a form that posts to the LogIn() action method of the Account controller. Note that the <form> tag uses the asp-route-returnUrl tag helper to specify a value for the returnURL query string parameter. Within the form, the code uses <div> elements to display five rows.

The first two rows use the asp-for and asp-validation-for tag helpers to bind to the Username and Password properties of the view model. That way, any property-level validation messages are displayed next to the corresponding <input> element.

The third row displays the Remember Me check box and uses the asp-for tag helper to bind it to the RememberMe property of the view model. By default, this box is unchecked. As a result, the app uses a session cookie for authentication. However, if the user checks this box, the app uses a persistent cookie for authentication.

The fourth row displays a Log In button that submits the form to the LogIn() action method for POST requests that's shown in the next figure. If the user enters valid data, this action method logs the user in. Otherwise, it displays the Account/Login view again with appropriate validation messages.

The fifth row displays a link to the Register() action method for GET requests. This action method displays the Register page shown earlier in this chapter. That way, a user who isn't registered can click this link to jump directly to the Register page.

The LogIn() action method for GET requests

```
[HttpGet]
public IActionResult LogIn(string returnURL = "")
{
    var model = new LoginViewModel { ReturnUrl = returnURL };
    return View(model);
}
```

The Login view

```
@model LoginViewModel
@{
    ViewBag.Title = "Login";
}


<h2>Login</h2>

<div asp-validation-summary="ModelOnly" class="text-danger"></div>
<form method="post" asp-action="LogIn"
      asp-route-returnUrl="@Model.ReturnUrl">
    <div class="row mb-2">
        <label class="col-form-label col-md-2">UserName:</label>
        <div class="col-md-4">
            <input asp-for="Username" class="form-control" />
        </div>
        <div class="col">
            <span asp-validation-for="Username" class="text-danger"></span>
        </div>
    </div>
    <div class="row mb-2">
        <label class="col-form-label col-md-2">Password:</label>
        <div class="col-md-4">
            <input type="password" asp-for="Password"
                   class="form-control" />
        </div>
        <div class="col">
            <span asp-validation-for="Password" class="text-danger"></span>
        </div>
    </div>
    <div class="row mb-2">
        <div class="col offset-md-2">
            <input type="checkbox" title="Remember Me" asp-for="RememberMe"
                   class="form-check-inline" />
            <label>Remember Me</label>
        </div>
    </div>
    <div class="row">
        <div class="col offset-md-2">
            <button type="submit" class="btn btn-primary">Log In</button>
            <a asp-action="Index" asp-controller="Home"
                   class="btn btn-primary">Cancel</a>
        </div>
    </div>
    <div class="row">
        <div class="col offset-md-2">
            Not registered?
            <a asp-action="Register">Register as a new user</a>
        </div>
    </div>
</form>
```

Figure 16-14   The Account/Login view

The LogIn() action method for POST requests

Figure 16-15 shows the LogIn() action method for POST requests. But first, it summarizes the PasswordSignInAsync() method that's used by this action method. This method is an asynchronous method that works much like the other asynchronous methods described earlier in this chapter.

The LogIn() action method shows how to use this method. To start, the declaration for this action method is coded with the async keyword and returns a Task<IActionResult> object as described earlier in this chapter. Then, within the action method, the code starts by checking whether the model state is valid. If not, it adds a model-level validation error that says "Invalid username/password", and it passes the view model to the Account/Login view so it can display validation messages. In most cases, that's adequate validation for a Login page.

On the other hand, if the model is valid, the code calls the PasswordSignInAsync() method of the private signInManager property and passes it the username, the password, and the value of the RememberMe property. In addition, it passes a Boolean value of false as the fourth argument. That way, the user is not locked out if the sign in operation fails. In most cases, that's adequate. However, if you want to make your page more secure, you can set this argument to true.

If the sign-in operation succeeds, the code checks that the string for the ReturnURL property of the view model is not null or empty and that it contains a local URL. If both of these conditions are true, this code redirects to the URL specified by the ReturnURL property. Otherwise, the action method redirects to the Home page. Here, checking that the ReturnURL contains a local URL helps to protect against a hacker redirecting the browser to a malicious website.

Another method of the SignInManager class

Method	Description
PasswordSignInAsync(username, password, isPersistent, lockoutOnFailure)	Logs in a user and returns an IdentityResult object. When lockoutOnFailure is set to true, Identity locks the user out if the sign in fails.

The LogIn() action method for POST requests

```
[HttpPost]
public async Task<IActionResult> LogIn(LoginViewModel model)
{
    if (ModelState.IsValid)
    {
        var result = await signInManager.PasswordSignInAsync(
            model.Username, model.Password, isPersistent: model.RememberMe,
            lockoutOnFailure: false);

        if (result.Succeeded)
        {
            if (!string.IsNullOrEmpty(model.ReturnUrl) &&
                Url.IsLocalUrl(model.ReturnUrl))
            {
                return Redirect(model.ReturnUrl);
            }
            else
            {
                return RedirectToAction("Index", "Home");
            }
        }
    }
    ModelState.AddModelError("", "Invalid username/password.");
    return View(model);
}
```

Figure 16-15   The LogIn() action method for POST requests

How to work with roles

So far, you've learned how to allow a user to log in. As a result, you can restrict access to users who are logged in. For example, you might want to restrict access to the Cart page so any user who is logged in can view it.

However, you may also need to restrict access to users who are members of a specified role. For example, if your website has an Admin area, you might want to restrict access to users who are members of the Admin or Manager role. The figures that follow show how to do that.

Properties and methods for working with roles

Figure 16-16 shows some of the properties and methods you can use to work with users and roles. To work with roles, you can use the properties and methods of the RoleManager class. For example, you can create, update, or delete a role. You can find a role by id or name. And you can get a collection of all roles.

Once you've created a role or two, you can use the properties and methods of the UserManager class to work with users and roles. For example, you can add a user to a role or remove a user from a role. You can find a user by id or name. You can check whether a user is in a specified role. You can get a collection of role names that the specified user belongs to. And you can get a collection of all users.

The first code example shows how to loop through all users and their roles. To do that, this code uses the Users and Roles collections that are available from the UserManager and RoleManager classes. Within the inner loop, this code uses the IsInRoleAsync() method to check whether the current user is a member of the current role. If so, you can perform some processing.

The second and third examples show how to use a RoleManager object to create and delete a role. Here, the second example uses the CreateAsync() method to create a role named Admin. Then, the third example uses the FindByIdAsync() method to find a role by its ID. Then, it uses the DeleteAsync() method to delete the role that matches that ID.

The fourth and fifth examples show how to use a UserManager object to add a user to a role and remove a user from a role. Here, the fourth example uses the FindByIdAsync() method to get the user with the specified ID. Then, it uses the AddToRoleAsync() method to add that user to the role named Admin. For this to succeed, the role named Admin must already exist.

The fifth example also uses the FindByIdAsync() method to get a user with the specified ID. Then, it uses the RemoveFromRoleAsync() method to remove that user from the Admin role.

When you use the methods shown in this figure, it's common to check whether the operation succeeded. Then, you can perform some processing if the operation succeeded or you can handle the error if the operation didn't succeed. In this figure, the last four examples show the if statement that checks whether

Some of the properties and methods of the RoleManager class

Property/Method	Description
`Roles`	Returns an IQueryable object of roles.
`FindByIdAsync(id)`	Returns an IdentityRole object for the specified role ID.
`FindByNameAsync(name)`	Returns an IdentityRole object for the specified role name.
`CreateAsync(role)`	Creates a role and returns an IdentityResult object.
`UpdateAsync(role)`	Updates a role and returns an IdentityResult object.
`DeleteAsync(role)`	Deletes a role and returns an IdentityResult object.

More properties and methods of the UserManager class

Property/Method	Description
`Users`	Returns an IQueryable object of users.
`FindByIdAsync(id)`	Returns an IdentityUser object for the specified user ID.
`FindByNameAsync(name)`	Returns an IdentityUser object for the specified username.
`IsInRoleAsync(user, roleName)`	Returns a Boolean value that indicates whether the user is in the specified role.
`AddToRoleAsync(user, roleName)`	Adds the specified user to the specified role.
`RemoveFromRoleAsync(user, roleName)`	Removes the specified user from the specified role.
`GetRolesAsync(user)`	Returns a collection of role names for the specified user.

Code that loops through all users and their roles

```
foreach (User user in userManager.Users) {               // all users
    foreach (IdentityRole role in roleManager.Roles) {  // all roles
        if (await userManager.IsInRoleAsync(user, role.Name)) {
            // perform some processing if user is in role
        }
    }
}
```

Code that creates a role named Admin

```
var result = await roleManager.CreateAsync(new IdentityRole("Admin"));
if (result.Succeeded) { ... }
```

Code that deletes a role

```
IdentityRole role = await roleManager.FindByIdAsync(id);
var result = await roleManager.DeleteAsync(role);
if (result.Succeeded) { ... }
```

Code that adds a user to the role named Admin

```
User user = await userManager.FindByIdAsync(id);
var result = await userManager.AddToRoleAsync(user, "Admin");
if (result.Succeeded) { ... }
```

Code that removes a user from the role named Admin

```
User user = await userManager.FindByIdAsync(id);
var result = await userManager.RemoveFromRoleAsync(user, "Admin");
if (result.Succeeded) { ... }
```

Figure 16-16   Properties and methods for working with roles

the operation succeeded, but it doesn't show any of the processing for these if statements. Instead, these examples just use an ellipsis (...) to show that you could perform some processing here.

The User entity and view model

Now that you know how to use the properties and methods for working with roles, you're ready to learn how to create a Manage Users page like the one shown in figure 16-17. This page lets you create and delete the Admin role, create and delete users, add users to the Admin role, and remove users from the Admin role. In this figure, the Manage Users page displays three users. Two of the users don't belong to any role, and the third user belongs to the Admin role.

Notice here that the Add To Admin and Remove From Admin buttons are included for each user, regardless of whether the user has been added to the Admin role. If that's not what you want, you can add Razor if statements to the view so these buttons are displayed only when appropriate.

Before creating this Manage Users page, you need to update the User entity class so it includes a RoleNames property that can store the names of all roles that the user belongs to. This provides an easy way for the User/Index view to display all roles for a user. When you code the RoleNames property, you need to add the NotMapped attribute so EF doesn't create a RoleNames column in the AspNetUsers table.

In addition, you need to create a User view model that stores a collection of User and Role objects. This provides an easy way for the view to access the users and roles that it needs to display.

For now, the Manage Users page only works with a single role named Admin. However, both the User entity and User view model classes are coded in a way that allows them to work with multiple roles if necessary. As a result, if you ever need to update this view to work with multiple roles, these classes are ready for it.

The Manage Users page

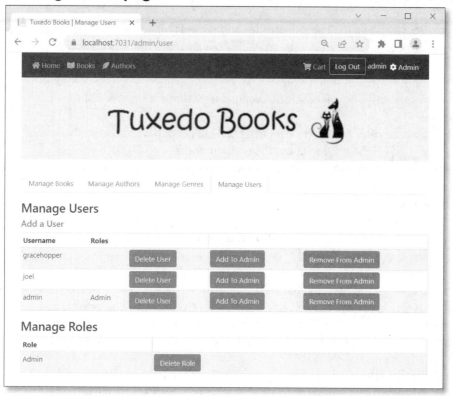

The updated User entity

```
using System.ComponentModel.DataAnnotations.Schema;   // for NotMapped
...
public class User : IdentityUser
{
    [NotMapped]
    public IList<string> RoleNames { get; set; } = null!;
}
```

The User view model

```
using Microsoft.AspNetCore.Identity;
...
public class UserViewModel
{
    public IEnumerable<User> Users { get; set; } = null!;
    public IEnumerable<IdentityRole> Roles { get; set; } = null!;
}
```

Description

- The Manage Users page lets you add and delete users, add and remove users from the Admin role, and delete the Admin role.

- If the Admin role doesn't exist, this page displays a button that you can click to create it.

Figure 16-17   The User entity and view model

The User controller and its Index() action method

Figure 16-18 shows the User controller and its Index() action method. Here, the User controller is decorated with an Authorize attribute that only allows users of the Admin role to access this page. That's typically what you want for a production app. However, when you're developing this page, you can comment out this attribute until you successfully create a user that's a member of the Admin role.

The User controller begins by declaring private properties named userManager and roleManager. Then, the constructor for the User controller initializes these properties to instances of the UserManager and RoleManager classes. That way, the entire controller can use the private properties to easily access these objects.

Since the Index() method calls asynchronous methods, it includes the async keyword and returns a Task object. Within this method, the first statement creates a list of User objects named users. Then, the code loops through all users.

Within this loop, the first statement gets a list of all role names that the user is a member of and assigns that list to the RoleNames property of the User object. This works because the call to the GetRolesAsync() method returns an IList<string> object, and that's also the type of the RoleNames property of the User object. Then, the second statement adds the updated User object to the list of User objects named users.

After the loop, the code creates the User view model and initializes its Users and Roles properties. To do that, it assigns the list of User objects named users to the Users property. Then, it uses the RoleManager object to assign its Roles property to the Roles property of the view model.

Finally, the Index() method passes the view model to the view. This renders the User/Index view that's presented in the next figure.

The User controller and its Index() action method

```
using Microsoft.AspNetCore.Mvc;
using Microsoft.AspNetCore.Authorization;
using Microsoft.AspNetCore.Identity;
using Bookstore.Models;
...
[Authorize(Role = "Admin")]
[Area("Admin")]
public class UserController : Controller
{
    private UserManager<User> userManager;
    private RoleManager<IdentityRole> roleManager;

    public UserController(UserManager<User> userMngr,
        RoleManager<IdentityRole> roleMngr)
    {
        userManager = userMngr;
        roleManager = roleMngr;
    }

    public async Task<IActionResult> Index()
    {
        List<User> users = new List<User>();
        foreach (User user in userManager.Users)
        {
            user.RoleNames = await userManager.GetRolesAsync(user);
            users.Add(user);
        }
        UserViewModel model = new UserViewModel
        {
            Users = users,
            Roles = roleManager.Roles
        };
        return View(model);
    }

    // the other action methods
}
```

Figure 16-18   The User controller and its Index() action method

The User/Index view

The User/Index view shown in figure 16-19 begins by identifying the UserViewModel class as its model. Then, the view sets the title of the page in the ViewBag and displays a heading for the page.

After that, it includes an Add link that calls the Add() action method of the User controller. This action method displays a User/Add view that you can use to add a user. However, this chapter doesn't present the code for this action method and its view because it works much like the Account/Register view presented earlier in this chapter. In fact, the Add() action method and the User/Add view use the RegisterViewModel presented earlier in this chapter.

After the Add link, the User/Index view displays the header row of a table. Then, a Razor if statement checks whether any User objects exist in the view model. If not, it displays a row that indicates that there are no user accounts. Otherwise, it loops through all the User objects.

Within the loop, the code creates one row for each user where each row has five columns. The first column displays the username. The second column displays any roles that the user is in. To do that, the code for this column uses a Razor foreach statement to loop through all roles for the user.

The next three columns display buttons that you can use to work with each user. The third column displays a button that you can use to delete the user. This button calls the Delete() action method and passes the user's ID as a route parameter. The fourth and fifth columns work similarly, but they display buttons that you can use to add the user to the Admin role or remove the user from the Admin role. These buttons call the AddToAdmin() and RemoveFromAdmin() action methods of the User controller.

Note that to make this app more efficient, you could display the Add To Admin button only if the user isn't already a member of the Admin role. To do that, you could code the <form> element for the column within a Razor if statement like this:

```
@if (!user.RoleNames.Contains("Admin"))
```

Similarly, you could display the Delete From Admin button only if the user is a member of the Admin role.

The User/Index view

```
@model UserViewModel
@{
    ViewData["Title"] = " | Manage Users";
}

<h1 class="mb-2">Manage Users</h1>

<h5 class="mt-2"><a asp-action="Add">Add a User</a></h5>

<table class="table table-bordered table-striped table-sm">
    <thead>
        <tr><th>Username</th><th>Roles</th><th></th><th></th><th></th></
tr>
    </thead>
    <tbody>
    @if (Model.Users.Count() == 0)
    {
        <tr><td colspan="5">There are no user accounts.</td></tr>
    }
    else
    {
        @foreach (User user in Model.Users)
        {
        <tr>
            <td>@user.UserName</td>
            <td>
                @foreach (string roleName in user.RoleNames)
                {
                    <div>@roleName</div>
                }
            </td>
            <td>
                <form method="post" asp-action="Delete"
                      asp-route-id="@user.Id">
                    <button type="submit" class="btn btn-primary">
                    Delete User</button>
                </form>
            </td>
            <td>
                <form method="post" asp-action="AddToAdmin"
                      asp-route-id="@user.Id">
                    <button type="submit" class="btn btn-primary">
                    Add To Admin</button>
                </form>
            </td>
            <td>
                <form method="post" asp-action="RemoveFromAdmin"
                      asp-route-id="@user.Id">
                    <button type="submit" class="btn btn-primary">
                    Remove From Admin</button>
                </form>
            </td>
        </tr>
        }
    }
    </tbody>
</table>
```

Figure 16-19   The User/Index view (part 1)

After the table of users, the User/Index view uses a Razor if statement to check whether any Role objects exist in the view model. If not, it displays a form that contains a button that you can use to create the Admin role. Clicking this button calls the CreateAdminRole() action method of the User controller.

On the other hand, if one or more roles exist, this code displays a table that has one row for each role. Here, each row has two columns. The first column displays the name of the role. Then, the second column displays a button that you can use to delete the role. This button calls the DeleteRole() action method of the User controller and passes the role's ID as a route parameter.

The User/Index view (continued)

```
<h1 class="mb-2">Manage Roles</h1>

@if (Model.Roles.Count() == 0)
{
    <form method="post" asp-action="CreateAdminRole">
        <button type="submit" class="btn btn-primary">
        Create Admin Role</button>
    </form>
}
else
{
    <table class="table table-bordered table-striped table-sm">
        <thead>
            <tr><th>Role</th><th></th></tr>
        </thead>
        <tbody>
            @foreach (var role in Model.Roles)
            {
                <tr>
                  <td>@role.Name</td>
                  <td>
                    <form method="post" asp-action="DeleteRole"
                            asp-route-id="@role.Id">
                        <button type="submit" class="btn btn-primary">
                        Delete Role</button>
                    </form>
                  </td>
                </tr>
            }
        </tbody>
    </table>
}
```

Figure 16-19   The User/Index view (part 2)

Other action methods of the User controller

Figure 16-20 shows the action methods of the User controller that are called by the buttons of the User/Index view. For example, if you click the Delete button for a user, the app calls the Delete() action method to delete the specified user. Similarly, if you click the Add To Admin button, the app calls the AddToAdmin() action method.

The Delete() action method accepts the user's ID as a parameter. Then, the code gets a User object for the user with that ID and checks whether this User object is null. If not, the code attempts to delete the user. If the delete operation fails, the code loops through all errors and creates an error message that it adds to TempData with a key of "message". For the Bookstore website, this causes the layout to display the error message across the top of the Manage Users page. If the delete operation succeeds, the Manage Users page displays the remaining users and roles for the app.

The Add() methods for GET and POST requests aren't shown here. That's because they are almost identical to the Register() methods you saw in figures 6-11 and 6-12.

The AddToAdmin() action method also accepts the user's ID as a parameter. Within the method, the first statement gets an IdentityRole object for the role named Admin. Then, the code checks whether that IdentityRole object is null. If so, it adds an error message to TempData with a key of "message" and redirects to the User/Index view. This displays an error message across the top of the Manage Users page that indicates that the Admin role doesn't exist and needs to be created. However, if the Admin role exists, this method finds the User object with the ID parameter. Then, it adds this user to the Admin role.

The RemoveFromAdmin() action method works much like the AddToAdmin() action method. However, removing a user from a role that doesn't exist doesn't cause an error. As a result, there's no need to check whether the Admin role exists in this method. So, this method just finds the User object that matches the ID parameter, removes that user from the Admin role, and redirects to the User/Index page.

The DeleteRole() action method accepts the role's ID as a parameter. Within this method, the first statement gets the IdentityRole object with the ID parameter. Then, this method deletes this role and redirects to the User/Index page. Note that if a role contains users when it's deleted, the users are simply removed from that role. They're not deleted.

The CreateAdminRole() action method doesn't accept any parameters. It just creates the Admin role and redirects to the User/Index page.

As you review these methods, you should realize that the ones with "Admin" in their names are hard-coded to work with a role named Admin. For the Bookstore website, that's adequate since it only supports the Admin role. However, if you need to support multiple roles, you could rename and refactor these methods to work with multiple roles. For example, you could rename CreateAdminRole() to CreateRole() and refactor it to accept an argument that specifies the name of the role to create.

Other action methods of the User controller

```
[HttpPost]
public async Task<IActionResult> Delete(string id)
{
    User user = await userManager.FindByIdAsync(id);
    if (user != null) {
        IdentityResult result = await userManager.DeleteAsync(user);
        if (!result.Succeeded) { // if failed
            string errorMessage = "";
            foreach (IdentityError error in result.Errors) {
                errorMessage += error.Description + " | ";
            }
            TempData["message"] = errorMessage;
        }
    }
    return RedirectToAction("Index");
}

// the Add() methods work like the Register() methods from 16-11 and 16-12

[HttpPost]
public async Task<IActionResult> AddToAdmin(string id)
{
    IdentityRole adminRole = await roleManager.FindByNameAsync("Admin");
    if (adminRole == null) {
        TempData["message"] = "Admin role does not exist. "
            + "Click 'Create Admin Role' button to create it.";
    }
    else {
        User user = await userManager.FindByIdAsync(id);
        await userManager.AddToRoleAsync(user, adminRole.Name);
    }
    return RedirectToAction("Index");
}

[HttpPost]
public async Task<IActionResult> RemoveFromAdmin(string id)
{
    User user = await userManager.FindByIdAsync(id);
    await userManager.RemoveFromRoleAsync(user, "Admin");
    return RedirectToAction("Index");
}

[HttpPost]
public async Task<IActionResult> DeleteRole(string id)
{
    IdentityRole role = await roleManager.FindByIdAsync(id);
    await roleManager.DeleteAsync(role);
    return RedirectToAction("Index");
}

[HttpPost]
public async Task<IActionResult> CreateAdminRole()
{
    await roleManager.CreateAsync(new IdentityRole("Admin"));
    return RedirectToAction("Index");
}
```

Figure 16-20   Other action methods of the User controller

The code that restricts access

Figure 16-21 shows the code that restricts access to some pages of the Bookstore website. To start, the first example shows the using directive for the namespace that contains the Authorization attributes that you can use to restrict access. Then, it shows how to apply these attributes to some of the controllers of the Bookstore website.

The second example shows the Authorize attribute that's applied to the Cart controller and all of its action methods. This attribute restricts access to all of the Cart pages to users that are logged in. As a result, if you are not logged in and you attempt to access any Cart page, the app redirects you to the Login page. At this point, you must log in to access the Cart page. Of course, if you haven't registered yet, you must register before you can log in.

The third example shows the Authorize attribute that's applied to the Book controller in the Admin area. However, this attribute is also applied to other controllers in the Admin area such as the Author, Genre, and User controllers. This Authorize attribute restricts access to users who are members of the Admin role. As a result, if you are logged in as a user who is not a member of the Admin role and you attempt to access one of these Admin pages, the app redirects to this URL by default:

`/Account/AccessDenied`

For this to work, you can add an action method named AccessDenied() to the Account controller as shown in the fourth example. This method can just return an Account/AccessDenied view like the one shown in the fifth example. Of course, if you log in as a user that's a member of the Admin role, you can access the Admin pages.

The using directive for the Authorization attributes

```
using Microsoft.AspNetCore.Authorization;
```

The Cart controller requires users to be logged in

```
[Authorize]
public class CartController : Controller {
    ...
}
```

Controllers in the Admin area require users to be in the Admin role

```
[Authorize(Roles = "Admin")]
[Area("Admin")]
public class BookController : Controller {
    ...
}
```

The AccessDenied() action method of the Account controller

```
public ViewResult AccessDenied()
{
    return View();
}
```

The code for the Account/AccessDenied view

```
@{
    ViewBag.Title = "Access Denied";
}
<h2>Access Denied</h2>
```

The Account/AccessDenied view

Description

- If you are not logged in and you attempt to access the Cart or Admin pages, the app redirects you to the Login page.
- If you are logged in as any user, you can access the Cart pages.
- If you are logged in as a user that's in the Admin role, you can access the Admin pages. Otherwise, the app redirects you to the AccessDenied view.

Figure 16-21   The code that restricts access

How to seed roles and users

Figure 16-22 presents some skills that you can use to seed your database with some initial roles and users. In particular, it shows how to create a user named admin that you can use to access the pages in the Admin area of the Bookstore website.

To start, you can create a static asynchronous method like the CreateAdminUserAsync() method shown in the first example. This method accepts a parameter named provider of type IServiceProvider.

Within the method, the first two statements use this parameter to get the UserManager<User> and RoleManager<IdentityRole> objects that the method needs to work with users and roles. Then, the code creates three string variables that store a username of admin, a password of Sesame, and a role name of Admin.

Next, this code checks whether the specified role already exists. If it doesn't, this code creates the role. Then, the code checks whether the specified username already exists. If it doesn't, this code creates a User object and stores the username in it. Then, it creates the user. If this operation succeeds, the code adds the user to the Admin role.

To execute the CreateAdminUserAsync() method, you can call it from the Program.cs file, passing it the IServiceProvider object it needs. Note, however, that you can't pass it the Services property of the app variable. If you do, you'll get the following error message when the method tries to use the service provider to create a RoleManager object:

```
Cannot resolve scoped service ... from root provider.
```

Instead, you can use the CreateScope() method of the IServiceScopeFactory interface to control the scope, as shown in the second example.

As you review this code, note that it only creates one role named Admin and one user with a username of admin and a password of Sesame. However, if necessary, it would be easy to modify this code to create multiple roles and users. For example, you could store all role names in a list and loop through the list to create each role. Similarly, you could store all username/password combinations for a specified role in a dictionary and loop through each key/value pair to create all of the users for that role.

A static asynchronous method that seeds an Admin role and user

```
using Microsoft.AspNetCore.Identity;

namespace Bookstore.Models
{
    public class ConfigureIdentity
    {
        public static async Task CreateAdminUserAsync(
        IServiceProvider provider)
        {
            var roleManager =
                provider.GetRequiredService<RoleManager<IdentityRole>>();
            var userManager =
                provider.GetRequiredService<UserManager<User>>();

            string username = "admin";
            string password = "Sesame";
            string roleName = "Admin";

            // if role doesn't exist, create it
            if (await roleManager.FindByNameAsync(roleName) == null)
            {
                await roleManager.CreateAsync(new IdentityRole(roleName));
            }

            // if username doesn't exist, create it and add to role
            if (await userManager.FindByNameAsync(username) == null)
            {
                User user = new User { UserName = username };
                var result = await userManager.CreateAsync(user, password);
                if (result.Succeeded)
                {
                    await userManager.AddToRoleAsync(user, roleName);
                }
            }
        }
    }
}
```

Code in the Program.cs file that calls the method

```
var app = builder.Build();
...
app.UseAuthentication();
app.UseAuthorization();

var scopeFactory = app.Services.GetRequiredService<IServiceScopeFactory>();
using (var scope = scopeFactory.CreateScope())
{
    await ConfigureIdentity.CreateAdminUserAsync(scope.ServiceProvider);
}
...
app.Run();
```

Description

- If you need to seed your database with some initial roles and users, you can create a static asynchronous method to do that and then call that method in the Program.cs file.

- For this to work, add code to the Program.cs file as shown here to control the scope that the method is called in.

Figure 16-22   How to seed roles and users

More skills for working with Identity

At this point, you have learned how to restrict access to the pages of the Bookstore website. In addition, you have learned how to create a Manage Users page that you can use to view and modify the users of an app and to control whether they are members of the Admin role. However, there are many more skills for working with Identity that you should be aware of. The next two figures describe a couple of them.

How to change a user's password

If you need to change a user's password, you can use a view like the Change Password view shown in figure 16-23. Here, the Change Password view displays the username but doesn't allow you to change it. In addition, it displays text boxes that let you enter the old and new passwords for the user and confirm the new password.

The view model for the Account/Change Password view includes properties for storing the username, the old password, the new password, and the confirm password. In addition, it uses data attributes to provide data validation for the old, new, and confirmation passwords. Here, no data validation is required for the username since the app always sets it correctly and it can't be changed. Similarly, the data validation for the old password is minimal because the most important part of its validation is whether it matches the password that's stored in the database. However, the data validation for the new and confirmation passwords is the same as it is for the Account/Registration view.

This figure doesn't show the code that adds the Change Password link to the navbar, because it's similar to the layout code you saw earlier. Similarly, it doesn't show all the code for the Account/ChangePassword view, because it's similar to the code for the Account/Register view that you saw earlier. However, it does show the HTML for the Username field so you can see that it uses the readonly attribute to keep the user from changing the username.

The Account/Change Password view

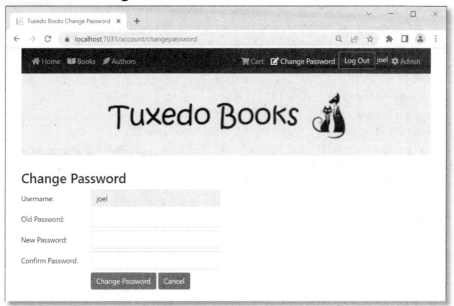

The ChangePassword view model

```
using System.ComponentModel.DataAnnotations;

namespace Bookstore.Models
{
    public class ChangePasswordViewModel
    {
        public string Username { get; set; } = string.Empty;

        [Required(ErrorMessage = "Please enter your password.")]
        public string OldPassword { get; set; } = string.Empty;

        [Required(ErrorMessage = "Please enter your new password.")]
        [DataType(DataType.Password)]
        [Compare("ConfirmPassword")]
        public string NewPassword { get; set; } = string.Empty;

        [Required(ErrorMessage = "Please confirm your new password.")]
        [DataType(DataType.Password)]
        [Display(Name = "Confirm Password")]
        public string ConfirmPassword { get; set; } = string.Empty;
    }
}
```

The HTML for the Username field in the Account/ChangePassword view

```
<div class="row mb-2">
    <label class="col-form-label col-md-2">Username:</label>
    <div class="col-md-4">
        <input asp-for="Username" class="form-control" readonly />
    </div>
</div>
```

Figure 16-23   How to change a user's password (part 1)

Part 2 of figure 16-23 presents the ChangePassword() action methods for GET and POST requests. The ChangePassword() method for GET requests creates a new ChangePasswordViewModel object, sets its Username property, and passes the object to the view. To set the user name, it uses the User property of the controller to access the authenticated user. Then, it uses the Identity and Name properties to get the username of that user. This User property is similar to the User property of the layout view that you saw earlier.

The ChangePassword() action method for POST requests receives an instance of the ChangePassword view model, which contains the old, new, and confirmation passwords entered by the user. This action method begins by checking whether the model state is valid. If not, it displays the view again with the appropriate validation messages.

However, if the model state is valid, it uses the username that's available from the view model to get the User object from the database. Then, it uses the ChangePasswordAsync() method to change the password for the User object from the old password to the new password. If this operation succeeds, the code redirects to the Home/Index page. Otherwise, it adds model-level errors to the ModelState property and displays the Account/Change Password view with the model-level validation errors.

The ChangePassword() action method for GET requests

```
[HttpGet]
public IActionResult ChangePassword()
{
    var model = new ChangePasswordViewModel {
        Username = User.Identity?.Name ?? ""
    };
    return View(model);
}
```

The ChangePassword() action method for POST requests

```
[HttpPost]
public async Task<IActionResult> ChangePassword(
    ChangePasswordViewModel model)
{
    if (ModelState.IsValid)
    {
        User user = await userManager.FindByNameAsync(model.Username);
        var result = await userManager.ChangePasswordAsync(user,
            model.OldPassword, model.NewPassword);

        if (result.Succeeded)
        {
            TempData["message"] = "Password changed successfully";
            return RedirectToAction("Index" , "Home");
        }
        else
        {
            foreach (IdentityError error in result.Errors)
            {
                ModelState.AddModelError("", error.Description);
            }
        }
    }
    return View(model);
}
```

Figure 16-23   How to change a user's password (part 2)

How to add more user registration fields

The Account/Register view presented earlier in this chapter only requires two fields: username and password. But what if you wanted to require more fields for a user to register? For example, what if you also wanted to require the user to enter a name, an email address, or a birth date? In that case, you can use the technique described in figure 16-24 to add those fields.

If you want to add a registration field that's available from the IdentityUser class, you can just add it to the Register view model. That's because the AspNetUsers table already contains the column needed to store the field.

For instance, the IdentityUser class presented earlier in this chapter includes an Email property that's inherited by the User class shown in this figure. As a result, you don't need to add an Email property to the User class. Instead, you only need to add the Email property to the Register view model as shown in this figure. When you do, you can use the DataType attribute to validate the email address field. This works much like using the DataType attribute to validate the password field.

However, if you want to add a registration field that isn't available from the IdentityUser class, you can add a property to the User class. Then, you need to add a migration that contains the code for adding the new column in the AspNetUsers table, and you need to update the database.

For instance, the FirstName and LastName properties are not available from the IdentityUser class, so the User class shown in this figure adds those properties. To add the corresponding columns to the AspNetUsers database, you can use the Add-Migration command to add a migration for those columns to the project. Then, you can use the Update-Database command to execute that migration and add the columns to the database.

After the database is ready to handle the new registration fields, you need to modify the Registration view model and view to work with the new fields. For instance, the Registration view model shown in this figure adds the FirstName and LastName properties along with data attributes for validation. Although this figure doesn't show the code for the view, you should be able to modify the existing Account/Register view to add the rows that get the Email, FirstName, and LastName fields from the user.

The updated User class

```
public class User : IdentityUser
{
    // need to be added to DB
    public string FirstName { get; set; } = string.Empty;
    public string LastName { get; set; } = string.Empty;

    [NotMapped]
    public IList<string> RoleNames { get; set; };
}
```

The updated Register view model

```
public class RegisterViewModel
{
    [Required(ErrorMessage = "Please enter a username.")]
    [StringLength(255)]
    public string Username { get; set; } = string.Empty;

    [Required(ErrorMessage = "Please enter a first name.")]
    [StringLength(255)]
    public string Firstname { get; set; } = string.Empty;

    [Required(ErrorMessage = "Please enter a last name.")]
    [StringLength(255)]
    public string Lastname { get; set; } = string.Empty;

    // from IdentityUser class
    [Required(ErrorMessage = "Please enter an email address.")]
    [DataType(DataType.EmailAddress)]
    public string Email { get; set; } = string.Empty;

    [Required(ErrorMessage = "Please enter a password.")]
    [DataType(DataType.Password)]
    [Compare("ConfirmPassword")]
    public string Password { get; set; } = string.Empty;

    [Required(ErrorMessage = "Please confirm your password.")]
    [DataType(DataType.Password)]
    [Display(Name = "Confirm Password")]
    public string ConfirmPassword { get; set; } = string.Empty;
}
```

Description

- If you want to add a registration field that's available from the IdentityUser class, you can just add it to the Register view model. That's because the AspNetUsers table already contains the column needed to store the field.
- If you want to add a registration field that isn't available from the IdentityUser class, you can add a property to the User class. Then, you need to add a migration for the new column in the AspNetUsers table, and you need to update the database.
- After the database is ready to handle the new registration fields, you need to modify the Registration view model and view to work with the new fields.

Figure 16-24   How to add more user registration fields

Perspective

Now that you've read this chapter, you should understand how to use Authorization attributes to restrict access to the pages of your web app. In addition, you should understand how to use ASP.NET Core Identity to authenticate users and allow users with appropriate authorization to access those restricted pages.

There's still plenty more to learn about authorization and authentication, though. For example, if you have serious security concerns for your app, you may want to learn more about locking a user out after failed login attempts. Or, you may want to implement two-factor authentication. Whatever your authentication and authorization requirements are, this chapter should provide you with a solid foundation in these topics.

Terms

authentication	OWIN (Open Web Interface for
authorization	.NET)
Windows-based authentication	role
individual user account authentication	asynchronous method
authentication cookie	thread
	synchronous method

Summary

- If you want to limit access to all or part of your app to authorized users, you can use *authentication* to verify each user's identity.

- Once you have authenticated a user, you can use *authorization* to check if the user has the appropriate privileges to access a page.

- *Windows-based authentication* requires that you set up a Windows user account for each user. Then, you use standard Windows security features to restrict access to all or part of the app.

- *Individual user account authentication* uses a login page that typically requires the user to enter a username and password. ASP.NET Core displays this page automatically when it needs to authenticate a user who's trying to access the app.

- To be authenticated, the user request must contain an *authentication cookie*. By default, this cookie is stored as a session cookie, but it can also be stored as a persistent cookie.

- ASP.NET Identity is based on *OWIN (Open Web Interface for .NET)* middleware, which is an open-source project that defines a standard interface between .NET web servers and web apps.

- *Roles* let you apply the same access rules to a group of users.

- An *asynchronous method* can return control to the calling code before it finishes executing. This allows the calling code and the asynchronous method to execute simultaneously. To make this possible, an asynchronous method typically runs in a different *thread* than the calling code.

- A *synchronous method* typically runs in the same thread as the calling code. As a result, it must finish executing before the calling code can continue.

Exercise 16-1   Review and improve the Bookstore web app

In this exercise, you'll review the authentication code in the Bookstore web app, update the database to include the Identity tables, test the authentication and authorization functionality, and add an admin user and some custom fields.

Review the code

1. Open the Ch16Ex1Bookstore app in the ex_starts folder.

2. In the Views/Shared folder, open the _Layout file. In the Bootstrap navbar, note the Razor code that uses dependency injection and the SignInManager class to determine whether a user is logged in.

3. In the Models/DomainModels folder, open the User entity class. Note that it inherits the IdentityUser class and adds a RoleNames property that isn't mapped to the database.

4. In the Models/ViewModels folder, open the RegisterViewModel and Login-ViewModel classes. Note the properties that these view models provide.

5. In the Controllers folder, open the AccountController class. Note that it gets UserManager and SignInManager classes by dependency injection and uses asynchronous action methods.

6. In the Controllers folder, open the CartController class. Note that it's decorated with the Authorize attribute.

7. In the Areas/Admin/Controllers folder, open the Book controller. Note that it's decorated with the Authorize attribute and specifies the Admin role.

Add the Identity tables to the database

8. In the Models/DataLayer folder, open the BookstoreContext file. Update it to inherit the IdentityDbContext<User> class. Be sure to also adjust the OnModel-Creating() method as described in figure 16-5.

9. Display the Package Manager Console (PMC) window and use the Add-Migration command to add a migration named AddIdentityTables. Then, review the migration file that's generated by this command.

10. Still in the PMC, run the Update-Database command to create the Identity tables. If you encounter errors at this step, you can start over by running the Drop-Database command. Then, you can run the Update-Database command again.

Test the Cart and Admin pages

11. Run the app and click the Cart link. It should redirect to the Login page.

12. Click the "Register as a new user" link and enter the fields necessary to register with the app. This should log you in.

13. Click the Cart link again. This should display the Cart page.

14. Click the Admin link. This should display a message that indicates that access is denied for that page.

15. Click the Log Out button. This should log you out.

Seed an admin user and role

16. In the Models/DataLayer/Configuration folder, open the ConfigureIdentity class and add a static asynchronous method named CreateAdminUserAsync() as described in figure 16-22.

17. In the Program.cs file, after the code that adds authentication and authorization, call the static CreateAdminUserAsync() method within code that controls its scope as described in figure 16-22. Since it's an asynchronous method, be sure to use the await keyword with this method call.

18. Run the app again and log in with a username of "admin" and a password of "Sesame". Then, click the Admin link. This should display the Admin page.

19. Navigate to the Manage Users page. This should display the user you added earlier in this exercise. Experiment with this page. For example, you might want to add the user you created earlier in this exercise to the Admin role.

Add fields to the Registration page

20. In the Models/DomainModels folder, open the User entity class and add string properties named FirstName and LastName.

21. Open the Package Manager Console (PMC) and add a new migration for these new registration fields.

22. Use the PMC to update the database. This should add FirstName and LastName columns to the AspNetUsers table in the database.

23. In the Sql Server Object Explorer, navigate to the AspNetUsers table and expand the Columns folder to confirm that this table now has FirstName and LastName columns.

24. In the Models/ViewModels folder, open the RegisterViewModel class and modify it to add the Firstname, Lastname, and Email properties as shown in figure 16-24.

25. In the Controllers folder, open the Account controller and find the Register() action method for POST requests. In this method, update the code to add the Firstname, Lastname, and Email values to the User object.

26. In the Views folder, open the Account/Register view and add fields for the Firstname, Lastname, and Email properties.

27. Run the app and register a new user.

17

How to deploy ASP.NET Core MVC apps

When an app is complete, you'll need to deploy it to the server where it will be accessed by users. To do that, you can use Visual Studio's publish feature. In this chapter, you'll learn how to use the Publish wizard to create publish profiles. Then, you'll learn how to publish to two specific targets: the file system and Microsoft's Azure.

How to work with Visual Studio's publish feature

Deployment refers to the process of copying an ASP.NET Core web app from the development system to the production server where it can be accessed by users. An app can also be deployed to a test server so it can be tested in a different environment before it goes live. Visual Studio provides a *publish* feature for deploying, or *publishing*, web apps.

How work with publish profiles

Visual Studio's publish feature allows you to publish to various targets, such as the file system, a web host, or Azure. To do that, Visual Studio uses *publish profiles* that store deployment information.

Each app can have more than one publish profile. For instance, an app could have a publish profile for a folder to publish to a test environment on the local file system. It could also have a publish profile for a hosting provider to publish to the production environment.

Visual Studio provides a Publish window that you can use to work with the publish profiles for an app, as described in figure 17-1. For example, you can add, edit, and delete publish profiles as described in this figure. In addition, you can rename a profile.

The technique you use to add a publish profile depends on whether the app already contains profiles. If not, the Publish window will look like the first one shown in this figure. Then, you can click the Add a publish profile link to add a profile. By contrast, if the app already contains one or more publish profiles, the Publish window will look like the second one shown in this figure. Then, you can click the New button to add a new profile.

Once you add one or more profiles, you can use the dropdown at the top of the Publish window to select the profile you want to work with. In this figure, the selected profile is for deploying the Future Value app to Azure. You can see some of the settings for this profile in the bottom portion of the window.

When you're ready to deploy an app, you click the Publish button. You'll learn more about what happens when you click this button as you progress through this chapter.

To edit, delete, or rename a profile, you select the appropriate option from the More actions dropdown. When you select the Edit option, a Publish dialog is displayed that lets you change the publish settings. You can also display this dialog by clicking on one of the pencil icons or on the Show all settings link in the Settings section.

The message area in the Publish window displays the status of the selected publish profile. For example, it can indicate that the profile is ready to be published, that a publish succeeded, or that a publish failed. Here, the message indicates that the publish succeeded on a specific date. Once you've published a profile, the message area will also include an Open link whose function depends on the type of deployment.

A Publish window with no publish profiles

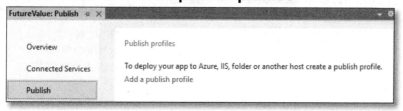

A Publish window with a profile that's been published

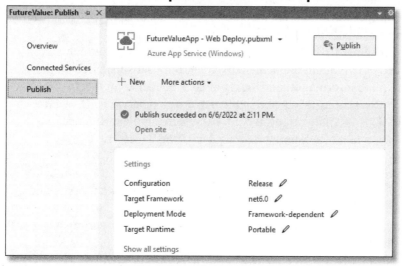

Two ways to open the Publish window

- Select the Build→Publish <project name> command from the Visual Studio menu.
- Right-click the project in the Solution Explorer and select Publish….

How to add a new publish profile

- If the project has no publish profiles, click on the Add a publish profile link.
- If the project has existing publish profiles, click the New button.

How to edit a publish profile

- Select the publish profile from the dropdown at the top of the window. Then, select Edit from the More actions dropdown and make the necessary changes.

How to rename a publish profile

- Select Rename from the More actions dropdown and enter a new name in the dialog that's displayed.

How to delete a publish profile

- Select a publish profile from the dropdown at the top of the window. Then, select Delete from the More actions dropdown and click the Yes button in the Confirm delete profile dialog that's displayed.

Figure 17-1   How to work with publish profiles

How to work with the Publish wizard

Visual Studio uses wizards to walk developers through multi-step processes like deploying an app. A *wizard* is a series of dialogs that let you perform tasks in a set order. Usually, the steps that a wizard displays depend on the choices made in earlier steps in the wizard.

Figure 17-2 shows the first step of the Publish wizard. This step asks you to select the target you want to publish to. In this chapter, you'll learn how to create publish profiles for the Folder and Azure targets. A brief description of the other targets follows. For more information on deployment in Visual Studio, you can start with the overview that's presented at the URL in this figure.

The Docker Container Registry target lets you publish to a Docker container, which is an isolated environment that's not dependent on what's installed on the host. You can find more information on Docker at docs.docker.com.

The FTP/FTPS Server target lets you publish to a web host via *FTP*, or *File Transfer Protocol*. This is a network protocol for transferring files from one computer to another, and it is a common way of deploying a web app to a web host.

The Web Server (IIS) target lets you publish to a web host that uses *IIS*, or *Internet Information Services*. IIS is Microsoft's general-purpose web server, and it is used by many web hosts.

The Import Profile target lets you create a publish profile by importing a .publishsettings file. You can get a .publishsettings file from a web host or Azure, and doing that can simplify the process of creating a publish profile.

The first step of the Publish wizard

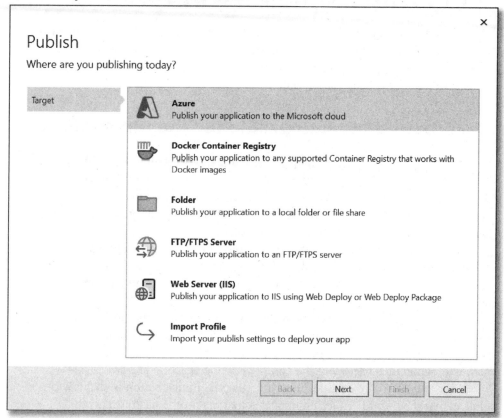

A URL for more information about deployment in Visual Studio

https://docs.microsoft.com/en-us/visualstudio/deployment/deploying-
applications-services-and-components

Description

- When you click on the Add a publish profile link or the New button in the Publish window, the *Publish wizard* starts and the Target step is displayed.

- If your application doesn't have any publish profiles yet, this wizard may start automatically when you open the Publish window.

- Visual Studio uses wizards to walk you through multi-step processes, such as deploying your application.

- The target you select in the first step of the Publish wizard determines the next steps that the wizard displays.

Figure 17-2   How to work with the Publish wizard

How to publish to the file system

The simplest way to publish an app is to select the Folder target to publish to a local or network folder of the file system. You might choose this target if you want to precompile an app in a staging area and then use an FTP program to move it to a test or production server.

How to create a publish profile for the file system

Figure 17-3 shows the next step of the Publish wizard after the Folder target is selected in the first step. In this step you enter the path to the folder where the files are to be published. By default, the wizard publishes to a location in the bin\Release folder for the app. If that's not what you want, you can click the Browse... button to navigate to a different folder.

In addition to selecting existing directories, you can create new ones. In this example, for instance, the bin directory exists, but the Release, net6.0, and publish directories do not. Instead, they will be created when the app is published.

This wizard step also provides information on how you should enter the file path for local folders and network, or shared, folders. For a local folder, you provide either a full path or a relative path. For network folders, you begin the path with \\ and then use either the computer name or its IP address.

After you enter a folder location, you click the Finish button to display the final step of the wizard. This step indicates that the profile has been created. Then, you can click the Finish button to return to the Publish window, which should display a "Ready to publish" message.

How to deploy to a publish folder

Figure 17-3 also presents the steps for deploying an app that's ready to publish. To do that, you simply click the Publish button. Then, a spinner icon and a 'Publishing to Folder' message will display in the message area, along with a Cancel link you can click to cancel the deployment. In addition, the deployment progress will show in the Output window.

When the deployment is complete, a "Publish succeeded" message is displayed that includes the date and time. An Open folder link also appears below the success message. You can click on that link to view the deployed files.

How to change the publish folder

Finally, figure 17-3 presents the steps for changing the folder where the files will be published. To do that, you edit the profile as described in figure 17-1. Then, you display the Connections tab, change the path in the Target location textbox, and click the Save button.

The dialog for specifying a folder location

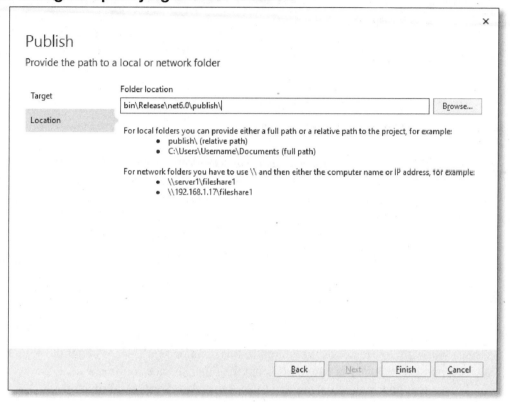

How to create the publish profile

1. Enter the path of the folder you want to publish to in the Location step.
2. Click the Finish button, then click the Close button in the Finish step that's displayed.

How to deploy to the publish folder

1. In the publish profile, click the Publish button. The progress will be displayed in the Output window.
2. To see the published files, click on the Open folder link when deployment is complete.

How to change the publish folder

1. Select Edit from the More actions dropdown.
2. Click on Connection.
3. Change the Target location and click Save.

Description

*   The simplest publish method is to publish to a local or network folder.

Figure 17-3   How to publish to the file system

How to publish a simple app to Azure

As you've seen, the Publish wizard provides several options for deploying your app to a remote web host. In this chapter, you'll learn how to publish to Azure, which is Microsoft's cloud. To start, you'll learn how to deploy a simple app that doesn't use a database to Azure.

How to get started with Azure

Azure is Microsoft's *Platform as a Service (PaaS)* offering. PaaS provides a complete development and deployment environment in the cloud. Using a cloud-based product like Azure lets you avoid having to purchase and maintain on-site hardware and software.

Figure 17-4 presents a URL for a website where you can sign up for a free trial of Azure. Once your free trial is over, Azure has a pay-as-you-go model where you are charged for the resources that your subscription uses.

To publish your app to Azure using Visual Studio's Publish wizard, you must log in to Visual Studio with the same credentials that you used when you signed up for Azure. Then, you can select the Azure target in the Publish wizard to display the dialog that's shown here. This dialog lets you choose the Azure service you want to use to host your app. In this chapter, you'll learn about the Azure App Service, but you can learn about the other services online.

Notice that you can publish an app to an Azure App Service running on either Windows or Linux. For the purposes of this section, you can select either of these options. However, you might notice some slight differences between apps running on these two operating systems. For instance, the Future Value app uses the ToString() method of the String object with the "C2" format string to display the future value as currency. In a Windows-based Azure app, this works as expected. But in a Linux-based Azure app, the dollar sign may not display properly. In most cases, though, simple apps should work correctly with either app service.

The website to sign up for a free trial of Azure

https://azure.microsoft.com/en-us/free/dotnet/

The dialog for selecting an Azure service

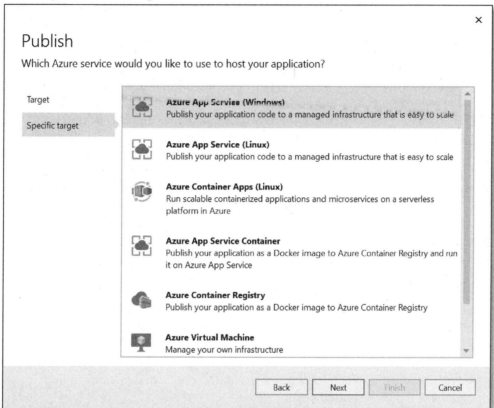

Description

- Azure is Microsoft's cloud-based *Platform as a Service (PaaS)* offering. You can sign up for a free trial of this service.
- To publish an app to Azure, you must log in to Visual Studio with the same Microsoft account that you used to sign up for Azure.
- To create a publish profile for an Azure App Service, you can choose either the Windows-based option or the Linux-based option from the Specific target step of the Publish wizard.

Figure 17-4   How to get started with Azure

How to create a publish profile for an Azure App Service

When you select the Azure App Service (Windows) or Azure App Service (Linux) option shown in the last figure, the next step of the wizard is displayed as shown in figure 17-5. Note, however, that if you haven't signed up for an Azure account or you aren't signed in, you will be asked to do that before the controls in this dialog are displayed.

Once you are signed in to your Azure account, this dialog will show the name of your subscription and any App Service instances that you've created. Of course, if this is the first Azure app you've published, the App Service instances list box will be empty as shown here. To create a new app service, you click the plus sign above the list box to display the Create new App Service dialog. Here, the Name value is the name of the Azure App Service you're creating and the Subscription name value is the name of your Azure subscription.

The Resource group value is the name of the Azure resource group that will be created when you deploy your app. A resource group in Azure is a container that holds all the resources for an app. This makes it easier to maintain your app.

Finally, the Hosting Plan value is the name of the Azure App Service plan that will be created when you deploy your app. In Azure, an app always runs in an Azure App Service plan that defines a set of computer resources and is analogous to a server farm.

Visual Studio generates default values for all four of these fields. However, these values are typically based on the app name and the current date, which can produce unwieldy values like "FutureValue20220603170932". Because of that, you'll typically want to change the generated values so they're more user friendly like the ones shown here.

Once the dialog is complete, you click the Create button to begin the process of creating the app service, the app service plan, and the resource group that will contain them both. This process can take a few seconds, and you'll see a progress bar in the lower left corner of the dialog. When it's done, you're returned to the Publish wizard where the resource group you just created is included in the App Service instances list box and is selected by default.

To create the publish profile, you click the Finish button. Then, the progress will be displayed in the dialog, and a success message will display when the creation is complete. If you don't want this message to be displayed in the future, you can check the Automatically close when succeeded checkbox. Finally, click the Close button to see the newly created publish profile in the Publish window.

The dialogs for creating an Azure App Service publish profile

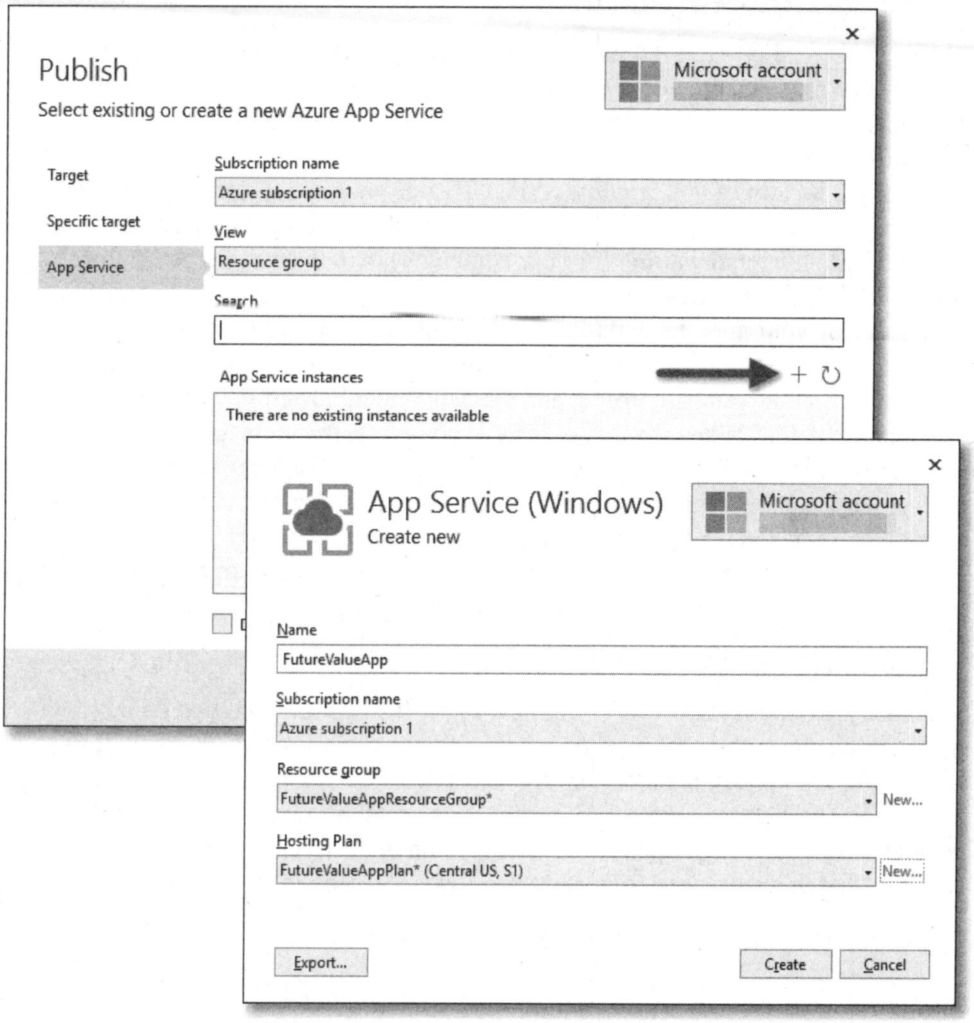

How to create a publish profile for an Azure App Service

1. In the Specific target step of the Publish wizard, select Azure App Service (Windows) or Azure App Service (Linux).

2. In the App Service step that's displayed, click the plus sign above the App Service instances list box (see the arrow above).

3. In the Create new App Service dialog that's displayed, accept the default values or change them as necessary. To change the Resource group or Hosting Plan, select a different item from the dropdown or click the New… link to create a new item.

4. Click the Create button. This will return you to the App Service step, and the new app service will be selected in the App Service instances list box.

5. Click the Finish button. When the creation process is complete, click the Close button. This will return you to the Publish window, and the new publish profile will be displayed.

Figure 17-5   How to create a publish profile for an Azure App Service

How to deploy to the Azure App Service

Figure 17-6 shows the Publish window after a publish profile for an Azure App Service has been created. Here, the message area displays a message that the app is ready to publish. Below that, you can see some of the configuration settings for the publish profile.

Near the bottom of this window is the URL for your new Azure App Service. If you click on this link, a website will be displayed with a message that your web app is running and waiting for your content. This indicates that your Azure App Service is set up, but your app hasn't been deployed to it yet.

To deploy your app, you simply click the Publish button. Just as when you deploy to a folder, a spinner icon and a publishing message will display in the message area of the publish profile, and the deployment progress will show in the Output window. When the deployment is complete, the message will change to "Publish succeeded". In addition, an Open site link will appear below the success message that you can click on to navigate to the Azure website. This links to the same URL as the one near the bottom of the window.

Finally, the newly deployed app will display in the browser. In this figure, for example, you can see the Future Value app after it has been deployed to Azure and opened in the browser. Note that the URL in the address bar is the same as the URL shown in the publish profile.

After your app is deployed, it's simple to deploy changes. All you do is save your changes in Visual Studio, open the Publish window, select the publish profile, and click the Publish button. As before, you'll see a progress message in the message area and progress information in the Output window. Also as before, the updated web app will open in a browser when deployment is complete. Note, however, that you may need to refresh the browser to see the changes you made.

An Azure App Service publish profile that's ready to publish

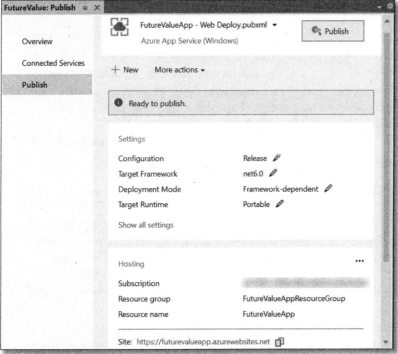

The Future Value app in a browser

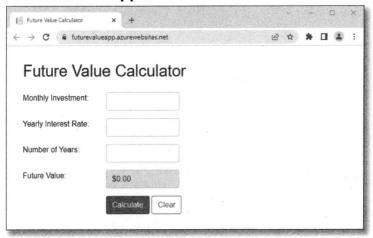

Description

- To deploy to the Azure App Service, select the publish profile in the Publish window and click Publish.

- The publish progress will be displayed in the Output window. Once the app is deployed, it will open in a browser.

- To deploy changes to the app, save the changes and click Publish again. You may need to refresh the browser to see the changes.

Figure 17-6   How to deploy to the Azure App Service

How to publish a data-driven app to Azure

In addition to deploying simple apps like the Future Value app to Azure, you frequently need to deploy apps that use a database. To illustrate how that works, the topics that follow show you how to deploy the Movie List App that you saw in chapter 4 to Azure. As you saw in that chapter, this app uses EF Core and migrations to work with a MovieList database.

How to add an Azure SQL Database to a publish profile

In the last section, you learned how to use the Publish wizard to create a publish profile for an Azure App Service. You use this same procedure to create a publish profile for an app that uses a database. If your app uses migrations, however, you need to be sure to use the Windows-based Azure App Service. That's because the Linux-based App Service doesn't always work correctly with migrations.

Once you've created the publish profile, you need to add the database to that profile before you deploy the app. To do that, you use the Service Dependencies section of the Publish window as shown in figure 17-7. For the Movie List app, this section has a dependency item labeled SQL Server Database. Note that when you first create your publish profile, it may take a moment for this item to appear on the screen.

From this section, you can click the menu button and select Connect to display the Connect to Dependency dialog. From this dialog, you select the Azure SQL Database option and then click the Next button to display the Connect to Azure SQL Database dialog, also shown in this figure. To connect to a database, you click the plus sign above the SQL databases table. When you do, the Create new Azure SQL Database dialog shown in part 2 of this figure is displayed.

The Service Dependencies section of a publish profile

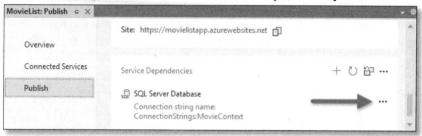

The Connect to dependency and Connect to Azure SQL Database dialogs

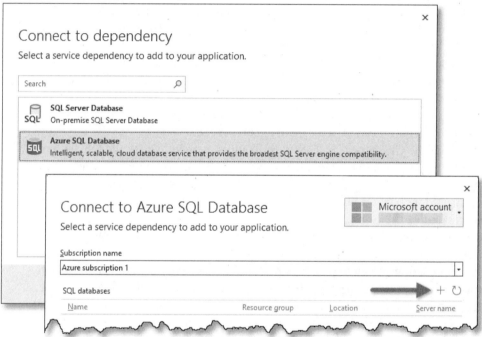

How to add an Azure SQL Database to a publish profile

1. Create a publish profile for the data-driven application as described previously. Be sure to use the Azure App Service (Windows) option, as migrations don't always work with Linux. Also, make sure to add a new resource group rather than re-using an existing one.

2. When the profile is ready to publish, scroll down to the Service Dependencies section of the profile and click the menu button (…) to the right of the SQL Server Database item (see the arrow above) and select Connect.

3. In the Connect to Dependency dialog that's displayed, select Azure SQL Database and click the Next button.

4. In the Connect to Azure SQL Databases dialog that's displayed, click the plus sign above the SQL databases table (see the arrow above) to display the Create New Azure SQL Database dialog (see part 2).

Figure 17-7   How to add an Azure SQL Database to a publish profile (part 1)

The Create new Azure SQL Database dialog displays a default database name that's based on the database used by your app. If a database with this name already exists, the dialog will display an error message indicating that the name is already in use. In that case, you can change the database name to one that isn't in use.

Next, you need to be sure that the resource group that's selected is the same as the resource group you created for the publish profile. After that, you're ready to create the database server that will host this new database. To do that, you click the New… link (not visible here) to the right of the Database server text box. This displays the Create new SQL Server dialog, also shown in this figure.

In this dialog, you can accept the default database server name or enter another name. If someone else has already used the default database server name, for example, you'll need to change it. Once again, the dialog will display an error message if the name isn't available.

You also need to enter an Administrator username and password in this dialog, and you need to confirm the password. As you start to enter the name and password, the dialog will display messages telling you the criteria that must be met for them to be valid. Be sure to make a note of the username and password you use, as you'll need to enter them again.

When the Create new SQL Server dialog is complete, click the OK button. This takes you back to the Create new Azure SQL Database dialog, where the Database server, Database administrator user name, and Database administrator password text boxes now display the values you entered in the Create new SQL Server dialog.

At this point, you can click the Create button to create your Azure database. When this process is complete, you'll be returned to the Connect to Azure SQL Database dialog shown in part 1. Now, though, the newly created database will appear in the SQL databases table. Then, you can select the database and click the Next button to display the connection string section of the Connect to Azure SQL Database dialog. There, you can enter the username and password you created previously, click the Finish button, and then click the Close button. When you're returned to the Publish window, the Service Dependencies section of the publish profile will show that you have an Azure SQL database connected to the publish profile.

The dialogs for adding a SQL Server database to a publish profile

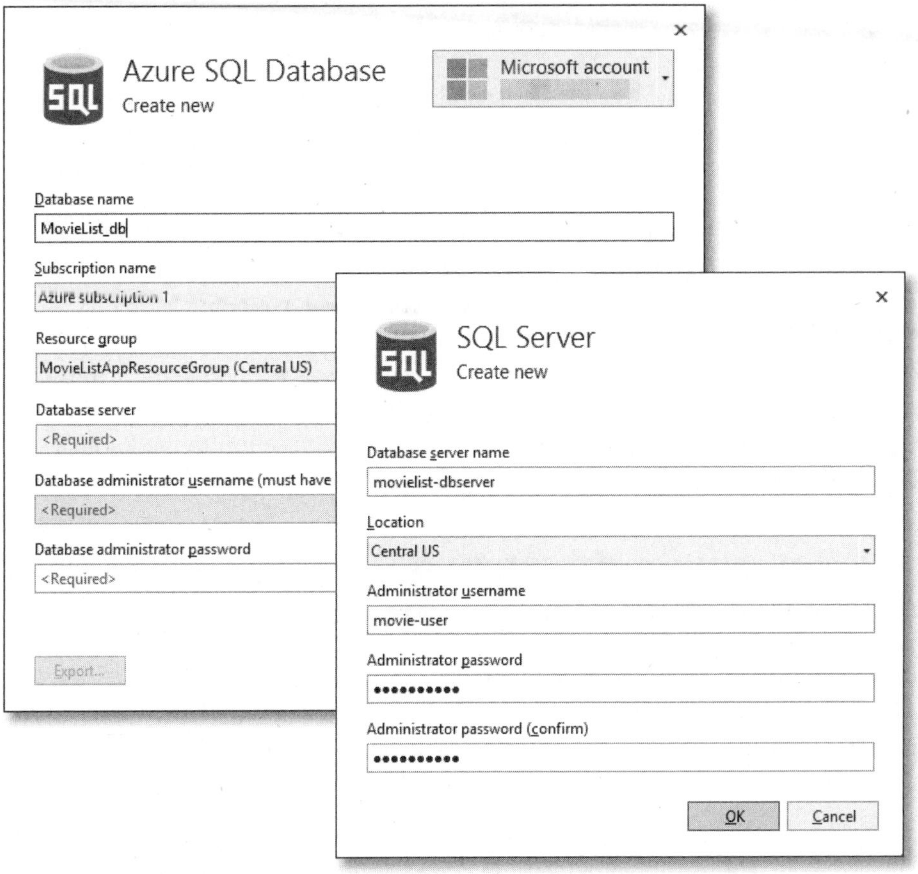

How to add an Azure SQL Database to a publish profile (continued)

5. In the Create new Azure SQL Database dialog, specify the database name.

6. Make sure the resource group you added for this application is selected.

7. Click the New… link to the right of the Database server textbox.

8. In the Create new SQL Server dialog that's displayed, specify the server name. If the default name isn't available, change it to one that the dialog will accept.

9. Enter an Admin username and password, and make a note of them for later. Click OK to return to the Create new Azure SQL Database dialog.

10. Click Create to create the Azure database and return to the Connect to Azure SQL Database dialog.

11. Select the database and click Next to display the next Connect to Azure SQL Database dialog.

12. Enter the username and password from step 9, accept the default connection string and Save option, and click the Finish button.

13. When the dependency configuration progress is complete, click the Close button to return to the publish profile, where a connected Azure SQL Database is now displayed.

Figure 17-7   How to add an Azure SQL Database to a publish profile (part 2)

How to configure a connection string and migrations in a publish profile

Even after you create an Azure SQL Database and connect it to the publish profile for your app, you're still not ready to deploy the app. Before you do that, you have to configure the connection string and migrations in the profile as shown in figure 17-8.

To configure the connection string and migrations, you edit the publish profile. An easy way to do that is to click the Show all settings link for the profile to display the dialog shown in this figure. Then, you can expand the Database and Entity Framework Migrations sections and select the check box in each section. That way, the app will use the specified connection string when it's run, and it will apply the specified migration when the app is deployed. When you're done, you can click the Save button to save the changes and return to the Publish window. At this point, you're ready to deploy the app.

How to deploy a data-driven app to the Azure App Service

To deploy a data-driven app to the Azure App Service, you use the same technique you use to deploy any other app. That is, you simply click the Publish button in the Publish window. Once the app has been deployed, it's displayed in your browser. In figure 17-8, for example, you can see the Movie List app in a browser.

The procedure for deploying changes made to a data-driven app to the Azure App Service is also the same as for any other app. That includes changes made to the database using new migrations. After applying the new migrations, just open the Publish window, select the correct publish profile, and click the Publish button. Remember that before you see the changes you made, you may need to refresh the browser.

The dialog for editing the settings for a data-driven app

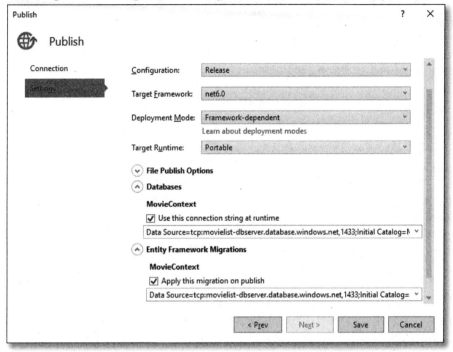

How to configure the connection string and migrations

1. In the publish profile, click on the Show all settings link and wait for the 'Discovering Data Contexts...' spinner icon to stop.

2. Expand the Databases section and select the Use this connection string at runtime check box.

3. Expand the Entity Framework Migrations section and select the Apply this migration on publish check box.

4. Click the Save button to return to the publish profile.

The Movie List app in a browser

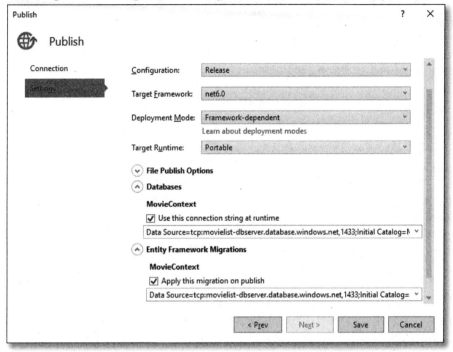

Figure 17-8   How to configure a connection string and migrations in a publish profile

How to work with an Azure app

Once you deploy an Azure App Service, you may need to work with it from Azure. To do that, you use the Azure portal. The topic that follows introduces you to this portal to give you a general idea how it works. Then, the next topic shows you how to delete an Azure app, which is something you may need to do when you deploy App Services from Visual Studio.

An introduction to the Azure portal

The first screen in figure 17-9 shows the home page for the Azure portal. You can get to this page using the URL at the top of this figure. Note that if you didn't choose to stay signed in to Azure when you created your account or you have signed out, you will need to sign in before you can see the home page.

As you can see, the home page provides access to all of the different types of services Azure provides. For example, you can click on the Resource groups icon to display a list of the resource groups you've created, you can click the App Services icon to display a list of the app services you've created, and you can click on the SQL databases icon to display a list of the SQL databases you've created. Note that when you first display the home page, you may not see the service you want. In that case, you can click the More services icon to display additional services.

The second screen in this figure shows the Resource groups page that's displayed when you click on the Resource groups icon. Here, you can see the resource groups for the Future Value and Movie List apps that you learned how to deploy to Azure in this chapter. To manage your resource groups, you can use the links at the top of this page. When you deploy apps from Visual Studio, however, you more likely to work with an individual resource group by clicking on its icon. Then, information about that group is displayed, and you can manage that item or display information about the individual resources in the group. If you practice this for a few minutes, you shouldn't have any trouble understanding how it works.

The URL for the Azure portal home page

```
portal.azure.com/#home
```

The Azure portal home and Resource groups pages

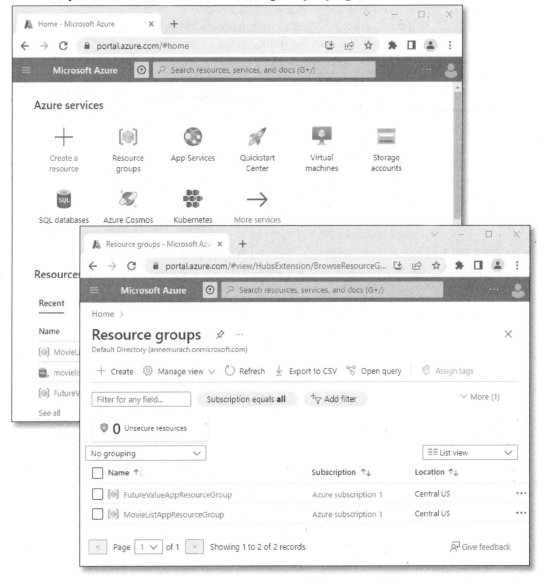

Description

- The Azure portal lets you manage the apps that you've deployed to Azure.
- The home page displays all the service types that Azure provides. You can click on any of these icons to display a page that lists the items of that type that you've created.
- Once you display a page with a list of items, you can use the icons and links on that page to get more information or to manage an item.

Figure 17-9   An introduction to the Azure portal

How to delete an Azure App Service

One of the things you're most likely to do after you've deployed an Azure App Service is to delete it. For example, if you have trouble getting a publish profile to work, you may want to delete the App Service, delete the publish profile as described in figure 17-1, and then recreate the profile. The easiest way to delete an app service is to use the Azure portal to delete the resource group that contains files for the app. That includes the app service itself, as well as the app service plan, the database, and the database server,

Figure 17-10 presents the procedure for deleting a resource group using the Azure portal. To start, you need to use the Azure portal to display the resource group you want to delete as shown in the first screen in this figure. By default, the Overview section of the page should be displayed. Then, you can click the Delete resource group link at the top of the details pane. When you do, a warning message is displayed to confirm the deletion, as shown in the second screen in this figure. Here, you can see that this message includes a list of the resources in the group.

If you do want to delete the resource group, you need to enter its name in the text box that's provided and then click the Delete button. This action can take several seconds to complete, and you may need to refresh the browser to update the list of resource groups.

The warning in the Azure portal when you delete a resource group

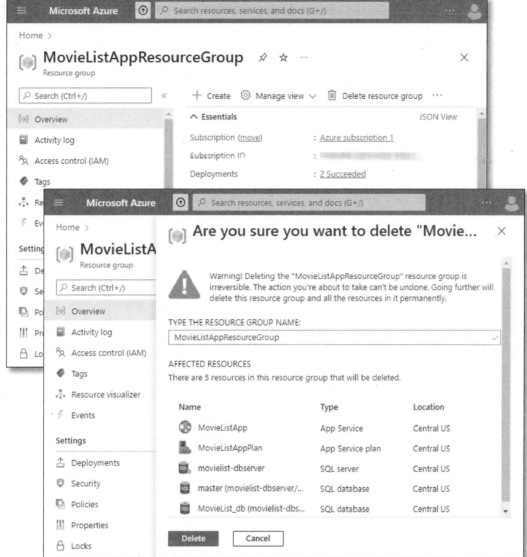

How to delete an Azure resource group

1. Log in to Azure, display the resource groups, and click on the resource group you want to delete.

2. In the details pane of the Overview section for the resource group, click the Delete resource group link. A warning message asking you to confirm the deletion will be displayed.

3. Enter the name of the resource group in the text box that's provided and then click the Delete button.

Figure 17-10   How to delete an Azure resource group

Perspective

This chapter has presented the basic skills for using Visual Studio's publish feature to deploy apps to the file system and to Microsoft Azure. It has also presented a brief introduction to the Azure portal, which you can use to work with the apps you deploy to Azure. However, there's much more to know about deploying apps, including other tools and techniques you can use. Even so, this chapter should get you off to a good start.

Terms

deploy	File Transfer Protocol (FTP)
publish	Internet Information Services (IIS)
publish profile	Azure
wizard	Platform as a Service (PaaS)

Summary

- Visual Studio allows you to *publish*, or *deploy*, apps to various targets, such as the file system, a hosting provider, or *Azure*, Microsoft's cloud platform.

- Visual Studio provides a Publish window that lets you work with the *publish profiles* for an app.

- Visual Studio uses *wizards* to walk you through multi-step processes. You can use the Publish wizard to create publish profiles.

- *File Transfer Protocol*, or *FTP*, is a network protocol for transferring files from one computer to another. This is a common way of deploying a web app to a hosting provider.

- *Internet Information Services*, or *IIS*, is Microsoft's general-purpose web server. It's used by many hosting providers.

- Azure is Microsoft's *Platform as a Service*, or *PaaS*, offering. It provides a complete development and deployment environment that's in the cloud.

Before you do the exercises for this chapter...

The last three exercises for this chapter require an active Azure account. So, before you can do these exercises, you need to sign up for an Azure free trial as described in figure 17-4, and then log in to Visual Studio with your Azure credentials. If you don't want to sign up for an Azure account, you can still do the first exercise.

Exercise 17-1   Publish the Future Value app to the file system

1. Open the Ch17Ex1FutureValue app in the ex_starts folder.

2. Open the Publish window to start the Publish wizard. If the wizard doesn't start automatically, click on the Add a publish profile link.

3. Select the Folder target and accept the default folder path or use the Browse... button to select a new one.

4. Click the Finish button. In the Finish step that's displayed, click the Automatically close when succeeded checkbox if you don't want the Finish step to be displayed in the future. Then, click the Close button.

5. Click the Publish button to deploy the files to the target folder.

6. When deployment is complete, click on the Open folder link to view the deployed files.

Exercise 17-2   Publish the Future Value app to Azure

Create the publish profile and deploy the app

1. If the Ch17Ex1FutureValue app in the ex_starts folder isn't already open, open it.

2. Open the Publish window if it isn't already open, and then start the Publish wizard by clicking on the New button.

3. Select the Azure target and then the Azure App Service (Windows) or Azure App Service (Linux) specific target.

4. Use the procedure described in figure 17-5 to complete the publish profile by creating an app service, app service plan, and resource group in Azure.

5. When the publish profile is complete, click on the URL for the web app in the Publish window to see the message that's displayed.

6. Click the Publish button to deploy the app to Azure.

7. When the Azure web app opens in the browser, test it with valid and invalid data to make sure it works correctly.

8. When you're done, close the browser.

Update the app and deploy the changes

9. Open the layout view, add a footer with this message "Deployed to Azure on *mm/dd/yyyy*", and save your changes.

10. In the publish profile, click the Publish button. When the web app opens in the browser, see if the new footer is displayed. If it isn't, click the browser's refresh button to display it.

11. When you're done, close the browser.

Exercise 17-3   Publish the Movie List app to Azure

1. Open the Ch17Ex3MovieList app in the ex_starts folder.

2. Open the Publish window to start the Publish wizard. If the wizard doesn't start automatically, click on the Add a publish profile link.

3. Select the Azure target and the Azure App Service (Windows) specific target.

4. Use the Publish wizard to create an app service, app service plan, and resource group in Azure as described in figure 17-5.

5. Add an Azure SQL Database to the publish profile as described in figure 17-7.

6. When the publish profile is complete, configure the connection string and migrations for the publish profile as shown in figure 17-8.

7. Click the Publish button to deploy the app to Azure.

8. When the Azure web app opens in the browser, test it by adding a new movie, editing that movie, and then deleting the movie you added.

9. When you're done, close the browser.

Exercise 17-4   Delete the Azure apps

1. Go to the Azure portal, and navigate to the Resource groups section.

2. Click the link for the FutureValueAppResource Group to display the information for that group.

3. Complete the procedure in figure 17-10 to delete the resource group. If necessary, click the Refresh icon to refresh the display so the resources are no longer displayed.

4. Return to the Resource groups section, click the link for the MovieListApp-ResourceGroup, and then delete that resource group.

18

How to use Visual Studio Code

This chapter shows how to use Visual Studio Code (also known as VS Code) with this book. This source code editor is an increasingly popular alternative to the Visual Studio IDE that has been presented so far in this book. Although VS Code doesn't provide as many features as the Visual Studio IDE, some programmers prefer the simplicity and speed that VS Code provides.

How to work with existing projects

This chapter begins by showing how to work with existing projects, such as the projects for this book that you can download from murach.com. These projects were originally created with the Visual Studio IDE, but it's easy to use VS Code to work with them. But first, if VS Code isn't already installed on your system, you need to install it.

How to install VS Code

Installing VS Code is similar to installing Visual Studio as described in appendixes A (Windows) and B (macOS). The main difference is that you begin by searching the internet for "Visual Studio Code download". Then, you download the installer file, run it, and respond to the resulting dialog boxes.

How to open and close a project folder

Once you have installed VS Code, you can start it and use it to open any existing projects. This includes projects that were created by the Visual Studio IDE. Figure 18-1 shows how to open a Visual Studio project with VS Code.

To do that, you can use the File→Open Folder item that's available from the menu system. Then, you can use the resulting dialog to select the folder for the project. For example, to open the Future Value app from chapter 2, you select the FutureValue folder for the project that's within the Ch02FutureValue folder for the solution. This is possible because VS Code doesn't need a solution or project file to store configuration information like Visual Studio does. Instead, when you open a project folder, VS Code provides access to all the source code files and other resources that it contains.

Once you've opened a project folder, VS Code displays its folders and files in the Explorer window that's on its left side of the main window. In addition, VS Code may prompt you with dialogs like the ones described in this figure. If you encounter dialogs like this, you typically want to respond with an affirmative answer such as Yes or Restore.

If you use the dialog described in this figure to add the required assets, VS Code creates a new subfolder named .vscode. This folder typically contains two JSON files named launch.json and tasks.json, and these files contain the configuration VS Code needs to run a project as described later in this chapter.

When you use VS Code to open a folder, it's important to close the folder when you're done with it. To do that, you can use the File→Close Folder item that's available from the menu system.

Most of the time, that's all you need to use VS Code to work with an existing Visual Studio project. However, if you need to work with a Visual Studio solution that contains multiple projects, or if you want to save special configurations and settings related to your projects, you can use the File→Save Workspace As item to save a configuration file. Then, if you want, you can use the File→Add Folder To Workspace item to add a second project folder to the

A typical message after opening a Visual Studio project

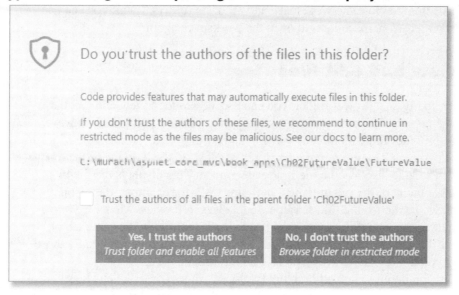

Do you trust the authors of the files in this folder?

Code provides features that may automatically execute files in this folder.

If you don't trust the authors of these files, we recommend to continue in restricted mode as the files may be malicious. See our docs to learn more.

C:\murach\aspnet_core_mvc\book_apps\Ch02FutureValue\FutureValue

☐ Trust the authors of all files in the parent folder 'Ch02FutureValue'

Yes, I trust the authors
Trust folder and enable all features

No, I don't trust the authors
Browse folder in restricted mode

How to open a project folder

1. Select File→Open Folder from the menu system.

2. Use the resulting dialog to select the folder that contains the Visual Studio project. For the Future Value app from chapter 2, you can select this folder:

   `\murach\aspnet_core_mvc\book_apps\Ch02FutureValue\FutureValue`

3. Click Select Folder.

How to deal with errors and messages after opening a Visual Studio project

- If you get a dialog asking if you trust the authors, click "Yes, I trust the authors". You can also check the "Trust the authors…" checkbox to avoid this message in the future.

- If you get a dialog that indicates that "Required assets to build and debug are missing" and asks if you would like to add them, click Yes. This adds a .vscode subfolder to your project folder that contains .json files with VS Code configurations.

- If you get a dialog that says "There are unresolved dependencies", click Restore.

- If VS Code still displays messages, including underlined code, close VS Code and start it again. The problems should go away when VS Code rereads its configuration files.

How to close a project folder

- Select File→Close Folder from the menu system.

Description

- *Visual Studio Code* (also known as *VS Code*) is a *source code editor*, which is simpler than an integrated development environment (IDE) like Visual Studio.

- To open a Visual Studio project with VS Code, you can open the folder for the project.

Figure 18-1   How to open and close a project folder

workspace. When you're done with the workspace, you can use the File→Close Workspace item to close the workspace and all of its folders. Later, you can use the File→Open Workspace item to open the workspace again.

How to view and edit files

After you open a project folder, you can use VS Code to view and edit the files in the project. This works much like using the Visual Studio IDE. However, VS Code provides three modes for viewing and editing files.

When you click on a file in the Explorer window on the left side of the main window, VS Code displays the file in Preview mode. This displays the file in a tab with the name of the file in italics. In figure 18-2, for example, the second tab displays the file for the FutureValueModel class in Preview Mode. If you click on the name of a different file, VS Code loads that file in the same tab of the editor. This is an excellent way to quickly view various files, especially those files that you don't want to keep open for a long time.

When you double-click a file in the Explorer window or make changes to a file in preview mode, VS Code displays the file in Standard Mode. This displays the file in a tab with the name of the file in normal, non-italic font. In this figure, for example, the first tab displays the file for the HomeController class in Standard Mode. While Preview Mode is ideal for switching between multiple files and spending a short time in each of them, Standard Mode is designed to be used for files that you want to keep open indefinitely.

Zen Mode removes all user interface components and only displays the editor. Some developers feel that the lack of user interface distractions helps them focus on the code and leads to greater productivity.

Note that the screen shown here, as well as those shown throughout this chapter, use one of VS Code's light color themes. Specifically, they use the Light (Visual Studio) color theme so they look similar to the Visual Studio screens you've seen throughout this book. If you want to change the color theme, you can select File→Preferences→Color Theme from the VS Code menu and then select the theme you want.

VS Code with files in Standard and Preview Modes

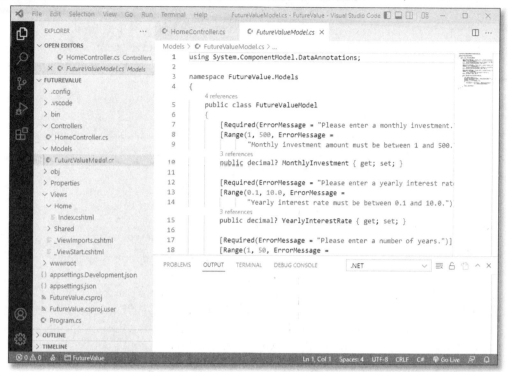

Three modes for viewing files

Mode	Useful for...
Preview	Switching between files to quickly view them.
Standard	Opening a file indefinitely for viewing and editing.
Zen	Focusing on editing a file's code without distraction of other interface elements.

Description

- To preview a file, click on it in the Explorer window. This displays the file in a tab in the editor with the name of the file in italics, indicating that you are in Preview Mode. If you click another file, VS Code reuses the tab.

- To open a file, double-click on it in the Explorer window. This displays the file in a tab in the editor with the name of the file in normal font style, indicating that you are in Standard Mode.

- To work on a file in Zen mode, open the file, click inside it, press Ctrl+K, release both keys, and immediately press Z for Zen. This displays the file in the editor without any other parts of the VS Code interface. To exit Zen Mode, press the Esc key *twice*.

Figure 18-2   How to view and edit files

How to run and stop a project

You can run an app in several ways from within VS Code. For example, you can select the Run→Start Without Debugging item from the menu system. However, you can also press Ctrl+F5 to accomplish the same task. This works much like it does for the Visual Studio IDE.

When you run a web app like the ones shown throughout this book, VS Code starts the web server and begins listening for requests issued for your web app. This is shown by the output that VS Code displays in its Debug Console. In figure 18-3, for example, the Debug Console below the editor shows that it is starting the Kestrel web server and listening for requests here:

```
https://localhost:7091
```

In addition, VS Code automatically starts the web browser that's set as the default for your system and navigates to the URL shown above. This displays the web app in your default browser. For example, if you use VS Code to run the Future Value app from chapter 2, it automatically displays that app in a browser as shown in this figure.

Note that if this is the first time you've run one of the apps for this book, a message may be displayed asking if you want to trust the ASP.NET Core SSL certificate, which is used to secure the localhost server. Trusting this certificate allows you to test your app locally on your own machine without your browser displaying this message. Or, if you prefer, you can tell the browser to ignore the warnings and proceed anyway.

You can also stop an app in several ways from within VS Code. For example, you can click the Stop button in the toolbar that's displayed across the top of the main window. Or, you can press Shift+F5. This stops the Kestrel server, but doesn't close the web browser. Conversely, closing the web browser doesn't stop the server.

VS Code with the app running in a browser

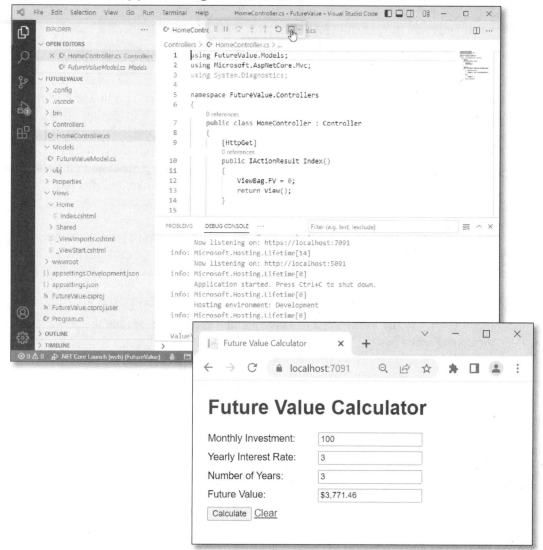

Description

- To run an app in the browser that you've set as the default for your system, press Ctrl+F5. This starts the app without debugging and automatically launches the browser.

- To stop an app, press Shift+F5 or click the Stop button in the toolbar.

- When VS Code runs the app on the Kestrel server, it uses the Debug Console window to display information about the server including the ports that it is using.

- If you get messages about trusting and installing an SSL certificate, you can click Yes. And if a web page is displayed indicating that the connection is not private, you can click the link to proceed.

Figure 18-3   How to run and stop a project

How to create the database for a project

If you run a project and you get an error message like the one that's shown at the top of figure 18-4, it's probably because you need to create the database that the project uses. To use VS Code to create the database for a project, you can use its Terminal window. This window provides access to a *command-line interface (CLI)* that allows you to execute commands by entering a line of text at the command prompt.

If the CLI tools for .NET EF Core aren't already installed on your system, you can follow the first procedure shown in this figure to install them. If these tools are installed on your system, but out of date, you'll get a message in the Terminal window to update them. To do that, you can follow the first procedure as well, with one change. You'll need to type the command 'update' rather than the command 'install'.

Once the CLI tools for .NET EF Core are installed on your system, you can use the second procedure to execute a .NET EF Core command that creates the database. This works much like the Update-Database command that's described in chapters 4 and 12.

After you've used VS Code's Terminal window to create the database for a project, you can run the app again. This time, the app should be able to access the database and run successfully.

The error message that's displayed if the database hasn't been created

A command prompt for the MovieList app from chapter 4

How to install the CLI tools for .NET EF Core

1. Display the Terminal by selecting Terminal→New Terminal.
2. At the command prompt, enter this command:

```
dotnet tool install --global dotnet-ef
```

How to create the database for a project

1. Display the Terminal by selecting Terminal→New Terminal.
2. At the command prompt, enter this command:

```
dotnet ef database update
```

Description

- If a project uses a database, you may need to create the database before the project can run successfully.
- A *command-line interface* (*CLI*) allows you to execute commands by entering a line of text at the command prompt.
- When you use VS Code, you often need to use the command line provided by the Terminal window to execute CLI commands such as the .NET EF Core commands.
- Before you can use the .NET EF Core commands, you need to install the CLI tools for EF Core. You only need to do this once.

Figure 18-4   How to create the database for a project

A summary of .NET EF Core commands

Figure 18-5 starts by reviewing the command that you need to install the CLI tools for .NET EF Core. Then, it presents five of the .NET EF Core commands. If you've read chapters 4 and 12, you should realize that these commands correspond to the PowerShell commands that are available from Visual Studio's Package Manager Console (PMC). That's because the CLI commands just provide a different way to access the same EF Core commands as the PMC.

When you use a CLI command for .NET EF Core, you preface the command with dotnet ef. For example, you can update the database by entering this command:

```
dotnet ef database update
```

In addition, you may sometimes need to include an argument after the name of the command. For example, to add a migration named Initial, you can enter this command:

```
dotnet ef migrations add Initial
```

If you understand how to use the PowerShell commands described in chapters 4 and 12, you shouldn't have much trouble understanding how to convert most of those commands to CLI commands. However, some commands require several arguments that you must specify as well as one or more options that you can specify. As a result, it can take some effort to figure out how they work.

In this figure, for instance, the last example presents the dbcontext scaffold command. This command begins by specifying two required arguments. The first one specifies that the connection string is stored in the appsettings.json file with a name of BookstoreContext. The second one specifies that the DbContext provider is EF Core for SQL Server.

After the two required parameters, this example uses an option to specify the output directory like this:

```
--output-dir Models/DataLayer
```

Here, the output directory is the DataLayer subfolder of the Models folder. In addition, to make this option easy to read, it uses two dashes to specify the long version of the option's name. However, you can use a single dash and a short version of the option's name like this:

```
-o Models/DataLayer
```

After the first option, the second option specifies that the command should use attributes (not the Fluent API) to configure the model whenever possible. And the third option specifies that the command should overwrite any existing files. Again, both of these options use two dashes and the long version of the name, although they could use a single dash and the short version of the name.

For more information about the commands shown in this figure, including detailed descriptions of their arguments and options, you can use the URL provided in this figure. Or, you can search the internet for "dotnet ef commands".

A command that installs the CLI tools for .NET EF Core

```
dotnet tool install --global dotnet-ef
```

Some of the .NET EF Core commands (prefix with dotnet ef)

Command	Description
`migrations add`	Adds the migration file with the specified name.
`migrations remove`	Removes the last migration file from the Migrations folder. Only works with migrations that have not yet been applied with the database update command.
`database update`	Updates the database to the last migration or to the migration specified by the optional name argument.
`database drop`	Deletes the database.
`dbcontext scaffold`	Generates DB context and entity classes from an existing database. This command uses arguments to specify the connection string and database context provider. In addition, it provides other options that control how this command works.

Two commands that add migrations

```
dotnet ef migrations add Initial
dotnet ef migrations add Genre
```

A command that updates the database to the last migration

```
dotnet ef database update
```

A command that updates the database to the specified migration

```
dotnet ef migrations update Initial
```

A command that removes the last migration

```
dotnet ef migrations remove
```

A command that drops the database

```
dotnet ef database drop
```

A command that generates DB classes from an existing database

```
dotnet ef dbcontext scaffold name=BookstoreContext
Microsoft.EntityFrameworkCore.SqlServer --output-dir Models/DataLayer
--data-annotations --force
```

Description

- The command-line interface (CLI) for .NET EF Core can access all of the same EF Core functionality as Visual Studio's Package Manager Console (PMC).

- For more information about the arguments and options for these commands, you can view the online documentation here:

  `https://docs.microsoft.com/en-us/ef/core/cli/dotnet`

Figure 18-5   A summary of .NET EF Core commands

How to start a new project

So far, you have learned how to use VS Code to open an existing project such as a project created by Visual Studio. That allows you to work with Visual Studio projects like the ones included with the download for this book. Now, you'll learn how to use VS Code to start a new project.

How to create a new project

Figure 18-6 shows how to use VS Code to create a new project for an ASP.NET Core MVC web app. To start, you can use your operating system to create a root folder to store the project. Then, you can use VS Code to open that root folder as described earlier in this chapter. When you do, VS Code should display the empty root folder in its Explorer window.

After you use VS Code to open the empty root folder, you can open a Terminal window and use the CLI to execute a command that creates the starting structure for the app. In this figure, the command in step 5 creates a new project that's based on the ASP.NET Core Web App (Model-View-Controller) template that's described in chapter 2.

However, if you wanted to create a new project that's based on the ASP.NET Core Empty template, you could enter a command like this:

```
dotnet new web
```

This template also works as described in chapter 2.

The command-line interface (CLI) can access all of the same templates as Visual Studio. The table in this figure only shows the two templates presented in this book. For a complete list of templates, you can use the URL provided in this figure, or search the internet for "dotnet new command".

After you use a template to create the starting folders and files for a new project, you can work with it like any other project. For example, you can run the project, edit existing code, add new code files, and so on.

How to add NuGet packages to a project

When you want to add a NuGet package to a VS Code project, you can use the CLI to do that. For example, to create a new project that uses EF Core to work with a SQL Server database, you typically want to use the commands shown in figure 18-6 to add the packages that a project needs to work with EF Core.

How to create a new project for an ASP.NET Core MVC web app

1. Use your operating system to create a new root folder for your project.

2. Start VS Code.

3. Select File→Open Folder and use the resulting dialog to select the root folder for the project.

4. Select Terminal→New Terminal to open a Terminal window.

5. Enter the following command:

```
dotnet new mvc
```

Two templates you can use to create ASP.NET Core projects

Template name	CLI argument
Web App (Model-View-Controller)	mvc
Empty	web

How to use the CLI to add NuGet packages for EF Core to the project

```
dotnet add package Microsoft.EntityFrameworkCore.SqlServer
dotnet add package Microsoft.EntityFrameworkCore.Design
```

Description

- The command-line interface (CLI) can access all of the same templates as Visual Studio. The table in this figure shows both of the templates presented in this book.

- For more information about the templates available with the new command, you can view the online documentation here:

  `https://docs.microsoft.com/en-us/dotnet/core/tools/dotnet-new-sdk-templates`

- The dotnet add package command adds a NuGet package reference to the project file and then runs the dotnet restore command to install the package.

- After creating a new project, you may need to close the project folder and open it again to get VS Code to display the dialog that asks if you want to add required assets for building and debugging a project. Then, you can click Yes to add these assets. These assets allow you to run a project as described earlier.

Figure 18-6   How to create a new project and add NuGet packages to it

How to work with the folders and files

When you open an existing project, all the folders and files you need to work with may already exist. In that case, you can use VS Code to view and edit these folders and files as described earlier in this chapter.

However, when you create a new project, you typically need to work with the project's folders and files as described in figure 18-7. For example, to add a folder to the main folder for the project, you can point to the name of the project and click the New Folder button that's displayed to the right of the name. To add a folder to any other folder, you can right-click on the folder in the Explorer and select New Folder. Either way, you can enter a name for the folder after clicking New Folder.

Once a folder exists, you can add a file to the folder by right-clicking on it and selecting New File. Then, you can enter the name for the file. When you enter a name for a file, you should include an extension that identifies the type of file that you're creating. For example, you can use an extension of .cs for C# files, .cshtml for Razor view files, .css for CSS files, .js for JavaScript files, and so on.

When you use VS Code to add a new file, it doesn't generate any starting code for the file. As a result, you must enter all the code for the file yourself. Or, if you prefer, you can copy and paste some starting code from another file. For example, if you create a new file for a controller, you might want to copy some starting code from another controller and paste it into the new controller. Then, you can edit that code so it works for the new controller.

If you're used to relying on the code that's generated by Visual Studio, this might seem intimidating at first. But once you get used to it, you might begin to prefer the simplicity of the blank file that's provided by VS Code.

VS Code after a new project is created with the MVC template

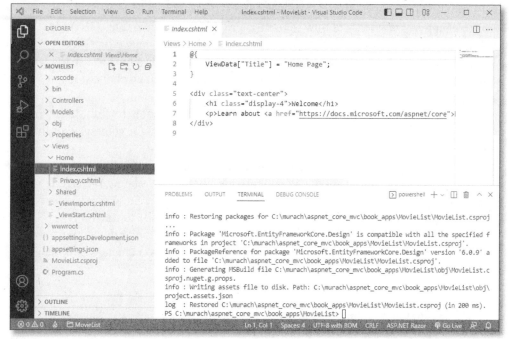

Description

- To add a folder to the project folder, you can point to the name of the project and click the New Folder icon that's displayed to its right. Then, you can enter a name for the folder.

- To add other folders, you can right-click on a folder in the Explorer window and select New Folder. Then, you can enter a name for the folder.

- To add a file, you can right-click on a folder in the Explorer window and select New File. Then, you can enter the name for the file, including its extension.

- Unlike Visual Studio, VS Code doesn't generate any starting code for new files. As a result, you must enter all code for new files yourself.

- To rename a folder or file, right-click on the folder or file and select Rename. Then, edit the name.

- To delete a folder or file, right-click on the folder or file and select Delete.

Figure 18-7   How to work with the folders and files

How to install and manage client-side libraries

In chapter 3, you learned how to use the graphical user interface (GUI) for LibMan that's available from Visual Studio to install and manage client-side libraries such as Bootstrap and jQuery. Now, figure 18-8 shows how to use the command-line interface (CLI) for LibMan to install and manage client-side libraries.

To start, the first example shows how to install the CLI tools for LibMan. You only need to do this if these tools aren't already installed on your system. In other words, you only need to run this command once.

After you install the CLI tools for LibMan, you can create the libman.json file that stores information about each client-side library that's being managed. Again, you only need to do this once.

After you create the libman.json file, you can use VS Code to open this file. Then, you can edit this file so it includes the name, version number, and destination for each client-side library. For example, when you create the libman. json file, it usually generates this JSON code:

```
{
  "version": "1.0",
  "defaultProvider": "cdnjs",
  "libraries": []
}
```

Within the square brackets, you can add one or more libraries, separated by commas. In this figure, for example,

```
"libraries": [
    {
      "library": "twitter-bootstrap@5.1.0",
      "destination": "wwwroot/lib/bootstrap/"
    }
]
```

specifies that LibMan should install version 5.1.0 of the Twitter Bootstrap library in the wwwroot/lib/bootstrap/ folder for this project.

After you've edited the libman.json file so it specifies the client-side libraries that you want to use, you can install or update that library by running the libman restore command. Or, if you want to delete all client-side libraries managed by LibMan, you can run the libman clean command.

If necessary, you can manually delete folders that contain client-side libraries that you don't want to use. To do that, you typically begin by expanding the wwwroot/lib folder to view the folder for the library. Then, you can right-click on the library's folder, select Delete, and respond to the resulting dialog.

VS Code using the CLI tools for LibMan to install client-side libraries

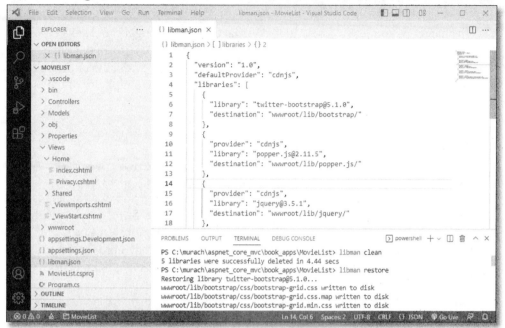

A command that installs the CLI tools for LibMan

```
dotnet tool install --global Microsoft.Web.LibraryManager.Cli
```

How to create a libman.json file for a project

1. At the Terminal command prompt for the project, enter this command:
    ```
    libman init
    ```
2. Press Enter to accept the default provider of CDNJS.

How to use LibMan to install client-side libraries

1. Open the libman.json file and edit it to include the client-side libraries you want to install as described in chapter 3.
2. At the Terminal command prompt, enter this command:
    ```
    libman restore
    ```

How to delete all client-side libraries installed by LibMan

*   At the Terminal command prompt, enter this command:
    ```
    libman clean
    ```

Description

*   The command-line interface (CLI) can use LibMan to manage client-side libraries in a way that's similar to the graphical user interface (GUI) for LibMan that was presented in chapter 3.

Figure 18-8   How to install and manage client-side libraries

How to debug a project

In chapter 5, you learned how to use Visual Studio's debugger to debug a project. Now, you'll learn how to use VS Code's debugger to perform the same task. These two debuggers work similarly, though the VS Code debugger doesn't provide as many features. Still, some programmers prefer the simplicity of the VS Code debugger.

How to set a breakpoint

Figure 18-9 shows how to use VS Code to set a *breakpoint* in an ASP.NET Core app. To start, you can set a breakpoint before you run an app or as an app is executing. However, a web app ends after it generates a page. So, if you switch from the browser to VS Code to set a breakpoint, the breakpoint won't be taken until the next time the page is executed. As a result, if you want a breakpoint to be taken the first time a page is executed, you need to set the breakpoint before you run the app.

After you set a breakpoint and run the app, the app enters *break mode* before it executes the statement that contains the breakpoint. In this figure, for example, the app will enter break mode before it executes the statement that saves changes to the database. Then, you can use the debugging features to debug the app.

In some cases, you may want to set more than one breakpoint. You can do that either before you begin the execution of the app or while the app is in break mode. Then, when you run the app, it stops at the first breakpoint. And when you continue execution, the app executes up to the next breakpoint.

Once you set a breakpoint, it remains active until you remove it. In fact, it remains active even if you close the project and open it again later. If you want to remove a breakpoint, you can use one of the techniques presented in this figure.

If you don't want to remove a breakpoint completely but you don't want to stop on it, you can disable it by right-clicking on it and selecting the Disable Breakpoint item. Then, if you later want to stop on that breakpoint, you can enable it by right-clicking on it and selecting the Enable Breakpoint item.

One easy way to enable and disable breakpoints is to use the Run menu. This menu includes items that let you enable or disable all breakpoints.

The Movie controller with a breakpoint

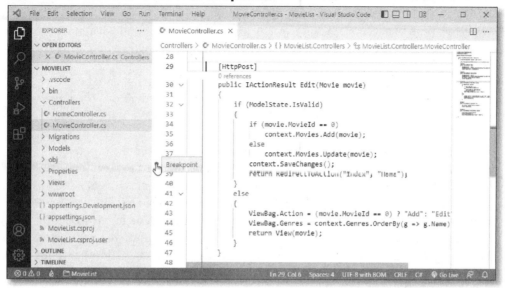

How to set and remove breakpoints

- To set a breakpoint, click in the margin indicator bar to the left of the line number for a statement. This highlights the statement and adds a breakpoint indicator (a red dot) in the margin.
- To remove a breakpoint, click the breakpoint indicator.
- To remove all breakpoints, select Run→Remove All Breakpoints.

How to enable and disable breakpoints

- To disable a breakpoint, right-click it and select Disable Breakpoint.
- To enable a breakpoint, right-click it and select Enable Breakpoint.
- To disable all breakpoints, select Run→Disable All Breakpoints.
- To enable all breakpoints, select Run→Enable All Breakpoints.

Description

- When ASP.NET Core encounters a *breakpoint*, it enters *break mode* before it executes the statement on which the breakpoint is set.
- You can set and remove breakpoints before you run an app or while you're in break mode.
- You can only set a breakpoint on a line that contains an executable statement.

Figure 18-9   How to set a breakpoint

How to work in break mode

To work in break mode, you must run your app with debugging using one of the techniques shown in this figure. Then, you can test your app. When the app hits a breakpoint, it enters break mode.

Figure 18-10 shows the Movie controller of the Movie List app in break mode. In this mode, the next statement to be executed is highlighted. Then, you can use the debugging information that's available to try to determine the cause of an exception or a logical error.

One way to get information about a variable is to view it in the Variables window that's displayed on the left side of the main window. This window displays information about the variables within the scope of the current method. If the code in a controller is currently executing, this window also includes information about the controller and all of its properties such as its ViewBag property. In this figure, for example, the Variables window shows the data for the Movie object that's stored in the variable named movie. This includes the values for its properties such as its Genre property, whose value is null.

Below the Variables window, the Watch window lets you specify an expression that you want to watch. For example, the Watch window in this figure includes an expression that displays the Name property of the Movie object. To add an item to a Watch window, you hover the mouse pointer over the title bar for this window to display an Add (+) button. Then, you click on the Add (+) button and enter the expression you want to watch.

Once you're in break mode, you can use the Step Into, Step Over, and Step Out buttons that are available from the Debug toolbar to control the execution of the app. Or, you can use the shortcut keys for these buttons. For example, the tooltip in this figure shows that the Step Into button has a shortcut key of F11.

To execute the statements of an app one statement at a time, you can use the Step Into button. Each time you use this button, the app executes the next statement and returns to break mode. That way, you can check the values of variables and properties as you step through code one statement at a time. The Step Over button is similar to the Step Into button, but it executes the statements in called methods without interruption (they are "stepped over").

The Step Out button executes the remaining statements in a method without interruption. It's common to use this button if you've stepped into a method that you don't want to step through. In that case, you can use the Step Out button to execute the rest of the statements in the method. Then, the app enters break mode before the next statement in the calling method is executed.

The Continue button continues execution of the app with debugging. As a result, the app continues to run unless it hits another breakpoint and enters break mode again.

When you're done debugging, you can click the Stop button on the far right side of the Debug toolbar. Or, you can press Shift+F5. This works the same as stopping an app when you run it without debugging as described earlier in this chapter. Then, you can click the Explorer button on the far left side of the window to display the Explorer window instead of the debugging windows.

The Movie List app in break mode

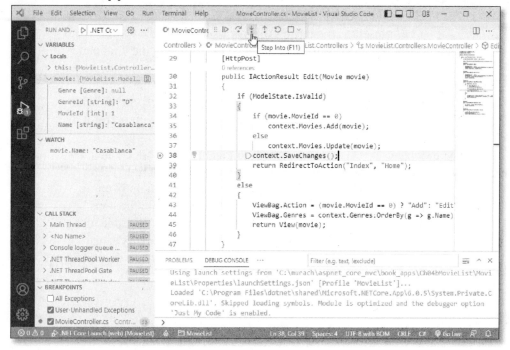

Two ways to run an app with debugging

- Press F5.
- Select Run→Start Debugging.

Description

- When you enter break mode, the debugger highlights the next statement to be executed. In addition, it displays the debugging windows on the left side of the main window, and it displays the Debug toolbar across the top of the main window.
- You can use the Step Into (F11), Step Over (F10), and Step Out (Shift+F11) buttons of the Debug toolbar to execute one or more statements and return to break mode.
- You can use the Continue (F5) button of the Debug toolbar to continue running the app with debugging.
- You can use the Variables window to view information about the variables and properties within the scope of the current method.
- You can use the Watch window to view the values of expressions that you specify.
- When you're done with the debugging windows, you can display the Explorer window again by clicking the Explorer icon in the vertical toolbar on the far left side of the main window.

Figure 18-10   How to work in break mode

Perspective

This chapter has presented the basic skills for using VS Code to work with ASP.NET Core MVC apps. This includes many skills for using the command-line interface (CLI) tools to work with ASP.NET Core. If you've already been using Visual Studio to work with ASP.NET Core MVC apps as described in this book, you shouldn't have any trouble using VS Code to perform the same tasks. And if you experiment with VS Code, you may find that you prefer it to Visual Studio for some tasks.

On the other hand, if you skipped straight to this chapter from chapter 1 and you don't have experience with Visual Studio, it might be a little more difficult for you to get started with VS Code. Still, with a little help from this chapter, you should be able to use VS Code to create and run the apps described in this book. For example, you should be able to use VS Code to create and run the Future Value app described in chapter 2. Similarly, you should be able to use VS Code to create and run the Movie List app described in chapter 4. And so on.

Terms

Visual Studio Code	command-line interface (CLI)
VS Code	breakpoint
source code editor	break mode

Summary

- *Visual Studio Code* (also known as *VS Code*) is a *source code editor*, which is simpler than an integrated development environment (IDE) like Visual Studio.

- A *command-line interface* (*CLI*) allows you to execute commands by entering a line of text at the command prompt.

- When ASP.NET Core encounters a *breakpoint*, it enters *break mode* before it executes the statement on which the breakpoint is set.

Exercise 18-1   Experiment with VS Code

In this exercise, you'll open and run some projects that are included with the download for this book, and you'll debug some code.

Run the Future Value app from chapter 2

1. In Visual Studio Code, open the FutureValue folder that's in the book_apps/ Ch02FutureValue folder.

2. If you get any dialogs about trusting authors, missing assets, or unresolved dependencies, click on the appropriate buttons to trust the authors, add the assets, and resolve the dependencies.

3. Double-click on the file for the HomeController class to open it in Standard Mode. Note that its filename is displayed in a normal font on its tab.

4. Click on the file for the FutureValueModel class to view it in Preview Mode. Note that its filename is displayed in italics on the tab.

5. Click on the file for the Home/Index view to view it in Preview Mode. Note that it reuses the tab that was used by the FutureValueModel class.

6. Press Ctrl+K, release both keys, and immediately press Z to enter Zen Mode. Note that this removes all user interface components except the editor. Then, press Esc twice to exit Zen mode.

7   Press Ctrl+F5 to run the project without debugging. This should display some messages in the Debug Console and automatically start the app in the default web browser for your operating system.

8. In your browser, use the app to calculate a future value. Then, close the browser.

9. In VS Code, click the Stop button to stop the app. Then, close the project folder.

Run the Movie List app from chapter 4

10. Open the MovieList folder that's in the book_apps/Ch04bMovieList folder.

11. If you get any dialogs about trusting authors, missing assets, or unresolved dependencies, click on the appropriate buttons to trust the authors, add the assets, and resolve the dependencies.

12. Use VS Code to view some of the source code files for the Movie List app. Note that it contains files for working with a database named Movies.

13. Display the Terminal window.

14. Use the dotnet tool install command to install the CLI tools for .NET EF Core.

15. Use the dotnet ef database update command to make sure the Movies database has been created.

16. Press Ctrl+F5 to run the project without debugging. This should display some messages in the Debug Console and automatically start the app in the default web browser for your operating system.

17. In your browser, use the app to view some movies and add a movie. Then, close the browser.

18. In VS Code, click the Stop button to stop the app. Then, close the project folder.

Set a breakpoint and step through code in the Future Value app

19. Open the FutureValue folder again, then open the FutureValueModel.cs class. Place a breakpoint at the first line of the CalculateFutureValue() method.

20. Press F5 to run the project with debugging.

21. In your browser, use the app to calculate a future value. When VS Code goes into break mode, step through the code line by line and inspect the variable values in the Variables window.

22. After you step into the for loop, click Continue to continue execution.

23. Return to the browser and view the future value calculation. Then, close the browser.

24. In VS Code, click the Stop button to stop the app. Then, close the project folder.

Exercise 18-2 Create the Future Value app

In this exercise, you'll create the Future Value app from chapter 2 from scratch.

1. Use your operating system to create a folder named Ch18Ex2FutureValue_sol in the ex_solutions folder. Within that folder, create a subfolder named FutureValue.

2. Use VS Code to open the FutureValue subfolder.

3. If you get a dialog about trusting authors, click the appropriate button to trust the authors.

4. Start a Terminal window.

5. Use the dotnet new mvc command to add the files for the ASP.NET Web App (Model-View-Controller) template.

6. Close the project folder and open it again. This should display a dialog that asks if you want to add required assets for building and debugging, and you should click Yes. This should add the .vscode folder to your project.

7. Press Ctrl+F5 to run the project without debugging. This should display some messages in the Debug Console and automatically start the app in the default web browser for your operating system.

8. In your browser, view the page that's displayed by the template for the MVC web app. Then, close the browser.

9. In VS Code, click the Stop button to stop the app.

10. In the Models folder, add a file named FutureValueModel.cs and enter the code for the FutureValueModel class that's shown in chapter 2. To do that, you can copy the code from the Ch02FutureValue app that's in the book_apps folder.

11. Open the HomeController.cs file and enter the code for the Home controller that's shown in chapter 2. Again, you can copy this code from the app for chapter 2 if you want.

12. In the wwwroot/css folder, open the site.css file and enter the code for the custom CSS file that's shown in chapter 2.

13. Open the _Layout.cshtml file and enter the code for the layout that's shown in chapter 2.

14. Open the Home/Index.cshtml file and enter the code for the Home/Index view that's shown in chapter 2.

15. Press Ctrl+F5 to run the project without debugging. This should start the app and display it in the default browser for your operating system.

16. In your browser, use the app to calculate a future value. Then, close the browser, stop the app, and close the project folder.

Appendix A

How to set up Windows for this book

This appendix shows how to install the software that we recommend for developing ASP.NET Core MVC web apps on a Windows system. Then, it shows how to install the source code and create the databases for this book.

As you read this appendix, please remember that most websites are continually updated. As a result, some of the procedures may have changed since this book was published. Nevertheless, these procedures should still be good guides to installing the software. And if there are significant changes to these setup instructions, we will post updates on our website (www.murach.com).

How to install Visual Studio

Figure A-1 shows how to install the Community edition of the Visual Studio IDE (Integrated Development Environment). To do that, you download the setup program from the website address shown in this figure. You can also search the internet for "Visual Studio Community download" and then download the setup program from any website that provides for that. Then, you run the executable file that's downloaded.

When the setup program runs, it will display a page like the one shown in this figure. Then, you can follow the steps summarized here to install Visual Studio. To start, you select the workload you want to install. The workload you select determines the components that are installed. To develop ASP.NET Core MVC apps, for example, you select the "ASP.NET and web development" workload. Then, the required components are listed under the Included heading at the right side of the page.

In addition to the required components, a number of optional components are installed by default. In most cases, you'll just accept the defaults. If you know that you won't use a component, though, you can deselect it. Then, if you need it in the future, you can run the setup program again to install it.

You can also select and deselect individual components from the Individual components tab. When you first display this tab, the components that will be installed based on the selections on the Workloads tab will be selected. That includes the .NET 6.0 Runtime, the .NET SDK, the NuGet Package Manager, and SQL Server Express 2019 LocalDB. Although you'll want to install the .NET 6.0 Runtime, the .NET SDK, and the NuGet Package Manager, you can deselect SQL Server Express 2019 LocalDB if it's already installed on your computer. In addition, you may want to add components. For example, if you want to develop web apps that target .NET Core 3.1, you can select the ".NET Core 3.1 Runtime" component.

Once you've selected the components you want to install, you click the Install button to start the installation. Then, Visual Studio displays a window that shows the installation progress. When the installation completes, Visual Studio is started by default and you're asked to sign in to or create your Microsoft account. You'll also be asked to set the default environment settings for Visual Studio.

Note that the procedure in this figure installs the current version of Visual Studio, which was Visual Studio 2022 at the time of this printing. However, this book should work equally well with later versions of Visual Studio.

The main page for installing Visual Studio Community

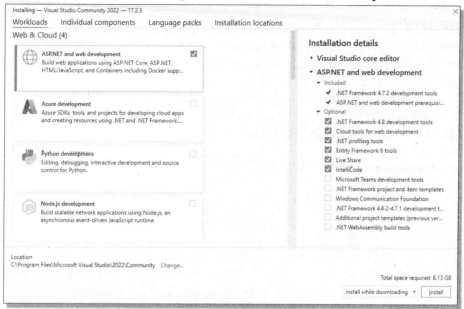

The download page for Visual Studio Community

`https://www.visualstudio.com/vs/community/`

How to install the Visual Studio IDE

1. Download Visual Studio Community from the website address shown above, and then run the downloaded executable file.
2. To install the default features for ASP.NET Core development, select the "ASP.NET and web development" workload. Then, deselect any optional features you don't want to install.
3. Click the Install button to start the installation.
4. When the installation is complete, Visual Studio is started by default and you'll be asked to sign in and set the default environment settings.

Description

- Visual Studio Community is a free IDE (Integrated Development Environment) that you can use to create ASP.NET Core MVC apps.
- By default, the Visual Studio 2022 setup program installs the most current version of .NET Core, as well as SQL Server 2019 Express LocalDB. If that's not what you want, you can display the Individual components tab and select just the components you need.
- For more information about installing and using Visual Studio, you can refer to the Visual Studio website.

Figure A-1   How to install Visual Studio

How to install the source code for this book

Figure A-2 shows how to download and install the source code for this book. This includes the source code for the web apps that are presented in this book. In addition, it includes the source code for the starting points and solutions for the exercises that are presented at the end of each chapter.

When you finish this procedure, the book apps, exercise starts, and exercise solutions should be in the folders shown in this figure. Then, you can review the apps that are presented in this book, and you'll be ready to do the exercises in this book.

The Murach website

www.murach.com

The folder that contains the Visual Studio projects

C:\murach\aspnet_core_mvc

The subfolders

Folder	Description
book_apps	The web applications that are presented throughout this book.
ex_starts	The starting points for the exercises at the end of each chapter.
ex_solutions	The solutions to the exercises.

How to download and install the files for this book

1. Go to www.murach.com.
2. Go to the page for *Murach's ASP.NET Core MVC (2nd Edition)*.
3. If necessary, scroll down to the FREE Downloads tab. Then, click on it.
4. Click the DOWNLOAD NOW button for the zip file for Windows. This should download a file named mvc2_allfiles.zip.
5. Find the zip file on your computer and double-click on it. This should extract the folders and files for this book into a folder named aspnet_core_mvc.
6. If necessary, use Explorer to create the Murach folder directly on your hard disk.
7. Use Explorer to move the aspnet_core_mvc folder into the Murach folder.

Description

- We recommend that you store the files for this book in the folders shown above.
- You may also want to make a second copy of the ex_starts folder as a backup. Then, if you want to go back to the original version of the starting code for an exercise, you'll have it.

Figure A-2   How to install the source code for this book

How to create the databases for this book

To verify that the software and source code has been installed correctly on your system, you can use Visual Studio to open one of the apps and run it. However, if you run an app and its database hasn't been created yet, you'll get an error message like the one shown at the bottom of figure A-3. This error message indicates that the app can't open the database.

To fix this issue, you can use the procedure shown in this figure to create the database for the app. In this figure, the procedure is for the Movie List app that's described in chapter 4 and the Movies database that it uses. The Movie List app is the first app in this book that uses a database.

Note that if this is the first time you've run one of the apps for this book, a message may be displayed asking if you want to trust the ASP.NET Core SSL certificate, which is used to secure the localhost server.

This figure also lists other apps that use other databases. If you want, you can use the procedure shown in this figure to open these apps now and create their databases too. That way, you won't get an error when you run these apps later. However, if you prefer, you can wait until later to create these databases.

The Package Manager Console (PMC) window in Visual Studio

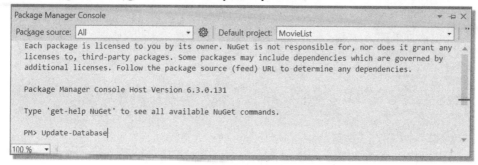

How to create the Movies database and run the Movie List app

1. Start Visual Studio.

2. Select the File→Open→Project/Solution command and use the resulting dialog to open the solution (.sln) file that's in this folder:

    /murach/aspnet_core_mvc/book_apps/Ch04bMovieList

3. Select the Tools→NuGet Package Manager→Package Manager Console command to display the Package Manager Console.

4. At the command prompt, type "Update-Database" and press Enter. Since the project for this app already contains the database migration files, this should create the database.

5. Press Ctrl+F5 to run the app. If this displays a list of Movies in a browser, the Movies database has been created. (If you get messages about trusting and installing an SSL certificate, you can click Yes. And if a web page is displayed indicating that the connection is not private, you can click the link to proceed.)

Other apps that you can use to create other databases

App name	Database name
Ch04aMovieList	Movies_simple
Ch07GuitarShop	GuitarShop
Ch08aNFLTeams	NFLTeams
Ch10bToDoList	TaskList
Ch11Registration	Registration
Ch13Bookstore	Bookstore

The error message that's displayed if the database hasn't been created

`Cannot open database "Movies" requested by the login. The login failed.`

Description

*   Many of the apps in this book work with data that's stored in SQL Server Express LocalDB databases. If you run an app and its database hasn't been created yet, you'll get an error message like the one shown above.

*   To create a database that's used by one of these book apps, you can open the app and run the "Update-Database" command from the Package Manager Console.

Figure A-3   How to create the databases for this book

Appendix B

How to set up macOS for this book

This appendix shows how to install the software that we recommend for developing ASP.NET Core MVC web apps on macOS. Then, it shows how to download the source code for this book, and it describes some of the differences between the Windows and macOS downloads.

As you read this appendix, please remember that most websites are continually updated. As a result, some of the procedures may have changed since this book was published. Nevertheless, these procedures should still be good guides to installing the software. And if there are significant changes to these setup instructions, we will post updates on our website (www.murach.com).

How to install Visual Studio

Figure B-1 shows how to install the Visual Studio IDE (Integrated Development Environment) on macOS. To do that, you download the installer program from the website address shown in this figure. Then, you can run the dmg file that's downloaded. When the dialog shown in this figure is displayed, make sure to select the .NET option. This installs Visual Studio as well as all of the necessary software for developing ASP.NET Core MVC apps.

The Visual Studio for Mac Installer

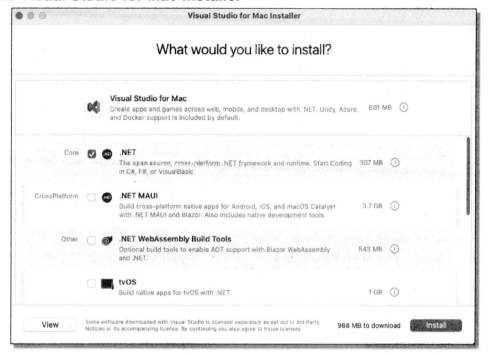

The download page for Visual Studio for Mac

https://www.visualstudio.microsoft.com/vs/mac/

How to install the Visual Studio IDE

1. Find the download page for Visual Studio for Mac by going to the URL above or by searching the internet for "Visual Studio for Mac download".

2. Click the appropriate Download button to download the installer program for Visual Studio for Mac to your hard disk. This installer program should be a dmg file.

3. Run the installer program and respond to the resulting dialogs. When the dialog above is displayed, be sure to select the .NET option.

Description

*   Visual Studio is a free IDE (Integrated Development Environment) that you can use to create ASP.NET Core MVC web apps.

*   For more information about installing and using Visual Studio, you can refer to the Visual Studio website.

Figure B-1   How to install Visual Studio

How to install the source code for this book

Figure B-2 shows how to download and install the source code for this book. This includes the source code for the web apps that are presented in this book. In addition, it includes the source code for the starting points and solutions for the exercises that are presented at the end of each chapter.

When you finish this procedure, the book apps, exercise starts, and exercise solutions should be in the folders shown in this figure. Then, you can review the apps that are presented in this book, and do the exercises that are at the end of each chapter.

However, you should know that the source code in the zip file for macOS has been modified to work with macOS as described in the next figure. As a result, this source code doesn't match the code that's presented in the book exactly. Still, most of the code matches the code in the book, the most significant differences are described in the next figure, and we've used comments in the code to identify the rest of the differences. So, you shouldn't have much trouble using macOS to work with the downloadable source code for this book.

The Murach website

www.murach.com

The folder that contains the Visual Studio projects

~/Documents/murach/aspnet_core_mvc

The subfolders

Folder	Description
book_apps	The web applications that are presented throughout this book.
ex_starts	The starting points for the exercises at the end of each chapter.
ex_solutions	The solutions to the exercises.

How to download and install the files for this book

1. Go to www.murach.com.
2. Go to the page for *Murach's ASP.NET Core MVC (2nd Edition)*.
3. If necessary, scroll down to the FREE Downloads tab. Then, click on it.
4. Click the DOWNLOAD NOW button for the zip file for macOS, and respond to the resulting pages and dialogs. This should download a zip file named mvc2_allfiles_macos.zip.
5. Use Finder to locate the zip file on your hard disk, and double-click on it. This should extract the folders and files for this book into a folder named aspnet_core_mvc.
6. If necessary, use Finder to create the murach folder in your Documents folder.
7. Use Finder to move the aspnet_core_mvc folder into the murach folder.

A note about right-clicking

- This book sometimes instructs you to right-click, because that's common in Windows. On macOS, you can hold down the Ctrl key and click instead of right-clicking.

A note about the download file for macOS

- Two zip files are available for this book from murach.com. The zip file for Windows contains the source code that matches the code presented throughout this book. The zip file for macOS has been modified to work with macOS. As a result, its source code doesn't match the source code in the book exactly. The most significant differences are described in figure B-3.

Description

- We recommend that you store the files for this book in the folders shown above.
- You may also want to make a second copy of the ex_starts folder as a backup. Then, if you want to go back to the original version of the starting code for an exercise, you'll have it.

Figure B-2   How to install the source code for this book

Problems and solutions when using macOS with this book

Figure B-3 presents some problems that you may encounter when using macOS to work with this book. It also presents solutions to those problems. In most cases, these problems have already been fixed in the downloadable source code for this book. Still, you need to understand these problems and their solutions if you're creating web apps from scratch.

For example, if you create the Movie List app from scratch as described in chapter 4, you need to use SQLite, not SQL Server Express LocalDB. That's because macOS doesn't support LocalDB. To use SQLite, you can add the appropriate NuGet packages shown in the first problem/solution example. To do that, you can select Project→Manage NuGet Packages and use the NuGet Package Manager as described in chapter 4. Then, you can modify the Program.cs file so it uses SQLite, not SQL Server. Finally, you can modify the appsettings.json file so it specifies the filename of the SQLite database.

This works because SQLite doesn't use a database server. Instead, it uses a client-side library to work with a database file. When creating a SQLite database file, it's common to give that file an extension of .sqlite. In step 3 of the first example, for instance, the database file is named Movies.sqlite.

Unfortunately, Visual Studio for Mac doesn't support the Package Manager Console (PMC) PowerShell commands presented throughout most of this book. As a result, if you need a PowerShell command, you'll have to use the equivalent command-line interface (CLI) command. Most of these CLI commands are described in chapter 18. For example, if you want to create the database for the first Movie List app from chapter 4, you can use the CLI commands shown in the second problem/solution example. To do that, you can start the Terminal program. Then, you can use it to enter the CLI commands. However, before you execute CLI commands that are specific to a web app, you need to use the cd command to change the current directory to the directory that stores the web app as shown in step 3.

Most of the time, SQLite can perform the same tasks as SQL Server Express LocalDB. However, LocalDB provides some features that aren't supported by SQLite. As a result, in some cases, you may need to modify your code so it only uses features that are supported by SQLite. For instance, the third problem/solution example shows that the Bookstore app from chapter 13 uses code that can't be translated by SQLite. To fix this, you can modify the code so it uses a different technique get a book at random. If the source code for our apps contains minor fixes like this, it also includes a comment like the one in this example that identifies the change.

Problem: **macOS doesn't support SQL Server Express LocalDB**

Solution: **Convert the app to use SQLite instead of LocalDB**

Example: **The Movie List app from chapter 4**

1. Install the following EF Core NuGet packages for working with SQLite, not SQL Server:
   ```
   EntityFrameworkCore.Sqlite
   EntityFrameworkCore.Design
   ```

2. In the Program.cs file, use SQLite, not SQL Server. To do that, call the UseSqlite() method, not the UseSqlServer() method, from the options for the DbContext like this:
   ```
   options.UseSqlite(builder.Configuration.GetConnectionString("MovieContext"))
   ```

3. In the appsettings.json file, code a database connection string that looks like this:
   ```
   "MovieContext": "Filename=Movies.sqlite"
   ```

Problem: **Visual Studio for Mac doesn't support PowerShell commands**

Solution: **Use CLI commands instead as described in chapter 18**

Example: **Create the database for the Movie List app from chapter 4**

1. Start the Terminal program.

2. If necessary, install the .NET EF tools. To do that, enter this command:
   ```
   dotnet tool install --global dotnet-ef
   ```

3. Change the current directory to the directory for the project that contains the database:
   ```
   cd ~/Documents/murach/aspnet_core_mvc/book_apps/Ch04bMovieList/MovieList
   ```

4. Create the migration file named Initial. To do that, enter this command:
   ```
   dotnet ef migrations add Initial
   ```

5. Create the database by running its migration files. To do that, enter this command:
   ```
   dotnet ef database update
   ```

Problem: **Some SQL Server features aren't available from SQLite**

Solution: **Modify your code so it doesn't use those features**

Example: **The Bookstore app from chapter 13**
```
// get a book at random - updated for SQLite
int bookID = new Random().Next(1, data.Count + 1);
Book random = data.Get(bookID);
```

Figure B-3   Problems and solutions when using macOS with this book

How to install and use DB Browser for SQLite

When you use Windows, Visual Studio includes a SQL Server Object Explorer window that allows you to view the SQL Server Express LocalDB databases on your system. When you use macOS with this book, the SQL Server Object Explorer window isn't available from Visual Studio. In addition, you will be using SQLite databases, not SQL Server databases, as described in the previous figure. As a result, to view the SQLite databases on your system, you may want to install DB Browser for SQLite as described in figure B-4.

Once you've installed this program, you can use it to view SQLite databases. To do that, you just open the database file that's in the app's root folder. In this figure, for example, the second procedure shows how to open the Movies.sqlite file for the database of the Movie List app presented in chapter 4. Then, it shows how to view the data in the Movies table. This is often helpful when you need to make sure that a table exists and contains the correct data.

The download page for DB Browser for SQLite

http://sqlitebrowser.org/dl/

How to install DB Browser for SQLite

1. Find the download page for DB Browser for SQLite. The easiest way to do that is to search the internet for "DB Browser for SQLite download".

2. Follow the instructions on that web page to download the installer file. This installer file should be a dmg file.

3. Find the installer file on your system and run it.

4. Accept the default options.

DB Browser for SQLite after viewing the Movie table

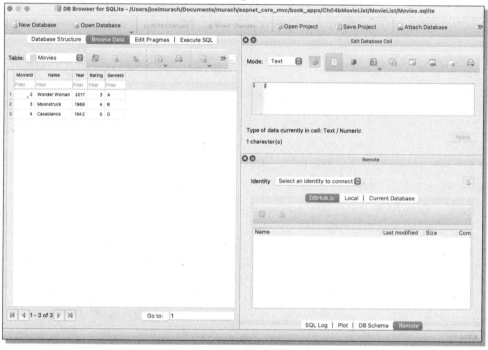

How to view the Movies database from chapter 4

1. Start DB Browser for SQLite.

2. Click the Open Database button. Then, use the resulting dialog to select the SQLite database file that's located here:

   `~\Documents\murach\aspnet_core_mvc\Ch04bMovieList\MovieList\Movies.sqlite`

3. In the main panel, click the Browse Data tab.

4. Use the drop-down list at the top of the main panel to select the Movies table. This should display all data that's stored in the Movies table.

Figure B-4   How to install and use DB Browser for SQLite

Index

! operator, 140, 141
    with EF Core, 446-448
* symbol (@addTagHelper), 606-607
.NET, 14-15
.NET Core, 14-15
.NET EF Core commands, 738-739
.NET Framework, 14-15
? operator, 292-294
? : operator, 238-239
@addTagHelper directive, 56-57, 606-607
@inject directive, 570-571
@model directive, 28-29, 58-59, 258-259
@Model property, 28-29, 58-59, 258-259
@section declaration, 276-277
@using directive, 56-57
    for Models namespace, 258-259
_Layout.cshtml file, 68-69, 244-245
_ViewImports.cshtml file, 56-57, 240-241, 244-245
    importing Models namespace, 258-259
    @addTagHelper, 606-607
_ViewStart.cshtml file, 68-69, 240-241, 244-245
    that sets the default layout, 268-269
\<a\> element, 246-247, 252-253
\<option\> element, 262-263
\<select\> element, 262-263
\<table\> element, 266-267

A

AAA pattern, 576-577
Absolute URL, 252-253
Access, restricting, 654-655, 690-690
Account controller, 664-665
Action, 26-27, 44-45
    coding, 208-209
Action method, 44-45
    accessing arguments in URL segments, 214-215
    for changing a password, 696-697
    for displaying users and roles, 682-683
    for logging in a user, 676-677
    for logging out a user, 670-671
    for registering a user, 670-671
    restricting access, 654-655
    with dependency injection, 568-569
    with strongly-typed view, 60-61

Action result, 26-27
action token (Route attribute), 216-217
ActionResult class, 288-289
    subtypes for redirection, 310-311
ActionResult object, returning, 290-291
active class (Bootstrap), 118-119, 120-121, 123
Add() method (DbSet), 150-151, 484-485
Add-Migration command (PowerShell), 146-147, 164-165, 452-455
    for adding Identity tables, 658-659
AddControllersWithViews() method (Program.cs), 30-31, 48-49, 204-205
    for enabling TempData, 315
AddDbContext() method (ModelBuilder.Services), 144-145
AddHttpContextAccessor() method (IServiceCollection), 561-562
AdditionalFields property (RemoteAttribute), 428-429
AddMemoryCache() method (Program.cs), 332-333
AddModelError() method (ModelStateDictionary), 412-413
AddMvc() method (Program.cs), 204-205
AddRouting() method (Program.cs), configuring URLs, 170-171
AddScoped() method (IServiceCollection), 561
AddSession() method (Program.cs), 332-333
AddSingleton() method (IServiceCollection), 561
AddToRoleAsync() method (UserManager), 678-679
AddTransient() method (IServiceCollection), 560-561
AddValidation() method (IClientModelValidator), 424-426
Admin area (Bookstore website), 548-553
Admin folder (Bookstore website), 508-509
Admin page (Bookstore website), 504-505
Alert (Bootstrap), 120-121
alert class (Bootstrap), 120-121
alert-*context* class (Bootstrap), 120-121
alert-dismissible class (Bootstrap), 120-121
alert-link class (Bootstrap), 120-121
AllAttributes property (TagHelperContext), 620-621
AllowAnonymous attribute, 654-655
Anonymous type, 482-483
App
    configuring for dependency injection, 560-562
    configuring to use session state, 332-333
    running with debugging in VS Code, 748-749
    starting folders and files, 240-241
Append() method (Cookies), 356-357

C

V

W

w class (Bootstrap), 106-107
WAN, 4-5
warning class (Bootstrap), 110-111
Watch window
    Visual Studio, 194-195
    VS Code, 748-749
Web app, 4-5
    configuring, 40-41
    debugging, 180-181, 192-197
    running, 50-52, 180-181
    starting, 38-39
    testing, 180-189
Web App MVC template, 38-39
Web browser, 4-5
Web page, 4-5
    dynamic, 8-9
    static, 6-7
Web server, 4-5
WebApplicationBuilder object (dependency injection), 560-561
Where() method (LINQ), 148-149, 480-481
Wide area network (WAN), 4-5
Wildcard symbol (@addTagHelper), 606-607
Windows PowerShell, 22-23
Windows-based authentication, 648-649
Windows-based Azure app, 710-711
WithMany() method (Fluent API), 457
    many-to-many relationship, 462-463
    one-to-many relationship, 459
WithOne() method (Fluent API), 457
    one-to-many relationship, 458
    one-to-one relationship, 461
Wizard, 706-707
Workload (Visual Studio), 754-755
Wrapper class (session state), 340-341
wwwroot folder, 240-241

XYZ

xUnit framework, 572-573
Zen mode (VS Code), 732-733

100% Guarantee

When you order directly from us, you must be satisfied. Try our books for 30 days or our eBooks for 14 days. They must work better than any other programming training you've ever used, or you can return them for a prompt refund. No questions asked!

Mike Murach, Publisher   *Ben Murach, President*

Related Book

Have you mastered HTML and CSS?

The more you know about HTML and CSS, the more productive you'll be as a server-side developer. That's why *Murach's HTML and CSS* is a perfect companion to our ASP.NET book.

Books for web developers

Murach's HTML and CSS (5th Ed.)	$59.50
Murach's JavaScript and jQuery (4th Ed.)	59.50
Murach's PHP and MySQL (4th Ed.)	59.50

Books for database programmers

Murach's MySQL (3rd Ed.)	$57.50
Murach's Oracle SQL and PL/SQL (2nd Ed.)	54.50
Murach's SQL Server 2019 for Developers	59.50

Books for Python, Java, C++, or .NET developers

Murach's Python Programming (2nd Ed.)	$59.50
Murach's C++ Programming (2nd Ed.)	59.50
Murach's Java Programming (6th Ed.)	59.50
Murach's C# (7th Ed.)	59.50
Murach's ASP.NET Core MVC (2nd Ed.)	59.50

Books for Data Analysis

Murach's R for Data Analysis	$59.50
Murach's Python for Data Analysis	59.50

Prices and availability are subject to change. Please visit our website or call for current information.

We want to hear from you

Do you have any comments, questions, or compliments to pass on to us? It would be great to hear from you! Please share your feedback in whatever way works best.

 www.murach.com

 1-800-221-5528
(Weekdays, 8 am to 4 pm Pacific Time)

 murachbooks@murach.com

 twitter.com/murachbooks

facebook.com/murachbooks

 linkedin.com/company/
mike-murach-&-associates

 instagram.com/murachbooks

The software for this book

- Visual Studio 2022 with the ".NET Core" workload. For Windows, this workload includes
    - .NET 6
    - ASP.NET Core MVC 6
    - C# 10
    - A built-in web server called Kestrel
    - A built-in database server called SQL Server Express LocalDB

  For macOS, this workload doesn't include SQL Server Express LocalDB because that server isn't available for macOS. Instead, you can use SQLite database files, which don't require a database server.
- For information about installing Visual Studio with the ".NET Core" workload, please see appendix A (Windows) or appendix B (macOS).

The downloadable files for this book

- The source code for all of the applications presented in this book.
- Starting points for the exercises in this book so you can get more practice in less time.
- Solutions for all of the exercises in this book so you can check your work on the exercises.
- For information about downloading and installing these applications, please see appendix A (Windows) or appendix B (macOS).

www.murach.com